On the Road of the Winds

On the Road of the Winds

AN ARCHAEOLOGICAL HISTORY

OF THE PACIFIC ISLANDS

BEFORE EUROPEAN CONTACT

Patrick Vinton Kirch

UNIVERSITY OF CALIFORNIA PRESS

Berkeley   Los Angeles   London

Frontispiece: Restored *Moai* (statue) on Rapa Nui, with replicated obsidian and coral eyes. (Photo by Thérèse Babineau.)

University of California Press
Berkeley and Los Angeles, California

University of California Press, Ltd.
London, England

Library of Congress Cataloging-in-Publication Data

Kirch, Patrick Vinton.
    On the road of the winds: an archaeological history of
the Pacific Islands before European contact / Patrick
Vinton Kirch.
        p.   cm.
    Includes bibliographical references and index.
    ISBN 0-520-22347-0 (alk. paper)
    1. Prehistoric peoples—Oceania. 2. Oceania—
    Antiquities. I. Title.
    GN871.K575 2000
    995—dc21   99-36664
                                                      CIP

Printed and bound in Canada

08   07   06   05   04   03   02   01   00   99
10   9   8   7   6   5   4   3   2   1

The paper used in this publication meets the minimum
requirements of ANSI/NISO Z39.48-1992 (R 1997)
(Permanence of Paper)

For

DOUGLAS E. YEN

whose outstanding ethnobotanical

researches continue to influence

interpretations of Pacific prehistory

The publisher gratefully acknowledges the generous contribution to this book provided by the Moore Family Foundation.

Contents

List of Maps

List of Figures

List of Tables

Preface

Born and raised on one Pacific island, I have spent three decades of my adult life exploring, living on, studying, and seeking to understand a plethora of others, especially the history and culture of their inhabitants. While my own ancestry is ultimately European, I sometimes feel that the Pacific is in my blood. This is, naturally, but a metaphor. Yet the many years spent living and working with Pacific islanders, learning to speak more than one of their indigenous languages, and adapting my behavior to fit their cultural canons have—I hope—engendered a certain empathy beyond that typically associated with dispassionate social science. This book is my attempt to distill a lifetime of study—and the insights gained through much tedious sifting of often minute strands of evidence by myself and innumerable colleagues—into a coherent whole, a synthesis for those whose curiosity would take them on an intellectual voyage into the Oceanic past.

Mine is but one of many constructions that could be made from the formidable array of archae-ological, historical linguistic, ethnographic, and human biological evidence concerning the Oceanic past, assembled by scholars over more than two centuries. It is necessarily personal in the emphasis I accord particular times, places, and concepts. Despite my acceptance of the idea that history (or "prehistory") is constructed rather than reconstructed (as might have been said three decades ago, during the heyday of the "New Archaeology"), I do not subscribe to the ultrarela-tivist stance of some late-twentieth-century social scientists. Although each new generation of archaeologists and prehistorians inevitably rewrites the past in their own terms, I prefer to see this, in Paul Veyne's (1984) words, as a process of "lengthening the questionnaire," of constructing multiple, rather than single, historical plots.

With each new generation the empirical base of archaeology advances, constraining what the next generation of scholars may construct of the past. Thus I agree with Ernst Mayr (1997:83) when he claims that science *does* advance, despite false starts and wrong-minded diversions along the way. Just as Mayr can rightly claim that our understanding of the cell in biology has truly progressed since its first recognition by Robert Hooke in 1667, so our knowledge of Pacific archaeology and long-term history has without question improved throughout the course of the nineteenth and twentieth centuries. The many surveys and excavations of Pacific archaeological sites, enhanced by the patient laboratory analyses of artifacts and other material traces, increasingly improve our ability to come to grips with the human past of Oceania. That does not mean that our current knowledge and understanding constitute "truth" in any absolute sense; it *does* mean that our models of what happened in the past are now a better approximation of that historical reality. Was there a "real past"? Yes, but we shall never know it definitively, as it exists only as material traces in the present. Thus for epistemology.

Peter Bellwood authored the last attempt at a general synthesis of Oceanic prehistory two decades ago: *Man's Conquest of the Pacific* (1979). Still useful as a guide to the literature and the interpretations of its time, Peter's book is long out of date, an encouraging sign of how our knowledge base has increased; it is long out of print as well. Despite the obvious need for a suitable replacement for his opus, I long refrained from undertaking such a work myself. Once committed to the task, however, I found it both stimulating and challenging to grapple with the problems of condensing such a broad field, one that has in recent decades grown by leaps and bounds. To compress within the covers of a 448-page book the panoply of archaeological and anthropological minutiae with which the scholar ordinarily concerns himself is impossible. How to sort and prioritize? What is truly significant? And what can be eliminated? Asking these questions forced me to confront more fundamental issues: underlying

assumptions about the very nature of the field, what we think we know, the often-unstated yet subtle organizing categories by which we conduct our research. In the end, the act of writing this book proved far more intellectually engaging than at first I imagined it might be.

I first participated in Pacific archaeological fieldwork thirty-five years ago, as part of a 1965 Bishop Museum team investigating rockshelter sites in Kona and Ka'u, Hawai'i, and I published my first professional article in 1970. When I came into the field as a young student in the mid-1960s, Jack Golson, Roger Green, Doug Yen, and others in Pacific archaeology were inspiring a renaissance in perspective and approach, as well as moving beyond (while not dispensing with) questions of cultural origins and migrations. Their work encompassed the then-new "settlement pattern" approach, questions of human ecological adaptations, and problems of sociopolitical evolution in island societies. Since then, I have been privileged to participate in many key developments and advances in Pacific prehistory, such as those that came out of the Southeast Solomons Culture History Program of the 1970s and the Lapita Homeland Project of the 1980s. Fieldwork has taken me across the breadth of the Pacific, from the Mussau Islands of Papua New Guinea to Rapa Nui, with stays between these geographic extremes in Palau (Belau), Yap, Majuro, Arno, Kolombangara, Nendö, Vanikoro, Tikopia, Anuta, Futuna, Alofi, 'Uvea, Niuatoputapu, Vava'u, Ofu, Olosega, Ta'u, Mangaia, and all of the main islands of Hawai'i except Ni'ihau. My research has encompassed high islands and atolls, islands tropical and subtropical, ones large and small, and spanned the classic ethnographic regions of Melanesia, Micronesia, and Polynesia. I trust it not untoward to claim that this diversity of field experiences lends me sufficient geographic and cultural background with which to undertake the synthesis attempted here, incorporating as well the work of a great many other field researchers. The comparative approach has long been a cornerstone of anthropology, and the opportunities to compare the archaeological records of so many diverse islands have been inspirational. Still, this book is as much a synthesis of the work and insights of innumerable others, some of whom I have been privileged to know as colleagues and friends, others only as academic ancestors whom I have met through the legacy of their scholarship.

Organizing this book—structuring it into chapters and subheadings—was perhaps the most agonizing part of writing. Early on, I experimented with less conventional schemes, with various topically organized outlines. In the end, I rejected these approaches in favor of an outline based partly on time and largely on space. Though more conventional in structure, this plan in my view allows for better presentation of the "facts" of prehistory as we currently conceive them, enabling them to be more readily accessed by students as well as other professionals seeking an introduction to the long-term history of the Pacific. But I am fully cognizant that "facts" exist— or at least can be interpreted—only within the context of theory, and I have tried to relate archaeological evidence to contemporary theoretical issues and debates wherever possible. My final chapter is an attempt to canvass what I see as some of the grand themes in the prehistory of the Pacific, issues that in the end transcend place and time, and go to the core of anthropology and history at large.

For more than twenty years I have taught Pacific archaeology and prehistory to undergraduates and graduate students at the Universities of Hawai'i, Washington, and California at Berkeley. Admittedly frustrated by the lack of a suitable introductory text that covered the entire Pacific

field, I had not thought of writing such a book myself. Too many other high-priority projects were always to the fore; the undertaking of a general synthesis seemed something that could wait for a more leisured time. William Woodcock, formerly of Princeton University Press, convinced me otherwise, and without his urging I would still be thinking of this as a far-off project. Still, it took four years before I was able to find the appropriate time to concentrate on its writing.

A year-long fellowship (1997–98) at the Center for Advanced Study in the Behavioral Sciences (CASBS), Palo Alto, provided invigorating freedom from normal academic duties. I am grateful for the financial support provided by the National Science Foundation (Grant No. SBR-9601236), which partially supported my fellowship at the Center, and to the University of California at Berkeley for the grant of a year's sabbatical leave. I especially thank Neil Smelser, director of the CASBS; Robert Scott, associate director; and their wonderfully supportive staff. Librarians Joy Scott and Jean Michel cheerfully tracked down obscure references and obtained rare volumes through interlibrary loans. Virginia MacDonald graciously word-processed my editorial corrections to several drafts. Susan Beach's delicious lunches helped too! And the stimulating intellectual atmosphere generated by my fellow colleagues of the Center's Class of 1997–98 made the experience especially memorable.

Several colleagues were generous enough to read and comment on one or more draft chapters. I especially thank Roger Green and Kent Lightfoot for reading the entire manuscript. Jim Allen, Steve Athens, Chris Gosden, Laura Nader, Barry Rolett, Matthew Spriggs, and David Steadman commented on specific chapters. They have saved me from making many errors, and I am most appreciative of their collegial efforts. I also thank the following colleagues for graciously giving me permission to use their photographs or illustrations: Jim Allen, Wal Ambrose, Steve Athens, Janet Davidson, John Flenley, José Garanger, Jack Golson, Roger Green, Geoff Irwin, Pat McCoy, William Morgan, Barry Rolett, Christophe Sand, Yosi Sinoto, Jim Specht, Matt Spriggs, Robert Suggs, Joanne Van Tilburg, Paul Wallin (for the Kon-Tiki Museum), Marshall Weisler, and Peter White.

At the University of California Press, Director Jim Clark and Executive Editor Doris Kretschmer enthusiastically accepted my book manuscript and made its production a high priority. I also thank Nicole Hayward for her superb design and Peter Strupp for his meticulous copyediting.

It gives me distinct pleasure to dedicate this book to Douglas E. Yen, who over three decades has been by turns mentor, co-fieldworker, and colleague, as well as friend and confidant. We have shared never-to-be-forgotten field experiences in Makaha, Halawa, Kolombangara, Anuta, Tikopia, and Kahikinui, as well as evenings at various watering holes from Nanakuli to Honiara. Doug's ceaseless adherence to the sound scientific principle of always being alert to the unsuspected alternative hypothesis has more than once been an inspiration. His influence on my generation of Pacific archaeologists has been legion.

Patrick Vinton Kirch
Palo Alto

Introduction

Mine is the migrating bird
winging afar over remote oceans,
Ever pointing out the sea road of the Black-heron—
the dark cloud in the sky of night.
It is the road of the winds
coursed by the Sea Kings to unknown lands!

Polynesian voyaging chant (Stimson 1957:73)

In March 1896, an English gentleman-adventurer by the name of F. W. Christian arrived at a place called Madolenihmw, on the southern coast of Pohnpei Island in Micronesia. Having spent some years in Samoa (where he was a neighbor of Robert Louis Stevenson), Christian had heard from that equally famous teller of South Sea tales, Louis Becke, that there existed on Pohnpei "an ancient island Venice shrouded in jungle." Christian had now made his way to Nan Madol at Madolenihmw, which he was about to explore, map, and photograph, exposing its wonders to the Western world. Relating his first visit to the Nan Madol ruins, Christian wrote: "Passing the southern barricade of stones, we turned into the ghostly labyrinth of this city of the waters, and straight-away the merriment of our guides was hushed, and conversation died down to whispers" (1899:78). The immensity of the ancient town and its stonework, laced with canals, overwhelmed him. "Above us we see a striking example of immensely solid Cyclopean stone-work frowning down upon the waterway, a mighty wall formed of basaltic prisms" (1899:79). Uncertain what to make of these vestiges of the "long, long ages," Christian evoked comparisons with "the semi-Indian ruins of Java, and the Cyclopean structures of Ake, and Chichen-Itza in Yucatan" (1899:80). Almost a century later, archaeological excavations at Nan Madol would reveal the gradual growth of this amazing site over nearly two thousand years, its megaliths telling a story of the in situ rise of an island civilization.

Nan Madol is but one of thousands of archaeological sites dispersed across the Pacific islands, a priceless material record of the long-term history of their indigenous peoples and cultures. Although one of the largest and most dramatic sites, Nan Madol is not the most famous; the gargantuan statues of Easter Island (Rapa Nui) would surely claim that distinction. They too testify to the rise of another island civilization, which, overshooting its resource base and damaging its fragile ecology, descended into the darkness of social terror. Other Pacific archaeological sites, while known primarily to scholars, are no less significant on the scale of world history. Kuk, a stratified succession of clay layers in the swampy floor of a New Guinea Highlands valley—and the antithesis of an impressive stone construction like Nan Madol—has produced clues to some of the earliest horticultural activities anywhere in the world, at about 7000 B.C. At Matemkupkum rockshelter on New Ireland, excavations yielded fishbones and shellfish dating back 35,000 years, some of the first evidence for exploitation of coastal marine resources by modern *Homo sapiens*. Then too, one could invoke the small rectangular temples of neatly stacked stone surmounting the rocky summit of Necker Island in the northwest Hawaiian chain, an island only 24 hectares in area and lacking any soil to speak of, yet covered with archaeological vestiges of former Polynesian voyagers, who came and went long before Europeans ever ventured into Pacific waters.

These examples hint at the diversity and richness of the Oceanic archaeological record, a legacy that has been thoroughly explored, studied, and properly interpreted only in the second half of the twentieth century. In the process, questions that scholars have posed and puzzled over for two centuries and more—Where did the Pacific islanders come from? How did they discover and settle the thousands of islands? Why did they build great constructions like Nan Madol, or carve the Easter Island statues?—are finally being answered. This book chronicles the efforts of archaeologists to discover and understand the archaeological record of the Pacific islands, offering a contemporary synthesis of what we have found.

My title—*On the Road of the Winds*—is meant to evoke more than just a single or simple metaphor regarding the peoples of the far-flung Pacific islands and their remarkable history. Countless voyages "on the road of the winds" underwrote the discovery and settlement of the myriad Oceanic islands. Some were short, others of great duration and hardship, most often made toward the east, hence upwind along countless trackways stretching away into the dawn. Ultimately, then, the origins of the Pacific islanders trace back to the west, to a period when cyclically rising and falling ice-age seas wrought great changes in the coastal configurations of the Southeast Asian and Australian continents. As the dates for earliest human movements into this Australasian realm are pushed farther back in time, we approach another kind of dawn: the very appearance of early modern humans (*Homo sapiens sapiens*) and their initial expansion out of Africa, across the face of the Old World. Then too, my title invokes not just voyages undertaken by Oceanic peoples themselves—whether by raft, dugout, or double-hulled sailing canoe—but also another kind of voyage: the intellectual voyage of exploration and discovery of the Oceanic past, a past encoded not in written texts, but in potsherds and stone tools unearthed from island middens, in the relationships among Pacific island languages, in the cultural and biological variation of hundreds of Oceanic societies and populations dispersed over one-third of the earth's surface, from New Guinea to Easter Island, from Hawai'i to New Zealand. Voyages both real and imagined—the voyages of history and intellectual voyages of the mind—are the concern of the chapters to follow.

Like all other peoples, Pacific islanders possess their own indigenous forms of history, accounts of ancestors passed down through chants, songs, and oral traditions.[1] These too speak of voyages, many of epic proportions. There is, for example, the saga of Rata, whose great double-hulled canoe, *The-Cloud-Overshadowing-the-Border*, carried Rata and his mother North Tahiti—after many harrowing adventures—back home to Great Vava'u in Upper Havaiki. The famous canoe *Lomipeau* transported on her deck the massive hewn limestone slabs with which to build Paepaeotelea (the tomb of Telea), from 'Uvea Island to the Tongan chiefly capital of Mu'a. The voyages of "the tropic bird people" led by Koura, in the canoe *Te-Buki-ni-Benebene* ("The-tip-of-a-coconut-leaf"), colonized the atolls known today as Kiribati. Such indigenous traditions provide one source of knowledge regarding the Oceanic past, a valuable resource for the insights they provide into cultural motivations. It is an insider's history. Western scholars have long drawn upon the historical traditions of Pacific islanders, and indeed these offered primary evidence for many late-nineteenth- and early-twentieth-century syntheses.[2] But as the human sciences have matured in the twentieth century, we have developed sophisticated methods for extracting historical information from diverse sources lying outside the boundaries of either traditional oral or written histories, sources that open windows on the deep past of "the peoples without history."[3]

This book is a history (or "prehistory" in the usual sense) based on such nontraditional "texts"—an explicitly anthropological history that privileges the *archaeological* record of human material culture (using that term in the broadest sense to include aspects of culturally altered landscapes as well as artifacts per se). It is also a history that draws upon the collaborative evidence of historical linguistics, comparative ethnography, and bio-

logical anthropology. Such works usually fall under the rubric of "prehistory," a term some find increasingly problematic, implying some kind of vague yet fundamentally qualitative difference between document-based history and a history in which the unwritten "text" consists of diachronically meaningful variation and patterning in the world at large. Let us call it, then, an anthropological and archaeological history, and one in which such traditional disciplinary boundaries are consciously disregarded.[4]

Using an elegant metaphor of history as a ceaseless progression of waves of different amplitude, French historian Fernand Braudel (1980) called the longest of these the *longue durée*. This is the "long run" of history, of deep time. It tracks the underlying rhythms of production, the fundamental structures of society, the seemingly imperceptible fitting of culture to nature, and the manipulation of nature to reproduce culture. In writing his famous opus on another ocean, *La Méditerranée*, Braudel followed the lead of his mentor Marc Bloc by incorporating varied nondocumentary sources of evidence, for the history of the *longue durée* is as much inscribed in the very fabric of the land, and in the patterns of culture, as it is in the written word. Recently, many archaeologists and prehistorians have come to view what they do as the writing of such long-term histories, the unearthing of the *longue durée*.

The deep, strong currents of the *longue durée* are akin to the great transoceanic swells that sweep the Pacific Ocean from continent to continent. To take the measure of their wavelength requires that we move beyond the constraints of a narrow documentary history, or even of a particularistic archaeology. A *holistic* perspective is called for, one that brings to bear the clues derived as much from the study of *synchronic* linguistic, cultural, and biological variation as from the direct, materialist, properly *diachronic* evidence of archaeology.

In Chapter 1, when the intellectual history of Oceanic historical anthropology is reviewed, we shall see that a great many naive assumptions long hindered scholars from appreciating the *longue durée* of the Pacific islanders. Scholarly opinion held that people had come only lately to the islands, that their cultures were essentially changeless (and hence timeless), that nothing would be gained from the tedious work of archaeological excavation in island soils. Such assumptions have now been thoroughly overturned and debunked, and the Pacific islands have begun to take their rightful place in the annals of world history. Their *longue durée* is a rich story, one that our narratives are only beginning to describe—fascinating in its own right, but also replete with plots and themes whose historical significance resonates beyond local place and specific time.

This is where I would now take you, on a voyage to the islands of history.

Defining Oceania

Vasco Nuñez de Balboa gazed out, in 1513, across the Pacific Ocean; Ferdinand Magellan crossed it in 1520–21. By the late sixteenth century the Spanish were annually sailing from Acapulco to Manila and back to New Spain via the North Pacific,[5] yet Europeans had little real knowledge of the Pacific or its thousands of islands until nearly two centuries later, when the epic voyages of Captain James Cook (1768–80) definitively disproved the theory of a great *Terra Australis*, a southern continent. Cook for all intents and purposes created the modern map of the Pacific. Moreover, he and the gentlemen-naturalists who sailed with him (Joseph Banks, Sydney Parkinson, Daniel Carl Solander, Johann Reinhold Forster, and George Forster) initiated serious ethnographic inquiry into the peoples and cultures of the Pacific islands. These European explorers—part of the great intel-

lectual movement we call the Enlightenment—were amazed to find the myriad islands of the Great South Sea well populated by indigenous peoples, many (but not all) of whom spoke related languages. Moreover, these islanders were expert sailors and navigators. Tupaia, a Tahitian priest-navigator interviewed by Cook, named no less than 130 islands for which he claimed to know sailing directions (relying on stars and other natural phenomena) and relative distances.[6] Thus, long before the Spanish and later the French and English, other peoples had explored the vastness of the Pacific, discovered virtually every single one of its habitable islands, and founded successful colonies on most. A few settlements did not endure, but most burgeoned into often substantial populations, marked by "aristocratic" (i.e., chiefly) social structures. These latter societies—of which "Otaheite" was the *sine qua non*—intrigued and tantalized Enlightenment savants, including Jean-Jacques Rousseau and Denis Diderot, who mined the explorers' journals for evidence to support their provocative theories of the human social condition.

By the 1830s, the period of great exploratory voyages initiated by Cook, Bougainville, and others was coming to its conclusion. One of the last of the great naval commanders, the French voyager Dumont d'Urville, in his "Notice sur les Îles du Grand Océan" (1832), classified the peoples of the Pacific islands into three great groups. The first of these were the *Polynesians* ("many islands"),[7] a generally light-skinned people spread over the islands of the eastern Pacific, including Tahiti, Hawai'i, Easter Island, and New Zealand. In the western Pacific north of the equator, Dumont d'Urville defined another major group, the *Micronesians* ("little islands"), many of whom occupied small atolls. His third group, whom he called the *Melanesians* ("dark islands"), consisted of the generally darker-skinned peoples inhabiting the large islands of New Guinea, the Solomons, Vanuatu (then the New Hebrides), New Caledonia, and Fiji.

Although based on a superficial understanding of the Pacific islanders, Dumont d'Urville's tripartite classification stuck. Indeed, these categories—Polynesians, Micronesians, Melanesians—became so deeply entrenched in Western anthropological thought that it is difficult even now to break out of the mold in which they entrap us (Thomas 1989). Such labels provide handy geographical referents, yet they mislead us greatly if we take them to be meaningful segments of cultural history. Only Polynesia has stood the tests of time and increased knowledge, as a category with historical significance. Probably this is because the Polynesians were defined by Dumont d'Urville as much by their linguistic similarities as by perceived racial affinities. Hence, the Polynesians do form a meaningful unit for culture-historical analysis, what we may call a robust "phyletic unit" (see Chapter 7).

On the other hand, the labels Micronesia and, most particularly, Melanesia imply no such culture-historical unity. Indeed, whether we are looking at language, human biological variation, or culture, the peoples of Melanesia defy categorization, and they are among the most diverse and heterogeneous to be found in any comparably sized geographic space on earth. The historical processes underlying such great variety—which can only be disentangled through the holistic methods of anthropological history—will be exposed in the course of this book. Suffice it to say that when the terms *Melanesia* or *Micronesia* are used in the following pages, the reference will be *exclusively to geographic regions*, with no implied ethnolinguistic uniformity.

Dumont d'Urville's three groups, taken together, are generally understood to make up *Oceania* and usually exclude the islands of South-east Asia (the Indonesian and Philippine archipelagoes in particular). In some usages (e.g., Oliver 1989), Oceania includes Australia, although that is not the sense here. The exclusion of island Southeast Asia from Oceania, however, is another curious consequence of academic history, for anthropological (as well as linguistic and historical) scholarship in the Pacific islands and Southeast Asia has largely independent and separate traditions. This is unfortunate, for—as modern linguistic, comparative ethnographic, and archaeological studies (e.g., Bellwood et al. 1995; Swadling 1997b) show—there are close culture-historical relationships between the indigenous peoples of island Southeast Asia and the Pacific. Indeed, the great Austronesian language family spans both regions. However, island Southeast Asia has had a more complex historical overlay of cultural influence from the Indian subcontinent, which is not shared with the islands east of the Moluccas in Eastern Indonesia, and this has partly influenced the separateness of geographically focused scholarly traditions. For the purposes of this book, I largely confine my scope to *Oceania* as traditionally defined (excluding Australia and island Southeast Asia), although at times it will be necessary to look beyond its borders in order to understand fully aspects of Oceanic history and culture.

Two other geographical terms require discussion, for these are relatively new concepts, not yet familiar even to many anthropologists or historians who work in Oceania. These are *Near Oceania* and *Remote Oceania*, originally proposed by Roger Green (1991a) in reaction against the historical sterility of the "Melanesia" concept. As seen in Map 1, Near Oceania includes the large island of New Guinea, along with the Bismarck Archipelago, and the Solomon Islands as far eastward as San Cristobal and Santa Ana. This is not only the region of greatest biogeographic diversity within

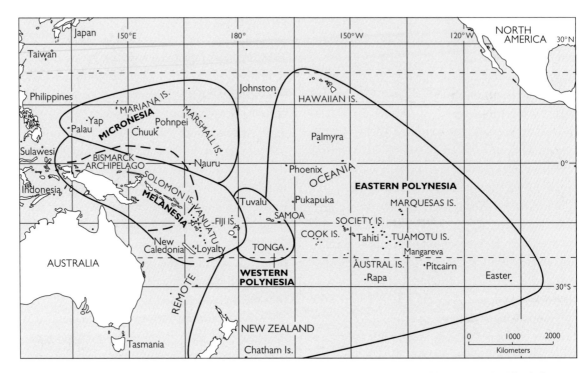

MAP 1 Oceania, showing the traditional cultural regions of Polynesia, Melanesia, and Micronesia. The heavy dashed line indicates the boundary between Near Oceania (to the west) and Remote Oceania (to the east).

Oceania, but also that which had human occupation beginning in the late Pleistocene (ca. 40,000 years ago or longer; see Chapter 3). Within Near Oceania, we find peoples who speak both Austronesian and Non-Austronesian (Papuan) languages. Remote Oceania includes all the Pacific islands to the north, east, and southeast of Near Oceania, yet its inhabitants speak exclusively Austronesian languages.[8] Archaeology confirms that the Remote Oceanic islands were not discovered or settled by humans until after about 1500 B.C., and in some cases as recently as A.D. 1000 (Green 1995). Thus the distinction between Near Oceania and Remote Oceania is not merely a geographic division, but one that consciously encapsulates two major epochs in the history of the Pacific islanders.

Linguistic, Human Biological, and Cultural Variation in Oceania

While primarily a work of *history*, this book also seeks an anthropologically grounded explanation for—and understanding of—the synchronic cultural, linguistic, and human biological variation exhibited throughout the modern Oceanic world. Thus a brief introduction to the dimensions of such variation is essential.[9] I begin with language. The indigenous peoples of Oceania speak roughly 1,200 extant or historically recorded languages. Of these, about 450 belong to the well-defined and geographically widespread *Austronesian* family (Map 2). The Austronesian languages (which in total number about 1,000) are found as far west as Madagascar, and they include most of the

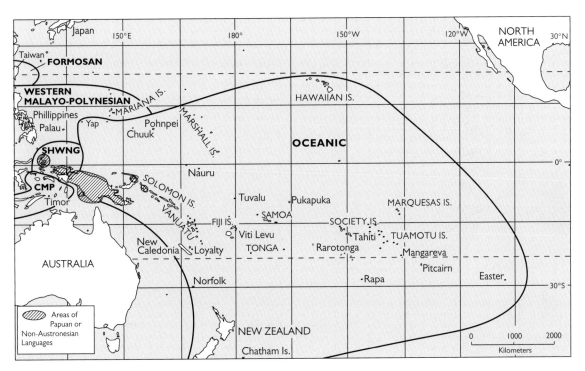

MAP 2 The distribution of the Austronesian and Non-Austronesian languages in Oceania. The Non-Austronesian languages are situated in the shaded areas, while the heavy lines delineate several major subgroups of Austronesian languages. SHWNG, South Halmahera–West New Guinea; CMP, Central Malayo-Polynesian.

languages of island Southeast Asia (including the aboriginal languages of Taiwan), the majority of languages spoken in Melanesia outside New Guinea, and all the languages spoken within Micronesia and Polynesia. Moreover, with few exceptions (in western Micronesia) the Austronesian languages spoken in Oceania all belong to one particular subgroup known as *Oceanic* (Pawley and Ross 1995). This linguistic distribution pattern proves to be of great culture-historical significance, as discussed further in Chapter 4.

On the large island of New Guinea, and in a few scattered locales elsewhere in Near Oceania (such as on New Britain and Bougainville Islands), the indigenous languages are *Non-Austronesian* or, as they are sometimes called, *Papuan* (Foley 1986).

There are an estimated 750 Papuan languages, but these emphatically do not form a single, coherent (i.e., "genetically related") language family, as with Austronesian. Rather, the linguistic diversity encompassed within the Papuan group is enormous, and several family-level groups (or "phyla") are included under this rubric. Many of the Papuan languages are nonetheless historically related (such as those of the Trans–New Guinea Phylum), even though not all of them may have descended from a common *ursprache* or proto-language. What is crucial is that in contrast to the Austronesian languages, the Papuan languages display significantly greater variation and diversity, with profound historical implications. In particular, there had to have been a substantially greater time depth for the differentiation of the Papuan languages, correlating with the much deeper time span of human occupation of New Guinea and Near Oceania, as archaeology has shown (see Chapter 3).

Although my emphasis is on archaeological evidence, I will at times refer to linguistic evidence, models, and interpretations. Perhaps to a greater extent than in any other major region of the world, in the Pacific archaeologists and historical linguists enjoy a fruitful collaboration. Our data and methods are different and our conclusions are derived independently, but both groups of scholars are concerned with cultural history (Pawley and Ross 1993, 1995). Significantly, historical linguistic work on Pacific languages utilizes the comparative method, a theoretically and empirically well-grounded set of techniques for establishing the "genetic" or historical relationships among a set of related languages, as well as for reconstructing the vocabularies (and associated semantic meanings) of various ancestral or proto-languages (Hoeningswald 1960, 1973; Trask 1996:202–40). Trask (1996:208) calls the comparative method "the single most important tool in the historical linguist's toolkit," and it must not be confused with other methods, such as lexicostatistics, that depend on crude statistical comparisons and may not yield accurate language family histories or relationships (e.g., Dyen 1965). As Pawley and Ross (1995:40–43) explain, the comparative method is based on neither typology nor statistics, but rather builds upon rigorous comparison of extensive sets of words or morphemes in groups of languages hypothesized to be historically related (cognate sets), thereby determining patterns of regular sound correspondences. Only when such patterns have been worked out does the historical linguist turn to the task of generating a "subgrouping model" or "family tree" of relationships among the languages under consideration. With such a model in hand, in which branches of

related languages are robustly marked by sets of shared innovations, one can then begin to reconstruct ancient vocabulary sets and their cultural domains. In this book, I will periodically refer to the subgrouping models of Pacific linguists, as well as to reconstructed proto-vocabulary, to assess independently how these stack up against the evidence of archaeology.

Turning to human biological variation, it is doubtless risky to summarize the great diversity of Pacific human populations in a few short paragraphs. Earlier in this century, pioneering physical anthropologists sought to classify the diverse populations of the Pacific into a small set of "races," such as Negroid, Negritoid, Australoid, or Polynesian (the latter being regarded as a "mixed race").[10] Modern biological anthropologists have shrived themselves of this kind of racial pigeonholing and endeavor to study "populations," using an array of both phenotypic (e.g., anthropometric, dermatoglyphic) and genetic (e.g., mitochondrial DNA, blood polymorphisms) characteristics. Whatever measures are used, the diversity within Oceanic populations is far from even.

The peoples who inhabit Polynesia, while displaying considerable differences in body form, are nonetheless a relatively homogeneous group when compared with other Oceanic populations. Along with the people of Fiji, the Polynesians generally link together robustly in statistical analyses. Populations distributed within Micronesia are somewhat more varied than those of Polynesia. Most diverse of all, however—*almost to the point of defying description*—are the populations distributed within the geographic area of Melanesia. "Melanesian" human biological diversity is immense, once having been described by Harvard anthropologist W. W. Howells as "so protean and varied as to resist satisfactory analysis" (1970:192). As with language, Melanesia (and particularly the part we call Near Oceania) proves to be the most diverse sector of the Oceanic world, and this is again an observation with considerable historical significance, since diversity frequently implies great time depth.

Yet the immense biological diversity found within Near Oceania is neither wholly random nor unpatterned. Recent investigations of genetic variation in this region (e.g., Friedlaender, ed., 1987; Hill and Serjeantson, eds., 1989; Lum and Cann 1998; Merriwether et al. 1999) indicate strong correlations between certain genetic markers and populations as defined on the basis of linguistic criteria (especially the distinction between Austronesian and Non-Austronesian speakers). For example, J. W. Froehlich (1987) used fingerprints (dermatoglyphs), which are highly heritable characters, to look at phylogenetic patterns among Solomon Island populations. He found that "despite an accumulation of . . . local effects, and with local relationships sometimes obscured by sampling variance, the fingerprint gene pools still reflect a broadly geographical and presumably historical distinction between [Non-Austronesian-] and [Austronesian]-speaking people" (1987:206). The same has recently been demonstrated for a particular 9-base-pair deletion in matrilineally inherited mitochondrial DNA (Merriwether et al. 1999). Thus the great biological heterogeneity of Melanesia is not without its underlying patterns, reflecting the deep and complex history from which they have arisen. Synchronic patterns of human biological variation in Oceania offer another kind of "text" from which history may be read, given appropriate conceptual and methodological tools.

Culturally, the peoples of Oceania also vary greatly, with similarities and differences that reflect patterns frequently cross-cutting the old categories of Melanesia and Micronesia, although again Polynesia (as with language) tends to hold up as a robust group of closely related cultures. Many aspects of culture are widely shared throughout Oceania, such as a subsistence economy typically based on tropical root, tuber, and tree-crop horticulture, augmented (for coastal dwellers and small-island populations) by fishing. Yet within these broad similarities much variation persists: in the emphasis accorded particular crops, in the mode of agricultural intensification, and in fishing techniques. Another aspect of overall similarity is undeniably an emphasis on watercraft and open-ocean voyaging. Yet even here, on close inspection of technological details one finds amazing diversity in the distribution patterns of lashing methods, sail types, and outrigger forms, yielding hypotheses concerning the historical development of sailing traditions (Haddon and Hornell 1936–38; Horridge 1987). For example, the extremely wide distribution of the Oceanic *lanteen sail* throughout the island Pacific strongly implies that this was the sail type used on the canoes of early Austronesian speakers when they rapidly dispersed across Remote Oceania beginning around 1200 B.C. (see Chapter 4). On the other hand, the restriction of the Oceanic *spritsail* to Eastern Polynesia shows this to be a later, and independent, development. Thus in ethnographically documented patterns of culture—as in language and biology—one may read fragments of the history of Pacific islanders.

Other aspects of Oceanic cultures are yet more varied: systems of kinship reckoning and descent, spiritual beliefs, and ritual practices. Descent reckoning, for instance, ranges from matrilineal systems, such as those found in parts of Melanesia (e.g., New Britain, New Ireland) and Micronesia (e.g., Truk), to patrilineal systems (e.g., those in southern Vanuatu and New Caledonia), to ambilineal or cognatic systems (which dominate in Polynesia but are also found elsewhere). A distinction between political organization based on principles of chiefship versus those of "big man–ship" was at one time thought to distinguish Polynesian from Melanesian cultures definitively (Sahlins 1963). More ethnohistorically and ethnographically informed work now suggests that true "big man" societies are typical of the Papuan-speaking groups of New Guinea, whereas Austronesian-speaking island Melanesians characteristically had some form of hereditary leadership (e.g., Guiart 1963; Scaglion 1996). But this is not the venue to rehearse a litany of cultural traits and their distributions. Suffice it to say that the cultural patterns practiced by the varied peoples of Oceania are the products of history, a history whose outlines are finally emerging through the insights of archaeology and historical anthropology.

About This Book

I close this introduction by addressing what this book is intended to cover, what I have chosen to emphasize, and what I have had to leave out. I am painfully aware of how much simply could not be mentioned in a book that takes as its scope such a vast segment of the world, encompassing more than 40,000 years of human history, perhaps 5,000 islands, and a panoply of peoples and cultures. I have authored entire books (Kirch 1984a, 1985a, 1997a) on topics covered here in a mere chapter or less, and colleagues have done the same for other regions (e.g., Davidson 1984; Spriggs 1997; White and O'Connell 1982). How to reduce the subtleties of data and argument, the complexities of history that have required entire scholarly monographs, to a few succinct pages? Yet grand syntheses are valuable—arguably essential—in an age of exponentially expanding information, not only in traditional print media but in cyberspace as well. Only a few committed scholars and students can possibly take the time to read and digest for themselves all the relevant articles,

chapters, monographs, and books underpinning a work such as this.

In the end, my choice of what to include and what to ignore—or at best to relegate to a footnote—has been dictated by my own predilections, my personal view of what is most interesting in Oceanic history. In this I have taken a broad, generalizing, and above all comparative perspective, for I believe that the long-term human history of Oceania, although inherently interesting in its own right, is worth studying for what it tells us more generally about the human career. This does not mean that I espouse an extreme positivist stance, such as that adopted by some proponents of the "New Archaeology" in the late 1960s and early 1970s. These scholars wrongly, in my view, pursued an experimental model of science (of which physics was the exemplar), claiming that archaeology could be a kind of *predictive* social science. Not at all. Archaeology and historical anthropology are *historical* sciences: they *retrodict* rather than predict, and they must take account of contingency and chance, as well as general principles and processes of human behavior and evolution. Thus our mode of explanation is properly the "historical narrative," guided by general principles of social science as constrained by empirical evidence (see Mayr 1982, 1997).[11] But as in our sister historical disciplines, generalization and comparison are also valid aims and goals; we can aspire to more than the documentation of the particular and the contingent. "History matters," it has been said, and I take that simple phrase to heart in the multiplicity of its connotations.

Hence I have tried to keep my writerly vision on the far horizon, while not neglecting too much the local particulars on which valid generalization and comparison must always build. This means, however, that some particulars, such as the details of artifacts and artifactually based sequences, will be touched upon only lightly. As in any part of the world, Oceania has a formidable literature dealing with the classification and analysis—both stylistic and functional—of the varied forms of material culture yielded up by its sites: in our case not only pottery, but also fishhooks, stone and shell adzes, ornaments, and other items. Such materials I have had to mention only briefly, with sufficient references to the specialized literature that those who wish to pursue the details can be guided to the relevant sources. Rather, I emphasize aspects of the archaeological record that I personally find of greater utility in comparative synthesizing: settlement patterns and their ideologically indexed architectural components, evidence for economic systems and their intensification, patterns of population growth, paleoenvironmental indications of land use and misuse, and material signals of interaction between island groups, whether over shorter or longer distances, to name a few.

The structure of this book and the coverage given to some regions and temporal periods also inevitably reflect the history and current state of archaeological research in Oceania. The Pleistocene period in Near Oceania, for example, has only been revealed through archaeological research since about 1985, and the number of excavated and well-published sites remains limited. Polynesia stands in striking contrast, because both surface and stratigraphic archaeology have a much longer history there, for which the published literature now runs to thousands of citations. Consequently, my treatment of the Pleistocene in Near Oceania is limited to a single chapter of modest length, whereas Polynesia commands two chapters. Near Oceania is not less intrinsically interesting; it

will simply require more decades of hard and concerted effort to build up an archaeological record comparable to that of Polynesia.

Such then are my biases, as well as the constraints imposed by the state of our knowledge. *Caveat lector.*

A Note on Dates and Time

Professional archaeologists agonize over the complexities of radiocarbon and other techniques of "absolute" dating, painfully aware that the conversion of such "dates" into actual calendar years is not straightforward, and in fact often problematic. Because this book is intended for a broad audience, I generally avoid representing time in radiocarbon years, although in some cases it is necessary (or important) to do so. Whenever radiocarbon years are given, these are "years before present" (B.P.), and a standard deviation is also provided if a specific age determination is being cited. In the tables of sites, time spans are also given as B.P. ages or ranges, since these are based on radiocarbon dates; the interested reader should consult the references provided in the tables for specific ^{14}C dates and calibrated age ranges. Otherwise, I have used the more familiar B.C./A.D. system for general time periods. The reader should bear in mind, however, that such "calendar" dates have usually been derived from radiocarbon age estimates and their calibrations, and therefore do not have the precision associated with dates derived from historical (written) texts. In most cases, general ages given for sites or phenomena have been rounded out to the nearest century.

CHAPTER I

Discovering the Oceanic Past

While this [excavation] was in progress, in May of 1950, word came of W. F. Libby's momentous discovery of a method for dating charcoal through measuring radioactivity. A sample of charcoal from a fireplace [in Kuli'ou'ou Rockshelter] ... was submitted ... revealing that the shelter had been occupied about A.D. 1004. This was the first radiocarbon date from any island in the Pacific and it opened up undreamed of possibilities for reconstructing the prehistory of the area.

Emory (in Emory et al. 1959:ix)

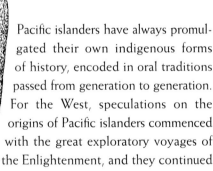

Pacific islanders have always promulgated their own indigenous forms of history, encoded in oral traditions passed from generation to generation. For the West, speculations on the origins of Pacific islanders commenced with the great exploratory voyages of the Enlightenment, and they continued as missionaries and other Europeans began to settle in the islands. In the late nineteenth century, the academic development of ethnology and archaeology had its local reflection in the founding of scholarly institutions in the Pacific. The kinds of evidence sought by scholars who have debated Oceanic prehistory have changed radically over the years; *archaeology* has come into its own only since World War II. Prior to E. W. Gifford's pioneering work in Fiji in 1947, most anthropologists were convinced that the Pacific islands lacked a stratified record of cultural change.[1] To appreciate fully our current understanding of Pacific prehistory and archaeology, some historical perspective is essential. This chapter traces the intellectual background to Pacific prehistory and archaeology over two centuries, providing a mirror for reflection on our own contemporary approaches and perspectives.

Enlightenment Voyagers

Within decades after Magellan crossed the Pacific in 1520–21, Spanish galleons annually plied the equatorial seaways from America to Guam (where the Spanish established a small settlement replete with stone forts) and on to Manila, returning to Acapulco via a tedious and often fatal North Pacific

passage. Seeking to extend Spanish imperial interests, Mendaña led his ill-fated expedition to colonize the Islands of Solomon in 1595. Dutch expeditions under the command of Schouten and Le Maire (in 1615), Tasman (in 1642), and Roggeveen (in 1721) advanced European geographic and cartographic knowledge of the Pacific Ocean. The motives for all of these early voyages were entirely commercial or imperial, and the explorers' journals give little hint of any intellectual curiosity regarding the "Other." Then, as the intellectual movement known as the Enlightenment gathered steam in the latter part of the eighteenth century, interest in the peoples of the Pacific exploded. Louis de Bougainville returned from Tahiti in 1769 with reports that set the salons of Paris buzzing, inspiring Denis Diderot (author of the famous *Encyclopédie*) to write his *Supplément au Voyage de Bougainville*, musing on social tolerance and sexual freedom. Jean-Jacques Rousseau based his concept of *l'homme naturel* on the Tahitian model. The peoples of the South Seas were suddenly incorporated within the Enlightenment project.

The three expeditions of Captain James Cook, under the joint patronage of the British Admiralty and the Royal Society of London, exemplify the Enlightenment voyage of discovery, whose goals were as much the advancement of natural science as the expansion of empire (Fig. 1.1). By the tragic third voyage (1776–80), Cook had seen more of the Pacific—interacting extensively and often sensitively with its inhabitants—than any prior European explorer. Cook was struck by the similarities he perceived among the peoples we now call Polynesians, whom he encountered on such widely separated islands as New Zealand, Easter Island, Tahiti, Tonga, and the newly discovered

Hawaiian group. Lying off Easter Island in 1774 while on his second voyage, Cook mused that "it is extraordinary that the same Nation should have spread themselves over all the isles in this vast Ocean from New Zealand to this island which is almost a fourth part of the circumference of the globe" (Beaglehole, ed., 1969:354). The high degree of relatedness in language was one line of evidence that Cook and his fellow voyagers particularly noticed. By the third voyage, Cook had outlined a theory of origins:

> From what continent they originally emigrated, and by what steps they have spread through so vast a space, those who are curious in disquisitions of this nature, may perhaps not find it very difficult to conjecture. It has been already observed, that they bear strong marks of affinity to some of the Indian tribes, that inhabit the Ladrones [Marianas] and Caroline Islands; and the same affinity may again be traced amongst the Battas and the Malays. When these events happened, it is not so easy to ascertain; it was probably not very lately, as they are extremely populous, and have no tradition of their own origin, but what is perfectly fabulous; whilst, on the other hand, the unadulterated state of their general language, and the simplicity which still prevails in their customs and manners, seem to indicate that it could not have been at any very distant period. (*Quoted in Howard 1967:46*)

The Enlightenment tradition of grand exploratory expeditions persisted after Cook well into the nineteenth century, under the command of such notables as La Pérouse, Vancouver, D'Entrecasteaux, Labillardière, Krusenstern, Kotzebue, Freycinet, and Dumont d'Urville (Fig. 1.2). It was Dumont d'Urville who burdened us with the tripartite classification of Pacific peoples as Polynesians, Melanesians, and Micronesians. The great expeditionary period culminated in 1838–42 with the United States Exploring Expedition under the command of Charles Wilkes, whose scientific results were published in a limited set of grand volumes. Volume 6, *Ethnography and Philology* by Horatio Hale (1846), deserves special notice. Like Cook, Hale was impressed with the linguistic connections among Pacific populations, and he developed a theory of Polynesian origins grounded in careful philological comparisons. As Howard (1967:50) comments, "on the basis of his research [Hale] concluded that the progress of emigration was from west to east, and that the Polynesians belong to the same race as that which peoples the East Indian Islands." Hale elaborated a putative sequence of migrations within Polynesia, with the Fiji group being the primary staging area:

> The original scene is probably on the Feejee Group. A party of Melanesians, or Papuans, arrive first at this group, and settle principally on the extensive alluvial plain which stretches along the eastern coast of Viti-levu. Afterwards a second company of emigrants, of the Polynesian race, perhaps from some island in the East Indies, called Bulotu, make their appearance, and finding the western coast unoccupied, establish themselves upon it. The two thus divide the land between them, and are known to one another as eastern people and western people, or Viti and Tonga. (*1846:178*)

In his reliance on linguistic comparisons, as well as his linking of Polynesian origins to the island Southeast Asian region, Hale prefigures contemporary scholarly debates regarding Pacific prehistory.

Outposts of Empire: Missionaries, Colonists, and Academic Beginnings

Well before the United States belatedly organized its own Exploring Expedition in 1838, the Pacific islands were under the sway of expanding

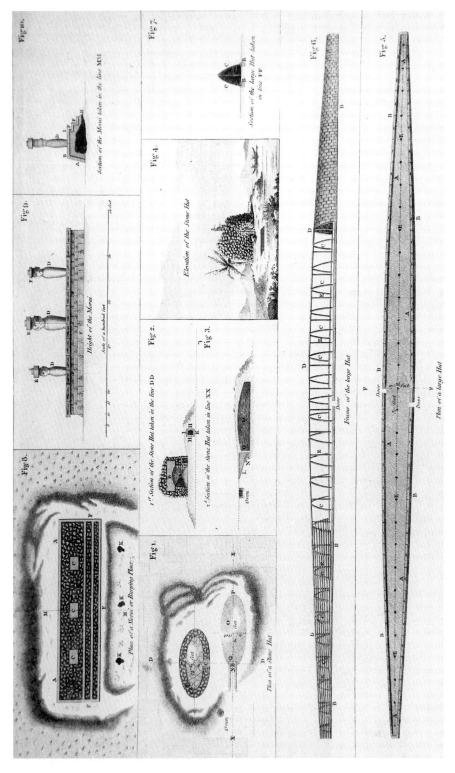

FIGURE I.2 "Geometrical Details of the Monuments of Easter Island," as recorded by the draftsman of La Pérouse's voyage around the world. This engraving, showing details of Easter Island *chu* temples and stone houses, is one of the earliest archaeological plans recorded for the Pacific. (Engraved 1798; collection of the author)

proselytizing, commercial, and imperial designs. The Société de Marie (French), London Missionary Society, and American Board of Commissioners for Foreign Missions (Boston) each had dispatched parties of missionaries to various (primarily Polynesian) destinations in Oceania. These purveyors of the faith took a great interest in the languages, cultures, and traditions of the peoples they endeavored to convert. Some, like William Ellis (1830), wrote substantial ethnographic tracts. Ellis's origin theory had the ancestral Polynesians migrating from Asia via the Bering Straits and down the western coast of North America, thereby avoiding the problem of how these peoples could "have made their way against constant tradewinds prevailing within the tropics" (Ellis 1830, II:48).

The missionaries established orthographies for indigenous languages, encouraging large numbers of Polynesians to become literate. Some Polynesians—such as David Malo and Samuel Kamakau in Hawai'i, Te Ariki Tara'are in Rarotonga, and Mamae in Mangaia—began to write down their own indigenous oral traditions and histories. Kamakau's *Ruling Chiefs of Hawaii* (1961) remains a remarkable record of indigenous political history, regularly consulted by archaeologists (e.g., Cordy 1996) and historical ethnographers (e.g., Kirch and Sahlins 1992).

Missionaries were hardly the only Whites to settle in the islands, as colonial outposts were established in New Zealand, Tahiti, Fiji, and elsewhere.[2] Among the colonial officials were Sir George Grey (who collected a wealth of Maori oral traditions), Basil Thompson (who wrote on both Fiji and Tonga), Abraham Fornander (a magistrate of the Hawaiian government), and S. Percy Smith (who recorded Rarotongan traditions). Fornander compiled a monumental collection of Hawaiian oral traditions (*Fornander's Collection of Hawaiian Antiquities and Folk-lore*, Thrum,

ed. [1916–20]) and authored a synthetic work, *An Account of the Polynesian Race* (1878). Based on his own reading of Polynesian oral traditions, Fornander proposed an elaborate theory of Polynesian origins:

> I think the facts collected . . . will warrant the conclusion that the various branches of the family . . . are descended from a people that was agnate to, but far older than, the Vedic family of the Arian race; that it entered India before these Vedic Arians; that there it underwent a mixture with the Dravidian race, which . . . has permanently affected its complexion; that there also . . . it became moulded to the Cushite-Arabian civilization of that time; that, whether driven out of India by force, or voluntarily leaving for colonizing purposes, it established itself in the Indian Archipelago at an early period, and spread itself from Sumatra to Timor and Luzon. (1878:159)

From island Southeast Asia, Fornander traced the Polynesian ancestors to Fiji, then to Samoa and Tonga, and finally to the far-flung islands of the eastern Pacific. Fornander's ideas carried great force in Polynesian studies, well into the early twentieth century.

Like Fornander, S. Percy Smith (1921) relied heavily upon Polynesian oral traditions, primarily those of Rarotonga (Cook Islands) and Taranaki (New Zealand). Smith postulated an Indian homeland for the Polynesians, and using genealogies he put unduly precise calendrical dates on events, such as a migration from Java to Fiji and then the Lau Islands between A.D. 0 and 450 (1921: 158–59), associated with the names of ancient chiefs such as Vai-takere and Tu-tarangi.

At the *fin de siècle*, as the fields of ethnology and anthropology were being formally defined in European and American universities, academic institutions also sprung up in leading Pacific cen-

FIGURE 1.3 The Bernice Pauahi Bishop Museum, shown here not long after its founding in 1889, became a leading research center for Polynesian archaeology and ethnology. The museum was constructed of local basalt blocks quarried on site. (Photo courtesy Bishop Museum Archives.)

ters (Rose 1980). In New Zealand, The Polynesian Society was established in 1892 "to promote the study of the Anthropology, Ethnology, Philology, History, and Antiquities of the Polynesian race," principally through the publication of a *Journal* bearing its name (which has been in continuous publication ever since). Equally significant was the founding, in 1889 at Honolulu, of the Bernice Pauahi Bishop Museum of Polynesian Ethnology and Natural History, a memorial to the last of the Kamehameha dynasty of ruling chiefs that incorporated their collection of Hawaiian ethnographic materials (Fig. 1.3). The Bishop Museum's first director, William T. Brigham (Fig. 1.4), held the post until 1919, authoring innovative monographs on Polynesian ethnology, including *Stone Implements and Stone Work of the Ancient Hawaiians* (1902). In New Zealand, the Dominion Museum in Wellington and the Otago Museum in Dunedin provided similar institutional bases for scholars such as Elsdon Best, who carried out important research on Maori *pa* fortifications (Best 1927).

In this premodern period of academic anthropology, archaeology (or the study of "antiquities")

was not yet distinguished from ethnology, and the same practitioners undertook both ethnographic work and museum studies of artifacts. They stressed systematic description and classification of material culture, as published in the Bishop Museum and Dominion Museum monographs. Some actual excavation, however, was undertaken. As early as 1872 Julius Von Haast in New Zealand excavated sites in South Island where prehistoric artifacts (Fig. 1.5) were comingled with the bones of extinct *moa* birds. This led to considerable digging in South Island sites and the amassing of museum collections of unearthed artifacts (generally lacking stratigraphic provenience). In 1913, John F. G. Stokes of the Bishop Museum excavated a stratified rockshelter on Kahoʻolawe in the Hawaiian Islands, recovering bone fishhooks and other objects. Unlike his contemporaries in New Zealand, Stokes recognized and followed the stratigraphy present in the Kamohio rockshelter, but his careful notes on these associations were ignored when J. G. McAllister (1933b) wrote up the site two decades later. Stokes (1991) also surveyed temple sites on Molokaʻi and Hawaiʻi,

FIGURE 1.4 William T. Brigham, the founding director of the Bishop Museum, with his staff about 1901. Left to right: A. M. Wolcott, assistant to the director; Alvin Seale, collector; J. J. Greene, printer; Brigham; William A. Bryan, ornithologist; J. F. G. Stokes, ethnologist. (Photo courtesy Bishop Museum Archives.)

in an effort to test Bishop Museum Director Brigham's theory of a two-stage development of Hawaiian religion (Dye 1989).

Another archaeological pioneer of the premodern period, Katherine Scoresby Routledge, led a remarkable expedition to Easter Island between 1913 and 1916 (see Fischer 1997:125–39). Routledge's description of her "research design" contrasts wonderfully with contemporary academic jargon: "When . . . we decided to see the Pacific before we died, and asked the anthropological authorities at the British Museum what work there remained to be done, the answer was 'Easter Island.' It was a much larger undertaking than had been contemplated; we had doubts of our capacity for so important a venture" (1919:3–4).

Not the least of her doubts concerned the extreme difficulty of getting to remote Easter Island, well off commercial steamship routes. "It was therefore decided, as Scoresby is a keen yachtsman, that it was worth while to procure in England a little ship of our own, adapted to the

purpose, and to sail out in her" (1919:4). The 90-foot *Mana* provided Routledge a base of operations as she carried out the first thorough exploration of Easter Island's unique statuary complex. Based on her field studies, Routledge correctly concluded that "various links connect the people now living on Easter Island with the great images," and that these were "the work of the ancestors" of the Polynesian-speaking Rapa Nui people (1919:291). Routledge published only a popular, but nonetheless invaluable, account of her fieldwork (1919), and for many years her original notes were feared lost. (Routledge herself was tragically committed to a mental institution during her later years.) Her notes have been relocated and constitute a mine of ethnographic as well as archaeological data.

Anthropological interest in Oceania was intense at the *fin de siècle*, marked by what Welsch (ed., 1998:565) calls the "expedition period" of ethnological research. Among the great expeditions of this age were the duly famous Cambridge Torres

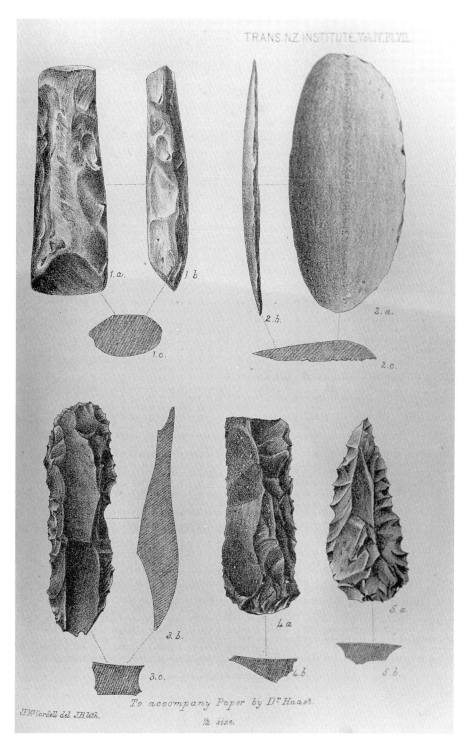

1. a.   *1. b.*

2. b.   *2. a.*

1. c.

2. c.

3. b.

4 a   *5. a.*

3. c.   *4. b.*   *5. b.*

To accompany Paper by Dr Haast.

JFMcCordell del. JB lith.

½ size.

FIGURE 1.5 Prehistoric artifacts found by Julius Von Haast in association with *moa* bones in New Zealand. (From Von Haast 1872.)

Straits Expedition led by A. C. Haddon (Herle and Rouse, eds., 1998), the ethnographic survey of Papua led by C. G. Seligman (1910), the Percy Sladen Trust Expedition under W. H. R. Rivers (1914),[3] and the Joseph N. Field South Pacific Expedition directed by A. B. Lewis (Welsch, ed., 1998). All of these expeditions focused on Melanesia, while the German Hamburg (*Peiho*) Expedition spanned Melanesia and Micronesia (Thilenius 1902). Despite early emphasis on Melanesia, the focus of most ethnographic and archaeological work soon shifted to Polynesia, and it would remain there as far as archaeology is concerned until recently.

Over the first two decades of the twentieth century, Pacific anthropology gradually took on the scholarly apparatus of academia, increasingly dominated by younger investigators credentialed with doctoral degrees (Harvard awarded its first Ph.D. degree in anthropology in 1894). Anthropology in these early years had a strong historical orientation, promulgated by such leaders as Franz Boas at Columbia, Roland Dixon at Harvard, and Alfred Kroeber at Berkeley (Stocking 1982). Another major figure, Edward Sapir, laid out the methodological basis for historical anthropology in his classic work *Time Perspective in Aboriginal American Culture* (1916). Although archaeological evidence played a role in Sapir's scheme, it was subordinated to comparative ethnography and linguistics, a bias that influenced Pacific historical reconstruction until after World War II. This relegation of archaeology to a minor role reflects the absence of a method for independent dating or temporal control (radiocarbon dating was not invented until the late 1940s). As Bruce Trigger (1989) observes, Americanist archaeology during the first half of the twentieth century was absorbed in developing methods—such as time-sensitive artifact classification and seriation—for reconstructing cultural sequences in the absence

of corroborating historical texts (such as Old World hieroglyphics or cuneiform tablets). The Pacific islands lacked not only written texts but also pottery, leaving only monumental architecture and stone tools as the main objects of archaeological study (e.g., Best 1927; Brigham 1902; Routledge 1919).

"The Problem of Polynesian Origins"

The year 1920 marked a watershed in Pacific anthropology. Herbert E. Gregory, Silliman Professor of Geology at Yale University and chairman of the Committee on Pacific Investigations of the National Research Council, had just been appointed director at the Bishop Museum in Honolulu. Gregory brought to his new post an academic association with Yale and $40,000 (a substantial sum of money at the time), donated to the university by a stockbroker alumnus, Bayard Dominick, and designated for Polynesian research (Gregory 1921:13). Gregory convened the first Pan-Pacific Science Conference in Honolulu, which drew up a set of *Recommendations for Anthropological Research in Polynesia*, including archaeology (Rehbock 1988). "Since Polynesian archaeology is in most respects a virgin field, the first problem is to make island surveys. . . . Such a survey should not only reveal the content of the archaeology for the island examined but should give hints of time relations and local variations" (Gregory, ed., 1921:117).

With ample Yale funds at his disposal, Gregory implemented the Bayard Dominick Expeditions to make good on the recommendations of the Pan-Pacific Science Conference and thus resolve "the problem of Polynesian origins" (Gregory 1921:13–15). Four field teams, consisting of young and energetic graduate students from elite American universities, were rapidly assembled and dispatched to the Marquesas, Tonga, Australs, and

Hawai'i. Each team included an ethnologist to study social organization and religion, and an archaeologist to attend to stone structures and material culture, "with necessary interpreters and assistants . . . stationed at strategic points to make the studies necessary to establish standards of physical form, material culture, traditions, and language of the Polynesians" (1921:14). The teams were furnished with calipers and standardized "anthropometrical cards on which to record the physical characteristics of as large a number as possible of the native inhabitants of the islands under study" (Hiroa 1945:45). These "somatological" data were to be worked up by Louis R. Sullivan and, later, Harry Shapiro of the American Museum of Natural History. In short, the Bayard Dominick Expeditions implemented the first modern, *holistic* anthropological study of Polynesia, following Sapir's (1916) proposed methodology for historical reconstruction.

In retrospect, archaeology played a subordinate role in the Bayard Dominick Expeditions. In the Marquesas, Ralph Linton precipitately decided that the islands "offer few opportunities for archaeological research; . . . no opportunity was afforded for the gradual accumulation of stratified deposits and so far as known no kitchen middens or shell heaps exist in the islands" (1925:3). Linton made this negative assessment without having put a spade in the ground, for decades later the Marquesas would prove to have one of the richest archaeological records of any Polynesian archipelago (Suggs 1961). John F. G. Stokes, more attuned to the potential of archaeology and already seasoned by fieldwork in Hawai'i, led the Austral Islands team and surveyed fortified village sites on Rapa Island (Fig. 1.6). Unfortunately, he was slow to produce his monograph, and after a falling out with Director Gregory, Stokes's manuscript (Stokes, ms. a) was shelved in the museum's archives, where it has languished to this day.

In Tonga, William C. McKern was only slightly less pessimistic: "On first consideration, the archaeological outlook in Tonga is not promising. The student finds here a mottled field, poor in stratified deposits attributable to human sources, but rich in artificial monuments of earth and stone" (1929:4). But McKern, at least, tried to dig, and he was rewarded with the discovery of pottery, previously unknown in Tonga. "At several scattered places [pottery] was found, in stratified deposits, occurring most plentifully in strata free from evidence of European contact" (1929:116). Yet, stymied by the lack of a method for ceramic dating, McKern mistakenly interpreted his sherds as a variant of late prehistoric Fijian pottery, with no great time depth. Had McKern been aware of nearly identical pottery found by a Belgian priest (Meyer 1909) on tiny Watom Island, 4,500 kilometers to the west, he might have realized that his Tongan potsherds were actually of considerable antiquity, holding clues to the earliest phase of human settlement in Remote Oceania (the Lapita cultural complex; see Chapter 4). However, the opportunity was missed, and the task of reconstructing Pacific prehistory was handed over to the ethnologists.

Edward S. C. Handy, head of the Marquesan party of the Bayard Dominick Expeditions, quickly rose to prominence in Polynesian studies. Ignoring the limited evidence of archaeology (and Sapir's careful methodology), Handy promulgated a theory of Polynesian origins and migrations, but one little improved over the earlier efforts of Abraham Fornander and S. Percy Smith. Based on his Tahitian ethnographic data, Handy laid out a complex diffusionist scheme, in which various Polynesian culture "traits" were correlated with "Brahmanical" and "Buddhistic" cultures from India, Indo-China, Malaysia, and China (Handy 1930a; see also Linton 1923).

Handy's and Linton's views did not go down well with all ethnologists, for some were increasingly

FIGURE 1.6 Bishop Museum ethnologist John F. G. Stokes and his wife on the dock at Rapa Island in 1920, during the Bayard Dominick Expedition. Stokes was a pioneer in Polynesian archaeology, in many respects ahead of his time. (Photo courtesy Bishop Museum Archives.)

uncomfortable with the diffusionist paradigm promoted by certain German scholars such as Fritz Gräbner (1905) of the *Kulturkreise* school (see Harris 1968:382–92), which was at odds with the careful historical particularism of Franz Boas and Edward Sapir.[4] In a work whose sophisticated culture theory was ahead of its time, Edwin Burrows (1938) argued that differences between Western Polynesian and Eastern Polynesian cultures had resulted from in situ cultural processes, such as local development and the abandonment or rejection of ideas; decades later, archaeology would lend support to Burrows's ideas. Ralph Piddington, the posthumous editor of Robert W. Williamson's (1924) voluminous comparative works on Polynesian social organization and religion, also attacked Handy's diffusionist history.[5] But Piddington likewise failed to grasp that archaeology could contribute more directly to knowledge of the past.[6] His view was that archaeology had "failed to produce any integrated body of historical conclusions," and that this was

> partly due to the fact that the types of culture revealed by archaeological investigation in Polynesia do not vary greatly from those which were prevalent when the islands were first discovered. . . . This means, in effect, that there are definite limits to what archaeology can add to our knowledge of Polynesian material culture; and that it implies for the most part nothing more than a duplication of [ethnographic] information already available. There is therefore little hope of the emergence of any series of culture types such as have been established in other parts of the world. (*Piddington 1939:334–35*)

FIGURE 1.7 Bishop Museum ethnologist Kenneth P. Emory (center), member of the Hawaiian team of the Bayard Dominick Expedition, during excavations at the Hanakauhi group of structures in Haleakala Crater, Maui Island, 1920. This was Emory's first field project in Polynesia. (Photo courtesy Bishop Museum Archives.)

Underpinning this bold but erroneous statement was the unquestioned rejection of any in situ cultural change or development in Pacific island cultures. Archaeology, in Piddington's narrow vision, revealed material vestiges that merely duplicated what was already documented ethnographically. No stratified record of cultural change existed. All was static and timeless in Oceania; truly, these were "peoples without history."

Remarkably, given this stultifying perspective, a certain amount of basic field archaeology was accomplished in the Pacific before World War II, mostly in Polynesia. Kenneth P. Emory (Fig. 1.7), Wendell C. Bennett, J. G. McAllister, and others mapped and recorded stone structures in Hawai'i, the Society Islands, the equatorial atolls, and elsewhere, and used these data to advocate historical hypotheses regarding Polynesian migrations (Bennett 1931; Emory 1921, 1924, 1928, 1933,

1934a, 1934b; McAllister 1933a, 1933b). In Micronesia, Laura Thompson (1932) synthesized collections excavated by two amateurs on Guam and other Marianas Islands. Yet, despite continued excavations in New Zealand (e.g., Duff 1942; Lockerbie 1940; Skinner 1923–24), virtually all Pacific archaeology prior to World War II was restricted to surface survey, and to the description and classification of material culture.[7]

Physical anthropologists of the 1920s and 1930s also weighed in on the debates concerning Polynesian origins. Harvard's Roland Dixon (1929) regarded the Polynesians as a mixture of several migratory "waves" (including Australoids, Oceanic Negroids, Caucasics, and Mongoloids), each with their own distinctive somatic characteristics. Similarly, Louis Sullivan (1924), who tabulated and analyzed the anthropometric observations obtained by the Bayard Dominick field parties, wrote that "Anthropologists have disagreed on the racial affinities of the Polynesians. Some have classified them as Mongols, others have classified them as Caucasians, while still others have maintained that they are a separate race. This in itself is strong evidence that *the Polynesians are a badly mixed people* for whenever there has been a general disagreement as to the racial affinities of any group it has been found almost invariably that the group was a non-homogeneous group" (1924:22, emphasis added).

From the perspective of modern population biology such statements—antiquated at best, perniciously racist at worst—are representative of the typological ("pigeonholing") thinking of this period. In the decades leading up to World War II, they helped to fuel White American views on racial purity and the desirability of restricting alien immigration, especially of "Asiatic races."[8] One outcome of this attitude was a particular shaping of the historical theories of the prominent Polynesian scholar Te Rangi Hiroa.

Te Rangi Hiroa and the "Micronesian Route" to Polynesia

Te Rangi Hiroa (Sir Peter Buck[9])—one of the most prominent Polynesian scholars of the mid-twentieth century (Fig. 1.8)—was raised in a bicultural world, learning the language and customs of his Maori mother while aspiring to the cultural institutions of his Irish father.[10] Born in 1877,[11] Hiroa attended Te Aute College, an Anglican boarding school for the children of the Maori elite, earning his medical degree at Otago Medical School in 1910. Government service as medical officer to the Maoris, and a term in the New Zealand parliament, were interrupted by his enlistment with the much-feted Maori regiment, which barely survived the debacle at Gallipoli. Even before the Great War, Hiroa was becoming

FIGURE 1.8 Te Rangi Hiroa (right) and Kenneth P. Emory (left) of the Bishop Museum at the investiture stone of Hauvivi *marae*, part of the Taputapuatea complex on Ra'iatea Island, during the Mangarevan Expedition of 1934. (Photo courtesy Bishop Museum Archives.)

entranced with ethnological research, and he published his first paper in the *Journal of the Polynesian Society* in 1910. Having made his name in New Zealand ethnography, Hiroa accepted an appointment to the Bishop Museum staff in 1927 and began to carry out field studies in tropical Polynesia. After he had served a stint as Bishop Museum Visiting Professor at Yale University in 1932–34, the museum's trustees invited Hiroa to take up the position of director upon the retirement of Herbert Gregory in 1936.

By the late 1930s, Hiroa was an internationally respected authority on Polynesian cultures, and as director of the Bishop Museum he held a prominent academic position (the director also carried the title of professor at Yale University). Yet Hiroa found himself a part-Polynesian in a society shackled by ideas of innate differences between human "races." He was proud of his Maori ancestry, yet painfully aware that many Whites viewed the Polynesians as inferiors, classified by some anthropologists (such as Sullivan and Dixon) as a "badly mixed race" incorporating both "Negroid" and "Mongoloid" elements.[12] Despite his academic fame (as well as his wartime and political service), Hiroa had failed to garner for himself the ultimate form of recognition from his mother country: a knighthood (Sorrenson, ed., 1986–88, III:262; see also Condliffe 1971:197–98).[13] This led him to seek American citizenship, but here too he ran up against racial prejudice, for to many Americans Polynesians were "Mongoloids," part of the feared "Yellow Peril."[14]

In this social and political context, Hiroa was cautiously developing a new theory of Polynesian origins, not surprisingly one that avoided any association between the Polynesian people and the dark-skinned inhabitants of Melanesia (then classified as "Oceanic Negroids"). Most theories of the time traced Polynesian migrations through Melanesia, implying that the Polynesians had a Melanesian "racial" component. As early as 1930, in reviewing River's *History of Melanesian Society*, Hiroa wrote to his friend Sir Apirana Ngata that "if you can cut out any survivals of Melanesian influence on [Polynesian] social organization so much the better" (Sorrenson, ed., 1986–88, II:78).[15] In 1938, Hiroa published his mature theory in a book intended for a broad audience: *Vikings of the Sunrise* (1938a). The endpapers comprise a map of the Pacific with arrows, bearing the caption: "The Polynesian Triangle with the northern Micronesian route and the rejected southern Melanesian theory." To avoid any taint of contamination with Melanesia, Hiroa now made the ancestral Polyne-

sians migrate from island Southeast Asia through the atolls of the Caroline and Kiribati archipelagoes. He invoked the anthropometric studies performed by the Bishop Museum, claiming that "the master mariners of the Pacific must be Europoid for they are not characterized by the woolly hair, black skins, and thin lower legs of the Negroids nor by the flat face, short stature, and drooping inner eyefold of the Mongoloids" (1938a:16).[16] Hiroa put his case as follows:

> In light of recent comparative study of the material cultures and social organizations of Melanesia and Polynesia, it seems improbable that the great migrations into the Pacific passed through Melanesia. In general the Polynesians are physically very different from the Melanesians. Had they stopped at Melanesian islands to refit their ships and gather new supplies, it is probable that racial intermixture would have taken place and that Negroid characteristics would appear consistently among Polynesians. . . .
>
> Strong support in favor of the Micronesian route lies in the positive evidence against the route through Melanesia. It is unfortunate that the original population of Micronesia had been overlain by Mongoloid elements that crept in after the ancestors of the Polynesians had passed through. Yet, in spite of the imposition of a new language throughout the area, numerous Polynesian words occur to mark the ancient trail. (*1938a:41, 45*)

Although Hiroa made it appear that the weight of evidence supported his Micronesian route theory, in fact there were problems. One of the most serious, which Hiroa himself recognized, was that the source of the Polynesian horticultural complex lay in Melanesia and could not be derived from the Micronesian atolls (1938a:307, 1945:13). Moreover, the sophisticated stone tool industries of Polynesia would have to be reinvented after a period of adaptation to shell technology in Micronesia.[17] To resolve

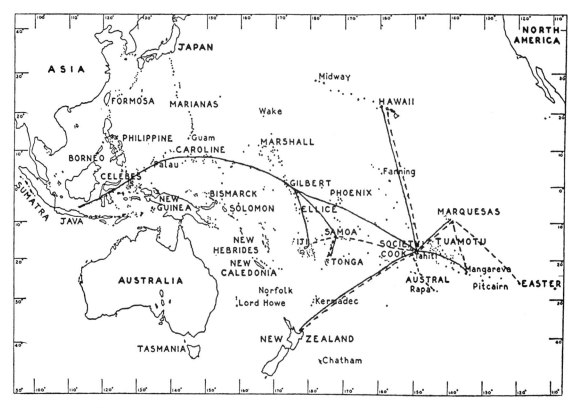

FIGURE 1.9 Te Rangi Hiroa's theory of Polynesian origins, depicting the posited "Micronesian route" of migrations. The dashed lines indicate secondary migrations. (From Hiroa 1944.)

these problems, Hiroa had the Polynesians re-acquire food plants and domestic animals from the Melanesians in Fiji, via Samoa and Tonga: "I am not an ethnobotanist, but I feel that, though the Polynesians traveled into central Polynesia by the Micronesian route, such important food plants as the breadfruit, banana, yam, and finer taro were carried from Indonesia to New Guinea and relayed by Melanesians to their eastern outpost at Fiji. . . . The richer food plants which reached Fiji had to be relayed to central Polynesia through volcanic islands. The first relaying station in western Polynesia was provided by Samoa or Tonga" (1938a:307–8). It was not a parsimonious explanation, but for Hiroa it was

essential if his Micronesian route was to be upheld.

Vikings of the Sunrise was intended for a wide public audience, whom Hiroa (publishing under his English name Peter H. Buck) wished to win over to the idea that the Polynesians were "Europoids." But he also laid out his theory in a dense scholarly monograph on Cook Islands material culture (1944; see also Hiroa 1945:12–13). There, in a lengthy discussion, he rejected Handy's "two-strata" theory and advanced his own proposition that the diversity of Polynesian cultures had originated from a single "Early Polynesian" stock, which had come into the Pacific from Indonesia via Micronesia (Fig. 1.9). Like Burrows (1938),

Hiroa realized that the subsequent differentiation of Polynesian cultures resulted from a variety of internal cultural processes.

I have dwelt at length on Te Rangi Hiroa both because he was *the* prominent authority on Polynesia in the mid-twentieth century and because his work demonstrates how any scholar's sociopolitical context can influence the development of his or her ideas. The "Micronesian route" theory—never well supported by empirical evidence—would fall completely once stratigraphic archaeology and modern comparative linguistics were brought to bear on the problem after World War II.[18] Relying almost exclusively on comparative ethnographic data—especially material culture—Hiroa was nonetheless able to mount a convincing argument. His work marks the culmination of the period of ethnographic domination of Pacific prehistory, with archaeology a mere bystander.[19]

The Discovery of Time Depth and Culture Change

World War II focused unprecedented attention on the Pacific, as thousands of American GIs fought their way through the jungles of Guadalcanal and other exotic locales. Partly as a result of this heightened interest in the Pacific, at war's end several regional anthropological programs were launched. While Pacific anthropology in the first half of the twentieth century had been dominated by ethnography, archaeology rapidly came into its own soon after midcentury. Professor Edward W. Gifford of the University of California, Berkeley, who as a young ethnologist had led the 1920 Bayard Dominick Expedition to Tonga, decided in 1947 to turn his hand to archaeology. Convinced by the prevailing views of Hiroa and others that there was no cultural stratification in Polynesia, Gifford chose to tackle Fiji:

As tropical Polynesia has yielded archaeologically only the early phase of the local cultures which were flourishing at the time of discovery, I decided to look farther west for a succession of cultures. Fiji seemed a likely place, and moreover I reasoned that it might show traces of early Polynesians, if they had come via Fiji. Also, I reasoned that large islands rather than small ones would be likely to produce a succession of cultural horizons; early colonizers would presumably be attracted to large land masses rather than to small ones. Hence Viti Levu, of more than 4,000 square miles area, was selected. (1951:189)

Gifford explored Viti Levu for six months, discovering 38 sites and excavating two, Navatu and Vunda (see Chapter 5), both well stratified and containing a sequence of changing pottery styles. Gifford was uncertain of the ages of these sites, but based on external stylistic comparisons he thought the stratigraphically earlier materials might correlate with "the Bronze Age of southeastern Asia via Borneo and the Solomons" (1951:237). The modern period of Pacific archaeology was launched.

Buoyed by his Fijian results, Gifford organized a second Pacific archaeological expedition in 1952, this time to the large island of New Caledonia (Gifford and Shutler 1956). Willard Libby's pathbreaking method of radiocarbon dating had just been developed, and Gifford seized the opportunity to date charcoal samples from his New Caledonian sites, as well as previously excavated samples from Fiji. At a place called Lapita on New Caledonia's west coast, Gifford and his student Richard Shutler, Jr. (Fig. 1.10) found a distinctive kind of stamped pottery, which Gifford recognized as nearly identical with the sherds that his Bayard Dominick Expedition coworker McKern had found in Tonga in 1920. What truly astounded Gifford, however, was the age of the associated charcoal samples as dated by [14]C: 2800 ± 350 B.P.

FIGURE 1.10 Professor Edward W. Gifford (center left) of the University of California and his graduate student assistant Richard Shutler, Jr. (center right), assisted by local workers, during their 1952 expedition to New Caledonia. It was during this expedition that the site of Lapita was discovered. (Photo courtesy P. A. Hearst Museum of Anthropology.)

Suddenly all the old assumptions about shallow time depth for Pacific island cultures seemed to crumble away; Gifford's excavations revealed just the kind of cultural stratification that Piddington and others had claimed did not exist. Here was a type of finely decorated pottery showing an early connection between Melanesia and Polynesia, quite contrary to Hiroa's "Micronesian route" theory. Indeed, what soon came to be called the "Lapita" pottery style crossed the boundary separating Melanesia and Polynesia, and it would in time force even the ethnologists to rethink fundamental categories they had inherited from the time of Dumont d'Urville (e.g., Thomas 1989).

At about the same time (1949–50), Alexander Spoehr of the Field Museum of Natural History in Chicago explored the archaeology of the Marianas Islands on the western fringe of Micronesia (Spoehr 1957). He too found well-stratified sites enmeshed in a ceramic sequence, as well as stone architecture that could be fitted into the later part of the cultural sequence (see Chapter 6). Spoehr took advantage of the new radiocarbon dating method to obtain a basal date of 1527 ± 200 B.C. from the Chalan Piao site on Saipan. He boldly argued that while the "reconstruction of Oceanic prehistory" had previously drawn on other branches of anthropology, "it is very largely on the data of archaeology that future knowledge of Oceanic culture history must be built" (1957:17). Appointed to succeed Hiroa as the director of the Bishop Museum after the latter's death in 1951, Spoehr was soon in an influential position to advance that research agenda.[20]

Indeed, less than a year before Te Rangi Hiroa passed away from cancer, the Bishop Museum's Kenneth P. Emory (by then a seasoned veteran of Pacific anthropology) had been the first to heed Willard Libby's call for charcoal samples from Pacific Island sites.[21] Emory, engaged in excavating the Kuli'ou'ou Rockshelter on O'ahu Island, sent Libby a sample from a hearth at the base of the shelter's cultural deposit: "On February 19, 1951, Buck [Hiroa] called Kenneth to his office and read aloud a letter just received from Chicago. Libby had dated Kenneth's sample of charcoal from the cave at Kuliouou at A.D. 1004, plus or minus 180 years. It was the first carbon date for Polynesia. 'Boy, was I excited,' said Kenneth later. 'Immediately it opened a whole new vista of possibilities'" (Krauss 1988:338).

Backed by the arrival of Spoehr at the Bishop Museum in 1953,[22] Emory launched a major program in Hawaiian archaeology, excavating sites throughout all the main islands, leading to the definition of a sequence based not on pottery—which was absent from Eastern Polynesia—but on changes in bone and shell fishhook styles (Emory et al. 1959).

But Emory in Hawai'i was not the only ethnologist-turned-archaeologist now searching for new evidence with which to reconstruct the Polynesian past. A decade earlier, Roger Duff had commenced excavations at Wairau Bar in New Zealand, which contained both habitation deposits and burials.[23] Duff opened his classic monograph on the Wairau Bar site with this notable statement: "The student of the ethnography of Polynesia has at hand a remarkable human laboratory in which to study whatever laws determine the evolution of human culture in time and space." He observed that if human culture had "remained static one might have expected the culture of any one island to have remained exactly like that of any other" (1950:1). Obviously, this had not been the case in the Pacific, even though the ethnologists had attempted to explain cultural differences as the result of successive migrations, or "waves" of people. But in New Zealand, Duff and his colleagues, such as E. D. Skinner and L. Lockerbie, discovered direct archaeological evidence of local cultural change, in part due to adaptation to the temperate conditions of these islands. Duff concluded that "the major contribution of this study to the theory of Polynesian cultural change is the demonstration that the culture may alter by a continuous and mainly self-motivated process of change" (1950:12). At last, *cultural change and process* were being integrated into Pacific archaeological and anthropological research.

In considering this rejuvenation of Pacific archaeology immediately following World War II, one cannot overplay the significance of radiocarbon dating.[24] An independent, scientific means had been developed whereby cultural materials could be directly dated, freeing archaeologists from hazy guesswork based on presumed stylistic correlations, often over vast geographic distances. Moreover, the ages produced by the first dated samples from New Caledonia, Saipan, and O'ahu were in excess of what orthodox ethnographic theories had predicted. Henceforth, Pacific prehistory belonged to archaeology, augmented by historical linguistics, another developing field in the post–World War II era. The dominance of comparative ethnology and the diffusionists was a thing of the past.

The Search for Polynesian Sequences

Inspired by the successes of Gifford, Spoehr, Emory, and Duff, other researchers joined the Pacific archaeological scene during the 1950s. Despite the exciting finds from Fiji, New Caledonia, and the Marianas, the greatest focus remained on Polynesia. Emory, soon joined by Yosihiko Sinoto (Fig. 1.11) and William J. Bonk, concentrated on the excavation of stratified rockshelters and sand dunes throughout the Hawaiian Islands. After 1960, Emory and Sinoto (1965) extended their research to the Society Islands and the Marquesas. In New Zealand, Duff's pioneering efforts were soon augmented as the department of

FIGURE 1.11 Kenneth P. Emory and Yosihiko Sinoto excavating at the Pu'u Ali'i sand dune site, South Point, Hawai'i, in the early 1950s. They are kneeling on an exposed pavement of basalt cobbles, examining a remnant baulk of the overlying cultural deposit. (Photo courtesy Y. H. Sinoto.)

anthropology at the University of Auckland appointed its first academic archaeologist. Jack Golson, a graduate of Cambridge University, brought to New Zealand a materialist tradition of archaeology stemming from his mentors V. Gordon Childe and Graham Clarke. Golson quickly set out to professionalize and upgrade the standards of excavation in New Zealand, organized the New Zealand Archaeological Association, and published several key papers outlining the prehistoric cultural sequence in these large islands (Golson 1959; see also Groube 1993b).

The continuing focus on Polynesia (rather than Melanesia to the west) was reinforced by worldwide attention to the 1947 *Kon-Tiki* balsa raft adventure of Thor Heyerdahl, a young Norwegian zoologist who tirelessly promoted his theory that the Polynesians had originated not in the west, but from the Americas (Heyerdahl 1952).[25] The successful drifting of *Kon-Tiki* from Peru to Raroia in the Tuamotus caused an international sensation, and in 1955–56 Heyerdahl led a second expedition into southeastern Polynesia, this time on a converted Greenland trawler equipped for archaeological research and staffed with four professional archaeologists (E. Ferdon, W. Mulloy, A. Skjølsvold, and C. Smith). The main objective of the "Norwegian Archaeological Expedition to Easter Island and the East Pacific" was Rapa Nui, but work was also carried out on Rapa Iti and Ra'ivavae in the Australs, and on Hiva Oa in the Marquesas. On Easter Island, the team concentrated on vestiges of the statuary cult (Fig. 1.12), with surveys and excavations at the Rano Raraku statue quarry and at several temples sites (including the Ahu Vinapu complex), in large part because Heyerdahl had proposed that similarities between Easter Island architecture and statues and those found in parts of South America supported his migration theory. Less attention was paid to habitation sites or other mundane archaeological features. The results of the Norwegian Expedition were splendidly published in two handsome, well-illustrated volumes (Heyerdahl and Ferdon, eds., 1961, 1965), still a landmark in Polynesian archaeology.

FIGURE 1.12 Statue 295 in the Rano Raraku Quarry, Rapa Nui, after the completion of excavations by the Norwegian Archaeological Expedition in 1956. (Photo courtesy Kon Tiki Museum, Oslo.)

machine, for they showed up off Easter Island in A.D. 380, led by a post–A.D. 750 Incan god-hero, with an A.D. 750 Tiahuanaco material culture featuring A.D. 1500 Incan walls, and not one thing characteristic of the Tiahuanaco period in Peru or Bolivia. This is equivalent to saying that America was discovered in the last days of the Roman Empire by King Henry the Eighth, who brought the Ford Falcon to the benighted aborigines. (*Suggs 1960:224*)

Heyerdahl did not fare much better in the scholarly press. Golson, reviewing the first volume of scientific results of the Norwegian Expedition, convincingly showed that "the changes in *ahu* architecture and function which provide a useful if limited framework for the periodisation of Easter Island prehistory need not be ascribed to the arrival of different populations on the island" (Golson 1965:78). Rather, all of the archaeological evidence uncovered by the Norwegian Expedition could readily be interpreted as supporting a more conventional view that the island had been settled by ancestral Polynesians from the west, with subsequent internal cultural developments on Easter Island itself.

While the Norwegian Expedition was at work on Easter Island, Robert Suggs was carrying out the first stratigraphic excavations in the Marquesas Islands of Eastern Polynesia, recovering a long cultural sequence revealed in a number of well-stratified sites (Fig. 1.13). Whereas Emory, Golson, and the Norwegian Expedition had all largely focused on artifact sequences (what is often termed the "culture history" paradigm in archaeology; see Trigger 1989), Suggs's trend-setting research reflected changing agendas in American anthropology. In the post–World War II era, an evolutionary perspective had arisen under the influence of such scholars as Julian Steward and Leslie White, as had an interest in human ecology (see

What the Norwegian Expedition failed to do, however, was convince anyone of the veracity of Heyerdahl's South American origins hypothesis. American archaeologist Robert C. Suggs lost no time in leveling a searing attack on Heyerdahl in his widely read synthesis, *The Island Civilizations of Polynesia* (1960). After reviewing the numerous inconsistencies in data and theory, Suggs parodied Heyerdahl's claims to have proved his raft theory:

Heyerdahl's Peruvians must have availed themselves of the classical device of science fiction, the time

FIGURE 1.13 Robert C. Suggs cleaning a test excavation face at the Ha'atuatua dune site in the Marquesas Islands, on the day he discovered the site in 1956. The Ha'atuatua site revealed the earliest period of Eastern Polynesian occupation. (Photo courtesy R. C. Suggs.)

Harris 1968:643–87). Although Suggs did not neglect artifact classification and seriation, he was intrigued by broader anthropological questions of culture change: "I wanted to collect comparative information on much more general topics. How did various kinds of ancient temple architecture in Polynesia fit in with the religious philosophies of the natives? Was there evidence of warfare on other islands? If so, did the situations resemble that which had evidently arisen on Nuku Hiva during the period when so much of the population had sought shelter in caves in the remote reaches of the island? How did the village

plans in various Polynesian societies fit with the social organization of these groups?" (1962:222).

Suggs's (1961) Marquesan sequence did not merely consist of lists of artifact types, but constituted a model for the evolution of Marquesan culture over time, in relation to island ecology and human demography (Fig. 1.14). His research meshed well with changing perspectives in Oceanic cultural anthropology, which had by now abandoned the old comparative ethnographic approach of Handy and Hiroa in favor of controlled comparisons and the study of *culture process*. This evolutionary perspective was exemplified in the work of such influential anthropologists as Ward Goodenough (1957), Marshall Sahlins (1958), and Irving Goldman (1970).

Broadening Research Horizons

By the 1960s, the research agendas of Pacific archaeologists and anthropologists had broadened beyond issues of cultural origins and defining artifact-based sequences. A major innovation was the development of "settlement pattern" archaeology, first applied in Polynesia by Roger C. Green (Fig. 1.15), who had been trained in this approach by Gordon Willey at Harvard (Golson 1996a).[26] First in his study of the 'Opunohu Valley on Mo'orea (Society Islands; Green 1961; Green et al. 1967), and then in a major multiyear project focused on Western Samoa (Green and Davidson 1969, 1974), Green demonstrated the power of a settlement pattern perspective. Rather than concentrate exclusively on artifact-rich sites, Green attempted to incorporate all aspects of an archaeological landscape (Fig. 1.16). He argued that "with the development of settlement pattern studies in archaeology and increasing concern with delineating the social aspect of the data recovered from sites as well, the day has passed when such monuments or their structural features can afford

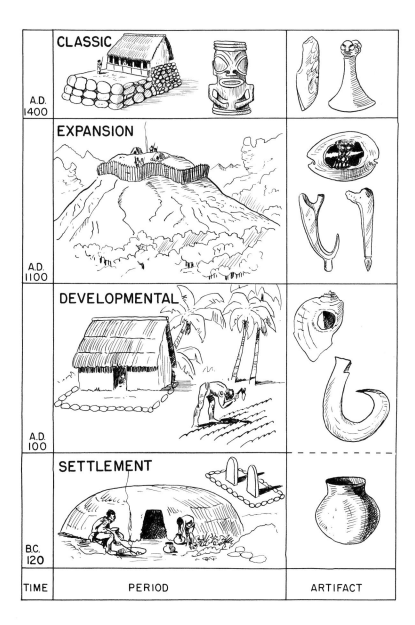

TIME	PERIOD	ARTIFACT
A.D. 1400	**CLASSIC**	
A.D. 1100	**EXPANSION**	
A.D. 100	**DEVELOPMENTAL**	
B.C. 120	**SETTLEMENT**	

FIGURE 1.14 Robert Suggs's cultural sequence for the Marquesas Islands, as graphically summarized by American Museum artist Nicholas Amorosi. Suggs defined his cultural periods as much in terms of settlement patterns and population dynamics as in terms of artifact types. (Courtesy R. C. Suggs.)

to be treated only as contexts for portable artifacts and not as artifacts in their own right" (1967b: 102). Settlement pattern studies became the norm in Polynesia, as archaeologists recognized their potential to yield insights regarding prehistoric social and political organization (Cordy 1985b). By the late 1960s and early 1970s, such studies were being carried out in Hawai'i (e.g., Kirch and Kelly 1975; Tuggle and Griffin 1973), New Zealand (Groube 1964, 1965), Easter Island (McCoy 1976), and the Marquesas (Bellwood 1972; Kellum-Ottino 1971).

Initially intended to shed light on prehistoric social relations and community structure, in

FIGURE 1.15 Roger C. Green in the field in Western Samoa, 1960s. (Photo courtesy R. C. Green.)

Polynesia the settlement pattern approach rapidly acquired an additional ecological orientation. Combined with the recovery and analysis of faunal and floral materials (e.g., Kirch 1973; Shawcross 1967, 1972), settlement pattern studies began to encompass agricultural field systems and other evidence for economic production. Ethnobotanist Douglas E. Yen played a major role in such work, collaborating with archaeologists in a pioneering study of prehistoric irrigation in the Makaha Valley, O'ahu, that yielded the first stratified evidence for agricultural change in Polynesia (Yen et al. 1972). Archaeological remains of agricultural systems, and the identification of preserved plant remains, were increasingly incorporated into Pacific research.[27]

Government institutions came to exercise increasingly critical influence on U.S. science during the cold war era. With the successful conclusion of World War II, American research universities and institutions (including the major natural history museums) began to receive unprecedented infusions of federal funds, owing in part to a plan conceived by Vannevar Bush, architect of the newly constituted National Science Foundation (NSF). As early as 1951, a subcommittee on Pacific archaeology of the National Research Council recommended a program for Micronesian archaeology, and a similar program for Polynesian archaeology was put forward in 1953 (Emory 1962:1; Spoehr 1954:24).[28] Throughout the 1950s, expanding field research in Pacific archaeology was still funded largely through private funds and grants, but this changed dramatically in 1962, when the Bishop Museum received its first NSF grant for Pacific archaeology (Emory 1962; Force 1964:19, 29; Spoehr 1962:13–14). With $77,220 for a three-year period, the museum dispatched field expeditions to Rarotonga, Pitcairn, Western Samoa, and American Samoa, including representatives of Auckland University, the Canterbury Museum, and the Otago Museum (New Zealand). Alex Spoehr, who would soon turn the reins of the Bishop Museum over to his protégé Roland Force, summed up the role of the NSF and other federal agencies in Pacific research:

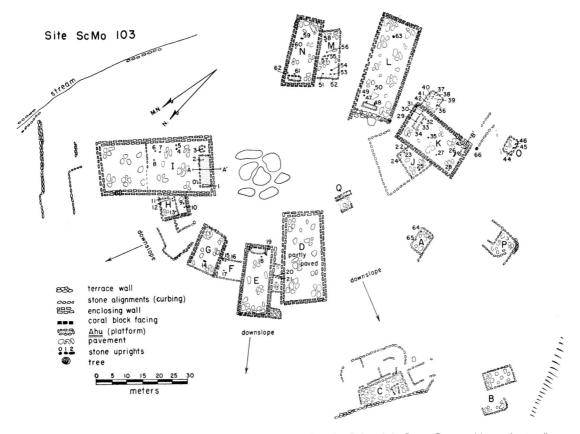

FIGURE 1.16 The settlement pattern approach to archaeology, introduced to Polynesia by Roger Green, paid attention to all classes of sites and not merely to artifact-rich deposits. This map of a *marae* or temple complex in the 'Opunohu Valley, Mo'orea, was prepared as part of Green's settlement pattern survey in 1961. (From Green et al. 1967.)

"The financial resources required for reasonably large scale research are beyond the means of any single institution. In the United States, federal support of basic research is becoming more and more necessary" (1962:3).

The Bishop Museum implemented its second three-year program of "Polynesian culture history" in 1965 (Force 1965), with increased NSF funding of $274,554 again supporting an international group of investigators, now incorporating historical linguistics and ethnobotany along with archaeology. The impact of this infusion of federal research funds cannot be underestimated, and

many of the advances in Polynesian archaeology of the 1960s stem directly from these programs. Moreover, the NSF has continued to fund Pacific archaeology, such as the multi-institutional Southeast Solomon Islands Culture History Program (SSICHP; Green and Cresswell 1976; Yen 1982), and many grants for projects ranging from Papua New Guinea to Hawai'i.

Another field of innovation with important influence on archaeology has been historical linguistics. In the 1930s, German linguist Otto Dempwolff (1934–38) laid the foundations for formal comparative analysis of Austronesian languages in the Pacific, and after World War II a number of young linguists (such as Bruce Biggs, Isidore Dyen, Sam Elbert, and George Grace) took up the field. By the early 1960s, they had shown that the Polynesian languages indeed formed a discrete subgroup within the Austronesian family, and that these were most closely related to other languages in island Melanesia and Micronesia, forming an "Eastern Austronesian" or "Oceanic" subgroup. At the same time, Emory (1946, 1963) and Pawley (1966) elaborated the internal subgrouping or classification of the Polynesian languages, which Green (1966) correlated explicitly with the newly elucidated archaeological sequences. The productive engagement of archaeology with historical linguistics in the Pacific has continued to the present (Pawley and Ross 1993, 1995; eds., 1994; Ross et al., eds., 1998).

Beyond Polynesia: Archaeology in Melanesia and New Guinea

Although Gifford and Spoehr specifically targeted *western* Pacific archipelagoes (Fiji, New Caledonia, the Marianas) in their post–World War II efforts to revitalize Pacific archaeology, most research in the 1950s and 1960s continued to focus on Polynesia. Perhaps this was an inevitable consequence of the need to achieve consensus on the old "problem of Polynesian origins," based on the new methods of stratigraphic excavation and radiocarbon dating. But Jack Golson saw the necessity of renewed work in Melanesia and seized the opportunity presented by an offer of appointment to the faculty of the Australian National University (ANU) in Canberra in 1961.[29]

From his new base at ANU, Golson mapped out a series of long-term projects that would add immensely to our knowledge of Melanesian prehistory (see Golson 1996b).[30] In the late 1950s,

Ralph and Susan Bulmer had excavated two rockshelters in the New Guinea Highlands, outlining a speculative prehistoric sequence (Bulmer and Bulmer 1964). Following up on these leads, Golson sent his student J. Peter White to the highlands, where additional rockshelters were located and excavated. Other students were dispatched to locations that Golson judged would be key to expanding our knowledge of Melanesian prehistory: Peter Lauer to the D'Entrecasteaux Islands, Brian Egloff to Collingwood Bay on the northeastern New Guinea coast, and Ron Vanderwal and Geoff Irwin to the Papuan coast.[31] The emerging importance of the Lapita cultural complex—about which Golson himself authored several key papers (Golson 1963, 1971, 1972a, 1972b)—was not neglected. Jim Specht re-excavated the Watom Lapita site, Jens Poulsen dug several Lapita middens on Tongatapu, and Colin Smart investigated sites in New Caledonia.[32]

Jim Allen, who had studied Australian historical archaeology under Golson, was appointed to the first faculty position in archaeology at the new University of Papua New Guinea in 1969. From this base, Allen carried out important work at Nebira and Motupore near Port Moresby, and he continued to play a major role in Melanesia after returning to ANU as a member of Golson's department. Independently, French archaeologist José Garanger (1972a) explored the archaeology of central Vanuatu, discovering a ceramic horizon—which he named Mangaasi after its type site—that seemed to follow or replace the Lapita ceramic horizon in parts of island Melanesia. Garanger opened up a new interpretive realm at the interface of archaeology and oral traditions by discovering the material veracity of certain indigenous Vanuatu narrative histories, such as that pertaining to the famous chief Roy Mata (see Chapter 5). Similar correlations between oral tra-

FIGURE 1.17 Excavations in the deeply stratified Sinapupu sand dune site on Tikopia Island during the 1978 phase of the Southeast Solomons Culture History Program revealed three thousand years of continuous occupation. (Photo by P. V. Kirch.)

ditions and the archaeological record would soon be demonstrated by Kirch and Yen (1982) in their work on the Polynesian Outlier of Tikopia.

By the close of the 1960s, this spate of new fieldwork in New Guinea and the Melanesian islands was finally drawing attention away from Polynesia, to the western archipelagoes of the Pacific. Roger Green, who had authored several archaeologically based syntheses of Polynesian origins (Green 1966, 1967a, 1968), was increasingly convinced that the Lapita ceramic complex held essential clues to the deeper origins of the pre-Polynesians, as well as to the peoples of island Melanesia. In 1970, Green and Douglas

Yen obtained NSF support for "an interdisciplinary investigation of the prehistory of the Southeast Solomon and Santa Cruz Islands" (Green 1976d:9). Their research design combined fundamental culture-historical work with current theoretical perspectives from "processual" archaeology, including an emphasis on ecological diversity, economic systems, and interisland exchange networks. In 1971–72, this project put field teams on Kolombangara, Ulawa, Uki, San Cristobal, Santa Ana, Santa Cruz (Nendö), the Reef Islands, and Anuta, precipitating a veritable outpouring of research results. The SSICHP was so successful that NSF funded a second two-year phase in

FIGURE 1.18 The Talepakemalai site in the Mussau Islands of Papua New Guinea, discovered during the Lapita Homeland Project and shown here during the second season of excavations in 1986, yielded the first evidence for a stilt-house settlement pattern during the Lapita period. (Photo by P. V. Kirch.)

1977–78, which extended fieldwork to Vanikoro, Tikopia (Fig. 1.17), and Taumako, and continued work in Nendö and the Reef Islands.[33] Between the work of Golson and his ANU students, and that of the Southeast Solomons project, the prehistory of New Guinea and island Melanesia was finally taking shape.

Green and Yen's Southeast Solomons project demonstrated the effectiveness of coordinated, multi-institutional research programs. This was the model that Jim Allen (1984a) consciously adopted when he organized the Lapita Homeland Project (LHP), focusing on the Bismarck Archipelago. The Bismarcks were known to have Lapita sites (such as Watom and Ambittle), but otherwise their prehistory was largely a blank, although there was a suggestion from Misisil rockshelter on New Britain that they might have a deeper Pleistocene history (Specht et al. 1981). In 1985, LHP team members (including the author) carried out surveys and

excavations on New Britain, New Ireland, Watom, Nissan, Manus, and Mussau (Fig. 1.18), not only expanding our knowledge of Lapita sites (Gosden et al. 1989) but also pushing the prehistory of the Bismarck Archipelago back to 33,000 B.P. (Allen et al. 1989; Allen and Gosden, eds., 1991). Such dates had been known for Australia and New Guinea, but this was the first demonstration that early humans had expanded into the Near Oceanic islands during the Pleistocene.

Island Melanesia has continued as the scene of much exciting fieldwork in the 1990s, as members of the LHP built on initial results to extend their research in New Britain, Mussau, Manus, and elsewhere. In New Caledonia, French archaeologists—including Daniel Frimigacci, Jean-Christophe Galipaud, and Christophe Sand—expanded on the pioneering work of Gifford and Golson to clarify our knowledge of southern Melanesian prehistory (see Chapter 5). And important new research is currently being carried out in the Western Solomons (P. Sheppard, pers. comm., 1998) and by several teams in Vanuatu. Melanesia, long neglected, at last has an archaeological record of its own, one in many respects deeper and richer than that of Polynesia.

Not an Ivory Tower: Public Archaeology in the Pacific

From the first decades of the twentieth century—when anthropology and archaeology achieved formal status as academic disciplines—until the 1960s, virtually all archaeological research in the Pacific was carried out by museum- or university-based scholars. In the United States (including Hawai'i), things began to change in the 1960s and 1970s as new federal and state laws encouraged and mandated the recovery and preservation of archaeological materials, both in connection with public works and, often, for privately financed developments (Green and Doershuk 1998). Although many museums and university departments began to undertake such "contract archaeology" (or "cultural resource management" [CRM] archaeology, as it has become known), these changes also spawned the rise of independent archaeological contractors. Initially, CRM archaeology in the Pacific was confined to Hawai'i and to other U.S. territories including American Samoa and Guam. However, the New Zealand government soon adopted similar laws, and in Micronesia the U.S. federal statutes began to be applied in the Trust Territory of the Pacific Islands, and later by the independent governments of Palau, the Northern Marianas, the Federated States of Micronesia, and the Marshall Islands (see Cordy 1980, 1982). Indeed, the expansion of archaeological work throughout Micronesia over the past two decades has been almost entirely the result of the CRM movement.

The rise of CRM archaeology in Hawai'i, New Zealand, Micronesia, and to some extent elsewhere in the Pacific has had several consequences. A huge infusion of funds for archaeological work (in the case of Hawai'i, totaling several million U.S. dollars per year), far exceeding what has ever been available for archaeological research either from private funding sources or from federal research agencies such as the NSF, has produced a vast outpouring of survey and excavation data. Results are frequently reported in limited-distribution documents, however, and are rarely published in traditional academic journals or monographs, resulting in a "gray literature." Synthesis lags behind fieldwork and data reporting. The inevitable linking of archaeology with land development has also led to some conflicts between archaeologists and indigenous peoples, as in Hawai'i (see Spriggs 1989b, 1991c; Kirch 1999). Nonetheless, CRM archaeology has resulted in a greatly expanded pace of archaeological research in some regions (especially Hawai'i, American Samoa, and parts of Micronesia) and despite its growing pains has made significant contributions.

In the postcolonial world of the Pacific, the very practice of archaeology (as well as anthropology) is constantly critiqued, discussed, and renegotiated. Some indigenous activists have called for a halt to archeological work, seeing it as a legacy of White colonialism. Haunani-Kay Trask, for instance, has called for a stop to "all anthropology and archaeology on Hawaiians." She writes: "There should be a moratorium on studying, unearthing, slicing, crushing, and analyzing us" (1993:172). Others, such as Joseph Kabui, former premier of Bougainville Province (Papua New Guinea), regard archaeology positively and look to archaeological findings in their search for national identity (Spriggs 1992b: 269). Certainly, as this historical overview shows, archaeology in the Pacific has—with a few notable exceptions such as Te Rangi Hiroa—been primarily the work of nonindigenous scholars. But things are rapidly changing as we enter the twenty-first century. Indigenous Maori, Hawaiian, Fijian, New Guinean, Kanak, and other Pacific islanders are themselves studying archaeology and becoming involved in its practice. As Jack Golson writes in his retrospective on 35 years of research in New Guinea:

> Today teaching and training in archaeology at the University in Port Moresby are in the hands of Papua New Guineans, John Muke and Joe Mangi, who were students of Les Groube. At the National Museum there is Nick Araho, a co-worker of Pamela Swadling in her Sepik research, and a new appointee to undertake salvage work, Herman Mandui. They are all well-known to those of us who have worked in their country over recent years, and we to them. It is to be hoped that these relationships will provide a basis for partnership in the important next stage of archaeological research. *(1996b:174)*

Along with the Papua New Guinea archaeologists named by Golson, we could add other indigenous scholars, such as Lawrence Foanaota, John Keopo, and Kenneth Roga in the Solomon Islands; Jacques Bolé, André Ouétcho, and Francis Wadra in New Caledonia; Ralph Regenvunu in Vanuatu; Sepeti Matararaba and Tarisi Sorovi-Vunidilo in Fiji; Peter Adds, Des Kahotea, Nepia Stewart, Nick Tupara, Dean Whiting, and others in New Zealand; Mauricio Rufino in Pohnpei; Erika Radewagen and Epi Suafo'a in American Samoa; and Kehau Cachola-Abad, Koa Hodgins, Kathy Kawelu, Hanna Springer, and others in Hawai'i. With them, the future of Pacific islands archaeology is sure to take on new dimensions and explore uncharted waters.

Contemporary Approaches to Pacific Prehistory

In this chapter I have traced some of the main intellectual themes and strands that run through the history of archaeology and historical anthropology in the Pacific. The ways in which scholars have looked at Pacific prehistory, their assumptions about time depth and cultural processes, the kinds of evidence they sought or were willing to entertain, all of these have changed dramatically over two centuries. A popular aphorism says that hindsight has 20/20 vision; it is easy to look back at the flawed assumptions underpinning the diffusionist paradigm of the early twentieth century and find them wanting. Putting our present assumptions, methods, and theories under critical scrutiny is more difficult. How our own contemporary research and writings will be judged by future generations only time itself will reveal.

Pacific archaeology is not without its debates, its differing academic camps, its squabbles over data, method, and interpretation (Kirch and Weisler 1994). Some of these focus on historical particulars and reflect an inadequate empirical record, such as the ongoing controversy regarding the settlement chronology for Eastern Polynesia (see Chapter 7). Such issues will eventually be resolved by further excavations, additional radiocarbon dates, and more and finer-grained research in general. Other debates reflect wider theoretical differences in the field of archaeology at large, such as the contrasting archaeological paradigms encapsulated by the terms *processual* and *postprocessual* (Trigger 1989). Still other issues center on matters of interpretation, such as whether the Lapita cultural complex in Near Oceania reflects a major intrusion of Austronesian-language speakers or alternatively was an indigenous development within New Guinea and the Bismarck Archipelago (see Chapter 4). These, in turn, often hinge on larger matters of methodological and theoretical perspective: those favoring the "Lapita-as-intrusive" position are typically "holistic" anthropologists who invoke historical linguistic and human biological evidence in addition to archaeological data, while the "Melanesian indigenist" camp largely restrict their approach to material remains (see Kirch 1997a).

Still other controversies and differences of approach stem from how one views the Pacific islands as a theater for anthropological research. Since at least 1950, many scholars have alluded to the "laboratory-like" aspects of Pacific islands and their human populations and cultures, suggesting that in the Pacific one has a kind of "natural experiment" of cultural differentiation and adaptation (e.g., Duff 1956; Goldman 1970; Goodenough 1957; Kirch 1984a; Sahlins 1958). Although none of these anthropologists ever took this laboratory metaphor so far as to seriously conceive of Pacific islands as closed systems, lately we have been admonished that the "myth of the primitive isolate" has set back Pacific prehistory (Terrell et al. 1997).[34] In truth, Pacific archaeologists have been studying interaction among island societies for a long time (see Kirch 1986b:2), and *both isolation and interaction* are fundamental concepts for the interpretation and understanding of culture change in Oceania. Yet another, related debate entails contrasting *phylogenetic* versus *reticulate* models of cultural differentiation (Bellwood 1996a; Kirch and Green 1987, in press). Neither model is necessarily superior, and indeed they need not be opposed; both have value, depending on the research questions one wishes to tackle.

I mention these academic debates not to claim the high ground for any particular viewpoint, for only time will reveal what survives and what ends up on the midden heap of intellectual history. I, for one, would be sad to see the day dawn when we think we know all the answers, for half the fun lies in pursuing new questions. My intention is merely to show that the field of Pacific archaeology—as always—is in flux. That, after all, makes the pursuit of it stimulating and worthwhile.

CHAPTER 2

The Pacific Islands as a Human Environment

In no other ocean has it been as difficult for a bit of land to be entirely surrounded by water. In no other has it been as difficult for a piece of the earth's crust to raise its head above the water to become an island. The wonder is not that most islands are small and scattered but that there are so many of them, for the Pacific Ocean contains more islands than all the rest of the world's oceans combined.

Thomas (1963:7)

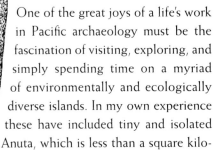

One of the great joys of a life's work in Pacific archaeology must be the fascination of visiting, exploring, and simply spending time on a myriad of environmentally and ecologically diverse islands. In my own experience these have included tiny and isolated Anuta, which is less than a square kilometer in land area and just 80 meters high, yet the permanent home of about 160 Polynesians; the semi-atoll formed by Eloaua and Emananus, whose reefs and lagoon harbor an almost indescribable array of marine life; Mangaia, with its fortresslike escarpment of upraised pinnacle karst encompassing an ancient, highly eroded volcano; the vast, elongated island of New Caledonia, its ancient rocks and metallic soils a remnant of archaic Gondwanaland; and Moloka'i, whose majestic windward cliffs rise 1,200 meters sheer from the sea, gapped by lush amphitheater-headed valleys with hundreds of waterfalls cascading down their slopes (Fig. 2.1). The contrasts inherent in just these five examples testify to an amazing diversity of Pacific island environments. Such contrasts stem from varied geological origins that have raised islands from the oceanic depths, from different ages, from the varied work of wind and water on landforms, and from biological processes of dispersal, colonization, and evolution that have cloaked Pacific islands in a rich flora and fauna, distinct from those of continents.

In spite of tremendous diversity, some patterns and processes are common to all oceanic islands. Islands can be classified into several major geological types, and important biogeographic trends across the Pacific account for much of the varia-

FIGURE 2.1 Dramatic sea cliffs along the windward coast of Moloka'i were created by massive landslides. Deep amphitheater-headed valleys slice into the central mountain range. (Photo by P. V. Kirch.)

tion in island biota. In this chapter I review these patterns, trends, and processes, providing a background for understanding the human settlement of the Pacific. The story of the movement of *Homo sapiens*, first out onto the larger islands and archipelagoes of Near Oceania, then in more recent times into the vast reaches of Remote Oceania, eventually to discover virtually every habitable speck of land, cannot be fully appreciated without some understanding of these key environmental variables. Winds and currents, along with island

distances, have influenced the development of navigational methods and seafaring skills. Limitations in natural plant and animal foods helped to shape the subsistence economies of Pacific peoples, and variations in soil, rainfall, and climate necessitated adaptations to their horticultural practices. The availability or absence of natural materials—basalt, chert, obsidian, shell, plant fibers, and the like—played a role in the development of material culture. None of this is to say that the lifeways or culture of Pacific islanders, any more than that of other peoples, was "determined" by their natural environments. On the contrary, humans everywhere actively modify and shape their world, yet they do so within certain constraints—and sometimes challenges—posed by the environments they inhabit. Moreover, in the islands of Remote Oceania, many of which were biologically isolated before the coming of humans, the advent of people often had a dramatic effect on the island ecosystems themselves. Thus the study of the Pacific islands as an environment for humans does not consist merely in the cataloging of a static "stage set" for the grand cultural play. The setting itself is dynamic through both time and space, and a great deal of this dynamism has been driven by the actions of men and women acting out their lives, making their choices on a daily basis, cumulatively over the centuries.

Origins and Development of Pacific Islands

The geological origins of the Pacific islands mystified scientists of the nineteenth and early twentieth centuries. The possibility that a great Pacific continent had formerly existed, only to sink beneath the sea, was entertained by various scholars and provided the basis for one of the more bizarre theories on the origins of Pacific peoples.[1] The theory of plate tectonics is surely one of the great triumphs of later twentieth-century science, revealing that the earth's crust consists of shifting plates separated by boundaries, themselves variously zones of spreading or of subduction.[2] Along the spreading zones, outpourings of magma constantly create new crust, especially along the East Pacific Rise. At the subduction zones, one plate downthrusts beneath another, and the oceanic crust plunges to great depths to be reabsorbed into the earth's mantle, and partly to reappear as molten lava on the sur-

face through island-arc volcanism, such as along the Kermadec-Tonga Trench.

A tectonic map (Map 3) reveals that the center of the Pacific basin consists of a vast crustal sheet, the Pacific Plate. Originating along its eastern margin, the Pacific Plate extends from the Pacific-Antarctic Ridge up through the East Pacific Rise (on which Easter Island sits) and follows the western coast of North America. As new oceanic crust is continually created along this lineament, the Pacific Plate ever so slowly yet relentlessly moves toward the northwest (arrows on Map 3). At its western margins the Pacific Plate is "consumed" by being downthrust into a complex series of subduction zones, marked by deep oceanic trenches. These include the Kermadec-Tonga Trench, the New Britain Trench, the Palau Trench, the Mariana Trench (notable for having the deepest spot in the earth's oceans), the Japan and Kuril Trenches, and the Aleutian Trench. The sinuous line formed by these trenches has long been known as the "Andesite Line" because the rocks found in islands to the west are predominantly andesitic, whereas islands on the Pacific Plate are dominated by basaltic lavas. To the west of these trenches lies not just one plate, but a maze of interlocking smaller plates.

Strings of island-arcs define the western margins of the Pacific Plate, formed by a characteristic kind of volcanic activity. As geographer Patrick Nunn describes the process, "The magma involved in island-arc volcanism derives from melting of subducted ocean crust. . . . The melting of the crust is the consequence of being heated through burial and from friction along the contact with the buoyant plate" (1994:34). Such plate margin volcanism has formed the extensive Tonga, Vanuatu, and Solomon archipelagoes. The complex geological history of island-arcs can include successive stages of active volcanism, erosion, subsidence, and formation of marine limestones and

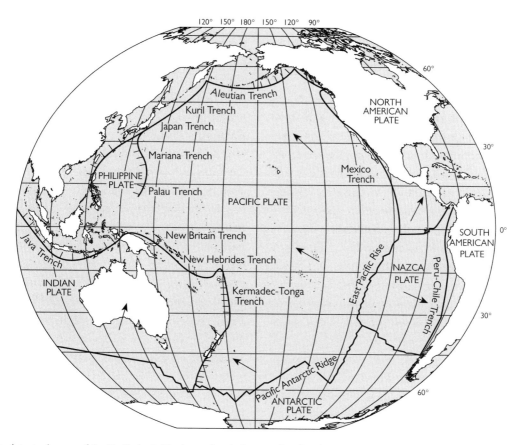

MAP 3 A tectonic map of the Pacific basin. The heavy lines indicate major plate boundaries, and the general directions of plate movement are indicated by the arrows. (Adapted from Oliver 1989.)

other sedimentary deposits, producing islands with complex structures of volcanic, meta-volcanic, and sedimentary rocks.

The western margin of the Pacific also incorporates plate fragments derived from the ancient supercontinent of Gondwana, which began to break apart 100 million years ago. New Caledonia is one such Gondwanaland fragment, parts of New Zealand another; both broke off from Australia about 80 million years ago and began a slow, isolating drift to the east. Their origins in the ancient southern supercontinent account for unique aspects of the biota of these islands, such as archaic conifer trees and many species of large

geckos on New Caledonia.[3] New Guinea too has a highly complex geological history—also reflecting its Gondwanaland origins—and includes rocks ranging in age from Cambrian or even older formations, up to recent Pleistocene volcanics (Brookfield and Hart 1971:26–29).

Pacific Plate islands have a different origin mechanism from those of island-arcs. These mid-plate or intraplate islands typically originate from a "hot spot" or thermal plume of magma arising from deep in the mantle. Such hot spots are stationary within the mantle, and thus the slowly migrating lithosphere of the Pacific Plate gradually moves over them.[4] This movement is sufficiently slow that there is time for new islands to be created by successive eruptions and extrusions of lava beginning with a rupture on the sea floor, piling up a volcanic mass that eventually rises above the ocean. In time, the new island moves off the hot spot as it is carried along by the conveyor belt of the crustal lithosphere. A new island then begins to form over the same more or less stationary hot spot. Over a period of tens of millions of years, an entire linear chain of volcanic islands successively rises from the ocean depths. Midplate islands in such linear chains typically pass through the following evolutionary stages: (1) initial volcanism and shield building; (2) subsidence due to point-loading of the thin oceanic crust; (3) subaerial erosion by streams, waves, and wind; (4) often, a late stage of renewed volcanism, typically pyroclastic; (5) continued erosion and reduction of the island's mass; (6) formation of extensive coastal reefs, if the island is within the tropical to subtropical regions; (7) complete erosion and subsidence of the volcanic cone, resulting in the formation of a coral atoll; and (8) eventual drowning of the island, forming a submerged seamount.

The textbook example of such a midplate linear island chain is the Hawaiian-Emperor Archipelago, extending from the island of Hawai'i (where the originating hot spot is located), up through the main "high" volcanic islands such as O'ahu, and continuing through the remnant volcanic pinnacles and coral atolls of the Northwestern Hawaiian chain, and finally with the submerged Emperor seamounts that end in Meiji Seamount, a total distance of 3,942 kilometers.[5] The Hawaiian chain is continually being created by the stationary magma plume situated in the southeast (where a new island, named Loihi, is being constructed today off the coast of Hawai'i), and eventually its submerged islands end their evolutionary cycle with subduction into the Kuril

Trench. Based on potassium-argon dating of islands along this lineament, the entire life cycle of a Hawaiian island takes something like 75–80 million years, during which perhaps only the first 8–15 million are above water.

Most islands on the Pacific Plate are oriented along such linear chains, including the Marquesas, Society Islands, Tuamotus, Australs–Southern Cooks, and Samoa.[6] As a consequence of their evolutionary cycle, the degree of weathering and hence landform development that midplate islands undergo varies with geological age. For example, in the main Hawaiian Islands the new island of Hawai'i (with surface rocks less than 0.3 million years old) has been weathered very little, and most of its surface lacks streams or deeply developed soils. At the other end of the chain, Kaua'i (ca. 5.1 million years old) is deeply eroded by streams, boasting a valley topography with rich soils and a coastline protected by extensive coral reefs. Such contrasting landforms were of great consequence to colonizing Oceanic peoples who, with their horticultural subsistence economy, preferred environments with ample water and good soils, as well as developed reefs and lagoons in which they could fish. This environmental gradient played an important role in the political dynamics of the late prehistoric Hawaiian chiefdoms (see Chapter 8). The Oceanic peoples themselves were keen observers of geological differences between islands, and they had their own folk theories about island origins. The Hawaiians, for example, clearly recognized that their archipelago had originated progressively from the southeast, the abode of the volcano goddess Pele. The marvelous Pele-Hi'iaka cycle of Hawaiian mythology (Beckwith 1970) explicitly refers to Pele moving her home from Kaua'i successively to the other islands, to end up at her present residence in the crater of Halemaumau on Hawai'i.[7]

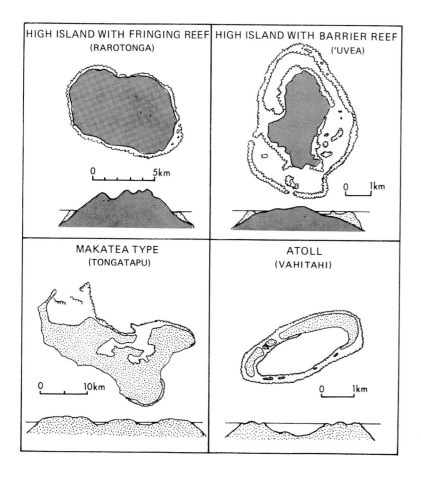

FIGURE 2.2 Examples of the principal geological types of islands. (After Kirch 1984a.)

Types of Islands

Different geological origins of island-arc and midplate islands provide one basis for classifying Pacific islands; another important variable is that of changes in an island's landform resulting from submergence and the formation of coral reefs, or by later emergence of reefs. Geographers (e.g., Thomas 1963) have long used a simple four-part classification of Pacific islands that is extremely useful for understanding the varied island environments to which Pacific peoples adapted. The four island types are: (1) island-arc islands, formerly referred to as "continental" islands; (2) high islands of midplate hot spot origin; (3) coral atolls, formed on volcanic masses that have subsided beneath the ocean's surface; and (4) makatea islands, in which coral atoll or reef formations have been uplifted or have emerged through tectonic activity. The last three types of islands are illustrated in Figure 2.2. This handy classification will be used throughout this book, and the key features of each island "type" are succinctly discussed here.

Island-Arc Islands Formerly labeled "continental" islands because they sometimes incorporate ancient continental rocks, island-arc islands are among the largest islands in the Pacific, concentrated along the western margins of the Pacific basin.[8]

FIGURE 2.3 Anuta Island in the southeastern Solomons group is one of the smaller high islands in the Pacific, but nevertheless home to about 160 Polynesians. (Photo by P. V. Kirch.)

They include New Britain and New Ireland of the Bismarck Archipelago, the Solomon Islands, Vanuatu (formerly the New Hebrides), New Caledonia, Fiji, and New Zealand. Often large in scale, such islands exhibit varied habitats. On large islands such as New Britain, one finds interior-dwelling peoples who have no direct experience of the coast or the sea, although they trade with coastal populations. Because of their complex geological histories, these islands offer a wider range of lithic resources utilized by ancient Pacific peoples to manufacture stone tools. Rhyolite, dacite, various metavolcanic rocks, chert, and in certain locations high-quality obsidian are to be found in such island-arc locations.[9]

High Islands   High islands are islands of midplate hot spot origin still in the earlier stages of their evolutionary cycle, before subsidence and erosion have done their work. They will eventually sink beneath the ocean surface to become atolls or seamounts. Tahiti, Rarotonga, Tutuila, and Pohnpei are typical examples of high islands. Most high islands consist of basalt, a hard, dense stone extensively used by Pacific peoples to make adzes and other implements. These islands range considerably in size, from Hawai'i at 10,458 square kilometers down to diminutive Anuta, only 0.8 square

kilometer in land area (Fig. 2.3). They also vary greatly in landform, depending to a large degree on age and hence extent of erosion. Geologically younger islands often lack watercourses, whereas older islands are deeply dissected by stream valleys. Some high islands, such as ethnographically famous Tikopia, consist of volcanic cones with lakes in their exploded craters.

When they are still young, high islands lack developed coral reefs and typically have wave-cut cliffs along their shorelines. In time, reefs develop along the shores of high islands, first as fringing reefs and later, as the island continues to subside, in the form of barrier reefs separated from the main island by a lagoon (Fig. 2.4). However, coral reefs are confined to the tropical and subtropical waters, because reef-building corals will not grow north or south of about 24° latitude. Gaps in the reef exist wherever there is substantial freshwater runoff, as at the mouths of large stream valleys.

Atolls   The stages in the formation of a coral atoll were originally worked out by Charles Darwin (1842), although he failed to account for the underlying geological mechanism of subsidence, now explained by plate tectonics. As islands migrate westward on the relentlessly moving Pacific Plate, they gradually subside and, in com-

FIGURE 2.4 The high island of Niu-atoputapu in the northern Tongan group is surrounded by an extensive barrier reef and lagoon. In the distance looms Tafahi Island, a young volcanic cone lacking reefs. (Photo by P. V. Kirch.)

bination with the erosion of their subaerial surfaces by wind and water, are slowly reduced. Reefs begin to develop around the island's margin, so that in time an older high island will have a small volcanic core surrounded by a lagoon and barrier reef, as in Mo'orea or Aitutaki Islands. Eventually this remnant volcanic core also becomes submerged, and only a ring of coral reef remains above the ocean, since coral will continue to grow upward in the photic zone of the ocean. Coral heads and sand generated by storms and biological processes accumulate at places on the reef to form islets, called *motu* after their Polynesian name. The stages in atoll development are diagrammed in Figure 2.5.

Atolls are among the most precarious environments settled by Pacific peoples.[10] At most, atoll *motu* are only 2–3 meters above sea level, vulnerable to inundation by waves and storm surges during cyclones. There are no streams, but atoll-dwellers have learned that a thin lens of fresh water (the Ghyben-Herzberg aquifer) floats on the heavier salt water within the sandy body of *motu* and can be tapped by excavating shallow wells. Certain crops, such as the giant swamp taro (*Cyrtosperma chamissonis*) can be cultivated in pits

dug down to expose this freshwater lens. However, cultivation on atolls is risky, and many crops simply will not tolerate the saline conditions. On the other hand, atolls are remarkable for their rich marine resources, and atoll peoples tend to be at home as much on and in the sea as on the land. Since atolls lack stone of any kind, their inhabitants have also had to adapt their material culture, using coral and various species of shell, such as the giant clam (*Tridacna gigas*), to make adzes and other tools.

Makatea Islands   When an atoll, or an old high island surrounded by a barrier reef, becomes elevated above sea level it forms what is called a *makatea* island. *Makatea* is a Polynesian word meaning "white stone" (reef limestone), and it is also the proper name of an island of this type in the Tuamotu Archipelago. Makatea islands are formed by tectonic uplift at plate margins, or by "lithospheric flexure," in which a new volcanic hot-spot island point-loads the thin oceanic crust, causing an upwarping at a certain distance from the hot spot.[11] For example, the heavy mass of Rarotonga in the southern Cook Islands caused a warping of the oceanic crust in its vicinity, elevating

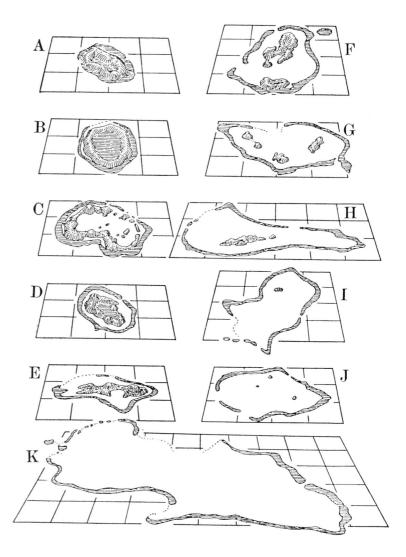

FIGURE 2.5 Stages in the development of an atoll, illustrated by block diagrams of various near-atolls and atolls. A, Naiau; B, Kambara; C, Fulanga; D, Tuvutha; E, Namuka; F, Ongea; G, Yangasa; H, Oneata; I, North Argo; J, Reid; K, Great Argo. (After Davis 1928.)

several nearby islands as much as 80 meters above sea level. Mangaia was one of those elevated, and its former barrier reefs now form a limestone rampart up to 2 kilometers wide, riddled with solution caverns used by the Mangaian people as fortress refuges and as burial places. Some makatea islands are marginal environments for human habitation, lacking surface water (rainfall disappears immediately into the spongelike karst) and even soil for cultivation. One such is Hender-son Island, yet prehistoric Polynesians managed to maintain a settlement there for 600 years (see Chapter 8).[12]

Climatic Factors in the Pacific

Pacific island climates span the humid tropics to the temperate zones (in New Zealand), but most of the islands we will consider in this book lie within the tropical to subtropical range. On some

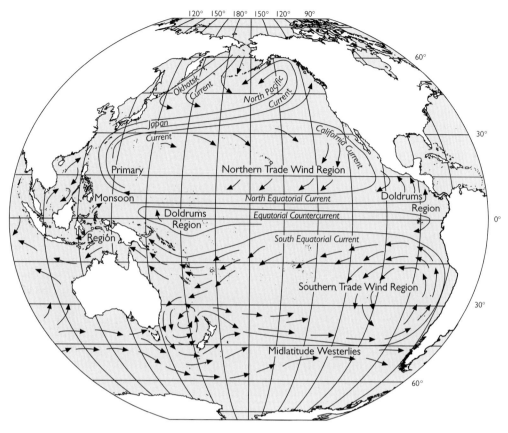

MAP 4 The dominant wind and current directions in the Pacific Ocean. (Adapted from Oliver 1989.)

islands, high mountains create microclimates, as on Hawai'i and Maui, where the higher elevations span humid temperate to alpine and tundra environments. The summits of both these islands receive regular snowfalls during the winter months, and Mauna Kea on Hawai'i was capped by a small glacier during the late Pleistocene.[13] New Guinea too not only had Pleistocene glaciers but also, as befits its larger land mass, exhibits even greater altitudinal climate differences.

Knowledge of the wind and current systems of the Pacific basin is essential to understanding human history in this region, for they had great effects on voyaging and settlement, as well as important influences on island ecology.[14] A wind and current map of the Pacific (Map 4) reveals two great gyres or circulation cells, one each in the Northern and Southern Hemispheres. Both of these flow from east to west across the equatorial region (the intertropical convergence zone); the northern gyre thus flows clockwise while the southern gyre flows counterclockwise. Given that the prevailing winds and currents are from the east throughout the main zone of tropical islands, Pacific navigators had to develop strategies for sailing from west to east, a topic considered in more detail in Chapter 7. There is some temporal variation, however, and the trade winds dominating

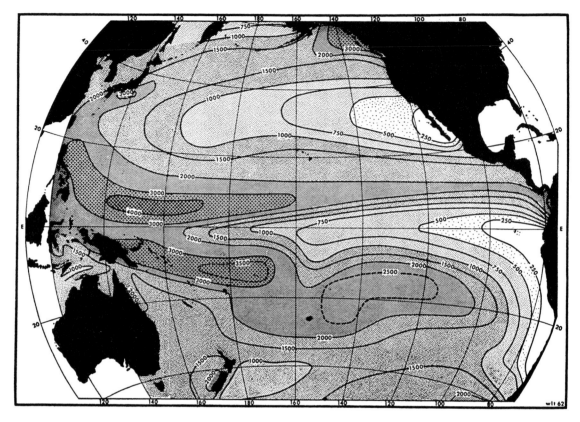

FIGURE 2.6 Average rainfall distribution (in millimeters) over the Pacific Ocean. (From Thomas 1963.)

the eastern Pacific are concentrated between May and September. In the western Pacific, there is a stronger seasonality between trade wind and monsoon seasons, influenced by the cyclic heating and cooling of the nearby Asian and Australian land masses.

The persistent trade winds, coming as they do year after year from the same direction, have a major environmental effect on high islands in their path. As moisture-laden trades flow across the windward side of a high island, they are heated and rise, resulting in heavy rainfall (known as orographic precipitation). The island's leeward side remains in a rain shadow, with significantly reduced rainfall. Over time, greater windward rain-

fall results in accelerated stream erosion and the creation of broad, amphitheater-headed valleys, while leeward landforms remain relatively dry and undissected. Vegetation is also affected, with lush rainforests on windward slopes and dryland shrub or parkland on leeward slopes. These windward-leeward contrasts were an important consideration to Oceanic peoples in establishing their settlements and gardens. Not surprisingly, the Polynesians developed a terminology for this windward-leeward axis, *tonga/tokerau*, which they carried with them throughout their colonizations.[15]

To horticultural peoples such as those of Oceania, rainfall is critical to the sustenance of life. A map of rainfall over the Pacific (Fig. 2.6) shows a gradual decline from west to east, with the Melanesian archipelagoes of the Bismarcks and Solomons receiving the greatest rainfall. However, there is sufficient rainfall throughout the zone of most islands to make horticulture feasible. The exceptions are along the equator (the Kiribati and Tuvalu Archipelagoes) and in northern Micronesia, where, for example, certain of the Marshall Islands suffer from periodic drought, making habitation tenuous.

We cannot leave the topic of climate without briefly discussing El Niño and the Southern Oscillation, terms that have become familiar to many people due to the effect of the process on contemporary patterns of rainfall or drought in North and South America as well as Australia. The El Niño–Southern Oscillation (ENSO) process consists of a periodic thermodynamic redistribution of energy over the Pacific basin, resulting from differential heat buildup in the western Pacific. During an ENSO event, the normal aridity of the western-central Pacific is broken by periodic heavy rainfall episodes, trade winds decrease in intensity, and there is a significant eastward flow of warm water. ENSO events can have dramatic consequences for particular islands, including droughts in the western and central Pacific, and heavy rains, floods, and increased cyclone frequency in the eastern Pacific. Fish populations, and the seabird colonies that depend on them for food, are sometimes devastated. Paleoclimatologists are only beginning to develop a historical record of ENSO activity over the past several thousand years, but these events presumably had serious impacts on Pacific island populations in the past.[16]

Island Life and Biogeography

When a new volcanic island emerges above the ocean swells (as Fenua Fo'ou has done in recent years in Tonga), it consists merely of barren rock and cinder—but not for long. Plant colonization begins surprisingly quickly, with floating seeds washed ashore by the waves, or with tiny seeds passed through the digestive tracts of visiting birds. Insects and spiders arrive either under their own power or passively dispersed on high-altitude winds. Seabirds may colonize an island even if it is still relatively barren of plant life. Over a few hundred thousand years, the new island will have acquired a significant biota, its slopes cloaked in trees, shrubs, and herbs, inhabited by a diversity of invertebrates and of volant vertebrates (e.g., birds, fruit bats, or microbats).

Dispersal is one of the most fundamental aspects of Pacific biogeography.[17] Groups of plants and animals that are good dispersers (because, for example, their seeds float and remain viable in salt water, or because they are capable of over-water flight) have managed to colonize oceanic islands time and again. Other groups, such as most vertebrates, have found it generally impossible to get far beyond continental shores. Because of this, the biota of Pacific islands differs radically from that of continental regions, with certain groups well represented and others wholly lacking; biogeographers sometimes refer to this phenomenon as "disharmony."

Distance—both from mainland source regions and between stepping-stone islands that aid in the dispersal process—is a critical aspect of island biogeography. Examining a map of the Pacific, one sees that the majority of islands are clustered in the western sector and that interisland distances increase dramatically as one moves eastward. Due to this uneven clustering of islands, Asia and New Guinea have served as primary source areas for Pacific floras and faunas, with a much lesser contribution from the Americas. Moreover, the large archipelagoes closest to Asia and New Guinea, such as the Solomons and Vanuatu, have much more diverse biotas, in terms of the numbers of higher-order taxa represented (genera and families), than those in the central and eastern parts of the Pacific.

Another key aspect of island biogeography is the tendency for new species to evolve, especially through the process known as adaptive radiation. When a species of plant or animal succeeded in colonizing an isolated island, it often found itself without its former predators and in a position to exploit what ecologists call an empty niche. Generations descending from this original colonist would multiply and diverge as some offspring adapted and moved into different microhabitats. The classic textbook case of adaptive radiation is that of Darwin's Galápagos finches, but numerous other examples abound throughout Oceania, such as the achatinellid and amastrid land snails of Hawai'i or the cryptorhynchinid weevils of Rapa. Speciation on oceanic islands led to high degrees of endemism in certain islands and archipelagoes. In the Hawaiian Islands, for example, no less than 94 percent of all flowering plant species, and 13 percent of the plant genera, are endemic (i.e., found nowhere else in the world).

These aspects of island biogeography, whose complexities I have only touched upon, had important consequences for colonizing human populations. First, as people moved from the large Near Oceanic archipelagoes into Remote Oceania, they increasingly found the newly discovered islands lacking in many familiar plants and animals. Moreover, east of the Bismarcks, there were few indigenous plants with edible tubers or fruits; the would-be colonizers had to bring crop plants and other economic species with them. On the other hand, sizable populations of land birds and nesting seabirds offered a ready source of meat, a resource that was frequently hit very hard within the first few decades after human settlement.

Vegetation on Pacific islands varies tremendously according to island size and altitudinal range, but a few typical plant communities are noteworthy from the perspective of human use.[18] In the tropical Pacific, the immediate coastal or strand vegetation is everywhere similar, dominated by salt-tolerant trees such as *Pandanus*, whose leaves were widely used to weave mats; *Barringtonia asiatica*, whose fruit produces a poison used to catch fish; and the ubiquitous coconut palm (*Cocos nucifera*). A wild form of coconut had naturally dispersed at least as far as central Polynesia (Cook Islands) prior to human settlement, but domesticated varieties with their larger fruit were evidently carried by canoeloads of would-be colonists.[19] In the western Pacific, the coastal zone is often characterized by extensive mangrove (*Rhizophora* and other taxa) swamps, or by lowland swamps of the sago palm (*Metroxylon* spp.), which is harvested for its starchy pith. Moving away from the coast into the interior lowlands of island-arc or high islands, one encounters rainforest, eventually giving way to even wetter montane and cloud forests on the higher islands. On some islands, the lower and middle elevations are dominated by grasslands or fernlands, especially in the drier leeward zones. This is the case over large parts of Viti Levu in Fiji (Ash 1992) and on New Caledonia, as well as on some smaller islands, such as Futuna, Mangaia, or Mangareva (Fig. 2.7). These pyrophytic savannas, characterized by fire-tolerant *Miscanthus* grass or *Dicranopteris* ferns, often were the result of millennia of human activities, such as forest clearance and repeated burning.

Island faunas, as I have noted, are frequently disharmonic in comparison with those of nearby continental regions.[20] Within the Pacific, mammals are limited to a few marsupials (e.g., wallabies, wombats, cuscus) and to several genera of rats (*Rattus*, *Melomys*, *Uromys*), along with fruit bats

FIGURE 2.7 Large tracts in the interior of Futuna Island in Western Polynesia are covered in pyrophytic *Dicranopteris* fernlands, the result of former land use practices such as shifting cultivation. (Photo by P. V. Kirch.)

(Pteropodidae). Of these, only fruit bats dispersed into Remote Oceania, the marsupials and rats being restricted to the Bismarcks and Solomon Islands. Reptiles too are of fairly limited distribution, with the majority of species of snakes, frogs, diurnal lizards, and geckos being found in Near Oceania or in the larger island-arc archipelagoes. Because of their excellent dispersal abilities, many kinds of birds managed to colonize Pacific islands, where they account for the greatest diversity of vertebrates. Seabirds (including frigates, shearwaters, petrels, noddies, and boobies) and various kinds of land birds (megapodes, pigeons, fruit doves, rails, and parrots among them) were especially abundant on many oceanic islands at the time of first human arrival (Steadman 1989, 1995, 1997). Moreover, flightlessness developed in a repeated evolutionary process on many Pacific islands, especially in various genera of rails.

The richest terrestrial faunal diversity on Pacific islands was among the invertebrates, including insects and landsnails, but most of these were of little direct consequence or interest to people. However, a large and highly delectable land crab, *Birgus latro*, the "coconut robber" crab, was a prized food of islanders. The presence of certain insects—most of all the *Anopheles* mosquitoes, which are vectors for several kinds of *Plasmodium*, the cause of malaria—also had health implications for humans.

The Pacific islands were not rich in edible terrestrial species other than birds and fruit bats, and, as we have seen, their floras were particularly impoverished in terms of edible plants. Far more important sources of animal food were the reefs and lagoons surrounding most islands. The same general pattern of a west-to-east decline in diversity, as we have seen in terrestrial biota, holds for the fish and mollusks of the Indo-Pacific faunal province.[21] Thus the waters of the Bismarck Archipelago teem with several thousand species of fish, while remote Easter Island has a mere 126 species. Most important to Oceanic peoples were the inshore and benthic (bottom-dwelling) fish, in such families as the parrotfish (Scaridae), wrasses

(Labridae), tangs (Acanthuridae), squirrelfish (Holocentridae), jacks (Carangidae), and groupers (Serranidae). These were taken with an amazing variety of fishing techniques, including the use of hooks, nets, spears, traps, and poisons. Oceanic peoples also knew how to troll the open sea for pelagic fish such as tunas (Scombridae) and *mahi-mahi* (Corphyraenidae), but compared with the inshore reefs the open ocean is a relative desert, and the yield from pelagic trolling was fairly minor. Bivalves and gastropod mollusks of all kinds were collected from reef and lagoon floors, both to eat and in many cases to manufacture artifacts from their durable shells. Other important marine foods were sea urchins, octopus, crabs of many kinds, seaweeds, and marine turtles (especially the green sea turtle, *Chelonia mydas*).

The Microbiotic World and Human Populations

It may be a universal cognitive feature of *Homo sapiens* to think of the world primarily in terms of our own bodily scale, and this bias carries over even into scientific notions about human history. Thus we take great account of human interactions with macroscopic animals and plants (even when the evidence for these is sometimes microscopic, as with pollen grains used to identify ancient species of plants), but in general pay little attention to the vast microscopic world that not only surrounds us, but also lives *within* us. We need to step back from our modern, first-world perspective of relatively healthy populations, with ubiquitous medical care in which most infectious and epidemic diseases have been minimized or eliminated, to consider the role of parasitic and infectious diseases in prehistory. Archaeologists have paid too little attention to these matters, partly because the evidence for disease among prehistoric populations can be difficult to obtain.[22] How-

ever, the historically documented distribution of disease-causing microorganisms in the Pacific islands raises several important hypotheses regarding the impacts and effects of disease in Oceanic prehistory.

The same biogeographic patterns that hold for macroscopic biota in the Pacific also apply to the microscopic world. Thus the diversity of microorganisms drops off sharply between Near Oceania and Remote Oceania, as does the diversity of such disease-bearing vectors as *Anopheles* mosquitoes. Generalizing broadly, the archipelagoes of Near Oceania (and here we must extend the boundary to encompass Vanuatu as well) are replete with infectious and parasitic viruses, protozoa, bacteria, and other disease-causing microorganisms, whereas the islands of Remote Oceania are (or were, prior to the expansion of disease after Western contact) relatively disease-free. Anyone who has done fieldwork in both Near Oceania and Remote Oceania will have learned this difference for themselves, often the hard way. I have spent many months on islands in both regions, and whereas neither I nor my Western team members have ever suffered serious health problems in Remote Oceanic field sites, it has been quite the opposite story in the Solomon Islands, or in Mussau in the Bismarcks. There we have contracted malaria (at times life-threatening), ulcerating skin infections resistant to even broad-spectrum antibiotics, persistent respiratory ailments, and gut-racking intestinal infections. It is not just that we are "soft" Westerners unaccustomed to the rigors of the "bush." The indigenous villagers with whom we lived in close contact in the Solomons and Mussau are themselves beset with these same ailments, and they often exhibit high levels of anemia from endemic malaria.[23] In contrast, the indigenous peoples with whom I have worked in Remote Oceania generally enjoy good health, even where little or no modern medical care is available (see Howe 1984:47–50). Tellingly, the exceptions occur where the adoption of a Western diet and lifestyle has led to such new diseases as hypertension and diabetes.

Without doubt, the most significant parasitic disease preying on the human occupants of Near Oceania (again extending into Vanuatu) has been malaria, a highly debilitating and often fatal disease resulting from infection by one or more of several *Plasmodium* species. In historic times, *Plasmodium vivax, P. malariae,* and *P. falciparum* have been found throughout the low- to midaltitude elevations of New Guinea, the Bismarcks, the Solomon Islands, and Vanuatu. The first two of these have probably been in the region for as long as humans (Groube 1993a), whereas the more virulent and often fatal *P. falciparum* may have been introduced somewhat later in prehistory. At least five species of *Anopheles* mosquito are also present, providing the necessary vector. In a study of four Solomon Islands populations, Damon (1974) found that as many as two-thirds of the adults (in Kwaio and Baegu) had enlarged spleens and lowered hemoglobin as a consequence of high malarial infection rates. In contrast, both the *Plasmodium* parasite and the *Anopheles* vector are absent from all of Remote Oceania other than the Reef–Santa Cruz group of the southeastern Solomons, and Vanuatu. (Indeed, in some Remote Oceanic island groups such as Hawaiʻi, mosquitoes were entirely absent prior to European contact.) As we shall see in later chapters, this disjunct distribution of malaria probably had major consequences for the demographic history of human populations in the two regions.

Near Oceania is also replete with other kinds of infectious and parasitic microorganisms, many of which are little studied and not well documented in either the anthropological or the medical litera-ture. Epidemiological surveys of several human groups in the Solomon Islands, however, reported frequently high infection rates for such parasites as hookworm (nearly 45 percent of some populations) and intestinal parasites like *Entamoeba coli* and other species (causing amoebic dysentery), *Ascaris, Trichuris, Iodamoeba, Giardia,* and *Dientamoeba* (Damon 1974; Friedlaender and Page 1987). Brown (1978:60–61) refers to the "high incidence of enteric and respiratory disease" among the Highlands peoples of New Guinea, as well as the presence of various "parasite and worm infections." The pervasiveness of these diseases in Near Oceania presumably lowered the overall resistance levels of indigenous populations, thereby increasing the probability of mortality from malaria or other fatal diseases, especially among high-risk individuals (such as infants and pregnant women). While we must be cautious about overgeneralizing, it nonetheless seems certain that the distribution of diseases within the pre-European Pacific islands was far from uniform, and that the concentration and persistence of disease-causing microorganisms in Near Oceania had serious consequences for long-term human history.

Island Ecosystems

Just as island biotas differ in fundamental ways from those of continents, so island ecosystems also have their peculiar characteristics. The brilliant Pacific botanist Raymond Fosberg (1963a) drew attention to some of the key aspects of island ecosystems that are relevant to our understanding of the role of humans in adapting to—and frequently changing—Pacific environments. Fosberg delineated two features as "basic to insularity": *isolation* and *limited size.* Naturally, both of these are relative and become more significant as one moves from the larger and less isolated archipelagoes of

Near Oceania into the vastness of the central and eastern Pacific. Fosberg cataloged some of the consequences of isolation and limited size: "limitation in, or even absence of certain other resources; limitation in organic diversity; reduced inter-species competition; protection from outside competition and consequent preservation of archaic, bizarre, or possibly ill-adapted forms; tendency toward climatic equability; extreme vulnerability, or tendency toward great instability when isolation is broken down; and tendency toward rapid increase in entropy when change has set in" (1963a:5). The last two of these are of particular relevance to the human settlement and occupation of the Pacific islands, for insular ecosystems were more vulnerable than others to disturbance at human hands. As Fosberg put it, "Perhaps the thing that most distinguishes islands, at least oceanic islands . . . is their extreme vulnerability, or susceptibility, to disturbance" (1963b:559).

Oceanic ecosystems have never been static or changeless, and natural and cultural processes are always at work to foster change. I have already noted such short-term natural processes as ENSO events that trigger episodes of drought or high cyclone frequency. In various parts of the Pacific, volcanic eruptions have had dramatic consequences for human populations. In Melanesia, explosive eruptions have occurred within the period of human occupation in New Guinea, New Britain, the Manus Islands, and Vanuatu.[24] Some of these volcanic events blanketed vast areas with scalding ash and pyroclastic debris, doubtless killing many people and making human habitation impossible. The Kuwae eruption, which occurred in the mid-fifteenth century A.D., blew apart an originally larger island, creating a vast caldera between what are now Epi and Tongoa Islands in Vanuatu. This eruption, which is recorded in Vanuatu oral traditions, probably had some effect on world climate, and it is recorded in ash falls from

the South Pole dating to A.D. 1452 (Robin et al. 1994). About 300 years ago, Long Island off the northeast coast of New Guinea similarly exploded in a cataclysmic eruption, spewing 10 cubic kilometers of tephra westward across the interior of New Guinea, blanketing about 80,000 square kilometers with an average depth of 1.5 centimeters of airfall tephra; this momentous geological event is likewise recorded in oral traditions throughout the region (Blong 1982). In the Hawaiian Islands, volcanism is rarely explosive but no less significant for the Polynesian inhabitants, since large portions of Hawai'i Island (and some parts of Maui) have been extensively covered with lava flows since the time of initial human arrival (Somers 1991).

Longer-term dynamism comes from such changes as the subsidence and formation of atolls, tectonic uplift of makatea islands, and eustatically fluctuating sea levels. Sea level change, in particular, has had important consequences for human settlement of the Pacific. During the Pleistocene, sea levels were periodically as much as 100–120 meters lower than at present, facilitating movement of people into Near Oceania (Chapter 3). Sea levels rose rapidly during the early Holocene, and throughout much of the central Pacific they reached a level 1–1.5 meters higher than at present by about 4,000–6,000 years ago. Thus archaeological sites dating to this time period are frequently found on older beach terraces, sometimes a considerable distance inland from present coastlines (see Chapter 4).

With the arrival of humans, the dynamism of oceanic ecosystems acquired a new tempo, for as Fosberg correctly observed, insular environments are particularly susceptible to disturbance. I conclude this chapter with a brief review of the mounting archaeological and paleoecological evidence for human-induced changes to Pacific island environments.

Human Impacts on Island Ecosystems

It has not always been realized that Pacific islanders played an active role in modifying and molding their island worlds. Eighteenth-century voyagers to the Pacific helped to shape European notions of the "noble savage," *l'homme naturel*, living in a state of harmony with nature.[25] Arriving at Tahiti in April of 1768, the French navigator Louis de Bougainville thought himself "transported into the garden of Eden" (Smith 1985:42). As natural history studies gained sophistication in the nineteenth and early twentieth centuries, the role of humans in causing disturbance to island ecosystems became increasingly evident, but often this was attributed to changes that occurred after the arrival of Western peoples, who introduced a host of new plants and animals, many of them competitive and destructive (such as goats, sheep, and cattle), as well as new land use practices (large-scale plantation agriculture among them). Thus for most anthropologists, until relatively recently, the disturbances caused by indigenous populations in the Pacific were thought to be minor or insignificant. Social anthropologist George P. Murdock summed up the prevailing view when he claimed that even the colonization of islands by Polynesian agriculturalists resulted in "little net change in organic diversity" (1963:151).[26]

This Rousseauian view was based on unquestioned assumptions, untested with direct empirical evidence of environmental changes before and after the colonization of islands by indigenous Pacific populations. Evidence for pre-European anthropogenic change began to accumulate in the late 1960s and early 1970s, when archaeologists working in the Pacific started to shift their research agendas away from an emphasis on origins and cultural sequences to investigate ecological relationships between indigenous human populations and island environments. Working collaboratively with palynologists, avian paleontologists, geomorphologists, and other natural scientists, Pacific archaeologists have now amassed a substantial body of data, demonstrating that the nonindustrialized peoples of the Pacific often exerted major impacts on island ecosystems.[27] Indeed, this should not come as a surprise, given the inherent fragility or vulnerability of oceanic ecosystems (as Fosberg had pointed out), combined with the high human population densities observed on many Pacific islands and the intensive modes of land use practiced by Pacific peoples.

Human-induced changes on islands often commenced with the first arrival of would-be colonists, for these people usually were equipped to establish permanent settlements, which meant that they had to transport and transplant their crop plants and domestic animals. Moreover, voyaging canoes carried inadvertent "stowaways," such as the Pacific rat (*Rattus exulans*), whose bones show up in virtually every Pacific settlement site.[28] Rats, whose numbers soon increased in the absence of predators, may have had significant impacts on ground-nesting land bird and seabird populations. In addition to the rat, we have evidence for the accidental transport of geckos and skinks, certain species of garden snails (e.g., *Lamellaxis gracilis*), and various weeds (e.g., *Ludwigia octivalvis*).

The modification of island ecosystems began in earnest as native forests were cleared to make way for root-crop gardens and for orchards of tree crops. Oceanic peoples widely practice swidden or shifting cultivation, in which patches of forest are cut, allowed to dry, and burned prior to planting.[29] Under conditions of low population density it is possible for forests to regenerate, but more often than not the cleared land is gardened repeatedly and a highly transformed, "second-growth" vegetation comes to replace the

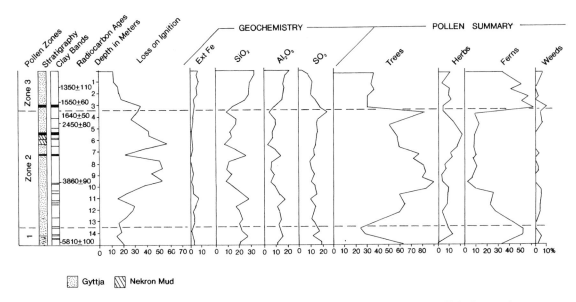

FIGURE 2.8 Summary pollen diagram for the TIR-1 sediment core from Veitatei Valley, Mangaia Island. This diagram shows a decrease in trees and an increase in *Dicranopteris* ferns beginning around 1600 B.P., associated with human activities.

original rainforest. On certain kinds of substrate, where soils are thin or poorly developed (as on many tropical islands), the removal of forest and repeated burning can seriously degrade a landscape, which then comes to be dominated by fire-resistant (pyrophytic) grasses or ferns. Other landscapes were, over time, thoroughly reworked by Pacific agriculturalists into highly intensive forms of land use. Examples of such "landesque capital–intensive" agriculture include the Highlands valleys of New Guinea, the vast irrigated systems and yam fields of New Caledonia, the extensive hill and ridge terraces of Palau, and the stone-faced taro pondfields of Hawaiian valleys.[30]

Evidence for vegetation changes resulting from such land use practices as shifting cultivation has now been obtained from a number of Pacific islands, primarily through the analysis of pollen grains (palynology) in sediment cores. Pollen sequences from sites in New Guinea, Van-uatu, New Caledonia, Fiji, Yap, the Cook Islands, the Society Islands, New Zealand, Easter Island, and Hawai'i all demonstrate major vegetation changes that can be linked to human land use actions.[31] A typical example is the pollen sequence obtained from the Veitatei Valley on Mangaia Island during our interdisciplinary paleoecology project in 1991 (Fig. 2.8). Prior to the arrival of humans, probably as early as 2,400–2,000 years ago, Mangaia had a significant forest cover on its volcanic interior, which later came to be dominated by *Dicranopteris* fern and scrub *Pandanus* savanna. The critical signal in this and most other Pacific island pollen sequences is the correlation between human arrival and the advent of significant burning (indicated by microscopic charcoal particles in the sediment samples). In the Mangaian case, there was virtually no burning on the island until the arrival of people, in this case Polynesian horticulturalists who used fire to help clear forest to make way for gardens.[32]

Easter Island presents a dramatic case of human-induced vegetation change, for this entire island was essentially deforested through hundreds of years of intensive land use.[33] Botanists who once thought that the island was a natural oceanic grassland "steppe" now realize that it was originally covered in forest dominated by an extinct species of giant palm (*Jubea* cf. *chilensis*), closely related to the Chilean oil palm. On Easter Island, the ultimate extinction of the palm and other woody plants had a further consequence: the inability to move or erect the large stone statues (see Chapter 8).

Forest clearance had additional consequences on certain islands, due to the exposure of steep hillslopes and accelerated erosion. Matthew Spriggs (1986) has shown that on the island of Aneityum in Vanuatu, a process of valley-bottom infilling and extension of the coastal plains began about 2,000 years ago, as a direct result of forest clearance and increased erosion rates on the interior hills and ridges. Similar sequences have been suggested for Futuna, Mo'orea, and O'ahu Islands, and the extensive iron sand dunes at the mouth of the great Sigatoka Valley on Viti Levu (Fiji) probably also owe their existence to land clearance and increased erosion rates in the interior.[34] In addition to sedimentation in valleys and on coastal plains, increased sediment loads in streams and rivers may have had effects on inshore marine ecology. In the Koné region of New Caledonia, for example, changes in the kinds of marine mollusks available through time are linked to changes in littoral substrates or turbidity resulting from erosion (Miller 1997). Vast tracts on both North and South Islands, New Zealand, were converted from temperate forest to open terrain, typically dominated by *Pteridium* ferns, as a consequence of human-ignited fires (Bussell 1988; Elliot et al. 1995; McGlone 1983; McGlone and Wilmshurst 1999).

Human impacts on islands were by no means limited to forest clearance and the development of savannas, or to erosion and valley-infilling. Dramatic evidence for human impacts on island ecosystems comes from the record of bird bones excavated from Pacific archaeological sites. David Steadman has analyzed such assemblages of bird bones from sites in Tonga, Tikopia, the Cook Islands, the Society Islands, the Marquesas, Henderson, Mangareva, and Easter Island, and his data are reinforced by other studies for Hawai'i and New Zealand. Case after case demonstrates that the Pacific islands before the advent of humans had a far richer bird fauna than that historically documented, with large populations of certain kinds of birds occupying oceanic islands at the time of initial human arrival.[35] On Easter Island, for example, Steadman's work shows that at least 25 species of seabirds and possibly 6 species of land birds were originally present, yet only one seabird species survives (barely) on the island today, and there are no endemic or indigenous land birds at all (Steadman et al. 1994; pers. comm., 1995). In New Caledonia, a large mound-building megapode (*Sylviornis neocaledoniae*) went extinct soon after the arrival of humans in the mid–second millennium B.C., as did other endemic fauna, including a terrestrial crocodile (Fig 2.9).

In 1989 and 1991, Steadman and I excavated a large rockshelter site on Mangaia Island, called Tangatatau. From the well-stratified ashy midden layers of this rockshelter, which had been occupied by Mangaians repeatedly for about eight centuries, we recovered a remarkable collection of bird bones, revealing a typical story of the reduction, local extirpation, and extinction of a large part of the island's original avifauna.[36] Among the bird species that were once present on the island, and which had been hunted, eaten, and their remains discarded in the shelter, were rails, crakes, a gallinule, a sandpiper, fruit doves, pigeons, and lorikeets. In all, a prehuman avifauna consisting of at least 19 land bird species and 12 seabird

FIGURE 2.9 Reconstruction of the extinct giant ground-dwelling megapode *Sylviornis neocaledoniae* and the extinct terrestrial crocodile *Mekosuchus inexpectatus*, both from the island of New Caledonia. (After Sand 1995.)

species was reduced during the period of Polynesian occupation to 5 land bird and 6 seabird species, many of these today holding on to a most precarious and endangered existence.

For no island group in the Pacific is the record of bird extinctions more dramatic than New Zealand. On these large subtropical to temperate islands, a marvelous array of bird life had evolved prior to the arrival of the first Polynesian settlers. Most distinctive were several genera and species of flightless birds known collectively by their Maori name, *moa*.[37] The biggest of these *moa*, *Dinornis giganteus*, stood almost 4 meters tall, probably the largest bird ever known to exist. However, New Zealand wildlife was not limited to the *moa*, and at least 37 native bird species and subspecies went extinct during the period of Polynesian settlement (Anderson 1997:280). By the time of European arrival, all 11 *moa* species had been completely eliminated. The larger *moa* were extensively hunted for food, especially on South Island, where some archaeological middens were

so packed full of *moa* bones that they were commercially mined in the late nineteenth and early twentieth century in order to make bone meal fertilizer! Equally important as a cause of the decimation of New Zealand's bird life was forest clearance for gardening, and clearance by fire for hunting, which has been estimated to have drastically reduced the native forest cover of the two main islands (McGlone 1983, 1989).[38]

Recognizing that indigenous Pacific peoples were responsible for significant changes to their island environments—as documented by mounting archaeological and paleoecological evidence—is not to single them out as environmentally insensitive eco-vandals. In my view, Pacific islanders were not more or less environmentally conscious than most other human groups; it is only our outdated Rousseauian notions that make it appear so. Pacific peoples certainly have a fond and often deeply emotional attachment to their island homes, and their songs and traditions frequently speak to the great beauty of these islands. It is also the case that traditional Oceanic societies practiced certain kinds of conservation practices and land management strategies, but these were generally aimed at conservation of resources for future use.[39] Yet the simple truth is that human populations everywhere live not in some idealized "state of nature," but in various forms of exploitative relationships with their environments. The impact of low-density hunters and gatherers may be *relatively* slight,[40] but the cumulative effects of high-density agricultural peoples on their landscapes are inescapably significant. Pacific islanders did much—with the "neolithic" technology at their disposal—to create viable subsistence economies on the islands they settled and to manage their resources wisely. That they were not always successful is a lesson that humanity today has yet to fully hear or heed.

CHAPTER 3

Sahul and the Prehistory of "Old" Melanesia

The Pleistocene evidence may open a window onto two different forms of the creation of time and space. The initial forms of colonisation created a spatially extensive and mobile world, in which the definition of groups and social identity would have been quite unlike anything we know of today. Spatially extensive and temporally long lasting, this world was then transformed in the glacial maximum to a way of life with different spatial and temporal rhythms.

Gosden (1993:134)

On the Huon Peninsula of northern Papua New Guinea, nature played the role of architect on a grand scale: a staircase created for a Wagnerian race of giants rises steeply from the Bismarck Sea, climbing hundreds of meters into the sky. Fantasy aside, the relentless tectonic engine of plate-margin uplift has raised a succession of coral reefs over the past 140,000 years. Each emerged reef appears like an abrupt step, and thanks to uranium/thorium (U/Th) dating, these stages can be accurately dated. In the 1980s, Les Groube and his students at the University of Papua New Guinea explored this giant staircase, finding numbers of stone implements called "waisted blades" on a reef terrace dated between 61,000 and 52,000 years ago. Actually, these tools are more like crude axes,

sometimes made from large river cobbles that had been split in half and further modified by flaking at their "waists," possibly to tie or haft them to wooden handles (Fig. 3.1). When Groube submitted for dating the volcanic ash from a layer associated with some of these implements, he obtained a thermoluminescence date of 60,000–40,000 years ago, cross-checking well with the U/Th dates on the reef terrace.[1] This makes the Huon site among the oldest manifestations of a human presence in the Australia–New Guinea region.

On our way to a third field season in the Mussau Islands in 1988, my graduate students and I visited Groube at his University of PNG laboratory at Boroko, just outside the capital of Port Moresby. One of the more colorful characters of Pacific archaeology, Les greeted us in rumpled

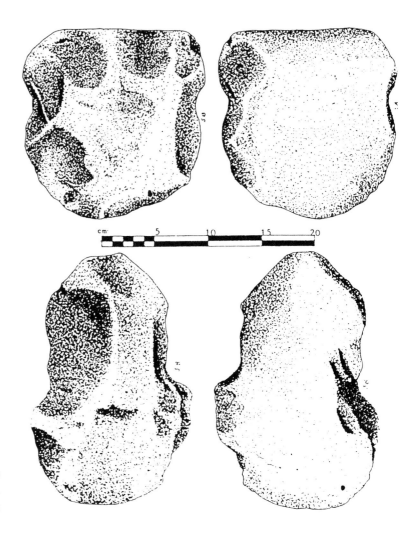

FIGURE 3.1 Waisted axes from the Huon Peninsula. (After Groube 1986.)

clothes and sandals, and proceeded to pull out several wooden trays filled with "waisted blades" while his lab mascot—a wiry tabby cat—rolled about on a heap of potsherds on the lab workbench. There is an indescribable thrill to holding in one's own hands a stone tool manufactured more than forty millennia ago (something on the order of 1,600–2,000 human generations). As we reverently passed the objects to each other—while Les described the geomorphological context that left no doubt as to their antiquity—we pondered what uses these massive implements

could have served in this remote time period, well before the invention of horticulture anywhere in the world.

Later, at the University staff club, Les told us of his own speculative interpretation of the Huon tools. Not being edge-ground, these implements could not have functioned as proper axes, but given their weight they might have been effective at smashing down forest undergrowth or for ring-barking trees. According to Groube, these tools "would be suitable also for some forms of more direct food procurement [such as] stages of sago production, for splitting cycad trunks, or for thinning *Pandanus* stands to promote ripening of the fruit" (1989:297). Groube observed that various natural food plants, such as "aerial yams, local bananas, swamp taro," and others (many of which were domesticated in Near Oceania), would thrive in areas where the dense rainforest canopy had been disturbed or opened up (1989:299). In short, the waisted axes of the Huon Peninsula may represent early stages in an evolutionary progression from forest foraging, through intermediate stages of food-plant promotion and forest management, leading ultimately to plant domestication and true gardening (1989:301–2).[2]

The Huon finds are among the critical and exciting new evidence, obtained over the past two decades, pertaining to the first great era in Pacific prehistory: the colonization of Australia, New Guinea, and the adjacent islands of Near Oceania by early humans, and the development—by generations of their descendants—of diverse cultures, languages, and biological populations. It is an era whose beginning date has been pushed back in time considerably from estimates of just twenty years ago, and about which there is still active debate. Although Pleistocene and early Holocene people did not venture into the Pacific beyond the southeastern end of the Solomons, this period is of greatest significance for regional prehistory. For it was here, in the area we call Near Oceania, that several fundamental cultural developments took place, especially the domestication of tropical crop plants and the origination of an oceanic mode of horticulture. It was also in Near Oceania that a later cultural synthesis would arise, out of the complex interactions of the original colonizers of Sahul (the peoples of "Old Melanesia") and groups of seafaring intruders from island Southeast Asia who spoke Austronesian languages. That story will be taken up in Chapter 4, but for now we must consider the Near Oceanic world

during the late Pleistocene, some 40,000–60,000 years ago.

The Pleistocene Geography of Sahul and Near Oceania

The great nineteenth-century naturalist Alfred Russel Wallace explored the Malay archipelago (what we today call Indonesia), drawing the attention of biogeographers to fundamental biological differences between the Australia–New Guinea region and Southeast Asia. Notable among such differences is the concentration of marsupials in the Australia–New Guinea region, with a concomitant near-total absence of other forms of terrestrial mammals. The boundary between the Asian and Australian faunal regions consists of a zone of smaller islands bearing the name "Wallacea," in honor of the great co-discoverer of the theory of natural selection.[3]

Wallace speculated that the key to understanding this disjunct faunal distribution would lie in "now-submerged lands, uniting islands to continents" (1895:9). He was right in that, with plate tectonic theory and knowledge of the geological evolution of the former Gondwanaland supercontinent, we now comprehend the long-term mechanisms for the patterns Wallace recognized. The deep-time history of Gondwanaland need not detain us, except to note that the Australian Plate separated from the rest about 40 million years ago, and its archaic biota thenceforth evolved on a separate trajectory. By the Pleistocene era the Australian Plate was in its modern position, separated from the Asian mainland by deep oceanic trenches in the Wallacean region.

New Guinea, Tasmania, and some smaller islands near Australia appear on a modern map as separate lands, yet were we to siphon off the world's oceans to a depth of only 130 meters below sea level, all these would suddenly be joined

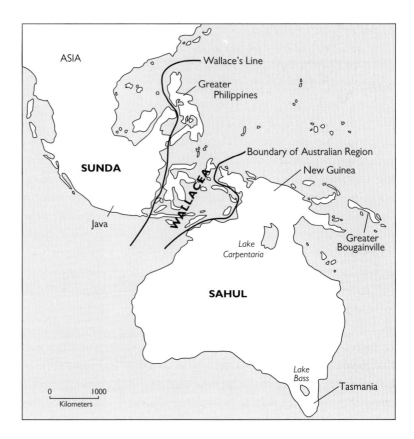

MAP 5 Approximate configuration of Sunda and Sahul during the Pleistocene. (Adapted from Spriggs 1997.)

to the greater Australian land mass. This, indeed, is just what happened at several intervals during the Pleistocene, the siphon being the uptake of oceanic waters into the vast ice sheets that repeatedly covered the world's high latitudes. A map of the Australian region during such a glacial maximum, such as Map 5, reveals the modern Arafura Sea between New Guinea and Australia as an extensive dryland plain (with the Gulf of Carpentaria as a lake at various times) linking New Guinea to Australia, and similarly, the Bass Strait as a land bridge to Tasmania. Biogeographers call this enlarged "Greater Australian" continent *Sahul* (Ballard 1993). On the western side of Wallacea, the vast Sunda shelf was also exposed as dry land, greatly expanding the Southeast Asian mainland. Nonetheless, the islands of Wallacea (primarily Sulawesi, Ambon, Ceram, Halmahera, and the Lesser Sundas) always remained an island world, imposing a barrier to the dispersal of terrestrial vertebrates, including early hominids.

To the north and east of New Guinea, the islands of Near Oceania (the Bismarcks and Solomons) were likewise never connected to Sahul by dry land, for deep-water trenches also separate these from the Australian Plate. This isolation gave rise to marked biogeographic patterns, for the diversity of marsupials, birds, and other life forms drops off rapidly as one leaves New Guinea and moves progressively through the Bismarck and Solomon Archipelagoes.

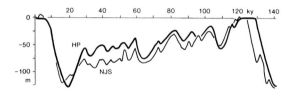

FIGURE 3.2 Fluctuating sea levels characterized the Pacific world during the late Pleistocene and Holocene. HP, Huon Peninsula curve; NJS, temperature-corrected isotopic sea level curve. (After Chappell 1993.)

The Pleistocene sequence of rising and falling global sea levels—linked to climatic cycles of glacial retreat and expanse—and the succession of transgressing and regressing shorelines that resulted from sea level change have been reconstructed thanks to the study of deep-sea cores combined with geomorphological study and radiometric dating of coastlines, such as that of the Huon Peninsula.[4] A sea level curve for the past 140,000 years (Fig. 3.2) indicates that the periods of greatest fall were at about 140,000 and 18,000 years ago. Between these two maximal periods, when the oceans dropped more than 100 meters, were less pronounced cycles with drops of 20–60 meters.

One might anticipate that the peopling of Sahul would correlate with one of these phases of greatest sea level lowering and maximal exposure of dry land. The archaeological evidence is against this, however, and it seems that human colonization of this region was most likely effected during the interval between 60,000 and 40,000 years ago, although some researchers would push the possible dates earlier. But the key point is that even when the oceans were at their lowest levels, there were always significant open-water gaps between the islands of Wallacea, and therefore the arrival of humans into Sahul necessitated over-water transport. This was also the case with the expansion of humans beyond New Guinea into the archipelagoes of Near Oceania. Herein lies one of the most exciting and intriguing aspects of Pacific prehistory: *that we are likely dealing with the earliest purposive voyaging in the history of humankind.*

Initial Human Arrival in Sahul and Near Oceania

Before considering the possibilities of Pleistocene watercraft and voyaging in the western Pacific, we must review the archaeological evidence for human arrival in Sahul and Near Oceania. More than 154 Pleistocene sites have now been discovered in Sahul and Near Oceania, and about 15 percent of these belong to the earliest time phase, greater than 30,000 years ago (Smith and Sharp 1993:52). Surprisingly, these early sites are *not* concentrated in the western parts of Sahul near the likely corridors of human entrée. In fact, they are distributed over virtually the entire geographic expanse of Sahul and Near Oceania, from Northern Australia to the Murray-Darling basin, from southern Tasmania to New Guinea, and even up to New Ireland. This evidence, painstakingly acquired by many archaeologists over the past two decades, demonstrates that having crossed the sea barriers separating Sahul from Asia for more than 40 million years, *Homo sapiens* populations rapidly spread out over these new lands. Moreover, these early modern humans were able to move into, exploit, and permanently inhabit a remarkable range of habitats, from the tundralike high latitudes of Tasmania, through the deserts of Australia, to the humid tropical rainforests of New Guinea and the Bismarcks.

Fixing a precise date for the first movement of *Homo sapiens* onto the Sahul continent is inadvisable, given the constantly changing archaeological picture.[5] A new claim for a possible age of 116,000–176,000 years ago from the Jinmium rockshelter in remote Northern Territory, using the thermoluminescence dating technique (Fullagar et al. 1996), is still highly controversial, as are possible dates on the order of 55,000 years reported for the Malakunanja site in Arnhem Land. We should be very cautious about these oldest age determinations, given that they exceed the technical limits of radiocarbon dating and depend on still-experimental methods. But the dating of the Huon Peninsula waisted axes to between 40,000 and 60,000 years seems solid, and there are now many firm radiocarbon dates from sites throughout the region at 35,000–36,000 years ago. For the time being, the conservative approach holds that initial entry into Sahul occurred *at least* 40,000 years ago, and that colonization of the entire Sahul–Near Oceanic area from Tasmania to New Ireland was accomplished by 35,000–36,000 years ago.[6]

Pleistocene Voyaging in Near Oceania

When Pleistocene-age dates for Australia began to be reported, first from Mulvaney's 1962 excavations at Kenniff Cave and then increasingly as the pace of archaeological research picked up, the probability of *purposive* voyaging—or of the *watercraft* to enable such voyaging—seemed unlikely for this remote time period. Some speculated that Sahul was settled by accident, with a few early humans (or even a single pregnant female!) drifting on floating logs over the Wallacean waterways. Now, however, the mounting (if indirect) evidence that these early colonists were capable of transporting themselves over open ocean for distances of 200 or more kilometers has become compelling, forcing a rethinking of the possibilities of Pleistocene-era watercraft. On reflection, this seems only appropriate, for the history of humankind in the Pacific must above all be a history of voyaging.

The evidence is entirely circumstantial, for no remains of rafts, dugouts, bark-boats, or the like have been preserved.[7] What then compels us to think that the colonists of Sahul and Near Oceania did not merely drift into their new lands by accident? The weight of statistical probability. If only a single open-water crossing were required, one could invoke Occam's Razor, or similar principles of parsimony, to argue that over the course of thousands of human generations, surely a few individuals would have made it by chance alone over the Wallacean divide into Sahul. But this was not the case, for—regardless of whether the early migrants followed a northerly route into Sahul via Sulawesi, Peleng, and Sula on into what is now Irian Jaya (or other variants thereof), or a southerly route via the intervisible chain of islands stretching from Java through Bali, Lombok, Sumbawa, Flores, Alor, and Timor onto the Arafura Shelf—not just one but *repeated* water crossings of 10–100 kilometers would have been required.

Such successive and successful crossings, over admittedly largely intervisible gaps between islands, got humans onto the Sahul continent. But the evidence does not end there. In 1981 Jim Specht reported the first Pleistocene-age radiocarbon date from New Britain, an island never connected to Sahul by dry land (Specht et al. 1981). A few years later, the Lapita Homeland Project uncovered firm evidence for the settlement of both New Britain and New Ireland at least 35,000 years ago. New Britain is visible from New Guinea, and New Ireland from the former, so one might again argue that an adventurous Sahulian saw opportunity on the horizon, set him- or herself adrift on a handy log, and hoped for the best. But then came the evidence from Kilu, a rockshelter on Buka Island in the Solomons with a first occupation dated to 29,000 years ago, which is *not* visible from New Britain.[8]

Suddenly the probability that people had gotten all the way out to the Solomons by a remarkable sequence of merely accidental "voyages" seemed quite low indeed. And then the clincher: an Australian National University team dug into the 4-meter depths of Pamwak Rockshelter on Manus (Fig. 3.3) and found that the Admiralty Islands too had been settled deep in the Pleistocene, by at least 13,000 years ago if not considerably before.[9] Matthew Spriggs, one of the excavators of Pamwak, puts the implications of this discovery this way:

> The settlement of Manus may represent a real threshold in voyaging ability as it is the only island settled in the Pleistocene beyond the range of one-way intervisibility. Voyaging to Manus involved a blind crossing of some 60–90 km in a 200–230-km voyage, when no land would have been visible whether coming from the north coast of Sahul or New Hanover at the northern end of New Ireland. These would have been tense hours or days on board that first voyage and the name of the Pleistocene Columbus who led this crew will never be known. The target arcs for Manus are 15° from New Hanover, 17° from Mussau, and 28° from New Guinea. (*Spriggs 1997:29*)

Once it was certain that Manus and Buka had been colonized in the Pleistocene, who could doubt that the first Sahulians were people comfortable around and on the water? And why not? Fish bones and shellfish remains from the Matenkupkum site on New Ireland are possibly the earliest evidence of marine resource exploitation anywhere in the world.[10]

While we can be confident in our newly won knowledge that early Pacific peoples were capable of open-ocean voyages, gaining real understanding of their vessels or their methods is another matter. Here we remain wholly in the realm of theory, although the carefully crafted studies of

FIGURE 3.3 Archaeological excavation in progress in the Pamwak rockshelter, Manus Island. (Photo courtesy Wal Ambrose.)

Geoff Irwin (1991, 1992, 1993) allow us to glimpse some of the possibilities. Irwin views the region extending from the Bismarck Archipelago through the main Solomon Islands as a great "voyaging nursery," sheltered from the tropical cyclone belts that lie to the north and south, and one in which "seasonal and predictable changes" in wind and current direction encouraged early voyagers to experiment with round-trip expeditions exploring and exploiting these mostly intervisible islands. An intrepid navigator might anticipate the prevailing winds and currents of the southern summer that would take his or her social group from a departure point in New Britain or New Ireland down through the Solomons chain as far as San Cristobal or Santa Anna and plan for an equally predictable return voyage in the southern winter. If such a group were at home exploiting the rich shellfish and fish of inshore waters, as well as the more limited marsupial, avian, and other resources of the rainforest, the trip might well be repeated on a regular basis. But here we come to the limits of theoretical speculation regarding this period, so remote from the world of known ethnography; a brief reimmersion into the "facts" of prehistory is appropriate.

Near Oceania during the Pleistocene

Archaeological knowledge of New Guinea, the Bismarcks, and the Solomons during the Pleistocene is still limited, with a total of only 21 known sites (Smith and Sharp 1993, Table 1; Spriggs 1997, Table 3.1), most of these rockshelters or caves.[11] The sites are enumerated in Table 3.1, and Map 6 shows the geographical locations of some of them. Not all of these have yet been thoroughly excavated or reported. With the exception of the Huon terraces, most of the New Guinea sites are located in the interior, mountainous Highlands. The dearth of coastal or lowland sites stems from the difficulty of finding exposed sedimentary contexts dating to the Pleistocene, due both to post-Pleistocene drowning of coastlines and to the modern prevalence of extensive mangrove swamps around the littoral perimeter of New Guinea. Thus the uplifted terraces of the Huon provide a uniquely preserved example of Pleistocene shorelines. The other nine sites listed in Table 3.1 are situated on the large islands of New Britain and New Ireland, and on more distant Manus and Buka. Since these two clusters of

Pleistocene sites—in the New Guinea Highlands and on the Melanesian islands—occur in radically different environmental settings, I discuss them separately, beginning with the Highlands.

The New Guinea Highlands   European exploration of the Highlands, which began in earnest only in the mid-twentieth century, stunned the anthropological world by revealing the unsuspected presence of at least a million people, living a more or less "neolithic" existence. Thanks to the work of several archaeologists—such as Jack Golson, Mary-Jane Mountain, and J. Peter White—we now know that people have been present in these intermontane valleys for more than thirty millennia.[12] Moreover, the very landscape of the Highlands, with its extensive grasslands, has been radically shaped by the cumulative actions of many human generations. Still, we have little more than a glimpse through the window of time into the lives and cultures of these early mountain dwellers, because direct evidence is limited to materials from a handful of excavated and published sites, such as the Kafiavana (Fig. 3.4) and Nombe rockshelters, and the open site of Kosipe. The material culture found in these sites consists largely of amorphous stone flake and core tools and, from some sites such as Kosipe and Nombe, "waisted blades" or axes similar to those from the Huon terraces (Fig. 3.5). Remains of animal bones and terrestrial gastropods collected for food provide limited evidence of diet and economy. Additional evidence for environmental change comes from pollen sequences from several Highlands swamp sites.[13]

The climate of the higher-altitude interior of New Guinea fluctuated during the late Pleistocene, in response to worldwide climatic changes. Between about 35,000 and 30,000 years ago, alpine shrub or grassland vegetation expanded considerably, and it persisted until perhaps 15,000 years

TABLE 3.1

Pleistocene Sites of Near Oceania[a]

Island	Site	Site Type	Age Range (Ka B.P.)[b]	References
NEW GUINEA	Batari	Cave	16.9; 8.2–0	White 1972
	Huon	Upraised terraces	40–60	Groube et al. 1986
	Kafiavana	Rockshelter	11–0	White 1972
	Kiowa	Rockshelter	10.4–0	Bulmer and Bulmer 1964
	Kosipe	Open site	26.5–7.2	White et al. 1970
	Kuk	Swamp site	30	Smith and Sharp 1993
	Lachitu	Rockshelter	35.4; 13.9–12.3; 9–5.6; 2–0.3	Gorecki et al. 1991
	NFX	Alluvial terrace	18.1	Watson and Cole 1977
	Nombe	Rockshelter	26.2–0	Gillieson and Mountain 1983; Mountain 1983; White 1972
	Seraba	Rockshelter	14–6	
	Wanlek	Alluvial terrace	15.1–12; 5.5–2.8	
	Yuku	Rockshelter	9.8–0	Bulmer and Bulmer 1964
NEW BRITAIN	Misisil	Cave	11; 9; 3.7–0	Specht et al. 1981
	Yombon	Open site	35; 14; 6.8–4.1; 2.7–0	Pavlides 1993; Pavlides and Gosden 1994
NEW IRELAND	Balof 2	Rockshelter	14–8.5; 3.5–0	White et al. 1991
	Buang Merabak	Rockshelter	31–20; 10.8–0	Leavesley and Allen 1998; Rosenfeld 1997
	Matenbek	Rockshelter	20–18; 8.5–7	Allen 1996
	Matenkupkum	Rockshelter	35.4–20; 16–10	Gosden and Robertson 1991
	Panakiwuk	Rockshelter	15–13; 10–8; 1.5–0	Marshall and Allen 1991
MANUS	Pamwak	Rockshelter	Pre-13; 13–12; 10–5; 2–0	Fredericksen et al. 1993
BUKA	Kilu	Rockshelter	29–20; 10–5.4; 2.5	Wickler and Spriggs 1988

[a] Data compiled from Smith and Sharp (1993) and Spriggs (1997).

[b] Age ranges in thousands of years (Ka), based on radiocarbon dates. Multiple age ranges indicate more than a single period of occupation or use.

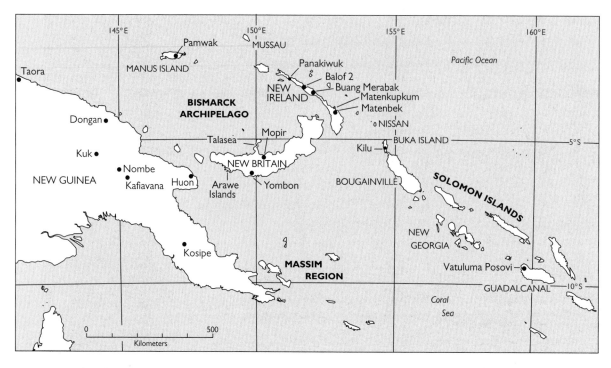

MAP 6 Near Oceania, showing the distribution of important Pleistocene and early Holocene archaeological sites.

ago, when the tree line began to rise significantly in response to climatic warming. The pollen cores suggest, however, that climatic factors were not the only influence on vegetation patterns, and there is good evidence that humans were igniting fires, and thus encouraging the spread of grasslands, beginning as early as 21,000 B.P. The evidence for anthropogenic burning lies in significant increases in carbonized particles in the cores as described by Haberle (1993:117), who refers to a "sustained anthropogenic disturbance episode" lasting from 21,000 to 8,000 years ago. The cultural reasons behind such human burning can only be guessed, but they might include the facilitation of hunting or forest clearance in order to encourage the growth and spread of economically useful plants, such as *Pandanus*. I have already mentioned Groube's hypothesis that early people in New

Guinea were actively managing plant resources, using waisted axes to open up forest canopy by trimming or ring-barking. Such cobble tools have been found at a number of the Highland sites, including Kosipe, which has been interpreted as "a seasonal site for the exploitation of mountain pandanus nuts and perhaps hunting of some of the upper forest megafaunal browsers" (Mountain 1991b:515).

The New Guinea Highlands during the Pleistocene were home to a remarkable range of marsupial megafauna, all becoming extinct by the early Holocene. Seven species of large, herbivorous marsupials have been identified, belonging to the wallaby genus *Protemnodon* or to the diprotodon family. According to Tim Flannery, these animals were "browsers of the forest and sub-alpine grassland," and while smaller than their

FIGURE 3.4 Kafiavana Rockshelter in the New Guinea Highlands, after excavation by J. Peter White. The site spans the terminal Pleistocene to Holocene periods. (Photo courtesy J. P. White.)

Australian megafaunal counterparts, they offered substantial food packages to Highlands hunters (1995:132). The largest of the extinct diprotodons weighed up to 200 kilograms and "was similar in form to the marsupial rhinoceros of Australia." There was also the "Huli beast" (*Hulitherium tomassetii*), "shaped much like a panda, with the same high forehead and forward-facing eyes," weighing in at about 100 kilograms. Bones of *Protemnodon, Thylacine, Diprotodon,* and various other

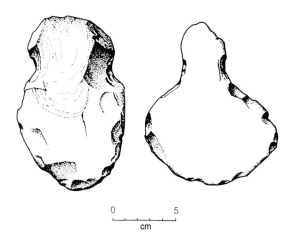

FIGURE 3.5 Stone tools from the Pleistocene occupation levels at Kosipe, New Guinea Highlands. (After White and O'Connell 1982.)

species have been recovered from Highlands sites such as Nombe, and these may have been among the prey targeted by early hunters. To what extent hunting was responsible for the extinction of these great beasts is debatable, although the combination of hunting and human-induced fires resulting in grassland expansion is likely to have been important, in conjunction with climatic changes. In the most detailed faunal analysis yet undertaken of a Pleistocene Highlands site, Mountain (1983, 1991a, 1991b) demonstrated important changes in the faunal evidence for hunting over the 20,000 years that this rockshelter was inhabited. In particular, at the end of the Pleistocene and into the early Holocene, there are significant increases in the numbers of smaller and medium-sized prey, such as birds, rodents, and fruit bats.

One yearns to know more about this fascinating and lengthy period in the early history of Near Oceania, but the evidence is simply too thin. We are left merely with a hazy picture of peoples adept at inhabiting a relatively cold, interior region

despite their minimal technology, insofar as that technology is reflected in the surviving record of stone and bone.[14] They may have hunted a range of now-extinct large marsupials, as well as other smaller fauna including birds, fruit bats, rodents, frogs, and dasyurids. By 21,000 years ago they were also burning the vegetation of their valleys, and quite possibly practicing forms of forest clearance and plant management aided by their waisted, split-cobble axes. Such early experiments in plant manipulation and management would lead, by the early Holocene, to the actual domestication of certain plants.

The Bismarck Archipelago and the Solomons   In 1985, the international Lapita Homeland Project (LHP) sent several teams of archaeologists into the field throughout the Bismarck Archipelago, in a coordinated effort to resolve some refractory issues surrounding the Lapita cultural complex (see Chapter 4).[15] Prior to the LHP, relatively little was known of the prehistory of this vast arc of islands: a handful of Lapita ceramic sites had been identified, the Balof 1 rockshelter on New Ireland had been dated to ca. 8000 B.P., and a single cave site called Misisil in the interior of New Britain had yielded a radiocarbon date that barely qualified as terminal Pleistocene. A year later, at the conclusion of the main field season of the LHP, Melanesian prehistory had to be rewritten. Excavations at four rockshelters (Fig. 3.6) on New Ireland (Balof 2, Buang Merabak, Matenkupkum, and Panakiwuk) had produced sequences well back into the Pleistocene, with the oldest from Matenkupkum coming in at 35,410 ± 430 B.P. (Allen and Gosden 1996:186). In the next few years, continued work by LHP members resulted in new Pleistocene finds at Matenbek on New Ireland, Yombon on New Britain, Kilu on Buka, and Pamwak on Manus (Table 3.1). All of this evidence is new, and since several sites are not yet been fully

FIGURE 3.6 Excavations in progress at the Matenbek site, New Ireland. (Photo courtesy Jim Allen.)

analyzed or reported, a detailed understanding of the 25,000 years of Pleistocene history represented in these sites lies in the future. Nonetheless, several tentative syntheses have been ventured, and we can at least rough out the framework of a prehistoric sequence for the Bismarcks-Solomons region from 35,000 to 10,000 years ago.[16]

Allen and Gosden opine that "crossing the Vitiaz Strait may have been a quick paddle for humans but it was a significant journey for Pacific history" (1996:185), for the Bismarcks were the first true Pacific islands to be colonized, beyond the shifting continental margins of Sahul. Establishing a viable existence on these islands required certain adaptations, given a steep decline in biogeographic richness as one moves off Sahul and into the island world. The numbers of plant and animal resources available to Pleistocene hunters

TABLE 3.2

Comparison of the Modern Faunas
of New Guinea and New Britain

(numbers of species)[a]

Faunal Group	New Guinea	New Britain
Anteaters	2	0
Tree kangaroos	4	0
Bandicoots	7	1
Wallabies	9	1
Phalangers	27	2
Birds	265	80

[a] Data from Allen and Gosden (1996).

and gatherers would have been noticeably reduced, as illustrated by a comparison of the modern faunas of New Guinea and New Britain (Table 3.2). Moreover, the islands lacked the now-extinct marsupial megafauna that had been available both in Australia and in the New Guinea Highlands during the period of initial human arrival.

From the initial LHP finds at the early coastally situated rockshelters such as Buang Merabak and Matenkupkum, it appeared at first that this adaptation to a true island existence might have been facilitated by a focus on the exploitation of littoral food resources (Gosden and Robertson 1991:43), in a kind of "strandlooping" economic mode. However, the discovery of chert flaking floors dated to 35,000–33,000 years ago at Yombon, in the interior of New Britain (35 kilometers from the coast), dispels any simple notion that the Pleistocene colonists of the Bismarcks confined their activities to the shoreline. Moreover, several rockshelters now close to the coast were situated a considerable distance inland during periods of lowered sea level.

In fact, the faunal evidence from the oldest Pleistocene sites in the Bismarcks suggests that people exploited a wide range of both terrestrial and inshore marine resources. Among the terrestrial animals represented in the faunal assemblages from these sites are a number of bird species (including some now extinct; Steadman et al. 1999), lizards, snakes, rats, and fruit bats. The coastal marine fauna includes a few fishbones (although no detailed reports are yet available on these) and a limited range of shellfish, such as the large reef gastropod *Turbo argyrostoma.* These marine foods could have been taken with simple methods, such as spearing, hand groping, and simple collecting, and there is as yet no material evidence for fishhooks or other sophisticated kinds of fishing devices.

A more open question concerns the kinds of plant foods that might have provided some balance to the diet of these early settlers. No hard-shelled nuts or other plant remains (including pollen) have yet been recovered from sites or levels predating 20,000 years ago. However, microscopic starch grains and raphides identified on stone tools from the Kilu site have been tentatively identified to the aroid genus *Colocasia* (of which the domesticated taro, *C. esculenta*, is a member), raising the possibility of wild tuber gathering.[17] Not only *Colocasia* but also the aroid genera *Cyrtosperma* and *Alocasia* may have been naturally present in the Bismarcks, along with the sago palm (*Metroxylon* spp.), and Spriggs (1997: 34) suggests that these could have been "possible staples . . . encountered by the first colonists." These are provocative hypotheses, but their testing requires more fine-grained field and laboratory research.

The lithic technology of the pre-20,000 B.P. period in the Bismarcks consists almost exclusively of simple flake and core tools of expedient or amorphous shapes (Fig. 3.7). These were made of locally available rocks, primarily fine-grained igneous or sedimentary types. There is no indica-

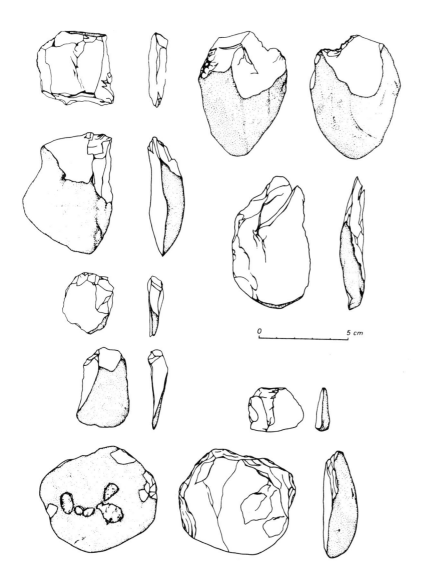

0   5 cm

FIGURE 3.7 Stone tools from the Matenkupkum Rockshelter on New Ireland. (After Allen et al. 1989.)

tion at this earliest period of the transport or exchange of stone resources over long distances.

Summarizing the period from ca. 35,000 to 20,000 years ago in the Bismarcks, Allen and Gosden write that the "meagre data imply population numbers large enough to create archaeological sites, but beyond this the sites themselves suggest only sporadic occupation. . . . We envisage this settlement to have involved small groups of mobile, broad-spectrum foragers" (1996:187). Gosden (1993:133) has called this a "world without any ethnographic parallel," emphasizing the challenge it poses to archaeological understanding. At about 20,000–18,000 years ago, however, things began to change in a manner that is detectable in the archaeological record of the Bismarcks. Two changes have captured the attention of prehistorians: (1) the appearance of bones of the Gray Cuscus, an arboreal marsupial (*Phalanger orientalis*), and (2) the presence of obsidian, deriving from the Mopir and Talasea sources on New Britain.[18] The cuscus bones are important because this species is not indigenous to the Bismarcks and is likely to have been purposively introduced by humans into the islands from its original habitat on New Guinea.[19] The obsidian, in a similar manner, indicates that people were no longer simply using local stone resources, but were transporting—directly or through trade or exchange networks—a valuable lithic material over distances of up to 350 kilometers (e.g., from Talasea to Matenbek, as measured by straight-line distance). Gosden points to the significance of these two changes: "instead of moving people to resources, resources were [now] moved to people" (1993: 133), perhaps signaling a shift in the way that islanders viewed their environment. Certainly, the possibility that watercraft and sailing abilities had undergone further development seems likely. It may be at around this time that the more remote Manus Islands were discovered, as the oldest levels in Pamwak (Fig. 3.3) date to something earlier than 13,000 B.P.

Other aspects of subsistence do not look much different in the period after 20,000 B.P. from that preceding. A mix of fish, shellfish, bats, rats, reptiles, and the newly imported *Phalanger* fills out the roster of faunal remains.[20] There may have been some evolution in material culture, however, for in addition to the imported obsidian there are hints at shell working. Some worked shell pieces from Matenbek look suspiciously like blanks or roughouts for simple fishhooks, but until the presence of finished hooks is confirmed archaeologically this remains speculative.

Given that the very existence of a Pleistocene archaeological record for island Melanesia is barely a decade old, we have made remarkable strides in our knowledge of regional prehistory. We have learned that the long centuries from that initial voyage across the Vitiaz Strait until the end of the Pleistocene were not without significant cultural changes. Filling out the record of change is the challenge lying ahead.

Cultural Innovations of the Early Holocene

If the pace of cultural change during the Pleistocene was so gradual as to be barely perceptible in the archaeological record, things began to change rapidly during the early Holocene, both in the New Guinea Highlands and in the coastal lowlands and islands. It is an open question whether the developments in these two regions proceeded independently, or whether they were influenced by exchanges of ideas (and human genes?). Likewise, prehistorians debate the extent of cultural and biological contacts between the peoples of Near Oceania and those of island Southeast Asia during the early to mid-Holocene. Near Oceania was certainly not hermetically sealed, and the supposed appearance of the pig by around 5000 B.P. in New Guinea suggests that contacts between Near Oceania and Southeast Asia were active. For the most part, however, the cultural developments of this period were indigenous to Near Oceania.

Plant geographers and ethnobotanists have long recognized that New Guinea and the adjacent Bismarcks are the probable place of origin for many tropical crops, because the wild ancestors of these plants are restricted in their natural distributions to this region.[21] Among these domesticates are the *Australimusa* bananas (which have an upright inflorescence and reddish-orange colored fruit), sugarcane (*Saccharum officinarum*), a tuber crop (*Pueraria lobata*), the ti plant (*Cordyline fruticosum*), probably breadfruit (*Artocarpus altilis*), a number of fruit- and nut-bearing trees (the *Canarium* almond, Tahitian Chestnut [*Inocarpus fagiferus*], *Barringtonia* spp., *Terminalia,* and others), as well as several aroids, including taro (*Colocasia esculenta*), "elephant-ear" taro (*Alocasia macrorrhiza*), and giant swamp taro (*Cyrtosperma chamissonis*). *Colocasia,* a major staple throughout Oceania, was once thought to be a Southeast Asian domesticate, but recent cytological research suggests multiple origins, one in the New Guinea region.[22]

Among the most exciting archaeological discoveries in Near Oceania over the past two decades have been those supporting this ethnobotanical hypothesis of a Near Oceanic center of early plant domestication and horticultural development.[23] These include archaeobotanical remains of crop plants, pollen and phytoliths, and the physical remains of field cultivation systems. Moreover, associated dates make it increasingly certain that these developments began in the early Holocene, as early as similar steps toward agriculture elsewhere in the Old World. Thus the Oceanic peoples can rightly claim to have played their own significant role in what is arguably the most fundamental cultural development in the history of modern *Homo sapiens:* the invention of—and ultimate dependence of human populations on—agricultural modes of production.

The New Guinea Highlands When Western explorers first entered the Highland valleys before World War II, they were amazed not only at the density of indigenous populations, but also at the marvelous ditched and raised-bed gardens that frequently covered hectare upon hectare of originally swampy valley bottoms.[24] Evidence for the antiquity and development of such Highlands cultivation systems did not, however, begin to emerge until the late 1960s, when Jack Golson began his long-term work at the now-famous Kuk plantation site in the Wahgi Valley near Mt. Hagen.[25] At an elevation of 1,550 meters above sea level, the swampy floor of the Wahgi was

being drained for a tea plantation in 1970 when Jim Allen observed a stratigraphic succession of often intercut older drains in the sidewalls of the new plantation drainage canals (Allen 1970). When subjected to detailed stratigraphic analysis combined with extensive areal excavations by Golson, these drains and associated features revealed a remarkable sequence of horticultural use of the Wahgi Valley floor over a period of some 9,000 years.

Golson has defined six phases of increasingly complex and intensive use of the Wahgi Valley floor at Kuk, but it is the earliest three phases which are of immediate interest to us here. Phase 1, dated to 9,000 years ago, consists of a series of "gutters, hollows, pits and stakeholes" of obvious human origin sealed beneath a telltale wedge of "grey clay" that blanketed the entire valley floor (Golson 1977:613). The exact function of these features has been vigorously debated, but they are clearly not habitation-related, and some kind of simple horticultural function seems most plausible. Moreover, the gray clay itself testifies to a period of accelerated erosion on the surrounding valley flanks that, in conjunction with pollen analyses, speaks to heightened levels of human disturbance, arguably from some form of incipient horticulture.

In Kuk phase 2 (6000–5500 B.P.), the evidence for active manipulation of the swampy valley floor becomes incontrovertible, with "at least four large channels" up to 2 meters wide and deep that were cut across the swamp to drain it (Fig. 3.8). Moreover, there are now also "circular clay islands of about a metre diameter" separated by intersecting channels. Such islands would have formed excellent raised beds for the cultivation of *Colocasia* taro, and possibly also *Australimusa* bananas or *Pueraria* tubers. By phase 3 (4000–2500 B.P.) the primitive raised beds of phase 2 had been replaced by true reticulate drainage systems that are

FIGURE 3.8 Archaeological section across a large drainage ditch (the dark infilled feature to the man's right), dating to about 3500 B.P., at the Kuk site. (Photo courtesy Jack Golson.)

undeniably the antecedents of the complex drainage systems ultimately witnessed by twentieth-century anthropologists.

Golson and his associates have made herculean efforts to determine what crops were grown in the Kuk swamp gardens in the earlier phases (for the latest phase there is no doubt that this was sweet potato; see Chapter 5). There is a hint, from phytolith evidence, of *Australimusa* bananas, which would be entirely reasonable, but in general the archaeobotanical evidence has proved intractable.

Douglas Yen (1991) believes that *Colocasia* taro, which seems to have been domesticated independently in Near Oceania, is the most likely candidate. The kinds of social and economic transformations that surely accompanied these early steps in the development of indigenous agriculture in the Highland valleys are as yet little in evidence, since few habitation sites of the early Holocene have been discovered or excavated. It would be premature to sketch any model of such changes, and it must suffice to underscore the tremendous importance of the Kuk sequence for Oceanic prehistory.

New Guinea Lowlands and the Islands   Nineteen sites ranging geographically from the northern New Guinea lowlands to the main Solomon Islands have yielded cultural materials dating to the early to mid-Holocene period (Table 3.3). Some of these are the upper levels of sites also producing Pleistocene-age assemblages, such as Pamwak and Panakiwuk rockshelters; others are strictly of Holocene age. Space precludes a site-by-site discussion, and I will focus only on two key aspects emerging from this period: evidence for horticulture and for advances in material culture, especially shell tool technology.[26]

Presently, portions of the north coast of New Guinea and the entire floor of the great Sepik-Ramu River drainages extending some 100 or more kilometers inland are dominated by dense, seasonally flooded swamps with *Nipa* palms, sago, mangrove, and other plants. Traveling by canoe or launch up the meandering Sepik today and viewing kilometer after kilometer of rank, saltwater, crocodile-infested swampland, one would think such an environment virtually primeval. Yet a mere 6,000 years ago the lower Sepik-Ramu was not swamp at all, but a vast inland sea or lagoon rich in marine and brackish-water resources, enticing people to settle along its shifting shorelines.

TABLE 3.3
Selected Sites of the Early to Mid-Holocene Period in Lowland New Guinea and Near Oceania

Island	Site	Site Type	Age Range (B.P.)[a]	References
NEW GUINEA	Dongan	Shell midden	5,690–5,830	Swadling et al. 1991
	Lachitu	Rockshelter	5,640	Gorecki et al. 1991
	Taora	Rockshelter	2,250–6,120	Gorecki et al. 1991
NEW BRITAIN	Apalo	Open site (waterlogged)	4,250–4,050	Gosden 1991a
	Lolmo	Cave	6,100–5,250	Gosden et al. 1994
	Misisil	Rockshelter	3,700	Specht et al. 1981
	Yombon	Open site	4,100–6,820	Pavlides 1993
NEW IRELAND	Balof 1	Rockshelter	7,450–recent	Downie and White 1978
	Matenbek	Rockshelter	8,500–7,000	Allen 1996
	Panakiwuk	Rockshelter	10,000–8,000; 1,500–recent	Marshall and Allen 1991
MANUS	Father's Water	Open site	?	Kennedy 1983
	Pamwak	Rockshelter	10,000–5,000; 2,000–recent	Fredericksen et al. 1993
	Peli Louson	Rockshelter	4,850	Kennedy 1983
NISSAN	Lebang Halika	Rockshelter	3,650–3,200	Spriggs 1991b
	Lebang Takoroi	Cave	6,100–3,800	Spriggs 1991b
BUKA	Kilu	Rockshelter	10,000–5,400; 2,500	Wickler and Spriggs 1988
	Palandraku	Wet cave	ca. 5,000	Wickler 1990
GUADALCANAL	Vatuluma Posovi	Rockshelter	6,285–4,415	Roe 1992, 1993
	Vatuluma Tavuro	Cave	4,230–3,650	Roe 1992, 1993

[a] Dates given are generally the oldest and youngest in a series of radiocarbon ages that may include more than those given here. Dates are listed as reported in the literature and may vary in terms of specific correction factors or calibrations.

Archaeologists Pam Swadling and Nick Araho of the Papua New Guinea National Museum, aided by geochronologist John Chappell, have determined the extent of this mid-Holocene embayment and its subsequent history of alluvial infilling, locating several settlement sites that help to fill in the picture of early economic developments in Near Oceania.[27]

The Dongan site, a marine shell midden now more than 15 kilometers inland on a tributary of the Ramu River, was once situated on or near the shores of the ancient inland sea. A test trench excavated into the eroding riverbank revealed occupation deposits radiocarbon dated between 5,690 and 5,830 years ago, and the waterlogged, anaerobic sediments contained well-preserved plant remains. Among the fruits, seeds, and nuts found by Swadling, Araho, and their team are many of the tree crops so important in indigenous Melanesian subsistence, including the *Canarium* almond, coconut (*Cocos nucifera*), betel nut (*Areca catechu*), candlenut (*Aleurites*), *Pangium edule*, *Pometia pinnata*, *Pandanus*, and several others (Swadling et al. 1991). This is the strongest evidence yet that the peoples of lowland Near Oceania had already taken significant steps toward the domestication of tree crops by the middle Holocene.[28]

From various sites in the Bismarcks and Solomons, evidence for indigenous arboriculture based on domesticated *Canarium* almond and other tree crops is also slowly accumulating. At Apalo on Kumbun Island off the southern New Britain coast, another waterlogged deposit dated to 4250–4050 B.P. (and thus predating the Lapita period) also yielded remains of *Canarium indicum*, coconut, *Aleurites*, *Terminalia*, *Pandanus*, *Pangium*, *Spondias*, and *Dracontomelon* (Spriggs 1997:79). On Nissan Island between the Bismarck and Solomon Archipelagoes, Spriggs recovered *Canarium*, *Pangium*, *Sterculia*, *Metroxylon*, *Burckella*, *Dracontomelon*, and *Terminalia* remains from levels of two rockshelters dated to the early second millennium B.C., again predating Lapita ceramic horizons. And, in two aceramic rockshelter sites on Guadalcanal Island in the main Solomons, Roe (1992, 1993) found *Canarium* nut charcoal and anvil stones used to crack open the hard-shelled nuts.

All of this evidence mounts a fairly strong case for indigenous development of a kind of subsistence system known as *arboriculture*, or orchard-based tree cropping. Whether taro or other root crops such as *Pueraria* were also cultivated at this period in the Near Oceanic lowlands and islands is not yet established. But tree crops such as *Canarium*, which is today distributed from Wallacea to Vanuatu, could have provided an important basis for subsistence. Moreover, *Canarium* and various other economically important trees would later become an essential component of subsistence economies not only in Near Oceania but also in the farther-flung islands of Remote Oceania.[29]

Other key cultural developments of the early to mid-Holocene period took place in material culture. Both Pam Swadling and Paul Gorecki have claimed that pottery was present in mid-Holocene contexts in their sites in the Ramu River region and on the Vanimo coast of New Guinea, respectively. There are unresolved questions, however, regarding the stratigraphic contexts and dating of these collections, and detailed site reports and ceramic analyses have yet to be published.[30] Until such details are provided, the extent of any pre-Lapita ceramic assemblages in Near Oceania remains uncertain.

What is clear, however, is that in the islands there was a mid-Holocene advance in shell-working technology, a critical adaptation to an insular and marine way of living. The sample of shell artifacts is still limited, but enough examples have been recovered from Pamwak (where there are edge-ground adzes or axes of *Tridacna* shell), Lolmo Cave (where the assemblage includes fishhooks and armbands of *Trochus* shell, and a *Conus* shell disc), Lebang Halika (*Tridacna* shell adzes, polished shell knives, and a *Trochus* fishhook), and the Guadalcanal rockshelters (*Trochus* armbands and cut shell) to dispel any doubts about the development of a complex shell-working technology. Both adzes and fishhooks are among the objects manufactured from shell, and these are two of the most fundamental implements in the classic oceanic tool kit: the adz for forest clearance and woodworking of all kinds, and the fishhook for exploitation of sea resources beyond what can be simply speared or gathered in the inshore shallows.

Of noneconomic aspects of life among these mid-Holocene occupants of Near Oceania we as yet know almost nothing. A few shell beads and armbands hint at a bodily aesthetic, but what of their forms of kinship address and social organization, their mythologies and cosmologies—all the things that make us uniquely human? The archaeological record is, for the present, mute, and I imagine that it will take the work of several more generations of archaeologists and historical anthropologists to even begin to draw back this veil of time. Matthew Spriggs sums up the situation elegantly: "That the early Island Melanesians had an aesthetic sense is obvious. They were after all modern humans like us. If they painted on cave walls the tropical climate would long ago have removed all traces. Other canvases for their art were likely to have been even more ephemeral. They had no fired pots to paint or incise. Their songs have gone" (1997:66).

A Paradox and a Hypothesis

Before leaving the topic of "Old" Melanesia I must draw attention to an apparent paradox of great consequence for the human history of Oceania. Given that humans have been in Near Oceania for at least 40,000 years, and also that this is a region of large and resource-rich islands, why did human populations never reach high density levels (except in the New Guinea Highlands), especially after the development of food-producing subsistence strategies in the early Holocene? The natural reproductive capacity of humans to increase rapidly has been understood at least since Thomas Malthus's classic essay, and even at the relatively low reproductive rates known for

hunting and gathering populations (perhaps 0.1% per year; Hassan 1981:200–3) a sizable population could easily have arisen in Near Oceania. Presumably the carrying capacity of the rainforests and littoral zones was not sufficient to support this kind of density with only a hunting and gathering economy, but then why did populations not suddenly burgeon after the domestication of various indigenous tree and root crops, as they did elsewhere in the world following the invention and adoption of agriculture? There is no evidence in the archaeological record for Near Oceania that human populations were ever very numerous or densely settled; if anything, the archaeological landscape of the early to mid-Holocene is particularly sparse.[31] Moreover, as we will see in later chapters, this situation contrasts strikingly with that in the Remote Oceanic islands, in which large and dense populations arose repeatedly on islands within only one to two-and-a-half thousand years. The demographic history of Near Oceania (except the New Guinea Highlands) thus stands apart from that of Remote Oceania.

This paradox is best explained by the pernicious effects of malaria, combined with other infectious diseases, as Les Groube (1993a) has suggested (see also Golson 1972b:29). The several species of malaria parasite (*Plasmodium*), along with their *Anopheles* mosquito vectors, are geographically confined to Near Oceania, along with the Reef–Santa Cruz Islands and Vanuatu. At least two species of *Plasmodium* (*P. vivax* and *P. malariae*) probably accompanied the first human colonizers of Sahul, or followed shortly thereafter, given the presence of genetic mutations in the blood systems of Near Oceanic populations that have been selected for because they confer partial resistance to the disease.[32] The more debilitating and frequently fatal *P. falciparum* may have entered the region later. Groube notes how endemic malaria (which is persistent, in contrast with epidemic diseases such as measles) might have regulated human population numbers, primarily through the continual mortality of individuals before they could reach reproductive age. Even with a case mortality of just 0.5 percent due to *P. vivax*, endemic malaria could have the effect of an 80 percent reduction in the rate of natural increase in the population (Groube 1993a:175–76). In addition to causing high mortality among infants and children, malaria can lodge in the placenta of a pregnant woman, "causing anaemia, foetal loss and death" (1993a: 174). Endemic malaria combined with other debilitating infectious diseases in adults can also lead to higher overall mortality rates.

In sum, Groube presents a hypothesis of fundamental significance in the long-term human history of Near Oceania. As he writes: "It is pointless to speculate too closely on unknown demographic variables in such a remote period. What is clear is that the natural increase rate appears to have been very low throughout the prehistory of Sundaland. Infections of *vivax* and *malariae* offer one possible check upon natural increase which could have been in operation from an early stage in the prehistory of the region" (1993a:177). The single obvious exception within Near Oceania is the New Guinea Highlands, where a large and dense population did develop in the fertile valleys, supported by intensive systems of food production. But the Highlands are generally above the altitude for *Anopheles* mosquitoes to survive, and malaria is either absent or has relatively little effect in the Highlands valleys (Brown 1978:60; Cattani 1992:304); they are the exception that proves the rule.

CHAPTER 4

Lapita and the Austronesian Expansion

We can propose for the S.W. Pacific some early community of culture linking New Caledonia, Tonga, and Samoa, antedating the "Melanesian" cultures of the first and ancestral to the historic Western Polynesian cultures of the other two. This community is expressed in terms of variants of the same pottery tradition.

Golson (1961:176)

The reddish-gold light of early morning streamed laterally through motionless coconut palms and *Pandanus* trees as the Eloaua village workmen and I headed up the narrow path toward our excavation at a place called Talepakemalai, in the Mussau Islands of Papua New Guinea. The sky was cloudless; I mused silently that it would be another scorching day in the breezeless excavation pit under a baking equatorial sun. Nothing hinted at any disruption in the normal routine of troweling away the waterlogged sands that for more than three thousand years had smothered and protected the remains of this ancient village of stilt-houses, which once fronted the lagoon at Talepakemalai. We took up our places, some at the screening platforms, others excavating. I asked Bauwa Sagila,

a middle-aged man whom I had found to be an alert and careful excavator, to work in one of the 1-meter grid units, while I took up my place in the adjacent square.

The work progressed steadily through the morning, sweat beginning to run in little rivulets off our brows as the tropical sun broke above the cool shade of the surrounding jungle. The point of my trowel revealed a cluster of reddish potsherds—still lying where they had settled in the shallow lagoon bed after being tossed off a stilt-house platform 3,500 years ago—and I began painstakingly to expose them for photographing. Out of the corner of my eye, I could see that Bauwa had uncovered a small, elongate object of heavy bone, which he had left in place, knowing that I would want to measure and plot its location. After I had taken the object's coordinates, Bauwa

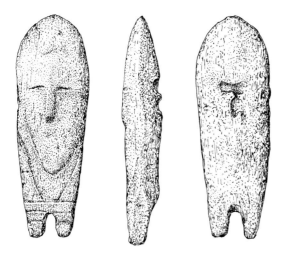

FIGURE 4.1 The carved anthropomorphic image, in porpoise bone, from Talepakemalai. (Drawing by Margaret Davidson.)

gingerly lifted the little piece of white bone, about 4 inches long, turning it over as he set it in his palm. Simultaneously, we caught our breath, two pairs of eyes riveted on the exquisitely carved, stylized human face that stared back emotionless, sunlight illuminating it for the first time since it had found its watery grave more than three millennia earlier (Fig. 4.1). Neither of us spoke; then Bauwa muttered in Melanesian pidgin, "God belong ol Lapita!"

The little "Lapita god" from Talepakemalai was just one of many discoveries we made in the course of three seasons of excavations in Mussau, part of the international Lapita Homeland Project, which commenced in 1985. As related in Chapter 1, Lapita sites first attracted the attention of Pacific archaeologists in the 1950s and 1960s, as it became evident that this cultural complex spanned the ethnographic divide between Melanesia and Polynesia. Synthesizing the emerging picture of Lapita in 1961, Jack Golson proposed that this ceramic complex represented a "community of culture" ancestral to

many of the later societies of *both* Melanesia and Polynesia. More than three decades of fieldwork after Golson made this radical proposal, the significance of Lapita for Pacific prehistory is more evident than ever. This chapter summarizes what we have learned of Lapita, and the role that the "Lapita peoples" played in the colonization of Remote Oceania.[1] First, however, let us review the Oceanic world on the eve of the Lapita phenomenon, between about 4,000 and 3,500 years ago.

The Human Landscape of Near Oceania at 2000–1500 B.C.

The first great epoch in the colonization of the Pacific commenced with Pleistocene human movements across the Wallacean waters into Sahul and—seemingly without pause—to the Bismarck and Solomon Archipelagoes beyond. After 30,000 years, perhaps longer, of local cultural development and change, especially in the early to mid-Holocene, a complex human landscape had emerged on the face of Near Oceania. We know far less than we would like to about this island world prior to the advent of the Lapita cultural complex at 3,500 years ago, but some patterns are discernible.

Human populations in Near Oceania were still small and scattered at this time, for the sites they left seem not to be numerous, nor are they extensive. There are no large permanent villages predating Lapita, and indeed most of our information comes from small, intermittently occupied rockshelters.[2] We might infer that individual social groups—whatever their kinship patterns and social organization—were also small, perhaps a few related families. Moreover, in settlement pattern there was a strong inland orientation, as opposed to a coastal focus, even though coastal resources were regularly exploited.

FIGURE 4.2 The large aroid plant *Alocasia macrorrhiza* is one of many tropical crops domesticated in Near Oceania. (Photo by P. V. Kirch.)

By the mid-Holocene the peoples who occupied island Near Oceania had developed new subsistence strategies that—while continuing to incorporate older patterns of hunting marsupials, reptiles, birds, and other small game, as well collecting forest products—now included food *production*. Edible roots, tubers, fruit, or nuts had been brought under human manipulation and control, domesticated through planting, tending, and selecting. These included some bananas (e.g., the *Australimusa* types with their upright inflorescences) and aroids (taro, *Colocasia*, and in the coastal lowlands, *Alocasia* and *Cyrtosperma*), sugarcane (*Saccharum officinarum*), and a range of tree crops (Fig. 4.2). These changes in subsistence were accompanied by new technologies in the working of shell and stone (as seen in the development of obsidian tools in sites near the main obsidian sources on New Britain). Adzes of *Tridacna* shell were probably used to clear small gardens, while fishhooks of *Trochus* shell allowed people to catch an expanded range of fish from reefs and inshore waters. The new shell technology was also applied to aesthetics, in the creation of beads and arm-rings.

Communication between the varied populations that occupied the islands of Near Oceania is evidenced by the movement of obsidian over considerable distances. Nonetheless, this was hardly a uniform human landscape culturally, linguistically, or biologically. Over 30,000 or more years, the indigenous peoples of Near Oceania had diversified. Linguistically, the Near Oceanic region is one of the most complicated in the world. Not including the Austronesian languages (which were introduced by the Lapita peoples), New Guinea and island Near Oceania encompass at least 12 distinct language families, with hundreds of mutually unintelligible languages.[3] These are loosely grouped under the rubric *Non-Austronesian* or *Papuan* languages, today concentrated in the interior of New Guinea, with scattered enclaves in the Bismarcks and Solomons (see Map 2). Such great linguistic diversity arose primarily through the long time depth of human occupation in Near Oceania, combined with geographic factors favoring isolation. As linguist William Foley, an expert on Papuan languages, puts it, "Fifty thousand years is a very long time, and if the present-day populations in the Sahul region descend directly from this period, then the extreme linguistic diversity found there, especially in New Guinea, finds a ready historical explanation" (1986:270).

The human landscape of Near Oceania was just as diverse biologically and culturally. Physical anthropologists have long noted the heterogeneity of Melanesian peoples, and while some of the diversity seen among the region's modern populations derives from gene flow with later Austronesian-speaking peoples, it is likely that the Near Oceanic populations already displayed substantial genetic variation by 4000 B.P. (Attenborough and Alpers, eds., 1992; Friedlaender 1987). Some populations within island Near Oceania had been in place sufficiently long to evolve genetic changes that were adaptive in a malarious environment, such as the α-thalassemia deletion.[4]

Just prior to the cultural events that turned this world of "Old" Melanesia upside down in the middle of the second millennium B.C., a natural disaster devastated parts of the Bismarck Archipelago. Mount Witori in New Britain erupted violently around 3,600 years ago (the W-K2 eruption), in what Matthew Spriggs describes as "one of the most massive eruptions to occur anywhere on earth during the time that modern humans have existed on the planet" (1997:76; see Machida et al. 1996). The explosion was probably heard hundreds of kilometers away, and a vast expanse of New Britain was blanketed in scalding, suffocating volcanic ash. At Mopir, locally exploited obsidian sources were buried under meters of ash fall. The full impact of the Witori eruption on the human landscape of the Bismarcks has yet to be determined archaeologically, but it was doubtless a pivotal event in regional prehistory.

Recent and ongoing research in West New Britain by Robin Torrence, Jim Specht, and others (e.g., Torrence and Boyd 1997; Torrence and Summerhayes 1997; Torrence et al. 1990, in press) has

begun to demonstrate the cultural discontinuities associated with the Witori eruption. The W-K2 tephra that blanketed much of New Britain (it reached as far as Lolmo Cave in the Arawe Islands, off the south coast) provides a distinct stratigraphic marker at 3600 B.P., with significant differences in site distribution patterns and artifact types below and above this bed. Below the W-K2 tephra, in the period dated to about 5,900–3,600 years ago, there are distinctive, well-worked obsidian tools with stemmed bases, presumably for hafting. Such stemmed tools are absent above the W-K2 tephra, with a shift to a more expedient lithic technology involving unretouched flakes. (This shift in lithic technology is also evident at the Yombon site in the interior of New Britain.) There are also changes in land use and settlement patterns, with evidence for high mobility before the W-K2 eruption, followed by more localized settlement, associated with coastal locations. Obsidian exchange, minimal prior to the W-K2 event, became substantial (and specialized) after it (Torrence and Summerhayes 1997:82). Notably, there are no ceramics in the archaeological contexts buried by the W-K2 tephra, whereas after this event "a highly decorated style of pottery called Lapita makes a sudden appearance in the Willaumez Peninsula" (Torrence et al., in press).

The Advent of Lapita

The Mount Witori eruption wrought havoc over much of Near Oceania, but its impact on the human landscape was negligible compared with cultural changes that commenced at almost the same time. Archaeologically, these are marked by the appearance of sites ranging from the Mussau Islands and Ambitle, to New Ireland, to the Arawe group off the southern coast of New Britain, and on to Nissan and Buka in the northern Solomons (Table 4.1). Several characteristics render these

TABLE 4.1
Selected Lapita Sites in the Bismarck Archipelago and Solomon Islands

Island	Site	Site Type	Age Range (B.P.)[a]	References
MUSSAU	Etakosarai (ECB)	Coastal midden	3,500–3,300	Kirch 1987; Kirch et al. 1991
	Etapakengaroasa (EHB)	Coastal midden	3,500–3,400	Kirch 1987; Kirch et al. 1991
	Epakapaka (EKQ)	Rockshelter	3,100–2,800	Kirch et al. 1991
	Talepakemalai (ECA)	Waterlogged coastal midden	3,550–2,700	Kirch 1987, 1988b; Kirch et al. 1991
WATOM	FAC, SDI, SAC, SAD	Coastal site complex	2,900–2,000	Green and Anson 1987, 1991; Green et al. 1989; Meyer 1909, 1910; Specht 1968a
AMBITLE	EAQ	Midden on old beach terrace	Undated	White and Specht 1971
NEW BRITAIN AND ARAWE ISLANDS	Apalo (FOJ)	Waterlogged coastal midden	3,000–2,700	Gosden 1989, 1991a; Gosden and Webb 1994
	Boduna (FEA)	Coastal midden	3,100–2,700	Specht 1974
	Kreslo	Sherd scatter on reef flat	Undated	Specht 1991
	Makekur (FOH)	Coastal midden	3,100–2,800	Gosden 1989, 1991a; Gosden and Webb 1994
	Paligmete (FNY)	Coastal midden	2,800–2,300	Gosden 1989, 1991a; Gosden and Webb 1994
DUKE OF YORK ISLANDS	Various sites (SDP, SEE, SEP, SET)	Coastal middens, somewhat disturbed	3,000–2,500	Lilley 1991a
NISSAN	Lebang Halika (DFF)	Rockshelter	2,800–2,400	Spriggs 1991b
	Yomining (DGD/2)	Rockshelter	3,000–2,700	Spriggs 1991b
BUKA	Kessa (DJQ)	Reef flat ceramic scatter	2,700?	Wickler 1995
	Sohano (DAA and DAF)	Reef flat ceramic scatters	Undated	Wickler 1995
NEW GEORGIA		Sherd scatters on reef flats	Undated	P. Sheppard (pers. comm., 1997)

[a] Age ranges given are approximations based on available series of radiocarbon dates. Refer to the references cited for individual radiocarbon dates associated with specific sites.

FIGURE 4.3 The dentate-stamped method of decoration is characteristic of Lapita pottery. (Photo by Thérèse Babineau.)

sites wholly different from anything preceding them in Near Oceania. First, they were good-sized settlements (in the case of Talepakemalai up to 80 or more hectares in extent), situated on coastal beach terraces or built out over the shallow lagoons as clusters of stilt-houses. Second, their occupants made, traded, and used large quantities of earthenware ceramics, of both plain and decorated varieties. The plain ware consisted largely of red-slipped globular jars with out-turned rims, while the decorated pottery was covered in finely executed motifs, many representing human faces, made by pressing small toothed ("dentate") stamps into the leather-hard clay before firing (Fig. 4.3). Third, the economic base had expanded from that of the preceding phase in Near Oceania, utilizing all of the tree crops that had been domesticated in this region, but also including pigs, dogs, and chickens. Fishing

strategies were sophisticated, and they employed a variety of fishhooks, including trolling lures for taking tuna and other pelagic fish on the open ocean.

The Lapita people were seafarers, venturing beyond coastal waters to move substantial quantities of pottery, obsidian, chert, oven stones, and other materials between their communities, frequently over hundreds of kilometers. Their material culture exhibits a greater range of tools, implements, and ornaments than any earlier sites in Near Oceania, including adzes in stone as well as shell, flake tools of obsidian and chert, shell scrapers and peeling knives, anvil stones, polishers, slingstones, shell rings of a variety of sizes and shapes, bracelet units, arm-rings, beads, discs, needles, awls, tattooing chisels, fishhooks, net sinkers, and other items. Archaeologists combine the sites exhibiting some or all of these characteristics under the rubric *Lapita*, the toponym of a site on the Foué Peninsula of New Caledonia, where the characteristic dentate-stamped pottery was excavated by Professor Edward W. Gifford in 1952 (see Chapter 1).

The distinctive Lapita pottery establishes these sites as having been occupied by closely related groups of people, sharing a common set of artistic rules and conventions, as are only found within a single culture (the pottery will be discussed in greater detail subsequently). Moreover, radiocarbon dates[5] indicate that the earliest Lapita sites in Near Oceania appear in a virtual instant of time (what archaeologists call "penecontemporaneous"). These radiocarbon dates calibrate to the century between about 1500 and 1400 B.C. (Kirch 1997a: 58). A century may not seem instantaneous to the layperson, but in archaeological time this is a short span indeed.

Despite some proposals over the past decade that the Lapita phenomenon in Near Oceania represents an indigenous, in situ development,[6] for many of us who have excavated and studied Lapita materials, the conclusion has become inescapable that these represent something entirely new and intrusive on the cultural landscape of this island world. To understand Lapita origins, however, we must broaden our geographic purview and assess developments to the west of Near Oceania, among the islands of Southeast Asia during the period between about 5,000 and 3,500 years ago.

Lapita Origins: The Austronesian Expansion

Until about 3000 B.C., the island world of Southeast Asia exhibited a human landscape not dissimilar from that of adjacent Near Oceania, and indeed there is no reason to think that there was any impermeable boundary between them.[7] Around the beginning of the third millennium B.C.,

however, ceramic-making peoples are first evidenced on the large island of Taiwan off the Chinese mainland, and over the course of the next 1,500 years, their descendants or closely related peoples expanded south and southeast, toward Near Oceania (Kirch 1995). On Taiwan, the earliest ceramic phase is the Ta-p'en-k'eng culture, succeeded around 2500 B.C. by several other cultures, some of which made not only ceramics and ground-stone adzes but also fishhooks and ornaments of *Trochus* and other shells. These people appear to have been horticulturalists, although more work must be done on the reconstruction of their subsistence economy. Around the same time, similar assemblages appear in the Philippines, such as in the Cagayan Valley (e.g., the Lal-lo and Magapit sites) in northern Luzon. Between 2500 and 2000 B.C., ceramic-using peoples expanded their distribution to Sulawesi and adjacent islands. At the Uattamdi rockshelter site on Kayoa Island west of Halmahera, red-slipped pottery nearly identical to Lapita plain ware, associated with a rich diversity of stone and shell artifacts, has been dated to about 1300–1000 B.C. (Bellwood 1998; Bellwood et al. 1998).

Peter Bellwood, who has synthesized the modern archaeological record of island Southeast Asia,[8] argues that this progression of ceramic-using cultures from Taiwan, through the Philippines, and into the equatorial islands of Southeast Asia represents the expansion of a particular ethnolinguistic group of people: the Austronesian speakers. The Austronesian language family is the most widely dispersed in the world, ranging from Madagascar to Rapa Nui (Easter Island), but its speakers are concentrated in island Southeast Asia and in the islands of the Pacific. Bellwood's contention that the archaeological record of an expansion of pottery-using, agricultural peoples out of Taiwan into island Southeast Asia and the Pacific correlates with the spread of the Austronesian

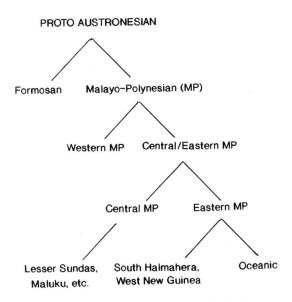

PROTO AUSTRONESIAN

Formosan   Malayo-Polynesian (MP)

Western MP   Central/Eastern MP

Central MP   Eastern MP

Lesser Sundas,   South Halmahera,   Oceanic
Maluku, etc.   West New Guinea

FIGURE 4.4 The subgrouping or "family tree" for the Austro-nesian languages. (After Kirch 1997a.)

speakers is shared not only by other archaeologists (e.g., Kirch 1997a; Spriggs 1995, 1997) but also by historical linguists who have studied the deep history of the Austronesian language family.[9] The archaeological model and its dating are remarkably consistent with the internal relationships or subgrouping (the "family tree"[10]) of the Austronesian languages as worked out through careful linguistic comparisons (Fig. 4.4).

Linguist Robert Blust, who has made a life's work of studying the historical relationships of the Austronesian languages and reconstructing their early culture history, summarizes the implications of the Austronesian "family tree" as follows:

> In accordance with the "principle of least moves" it follows that the most likely homeland of the AN [Austronesian] languages was on Taiwan, although it was not necessarily confined to that island. From Taiwan population expansion into the northern Philippines had begun by perhaps 5500 B.P. . . . From the southern Philippines the linguistic evidence

strongly suggests a split into two major population segments, a western one ancestral to Western [Malayo-Polynesian], and an eastern one ancestral to Central [Malayo-Polynesian]. [Central-Eastern Malayo-Polynesian] in turn evidently split into two streams, Central [Malayo-Polynesian] (CMP) moving southward into the central Moluccas and then westward through the Lesser Sunda Islands, and Eastern MP (EMP) moving eastward around the north coast of New Guinea and then splitting into South Halmahera–West New Guinea (SHWNG) and Oceanic (OC), the latter moving on into the insular Pacific, where it is associated archaeologically with the Lapita culture complex in the Bismarck Archipelago by at least 3600 B.P. *(Blust 1995:458)*

Archaeological evidence reveals that these expanding Austronesian peoples were horticulturalists, had domestic animals, knew how to fish the inshore and offshore waters, made red-slipped earthenware pottery, used ground-stone and shell adzes, and had a variety of other tools and implements in shell. Lexical reconstructions of the Proto Austronesian (PAN) and Proto Malayo-Polynesian vocabularies by linguists such as Blust greatly expand our knowledge of early Austronesian cultures. For example, these people had words for such important Indo-Pacific crops as taro (PAN *tales*),[11] coconut (*niuR*), banana (*punti*), and breadfruit (*kuluR*), and for the domesticated pig (*beRek*), chicken (*manuk*), and dog (*asu*). They lived in dwellings called *Rumaq* sometimes raised on posts (*SadiRi*), and their settlements included other house types, one of which (*balay*) was an open-sided building used at times for public gatherings. Significantly, given their rapid expansion over island Southeast Asia, the Austronesians were canoe-builders and navigators. Linguists Andrew and Medina Pawley (1994, 1998) have reconstructed early Austronesian terms for canoe parts and sailing, finding that speakers of these languages had outrigger canoes (*wag-ka*) with planks (*papan*), washstrakes (*[q]oRa*), and possibly carved end-pieces (*ijug*), and with platforms (*patar*) between hull and outrigger (*saman*). Such canoes had masts (*kayu-tuqur*) and were propelled by sails (*layaR*), or paddled (*pa-luja*), and were captained by expert seafarers (*tau-tasi[k]*).

These seafarers—who quite "instantaneously" appeared on the landscape of island Near Oceania in the mid–second millennium B.C.—were a branch of the Austronesian peoples. Their outrigger canoes must have been a novel sight in Pacific waters, and they established stilt-house settlements fringing the beaches of Mussau, New Ireland, and New Britain. Yet they were not the first inhabitants of these islands, and on these beaches we must envisage a meeting of cultures, between the immigrant seafarers who spoke an Austronesian language that we call Proto Oceanic and the diverse indigenous inhabitants of Near Oceania who spoke not one, but a plethora of Papuan (or Non-Austronesian) languages, and who were culturally and biologically quite varied. Out of these encounters—no doubt tentative and cautious at first—would come a cultural synthesis that changed the face of "Old" Melanesia.

The pottery excavated from the earliest Lapita sites in the Bismarck Archipelago is undeniably related to ceramics from contemporary or slightly older sites in Halmahera, Talaud, Sulawesi, and the Philippines (Kirch 1995). Yet the Lapita decorative style itself seems to be an innovation in Near Oceania, one of several traits that allow us to define Lapita as a "cultural complex" that emerged in the Bismarcks, out of a fusion of intrusive Austronesian and indigenous Papuan cultures. From the older indigenous occupants of Near Oceania, the Lapita peoples may have borrowed the concept of the earth oven, and they quickly adopted the cultivation of local tree crops, including the

Canarium almond. Intermarriage between the intrusive Austronesian speakers and the long-resident populations of Near Oceania is indicated by the incorporation of certain markers into the gene pool, particularly an α-thalassemia deletion that confers resistance to malaria.[12] Recognizing these and other indications of interaction between the immigrant Austronesian speakers and the indigenous Papuan language speakers of Near Oceania in the mid–second millennium B.C., Roger Green (1991a) proposed a "Triple-I Model" of immediate Lapita origins. "Triple-I" stands for the terms *intrusion, innovation,* and *integration,* recognizing that all three processes played a role in the emergence of the Lapita cultural complex within the Bismarck Archipelago.[13]

Lapita Dispersal into Remote Oceania

Leaving aside for the moment further details of the Lapita cultural complex (I will return to these later in the chapter), let us continue to trace the movements of the Lapita peoples in the southwestern Pacific. More than 200 radiocarbon dates have been obtained from Lapita sites ranging geographically from the Bismarck Archipelago to Samoa and Tonga (Table 4.2, Map 7), providing a firm basis for tracking the chronology and rate of population spread.[14] In Figure 4.5, these radiocarbon dates are summarized as cumulative probability distributions for four main geographic regions.

The earliest dates for sites with the distinctive Lapita style of dentate-stamped decoration range between 1500 and 1400 B.C. For the next two to three centuries, there was no expansion of Lapita populations beyond the immediate Near Oceanic region. Then, around 1200 B.C., a phase of long-distance voyaging and colonization commenced, with Lapita groups rapidly breaking through the invisible boundary of Near Oceania (at the southeastern end of the main Solomons chain), which

TABLE 4.2
Selected Lapita and Related Ceramic Sites in Remote Oceania

Island	Site	Site Type	Age Range (B.P.)[a]	References
SANTA CRUZ GROUP	Nanggu (SZ-8)	Coastal midden	3,200–3,100	Green 1976a, 1991b, 1991c
	Nenumbo (RF-2)	Coastal midden	3,200–1,900	Donovan 1973; Green 1974a, 1976a, 1978; Sheppard 1992, 1993; Sheppard and Green 1991
	Ngamanie (RF-6)	Coastal midden	2,800–2,500	Green 1976a, 1991b, 1991c
VANUATU	Erueti (Efate Island)	Midden on emerged beach terrace	2,300?	Garanger 1972a
	Malo Island (NHMa-7)	Midden on emerged beach terrace	3,100–3,000	Hedrick 1971; Spriggs 1990a
LOYALTY ISLANDS	Patho (Maré Island)	Coastal midden	2,500	Sand 1995
NEW CALEDONIA	Koumac (Boirra)	Midden on emerged beach terrace	2,500	Frimigacci 1975
	Lapita (Site 13)	Coastal midden	2,900–2,400	Frimigacci 1975; Gifford and Shutler 1956; Sand 1998a
	Vatcha	Coastal midden	2,800	Frimigacci 1974, 1975
VITI LEVU, FIJI	Naigani (VL21/5)	Midden on emerged beach terrace	3,100	Kay 1984
	Natunuku (VL1/1)	Coastal midden	3,200–3,100	Davidson and Leach 1993; Davidson et al. 1990; Mead et al. 1975
	Sigatoka (VL16/1)	Dunes at Sigatoka river mouth	2,400	Birks 1973
	Yanuca (VL16/81)	Rockshelter	2,900	Birks and Birks 1967
LAKEBA, FIJI	Qaranipuqa	Rockshelter	2,800	Best 1984
TONGATAPU	Moala's Mound (To.2)	Midden under mound	3,000	Poulsen 1987
	Pe'a (To.1)	Midden on emerged beach terrace	3,100	Poulsen 1987

(continued)

TABLE 4.2 (*continued*)

Island	Site	Site Type	Age Range (B.P.)[a]	References
HA'APAI GROUP	Faleloa (Foa Island)	Coastal midden	2,900	Shutler et al. 1994
	Tongoleleka (Lifuka Island)	Midden on emerged beach terrace	2,900	Dye 1988; Pregill and Dye 1989; Shutler et al. 1994
NIUATOPUTAPU	Lolokoka (NT-90)	Midden on emerged beach terrace	3,000–2,800	Kirch 1978, 1988a; Rogers 1974
FUTUNA	Asipani	Coastal midden buried under alluvium	2,800–2,400?	Sand 1993
	Tavai	Coastal midden buried under alluvium	2,100	Kirch 1981
SAMOA	Mulifanua (Upolu Island)	Submerged coastal site under reef	3,000	Green and Davidson 1974; Leach and Green 1989
	To'aga (Ofu Island)	Coastal midden	3,000–2,500	Kirch and Hunt, eds., 1993

[a] Age ranges given are approximations based on available series of radiocarbon dates. Refer to the references cited for individual radiocarbon dates associated with specific sites.

for 30,000 years or more had marked the limits of human existence in the Pacific. Lapita canoes began to ply waters where no humans had gone before, first to the islands of the Santa Cruz group, 380 kilometers southeast of San Cristobal, where they established small settlements along the coast of the main island of Nendö and on the small coral islets of the Reef Islands.

Other Lapita groups rapidly moved south, through the Banks Islands and into the main Vanuatu archipelago, in quick succession to the upraised makatea islands of the Loyalty group, and on to discover that great elongated remnant of Gondwanaland, La Grande Terre of New Caledonia. Numerous radiocarbon dates from sites distributed over New Caledonia and the Île des

Pins bracket the first Lapita settlement of the island between about 1200 and 1100 B.C., a date not statistically different from that for the settlement of the Santa Cruz group several hundred kilometers to the north (Sand 1996a, 1997).

Yet others undertook an awe-inspiring voyage or voyages due east from either the Santa Cruz or northern Vanuatu islands, sailing upwind against the prevailing trades and currents, to cross 850 kilometers of open, trackless ocean, with no stepping-stone islands in between, arriving in the Fiji archipelago. The earliest dates from Fiji come in at about 1100–900 B.C. (Anderson and Clark 1999), telling us that this eastward expansion into the heart of the central Pacific occurred more or less simultaneously with the southward expansion

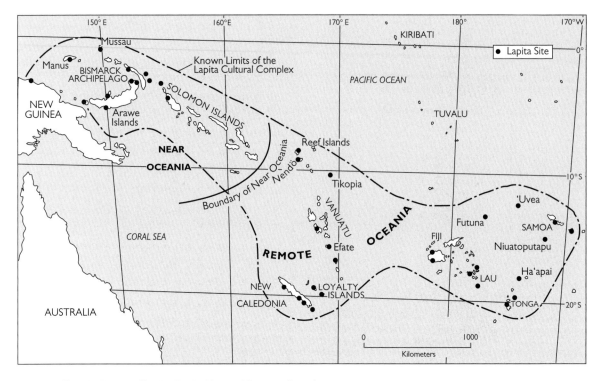

MAP 7 The distribution of Lapita sites in Near and Remote Oceania.

through Vanuatu into New Caledonia. From Fiji, there was rapid exploration eastward, via the numerous small islands of the Lau archipelago on to Tongatapu and 'Eua, and thence probably via the Ha'apai group of coral islands northward to Niuatoputapu and Samoa (Burley et al. 1999). Futuna and 'Uvea, between Fiji and Samoa, were also discovered and settled. The Manu'a Islands, at the extreme eastern end of the Samoan chain, have radiocarbon dates firmly establishing human settlement by 2950 B.P. The Tonga-Samoa chain of islands comprises the region known ethnographically as Western Polynesia, and the initial human colonization of these islands by Lapita peoples establishes Lapita as directly ancestral to later Polynesian cultures and societies.

With as much precision as the inherent error range of radiocarbon dating allows, we can conclude that the Lapita expansion out of Near Oceania into Remote Oceania—as far south as New Caledonia and as far east as Tonga and Samoa—was accomplished in two to three centuries. If we conceptualize the Lapita dispersal in directly human terms, these small groups of intrepid seafarers explored an ocean realm stretching across 4,500 kilometers during the course of perhaps 15–25 successive human generations (taking 20 years as the length of a reproductive generation). No doubt, the Lapita colonization of Remote Oceania ranks as one of the great sagas of world prehistory.

These were not merely voyages of discovery by itinerant sailors who came for a brief period and then returned to a homeland in the western Pacific.[15] Quite the contrary, these were purposeful voyages of discovery and colonization. The

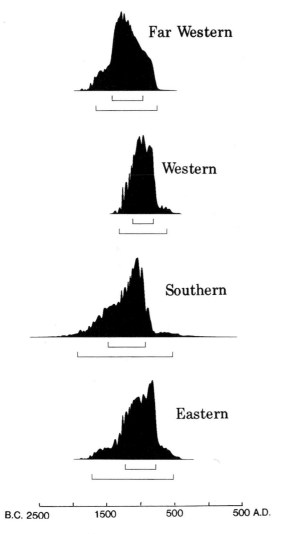

FIGURE 4.5 Lapita ^{14}C probability distributions for four major subregions of the western Pacific. (After Kirch 1997a.)

This sequence of island colonization raises fundamental anthropological questions, both demographic and social.

Demographically, this process of expansion—which established new, permanent settlements and yet continued to bud off colonizing daughter populations—would have required a high net population growth rate, presumably achieved by a combination of a high fertility or birth rate and a low morbidity or death rate. Otherwise, there simply would not have been a sufficient demographic head of steam to keep the process moving. Even so, colonizing populations were small, resulting in "genetic bottleneck" effects that can be detected in modern molecular variation among Polynesians (Flint et al. 1989; Martinson et al. 1993). Socially, we must ask: what motives impelled these people to keep exploring southward and eastward into the unknown waters of the Pacific? It could not have been the sometimes-cited "population pressure" of overcrowded islands, for many of the newly discovered lands were vast and uninhabited, and it would take centuries before large islands such as Efate or Viti Levu were densely populated. Rather than a "push" factor, we must invoke "pull" factors in trying to understand the Lapita expansion.[17] Initially, one kind of "pull" incentive that brought Austronesian speakers from southeast Asia into the Bismarck Archipelago might have been a search for new trading opportunities (such as obsidian). However, once the Lapita peoples left Near Oceania and ventured into uninhabited "oceanic outer space," trade seems an unlikely explanation.

Quite possibly, Lapita social structure played a key role in driving the engine of exploration and colonization. Linguistic reconstructions of Proto Oceanic words for kinship, social statuses, and the like reveal that these peoples put much emphasis on birth order.[18] Older and younger siblings were ranked, and inheritance of house sites, garden

earliest Lapita sites are permanent habitations, not temporary camps.[16] What we are witness to in the archaeological record of the Lapita expansion is successive groups of settlers, each in its turn founding a new colony on a previously uninhabited island. Within a generation or two, descendants of the group then repeated the scenario, setting out to find yet another new island.

lands, and other kinds of property, as well as such intangibles as ritual privileges and esoteric knowledge, passed from parents to first-born offspring. As I have written elsewhere, "In such societies, junior siblings frequently adopt a strategy of seeking new lands to settle where they can found their own 'house' and lineage, assuring their own offspring access to quality resources" (Kirch 1997a:65). Rivalries between older and younger brothers are a frequent theme in the myths of Polynesians,[19] who are direct descendants of one branch of the Lapita peoples. Peter Bellwood (1996b) has argued that such a "founder-focused ideology" is inherently characteristic of Austronesian-speaking peoples, and that discovery and settlement of a new island (or later, a new valley or part of an island) served to enhance founder rank. It may be in the realm of such social phenomena that a key to understanding the unprecedented Lapita expansion will be found. Of course, we cannot underestimate as well the importance of new voyaging strategies (such as upwind search-and-return voyages) and of improved watercraft, which provided the technological basis for such expansion (Irwin 1990, 1992).

Lapita in Linguistic and Biological Perspective

The arrival of pottery-making, seafaring peoples in the Bismarck Archipelago around 1500 B.C.—from whom the Lapita culture arose out of a synthesis of intruder and indigene—correlates closely with the inferred movements of the easternmost branch of the Austronesian language family, the *Oceanic* subgroup of Austronesian.[20] The Oceanic subgroup includes virtually all of the approximately 450 modern languages spoken by island peoples in Polynesia, Micronesia,[21] and all of the Melanesian islands within Remote Oceania (i.e., Fiji, Vanuatu, the Loyalty Islands, and New Caledonia). In Near Oceania, most of the lan-

guages of the Bismarcks and Solomons, and many languages along the coast of New Guinea, belong to the Oceanic subgroup. Map 2 shows the distribution of the Oceanic languages, and the distribution of Lapita sites is depicted in Map 7. The Lapita region forms a sort of core, out of which populations speaking Oceanic languages centrifugally expanded.

Some archaeologists are skeptical of—even hostile to—the idea of linking archaeological sites and cultures with specific ethnolinguistic categories such as "Oceanic." In part, this stems from a century or more of methodological abuses in the history of Indo-European studies in the Near East and Europe, some of them racially inspired (e.g., those by state-sponsored archaeologists during the Nazi era). Certainly, the correlation of archaeological and linguistic evidence requires caution, with attention to the different kinds of evidence each field commands. But archaeologists need not run and hide from linguistic reconstructions simply because they may not be trained in and thus mistrust the methods of their linguist colleagues. Not only in Oceania, but in other regions such as sub-Saharan Africa, good correlations are being made between particular phases in the archaeological record and the diversification of major groups of languages, frequently indicating a period of expansion of peoples with an agricultural economy.

In the case of the Oceanic languages and Lapita, the linkage is particularly well supported (Green 1997). This reflects the advanced state of Oceanic linguistic studies, in which decades of careful comparison have yielded a well-attested phylogeny or subgrouping model for the Oceanic languages and their position within the larger Austronesian family. One outcome has been to demonstrate that the Oceanic branch has no deep history of successive language "splits" such as would be expected had speakers of these languages

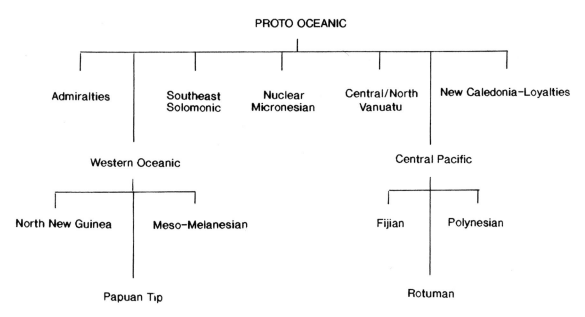

FIGURE 4.6 The subgrouping of the Oceanic languages. (After Kirch 1997a.)

been present for a long period in Near Oceania (as were the speakers of the highly diverse Papuan languages). Rather, the first-order branches or subgroups of Oceanic form a chainlike *linkage* (Fig. 4.6). To linguists, this implies that the Proto Oceanic speech community moved rapidly into the area east of Halmahera and as far as the Solomon Islands, quickly forming a dialect chain, along which communication continued for some time. Differentiation eventually occurred as links in this chain were severed, leading to the four or five major first-order subgroups of Oceanic witnessed in the area today.[22] This linguistic model resonates well with archaeological evidence for the rapid intrusion of a new population, coming out of island Southeast Asia around 1500 B.C., rapidly setting up new communities through the Bismarcks and Solomons. Moreover, archaeology provides evidence for constant trade and exchange among these communities, such as would be expected

among peoples who spoke related dialects (Green and Kirch 1997).

When we turn to Remote Oceania, the linkage between Lapita and Oceanic languages is more ironclad, because these are *foundation cultures* and *foundation languages*, respectively.[23] There is no evidence for any human occupation prior to Lapita, and all of the languages in this vast realm are exclusively Oceanic. We have no evidence for any language replacement, or for any other kind of intrusive population, within the Remote Oceanic area.[24] Moreover, the subgrouping model for the Oceanic languages spoken in Remote Oceania closely mirrors the sequence of island settlement as given by archaeology.[25]

Such correlations between archaeological and linguistic models of Pacific settlement allow both kinds of evidence to be used comparatively to cross-check each other and, in tandem with comparative ethnography, to construct more robust culture histories than would be possible through archaeology alone. For example, while archaeological evidence gives us the chronology of historical change, the nature of physical settlements and land use, much about technology and material culture, and a good deal about subsistence and diet, it is rarely able to provide nuanced reconstructions of social organization, ritual practice, or ideology. Through careful lexical and semantic reconstruction, on the other hand, linguists can offer much detail in such domains as kinship, social structure, the names of gods and spirits, and the parts of such items of perishable material culture as canoes (Ross et al., eds., 1998). Working collaboratively, archaeologists and historical linguists can produce far more sophisticated culture histories. Some of the most exciting work in recent Oceanic culture history results from such collaboration.[26]

The rapid movement of Austronesian-speaking populations from island Southeast Asia into Near Oceania, and then on into Remote Oceania, is reflected in the pattern of human biological variation in the Pacific. The morphological (i.e., phenotypic) and genetic evidence is too extensive to review in detail.[27] However, human geneticists such as Sue Serjeantson, A. V. Hill, and J. J. Martinson are confident that the movement of the Austronesian speakers into the Pacific left a "genetic trail" that can be traced in such features as blood groups, lymphocyte antigens, and immunoglobulins, as well as in DNA itself. For instance, there is a high degree of correspondence between a particular 9-base-pair deletion characteristic of island Southeast Asians, Polynesians, and Austronesian language–speaking populations in island Melanesia.[28] Lum and Cann (1998:116) have examined a large sample of Oceanic individuals for mtDNA variation, observing "significant correlations between genetic and linguistic distances when geographic distances are controlled." This

evidence strongly supports the idea of a "genetic trail" resulting from the intrusion of Austronesian-speaking populations some 3,500 years ago. Moreover, intermarriage and gene flow between the Austronesian speakers and the indigenous Papuan language speakers of Near Oceania are indicated in these genetic markers.[29] Martinson, for example, believes that the new molecular data indicate both that "a major component of the Polynesian gene pool was until recently located in island Southeast Asia," and that as the pre-Polynesian population expanded into island Melanesia, there was "enough exchange with the existing inhabitants of the region, for that population to acquire a 30% component of Melanesian nuclear markers" (1996:185).

In Chapter 3 I discussed the hypothesis that endemic malaria (probably in conjunction with other infectious diseases) regulated and suppressed indigenous human population growth in Near Oceania, even after the emergence of food production. We know from genetic evidence that the pre-Lapita peoples in Near Oceania had already developed an α-thalassemia condition and that they passed this on through marriage and gene flow with the intrusive Austronesian speakers. What is not known is the date of introduction of the far more debilitating and frequently fatal *Plasmodium falciparum* form of malaria, and whether this might have been carried into Near Oceania by the Austronesian newcomers. Clark and Kelly (1993) pointed to a Gm blood haplotype that also confers some resistance to malaria, and that is found primarily among Austronesian speakers in Southeast Asia and the Pacific, but which was apparently not present in the older Non-Austronesian–speaking groups. This led them to suggest that it may have been Austronesians who introduced malaria. While I agree with Groube (1993a) that *P. vivax* and *P. malariae* must have been in Near Oceania since the Pleistocene, it is conceivable

FIGURE 4.7 Lapita pottery was probably fired using an open-air method, as is still practiced in Fiji. This firing sequence was observed by the author in the Sigatoka Valley. (Photo by P. V. Kirch.)

that the intrusive Austronesian speakers might have brought *P. falciparum* with them. If so, the consequences for contact between the two groups would have been significant. At present, this is nothing more than a speculative hypothesis requiring a great deal more interdisciplinary research to sort out.

The Lapita Ceramic Series

It was the distinctive Lapita pottery that first led E. W. Gifford, and then Jack Golson, to affirm the significance of this prehistoric cultural complex, whose very existence seemed to run contrary to the logic of ethnographic models. Lapita ceramic assemblages are not uniform, and there were changes in manufacture, in vessel forms, and especially in decoration over time as the Lapita

peoples expanded into Remote Oceania. In a synthesis such as this, I cannot treat all of these variations and temporal changes.[30] However, there are commonalities to all Lapita ceramics, which can be grouped together under the rubric of the *Lapita Ceramic Series*.

Lapita pottery consists of handmade earthenware, manufactured without the aid of a wheel, but often using a paddle-and-anvil method of vessel wall thinning. The potting clays had beach or river sand added as temper.[31] We have no evidence of kilns, and pots were presumably fired in simple open blazes of coconut shells and wood, as is still done in some Oceanic societies (Fig. 4.7). Due to this method of rapid, low-intensity firing (with temperatures in the range of 600–700°C), the interior walls of Lapita vessels are often incompletely oxidized, leaving a telltale "sandwich" filling of dark, unfired clay while the outer surfaces are usually a reddish brown color.

Lapita pottery was made in a range of shapes, as shown in Figure 4.8 with examples from early Lapita assemblages in New Caledonia. The earliest known Lapita assemblages from Mussau and the Arawe Islands in the Bismarck Archipelago are dominated by open bowls supported by pedestals or ring-feet (a typically Southeast Asian vessel form), by flat-bottomed dishes with flaring sides, and by large globular jars with restricted necks and flaring rims (Fig. 4.9). The bowls and flat-bottomed dishes, along with some carinated jars, are decorated with elaborate dentate-stamped designs, while the globular jars are plain.

Although all Lapita ceramic assemblages consist of decorated and plain wares, the decorated pottery has especially captured the attention of archaeologists.[32] Lapita potters used several techniques to decorate the surfaces of bowls, dishes, and jars. Most often the leather-hard clay was impressed with stamps that had series of finely carved teeth; the process was thus referred to as "dentate-stamping." The stamps have not been archaeologically recovered, and they may have been carved in wood, bamboo, or possibly turtle shell (Ambrose 1997). In addition to dentate-stamping, Lapita potters used incision with a finely pointed tool, and they also modeled and carved vessel surfaces.

Dentate-stamping gives Lapita decoration its highly distinctive and unique character, for the following reason. The individual stamps each constitute a single *design element*, and these were then combined in highly regularized patterns to form larger *motifs* and *design fields*. While in theory the stamps could have been combined in an almost endless number of ways, they were in fact applied by the Lapita potters according to a set of artistic rules, constituting a "grammar" of Lapita design.

We will never know how the potters themselves thought or spoke of these designs, or the cultural rules for making them, but we can analyze and write a formal grammar of Lapita design through the use of a linguistic or structuralist approach (Mead et al. 1975). Such formal studies, and comparisons of motif catalogs from different Lapita sites, provide archaeologists with powerful tools for determining degrees of similarity between different Lapita ceramic assemblages.

That all Lapita ceramics share the same basic design code (which underwent various changes and transformations over time and space) is prima facie evidence that the peoples who made and used these vessels shared a common, culturally encoded aesthetic system. Although archaeologists are always cautious about equating pots with people, in the case of Lapita a common culture is strongly indicated, at least for the earliest stage. Of course, once the various descendant Lapita populations had expanded into Remote Oceania to become increasingly isolated from each other, local and regional changes occurred, leading to cultural differentiation. Over the course of several centuries, many cultures developed over the islands of the southwest Pacific, but most of these can be traced back to an ancestral Lapita pattern that began in Near Oceania.

When we examine the decorated component of Lapita assemblages over the entire ceramic series, there is a tendency for the most complex and finely executed decoration to occur in the oldest sites, especially in the Bismarck Archipelago, but also in the earliest sites in New Caledonia and Fiji. In the latter two archipelagoes, there was rapid simplification of the design system and range of motifs within a few centuries after Lapita settlement, leading to a virtual loss of decoration and leaving only the plain wares. Possibly the elaborately decorated vessels (which also required

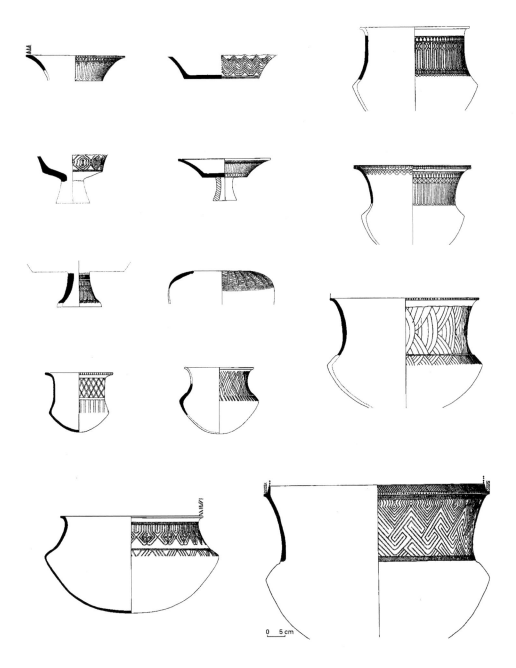

FIGURE 4.8 The varieties of Lapita vessel forms occurring in early Lapita sites in New Caledonia. (Diagram courtesy Christophe Sand.)

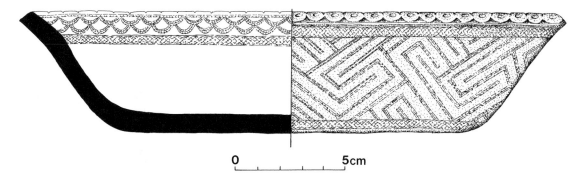

FIGURE 4.9 A ceramic dish, decorated with dentate-stamped designs, from the Talepakemalai Lapita site in the Mussau Islands. (Drawing by Margaret Davidson.)

considerable labor to produce) played a socially significant role in Lapita society and were not simply utilitarian objects. Indeed, temper and chemical analyses of the clay reveal that decorated vessels were exchanged between Lapita communities and thus may have been objects that circulated between communities whose members were linked by social and economic ties. Such linkages would have been critical in the early phase of Lapita expansion and island colonization, when small daughter populations may have wished to maintain connections with kinsfolk on "homeland" islands.[33]

Further evidence that the early, decorated pottery played a nonutilitarian role in Lapita society comes from an analysis of the motifs themselves. In the earliest assemblages, recently recovered from such sites as Talepakemalai, a large number of the motifs on Lapita bowls, dishes, and other kinds of vessels represent *human faces*.[34] The most figurative of these anthropomorphic representations have recognizable eyes, an elongated nose, curved upraised arms with five digits, a kind of "flame" headdress, and subsidiary emblems or motifs flanking the face (Fig. 4.10). Other examples are more geometrically figurative, and over time there was a progression to highly stylized representations, such as rows of eye motifs or stylized noses. But even these stylized transformations depicted human faces, and they would have been evident to participants within the cultural system.

What did these human faces on bowls and dishes signify to the Lapita peoples? Possibly they were representations of ancestors, the vessels functioning within a ritual system or cult of ancestors, as well as constituting objects of reciprocal exchange among related kinship groups. This would be in keeping with what historical linguists have reconstructed for Proto Oceanic societies, with an emphasis on founder ideology and birth-order rank. Indeed, a Proto Oceanic word for "ancestor" (*tumpu*) can be reconstructed, derived from the word *tumbuq*, meaning "to grow." As Jim Fox (1995) and other ethnographers have argued, the Austronesian peoples have deeply rooted concepts of "origin structures" and conceive of their social groups as growing and expanding like a tree or bush, with ancestors at the base or trunk. (Interestingly, this indigenous concept turns the

FIGURE 4.10 An anthropomorphic face design on potsherds from the Talepakemalai site in the Mussau Islands. (Drawing by Margaret Davidson.)

anthropological notion of "descent" groups on its head, for Austronesians see themselves as having "ascent" groups.)

It is conceivable that the decorated vessels were actually representations of ancestors, and that the act of decorating the pots was analogous to tattooing a human body.[35] We know that the Lapita peoples practiced tattooing, for tattoo chisels have been found in some sites, made up of rows of fine teeth, probably similar to the stamps used to decorate Lapita pottery. It does not require much of a stretch of the imagination to find the origins of the Lapita decorative style in the transference of an aesthetic system from one medium (the human body) to another (clay), especially since Oceanic art is of the *pervasive* type (as opposed to *partitive*), in which the same motifs and rules are applied to a diversity of artistic media.[36] Admittedly, these hypotheses cannot be "proved" to the satisfaction of hard-line positivists, but they are certainly reasonable and provide a consistent explanation for the role of the elaborately decorated Lapita ceramics, as well as their transformations over time.

At the eponymous site of Lapita (WKO-013A) at Koné, New Caledonia, Christophe Sand in 1995 discovered the eroding remnants of a pit (Fig. 4.11) containing two large, virtually intact Lapita pots and large sections of at least nine other vessels (Sand 1998a; Sand et al. 1998). These large carinated jars, intricately decorated (some with anthropomorphic face designs), were purposively interred in the pit, perhaps at the conclusion of some ceremony. Both of the intact pots had

FIGURE 4.11 Excavating the two large, in situ vessels at the site of Lapita (Site WKO-013A), at Koné, New Caledonia. (Photo courtesy Christophe Sand.)

pierced bases, which suggests some sort of ritual "killing" of these vessels. The Lapita "pottery pit" is thus far unique, but it hints at the social role of the decorated component of Lapita ceramics.

Not all Lapita pottery was decorated, and in many sites the majority of potsherds are of plain ware. These plain wares are of mostly different vessel shapes than the decorated pottery, largely globular jars with flaring rims or simple open bowls. Such vessels were likely used for storage, since there is little evidence that they were used for cooking over open fires (they lack the fire clouding and carbonized remains that result from such cooking). One possibility is that the larger globular jars with narrow necks were used to hold "flour" derived from the pith of sago (*Metroxylon*) palms. When kept dry, sago flour will keep for extended periods, and this food may have been essential to colonizing groups while their horticultural systems were being established.

Lapita Sites and Settlements

As with the ceramics, there was variation in Lapita settlements and important changes over time, but these differences can still be encompassed within a broad pattern. One fundamental similarity among Lapita sites is that they are all found along coasts, usually on beach terraces. At the time of Lapita expansion into Remote Oceania, sea levels in the southwestern Pacific were about 1–1.5 meters higher than at present, and many Lapita middens are situated on beach terraces that formed at that higher sea stand; such terraces are often now found some distance inland from present coastlines.[37] In Samoa, on the other hand, the Lapita site of Mulifanua lies beneath 2 meters of seawater and is capped by a cemented reef platform, because the island of 'Upolu has undergone rapid submergence.[38] In the Bismarck Archipelago, Lapita stilthouse villages built over reef flats either have been covered with prograding sands (but remain waterlogged) or exist as palimpsests scattered over reef flats (as at Kreslo on New Britain and the Roviana and Marovo Lagoons in the Western Solomon Islands).

That beaches and reefs were the favored location of Lapita settlements speaks to several aspects of their culture. Certainly they had a maritime orientation, and most sites are located across from or near a major pass in the adjacent reef, permitting ready canoe access to the open sea. In a careful environmental analysis, Dana Lepofsky (1988) showed that Lapita sites are also typically situated in close proximity to fresh water and to good gardening land. By situating their hamlets and villages on the beach—at the interface between land and sea—the Lapita peoples took full advantage of both terrestrial and marine resources. There is also the possibility, at least for the Near Oceanic area where stilt-house settlements may have been the norm, that they were trying to avoid undue exposure to swarms of malaria-bearing mosquitoes that inhabit the rainforest.

Lapita settlements also vary in size. We do not know the full extent of many sites, but good data on area are available from about 36 sites (Sheppard and Green 1991). The majority (about two-thirds of the sample) are smaller than 5,000 square meters, while another eight sites fall into the range between 9,000 and 15,000 square meters. There are three quite large sites in the sample, the most extensive being Talepakemalai (82 or more hectares in extent). Translating these numbers to a human scale, the smaller sites would be characterized as *hamlets*, generally with fewer than ten dwelling houses, and in some cases only one or two dwellings.[39] The midsized settlements could have accommodated between 15 and 30 dwellings and as many households, and thus they would begin to approximate what we could think of as a modest *village*. A very large site, such as Talepakemalai, could have incorporated as many as 150 households, although it is not certain that this entire site was ever occupied simultaneously, so the Talepakemalai village may have always been smaller. At any rate, we are for the most part referring to small-scale communities, a significant clue in assessing the nature of Lapita society.

Lapita settlements were constructed of wooden posts and rafters, with thatch probably made from sago leaf or *Pandanus* leaf—all materials that do not normally preserve in the archaeological record of the humid tropics. At Talepakemalai and some of the Arawe Islands sites, the waterlogged, anaerobic deposits preserved the bases of wooden house posts or stilts (Fig. 4.12), while the house platforms and thatched superstructures have disappeared. These Lapita sites in Near Oceania consisted of clusters of houses constructed over reef flats or the shores of lagoons, with stilts or pilings driven into the sand and coral rubble. Once Lapita peoples expanded into Remote Oceania, they abandoned such pile dwellings and began constructing their houses directly on the sandy beach terraces. One such house cluster at Nenumbo in the Reef Islands has been extensively excavated by Roger Green, revealing details of

FIGURE 4.12 Excavations at the waterlogged Talepakemalai site in the Mussau Islands exposed the anaerobically preserved bases of wooden posts, once supporting stilt-houses over a shallow reef flat. (Photo by P. V. Kirch.)

the household layout (Fig. 4.13).[40] A main house lay at the north end of the site, near a large earth oven. In the southern sector a mass of smaller postmolds and food storage pits delineates cook sheds; a deep pit nearby may have been a well dug to tap the coral islet's freshwater lens. The distribution of pottery corresponds with the structural layout of the site, with the decorated ceramics concentrated in the area of the main house, while in the cook shed area the pottery consists primarily of plain ware, especially large globular

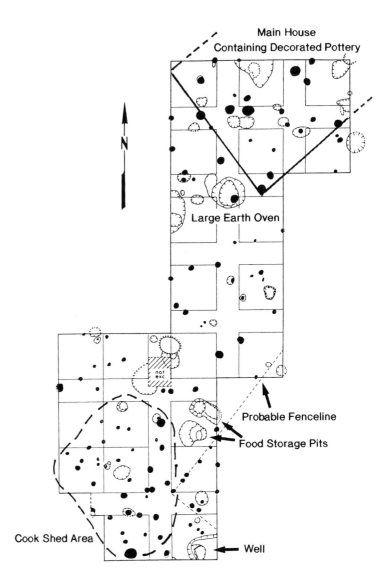

Main House
Containing Decorated Pottery

N

Large Earth Oven

not exc

Probable Fenceline

Food Storage Pits

Cook Shed Area

Well

FIGURE 4.13 Plan of the Nenumbo Lapita site in the Reef Islands, excavated by Roger Green. (After Kirch 1997a.)

jars. The artifact distribution pattern also reflects spatial differences, with concentrations of obsidian and chert tools in the area of the main house, and fishbone and shellfish remains in the cook shed area.

Drawing on archaeological as well as historical linguistic evidence, Roger Green and Andrew Pawley (1998) trace some key transformations in the houses and settlements of the Lapita peoples (or, speaking linguistically, the speakers of Proto Oceanic and its descendant languages). The original form of main dwelling house, probably raised on stilts as at Talepakemalai, would have been called *Rumaq*, a term found throughout island Southeast Asia and that persists in Near Oceania as well as in Micronesia. When we move into the Fiji–Western Polynesian region, however, we find that the dwelling house is called by variants of the

Proto Oceanic word *balay* (e.g., Samoan *fale*). Originally, the *balay* was some kind of open-sided building, not built on stilts but directly on the ground. When Lapita peoples moved eastward into Remote Oceania, they abandoned the style of dwellings on piles and adapted the *balay* for their dwellings. Thus the older term *Rumaq* dropped out of the vocabulary of these Remote Oceanic people. This is one example of how archaeological and linguistic evidence can collaboratively achieve a richer historical understanding.

Lapita Subsistence Economies

In resource-rich Near Oceania—with its abundance of marsupials, reptiles, birds, and wild plant foods as well as shellfish and inshore fishes—small groups of people were able to make a living as hunters and gatherers for tens of thousands of years. Not so in the biogeographically impoverished and faunally depauperate islands of Remote Oceania; it is true that wild populations of birds and fish were plentiful in lagoons and on reefs, but these fragile resources could be quickly decimated. Moreover, the central Pacific islands lacked wild plants with edible seeds, fruit, or tubers suitable for gathering, let alone for domestication. Thus an essential part of what made the Lapita peoples so successful as oceanic colonizers was not just their seafaring technology and navigational abilities but also their subsistence economies.

Wherever they sailed in Remote Oceania, Lapita groups came fully equipped to establish permanent settlements, carrying with them domestic animals and planting stocks of tuber, fruit, and tree crops, as well as a sophisticated knowledge of horticulture and plant manipulation. They transported and established the biotic and cultural components necessary to recreate in each new island precisely the kind of managed landscape they had just left behind. On a smaller scale, perhaps, but no less effectively, they practiced many of the same principles of "ecological imperialism" that Alfred Crosby (1986) has described for the historic expansion of European peoples. Ethnobotanist Edgar Anderson (1952) coined the phrase "man's transported landscapes" to refer to the ensemble of crops, weeds, animals, vermin, and other biota that accompany all human populations, but especially agricultural peoples as these expand into new territories. The transported landscapes of the Lapita peoples were a fundamental part of what made them—and in due time their descendants—able to settle virtually every speck of habitable land in the Pacific Ocean. The consequences for the island ecosystems of Remote Oceania were irreversible (see Chapter 2).

In the early years of excavations at Lapita sites, archaeologists vigorously debated whether Lapita populations subsisted merely by exploiting marine resources, moving rapidly from island to island like some manner of oceanic "strandloopers."[41] The accumulated evidence—ranging from the permanent nature of settlement sites, to plant-food preparation equipment, to the bones of domestic animals, and finally to the direct botanical remains of crop plants themselves—ultimately falsified this scenario. In addition, we have the corroboratory evidence of historical linguistics, which provides us with an extensive Proto Oceanic vocabulary, not just words for crop plants but also terms for swidden garden and for various aspects of horticultural practice.[42]

The roster of crop plants cultivated by Lapita gardeners—and successfully transported by them from island to island—runs to 28 species (Kirch 1997a, Table 7.2), of which at least 15 are attested by archaeobotanical remains and the rest by linguistic or other inferential evidence.[43] The list includes root or tuber crops such as taro (*Colocasia esculenta*) and yams (*Dioscorea alata* and other species), coconut (*Cocos nucifera*), bananas (*Musa* hybrids and *Australimusa*), and a wide variety of tree crops, bearing nuts (e.g., *Canarium* almond, *Terminalia* almond, Tahitian Chestnut [*Inocarpus fagiferus*]), starchy fruit such as breadfruit (*Artocarpus altilis*), and fleshy fruits (e.g., Vi Apple [*Spondias dulcis*], Malay Apple [*Eugenia malaccensis*]). As described in Chapter 3, some of these plants had been domesticated in Near Oceania, and they were one of the cultural elements contributed by the indigenous Papuan-speaking populations to the synthesis we call Lapita. Other crops, such as the Greater Yam (*D. alata*) and the *Eumusa* bananas, are of island Southeast Asian origin and were probably carried into the region by the intrusive Austronesian-speakers.

The waterlogged sands of Talepakemalai in Mussau—the same which bequeathed to us the little "Lapita god"—also yielded up more than 10,000 individual, well-preserved plant remains over three seasons of excavations. Similar finds have come from the Arawe Island sites excavated by Chris Gosden.[44] While soft, fleshy plants such as taro tubers or bananas were not preserved, we did find abundant remains of virtually all of the hard-shelled nuts, especially the delicious *Canarium* almonds whose shells had been cracked open and discarded by the hundreds around the Talepakemalai stilt-houses. Coconut shells, husked and cracked in half to extract the meaty flesh, were common in the anaerobic midden deposits; one coconut shell bore distinct traces, on its inner surface, of a serrated shell implement used to grate the meat. Grated coconut meat was most likely squeezed and strained to produce coconut cream, an essential ingredient of Oceanic cuisines. Another unique find was the fleshy key of a *Pandanus* fruit, with impressions of a row of human incisors on its proximal end, where these had stripped away the edible pulp. While we did not find direct evidence of taro or yams, peeling

knives of pearl shell were common; identical implements are used today by Mussau islanders to prepare root crops for cooking.

How did the Lapita people cultivate their crops, and what gardening techniques did they use? These questions are hard to answer through direct archaeological evidence. Gosden believes that erosional lenses of clay at the base of a hillslope on Pililo Island in the Arawe group are the telltale traces from clearing of the rainforest to make swidden gardens.[45] If we turn to the linguistic evidence for Proto Oceanic, there are at least 16 reconstructed words that apply to horticulture (Osmond 1998), including terms for a garden (**quma*), for yam mounds (**ta[p,b]puki*) and planting stocks (**[m]pula[m]pula*), and for various kinds of horticultural activity, such as clearing (**poki*), planting (**pasok*), weeding (**papo*), and harvesting (**sapu[t]*). The main horticultural implement was presumably the dibble or digging stick of wood (**waso*), a tool virtually ubiquitous among ethnographically documented peoples in Oceania.

Lapita horticulture was most likely based on a combination of permanent orchard gardens of perennial tree crops (quite likely situated in and around the villages themselves) and swiddens or shifting cultivations cut annually in the rainforest (or from second-growth forest once this was established) for the root and tuber crops. We have no evidence that complex systems of water control (irrigation or drainage) were used, although the Lapita peoples might have utilized naturally swampy areas to grow hydrophilic aroids such as *Colocasia* and *Cyrtosperma*. Contrary to earlier proposals, large-scale valley or hillside irrigation systems seem to have developed independently and later in the Pacific, and not as a result of agricultural "diffusion" out of Asia (see Chapters 5 and 7).[46] Nonetheless, the Lapita horticultural complex encompassed all of the essential crops and agronomic strategies that laid the foundation for the more elaborated horticultural and agricultural economies of later Oceanic societies.

The Oceanic peoples are ethnographically characterized as keeping a triumvirate of chickens, dogs, and pigs (Oliver 1989:217–28). These are all of Southeast Asian origin, part of the contribution of the early Austronesian speakers to the Lapita complex.[47] Pig bones are present (usually in small numbers) in some Lapita sites, but they are often outnumbered by chicken bones; dog bones are rare but definitely present. Although all three animals were kept by Lapita households, they were not major components of the diet. However, they were an important part of the Lapita "transported landscape," and in later societies that descended from Lapita colonists one or more of these animals (especially pigs) would at times become major prestige foods.[48]

While the successful colonization of Remote Oceania depended upon an ability to transport and establish horticulture, the Lapita peoples were hardly exclusively focused on the land. Theirs was a dual economy, reflected in their choice of beaches for settlements, and they extensively harvested the resources of reef, lagoon, and open sea. Most Lapita sites are dense middens full of a diversity of mollusk shells along with the bones of fish, sharks, rays, and turtles.[49] At Talepakemalai, each cubic meter of deposit we excavated yielded on average 30 kilograms of mollusk shells, including a diversity of clams and oysters, cones, spider conchs, cowries, and many other taxa. The fish bones are predominantly from inshore and reef-edge species, such as parrotfish, wrasses, surgeonfish, triggerfish, eels, and emperors, which is not surprising considering that the greatest biomass concentration on tropical reefs is in these inshore microhabitats. Bottom-dwelling (benthic) fishes, such as squirrelfish and groupers, are also represented. And although not common, the bones of large pelagic, carnivorous fish such as tunas

(Scombridae) are present in Lapita middens. Shark teeth and the bony vertebrae of sharks or rays, along with the plastron bones of the Green Sea Turtle (*Chelonia mydas*), are frequently present. At Talepakemalai, we recovered numerous porpoise bones, and the little "Lapita god" was carved from one of these (did it thus represent a deity of the sea?).

This diverse range of marine foods was doubtless obtained through a variety of methods and fishing strategies, including simple hand gathering and collecting on the reef, but also using nets, spears, fishhooks, and probably plant poisons.[50] Fishhooks manufactured from the stout shells of *Trochus niloticus* (or from *Turbo setosus*) have been found at a number of Lapita sites (Fig. 4.14). These include one type of hook for bottom fishing and another for open-sea trolling, as well as diminutive hooks of pearl shell probably intended for handline fishing on reefs.

Although the sea yielded the greatest range and quantity of their flesh foods, Lapita peoples also used such wild food resources as they could obtain on land. Their middens yield bones of sea- and land birds, particularly plentiful on central Pacific islands, such as in the Ha'apai group of Tonga. In New Caledonia, they found a large, flightless megapode bird (*Sylviornis neocaledoniae*) to hunt, as well as an endemic terrestrial crocodile (*Mekosuchus inexpectatus*).[51] In Fiji and Tonga, there were large iguanid lizards. Terrestrial crabs were also available on most islands, especially the highly prized coconut-robber crab (*Birgus latro*).

Lapita subsistence economy, based on a strategy of "transported landscapes" and on the intensive exploitation of naturally available resources, can be viewed from two perspectives. From the human viewpoint, it was highly successful and adaptive, permitting *Homo sapiens* to expand into a vast empty sector of the globe and to establish viable communities even on tiny coral islands. From

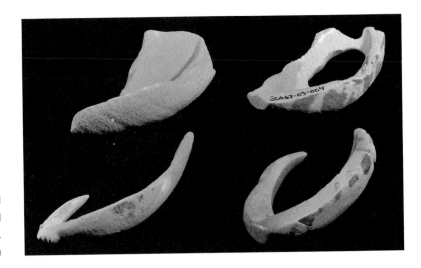

FIGURE 4.14 Unfinished and finished fishhooks of *Trochus* shell from the Talepakemalai Lapita site. (Photo by Thérèse Babineau.)

the perspective of the naturalist, however, the Lapita expansion was not without its irrevocable impact on the biota and ecology of these islands. In Chapter 2, I reviewed the accumulating evidence for prehistoric human impacts on inherently fragile and vulnerable island ecosystems. Although Lapita populations were not initially large, they frequently had a significant impact, especially on the smaller islands and islets. In Lapita sites of the Ha'apai group, David Steadman (pers. comm.) has found that a diverse collection of indigenous and endemic land birds (including parrots, rails, pigeons, and fruit doves) was swiftly exterminated, probably through direct predation for food and feathers, combined with forest clearance to make way for gardens. Also in Ha'apai, the endemic iguana was soon hunted to extinction, and in the Manu'a group of Samoa an endemic flightless megapode bird was similarly extirpated from the natural biota. Even on the extensive island of New Caledonia, the large flightless *Sylviornis* megapode and the terrestrial crocodile did not persist past the end of the Lapita period.[52] To chronicle these changes is not to impute some inherently destructive ethos to the Lapita people;

probably it could not have been otherwise if they were to convert these oceanic islands to sustainable *human* habitats. In the existential game between humans and nature, there are always trade-offs, and the myth of *l'homme naturel* is precisely that—a myth.

Exchange among Lapita Communities

One of the most fascinating aspects of the Lapita is the extensive and elaborate exchange between their communities. Ethnographically, Oceania is famous for the diversity and complexity of its many exchange networks (Hage and Harary 1991, 1996). It now seems that many of these historically documented systems may ultimately trace their genesis to systems of exchange that were first developed by the Lapita peoples.

Exchange is, fundamentally, a *social* phenomenon and in its purest form consists of the exchange of marriage partners, often in some formal symmetrical or asymmetrical pattern. But much exchange also involves a material component, and social and material manifestations may be complexly interwoven, as in some well-known

Oceanic systems (e.g., the *kula* exchanges of the Massim, or the red-feather money exchange network of the Santa Cruz group).[53] For the archaeologist, social aspects of prehistoric exchange must be inferred, usually only with difficulty, but at least some components of material exchange can be directly determined through the *sourcing* of raw materials, as well as through technological analysis of specialized production. For Lapita sites, it has been possible to source (or at least to characterize source variability in) the following kinds of materials: obsidian, chert, metavolcanic adzes, pottery (including clay and temper), and oven stones. Some shell objects also functioned as exchange valuables, based on evidence for their specialized production.[54] Some of these objects traveled long distances, particularly obsidian, which has been found as far as 4,500 kilometers distant from its quarries. This is the extreme case, however, and most exchanges were conducted over shorter distances, ranging from a few tens of kilometers up to 300 or 400 kilometers.

The large village site of Talepakemalai, in Mussau on the northern periphery of the Bismarck Archipelago, provides a case study for Lapita exchange. Talepakemalai was occupied for something like 500–700 years, and over this time we can track a number of significant changes and realignments in external exchange.[55] During the earliest phase (ca. 1500–1400 B.C.) the occupants of Talepakemalai received a significant range of materials originating outside the Mussau Islands. Obsidian was imported from two source areas in roughly equal quantities: from the Manus group to the west and from the Willaumez Peninsula on New Britain. Pottery, especially decorated vessels, originated in at least 12 different localities (or at least using 12 different clay sources), whose precise identities we have not been able to pin down, but that may include Manus, New Ireland, or some of the islands off the northern New Ireland coast

(e.g., Tabar, Lihir, Ambitle). Significant quantities of basalt and andesite rocks, for use in the village's earth ovens, were probably coming in by the basketload. In lesser quantities, chert (for flake tools) and metavolcanic adzes were also imported to Talepakemalai. Based on evidence for high-volume manufacture, and on a high ratio of discarded and unfinished rejects to finished artifacts, we also know that the Talepakemalai people made *Trochus*-shell fishhooks and various kinds of rings, beads, and other "shell valuables" from *Conus*, *Spondylus*, and other mollusks (Fig. 4.15). These shell objects provided at least one kind of export that balanced the numerous imports to Mussau. This exchange network—of which Talepakemalai was just one node—was quite complex, with much content diversity, encompassing many individual nodes, and with multiple, high-volume flows in and out of Mussau.

Some centuries later, the picture of exchange relationships at Talepakemalai had changed. Obsidian was still being imported, but now primarily from the closer Manus source. The number of foreign ceramic sources had dropped to perhaps six. Oven stones were still being imported, but probably not chert and metavolcanic adzes. On the export side, there is little evidence for the kind of high-volume shell object manufacture of the earlier period. In short, the network in which the Talepakemalai community participated had been reduced in its content and diversity, and in the number of nodes to which it was connected; the overall volume of exchange seems to have declined as well.

These changes at Talepakemalai reflect a simplification and perhaps a shrinking regionalization of long-distance exchange, a pattern repeated in other spheres of the Lapita world. This may be because exchange between Lapita communities was an essential social aspect of their colonization strategy, maintaining linkages between homeland

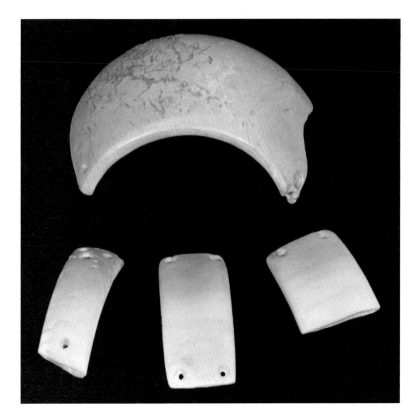

FIGURE 4.15 Carefully prepared sections of *Conus* shell, with holes drilled for line attachment or suspension, were among the various kinds of shell "exchange valuables" manufactured at the Talepakemalai Lapita site in the Mussau Islands. (Photo by Thérèse Babineau.)

and daughter communities (Kirch 1988c, 1997a). Over time, as new settlements grew and became more independent and less reliant on contacts back home, the need for such external exchanges—sometimes maintained by means of rather arduous voyages over open sea—would have waned. In their place, localized exchange networks sometimes developed, such as those on the island of New Caledonia or in the Fiji group.

Ancestral Oceanic Societies

For anthropologists, exchange leads logically to the question: what were Lapita, or more properly, Ancestral Oceanic *societies* like?[56] Assuredly, this is a matter requiring a great deal more work before anything approaching a full reconstruction is possible. But using the recently acquired data of archaeology, combined with insights from historical linguistics, it is possible to pose a few realistic hypotheses. Archaeological settlement size tells us that these were *small-scale* societies, in which individual communities ranged from perhaps only two or three households up to no more than 150 households at the most. But while they incorporated relatively small numbers of people, they were not egalitarian. Reconstructions of early Austronesian and Proto Oceanic kinship terms make it clear that there were critical distinctions based on gender, birth order, age, and affinity (marriage). The birth-order distinction between older and younger siblings of the same sex is noteworthy, for this suggests a key element of *ranking* within Lapita societies.

Linguistic reconstruction, augmented by comparative ethnography, also allows us to infer that the Ancestral Oceanic peoples organized themselves into sets of social groups they called *kainanga* (Hage, in press; Kirch and Green, in press; Pawley 1982). These were unilineal descent groups, comprising people who traced their origins back to a founding ancestor and who had rights of access to land by virtue of group membership. Historical linguists have reconstructed two key social status terms: Proto Oceanic *tala(m)-pat*, meaning "big, great person," and *aq adiki*, meaning "oldest or first-born child."[57] This correlates with a widespread and hence presumably ancient Austronesian emphasis on "origin structures," reflected in a term for "ancestor," *ta(m)pu*, which is based on the root term *tu(m)pu*, "to grow." All this is a part of the founder-ideology characteristic of Austronesian cultures in general, of which Bellwood (1996b) has written. Here then is further evidence for the importance of genealogical order and connectivity to ancestors, additional elements that contribute to a hypothesis of Lapita societies as *ranked*.

The archaeological evidence is consistent with such a reconstruction. Great emphasis was placed on the laborious decoration of certain ceramics that had a nonutilitarian function, and indeed may have been representations of ancestors. This pottery was exchanged among Lapita communities, along with a diverse assortment of other goods. In addition to such functionally useful items as obsidian, chert, and oven stone, exchange goods included a range of shell "valuables," artifacts of a kind known in ethnographic contexts to have circulated asymmetrically between exchange partners seeking to increase their relative prestige and rank.

What emerges is a picture of Ancestral Oceanic societies as being what anthropologists call "ranked," but not yet sufficiently complex or elaborated as to be termed "stratified" or "hierarchical." In keeping with current anthropological discussions, it may be best to use the term *heterarchical* for Lapita social organization.[58] In a heterarchical society, the fundamental social units (probably extended households)[59] are in a kind of economic competition with each other, emphasizing minor distinctions in prestige or wealth, particularly as these are played out through formalized exchange. Some groups may achieve higher rank than others, leading to a situation in which incipient chiefship—based on hereditary ranking principles—can readily emerge. As we will see in subsequent chapters, the various Lapita groups who expanded into the islands and archipelagoes of Remote Oceania were the founding populations from which the later, more complex societies of this vast region ultimately developed. Lapita social structure, as we presently conceive it, contains the necessary germs of ranking, and of intergroup competition based on economic exchanges, from which the diverse array of complex societies of Micronesia, Polynesia, and island Melanesia emerged over two to three thousand years of continuous social change.

Lapita: Transformations and Legacy

There is no real "end" to the Lapita period in Oceanic prehistory. Prehistorians do not use the term *Lapita* for sites or assemblages that continue in time beyond the end of the first millennium B.C., as a matter of culture-historical terminology; by that time the various ceramic styles had changed sufficiently that new labels are necessary. In fact, there was continuity between the founding Lapita populations in Remote

Oceania and those societies and cultures that follow them on archaeological time charts (Spriggs 1992a). Within Near Oceania there was continuity too, but here the matter was more complex, for the Lapita peoples continued to interact—and intermarry with—the older, indigenous Papuan language–speaking peoples. This led to far greater linguistic, cultural, and genetic diversity within Near Oceania, which will be discussed in Chapter 5. What may be fairly said of Lapita is that its outcome set the stage for the last great act of Pacific prehistory, and that its legacy is the modern ethnographic diversity of Oceania.

CHAPTER 5

The Prehistory of "New" Melanesia

All the chief social institutions of Melanesia, its dual organisation, its secret societies, its totemism, its cult of the dead, and many of its less essential customs, such as its use of money, its decorative art, its practice of incision and its square houses, have been the direct outcome of the interaction between different and sometimes conflicting cultures.

Rivers (1914, II:595)

The cultural synthesis between Austronesian-speaking "newcomers" and the older indigenous peoples of Near Oceania (the Papuan or Non-Austronesian speakers)—from which the remarkable Lapita expansion into Remote Oceania emerged—forever changed the cultural landscape of the region Dumont d'Urville dubbed "Melanesia" (Map 8). Whereas prior to 1500 B.C. humans had been confined to the intervisible archipelagoes west of Makira (San Cristobal) Island in the Solomons, they now rapidly colonized virtually every island within the southwestern Pacific. The verbal, cultural, and genetic interactions between Austronesian- and Non-Austronesian–speaking populations would lead to protean linguistic, cultural, and biological complexity. It is in this sense

that I use the terms "old" and "new" Melanesia, to speak of the periods prior to and after the emergence and expansion of Lapita.

To canvass the cultural developments that occurred throughout "new" Melanesia in the period following the Lapita expansion is a daunting task, given the enormous ethnographic diversity that emerged within this region over the past three millennia.[1] The task is rendered more difficult by the paucity of archaeological work in some areas, such as the Massim or the central Solomons. Even in archipelagoes where archaeologists have explored and excavated, well-analyzed sites and published sequences are still few and far between (Table 5.1). I have opted for a region-by-region approach, in which the particulars of what is known (and, as often, not known!) can be readily brought out. For each region, I emphasize

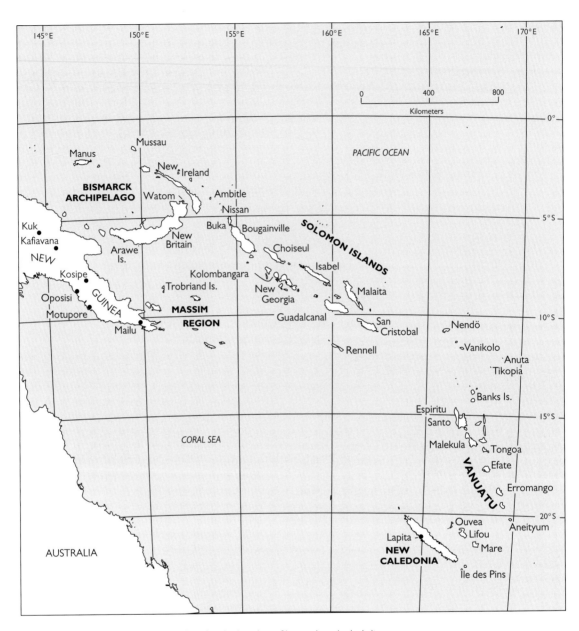

MAP 8 Island Melanesia, excluding Fiji, showing the location of key archaeological sites.

TABLE 5.1
Selected Non-Lapita Sites in Melanesia

Island/Group	Site (Island)	Site Type	Age Range (B.P.)[a]	References
BISMARCK ARCHIPELAGO	Boliu (Mussau)	Coastal midden	1,000–200?	Kirch et al. 1991
	Elunguai (Mussau)	Coastal midden	1,500–1,000	Kirch, ed., forthcoming
	Fissoa (New Ireland)	Coastal habitation	2,000–1,500	White and Murray-Wallace 1996
	Lasigi (New Ireland)	Coastal habitation	2,500–2,000?	Golson 1991b
	Lesu (New Ireland)	Mounds on coastal plain	2,500–2,000?	White and Downie 1980
	Sasi (Manus)	Midden under ash fall	2,100	Spriggs 1997
PAPUA-MASSIM	Collingwood Bay	Midden mounds	1,000–200	Egloff 1979
	Mailu	Village site, offshore island	2,000–200	Irwin 1985a
	Motupore	Village site, offshore island	800–300	Allen et al. 1997
	Nebira 4	Midden dump	2,000?	Allen 1972
	Oposisi	Midden	1,900–1,600	Vanderwal 1978
NEW GUINEA HIGHLANDS	Kuk	Swamp cultivation	9,000–200	Golson 1977
SOLOMON ISLANDS	Ndughore Valley (Kolombangara)	Ridgetop settlements; valley irrigation systems	300–100	Kirch and Yen (unpublished data)
	Panaivili (New Georgia)	Reef-flat sherd scatter	Undated	Reeve 1989
	Su'ena (Uki)	Coastal midden	900–100	Green 1976c
	Vatuluma Posovi	Rockshelter	6,400–2,200	Roe 1992, 1993
SANTA CRUZ GROUP	Anuta (site An-6)	Coastal (sand dune) midden	2,900–2,500, 1,440–100	Kirch and Rosendahl 1973
	Dai Village	Stone-walled village	500–100	McCoy and Cleghorn 1988
	Emo (Vanikoro)	Coastal (sand dune) midden	1,800–?	Kirch 1982c, 1983a
	Mateone	Dance circle and midden deposit	600–100	McCoy and Cleghorn 1988
	Sinapupu (Tikopia)	Coastal (sand dune) midden	2,900–250	Kirch and Yen 1982
VANUATU	Aneityum Islands	Various irrigation sites	950–recent	Spriggs 1981, 1986
	Ifo (Erromango)	Open settlement site	2,500–2,250	Spriggs and Wickler 1989

(continued)

TABLE 5.1 *(continued)*

Island/Group	Site (Island)	Site Type	Age Range (B.P.)[a]	References
	Mangaasi (Efate)	Midden site	2,500–2,200?	Garanger 1972a; Spriggs 1997
	Pakea (Banks Islands)	Midden mounds	2,200, 1,500–?	Ward 1979
	Ponamla (Erromango)	Open settlement site	2,700–2,500	Spriggs 1997
	Retoka (Efate)	Multiple burial site	650–400	Garanger 1972a; Spriggs 1997
LOYALTY ISLANDS	Hnakudotit (Mare)	Stone-walled fortification	1,800?	Sand 1995
NEW CALEDONIA	Col de la Pirogue	Irrigation complex	1,500–1,100	Sand 1995
	Oundjo	Coastal midden	900–recent	Gifford and Shutler 1956; Kirch et al., eds., 1997
	Potanéan	Coastal midden	1,700?	Gifford and Shutler 1956; Kirch et al., eds., 1997
	Tipalet	House mounds	Not dated	Sand 1995
FIJI ISLANDS	Navatu (Viti Levu)	Midden site	2,000–100	Gifford 1951
	Sigatoka (Viti Levu)	Dune site with ceramic levels; later burials	2,400–1,700, 700–500	Birks 1973; Burley 1997
	Ulunikoro (Lakeba)	Fortified village site	900	Best 1984
	Vunda (Viti Levu)	Midden site	1,100–100	Gifford 1951
	Wakaya Islands	Fortified village sites	650–100	Rechtman 1992

[a] Age ranges given are approximations based on available series of radiocarbon dates. Refer to the references cited for individual radiocarbon dates associated with specific sites.

aspects of the prehistoric record that are of special interest or have been more thoroughly studied. This approach makes for comparative unevenness, but in the current state of play in Melanesian archaeology, such is unavoidable. In the chapter summary, I discuss recurring themes of Melanesian prehistory.

Trading Societies of Papua and the Massim

When pioneering anthropologists such as Bronislaw Malinowski, C. G. Seligman, and F. E. Williams began systematically to explore and describe the indigenous cultures of southeastern New Guinea and the adjacent Massim Islands (comprising the D'Entrecasteaux, Trobriand, Woodlark,

FIGURE 5.1 High-volume production of pottery for trade characterized many of the coastal societies of Papua in the proto-historic period. (Photo courtesy Jim Allen.)

and Louisiade groups), they were struck more than anything else by the highly specialized systems of trade and exchange that dominated the lives of these peoples (Fig. 5.1). Malinowski made the *kula* network of the Massim—with its counter-circulating shell valuables (the ritual epiphenomena of a highly complex network circulating all manner of goods)—a textbook case of "primitive economics." Of equal interest were the loosely interconnected trade networks centered on the Mailu and Motu peoples of the southern Papuan coast, especially the annual *hiri* expeditions that sailed on large seagoing canoes called *lagatoi*, each voyage transporting as many as 30,000 clay pots from the Port Moresby area several hundred kilo-

meters westward, to the sago swamp–dwelling peoples of the Gulf, returning with quantities of sago palm flour sufficient to provide sustenance for months.[2] Many of these coastal and island trading peoples are Austronesian (Oceanic) speakers (although the Mailu and their trade partners in the Gulf are Non-Austronesians), which in itself suggests that their history may be linked to the Lapita expansion.

Beginning in the 1960s and 1970s, archaeological work in the vicinity of Port Moresby, as well as in the Mailu area, began to unearth a 2,000-year-long cultural sequence and to provide crucial evidence for the rise of specialized trading along the Papuan coast.[3] Less is known regarding the

Gulf end of this trading network. For the Massim and adjacent coast of northeast Papua (the Collingwood Bay area), the archaeological record is spotty, with few stratigraphic excavations.[4] Until renewed field research is undertaken, more questions than answers are apparent, but some hypotheses can be advanced regarding the long-term history of these trading societies.

The oldest known sites along the Papuan coast—such as Oposisi on Yule Island, Nebira 4 near Port Moresby, and Selai in the Mailu area— have radiocarbon ages placing them between about 1900 and 1600 B.P., after the end of the Lapita period (Fig. 5.2). Vanderwal characterized pottery from the lowest deposits at Oposisi as consisting of three vessel types (open bowls and two pot forms), well-fired and burnished, with frequent use of red slip and decorations (sometimes lime-infilled) made by "pressing the edge and sides of small shells" into the clay (1978:418). Many motifs are reminiscent of Lapita designs, as is the use of lime-filling and red slip. Vanderwal saw the early Oposisi assemblage as falling "within the Lapita tradition" (1978:424), and Jim Allen also regards the earliest Papuan coast cultures as derivative from Lapita, marking a phase of expansion of Austronesian-speakers.

On the north Papuan coast, in the Wanigela region of Collingwood Bay, Egloff (1979) found no in situ stratified deposits older than about 1,000 years, but he collected surface potsherds that he thought were older. In particular, his "Ceramic Group P" includes pedestaled bowls of striking Lapita affinity (Egloff 1979:70, Plate 8). At the time, little was known of Lapita sites in Near Oceania, and Egloff did not know that the pedestaled bowl was a dominant early Lapita form, leaving him to guess at possible connections to the Philippines or elsewhere in island Southeast Asia (1979:115). In light of our expanded knowledge of Lapita ceramics in the Bismarck Archipelago, a

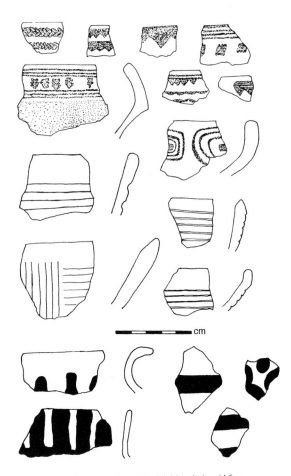

FIGURE 5.2 Potsherds from the Nebira 4 site. (After Allen 1972.)

direct connection between Egloff's Group P and Lapita seems probable (Fig. 5.3). Further fieldwork along the northeastern Papuan coast and/or in the Massim Islands may ultimately yield Lapita occupations.[5]

That these early populations were engaged in long-distance exchange or trade is evident, given the presence of Fergusson Island obsidian at several sites. Trochus-shell armbands were probably exchange items, and specialized manufacture of shell beads at Nebira 4 suggests that shell "valuables" continued to play a role in exchange, as

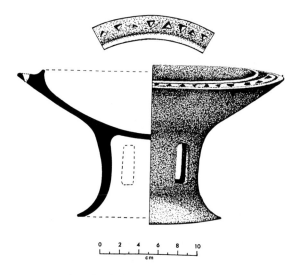

FIGURE 5.3 A pedestaled bowl from the Collingwood Bay region is strongly suggestive of Lapita connections. (After Egloff 1971.)

they had in the earlier Lapita networks (see Chapter 4). Using X-ray fluorescence analysis, Bickler (1997) demonstrates that Yule Island pottery was moving as far west as the Gulf of Papua during this early period. According to Allen (1982:202), there was increasing formalization of trade until about A.D. 800, when a "disruption" of socioeconomic systems occurred along the entire south Papuan coast.

After A.D. 800, the archaeological records from the Port Moresby (Motupore) and Mailu regions chronicle the rise of highly specialized trade networks, with loose linkages between them. Allen's extensive Motupore Island excavations document the history of this specialized trading center from about A.D. 1200 to 1700 (Fig. 5.4). The Motupore inhabitants engaged in high-volume pottery production for export and also manufactured small shell disc beads (Allen et al. 1997). They imported wallabies from the New Guinea mainland for food and probably sago flour and other perishable

foodstuffs. Chemical analyses of potsherds from the Popo site in the Gulf of Papua link Bootless Bay pottery with the Gulf sago producers. However, the ethnographically documented *hiri* system may be only the final phase in a long history of intensification and specialization of trade, dating back three or four centuries.

Irwin's research in the Mailu region showed that initially Mailu (an offshore island like Motupore) was only one of several pottery-making villages, enjoying no particular economic advantage. Over time, however, Mailu became increasingly specialized in ceramic manufacture, eclipsing nearby communities. Combined with a pattern of increased warfare and raiding—leading to changes in settlement patterns from coastal fringe to hilltop locations—Mailu became a central place in the area's trading system, by European contact achieving a total monopoly on pottery manufacture.

In the Massim, with no deeply stratified sites or continuous sequences, the picture is far from clear. The available data suggest that the *kula* of the "ethnographic present" has no great time depth and was preceded by more geographically extensive exchange networks. For example, while pottery in the Trobriands came historically from the Amphlett Islands, surface sherds collected from the Trobriands include ceramics deriving from the New Guinea mainland (Collingwood Bay) and from Goodenough Island. Thus Egloff concluded that prior to A.D. 1500 there was a wider system in place, with "increasing localization through time and a constriction of interaction in the north-western sector of the *kula* islands" (1978:434). Irwin (1983) suggests that the highly specialized Amphlett Islands pottery producers may be a recent phenomenon, perhaps analogous to the development of Mailu as a central place.

Although the data are too thin to attempt a more detailed reconstruction, or to trace the

FIGURE 5.4 Excavations at the well-stratified Motupore site, Papua New Guinea. (Photo courtesy Jim Allen.)

history of these changing systems, there is great potential for such work in the future. Archaeologists in Oceania have developed powerful methods of characterizing and sourcing obsidian, pottery, chert, and other materials, which permit quite sensitive analysis of interisland movements of materials.[6] With renewed field and laboratory work, the *kula* and related exchange systems of the Massim and Papuan coast, made famous by pioneer ethnographers Seligman and Malinowski, may yet see their long-term historical contours revealed.

The Late Holocene in Highland New Guinea

One part of Near Oceania that experienced only indirect impact from the incursion of Austronesian-speaking peoples, and from the emergence of the Lapita cultural complex, is the interior Highlands of New Guinea.[7] Nonetheless, the late Holocene period in the Highland valleys witnessed significant changes. Unfortunately, there are too few well-excavated and published sites dating to this period to provide a picture of regional variability *within* the Highlands, though such regional patterns will doubtless emerge through further work.[8] Yet a broad picture can be sketched.

In Chapter 3, I discussed the emergence in the Highlands, during the early Holocene, of incipient forms of cultivation involving drainage of the valley floors, probably based on the cultivation of *Colocasia* taro, along with other crops such as *Pueraria* tubers or *Australimusa* bananas. By the late Holocene, the Kuk swamp sequence shows that these systems had become quite sophisticated. Kuk Phase 4, dated to A.D. 1–800, is marked by a highly standardized grid of parallel and right-angle ditches enclosing square or rectangular plots. Bayliss-Smith and Golson argue that Kuk Phase 4 represents a new level of intensification based on taro cultivation. Indeed, it may mark a "Colocasian revolution" (1992:18). Whether a true "revolution" occurred may be debated, but the Phase 4 "agricultural base had the capacity to sustain a high density of pigs and people in stable, sedentary settlements and to permit regular exchange, in what was otherwise a quite empty landscape of degraded grasslands with shifting cultivation in scattered forest swiddens" (1992:18).

Environmental data—especially pollen sequences—reveal that agriculture in the Highlands was not restricted to the swampy valley floors; shifting cultivation was probably far more important overall, at least until the intensive developments of the past 1,200 years.[9] These pollen sequences chronicle deforestation and expansion of anthropogenic grasslands, and a consistent rise after about A.D. 1000 in the occurrence of ironwood (*Casuarina equisetifolia*) pollen. Golson observes that *Casuarina* is planted today "for its timber and its capacity for soil rehabilitation through nitrogen fixation," and he hypothesizes that its increased frequency in the past millennium marks the development of an indigenous silviculture. Yet in spite of such efforts, over the past few thousand years the net effect of human agricultural practices in the Highlands—especially shifting cultivation—was a cycle leading to ever more intensive forms of cultivation, and to increased investment in a built environment, in response to environmental degradation. To quote Golson, who has thought deeply about the evidence, "a model incorporating these elements would propose the continuing replacement of older forest by increasingly degraded secondary growth, as cultivation expanded to its local limits and turned back on itself in a tightening cycle of more frequent clearances separated by ever-shortening fallow periods, driven by the pressures of production" (1997:41).

Pigs are essential to Highlands economies. Ethnographically, pigs along with certain imported shell valuables are "accorded marked cultural value by Highlands prestige systems" (Kelly 1988:173). Claims for the presence of *Sus scrofa* in the Highlands as early as 8000 B.C. are based on rare single teeth or bones in dubious stratigraphic contexts.[10] More likely, the pig was not introduced to New Guinea until after about 3000 B.C., and indeed "pig bone is only sparsely represented in the Highlands archaeological record before perhaps the past 1,000 years" (Golson 1997:44). Thus the highly intensive systems of pig production—and exchange networks based on pig feasts—are a relatively new feature of Highland societies. Moreover, the systems so well documented ethnographically most likely owe their origins to an event that dates to a mere 300 years ago: the introduction of the sweet potato into the Highland valleys.

When Highland societies were first contacted by Whites earlier in this century, it was apparent that their high population densities were dependent on the high productivity of the sweet potato (*Ipomoea batatas*), a crop noted for abundant yields, tolerance of higher altitudes and cooler climates, and adaptability to nutrient-poor or depleted soils. Although the sweet potato was introduced into Eastern Polynesia in prehistoric times (see Chapter 7), there is no evidence that it had been transported westward into Melanesia or New Guinea prior to European expansion into the Pacific. Following Yen's (1974a) "tripartite hypothesis" of *I. batatas* distribution, the crop arrived in Southeast

Asia via two routes, one Portuguese (via the Atlantic and the Cape of Good Hope), the other Spanish (across the Pacific with the Manila Galleon trade). From the Indonesian islands adjacent to New Guinea, where sweet potatoes were present by the end of the seventeenth century, the crop found its way via indigenous networks of trade and exchange into New Guinea and the Highland valleys (see Swadling 1997b:161, 165, 282–83). There, given the cycle of increasingly intensive agricultural production that had emerged over the preceding millennia, the new crop was a godsend, its productivity spurring what James Watson (1965) first called an "Ipomoean revolution."

At Kuk, the final phase (A.D. 1750–1900) reflects this Ipomoean introduction, with a regularized grid and raised-bed cultivation. For the first time, habitations appear within the field system itself. The emphasis on the sweet potato had direct repercussions for pig production, since it is excellent pig fodder. To quote Golson, "In principle, the sweet potato, as prime pig fodder that could be grown over a wider range of soils and environments, extended possibilities for successful pig keeping and offered an opportunity for more men, through the labor of their wives, to enter previously restricted systems of exchange in which pigs were a central item" (1997:49).

A final aspect of late Holocene prehistory in the Highlands is external exchange or trade networks,[11] particularly those involving obsidian, stone axes, and shells. Watson (1986) analyzed 30 obsidian flakes from open sites in the Eastern Highlands, finding that most originated at a Talasea source on New Britain, although one flake came from Fergusson Island in the Massim. These materials moved over long distances, "probably in incremental steps rather than in a single trade trajectory" (Watson 1986:9). Fourteen stone axe quarries are documented within the Highlands,

and sourcing studies link surface-collected as well as excavated axes or axe fragments to the quarries. Burton (1987) demonstrated the appearance of specialized quarrying in the Tuman and Jimi areas, a pattern that may have emerged between about 500 B.C. and A.D. 500. When Whites first entered the Highlands, they noted that the inhabitants greatly prized various kinds of shells that were worked into ornaments, setting off a phase of intense inflation of these exchange valuables as the White entrepreneurs introduced unprecedented quantities of shell. The archaeological record of shell use and its role in exchange is still not well understood, although worked marine shells were recovered from Horizon VII in the Kafiavana rockshelter, dated to 8000 B.C. Small numbers of such objects are found in sites throughout the Holocene, but there is a tendency toward greater variety in more recent contexts.

The Bismarck Archipelago after Lapita

While archaeological work in the Bismarck Archipelago has concentrated on either Pleistocene-age or Lapita sites, a picture of the transition from Lapita to post-Lapita is tentatively emerging. No sudden or abrupt "end" to Lapita is evident. Rather, we see a gradual process of "settling in," accompanied by the development of local or regional cultural spheres. The early system of geographically widespread, highly interconnected, and complex exchanges that characterized the Lapita phase in the Bismarcks (see Chapter 4) was gradually transformed into several regional systems, as evidenced by the sequence from Mussau (Kirch 1990a, 1996a). This process of regionalization is reflected linguistically, in several primary clusters or subgroups of Oceanic languages, resulting from the breakup of the original Oceanic dialect chain, and later from the expansion of the Meso-Melanesian group in Bougainville and the Western Solomons region (Ross 1988, 1989).[12] These main, high-order Oceanic subgroups may indeed mirror regionalized exchange networks of the late first millennium B.C. They include a North New Guinea Coast Cluster, a Meso-Melanesian Cluster linking New Ireland and the northern-central Solomons, and a Papuan Tip Cluster (probably correlating with the expansion of Oceanic speakers into Papua and the Massim).

Spriggs (1997:152–61) reviews some cultural processes possibly accounting for the "end" of Lapita, not only in the Bismarcks, but also in the Remote Oceanic archipelagoes. In addition to (1) the contraction or specialization of trade and exchange networks (correlated with dialect differentiation), these include (2) local adaptation; (3) sociopolitical transformation, particularly that resulting from the breakdown of earlier prestige-good exchange systems; (4) absorption by indigenous, Non-Austronesian–speaking groups; and (5) secondary migrations. All of these factors probably played their roles in the transformation of a widespread Lapita "horizon" into the more highly localized and differentiated set of archaeological cultures, ranging from the Bismarcks right out to New Caledonia and Fiji. More elaboration of local archaeological sequences will be necessary to determine which processes were salient in any given region.

Using a classic archaeological approach of indexing cultural change through pottery styles, the transformation of Lapita into a varied set of local ceramic traditions can be traced in several localities in the Bismarcks. In Mussau, a major change occurs between about 1000 and 700 B.C., when the use of dentate-stamping began to decline precipitously, giving way to a high frequency of incising, and slightly later in time to other techniques such as end-tool impressing, punctation, fingernail impression, and shell-stamping (Fig. 5.5). There is no evidence to suggest that this ceramic

sequence represents anything other than style changes produced by the same people. By the mid-first millennium B.C. in Mussau, sites such as Epakapaka rockshelter (EKQ) exhibit little dentate-stamping, with the pottery made up largely of thin-walled, well-fired globular jars decorated with incised motifs, and with crenation or finger-pinching on their rims.[13]

The Mussau ceramic sequence is paralleled in other sites in the Bismarcks. On New Ireland, the Lesu (or Lossu), Lasigi, and Fissoa sites have yielded pottery similar to the late materials from Mussau.[14] At Lasigi, with radiocarbon dates between 2700 and 2300 B.P., some dentate-stamping is present, but much of the pottery is decorated with applied relief, and fingernail- or thumb-impressed designs. At Fissoa, applied and incised ceramics date between 2000 and 1500 B.P. On the small island of Watom between New Britain and New Ireland, the ceramic sequence begins with dentate-stamped Lapita and continues with incised, applied-relief, and fingernail-impressed (as well as plain) ceramics, as attested in the Kainapirina (SAC) and Vunavaung (SDI) sites.[15]

Ceramic production ceased altogether in many parts of the Bismarcks around the end of the first millennium B.C. This was the case in Mussau, which continued to import small quantities of plain ware ceramics from the Manus (Admiralty) Islands 250 kilometers to the west right up into historic times. In Manus, pottery production continued throughout the last 2,000 years, becoming specialized in local communities such as the small islands of Hus and M'Buke.[16] Ceramic production on New Ireland apparently ceased around 1500–1000 B.P. On the southern coast of New Britain, pottery use in the Arawe Islands stopped around 1,500 years ago. Occasional pottery was then imported into this region from mainland New Guinea (Sio Ware), where a pottery industry continued.

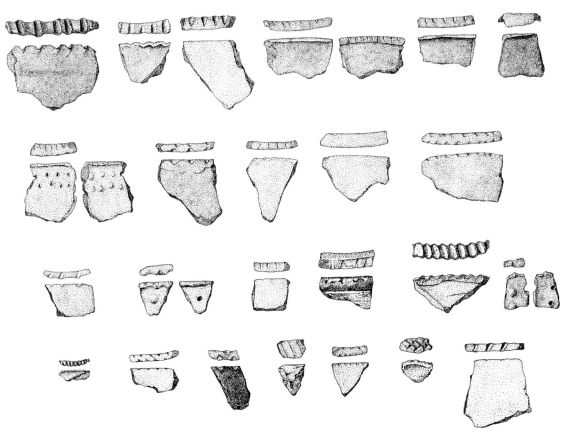

FIGURE 5.5 Potsherds from the Epakapaka Rockshelter site (EKQ) in Mussau with incised and punctate designs. (Drawing by Margaret Davidson.)

The last two millennia of Manus prehistory have yet to be well defined, but some features are noteworthy. Ambrose investigated the Sasi site on Lou Island, an important obsidian source.[17] Sasi, dating to 2100 B.P., is buried under a massive tephra and ash deposit up to 5 meters thick, resulting from an explosive eruption. The Sasi deposits, exposed by sea wave erosion, yielded pottery with incised, applied, and impressed decorations (another instance of late transformation of Lapita wares), along with obsidian blades, stone adzes, and other artifacts. Ambrose recovered from Sasi a small, flat, rectangular piece of bronze, which speaks to occasional contacts (direct or, more likely, indirect) with bronze-using peoples in island Southeast Asia, evidence paralleled by the discovery of Talasea obsidian in a site of similar age in Sabah (Borneo).[18]

Cultural change in Manus over the last 2,000 years remains to be worked out in detail, but Wahome (1997) has examined ceramic assemblages from 116 surface-collected and 10 excavated sites in the group. A correspondence analysis–based seriation of these assemblages yielded four main ceramic groups: (1) Lapita; (2) early post-Lapita from 2100 to 1650 B.P.;

(3) late post-Lapita from 1650 to 800 B.P.; and (4) late prehistoric, dating after 800 B.P. The early post-Lapita pottery is "largely distinguished . . . by the presence of shell impressions" (Wahome 1997:119), although some fingernail impressions are also present. Later-phase ceramics display "a diversification of the Early post-Lapita attributes and attribute combinations, lip and rim forms as well as an increase in the number of vessel forms" (1997:119). Wahome concludes that there is "no evidence for a total break from classic Lapita to post-Lapita" and indeed thinks that Manus parallels Mussau, Lasigi, and Watom with a transitional continuity from Lapita to what came after (1997:122). At the contact-period "ethnographic endpoint," the archipelago harbored a diversity of localized societies, many of them economically specialized. For example, McEldowney (1995) studied two contrastive groups, the fishing peoples of Andra islet off the northern coast of Manus and the highly intensive yam gardeners of Baluan Island off the south coast. On both islands, permanent facilities improved production efficiency; on Andra these were stone fish traps on the reef, while Baluan is covered in a reticulate grid of stone-walled garden enclosures.

Another kind of specialization occurred in the Vitiaz Strait region between mainland New Guinea (the Huon region) and New Britain, where the occupants of the tiny Siassi Islands operated as middlemen traders.[19] Lilley's (1986, 1988) archaeological investigation shows that trading connections have an antiquity extending back to Lapita times, but that the highly specialized system as known ethnographically dates only to the last few hundred years. This develops out of a "proto-system" operative at about A.D. 400, marked by the appearance of new ceramic styles and by evidence for cross-straits transfer of pottery, obsidian, and chert.

In Mussau, the last 1,000 years are imperfectly revealed through deposits on Boliu Island (site EKE) and elsewhere. Distinctive adzes made from *Terebra* shell, with the basal whorl ground down to form a concave cutting edge (Fig. 5.6), are first dated to A.D. 460–620 in the EHK site on Eloaua. Also common are *Tridacna*-shell adzes made from the dorsal region of giant clam shell valves, an artifact type rare or lacking in earlier Lapita contexts. *Terebra*-shell adzes appear in Solomon Islands and Vanuatu sites at about the same time, perhaps suggestive of some communication between the peoples in these regions. These distinctive artifacts might also signify communication with Micronesian societies to the north, where they are ubiquitous.[20] Economic changes in late-period Mussau sites include high frequencies of pig bone, suggestive of the rise of local, prestige exchange systems focused on competitive feasting.

A number of volcanic events in the Bismarcks during the last 2,500 years disrupted the region's human populations, including outright destruction of some groups and displacement of others. I have already mentioned the explosive eruption on Lou Island that buried the Sasi site around 2100 B.P. In the Hoskins area of West New Britain, there were major tephra-forming eruptions at roughly A.D. 200, 600, and 800 (Machida et al. 1996:77). The last produced a plinian tephra estimated at 20 cubic kilometers bulk volume, but even the lesser events deposited between 0.5 and 3 meters of pyroclastic products up to 50 kilometers away from the eruptive centers. At the northeastern tip of New Britain, Rabaul harbor resulted from a massive and violent eruption around A.D. 600. On Watom, 16 kilometers away, a tephra ashfall led to the temporary abandonment of the island. On New Britain itself, the Rabaul ignimbrite deposit is as much as 0.5 meter thick some 25 kilometers from the caldera. As Spriggs

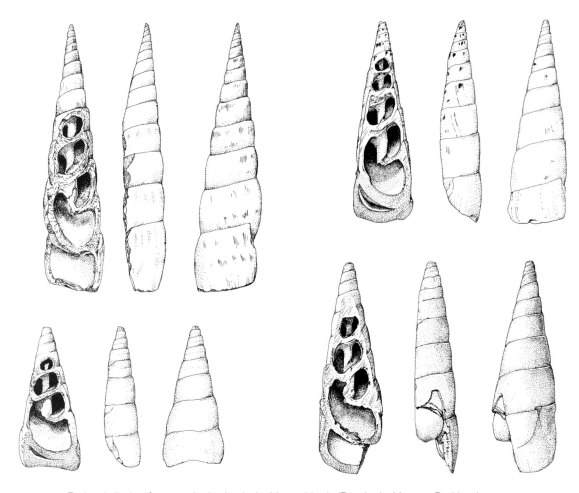

FIGURE 5.6 *Terebra*-shell adzes from post-Lapita sites in the Mussau Islands. (Drawing by Margaret Davidson.)

(1997:168) summarizes the effect of this massive eruption, "anyone remaining on the Gazelle Peninsula would have been killed, a fact seemingly confirmed by the oral traditions of the Tolai people of the Rabaul area . . . who say they moved there from New Ireland subsequent to the eruption."

The Solomon Islands

During several expeditions to the Solomon Islands in the 1970s, I sailed via government ship from the capital, Honiara, cruising through "The Slot"

made infamous during World War II, either northwest to the New Georgia group or southeast past Malaita and Makira to the remote Outer Eastern Islands. These little ships—packed to the rails with islanders coming and going from outlying villages, loaded with their pigs, chickens, and worldly goods parceled tightly in *Pandanus* sleeping mats—coasted along close to shore, stopping here and there to pick up sacks of copra and offload passengers. Watching the rainforest-cloaked landscape glide by, hour after hour, broken only by glimpses of small hamlets of sago leaf–thatched

TABLE 5.2
The Cultural Sequences of Buka and Nissan Islands[a]

Buka Sequence Phases	Dates B.P.	Nissan Sequence Phases	Dates B.P.
Pleistocene	29–10,000	(unoccupied)	
Early to mid-Holocene	10,000–3,200	Takoroi	ca. 4,900
		Halika	3,650–3,200
Early Lapita	3,200–2,500	Lapita	3,200–2,500
Late Lapita	2,500–2,200		
Sohano	2,200–1,400	Yomining	2,500–1,150
Hangan	1,400–800	Late Hangan	ca. 750
Malasang	800–500	Malasang	700–500
Mararing/Recent	500–0	Mararing/Recent	500–50

[a] After Wickler (1995, Table 1.1).

huts, I gained a perspective on these large islands totally different than the one I had looking down from a jet cruising at 30,000 feet. It is the perspective that early islanders themselves had, exploring these same seas and coasts by dugout and outrigger canoe. One feels diminished by the scale of these islands, noting how relatively underpopulated many of them are.

The main Solomon Islands extending from Bougainville through Choiseul, the New Georgia group, Santa Isabel, Guadalcanal, Malaita, to San Cristobal—encompassing a total land area of 31,080 square kilometers—occupy a critical geographic position in Oceania. Their prehistory holds a key to all of Melanesia. As noted in Chapter 3, the southeastern end of the Solomons marks the boundary of Near Oceania (and thus of "old" Melanesia), yet at present we have but a single Pleistocene site in evidence (Kilu on Buka Island). The situation is not much better for the Lapita period, with definitive sites known only from Buka,[21] although a few caves on Guadalcanal date to the same time period. For the post-Lapita period, our knowledge is only slightly improved, but still

highly uneven. Put bluntly, this vast archipelago has not enjoyed sufficient archaeological work—even of a reconnaissance nature—to begin to flesh out its prehistory. Large islands such as Choiseul, Santa Isabel, and Malaita are archaeological terra incognita. I stress this point on two counts: first, because any attempted synthesis must be subject to revision with the next field project, and second, as a plea for a heightened level of interest in and investigation of these critically important islands.

Some of the best current data from the Solomons come from its northwestern terminus in Buka, including Nissan Island, which lies halfway between the Bismarcks and the Solomons.[22] Thanks to the work of Jim Specht, Matthew Spriggs, and Steve Wickler, this is one of the few regions in Near Oceania where a semblance of a continuous archaeological sequence spans the pre-Lapita to early historic periods. Table 5.2 lists the cultural sequences for Buka (as revised by Wickler 1995) and Nissan. The phases in the two islands are to some degree correlated, in part reflecting the importation of Hangan-style pottery from Buka to

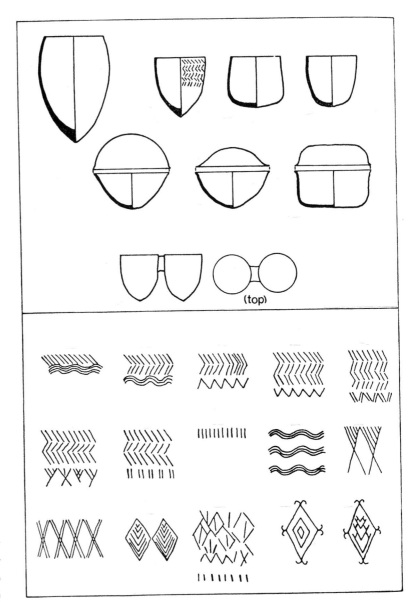

FIGURE 5.7 Modern pottery vessel forms and pottery motifs from Buka Island (not to scale). (From Specht 1972.)

Nissan. On Buka, the Sohano ceramic style represents a continuity out of late Lapita at around 200 B.C., much as there was continuity in post-Lapita ceramic styles in the Bismarcks. Around A.D. 600 another major ceramic style change occurred, marking the Hangan Phase, again a continuity from the previous phase, in turn giving way to the Malasang style (ca. A.D. 1200). The final Mararing/Recent style again reflects a transition from the Malasang style, so in aggregate we have a continuous pottery sequence linking Lapita with the "ethnographic present" (Fig. 5.7).

On Nissan the situation is slightly different, because there the Yomining Phase ceramics differ from the Sohano style of Buka; Spriggs (1997:170) suggests that Yomining ceramics were probably imported to Nissan from a source on New Ireland or one of the smaller islands off its coasts (e.g., Anir, Lihir, Tabar). According to Spriggs, on Bougainville, Sohano- and Hangan-style potsherds have been found as far south as Teop. Spriggs (1997:171) also reports that in the central Bougainville region he has recovered a "continuous ceramic and cultural sequence spanning the last 1500 years," with three successive pottery styles (which he labels Sivu, Asio, and Pidia); the details remain to be published. At the southern end of Bougainville, Irwin (1972) reports a pottery sequence from the Shortland Islands that parallels the Buka sequence. To go beyond ceramics to larger patterns of cultural and sociopolitical change poses a challenge; Wickler (1995) discusses changes in nonceramic artifacts and economic patterns, but more research is required.

Choiseul Island is virtually unknown archaeologically, but there has been limited work in the New Georgia group; a field project under the direction of Peter Sheppard of Auckland University promises to flesh out a sequence for this environmentally diverse set of islands.[23] Only a few Lapita sherds are yet known from New Georgia, but Panaivili in the Roviana Lagoon is a reef-flat ceramic site resulting from a Lapita-like stilt-house village. The incised, fingernail-impressed, and applied-relief ceramics have a late or immediately post-Lapita look to them, and a Lapita connection is suggested by shell artifacts and basalt adzes of typical Lapita forms. Sites of Lapita age will probably be discovered in New Georgia (and they will be stilt-house–type settlements on reef flats), and a continuity from Lapita to post-Lapita will likely be established for this area.

FIGURE 5.8 Ridgetop settlements in the Ndughore Valley, Kolombangara Island, frequently have stone-lined burial crypts containing multiple crania and various kinds of shell-exchange valuables. (Photo by P. V. Kirch.)

While such a sequence remains to be worked out, we do have some survey data for the late prehistoric and early postcontact periods, from Kolombangara and other islands. On Kolombangara, Doug Yen, Paul Rosendahl, and I surveyed and excavated hilltop, fortified village and hamlet sites in the Ndughore Valley in 1971. The habitation sites incorporated burial crypts containing human crania and substantial quantities of shell valuables (Fig. 5.8), reflecting prestige-goods exchange only partly described in the

ethnographic record (Hocart 1922). These residential sites were associated with extensive, tech-
nologically sophisticated pondfield irrigation in
the valley bottoms, a kind of landesque capital
intensification also found on parts of New Georgia
Island. The deeper history of this settlement-
subsistence system, involving fortification and
intensive agriculture, linked to a pattern of interisland raiding and the taking of "slaves," poses a fascinating research problem for future investigators.

On Guadalcanal Island, David Roe (1993)
reanalyzed materials originally excavated in
1966–68 at the Vatuluma Posovi rockshelter (also
known as Poha Cave) and excavated a small area
of undisturbed deposits, as well as conducting
excavations at two new sites, Vatuluma Tavuro and
Vatuluma Ngolu, all in the Poha Valley. Although
none of these sites was rich in artifacts (and all
lacked pottery), "the environmental material is
quite eloquent in its expression of human activity
in the Guadalcanal landscape" (Roe 1993:179).
Roe (1993:182–84) proposed a three-phase cultural sequence for northwest Guadalcanal, as
follows. In the Hoana Phase (6400–2200 B.P.),
people occupying the Vatuluma Posovi cave used
chert tools, along with fishhooks and arm-rings
of *Trochus* shells. Human impacts on the environment were "of a low level," and the subsistence
economy revolved around "hunting of forest taxa
and the collection of mollusks from mainly fresh
and brackish water environments," along with
some use of the *Canarium* almond (possibly the
wild species *C. salomonense*). Toward the end of
this phase, at around 3,000 years ago, there were
changes in the sources of chert used for tools, and
shell beads and fully polished stone adzes first
appear. Were these changes, as Roe suggests, "an
echo of changes known to be occurring both
north and south of the Solomons and associated
with the advent of Lapita?" (1993:182). Quite
probably.

In the succeeding Hamosa Phase (2200–1500
B.P.), a major period of impact on the local environment was initiated. Roe thinks it is likely that
there were "small open settlements" on ridge
crests, as known ethnohistorically, although no
such sites have been excavated. Sedimentary and
pollen evidence from the north Guadalcanal plains,
however, indicates increased erosion on the hillslopes and higher sedimentation rates on the
plains, as well as the establishment of extensive
Themeda australis grasslands (1993:183). The pig may
also have appeared at this time. Although preliminary, the evidence suggests that the Hamosa
Phase witnessed a phase of pioneering agricultural
economy.

In the final Moru Phase (1500–150 B.P.) on
Guadalcanal, inland forest areas were first occupied in a substantial manner, and caves and rockshelters near the coast were again utilized (Roe
1993:183). Agricultural intensification is indicated
by irrigation systems in the valleys in the Visale
area. According to Roe, "Within the last 500 years
there is evidence for a renewed assault on the
forest," and for the rise of the ethnographic distinction between "bush" and "salt-water" peoples,
with a corresponding diversification of economic
strategies. Roe's sequence for Guadalcanal is preliminary, based on a limited number of excavated
sites, but future research here and on other islands
of the central Solomons will doubtless expand
and refine his pioneering effort.

In the southeastern Solomons, a handful of sites
have been investigated on Ulawa, San Cristobal,
and Santa Ana, primarily during the first phase
of the Southeast Solomon Islands Culture History
Program (SSICHP), organized by Roger Green
and Doug Yen during the 1970s.[24] No Lapita
sites are known, although significant quantities of
Ulawa and Malaita chert in Lapita sites of the
Reef–Santa Cruz Islands raise the likelihood that
they will ultimately be found. A rockshelter on

Santa Ana, however, yielded calcareous-tempered plain ware ceramics dating to the early first millennium B.C., similar to the Kiki Ware of Tikopia and other late-Lapita plain wares. A deep midden site in Su'ena Village on Uki Island off the coast of San Cristobal, excavated by Roger Green, encapsulates a depositional sequence extending back to A.D. 1150. This was entirely aceramic, and it indicates that the use of pottery in the region ceased sometime prior to that date. The Su'ena midden yielded many chert adzes and a wide range of fishing gear, as well as finely decorated *Trochus*-shell armbands. Green remarks that "the important thing reflected by this assemblage is a high degree of general continuity between the most recent and the oldest items in the sequence" (1976c:191).

Leaving San Cristobal, and crossing 450 kilometers of open sea, one arrives in the Outer Eastern Islands Province, made up of the Santa Cruz group (Nendö, the Reef Islands, Utupua, and Vanikoro) along with Taumako and the Polynesian Outliers of Tikopia and Anuta. These islands were the focus of the SSICHP, and their prehistories are better known than those of the islands in the main archipelago.[25]

On Nendö (the largest island in the Santa Cruz group) and in the nearby Reef Islands, the archaeological record commences with Lapita sites dating to 1200–1000 B.C. Tikopia and Anuta were both colonized around 900 B.C., by peoples making and using late-Lapita plain wares. Excavations on Nendö Island by McCoy and Cleghorn (1988) demonstrated a continuous plain ware pottery tradition persisting to ca. 100 B.C., when as on Tikopia and Anuta (and probably in the Reef Islands), local production of pottery ceased. The later aceramic period on Nendö is partly known from the Mateone Dance Circle site in Graciosa Bay, and from the late Dai Village site on Te Motu Island (Fig. 5.9), as well as from an inland occupa-tion site (Naiavila) on the limestone plateau above Graciosa Bay (Yen 1976b). A marker of this later period is the *Terebra*-shell adz, also a feature of later prehistory in Mussau and in Vanuatu. Architecturally, stone-walled house foundations characterize the late period on Nendö, as well as unique, coral slab–outlined dance circles such as that at Mateone.

The high volcanic islands of Utupua and Vanikoro, south of Nendö, have enjoyed much less work. In 1978 I reconnoitered Vanikoro (Kirch 1983a) and test excavated the Emo site with its 1.9-meter-deep midden, extending back to A.D. 200. This midden contains incised pottery of nonlocal origin, nearly identical to the Sinapupu Ware of Tikopia and like it deriving from northern Vanuatu (Kirch 1982c). This trade ware falls in the Mangaasi tradition, evidence of once more extensive connections between Vanuatu and the Santa Cruz Islands. Also present in Vanikoro are *Tridacna*-shell adzes with stylistic features linking them to Vanuatu shell adzes of the post-Lapita period, but *Terebra*-shell adzes appear only late, in the proto-historic period.

Vanuatu

Vanuatu (formerly the New Hebrides), almost as extensive as the Solomons, is equally diverse ethnographically.[26] At the risk of sounding repetitive, we are once again ignorant about much of the prehistory of this vast archipelago. Pioneering field research by José Garanger (1972a) on Efate and adjacent islands of the central region established a Lapita presence at the base of a ceramic sequence that develops into a locally variable set of incised and applied-relief ceramics, under the rubric "Mangaasi" (Fig. 5.10). The toponymous Mangaasi site on Efate Island is stratigraphically complex (Fig. 5.11), subject to differing interpretations. Spriggs (1997:179–81,

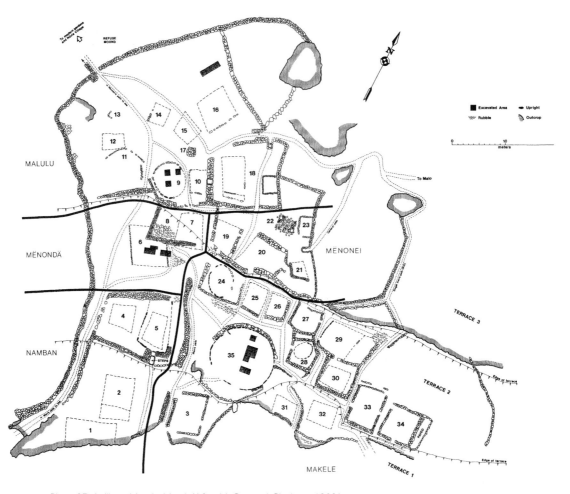

FIGURE 5.9 Plan of Dai village, Nendö Island. (After McCoy and Cleghorn 1988.)

Fig. 6.3) suggests that marine deposits sandwiched between cultural layers in the site represent tsunami or surge events derived from cataclysmic volcanic eruptions of Ambrym around A.D. 150, and later of Kuwae in A.D. 1452. While the main Mangaasi occupation, with its incised and applied-relief pottery, may date to 500–200 B.C., the cessation of pottery use on Efate remains unresolved. Spriggs notes that it had ceased by A.D. 1300 but that it may have stopped much earlier, by ca. A.D. 150 (1997:181). In northern Vanuatu, pot-

tery making continued into the "ethnographic present."[27] Correlating with the end of pottery production in the central islands is the appearance of the *Terebra*-shell adz, a discontinuous but widespread artifact of the past 1,000 years in island Melanesia and Micronesia.

Recently a joint research team from the Australian National University and the National Museum of Vanuatu has been carrying out renewed archaeological surveys and excavations, both on Efate (the main locus of Garanger's pioneering

FIGURE 5.10 Potsherds from the Mangaasi site (EF-17) on Efate Island, Vanuatu. (Photo courtesy José Garanger.)

FIGURE 5.11 The site of Mangaasi (EF-17) on Efate Island, Vanuatu, after the completion of excavations. (Photo courtesy José Garanger.)

work) and Malakula and Erromango (Bedford et al. 1998). On Erromango Island, the Ponamla and Ifo sites have revealed a ceramic sequence beginning with Lapita around 3,000 years ago and continuing over the next thousand years with "an early plainware phase . . . followed by incised and fingernail-impressed ware" (Bedford et al. 1998: 178). On Malakula, initial settlement was again by Lapita people, but the archaeological record currently reflects a long gap between this colonization phase and the appearance of "Late Malakulan" ceramics around 1000 B.P. and continuing to the ethnohistoric contact period. Summarizing their research to date, the ANU–National Museum team write that

The project has established that the archipelago was first settled by Lapita colonists some 3000 years ago and the ceramic sequences that followed evolved from the Lapita ceramic tradition and occurred in some sequences for up to 1000 years. Lapita dentate-stamped ceramics appear to have largely disappeared after several hundred years, to be proceeded by plainware material, which in turn is followed, at around 550 B.C., by decorated wares. On Erromango the decoration is dominated by fingernail impression and linear incision, and on Mangaas (Efate) by incision and applied relief. *(Bedford et al. 1998:189)*

As in parts of the Bismarcks and northern Solomons, then, new ceramic styles with mostly incised patterns, along with relief, appliqué, fin-gernail-impressed, and other forms of decoration, signal late transformations of Lapita wares. The Mangaasi ceramic complex of Vanuatu represents a similar development, and along with ceramic changes in New Caledonia to the south and in Fiji to the east it raises the question of whether these trends were entirely independent or instead reflect some degree of contact and hence shared ideology. This is an issue I will discuss further at the end of this chapter.

One of the most remarkable archaeological sites anywhere in Oceania is the burial ground on Retoka Island near Efate (Fig. 5.12), reputed in local oral traditions to be the grave of a chief named Roy Mata, famous for instituting a wide-spread peace in the region.[28] According to the traditions, when Roy Mata died his body was displayed in the villages under his suzerainty and then interred on Retoka Island along with the bodies of kinsfolk and of representatives of the various clans, some interred involuntarily. Retoka Island remains sacred to this day, and it can be visited only during daylight as it is thought to be inhabited by the spirits of the dead.

Led to the site by his informants who had related these traditions, Garanger excavated a burial ground (Fig. 5.13) with a single central, male skeleton—certainly Roy Mata himself—sur-rounded by a macabre tableau of paired male and female skeletons, the males supine on their backs in relaxed positions, the females clutching at their partners in positions that strongly suggest they were buried alive. As Spriggs says regarding the Roy Mata tradition, "The men had been drugged with very strong kava, a drink forbidden to women, and so were unconscious at the moment of burial, while the women were fully conscious when they were buried alive and in a state of complete terror as shown by their pitiable contortions preserved in death. One young female appears to have tried

to raise herself out of the ground after burial" (1997:211). The significance of the central burial (Roy Mata) is shown by its position at the base of two large upright slabs, with a young woman laid out at his feet, another man on his right, and a couple on his left. A bundle burial was interred between the outstretched legs of Roy Mata, pos-sibly the bones of one of his own ancestors. Radiocarbon dates place the site between 650 and 400 B.P.

The Retoka burials are richly ornamented with shell beads, pig tusks, and shell bands; differences in ornamentation patterns may reflect specific clan insignia. Roy Mata, an older man who had lost most of his teeth, had shell armbands on both arms, along with bracelets of *Ovula* shells, a bead necklace, a perforated *Spondylus* shell, and three whale-tooth beads. Rows of shell beads around his waist had presumably been attached to some kind of woven garment. On his wrists were pig tusk bracelets (produced by knocking out the upper incisors of pigs and allowing the lower incisors to grow in a circle), a practice known ethnographically. The Retoka site and Roy Mata's burial demonstrate the historical validity and per-sistence of an indigenous oral tradition hundreds of years old.[29]

The Roy Mata burial ground represents a level of sociopolitical control and hierarchy not evident in earlier time periods in island Melanesia. The unanswered question is whether this was the result of in situ social changes, or whether Roy Mata was an immigrant who introduced new social forms and was able to maintain them either by force or by persuasion. Garanger (1972a) thinks it likely that Roy Mata was a Polynesian immigrant, and Spriggs (1997:212) points out that the Retoka burial ground—with its evident sacrificial inter-ments—has parallels in a recently excavated chiefly burial mound on 'Uvea Island in Western Polynesia (see Chapter 7).

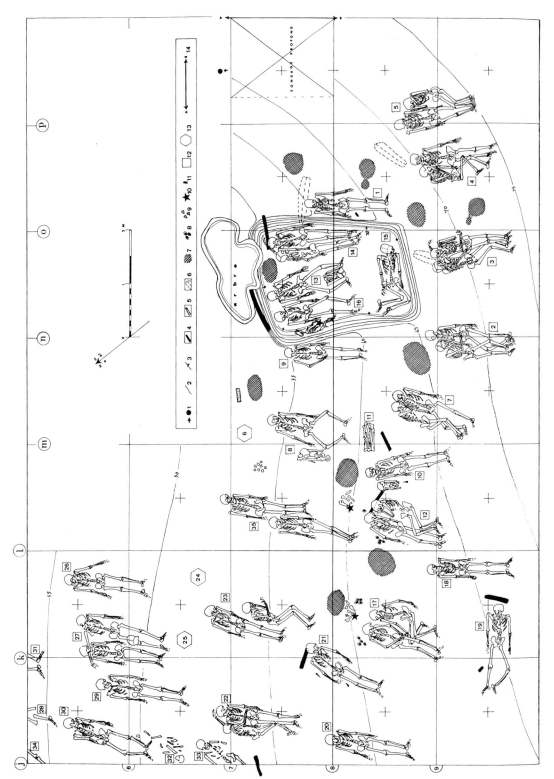

FIGURE 5.12 Plan of the Roy Mata burial site on Retoka Island. (From Garanger 1972a.)

FIGURE 5.13 The Roy Mata burial site. Note the prominent central burial with open legs, ornaments on the chest, and a secondary burial between the legs. (Photo courtesy José Garanger.)

As in the Bismarck Archipelago, massive volcanic eruptions devastated parts of the Vanuatu landscape within the period of human habitation, most notably the Kuwae eruption, which literally tore apart the southeastern part of Epi Island, separating it from Tongoa Island.[30] The Kuwae eruption ranks as one of the ten largest volcanic events anywhere in the world during the Holocene, probably larger in scale than the well-known Santorini eruption in the eastern Mediterranean around 3600 B.C., which destroyed the Minoan city of Thera, perhaps giving rise to the Atlantis myth. The highly violent Kuwae eruption, resulting from an interaction of hot magma with sea-

water, probably occurred in A.D. 1452, and it may be responsible for anomalies in the Greenland ice cores from A.D. 1452–60. Oral traditions refer to the Kuwae eruption, attributing its origin to a man named Tombuk or Toboka who, angry over being tricked into committing incest with his mother, in revenge used magic to cause the cataclysm (Spriggs 1997:212). The effects must have been greater than Tombuk ever intended, and while some people may have fled to Efate prior to the main explosive eruption, many others certainly were killed.

At the southeastern end of Vanuatu lies Aneityum Island, locus of an important study of environmental change and agricultural intensification

FIGURE 5.14 A prehistoric irrigation canal on Aneityum Island, after excavation. (Photo courtesy M. Spriggs.)

by Spriggs (1981, 1986). Although no Lapita occupation sites were discovered on Aneityum, a pollen core from Anauwau swamp studied by Hope and Spriggs (1982) exhibits a clear signal of human arrival on the island—disturbance to the rainforest and increases in charcoal particles—around 900 B.C., believed to reflect a Lapita colonization. From that initial settlement date until around A.D. 1000, shifting cultivation on the island's volcanic hillsides was the primary mode of subsistence production. As on some other islands, such as Futuna (Kirch 1994), centuries of swidden agriculture resulted in a degraded vegetation and heightened erosion rates, leading to alluvial valley infilling and progradation of the island's coastal flats. During the last millennium, these newly created alluvial soils began to be used for intensive forms of agriculture, particularly irrigated cultivation of taro. During the latest 300–400 years, especially, canals were constructed to cross the divides between separate drainage systems (Fig. 5.14). Spriggs traces the development of these irrigation systems in terms of transformations of Aneityumese sociopolitical systems:

The growth of chiefly power and the expansion of irrigation on the island went hand in hand. As a chief's prestige grew he would become more able to command labor to expand the conditions of agricultural production by the building of new canals and the extension of irrigation systems to the flatter areas of the coastal plains. It was the chief's power to appropriate surplus production for feasts in order to maintain his prestige which required the expansion of the irrigation systems. An expansion in one district or dominion would necessitate expansion in the others to match food presentations, taro for taro, up to the limits of the productive capacity of the island. (*Spriggs 1986:16*)

This sequence of late prehistoric agricultural intensification on Aneityum, like that in New Georgia, is one of several cultural developments in island Melanesia reflecting common processes of demographic and sociocultural change.

The Polynesian Outliers in Melanesia

In the usual tripartite cartographic dissection of Oceania, Polynesian societies are confined within a triangle whose apices are Hawai'i, New Zealand, and Easter Island. However, in addition to the more than 20 Polynesian societies found within the "Polynesian Triangle," another 18 societies whose members speak Polynesian languages and whose cultural practices include markedly Polynesian features are located geographically west of the triangle. These "Polynesian Outliers" are found on smaller islands and islets fringing the Melanesian island-arcs, but with two also in Micronesia.[31] The Outliers include perhaps the most anthropologically renowned island in all of Oceania: Tikopia, the subject of Sir Raymond Firth's classic studies.[32]

Early twentieth-century diffusionists such as Churchill (1911) saw in the Outliers a trail of Polynesian migration from Asia direct to the main Triangle. More astute observers, such as the German ethnographer Thilenius (1902), recognized that Outlier oral traditions spoke of origins in the east, often resulting from accidental or drift voyages from homelands in "Tonga" or "Rotuma."[33] Indeed, the very names of some Outliers were transferred from a homeland island to a new colony (e.g., Ouvea in the Loyalty group derived from 'Uvea, and Futuna in Vanuatu derived from Futuna in Western Polynesia). Thilenius hypothesized that "the populations of the northwestern Polynesian islands [the Outliers distributed along the Solomons chain] have arisen gradually from small beginnings through the landing of at most a single boat's crew and through rarer voyages of conquest" (1902:83). A high probability of drift voyages originating in Western Polynesia making successful landfall on one of the Outliers was demonstrated through computer simulations.[34]

Archaeological investigation of the Outliers commenced in the 1960s and early 1970s, with studies of Nukuoro (in Micronesia), Anuta, and Rennell-Bellona.[35] The second phase of the SSICHP (1977–78) included archaeological studies of Taumako and Tikopia in the outer Southeastern Solomons, but only the latter has been published (Kirch and Yen 1982). Fewer than half the Outliers have been investigated, and their sequences vary, but they consistently have a late Polynesian phase, sometimes as an intrusion overlying earlier non-Polynesian phases.[36]

Because its cultural sequence is well understood, I will focus on Tikopia, recognizing that the histories of other Outlier societies differ. Tikopia encapsulates many key aspects of Outlier history, including interactions between Polynesian and non-Polynesian populations.[37] A small (4.6 square kilometers) but topographically dramatic island—featuring steep volcanic hills rimming a deep crater lake (Fig. 5.15) that resulted from a cataclysmic eruption—Tikopia is home to about 1,500 Polynesian speakers, organized into four main clans (kainanga), each headed by a hereditary chief. Our work in 1977–78 revealed a well-stratified archaeological record, especially in the Sinapupu sand dune site at Faea, where up to 3.5 meters of continuous deposit encapsulated a 3,000-year sequence, yielding an abundance of artifacts as well as faunal materials. Excavations there and at several other sites, along with 20 radiocarbon dates, allowed us to outline a sequence of three prehistoric phases (Fig. 5.16).

Although the island may have been intermittently visited even earlier, permanent settlement began around 900 B.C., by people making pottery of the Lapita ceramic series.[38] The initial Kiki Phase lasted until about 100 B.C., and it bears the usual Lapita signature, such as a mixed horticultural-maritime economy and—at least in the earliest centuries—external exchange linkages including the importing of obsidian, chert, and metavolcanic adzes. Angling with one-piece fishhooks made of large *Turbo* shells (Fig. 5.17) was an important component of the island's subsistence economy. Around 100 B.C., several cultural changes

FIGURE 5.15 Tikopia consists of a volcanic cone with a central crater lake, resulting from an explosive eruption about 80,000 years ago. (Photo by P. V. Kirch.)

mark the beginning of the Sinapupu Phase, which persisted until about A.D. 1200. In material culture, the Sinapupu Phase is characterized by the absence of local pottery manufacture and by the importation of low frequencies of incised and painted pottery with close affinities in the Banks Islands or Northern Vanuatu.[39] Other artifact styles also changed, such as shell adzes, which show a distinctive tapered-butt form prominent in Vanuatu adzes of comparable age (Fig. 5.18). Evidence of linkages between Tikopia and islands to the south consists of substantial quantities of obsidian from the Vanua Lava and Gaua sources in the Banks Islands. In short, during the Sinapupu Phase, Tikopia was linked through regular long-distance exchange with populations in the Banks and northern Vanuatu Islands.

An abrupt cultural change again occurred around A.D. 1200, with the onset of the Tuakamali Phase and the intrusion of Polynesian-speaking populations from the east. Although contacts with the Banks Islands were not wholly abandoned (some obsidian continued to be imported), no ceramics are present in Tuakamali Phase sites. Distinctive Polynesian material culture appears at this time, such as basalt adzes brought on voyaging canoes from Samoa, 'Uvea, or other Western Polynesian Islands; the classic two-piece Polynesian trolling lure rig; and bone beads. Turtles and sharks—foods that had evidently been taboo

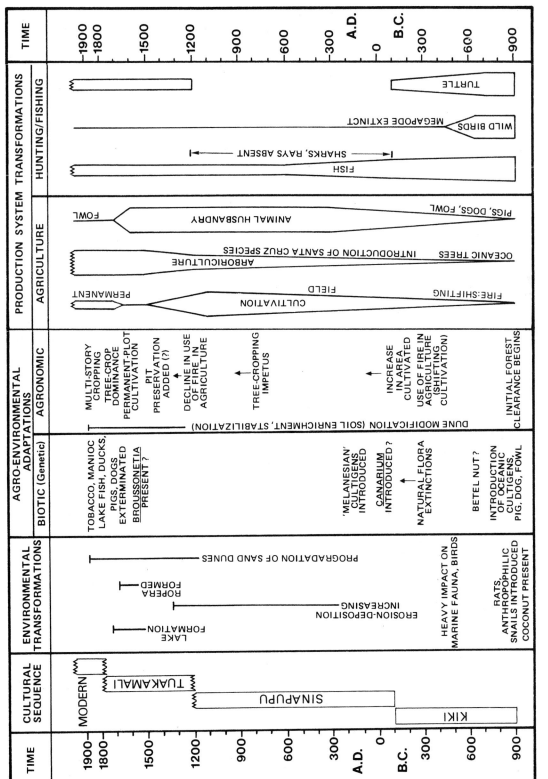

FIGURE 5.16 The cultural sequence of Tikopia. (From Kirch and Yen 1982.)

FIGURE 5.17 *Turbo*-shell fishhooks excavated from archaeological sites on Tikopia Island. Both finished hooks and stages of manufacture are illustrated. (Photo by P. V. Kirch.)

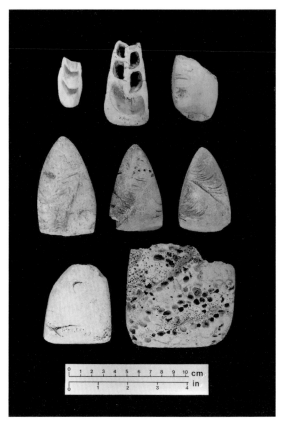

FIGURE 5.18 Tikopia *Tridacna*-shell adzes from the Sinapupu Phase (middle row) have a distinctive tapered and pointed butt similar to adzes from Vanuatu at the same time period. The upper row also illustrates two *Terebra*-shell adzes. (Photo by P. V. Kirch.)

during the preceding Sinapupu Phase but that are relished by Polynesian peoples—were once again captured and eaten.[40]

Tikopia oral traditions (Firth 1961) speak of multiple lineage origins in Western Polynesia, and archaeological evidence supports this. These traditions relate a series of internal social conflicts and upheavals, some spurred by ecological changes (in particular, the conversion of a marine embayment to the brackish crater lake) but others reflecting aggression by the Polynesian newcomers against the indigenous occupants. Archaeo-logical evidence testifies to the veracity of these traditions, such as the expulsion of the Nga Faea people, whose village site we mapped and excavated. However, although after A.D. 1200 Tikopia became culturally and linguistically a distinctly Polynesian place, there was no wholesale replacement of its original population. Genetic continuity is indicated by the presence in the modern Tikopia of at least one, and probably more, marker genes found in Vanuatu but not in Western Polynesia.[41]

Diminutive Anuta (only 80 hectares in area), 137 kilometers northeast of Tikopia, had regular social relationships with the latter, and an archaeological sequence that in some respects parallels that of Tikopia. Colonization of Anuta occurred around 900 B.C., with a group making calcareous sand–tempered pottery virtually identical to that found in Kiki Phase sites on Tikopia. Sometime between 500 B.C. and A.D. 580, this population either abandoned Anuta or was exterminated, possibly as a result of a cyclone that left a massive sand deposit in the main An-6 site. Anuta was unoccupied for some time, and then it was recolonized around A.D. 600, presumably by one or more Polynesian-speaking groups (Kirch 1982d).

In proto-historic times and into the ethnographically recorded "present," the populations of Anuta and Tikopia had regular contacts with non-Polynesian groups, such as the people of Vanikoro and Utupua, as well as those of the Banks Islands. Tikopian knowledge of a European shipwreck on Vanikoro provided clues to Peter Dillon in 1827, enabling him to resolve the mystery of the ill-fated La Pérouse expedition. On Vanikoro, various old songs in a seemingly Polynesian language—which the Vanikoro people themselves do not understand—provide another clue to wider contacts in the past.

Contact between Polynesian and Melanesian groups occurred not just in the Southeast Solomons but also in Vanuatu, the Loyalty Islands, and New Caledonia. Spriggs (1997:187–222) discusses the social and cultural effects resulting from interaction between Polynesian Outlier populations and the peoples of eastern Melanesia. Although this is not conclusive, both Garanger and Spriggs attribute the Roy Mata burial site to a Polynesian immigrant group. Although the five documented Polynesian Outliers in central and southern Vanuatu (Emae, Mele, Fila, Aniwa, West Futuna) have yet to be archaeologically investigated in any

detail, they may have had considerable cultural influences during the past 500 years of Vanuatu history. In the Loyalty Islands, a migration from 'Uvea in Western Polynesia resulted in the takeover of Ouvea Island by Polynesian speakers. Sand (1995:203–12) suggests that the Xetriwaan group of people with immediate origins in southern Vanuatu, who were influential both on Lifou and on La Grande Terre proper, may have had Polynesian associations. As Spriggs remarks, "the migrants inserted themselves within the indigenous economic systems and took them over from the inside" (1997:221). In other cases, such as Tikopia, there was a near-total cultural and linguistic (but not biological) replacement. Certainly, we have a great deal more to learn about the history of Polynesian-Melanesian interchange.

Ethnogenesis in La Grande Terre

At the southeastern terminus of Melanesia, 1,000 kilometers east of Australia, lies La Grande Terre (New Caledonia), a long, skinny remnant of ancient Gondwanaland stretching 400 kilometers from northwest to southeast (the total land area is 24,436 square kilometers).[42] Several smaller islands lie off its coasts, such as the Île des Pins to the southeast, while to the east the Loyalty Island chain, comprising Ouvea, Lifou, and Maré, lies about 100 kilometers distant. Ever since colonial "possession" was proclaimed in 1853, both La Grande Terre and the Loyalties have been under French control, but even prior to European influence the societies of the two island groups had close contacts and relationships.

New Caledonia's mountainous terrain and mineral-rich soils (it is one of the world's main sources of nickel) support a unique biota with Gondwanan roots. Interesting as this biota is to naturalists, it must have been an even more stunning world in the late second millennium B.C., when Lapita voyagers sailed their canoes through the island's marvelous barrier-reef lagoons and hauled ashore, to encounter such bizarre creatures as giant flightless megapodes, terrestrial crocodiles, varanid lizards, and large horned terrestrial turtles. These and other creatures, lacking any fear of the new bipedal predators, did not withstand the human onslaught for more than a few centuries, and we know them today only from subfossils and remains in archaeological contexts.[43] Unlike La Grande Terre, the Loyalty Islands consist of upraised makatea. Maré and Lifou have cliff-bound coasts and extensive flat plateaus with arable soils formed by decomposition of the limestone and organically enriched.

In this new and biotically strange land the Lapita colonists of La Grande Terre and the Loyalties—and the generations of descendants they spawned—gave rise to a remarkable diversity of societies and language groups.[44] While all of the languages spoken in these islands are of the Oceanic branch of Austronesian, there are no fewer than 37 distinct languages classified within some seven primary subgroups. And although there is much cultural homogeneity (in material culture, for example, or in subsistence practices), the islands' populations seem to have consciously differentiated among themselves sociopolitically and ethnically.[45] From the anthropological viewpoint, a fascinating aspect of New Caledonia is the degree of *ethnogenesis* that occurred within a mere three millennia.

This linguistic and cultural diversity intrigued the pioneer ethnographers, who were at a loss to explain it other than through numerous and repeated migrations by groups with varied ethnic and biological origins.[46] E. W. Gifford and his student Dick Shutler, Jr., carried out the first modern archaeological excavations on La Grande Terre in 1952 and, finding no evidence of a "prepottery cultural level," rejected any notion of a

"Paleolithic stage of culture" in the archipelago's history (1956:94). While this should have been the end of the matter, when Jack Golson as well as Luc Chevalier discovered earthen mounds or "tumuli" on the Île des Pins, with radiocarbon ages as old as 12,900 ± 450 B.P., the question of a preceramic, pre-Austronesian occupation was resurrected.[47] Moreover, the New Caledonian ceramic sequence was complicated by the presence not only of Lapita ware but also of a second, coeval pottery type (with paddle-impressed surfaces) called "Podtanéan."[48] Thus, until quite recently, New Caledonian prehistory has been regarded as "very poorly understood" (Bellwood 1979:262), an enigma in the otherwise clearly unfolding story of Western Pacific cultural history.

Thanks to an energetic group of French archaeologists—including Daniel Frimigacci, Jean-Christophe Galipaud, and Christophe Sand (all trained by José Garanger of the Sorbonne in Paris)—this situation has dramatically improved in recent years, as extensive excavations and surveys have been carried out throughout the archipelago.[49] Most scholars now accept that the tumuli were the work of extinct giant megapodes, heaps of earth (incorporating large terrestrial *Placostylus* gastropods) scraped up to incubate their eggs, as is the practice with other extant species of this genus.[50] Thus the initial human settlement of the archipelago was indeed by the Lapita peoples, as with other parts of Remote Oceania. Moreover, as Jean-Christophe Galipaud has convincingly demonstrated, Podtanéan pottery was made of the same clays and tempers as the decorated Lapita wares, and in some cases it is found in the same sites.[51] Rather than two distinct founding cultures, these represent the plain and decorated components of the Lapita ceramic series (see Chapter 4). With these enigmas resolved, archaeologists have been able to move on to far more interesting aspects of New Caledonian prehistory.

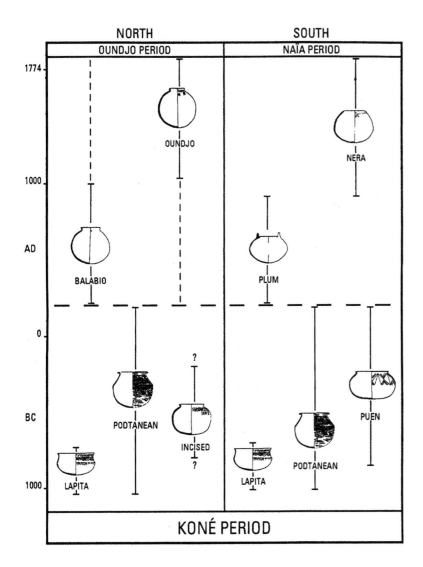

FIGURE 5.19 The cultural sequence of New Caledonia, as defined by ceramic styles, according to Sand (1996a).

In New Caledonia pottery continued to be produced and used throughout prehistory, into recent times (Fig. 5.19). Aside from their use to archaeologists as relative chronological markers, these New Caledonian ceramics offer a material index to the ongoing processes of ethnogenesis.[52] At the time of initial human colonization, Lapita (i.e., dentate-stamped pottery) and Podtanéan (plain and paddle-impressed) wares are found throughout the island, with little local variation. The dentate-stamped vessels did not persist more than a few centuries, paralleling Lapita ceramic change in other archipelagoes (see Chapter 4), while the plain or paddle-impressed Podtanéan wares continued to be produced for a thousand years or more. During the mid–first millennium B.C., we also see the appearance of two new styles of decorated pottery, in the northern and southern parts of La Grande Terre, respectively. In the north, incised designs were applied largely to globular vessels, while in the south the incised designs on such vessels are sufficiently distinctive to be distinguished as "Puen" ware.[53]

Early in the first millennium A.D., at the commencement of the Oundjo Period, the situation becomes more complex, with two distinct ceramic traditions: Balabio and Oundjo proper. Balabio ceramics, with a black paste and spherical vessel form, developed—according to Sand—out of the Podtanéan tradition. Toward the end of the first millennium A.D., the Balabio tradition was replaced by the Oundjo tradition, characterized by incised, stamped, and relief decorations on the upper parts of the globular pots, below the rim.[54] In the southern part of La Grande Terre, the Naïa Period is defined by a succession of the Plum and Nera ceramic traditions. The earlier Plum ceramics, whose incised decorations developed out of the Puen tradition (of the Koné Period), have distinctive handles. Noting the design similarities between Plum ceramics and a style of petroglyphs, Sand (1995:144) makes the intriguing suggestion that the latter might be interpreted as boundary markers, possibly a reflection of growing ethnolinguistic differentiation within the island. The later Nera tradition is marked by spherical vessels lacking everted rims, with simple decorations consisting of rows of nubbins and some incising. More than anywhere else within island Melanesia, the stylistic differentiation of New Caledonian pottery parallels the differentiation of its ethnolinguistic groups. Indeed, it seems likely that ceramics, as well as other forms of material culture, were actively manipulated by local peoples as symbols of ethnic identity.

This kind of social differentiation, it should be said, had as one underlying basis the growth and expansion of the archipelago's population (Fig. 5.20). The early Koné Period, with a dura-

tion of perhaps 1,200 years, witnessed the gradual expansion of human settlement throughout New Caledonia and the Loyalty archipelago, at first concentrated along the coasts and in the more horticulturally suited humid sectors, but toward the end of the period expanding into interior valleys. Sand (1995:112–13) estimates that by the close of the Koné Period the island's aggregate population had reached 50,000 persons. Stratigraphic evidence from the Bopope region indicates that by the first few centuries of the Christian era, even interior valleys were permanently occupied, with anthropogenically transformed landscapes.

Significantly, the earliest evidence for material signals of social transformation—specifically, indications of hierarchy, competition, and warfare—is found not on La Grande Terre but on the central plain of Maré Island. Two monumental stone structures, built of coral blocks weighing up to 5 tons each, were defensive sites or forts; the rectangular enclosure of Hnakudotit (site LMA016) incorporates 23,000 cubic meters of stone (Fig. 5.21). This remarkable construction dates to the first two or three centuries A.D. According to Sand (1995:133), these structures indicate the prior existence of a "political system . . . very different from that known ethnographically in New Caledonia." In my view, the ecological setting of these structures is telling: the upraised, karst limestone plateau of Maré Island, a "dry" and somewhat marginal environment for an agriculturally based economy. According to a model of contrastive "wet and dry" agroecological regimes first developed for Polynesia (Kirch 1994), it is in just such environments—where the choice of agricultural strategies is highly constrained toward labor-intensive short-fallow swidden—that competition for land and aggressive territorial warfare are most likely to arise. Thus it is not surprising to find these earliest material indications of competition

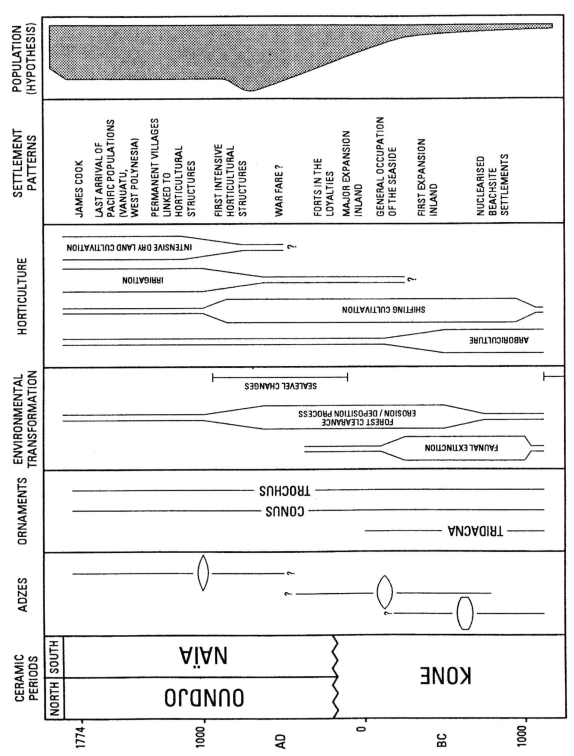

FIGURE 5.20
The cultural
sequence of
New Caledonia,
according to
Sand (1996a).

FIGURE 5.21 Stacked walls of limestone boulders make up the Hnakudotit fortification site on Maré, Loyalty Islands. (Photo courtesy Christophe Sand.)

and territorial marking on Maré, rather than on La Grande Terre, with the latter's much greater potential for alternative forms of intensification, such as terracing.

Yet if the first signals of ecological and/or demographic stress—and consequent sociopolitical response—arose on the makatea plateaus of the Loyalties, other kinds of intensification also soon appeared on the main island. La Grande Terre has long been noted by ethnobotanists for several kinds of *landesque capital* intensification[55] (i.e., those resulting in permanent landscape transformations). These include taro irrigation systems—the most extensive in all of Oceania—as well as *Dioscorea* yam mound systems.[56] Anyone who has viewed the magnificently sculpted hillsides of the Col de la Pirogue, with row upon row of descending terraces for taro planting irrigated by a complex network of canals and ditches (Fig. 5.22), must be impressed at the scale of landscape manipulation achieved by this preindustrial society.

Although much more work must be carried out, we are beginning to get some indications of the prehistory of these impressive landscapes.

Excavations in taro terraces (site WPT069) at the famous Col de la Pirogue irrigation complex near Nouméa yielded a radiocarbon age of A.D. 670–990, the oldest date for a Melanesian irrigation complex.[57] Other terraces gave more recent ages, within the last two or three centuries. The Païta data—if confirmed by future research—provide evidence that on La Grande Terre, as in Hawai'i, Futuna, and elsewhere, intensive, canal-fed irrigation was a development of the middle to later phases of island sequences, linked both to demographic pressures and to sociopolitical transformations.[58] Of equal note are vast areas of ancient dryland terracing and mounding that mark formerly intensive systems of "dry" cultivation, focused primarily on *Dioscorea* yams. The New Caledonian dryland systems rival in scale and complexity those of the New Guinea Highlands (Fig. 5.23). At Tiwaka, a single dryland system includes more than 150 large mounds, totaling at least 35 hectares. Mounds may be 1–3 meters high, 10 meters wide, and up to several hundred meters long. Unfortunately, these dryland systems have not yet been excavated or dated, and

FIGURE 5.22 Flights of formerly irrigated taro terraces, now covered in grasslands, at the Col de la Pirogue, New Caledonia. (Photo courtesy Christophe Sand.)

FIGURE 5.23 Aerial photo of ancient yam cultivation mounds on an alluvial plain at Tiwaka, New Caledonia. (Photo courtesy Christophe Sand.)

their history remains a problem awaiting further research.

New forms of inland habitation arose during the Oundjo and Naïa Periods, in close spatial association with the intensive agricultural systems. While the coastal regions—marked by extensive shell middens—continued to be occupied, the interior valleys and coastal plains came to be dotted with elevated house mounds, frequently organized in linear arrangements of 15 or more house mounds around a central alleyway. The plan of Tipalet (site ETO018) in the Bopope region (Fig. 5.24) shows such mounds on either side of an elongate plaza, with a substantially larger mound

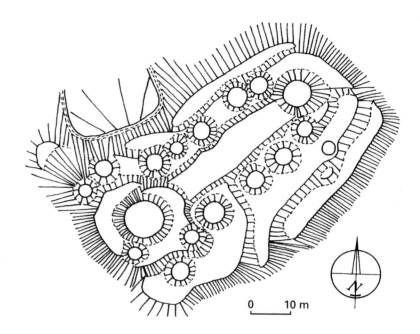

FIGURE 5.24 Plan of house mounds at Tipalet in the Bopope region of New Caledonia. (Courtesy Christophe Sand.)

at each end. Other habitation mound complexes reflect a hierarchy of mound sizes and heights, possible evidence for social stratification or at least for ranking of households. Few such complexes have been excavated, but a charcoal sample from the base of a mound at Pwapwadouhi yielded a calibrated radiocarbon age of A.D. 1290–1470.

In the view of Christophe Sand, "It is the intensification of horticulture which appears the most characteristic" of the Oundjo and Naïa Periods (1995:200). He accepts a primary causal role for demographic pressure but cautions that population growth by itself is too limiting an explanatory factor. Indeed, the very existence of these intensive agricultural systems—which are found throughout the interior valleys and plains of New Caledonia—provoked Sand to question long-held ethnographic notions concerning traditional Kanak societies (e.g., Guiart 1963). Rather than regarding the sociopolitical systems associated with these intensive systems of agricultural production as "weak chiefdoms," and the sites themselves as only

intermittently occupied by a peripatetic population, Sand asks instead whether the archaeological evidence might not better support an interpretation of "strong chiefdoms" bolstered by substantial surplus extraction and driven by prestige rivalry. The implications of Sand's arguments are profound, for they raise fundamental questions about the validity of much Melanesian ethnography as a guide to interpreting the past.

How can we account for the disparity between the New Caledonian archaeological record, which speaks to the former existence of highly complex sociopolitical formations, and the received twentieth-century ethnography, which refers at best to "weak" chiefdoms? The answer—still highly contentious—may lie in a demographic collapse of hitherto-unappreciated magnitude, immediately after European contact.[59] The crux of the argument is as follows. Based on a narrow reading of the available textual sources—and in particular favoring census data that did not become available until after missionization in the mid-nineteenth century (more than 60 years after initial European contact)—academic demographers have maintained that the precontact population of La Grande Terre never exceeded 50,000 persons. In contrast, archaeological data (while too thin to attempt regional population estimates) suggest that the latter figure is way too low to account for the density and intensity of the agricultural and residential landscape. In a case study of the Païta region near Nouméa, Sand (1995) shows that while the ethnologist Guiart estimated the maximum population at perhaps 1,200 persons, the archaeological vestiges of intensive terracing and habitation lead one to a conservative estimate of 8,000 persons, with a strong likelihood of double that number!

How to account for the disparity in estimates? Sand argues that not only the effects of diseases for which the indigenous Kanaks had no resistance, but also the political and military strategies of several decades of whalers, sandalwooders, and outright colonists, had far greater impacts than hitherto recognized. The French colonials pursued a strategy of outright destruction of agricultural infrastructure, leading to famine and social collapse. Sand's dissection of the arguments of Norma McArthur (1968) for low population densities deserves to be read by all anthropologists and historians working in Melanesia. In Sand's words, "To appreciate the extent of the demographic collapse is to revisit the autopsy of the destruction of a society" (1995:248). Sand presents us with a challenge, not just for La Grande Terre but also for many other islands and archipelagoes of the Pacific where the archaeological evidence of densely populated interior regions directly contradicts accepted historical demographic estimates (see Chapter 9 for further discussion). This is one of the most significant tasks that lies ahead for Pacific archaeology, not merely for its intrinsic intellectual interest but because

the "truth" is a matter of vital concern to the indigenous peoples of the Pacific.

Fiji: An Archipelago "in Between"

Fiji (Map 9) offers striking contrasts yet intriguing similarities with New Caledonia. The archipelagoes are of comparable scale (24,436 square kilometers for New Caledonia, 18,272 for Fiji) and have been inhabited for approximately the same length of time (they were both settled by Lapita peoples), but Fiji's history does not display the same emphasis on small-scale ethnolinguistic differentiation seen in La Grande Terre and the Loyalties. There is, to be sure, intra-archipelago diversity within Fiji, but this is more limited. For example, the Fijian peoples speak only two main dialects (Western and Eastern Fijian), while there is a third discrete language on isolated Rotuma Island.[60] Culturally, there were important differences between coastal and offshore island dwellers, and the "bush people" of the interiors of Viti Levu and Vanua Levu. In addition, the people of the Lau Islands had their own distinctive characteristics, in part derived from regular contact and interaction with Tonga.[61]

Anthropologists have never quite known how to deal with Fiji. It is a sort of "between" archipelago, situated geographically closer to Western Polynesia (with whose societies there were important historical interactions), yet usually classified as a "Melanesian" culture. Of course, such nineteenth-century classifications are of little real historical or analytical value, and perhaps the Fijian case is the best example (see the Introduction). Settled late in the second millennium B.C.—by what on all evidence was the same founding Lapita population that quickly colonized nearby Tonga and other Polynesian islands—Fiji thus shares an identical foundation culture with Western Polynesia. At the same time, Fiji continued in later millennia to

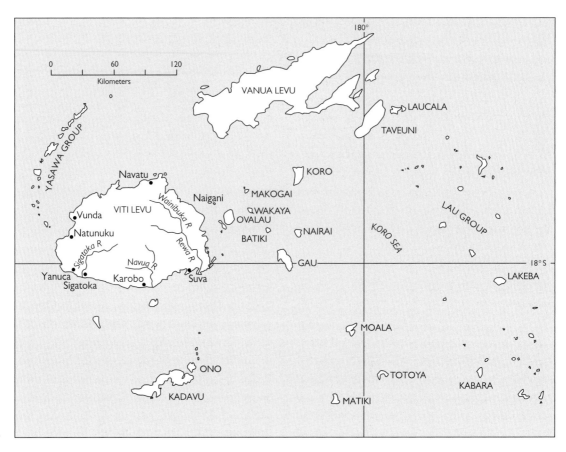

MAP 9 The Fiji archipelago, showing the location of key archaeological sites.

receive both genetic and cultural influences from the west (i.e., from "Melanesia"), inputs which in part set its historical trajectory apart from those of Tonga, Samoa, or Futuna. There is ample evidence—archaeological, linguistic, and cultural—that the peoples of Fiji, Tonga, Samoa, Futuna, Lau, and other smaller islands in this part of the central Pacific had regular exchanges (material, social, and genetic) throughout prehistory. Thus, in contrast to New Caledonia (which, while not wholly isolated, is set apart in its corner of the southwestern Pacific), Fiji was a sort of "between place"—a foyer of exchange and interaction.

E. W. Gifford (1951) pioneered excavation in Fiji, focusing his attention on the main island of Viti Levu. On his 1947 expedition, Gifford dug two sites: Navatu (site 17) on the north coast under the shadow of the imposing volcanic monolith Uluinavatu, an important place in Fijian origin traditions; and Vunda (site 26), near Lautoka. These sites yielded materials spanning the last two millennia of Fijian prehistory, while later excavations in the 1960s and 1970s at the Sigatoka dunes, the Yanuca rockshelter, Natunuku, and Naigani Island filled in earlier phases of the sequence.[62] For such a large archipelago, however, Fiji has had insufficient archaeological exploration, and large

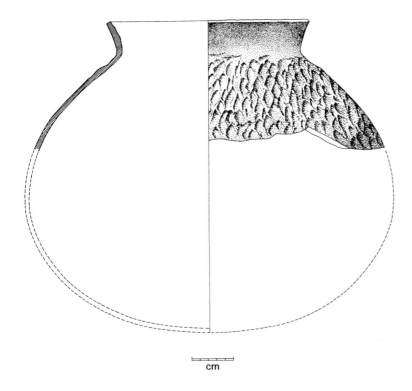

cm

FIGURE 5.25 A paddle-impressed pot from the Sigatoka dune site, Fiji. (After Birks 1973.)

regions remain uninvestigated. Important contributions include the work of geographer John Parry on archaeological landscapes of the Rewa and Navua deltas and of the Sigatoka River valley, Everett Frost's work on the hill fortifications of Taveuni Island, Robert Rechtman's study of forts on Wakaya Island, and Simon Best's research on Lakeba Island in the southern Lau group.[63] A number of current projects, such as a restudy of the Sigatoka dunes by an international team and of the Navatu and Natunuku sites by the Australian National University, should contribute further to our understanding of the archipelago's prehistory.

Gifford (1951:189) observed that pottery is the "chief characteristic of Fijian archaeology." As in New Caledonia, ceramics are found throughout the prehistoric sequence, and they continued to be manufactured after European contact.[64] From the ceramic sequences at Navatu and Vunda, Gifford defined an early period with "relief"-decorated sherds (Fig. 5.25) and a late period with dominantly "incised" sherds. Green (1963a) later showed that Gifford had missed the first third of the Fijian sequence, marked by pottery of the Lapita ceramic series, and renamed the phases as follows: Sigatoka (ca. 1200–100 B.C.), Navatu (100 B.C.–A.D. 1100), Vunda (A.D. 1100–1800), and, after European contact, the Ra Phase. This terminology has been adopted by most investigators and is described by Frost (1979).[65]

The Fijian archipelago was discovered as a part of the Lapita expansion into Remote Oceania (see Chapter 4) late in the second millennium B.C., probably between 1200 and 1000 B.C. From Fiji, the Lapita expansion continued—seemingly without significant pause—eastward into Tonga and Samoa, and contacts between these groups are indicated both in archaeological materials and by historical linguistic evidence.[66] As elsewhere in the Eastern Lapita region, dentate-stamped pottery rapidly declined, so that Sigatoka Phase assemblages of the first millennium B.C. consist largely of plain wares (with some paddle-impressing).

The transition from Sigatoka to Navatu Phases is fairly gradual in terms of the indications from ceramics, marked by an increase in carved-paddle impressions on globular vessels. As Shaw, Frost, and others argue, there is no reason to see such ceramic changes as other than internal stylistic developments. However, stylistic changes marking the boundary between the Navatu and Vunda Phases at roughly A.D. 1100 are more abrupt, with a whole new array of incised designs. Not surprisingly, archaeologists debate whether these changes reflect external influences, such as the movement or migration of a new group of people into Fiji at this time. Green, Bellwood (1979:264–65), and others consider such a population intrusion likely and point to close stylistic similarities between Vunda Phase ceramics and those of the Mangaasi complex of Vanuatu.[67] Vanuatu obsidian in rockshelters on Lakeba Island around 1700 B.P. supports this interpretation (Best 1984: 643). Others, such as Rechtman (1992), remain profoundly skeptical of explanations that invoke external influences and prefer to see all change in the Fijian sequence as stemming from internal dynamics. My own view is that some influence from Vanuatu around A.D. 1100 is likely, and may have been the impetus for ceramic style changes, but that other developments, such as the construction of fortified settlements, are best explained by internal demographic, economic, and sociopolitical change.

The cultural developments of the Vunda Phase—roughly the last thousand years—include fascinating parallels with New Caledonia in the extensive modification of landscapes for food production, yet striking differences in residential patterns. It is not certain when fortified villages began to be constructed in Fiji, but excavations in fortified sites on Taveuni and Wakaya Islands demonstrate that these were a dominant feature of the Vunda Phase. Perhaps the most common form is the "ring-ditch" style enclosing a cluster of habitation sites, these latter often elevated on earthen or stone-faced mounds. Terraced fortifications are present in more hilly topography. Figure 5.26 illustrates a particularly complex ring-ditch site at Lomolomo in the Sigatoka River valley. Ring-ditch fortifications are ubiquitous in low-lying terrain, as on the fertile deltas and flood plains of the Rewa, Navua, Sigatoka, and other drainages. Large numbers of fortified sites have been identified from aerial photographs, closely associated with extensive agricultural remains.[68] These include reticulate systems of raised beds and intervening ditches, called *vuci* in Fijian, used to grow *Colocasia* taro as well as giant swamp taro (*Cyrtosperma chamissonis*). In hilly areas such as the interior of the Sigatoka Valley, extensive pondfield terraces cascade down hillsides, similar to those in New Caledonia.[69] Such extensive agricultural modifications, as well as shifting cultivation, probably heightened erosion rates in the Sigatoka Valley, leading to increased sediment loads in the Sigatoka River and resulting in the formation of the massive dune field now located at the valley mouth, itself an important archaeological site (Dickinson et al. 1998).

The broader cultural processes associated with the construction of the literally thousands of fortified sites that appeared over the Fijian landscape in the Vunda Phase are also debated. Frost (1974, 1979) invoked the arrival of an immigrant population, bringing the new incised ceramic styles, who "clashed" with the indigenous people, leading to a major period of fort building and warfare. However, while the ceramic changes may indeed reflect

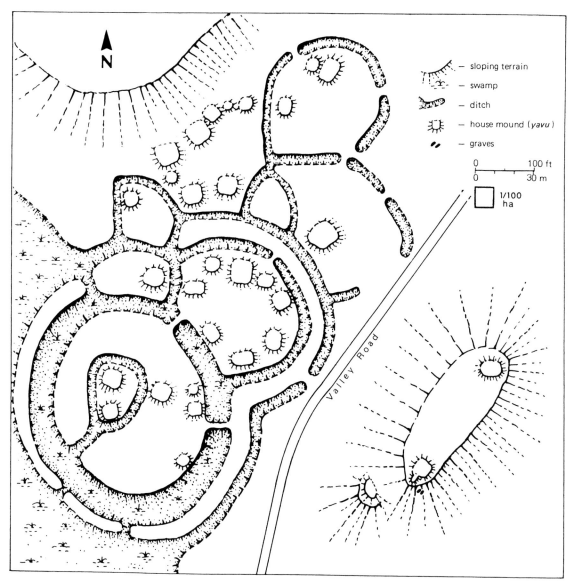

FIGURE 5.26 Plan of a village fortified with ring-ditches, at Lomolomo (site VL 16/57) in the Rewa Delta of Viti Levu, Fiji. (After Parry 1987.)

external influences at around A.D. 1100, they need not be directly linked to the settlement pattern changes, for which internal demographic, economic, and sociopolitical processes provide more likely explanations. Parry (1981, 1987) and Rechtman (1992) argue that the intensified landscape modifications of later Fijian prehistory are linked to increasing population density, competition for resources (especially prime agricultural lands), and an involutionary spiral of intergroup warfare.

Rechtman (1992:46–52) advocates a processual model of sociopolitical evolution for Fiji in which the origin of fortified sites is an "internal development," spurred in the first instance by population growth and by an increased need for resources. These processes led, after A.D. 1100, to interregional contact and conflict, marked both by fortification and by the proliferation of ceramic styles, the latter presumably as an index of increased social or ethnic differentiation. As conquest warfare became increasingly common, Rechtman believes that a shift occurred in leadership, from ideological control by sacred leaders to secular control based on force. A corollary of this change was the development of highly institutionalized cannibalism.

While some anthropologists are skeptical that cannibalism actually existed anywhere in the world, and the ethnographic or archaeological evidence for ritualized consumption of human flesh has often been discounted, the case for cannibalism in late Fijian prehistory seems particularly sound.[70] Gifford (1951:208) observed in his usual terse fashion that "man was the most popular of the vertebrate animals used for food," based on the faunal materials from the Navatu and Vunda sites. Recent reanalysis of Gifford's Navatu collections using modern criteria for evaluating cannibalistic practices confirms his view.[71] Rechtman carried out faunal and taphonomic studies of the human materials from Wakaya Island and is equally convinced that the archaeological evidence supports cannibalism as a major practice in later Fijian prehistory. Likewise, in his Lakeba Island sites, Best (1984:534) found that bones of *Homo sapiens* could be interpreted as "food remains," based on frequent charring, cut marks, and "the underrepresentation of hands, feet, and heads." Of course, the contact-period historical sources speak to the ritualized and extensive nature of Fijian anthropophagy, which until recent years has not been questioned. In my view, the significant issue is not whether the Fijians practiced cannibalism, but why

such practices should have become so pervasive and institutionalized. They may represent a kind of "competitive involution" in sociopolitical evolution parallel to that hypothesized for the Marquesas Islands (Kirch 1991b), where, as in Fiji, cannibalism is also evidenced archaeologically (see Chapter 7).

The island of Rotuma, 450 kilometers north of the main Fiji group, has a cultural history that on linguistic grounds should be as long as that of Viti Levu, but which remains little explored archaeologically.[72] However, in a methodologically path-breaking study utilizing a geographic information system approach to ecological and settlement pattern analysis, Ladefoged (1992) developed a model of interdistrict aggression and political integration in which the impetus for warfare and conquest arose in the more resource-poor parts of the island. It was from these eastern sectors that the *sau*, or highest-ranked political leaders of Rotuma, came in late prehistory and postcontact times. Ladefoged's model for Rotuma provides another supporting case for a more general model of "wet" and "dry" agroecological regimes in tropical Oceanic societies, as advocated by Kirch (1994) and further discussed in Chapter 9. The testing of these models in Viti Levu and elsewhere in the main Fiji group may prove insightful.

One of the most thorough archaeological studies within the Fiji archipelago is Best's (1984) investigation of Lakeba in the central Lau Islands. A nearly circular high island of 56 square kilometers, Lakeba, as did other Lau islands, had important proto-historic connections to Tonga. Best's survey of 209 sites and his excavations at six of these produced a cultural sequence commencing in the early Lapita period (ca. 1000 B.C.) that displays many of the key stylistic changes in ceramics found elsewhere in Fiji. Best suggests that population numbers were low in the early phase (settlement may even have been seasonal or intermittent for the first two centuries) but began to increase significantly in his Period II (ca. 500 B.C.), as marked by "a spectacular spread of sites across the landscape" (1984:592). Given this inland expansion, there is by A.D. 1 a perhaps not surprising degree of environmental degradation, with a "regime of inland burn-off."[73] A population maximum was reached by about A.D. 1000, by which time large forts such as Ulunikoro (site 101/7/47) were constructed. Thus, in the Lakeba sequence, the rise of both forts and cannibalism came after a phase of initial population expansion and possible overexploitation of agricultural resources.

Clark and Cole (1997) applied a coordinated program of archaeological survey and palynological analysis of sediment cores to construct a tentative cultural and environmental history of Totoya Island, in the Yasayasa Moala group southeast of Viti Levu. Initial settlement was again by people with Lapita ceramics, "perhaps close to 3000 years ago" (1997:150), at a period of higher sea level when the island's coastal benches had not yet prograded. Human-induced forest clearance began shortly after colonization, leading to the expansion of grasslands and secondary forest. Settlement was concentrated around the coastal areas until about 2000–1700 B.P., when there was a "significant move inland and the establishment of inland villages" (1997:152). Not surprisingly, this change in settlement patterns is coupled with another "round of substantial vegetation disturbance." Finally, in the second millennium A.D., the final decline of the inland forest—leading to extensive grasslands covering the central hills—corresponds to a period when hilltop forts were constructed at several locations. As Clark and Cole suggest, "The expansion of warfare on the island may have been related in part to a large population and pressure on limited resources" (1997:152).

While internal dynamics such as population growth and resource competition were surely key factors in the transformation of Fijian society over the course of three millennia, there were also external connections that linked Fijian populations with adjacent islands and archipelagoes. In Lapita sites of Fiji there is evidence for the movement of obsidian, chert, stone adzes, pottery, and other material items between islands, some from outside the Fijian archipelago itself. Fijian potsherds have occasionally been found in Tongan sites,[74] and in the proto-historic period there is ample ethnographic and oral traditional evidence for a complex network of exchange relationships linking Fiji with Tonga and Samoa.[75] The people of Lau, in particular, served as intermediaries between the chiefly lineages of Tonga and Fiji, and groups of Tongan canoe builders were allowed to take up residence in Lau in order to have access to large timber trees. Such regular and frequently systematized contacts no doubt facilitated the spread of innovations ranging from the material to the ideological, which account for parallel cultural developments in Fijian and Western Polynesian cultures.[76]

Summary

We have reviewed a diverse range of evidence for cultural changes in New Guinea and the islands of Melanesia over the past 2,500 years, the period following the remarkable Lapita expansion. The coverage—both geographical and topical—has of necessity been uneven, reflecting the current state of archaeological knowledge. I now draw attention to three themes that run through the prehistory of this vast region, cross-cutting geographical divisions. These are certainly not the only patterns that others may find of interest, but to my mind they are salient.

Change in Ceramic Sequences Archaeologists are interested in ceramic change, not only because pottery styles are sensitive temporal indicators and thus form the bases of chronology, but also because ceramic styles may indicate cultural connections over space and time. In Chapter 4 we saw the remarkable expansion of a well-marked ceramic style horizon—Lapita—from the Bismarck Archipelago as far as New Caledonia, Tonga, and Samoa. In this chapter I have reviewed the evidence for later changes in Lapita and post-Lapita ceramics throughout this region. In some localities, ceramics did not persist beyond about A.D. 1–200, although they were frequently imported from neighboring groups who continued to manufacture pottery. This is the case in both Mussau and Tikopia. More interesting, perhaps, are parallel style changes that occurred from the Bismarcks to Vanuatu and New Caledonia, and that are reflected to some degree in Fiji. These are the decline and abandonment of the classic Lapita dentate-stamped technique of decoration and its replacement primarily with incised designs, but also with designs executed using other techniques, such as end-tool impressing, fingernail impressing, relief, and appliqué. The Mangaasi ceramic complex of central Vanuatu was one of the first such post-Lapita ceramic groups to be identified, although Garanger (1972a) was uncertain of its relationship to Lapita proper. With the discovery of parallel sequences in Mussau, Manus, New Ireland, Watom, Nissan-Buka, and New Caledonia, however, we now know that Mangaasi is only one of a number of such ceramic transitions. The question thus arises whether these developments—most of which seem to occur in the period from about 2500 to 1800 B.P.—were in any way related.

One possibility is that similarities in these style changes reflect continued interisland and intersocietal contacts and thus the sharing of technical and stylistic innovations. But incising as a technique was certainly a part of the older Lapita design repertoire, and it is far less labor-intensive

than dentate-stamping. Thus the shift from dentate-stamping to incising throughout island Melanesia beginning around 500 B.C. and continuing until about A.D. 200 may simply reflect common responses on the part of potters to the changing social and economic roles and values of ceramics. As the initially widespread Lapita network began to break apart into a series of geographically less extensive, regional networks, the high value formerly placed on the elaborately decorated forms of Lapita pots could have decreased, and indeed the role of ceramics in exchange systems is likely to have declined. Since there is continuity in motifs from Lapita ceramics to the early phases of incised ("Mangaasoid" or Mangaasi-like) pottery, it may be that potters were no longer interested in, or willing to invest long hours in, decorating their pots.

The shift to incised pottery occurred later in Fiji than in the Melanesian archipelagoes to the west. This raises the question of whether the change in Fiji—which did not proceed, as elsewhere, directly from dentate-stamping to incising but rather via an intermediate phase dominated by paddle-impressed pottery—was the result of a population movement or intrusion, possibly from Vanuatu or New Caledonia. This is the position of Best (1984), Frost (1979), and Green (1963a), contested by others such as Rechtman (1992) who prefer to see the Fijian sequence in isolationist terms. Much more basic field and laboratory work must be done to fill out the ceramic sequences of Melanesia, and it will ultimately provide answers to the questions just posed. We must always keep to the fore, however, the view that ceramics have as much to tell us of cultural and social processes in the past as they do of chronology.

Development of Specialized Trade and Exchange Networks
Another recurrent theme in the prehistory of the "new" Melanesia concerns the rise of highly inten-

sified forms of external exchange, and of high-volume specialist trade.[77] Several examples are (often still incompletely) known from the archaeological record, including the coastal Papuan systems with their pottery-producing central places (Mailu or Motupore), the antecedents of the ethnographic *kula* in the Massim, the Siassi middlemen traders, the "red-feather money" network of the Santa Cruz Islands and Taumako, the mid–first millennium A.D. network(s) linking Tikopia and Vanikoro to northern Vanuatu, and networks in Fiji and the Lau Islands.

Arguably, all of these later exchange or trade systems developed out of antecedents that can ultimately be traced back to the Lapita cultural complex, itself marked by extensive exchange, including at times highly complex (multinodal) and geographically extensive systems. In the Lapita networks as we presently understand them, there was an important social or ritual component, reflected in the movement of such material items as elaborately decorated pottery and a range of finely made shell valuables. In some post-Lapita systems, this pattern was continued and elaborated. Shell valuables, for example, remained an important component of Papuan trading even after this shifted to high-volume ceramic production. And one cannot fail to mention the classic *kula* exchange in armshells and bead necklaces, material forms that may well trace their ultimate ancestry to Lapita shell valuables.

As societies in the archipelagoes of "new" Melanesia began to differentiate and diverge in the centuries following the initial Lapita diaspora, the original widespread exchange linkages retracted, to become regionalized or localized. Thus in Papua and the Massim, an earlier system that possibly linked both areas broke down into several regional networks (two of which focused on Motupore and Mailu) about A.D. 800. Jim Allen (1977, 1984b) developed a model of such transformations

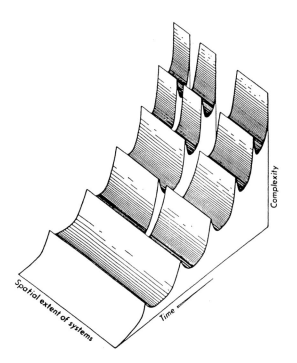

FIGURE 5.27 Allen's model of changing exchange network configurations in the Papua region. (After Allen 1984b.)

(Fig. 5.27), in which the spatial extent of networks decreases over time, as their complexity (or degree of specialization) increases. This model fits the Papuan data well; further work is required to test its validity for other sequences of changing exchange and trade in eastern Melanesia.

Landesque Capital Intensification and Sociopolitical Transformation   In the late phases from New Georgia, Santa Ana, Aneityum, New Caledonia, and Fiji, as well as in the New Guinea Highlands, there were parallel developments of highly intensive agricultural production systems, often accompanied by changes in settlement and residential patterns. The agricultural systems are all types that Blaikie and Brookfield (1987) term "landesque capital," involving the permanent transformation of a landscape through the construction of facilities such as terraces, canals, or walled garden plots. Once such transformations have been accomplished, landscapes may be put back into use even after periods of disuse or abandonment. Although they may have relatively high associated labor costs during construction, these systems have the benefit of conferring high yields, often at labor input levels that are considerably less than those seen with shifting cultivation and certainly with short-fallow swidden regimes.[78]

These intensive agricultural systems were something entirely new on the face of post-Lapita Melanesia. We have no evidence that the Lapita peoples themselves practiced anything other than classic shifting cultivation, or possibly the planting of naturally swampy areas in *Colocasia* or *Cyrtosperma* aroids. An older notion that the first Austronesian-speaking peoples who moved into Oceania brought with them Asiatic forms of terracing and irrigation technology does not stand up to scrutiny of either archaeological or linguistic evidence (Kirch and Lepofsky 1993).

Were the terraced, canal-fed irrigation systems of New Georgia, Aneityum, New Caledonia, and Fiji the result of interarchipelago communication and the diffusion of technological innovations, or were they independent but convergent responses to common sets of pressures or challenges? I am inclined to think the latter, seeing these intensive forms of agricultural practice as logical developments out of widespread agronomic and ethnobiological knowledge having an antiquity going back to Lapita, and perhaps earlier.

If this interpretation is correct, what were the "push" or "pull" factors, and the changing sociopolitical contexts, that led to these convergent agricultural developments? An underlying factor in all cases is probably to be found in population numbers and densities, but to put the full or even the primary onus on demography is unwarranted.

Environmental factors such as resource variability and degradation of landscapes through centuries of shifting cultivation are also salient factors, as both the New Guinea Highlands and Aneityum cases (and probably the New Caledonian one as well) suggest. Moreover, we cannot ignore the complex linkages between production for subsistence and "social" production (Brookfield 1972, 1984; Kirch 1994). As the societies of "new" Melanesia became larger, and gradually shifted from being heterarchical to hierarchical, elites benefited incrementally from the surpluses they could extract from intensive agricultural systems and put to social and political ends through competitive feasts or other means.

I have not dealt directly with the topic of sociopolitical transformation in post-Lapita Melanesia, largely because the state of our knowledge of prehistoric social formations remains for the most part rudimentary. But implicit in much of what I have discussed is the notion that the past two and a half millennia witnessed significant transformations of Melanesian societies, with small-scale "house" societies of the Lapita period (see Chapter 4) giving rise to large-scale aggregations under the control of elites whom early explorers, missionaries, and later ethnographers were frequently to label "chiefs."[79] The archaeological records of these islands hint at these changes, such as the massive forts of Maré Island, which must have taken centralized labor control to construct; the differentiated habitation mounds of later New Caledonian settlements, in which the residences of elites seem to be set off from or command higher elevations than those of commoners; or the elaborate funerary rites associated with Roy Mata. However, a sophisticated "social archaeology" that can tease out the evidence for such sociopolitical transformation is barely nascent in Melanesia at present, though it without doubt shows the greatest promise.

CHAPTER 6

Micronesia

In the "Sea of Little Lands"

Hidden in the jungle along the shores and in the well-watered interior lowlands of Guam are double rows of upright monuments associated with caps and accompanied by burials, potsherds, and stone and shell implements. These monument sites are called *latte* or *casas de los antiguos* by the natives, who believe that they are haunted by *Taotao Mana* (people of beforetime). The natives carefully avoid these sites.

Thompson (1932:8)

Micronesia—one of the three divisions of Oceania originally proposed by Dumont d'Urville—encompasses about 2,100 islands, most of which lie north of the equator but below latitude 20° N (Map 10). From west to east, the main archipelagoes are Palau (also known as Belau), the Marianas, the Carolines, the Marshalls, and Kiribati (formerly the Gilbert Islands). Tuvalu (formerly the Ellice Islands) lies between Kiribati and Western Polynesia–Fiji and will be considered here in relation to the early settlement of atolls, although its occupants speak Polynesian languages. Despite the great number of islands in Micronesia, in aggregate they total a mere 2,700 square kilometers of land in an ocean area of approximately 7.4 million square kilometers, and Guam alone accounts for 582 square kilometers. Thus an early explorer of Micronesia, F. W. Christian, dubbed it the "sea of little lands" (1899). Many Micronesian islands are atolls, comprising diminutive and low-lying islets encircling a lagoon (see Chapter 2). The Marianas chain and some of the Palau group consist of upraised makatea limestone, but outside these western archipelagoes there are only a few high and makatea islands. In the Carolines, Yap, Chuuk (formerly Truk), Pohnpei (formerly Ponape), and Kosrae (formerly Kusaie) are high volcanic islands. Isolated Nauru and Banaba are upraised makatea islands, as are several of the Marshalls.

The varied traditional cultures of Micronesia reflect different origins in western and central-eastern Micronesia, as well as distinctive adaptations to local environmental conditions, not to mention the underlying contingencies of history.[1]

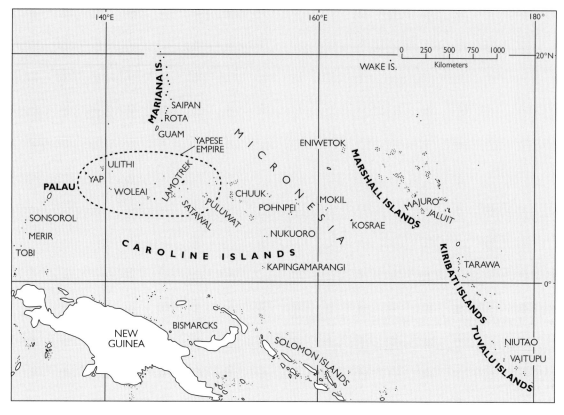

MAP 10 The islands of Micronesia.

All Micronesian peoples speak Austronesian languages, but not all of these belong to the Oceanic subgroup, a clue to their diverse origins. In contrast to Polynesia, Micronesia does not form a "monophyletic" cultural group, although its history is shallower and less complex than that of Near Oceania.

Despite important early archaeological work in Micronesia before and soon after World War II, the region remained neglected until recently.[2] Alexander Spoehr (1957) excavated in the Marianas in 1949–50, and E. W. Gifford made his third and final Pacific expedition to Yap in 1956 (Gifford and Gifford 1959). These pioneering studies, along with Osborne's (1966) extensive survey of Palau,

all focused on high islands. For reasons outlined by Davidson (1967b), archaeologists assumed that the atolls lacked stratified deposits, until she demonstrated through her fieldwork on Nukuoro that such views were unwarranted. Although in some areas (such as the Marshall Islands) periodic cyclones do destroy substantial segments of the archaeological record,[3] atolls have nonetheless proved to have often rich and surprisingly deep stratigraphic records.

Since the mid-1970s, Micronesia has seen a resurgence of archaeological work, primarily cultural resource management (CRM; see Chapter 1). Although CRM work frequently resides in a so-called "gray literature," some archaeologists have

MICRONESIA: IN THE "SEA OF LITTLE LANDS"

been diligent about publishing their results in scholarly journals (e.g., Athens 1980, 1984a; Athens and Ward 1995; Butler 1994).[4] Certainly our knowledge of Micronesian archaeology and prehistory would be more limited were it not for the heightened level of CRM funding of field activities, and there have been positive effects in related fields such as bioarchaeology (Hanson and Pietrusewsky, eds., 1997). Indeed, CRM research in progress on Babeldaob and other islands in Micronesia will improve our understanding of aspects of regional prehistory in the near future (Steve Athens, pers. comm., 1998). A list of selected archaeological sites in Micronesia is provided in Table 6.1.

Colonization and Early Settlement in Micronesia

Both archaeology and historical linguistics have put forward theories concerning the origins of Micronesian peoples and the directions of early settlement and dispersal through the region. Although some question whether the evidence of these two fields can productively be combined in culture-historical models (for example, Davidson 1988:91–93 with specific reference to Micronesia; cf. Intoh 1997:16), a convergence between the two is emerging (Rehg 1995). This is particularly so now that earlier uncertainties in the subgrouping of Oceanic languages have been resolved (Pawley and Ross 1993, 1995; Ross 1988, 1996b; Zobel 1997) and that deep and continuous archaeological sequences have been revealed for the central Caroline Islands and the Marshalls, and not just for the western Micronesian archipelagoes, as was the case a decade or more ago.

Linguistic evidence provides a working model that may be tested against emerging archaeological data for early settlement. Almost all of the Austronesian languages spoken in the Pacific

islands belong to its *Oceanic* subgroup. (See Figure 4.4 for a chart of the higher-order subgrouping of the Austronesian languages.) Significantly, two exceptions are found in Western Micronesia: Chamorro (in the Marianas) and Palauan (Yapese has in the past been claimed to be a third case).[5] Rather than being Oceanic, these belong to another high-order subgroup of Austronesian, *Western Malayo-Polynesian,* which includes a large number of languages today spoken in the Philippines and Indonesia. Indeed, the Western Micronesian languages may have their closest relations in the Philippine-Sulawesi region (Zobel 1997), although some propose possible links to the Formosan languages of Taiwan, particularly for Chamorro (Starosta 1995; cf. Reid 1999). Thus on linguistic evidence, the origins of the Palau and Marianas islanders are to be found in island Southeast Asia.

All of the other languages spoken throughout the Caroline, Marshall, and Kiribati archipelagoes belong to the Oceanic subgroup,[6] closely correlated with the Lapita expansion, since a Proto Oceanic dialect chain can arguably be correlated with the early phase of the Lapita cultural complex (see Chapter 4). With the exception of Yapese, all of these Micronesian languages fall together in a single subgroup of Oceanic—Nuclear Micronesian—which has its "center of genetic diversity" in the eastern part of Micronesia, "in the region of Kiribati, Kosrae, Pohnpei, and the Marshalls" (Jackson 1986; Pawley and Ross 1993:439). The Nuclear Micronesian group must have split off following the breakup of the Proto Oceanic dialect chain. This implies that the first settlement of central-eastern Micronesia should be from the region of the initial Lapita expansion, somewhere between the Bismarcks and the southeast Solomons-Vanuatu region. Indeed, the Nuclear Micronesian languages share features with the languages of the Southeast Solomons or Northern

167

TABLE 6.1
Selected Archaeological Sites in Micronesia

Island/Group	Site (Island)	Site Type	Age Range (B.P.)[a]	References
MARIANAS	Achugao Point (Saipan)	Coastal midden site	3,500+?	Butler 1994
	Chalan Piao (Saipan)	Midden site	3,500	Amesbury et al. 1996; Spoehr 1957
	Laulau (Saipan)	Rockshelter	3,500–3,000?	Spoehr 1957
	Taga (Tinian)	Megalithic *latte* site	Undated	Spoehr 1957
	Tarague Beach	Midden site	3,400–1,100	Athens 1986; Kurashina and Clayshulte 1983; Kurashina et al. 1984
PALAU	Bairulchau	Megalithic colonnade	1,800?; 285?	Osborne 1966, 1979; Van Tilburg 1991
	Melekeok	Megalithic sculptures	Undated	Osborne 1979; Van Tilburg 1991
	Ngerulmud Hill	Terraced site	2,200	Liston et al. 1998
	Uchularois	Cave site	1,200–600	Masse 1989, 1990
YAP	Pemrang	Midden	1,800–250	Gifford and Gifford 1959
CAROLINES	Bolipi site (Lamotrek)	Midden site	1,000	Fujimura and Alkire 1984
	Fais Island	Midden sites	1,700–recent	Intoh 1991, 1996
	Ngulu Island	Midden sites	1,700?	Intoh 1984
	Sabaig site (Lamotrek)	Midden site	1,000	Fujimura and Alkire 1984
CHUUK	Fefan	Coastal midden deposits (with ceramics)	2,000	Sinoto, ed., 1984
	Tol	Fortified hilltop sites	400–200	Takayama and Seki 1973
POHNPEI	Nan Madol	Megalithic settlement	2,000–300?	Athens 1990a; Ayres 1992; Bryson 1989; Hambruch 1911, 1936
	Sapwtakai	Megalithic settlement	700–300	Bath 1984a, 1984b

(continued)

TABLE 6.1 *(continued)*

Island/Group	Site (Island)	Site Type	Age Range (B.P.)[a]	References
KOSRAE	Lelu	Megalithic settlement	1,500–200	Cordy 1993; Hambruch 1919
MARSHALLS	Kwajalein	Midden site	2,200–2,000	Beardsley 1994
	Laura (Majuro)	Midden site	2,000–1,800	Riley 1987
	Maloelap	Midden site	1,900	Weisler 1999
TUVALU	Temei (Vaitupu)		900?	Takayama and Saito 1987; Takayama et al. 1987
NUKUORO		Midden sites	1,200–recent	Davidson 1967a, 1967b, 1992
KAPINGAMARANGI		Midden sites	700–recent	Leach and Ward 1981

[a] Age ranges given are approximations based on available series of radiocarbon dates. Refer to the references cited for individual radiocarbon dates associated with specific sites.

Vanuatu (Shutler and Marck 1975; but see Jackson 1986).

Internal subgroups within Nuclear Micronesian hint at the process of differentiation once Proto Nuclear Micronesian had split off from early Oceanic. Bender and Wang (1985) find five major branches of Nuclear Micronesian, these being Kiribati, Marshallese, and Kosraean (all single languages); a Pohnpeic subgroup with four languages; and a large Chuukic subgroup (centered on Chuuk) including perhaps 60 distinct speech communities, primarily on atolls. These five groups have been arrayed by Jackson (1986) and Rehg (1995) in a classic tree model, in which Kosraean, Kiribati, and Marshallese were the first to split off from a Proto Micronesian ancestor, while the Chuukic dialect chain and Pohnpeic both diverged from a Proto Chuukic-Pohnpeic ancestor.

Until recently, the Yapese language defied classification as either Oceanic or non-Oceanic Malayo-Polynesian (e.g., Bender and Wang 1985). Malcolm Ross (1996b) has now marshaled evidence to support a hypothesis that Yapese is an Oceanic language, subsequently influenced by at least four periods of borrowing, two of these from non-Oceanic languages. Such borrowing reflects Yap's key geographical position in Micronesia and concurs with archaeological evidence for the movement of people and things into Yap over long periods of time. Moreover, Ross suggests that Yapese is a highly conservative Oceanic language, one that diverged early and whose closest relationships are probably with the Admiralty Islands language group. If this proves to be true, then the first settlement of Yap may have been directly from the Bismarck Archipelago, during the second millennium B.C.

In short, the historical linguistic evidence requires at least a three-part sequence for the human settlement of Micronesia, with one group of people (but quite possibly more than one group) moving into the western archipelagoes directly from island Southeast Asia, and a second population (or closely related populations) moving up into the central-eastern islands from the Solomons-Vanuatu region as a northern prong of the Lapita expansion.[7] The Proto Nuclear Micronesian speech community was probably rapidly emplaced on more than a single island, and it may have constituted a dialect chain spanning at least the high islands (and probably some atolls) of the central-eastern Micronesian region. A third population seems to have moved directly from the Bismarck Archipelago into Yap. Further complexities arose later, for example with Yapese, which (lying at the interface between western and eastern-central groups) borrowed significantly from Nuclear Micronesian, thus masking its Proto Oceanic origins. Having briefly stated the model as derived from historical linguistics, let us examine the archaeological evidence.

The Western Archipelagoes In 1949–50, Alex Spoehr excavated at Chalan Piao on Saipan Island in the Marianas, recovering an oyster shell dating to 1527 ± 200 B.P. and demonstrating a long prehistory for western Micronesia—indeed one longer than some were willing to accept, for the date was later questioned more than once.[8] Renewed work at Chalan Piao in 1987, however, combined with excavations at other early deposits such as Tarague Beach on Guam and Achugao Point on Saipan, has produced expanded suites of radiocarbon dates in good cultural association, leaving no doubt that humans had colonized the Marianas by the late second millennium B.C., and probably before 1500 B.C.[9] Butler's excavations at Achugao

Point on Saipan (a fine example of high-quality CRM archaeology) revealed "an intact remnant of a very early occupation surface protected behind a section of raised fossil reef" (1994:15). The living surface, marked by pit features and postholes, was securely dated by five wood charcoal samples, the oldest of which is dated at 3490 ± 120 B.P. (calibrated to 1930–1630 B.C.). Rainbird (1994: 298) suggests that "the long curve of the [Marianas] archipelago perhaps provided a wide target for early navigators sailing eastwards" on voyages of discovery from the Philippines.

These early Marianas sites contain two kinds of ceramics, probably variants of the same ware. Spoehr (1957) labeled these Marianas Red and Lime-Filled, Impressed Trade Ware, although later work indicates that the second type was not a "trade" ware but locally manufactured. Amesbury et al. (1996:60–61) describe the Marianas Red pottery as a "thin-walled, often red-slipped or painted, calcareous sand-tempered [CST] pottery." The decorated sherds are of the same or similar paste (also CST) and have distinctive designs (circles, lines) that were impressed (or sometimes incised) into the surface and filled with white lime after firing.

Butler analyzed a sample of 3,649 potsherds (including 143 with decorations) from Achugao Point and defined two distinctive styles of "complex incised and stamped (impressed) decoration" (1994:23–33), which he labels Achugao Incised and San Roque Incised (Fig. 6.1). The first exhibits rectilinear patterns, "with the zones between the major elements packed with tiny, delicate punctations" (1994:27). San Roque Incised sherds (of which only 15 were found) consist of "bands of curvilinear garlands made by linking incised arches (half circles) with small stamped circles or large punctations placed at the junctions of the arch segments."

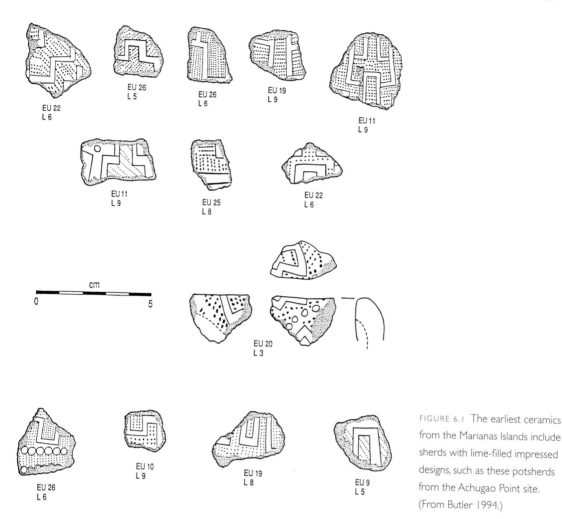

FIGURE 6.1 The earliest ceramics from the Marianas Islands include sherds with lime-filled impressed designs, such as these potsherds from the Achugao Point site. (From Butler 1994.)

Although both Marianas Red and the lime-filled decorated variants have been compared to Lapita assemblages, they are probably not directly related, but rather stem from a common, older tradition in island Southeast Asia (see Butler 1994:34; Kirch 1995). The impressed designs on the Marianas pottery differ from those characteristic of Lapita, yet are remarkably similar to motifs found on pottery in island Southeast Asia, such as that from the Sanga Sanga site in the Philippines (Spoehr 1973:184–91) and from the Kalumpang and

Minanga Sipakko sites in Sulawesi (Van Heekeren 1972:184–90, Fig. 46, Plates 101–2). The latter two assemblages, in particular, exhibit a style of incised designs with small punctations infilling spaces between the lines, similar to the early pottery from Achugao Point. In addition, the vessel forms, use of red slip, and calcareous temper that typify Marianas Red are all consistent with Philippines ceramic assemblages of the early to mid–second millennium B.C. (Bellwood 1985, 1987a). Other artifacts found in association with this early pottery, such as *Conus*-shell beads and *Conus* brace-lets, are known from contemporaneous Southeast Asian sites and also need not imply a direct Lapita connection. The Marianas archaeological record is consistent with the linguistic model of settlement directly from island Southeast Asia, most probably the Philippines region, and radiocarbon dating puts this roughly in the mid–second millennium B.C.

The island of Taiwan might be an alternative source for the first settlers in the Marianas (rather than the Philippines). Stanley Starosta (1995) argues that the Chamorro language is a "mid-level" offshoot from the Formosan language tree (itself a first-order branch of the Austronesian language family); if he is correct (this is by no means certain; see Zobel 1997), this thesis implies a population movement from Taiwan to the Marianas sometime after the initial split of Proto Formosan into its main Rukai, Tsou, and Sa'aroa branches.[10] The hypothesis is intriguing, for Taiwanese ceramic assemblages dating to the third and second millennia B.C. are remarkably similar to Marianas Red Ware and contain shell artifacts identical with early Micronesian forms (e.g., Li 1983; Tsang 1992; see also Kirch 1995). However, Lawrence Reid, a linguist with much knowledge of Austronesian languages in the Philippines, casts doubts on the hypothesis that Chamorro is a member of the Formosan group. Nonetheless, Reid argues that Chamorro did split off very early from other branches of the Austronesian family. His tentative conclusion is that "Chamorro is an Extra-Formosan language, but that it is a first order branch of the [Austronesian] family, separating from Proto-Extra Formosan, probably from the Northern Philippines, prior to the actual dispersal of the other branches of the family" (Reid 1999:49). Pending further linguistic and archaeological research, it might be well to keep open the alternative (and not necessarily mutually exclusive) hypotheses of

Taiwan and Philippine-Sulawesi sources for the initial Marianas population.

Direct archaeological evidence for settlement of the Marianas by 1500 B.C.—if not considerably earlier—is confirmed by paleoenvironmental evidence from sediment cores in Tipalao Marsh (Orote Peninsula) and in the Pago River Valley of Guam (Athens and Ward 1995; Ward n.d.).[11] The Tipalao Marsh cores encapsulate a record extending back to 7900 B.P., in which human arrival at 3550 B.P. is signaled by the appearance of charcoal particles, absent in deeper levels. By 2450 B.P. significant forest clearance was under way, and by 1400 B.P. extensive grasslands are evidenced in the pollen record. The Pago Valley core suggests a yet older date for human activities within the local drainage catchment, with the onset of burning (indicated by charcoal particle influx) dated to around 4300 B.P. Higher levels in the core are marked by reductions in forest trees and by increases in the fire-adapted fern *Gleichenia* (*Dicranopteris*) *linearis*, a classic signal of anthropogenic disturbance on oceanic islands. Notably, coconut (*Cocos nucifera*) pollen first occurs at the same time as the initial burning, hinting that this economic plant may have been a human introduction.[12] These paleoenvironmental data, reinforced by similar results from Palau and Yap, pose a challenge to field archaeologists, for they imply that humans had been in western Micronesia since the mid- to late *third* millennium B.C., despite a total absence of direct archaeological evidence older than about 1500 B.C.

In the Palau archipelago to the southwest, early ceramics like those in the Marianas are lacking,[13] and the earliest reported dates on archaeological materials cluster around 2000 B.P. (Masse 1990:220). The oldest known pottery, such as that from Uchularois Cave, consists of "a well constructed and heavily slipped and polished red-ware," absent from later sites. Masse (1990) takes this direct archaeological evidence at face value, arguing that humans arrived in Palau about 2,000 years ago, but his interpretation is being challenged by paleoenvironmental evidence.

Ward et al. (1998) recovered 22 sediment cores from sites dispersed around Babeldaob Island and have analyzed three of these for pollen content and charcoal particle influx. In all cores, there is evidence for "an apparently sudden increase in savanna/grasslands on Babeldaob Island by at least 3100 cal B.P. [where 'cal' denotes a 'calibrated' age, as opposed to a 'conventional' ^{14}C age], with some indication that the western side of Babeldaob may have experienced this change significantly earlier" (1998:5). These pollen changes are accompanied by substantial increases in the amount of charcoal particles, making it likely that this was an anthropogenic change. Moreover, pollen of two cultivated plants, coconut and betel nut palm (*Areca catechu*), first appears as early as 4229 cal B.P. in one core. Ward et al. argue that these data imply "the presence of humans on Palau at least by 3000 cal B.P., and possibly as early as 4200 cal B.P." (1998:6). I agree, although others will doubtless demur until direct archaeological evidence of human presence is established (cf. Spriggs and Anderson 1993).

In Yap, the oldest known archaeological assemblages date to about A.D. 1, at the Pemrang site tested by E. W. Gifford (Gifford and Gifford 1959) and later re-excavated by Jun Takayama (1982).[14] But as in Palau, recent palynological and paleoenvironmental evidence (Dodson and Intoh 1999) indicates a human presence on Yap beginning around 3300 B.P., marked by "a major period of forest destruction, accompanied by fire." Thus, as has happened in other Pacific archipelagoes in the past, the first third of the Yapese cultural sequence has probably yet to be archaeologically recovered.[15] This increases the likelihood that a similar situation obtains in Palau, and given the closer

proximity of Palau to the Philippines, it should not surprise us if future work confirms Athens's suspicion (pers. comm., 1998) that initial human settlement in western Micronesia occurred as early as 4600–4200 B.P. If this is true, at least one corner of the Remote Oceanic world witnessed human footprints a millennium prior to the Lapita diaspora.

The High Islands of the Carolines　Whereas in western Micronesia ceramics continued to be manufactured and used into the period of European contact, this was not so in central-eastern Micronesia, where pottery was entirely unknown. Archaeological work on Chuuk, Pohnpei, and Kosrae has now shown, however, that pots were at one time in use on the high islands of the Carolines, where suitable clays are available. The later decline in pottery use, and its ultimate abandonment in the Carolines, parallels similar changes in parts of island Melanesia and in Polynesia (see Chapter 7). The earliest ceramic assemblages from Chuuk, Pohnpei, and Kosrae along with associated material culture strongly support a hypothesis of one or more colonizing populations originating out of late Lapita cultures in island Melanesia, probably in the outer eastern Solomons.

Along the coast of Fefan Island in the Chuuk lagoon, deposits within the swampy intertidal zone (probably representing former stilt-house villages) yielded CST pottery along with *Tridacna*-shell adzes and numerous *Conus*-shell ornaments (Sinoto, ed., 1984). Radiocarbon ages of 2080 ± 90 and 2060 ± 80 B.P. are associated with these finds. The Fefan pottery consists of plain ware bowls or pots with constricted necks and slightly everted rims; the rims are sometimes decorated with crenations, while a few body sherds have incised lines. Overall, the pottery compares favorably with Kiki Ware from Tikopia, dated to 900–100 B.C.; with similar plain ware on Anuta, Nendö, and the Reef Islands;

and possibly with plain ware from Santa Ana, all in the southeast Solomons. All these assemblages are associated with *Tridacna*-shell adzes and *Conus*-shell ornaments, strengthening the case for a close connection between Chuuk and the southeast Solomons.

In Pohnpei and Kosrae, CST ceramics have been recovered from basal deposits underlying the artificial stone islands of Nan Madol and from similar contexts at the Lelu site.[16] In both cases, the peoples who used this pottery may have occupied stilt-house settlements, for as on Chuuk, the pottery-bearing deposits lie within the intertidal or subtidal zone.[17] Given the presence of Lapita stilt-house villages in Near Oceania, this is another connection between Lapita and early Caroline Islands cultures. The strongest evidence, however, is the CST pottery from levels dated to between 5 B.C. and A.D. 240 in Pohnpei (Athens 1990a:21), and between 108 B.C. and A.D. 244 in Kosrae (Rainbird 1994:299). That these dates accurately reflect initial colonization is indicated by pollen cores from Kosrae that date initial human disturbance to the island's vegetation, and the introduction of cultivated plants, to the same time as the pottery (Athens et al. 1996). Athens (1990a) characterizes the Nan Madol pottery as consisting of two main vessel forms: globular jars with everted rims and small bowls. Again, the Pohnpei and Kosrae CST ceramics are closest to late Lapita plain wares in the southeast Solomons (Santa Cruz group, including Tikopia and Anuta) or possibly in northern Vanuatu.[18]

In short, a strong case can be made on strictly archaeological grounds for deriving the initial settlement of the central Caroline high islands directly from late Lapita pottery-using populations in the southeast Solomons or immediately adjacent regions. This brings the archaeological evidence squarely into line with the hypothesis predicted from the linguistic relationships. Athens, who has

studied the early Caroline Islands finds closely, has reached the same conclusion:

> Regarding the origins of the Pohnpei settlers and, perhaps, those of Truk [Chuuk] and Kosrae, it appears that the best case can be made for a linkage with the late Lapita Plain Ware pottery tradition. . . . The chronology is consistent: it begins after 500 B.C. The pottery vessel shapes and decorative techniques are consistent: simple globular pots and bowls with perhaps some rim notching or punctation. Also, its location is consistent: late Lapita Plain Ware pottery is found in the southeast Solomon and New Hebrides Islands where linguistic data suggest the homeland for nuclear Micronesians is located. (*1990a:29*)

The Atolls   When we turn from the high islands to the atolls of the central Carolines, Marshalls, and Kiribati, some key environmental factors must be taken into consideration. Evidence has steadily accumulated that the mid-Holocene sea level in the tropical Pacific ranged from 1 to 1.5 meters higher than at present (i.e., during the period between roughly 2000 B.C. and A.D. 1).[19] Sea levels began to rise rapidly around 8000 B.C., from their last glacial maximum low of 100+ meters below present level, and continued to rise unabated for the next six millennia, successively drowning many makatea islands that had been exposed by the lowered sea levels of the terminal Pleistocene. Before atolls could form on these newly drowned makatea reefs, it was necessary for sea levels to stabilize and to remain stable for some time. This did not occur until sea level fell to its modern position, perhaps around A.D. 1. Thus the Micronesian atolls were in their initial stages of subaerial formation and stabilization when late Lapita populations began to explore the seaways north of the equator.

These newly formed atolls must have been tenuous environments for human colonization, with but the sparsest vegetation. Given that classic "atoll vegetation" is dominated by human-introduced plants, human manipulation of these environments was necessary to render them suitable as permanent abodes. From high-island bases on Chuuk, Pohnpei, and Kosrae, pioneers may have intermittently or seasonally exploited (or temporarily inhabited) atolls in the vicinity, introducing economically vital plants such as coconut and breadfruit and excavating cultivation pits to tap the freshwater aquifers (Weisler 1999). After generations of intermittent use, atolls might have yielded to permanent settlement, and the more far-flung islands could be inhabited.

While only a few Micronesian atolls have been accorded thorough archaeological study, those with stratified sequences exhibit little evidence of use earlier than about 2,000 years ago. In the Marshall Islands, for example, sites on Majuro and Maloelap date to around A.D. 100.[20] On Maloelap, Weisler (1999) has documented the excavation of a *Cyrtosperma* cultivation pit to 1910 B.P., coterminous with initial settlement. Beardsley (1994:161–62) reports a calibrated radiocarbon age of 167–124 B.C. from an early cultural deposit on Kwajalein Atoll. Other atolls were not settled until later, such as Ngulu, where the earliest date is 1150 B.P., Imwinyap at 1150 B.P., or Nukuoro at 1237 B.P. In short, atoll colonization was probably continuous, with the full spectrum of Micronesian atolls not occupied by humans until well into the last millennium.

A final comment on the correspondence between linguistic and archaeological models and evidence for Micronesian settlement is relevant. Bender and Wang (1985:83) posit that the central-eastern Micronesian islands were settled quickly, so that in linguistic terms there was "virtually no period of common Micronesian development, and thus no uniquely shared linguistic innovations, either within nuclear Micronesian or

between major branches of the putative subgroup." This fits well with the apparent "shallowness" of internal language subgrouping in Nuclear Micronesian, in contrast with the case for Polynesian languages (see Chapter 7). To me, the emerging archaeological evidence strongly supports this linguistic interpretation (cf. Davidson 1988; Intoh 1997).

Cultural Sequences in Micronesia

Archaeological pioneers in any region often seek to find the *earliest* materials, and their research emphasizes the *origins* of the region's peoples. Certainly this has been the case with Micronesia, but now that archaeology and linguistics are converging on a common historical scenario, more attention can be paid to other matters, such as the development of complex sociopolitical formations on some islands, or the rise of reticulated networks of interisland exchange linked by sophisticated maritime technology and navigational skills. For such theoretically exciting work to proceed, however, it is also necessary that basic cultural sequences be established in all of the main island groups, a phase of research that is only partially completed in Micronesia.

Spoehr's (1957) Marianas Islands sequence was based on ceramic chronology combined with architectural evidence for the construction, in later prehistory, of limestone-pillar structures termed *latte*. Spoehr demonstrated that over time there was a quantitative change in pottery assemblages from those dominated by Marianas Red to later ones containing only Marianas Plain Ware (Fig. 6.2). The *latte* structures, about which more will be said later, are dominantly associated with Marianas Plain Ware, which Spoehr attributed to the last 850 years. Spoehr's sequence has more or less stood up to subsequent work, although Hunter-Anderson and Butler (1995) propose subdividing Spoehr's

CHALAN PIAO

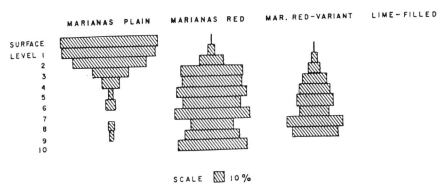

LAULAU ROCKSHELTER

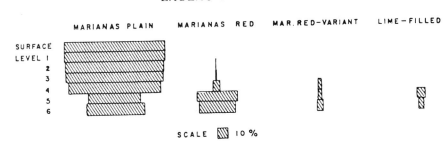

FIGURE 6.2 The seriation of major ceramic types in the Marianas Islands, as developed by Spoehr from his pioneering excavations. (After Spoehr 1957.)

long "Pre-*Latte*" phase into three phases (Early Pre-*Latte*, Intermediate Pre-*Latte*, and Transitional).[21]

For Palau, Osborne's speculative sequence was based on a dubious ceramic typology (1966, 1979) and has proved to be of no lasting value. Masse (1990) outlined an alternative sequence beginning with a "Colonial" Period from A.D. 1 to 650, continuing with a "Resource Intensification" Period (A.D. 650–1200), and followed by a "Rock Island Village" Period (A.D. 1200–1450), a "Transition" Period (A.D. 1450–1600), and finally a "Traditional" Period (A.D. 1600–1914). This sequence privileges Masse's data from the upraised "Rock Islands" south of the main island of Babeldaob. Recent CRM work on Babeldaob (Athens, pers. comm., 1998) suggests that extensive revisions of the Palauan sequence are likely, including pre–

2000 B.P. settlements.[22] One recent find is a distinctive "thin blackware" type of pottery predating the ubiquitous thick-walled and grog-tempered later Palauan pottery, and that may be associated with an early phase of inland (ridgetop) settlement on Babeldaob. At the Ngerulmud Hill site in Melekeok State, sherds of this thin blackware have been dated to 2180 ± 60 B.P. (Liston et al. 1998:59, 82). On Babeldaob, the interior ridges and hillsides were massively reworked with vast terrace complexes; these are discussed later in this chapter.

Recent palynological work suggests that the first third of the Yapese archaeological sequence remains to be uncovered (Dodson and Intoh 1999). While a rough ceramic sequence beginning with CST pottery and moving to a later Yapese "laminated ware" was demonstrated by Gifford and Gifford (1959) and confirmed by later work (e.g., Intoh 1988, 1990; Intoh and Leach 1985), the details of a full cultural sequence remain elusive. Yap has extensive stone architectural remains, some studied ethnoarchaeologically (e.g., Hunter-Anderson 1983, 1984; Pickering 1990), but there have been too few excavations to place the development of this architecture—let alone its significance for sociopolitical changes—in proper temporal perspective.

Chuuk's extensive lagoon (with an area of 2,125 square kilometers) encompasses a number of small high islands and even smaller islets, totaling 120 square kilometers of land. Thus far, archaeological work has concentrated primarily on Tol, Moen, and Fefan Islands.[23] King and Parker (1984:415–41) attempted a synthesis of the Chuuk sequence but could define only two periods, with an intervening "period about which at present we know virtually nothing," lasting from A.D. 500 to 1300. They named the early period the Winas Pattern, characterized by CST pottery (such as that recovered from the Fefan Island sites), as well as *Tridacna-* and *Cassis-*shell adzes, *Conus*-shell rings, and other kinds of shell ornaments. Settlements were confined to coastal locations, possibly with stilt-house villages. The later Tonnachaw Pattern, from A.D. 1300 until European contact, lacks pottery but has many kinds of artifacts known from ethnographic collections, such as *Cypraea*-shell breadfruit peelers, coral pounders, slingstones, and *Terebra*-shell adzes. Tonnachaw settlement patterns incorporated not only coastal residential sites but also interior residential and cookhouse sites, shell middens on ridges and hill summits, and stone-walled forts on high ridges or summits. The emphasis on ridgetop locations—whether deliberately fortified or not—speaks to the significance of warfare and raiding in the Tonnachaw phase (Rainbird 1996).

The best-defined sequence for any Micronesian island is that proposed by Ayres (1990) for Pohnpei, based on extensive work conducted over several years by his research team and by others.[24] Ayres's Pohnpei sequence is presented in Table 6.2. However, his early "Settlement and Adaptive Integration Phase" is speculative, and there is no firm evidence for human settlement on the island before about A.D. 1. In material culture, important changes include: (1) the decline in ceramic use and its abandonment by A.D. 1500, if not earlier; (2) the appearance of distinctive *Terebra-* and *Mitre-*shell adzes after about A.D. 1000;[25] and (3) the development of compound trolling lures of pearl shell, after about A.D. 1200. Of particular interest is the Nan Madol Phase, associated with the construction of this massive site, discussed at greater length later in this chapter.[26]

A sequence for Kosrae has not been formally defined, but it might parallel that for Pohnpei. Among the similarities are an early phase with pottery, the later abandonment of ceramics, and development of complex stone architecture (including a major chiefly residential center at Lelu), especially during the past 500 years. Athens et al. (1996) trace the history of an intensive "agroforest" or arboricultural subsistence system over 2,000 years of human land use on Kosrae, with breadfruit as a dominant tree crop. The transformation of the island's original vegetation into this agroforest occurred by 1550–1350 B.P., well before the later "rise of social complexity as evidenced by the Lelu megalithic ruins [which] was not accompanied by any perceptible change in cultigens or agricultural practices" (Athens et al. 1996:845).

For the Caroline and Marshall Islands, sequences for particular atolls can be constructed where extensive excavations have been carried out, as with Majuro, Kwajalein, and Arno atolls in the Marshalls or Ulithi, Woleai, and Lamotrek in the

TABLE 6.2
The Pohnpei Culture-Historical Sequence[a]

Phase	Characteristics	Time Range
Settlement and Adaptive Integration Phase	Inland forest clearance in Awak Valley; calcareous tempered pottery (CST) in use.	500 B.C.?–A.D. 1
Peinais Phase	Stone house foundations, breadfruit storage pits, pottery with rim notching, rare punctate and incised line designs; Nan Madol islets with some columnar basalt construction by A.D. 500–600.	A.D. 1–1000
Nan Madol Phase	Expansion and formalization of the Nan Madol complex and associated sociopolitical aspects (Deleur "Empire"), chiefly residential architecture, stylized tombs (*lolong*), pottery declining in use (increasingly plain ware) or absent.	A.D. 1000–1500
Isohkelekel Phase	Disintegration of the Deleur polity, Nahmwarki title in use, chiefly complexes and new style of meeting house (*nahs*); pottery use abandoned entirely.	A.D. 1500–1826
Early Contact Phase	Initial contact with the West; Nan Madol occupation continues but in a noncenter role.	A.D. 1826–1885
Historic Phase	Western contact and colonial governments.	A.D. 1885–present

[a] After Ayres (1990).

Carolines.[27] Weisler's (pers. comm., 1997) multi-year project focuses on the origins and transformation of prehistoric Marshallese society, with field studies on Ujae, Maloelap, Ebon, and Utrik atolls. With more than 50 radiocarbon dates, Weisler can now outline occupation sequences for these atolls extending back 2,000 years. The principal village sites (typically there is one main site situated on the largest islet of each atoll) have yielded artifact assemblages dominated by shell adzes (made from *Tridacna, Cassis, Conus,* and *Lambis* shells), *Spondylus*-shell beads, *Conus*-shell rings, and pumice abraders. Single-piece fishhooks and trolling lures of pearl shell are known for the past 1,000 years and may date earlier. None of the atolls has substantial stone architecture (other than low house alignments), and settlement patterns were highly stable.

It may be premature to compare these island sequences, but some parallel trends and differences suggest themselves. One difference is the persistence of pottery in western Micronesia and the abandonment of ceramics in the central-eastern islands. In both regions, specialized architecture developed in later time periods, although particular forms varied greatly from island to island (Morgan 1988). Major architectural traditions are confined to the high islands, presumably because only on the larger land masses did sizable populations (and population densities) arise. These architectural forms correspond to the rise of powerful and centralized chiefly polities, to be discussed subsequently. In contrast, atoll sequences display remarkable stability over time with little change, at least insofar as we can detect in their archaeological records.[28]

Tuvalu and the Polynesian Outliers in Micronesia

There are two exceptions to the generalization that all of the Micronesian islands east of Yap are inhabited by speakers of Nuclear Micronesian languages: the atolls of Nukuoro and Kapingamarangi, which lie to the south of the main Carolines, are both inhabited by Polynesian speakers. These islands are therefore counted among the "Polynesian Outliers" located outside the Polynesian Triangle, of which the Melanesian members were discussed in Chapter 5.

Until recently, it was thought that all of the Polynesian Outlier languages fell together in a single subgroup of Polynesian, known as "Samoic-Outlier" because it grouped the Outlier languages together with the Western Polynesian languages of Samoa and East Futuna (Pawley 1967). New linguistic research now suggests that while many if not all of the Outlier languages in the Solomons–Vanuatu–New Caledonia region are closely related to East Futunan, those of Kapingamarangi and Nukuoro fall into a different subgroup, closely related to the Ellicean language of Tuvalu (Marck 1997; W. Wilson 1985). Rather than having a single common origin, the Outlier populations probably had multiple origins, and the Micronesian Outliers may have derived from populations originally located in the Tuvalu group of atolls.

Tuvalu itself remains almost unexplored archaeologically. Takayama and Saito (1987; Takayama et al. 1987) excavated at Temei on Vaitupu Island, where they report finding "deeply stratified cultural deposits" containing pottery and two *Turbo*-shell fishhooks, with an associated shell radiocarbon date of around A.D. 1080, but no full report is available. (The pottery, based on petrographic analysis by William Dickinson, is of Fijian origin and was probably a trade item.) A model based on

the linguistic subgrouping of Polynesian languages suggests that Tuvalu—along with the Tokelau Islands, and possibly the Northern Cooks or some of the Equatorial Islands, or both—might have been colonized early in the first millennium A.D., corresponding with the breakup of a Proto Nuclear Polynesian speech community formerly confined to the Western Polynesian region (see Chapter 7). Once Tuvalu had been settled, it would have provided a source for drift voyages extending westward into Carolinean waters. More field research in Tuvalu to test this model would be desirable.

Intensive archaeological studies have been made of both Nukuoro and Kapingamarangi.[29] Davidson's pioneering atoll excavations on Nukuoro revealed well-stratified occupation deposits, rich in material culture and faunal remains. Although she originally thought that this sequence spanned 2,000 years, Davidson (1992) now puts initial occupation at around 1237 ± 55 B.P. Her excavations recovered a large assemblage (697 specimens) of pearl-shell fishhooks, with several forms that changed over time (Fig. 6.3). Takayama and Saito (1987) point out that the two *Turbo*-shell hooks from the Temei site in Tuvalu correspond to Davidson's Nukuoro Type I[a], adding one bit of archaeological evidence in support of a possible Tuvalu origin for the Nukuoro population. The Nukuoro excavations also produced many other kinds of shell and bone artifacts, including adzes of *Tridacna* and *Terebra* shells.

Davidson (1992:297) is pessimistic "about the ability of archaeologists to identify Polynesian arrival on Nukuoro," since she feels that "the point at which Nukuoro became a Polynesian Outlier is no closer to recognition." However, in light of the revised subgrouping of Outlier languages, and the model for a first millennium A.D. expansion of Proto Ellicean speakers into Tuvalu, there is no reason why the Nukuoro sequence should not be

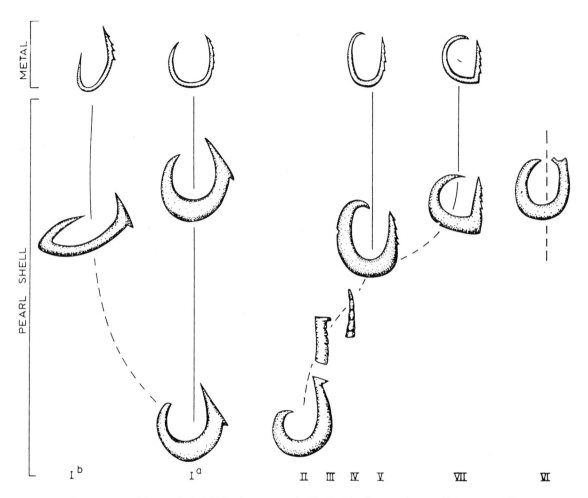

FIGURE 6.3 The sequence of changes in shell fishhook types revealed by Davidson's excavations on Nukuoro atoll. (From Davidson 1967b.)

regarded as "Polynesian" from bottom to top. None of the material culture in the Nukuoro sequence contradicts this hypothesis, especially since initial settlement would have been launched from a similar atoll environment. Such an interpretation eliminates the search for an elusive "point" at which Nukuoro became Polynesian.

Kapingamarangi Atoll has remarkably well-stratified cultural deposits, up to 4 meters deep on Touhou Islet, which was built up from a small sand cay to a substantial islet over about 700–1,000 years, partly by purposeful addition of sand and gravel retained by seawalls. The early part of the Touhou sequence reflects "transient occupation" much as suggested in my model of atoll settlement discussed earlier, with the formation of an "artificial islet" between A.D. 1300 and 1700, and finally a period of "intensive residential occupation" in the last 300 years (Leach and Ward 1981: 53–55). The Kapingamarangi artifact assemblage is not as rich as that from Nukuoro, but a similar range of types is represented, including *Tridacna*-shell adzes and one-piece shell fishhooks, as well as a massive form of trolling lure, possibly made from *Tridacna* shell.

Atoll Adaptations

A most peculiar kind of island—and often a precarious environment as well—an atoll requires critical adaptations if human existence is to be sustained.[30] In 1980, I spent several weeks on Arno in the Marshalls, supervising the first archaeological survey of that atoll by Tom Dye (Dye, ed., 1987). Living on such an island, one becomes intensely aware that the ocean is never more than a few meters—horizontally and, especially, vertically—distant. Walking across an atoll islet, from the calm lagoon beach with its fine sands to the wave-battered seaward coast with its coral rubble ramparts, takes no more than a few minutes. The roar of surf on coral is incessant, particularly at night, lying in one's hut after the sounds of the village have died down. Everything underfoot consists of coral in one form or another: coral reef, coral boulders, coral sand. There is no other kind of stone. The atoll soil itself is formed of calcareous sand, enriched only with organic matter, including the debris of human habitation.

On such tenuous heaps of coral and sand rimming productive lagoons and extensive reefs, the early Micronesian colonizers worked out a set of cultural adaptations enabling them not only to survive but also to live a satisfying life. The archaeological record of these adaptations is only now emerging. Obtaining fresh water is perhaps the single greatest challenge to atoll life, not only water to drink but also water to sustain crops. Traditional atoll subsistence in Micronesia typically focuses on a few main plants: coconuts (essential

for drinking fluid, nutritious "meat," and leaves used for plaiting and weaving) and *Pandanus* for food and leaves. Both of these are naturally adapted to the coralline, halophytic (high-salt) environment of the coastal strand. Also common are breadfruit (*Artocarpus altilis*) and giant swamp taro (*Cyrtosperma chamissonis*), neither of which is a strand plant in its natural state. Certain varieties of breadfruit can be grown on the larger atoll islets, where a substantial, rain-fed freshwater aquifer (the Ghyben-Herzberg aquifer) supplies the trees' roots with water. Swamp taro, on the other hand, must be cultivated in artificial pits excavated down to this aquifer, mulched with leaves and other organic debris (Fig. 6.4). This method of pit cultivation developed early in the sequence of atoll settlement, for Weisler (1999) has dated pit construction on Kaven Islet in Maloelap Atoll in the Marshalls to 1910 ± 70 B.P., contemporary with the oldest dates for habitation sites on the atoll.

Atoll islets are consummate man-made environments. In addition to digging *Cyrtosperma* pits, or on some atolls constructing seawalls for sand retention, humans have extensively modified both the physical and the biotic environments of atolls. Atoll vegetation is dominated by plants purposively introduced by humans, and most of the terrestrial fauna (such as rats, snails, and geckos) is also *synanthropic*, or human-associated.[31] Even atoll soils are anthropogenic. The richest soils on atoll islets are those that have formed on calcareous sands through centuries of continuous human habitation; they are essentially midden deposits that have been continually reworked through cultivation of abandoned house sites.

Lacking stone, atoll dwellers made extensive use in their material arts of shell, along with bone, wood, and vegetable materials (leaves, fibers). The Lapita peoples had already developed a sophisticated shell technology (see Chapter 4), which

FIGURE 6.4 Excavation through the berm of a *Cyrtosperma* cultivation pit on Maloelap, Marshall Islands. The man is standing on the edge of the pit, with *Cyrtosperma* plants behind him. (Photo courtesy Marshall Weisler.)

doubtless preadapted the first atoll colonists to survive without access to stone. But the range of material culture utilizing shell (and coral) expanded in atoll societies. Adzes were manufactured not just from giant *Tridacna* clams but also from *Terebra, Mitre,* and *Cassis* shells, and a diversity of forms developed. Fishhooks were made from pearl shells, not only one-piece angling hooks but also trolling lure rigs. Large helmet shells (*Cassis cornuta*) were adapted for use as containers (Dye, ed., 1987:362). Pestles and pounders for processing *Pandanus* were worked from coral heads or from reef limestone.

Other kinds of adaptation in social organization and in interisland relations and communications were equally essential to atoll existence.

In sailing and navigation, the Caroline islanders developed the most sophisticated outrigger canoe technology and star-compass systems known in Oceania (Fig. 6.5).[32] As Alkire (1965:171) points out, "Human survival on small islands often depends on a maximum exploitation of available resources. Emergencies [such as cyclone or tsunami damage, or drought] . . . may take large areas of the island out of production for extended periods of time." Such conditions encouraged interisland contacts, and even the dispersion of social units across more than a single island. The Carolinean system of long-distance voyaging was one kind of adaptation to the environmental hazards of life on atolls.

FIGURE 6.5 A sailing canoe of the central Caroline Islands, as drawn by the early-nineteenth-century French artist Louis Choris, who accompanied the Russian explorer Otto von Kotzebue. (Collection of the author.)

Later Prehistory in Western Micronesia

While questions of origins and cultural sequences have been put to the fore in Micronesian archaeology, prehistorians are increasingly engaged in reconstructing prehistoric sociopolitical systems. One might suppose that the accounts of early Western observers and later ethnographers would be sufficient to understand traditional Micronesian societies, but such is far from the case. In the Marianas Islands, Spanish contact began with Magellan in A.D. 1521, and by 1668 a permanent Spanish settlement was flourishing on Guam. Over the following two decades, the indigenous Chamorro people were reduced to a mere fraction of their original population, their settlement patterns forcibly disrupted as they were resettled in villages centered around newly constructed churches; their culture was irrevocably transformed. Elsewhere in Micronesia, contact was not as early or always as brutal in its consequences, but successive Spanish, German, Japanese, and American mercantile, missionary, and colonial incursions exacted their toll. Thus ethnographic accounts such as the monumental *Ergebnisse der Südsee-Expedition* (Thilenius, ed., 1913–36) document societies already transformed—sometimes radically—through decades or centuries of depopulation and sociopolitical upheaval. It therefore becomes the task of prehistory to inquire into the nature of these societies prior to Western intrusion, and into how they changed over the millennia.

Latte *and Social Complexity in the Marianas* Visually striking on the Marianas archaeological landscape are the numerous double rows of three to seven hewn limestone columns or uprights each, the columns often surmounted by carved capstones; these structures are called *latte* in the Chamorro language (Fig. 6.6). The columns and capstones (or capitals) were quarried from exposures of upraised reef limestone, and quarry sites with unfinished columns and capstones in situ have been recorded. A few eyewitness accounts from the early Spanish period associate *latte* with dwellings, such as that from the Miguel de Legaspi expedition of 1565: "Their houses are high, well kept and well made. [They] stand the height of a man off the ground, atop large stone pillars, upon which they lay the flooring" (quoted in Morgan 1988:119). *Latte* drew the attention of early investigators like Hornbostel (Thompson 1932) and Spoehr (1957), and they continue to attract archaeological work (Fig. 6.7), figuring prominently in debates on Chamorro sociopolitical organization.[33]

Latte sites, found on all of the main islands in the Marianas group, vary considerably in form, size, and layout, but they consistently follow the same basic pattern of two parallel rows of upright columns with a rectangular plan. Based on a sample of 234 *latte* sets on Guam, Graves (1986b, Table 5) showed that the number of columns ranges from 6 (3 per row) to 14 (7 per row), with the most common number of columns being 8 (152 sets or 65% of the sample). Butler's sample from the small island of Aguiguan is similar, although the mean number of columns there is 10 (1988, Table 9.1). In both samples, there was only a single site with 14 columns. Other features, such as the height of columns and the area encompassed by the rows, also vary. Smaller *latte* have shaft heights of less than 1 meter, but heights in the 2- to 3-meter range are not uncommon; the impressive House of Taga

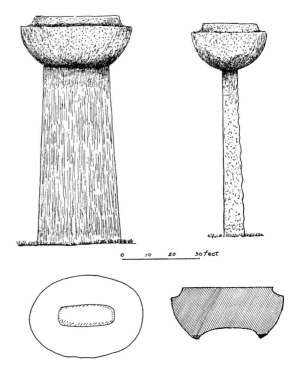

FIGURE 6.6 Profiles and plan of typical *latte* columns in the Marianas Islands. (After Thompson 1932.)

site on Tinian has columns 5.33 meters tall. The number of columns correlates with interior surface area, which ranges from about 18 square meters in small *latte* up to 61 square meters or more in the largest cases.

Latte sets typically occur in clusters, presumably representing hamlets or villages; Morgan (1988) illustrates several typical plans. Small clusters have only a few *latte* sets, whereas others such as the Mochong site have as many as 52 sets. The long axes of *latte* typically parallel the coastline, and there is some formality of community patterning. In the Taga site, the imposing House of Taga sits midway along a single alignment of *latte* structures, all parallel to the coast, and faces a single isolated *latte* seaward of it, the latter perhaps having some special function (Fig. 6.8). At Mochong,

FIGURE 6.7 The Tapony *latte* site on Guam, Marianas Islands. Note the row of standing uprights and the two large mortars in the foreground. (Photo courtesy Steve Athens.)

the largest *latte* (a 14-column structure) is likewise centrally situated.

Excavations at a number of *latte* complexes provide data on chronology and function. Graves (1986b) argues that *latte* are securely dated to as early as A.D. 1000–1100. The quantities of residential midden surrounding these structures—including Marianas Plain Ware potsherds, other artifacts, and shell and bone refuse—make it clear

that they were habitations. Numerous burials are directly associated with *latte*, primarily of adults with both sexes about equally represented. The nature of the perishable superstructures that *latte* supported is a matter of speculation, but some kind of A-frame structure seems likely. Figure 6.9 shows Morgan's conjectural reconstruction of such a pole-and-thatch building atop the truly monumental House of Taga *latte*.

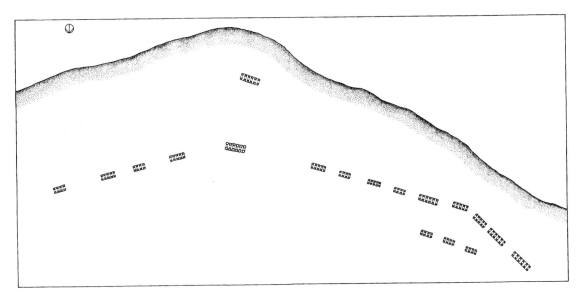

FIGURE 6.8 Plan of a typical *latte* site, with a linear arrangement of *latte* foundations running parallel to the coast. (From Morgan 1988.)

Latte sites provide significant archaeological evidence for the development of Chamorro social complexity during the last millennium. The nature of Chamorro society is debatable, with Thompson (1945) arguing for a three-class status hierarchy, and other scholars such as Cordy (1983) suggesting that only two classes (chiefs and commoners) were present. Early contact-period records are so vague as to permit either argument. Based on his comparative analysis, Graves inferred that *latte* were the residences of "high-ranking members of kin-based corporate groups, . . . [who] could have best afforded the expenditure of resources in support of the additional labor required to construct latte sets, labor most likely drawn from low-ranking families within the lineage as a form of solidarity and support" (1986b:149). Certainly such a model fits with known ideological uses of monumental architecture to differentiate social strata in other Oceanic societies. Drawing upon ethnographic data on the cultural significance of height in

Oceanic societies (greater height correlating with higher rank or with sacredness), Graves suggests that the construction of particularly large and high *latte* sets (such as the House of Taga) may reflect "the elaboration of another level of status ranking among a limited set of communities on Tinian and Rota" (1986b:153).

Graves's model has been challenged by Craib (1986), who argues that *all* residences in the late prehistoric period were raised on *latte* and that the use of these structures was therefore not confined to an elite class.[34] Indeed, Craib suggests the archaeological pattern of *latte* is consistent with "a society lacking a centralized authority and . . . instead, organized on a local autonomous level" (1986:173). Following Craib's lead, a concept of *heterarchy* or horizontal differentiation among local corporate groups—each competing with the others through ritual exchange—might provide a better model for late prehistoric Chamorro society than one of hierarchy. Moreover, Hunter-Anderson

FIGURE 6.9 Reconstruction of the House of Taga *latte* site. (From Morgan 1988.)

and Butler (1991:35) suggest that *latte* may have served "more than one function, simultaneously and over time." They argue that *latte* sets, when not used to support dwellings, may have been material symbols legitimizing land claims or places in which to bury deceased lineage members. We have

not heard the last word on this debate, and further fieldwork (especially extensive, fine-grained horizontal excavation) is called for.

The Terraced Landscapes of Palau   Moving southwest from the Marianas to Palau, one encounters

FIGURE 6.10 A terraced landscape at Airai, Babeldaob, Palau, showing a crown-and-brim arrangement surmounting a series of terraces. As is typical of many such terrace landscapes, the dominant vegetation consists of swordgrass and scrub *Pandanus*. (Photo by P. V. Kirch.)

totalizing transformations of volcanic landscapes, in which entire ridges, hills, and valley slopes were completely reworked and shaped (Fig. 6.10). It would be difficult to find a more complete transformation from natural to cultural, excepting perhaps the famous terraced landscapes of Ifugao country in the Philippines. The terraced landscapes of Palau—marvelous architectonic works—nonetheless remain an enduring puzzle of Oceanic prehistory, for little is certain regarding their construction or function.

The Palau terraces cover extensive areas on the principal island of Babeldaob, many of which were surveyed, and some later tested, by Osborne

(1966, 1979). Osborne describes the characteristic form of the upper hilltop terraces as follows:

At many of the larger sites is found an arrangement of the penultimate and ultimate terraces which conforms to a widespread pattern. The two superior terracings resemble a hat, and I have adopted the descriptive terminology therefrom. The final terrace remnant I have called the crown, and the next to the final one the brim. . . . A few crowns possess a central depression or pond which could have served as a water storage reservoir, or as a semisubterranean defensive or other structure. At one end of the crown is often seen the peak, a small embankment which runs the width of the crown. . . . They appear

FIGURE 6.11 Plan map of terraces inland of Ngchemiangel Bay, Palau. (From Morgan 1988.)

to be defensive, a small redoubt embankment or breastwork.

The brim and crown terraces contribute a spectacular quality to the Babeldaob skyline: when viewed from a distance they have the quality of Mexican pyramids. (*1966:151*)

Morgan (1988:4–13) used aerial photos combined with photogrammetric mapping to study a large complex of terraced hills above Ngchemiangel Bay; his map is reproduced here as Figure 6.11.

Based on the limited excavations of terraced sites to date, it has been suggested that terrace construction began around A.D. 500 and continued until perhaps A.D. 1400, with no significant construction after that date. Recent and ongoing CRM work on Babeldaob will doubtless yield a wealth of new data and radiocarbon dates to fur-

ther refine, and possibly revise, the chronology of terrace use and construction. The terraces were apparently already abandoned at the time of early European contact.[35] What purposes the terraces served has been vigorously debated. Potsherds lie everywhere on them, but often these are in reworked contexts such as terrace fill. Most likely, the terrace complexes had multiple functions and internal spatial differentiation. Many terraces—especially those cascading down hillsides—likely had an agricultural function, and the disposal of residential refuse from habitation terraces (perhaps as mulch?) may account for the widespread distribution of potsherds. The crown-and-brim arrangements seem to have had some defensive function, or possibly they were centers of ritual activity. In Melekeok State (east-central Babeldaob), Liston et al. (1998) identified and test-excavated a fortified ring-ditch site around the middle and upper slopes of Ngerulmud Hill, dating to around 2000 B.P. and associated with early thin blackware ceramics.

The form of sociopolitical organization that existed in Palau during the period of major terrace construction is also debatable. One might argue that only a centralized form of organization could have carried out such impressive earthworks, but it is entirely possible that local groups built these terraces incrementally over extended periods of time. A major excavation program on one or more terraced complexes, bringing to bear the interdisciplinary power of contemporary archaeological method, is needed to resolve these unanswered questions regarding Palauan terraces. Such a project will be labor-intensive and costly, for these are truly massive sites.

Although less pervasive than the ubiquitous terraces, a second category of monumental architecture in Palau also commands attention: anthropomorphic stone monoliths (Fig. 6.12), distributed primarily on Babeldaob, but also on Oreor (Koror) Island.[36] These range in size from small uprights only 40 cm in height to larger ones reaching 2.93 meters, and they are generally made of andesite. A variety of human face designs are represented, including an "owl" face, a "fanged mouth" face, and a "quadruped-face" combination. At Melekeok on the east coast of Babeldaob is a group of nine stone sculptures, known as the Great Faces. The single most impressive megalithic complex is Bairulchau near the northern tip of Babeldaob. Here, situated on a leveled plaza south of a large terraced crown, are 52 megaliths (Fig. 6.13). Twenty-five of these are arranged in a colonnade extending over 70 meters. These colonnaded stones have shallow grooves on their top surfaces, seemingly to receive horizontal wooden beams for some kind of immense structure. Morgan (1988:16) and Osborne (1979:178–80) both suggested that the Bairulchau

FIGURE 6.12 An "owl" face stone sculpture at NgerekIngong, Ngeremlengui State, Palau. (Photo courtesy J. Van Tilburg.)

colonnade represents an early version of the traditional Palauan *bai* or village council house. Also present on the Bairulchau site are six large carved Great Faces with rather demonic appearances. Osborne excavated at Bairulchau but obtained only two radiocarbon dates with widely differing ages (1800 ± 80 and 285 ± 80 B.P.), leaving the chronology of the site unresolved.

The chronology of the Great Faces and other megaliths, and their function(s) within prehistoric Palau society, remain conjectural and speculative. Oral traditions suggest they may be guardian deities, and one category of megalith is termed *chesuch* or "owl"; other names have sexual connotations. Van Tilburg (1991:57) sees the Palauan

FIGURE 6.13 The Bairulchau site on Babeldaob, with its megalithic carvings. (Photo courtesy J. Van Tilburg.)

sculptural tradition as "an integrated expression of local artistic concepts demonstrating formal and symbolic continuity as well as [a] transformation over time," and she believes that there are stylistic and iconographic connections between the megaliths and designs found on ethnographically documented *bai* council houses.

The "Yapese Empire"   Yap occupies an ambiguous position in Micronesian culture history. The Yapese language long defied classification as either Western Malayo-Polynesian or Oceanic, because it has extensively borrowed from both of these groups (Ross 1996b). This linguistic ambiguity is not surprising, for ethnographically Yap was the hub of an amazing long-distance communication network, referred to as the "Yapese Empire" (Hage and Harary 1991:17–18, 105–8; 1996:30–35). To the southwest, Yap was connected with Palau, where aragonitic limestone quarries produced the famous stone "money" essential to internal exchange relationships in Yap (Gilliland 1975). To the east, an elaborate communication structure linked the Gagil District of Yap with a succession of 14 Carolinean atolls, stretching from Ulithi all the way to Puluwat and Namonuito, a total distance of 1,200 kilometers. This exchange system, the *sawei*, has been characterized as "a bicultural system of tribute offerings, gift exchange, and disaster relief" (Hunter-Anderson and Zan 1996:1).

This system also resulted in considerable "male-based gene flow," as Lum (1998) has shown by analysis of molecular genetic variation in central and eastern Micronesia. Further long-distance exchange relations linked the Carolinean atolls with the Marianas archipelago (and thus indirectly with Yap).

The "Yapese Empire" was simultaneously a system of areal integration and a prestige-good exchange network, in which certain elite groups on Yap controlled the flow of goods necessary for their social reproduction. As Hage and Harary, who have studied the system from a graph-theory point of view, describe it:

> In the Yapese tribute system, 14 low, coral, islands and atolls stretching some 1,200 kilometers eastward were joined to the Gagil District of Yap by three types of gift relation. In the *pitigil tamol* relation, the low islanders paid tribute to the highest-ranking matrilineal chief of Gagil. In the *sawei* relation, individual low island matrilineages paid "rent" to individual Gagil patrilineages that owned (at least nominally) individual districts of the low islands. In a symbolic replication of intercaste relations, the low island tenants stood as "children" to their Yapese landlords and "fathers." In the *mepel* relation, low island matrilineages made religious offerings to Yapese ancestral ghosts. Tribute gifts consisted of woven fiber cloth, mats, coconut-fiber rope, and shell valuables. The *sawei* gift was reciprocated by "optional" Yapese gifts of food, including taro, yams, sweet potatoes, and bananas, craft goods, and raw materials such as basalt, timber, and turmeric, all of which were scarce or unavailable on the low islands.
> (*1996:31*)

The navigation and sailing technology enabling the *sawei* was controlled by the atoll-dwellers. The system had advantages both for the Gagil people of Yap, who used the externally obtained prestige goods to enhance their status locally, and for the atoll-dwellers, who needed access to high-island resources. What were the origins of this remarkable long-distance network? How long has it been in place, and has its configuration changed over time? Data from excavations on a number of atolls within the ambit of the "Yapese Empire" are beginning to provide tentative answers, although much more work is required.

On Ngulu Atoll between Yap and Palau, Intoh (1984) tested deeply stratified cultural deposits, the earliest of which predate A.D. 300. Connections with both Palau and Yap are indicated by potsherds of Palauan Ware, Yapese Early Calcareous Ware, Yapese Unlaminated Ware, and Yapese Laminated Ware. The Yapese pottery predominates, but a phase of regular contact with Palau between A.D. 800 and 1400 is also indicated. Intoh (1991, 1996) excavated as well on Fais Atoll to the east of Yap, where she found stratified deposits dating to ca. A.D. 300. She found a direct connection with Yap in about a dozen pieces of greenschist, a rock type occurring within the Micronesian area exclusively on Yap. The settlement of Fais was presumably from Yap, as a high-island origin is indicated by the presence of pig bone. Continuous contact with Yap is indicated by more than 800 potsherds of Yapese origin, including CST and later laminated wares.[37]

Descantes (1998) excavated on the Mogmog Islet of Ulithi Atoll, finding evidence for the importation of Yapese ceramics into Ulithi, beginning as early as the seventh century A.D. Using mineralogy and chemical composition analyses, Descantes was able to localize the Yapese ceramics to the Gachpar area. He also suggests that exchange contacts between Yap and Ulithi intensified around A.D. 1400.

Additional evidence from within the "Yapese Empire" network comes from Faraulep, Woleai, and

Lamotrek Atolls located farther to the east. Fuji-mura and Alkire (1984) test-excavated on these islands in 1975–76. Faraulep and Woleai produced only shallow deposits, suggesting a late proto-historic settlement, but Lamotrek had well-stratified deposits, with radiocarbon dates to A.D. 1000–1100 and possibly earlier. Pottery of both Yapese and Palauan origin was recovered from the Sabaig and Polipi sites on Lamotrek (Dickinson 1984). In the excavators' words, "Ceramic and stone materials, obviously of foreign origin, indicate that voyaging and trading ties have long existed . . . between Lamotrek and Yap, Palau, and Truk. Ties to all of these volcanic islands appear to be of equal antiquity, dating to at least A.D. 1200" (Fujimura and Alkire 1984:125).

Lingenfelter (1975) and Alkire (1980) offered explanations for the origins and function of the *sawei* system, seeing this alternatively as a matter of political power relations or as an economic system of tribute relations. Hunter-Anderson and Zan (1996) have critiqued their models, offering a new explanation. They see the *sawei* as having originated within Yap itself, where "competition over land in Yap gave rise to a cultural regime characterized by warfare, shifting defensive-offensive alliances among socioterritorial units, and conventions by which socioterritorial units communicated their worthiness as alliance partners" (1996:1). By assuming *sawei* obligations with the atoll-dwellers, the Gagil people purportedly strengthened their internal position in Yap, communicating their "worth as an alliance capable of supporting the large Carolinian dependency." While intriguing, Hunter-Anderson and Zan's model is no more compelling than the alternatives. Indeed, Descantes's recent work on the long-term history of exchange relationships between Ulithi and Yap highlights the need for a dynamic model, since the relations between

these two modes clearly changed in nature over time, from "infrequent gift-giving" early on to a later "formal and intensive exchange system" (1998:264).

For Yap Island, our current archaeological knowledge is too embryonic to trace the internal sociopolitical or economic transformations linked to the external prestige-good network. Labby (1976) advanced a model of changing modes of production (from initial shifting cultivation to intensified taro cultivation in swamps) linked to changes in social structure and land tenure, worthy of archaeological testing through a study of changing settlement patterns.[38] To date, however, work on Yapese settlement patterns has been entirely synchronic (ethnoarchaeological) or limited to minor tests of structures dating only to the proto-historic period (e.g., Hunter-Anderson 1983; Intoh and Leach 1985).

Nothing could seem more highly structured than the Yapese landscape, with its elaborate stone constructions, including stone house platforms and stone-paved terraces with backrests that serve as meeting areas, linked by networks of paved trails connecting plazas lined with aragonite disc "money" (*rai*) (Fig. 6.14). In 1977 I carried out a reconnaissance survey in the Rull and Kanify areas on Yap Island (Kirch 1977b). The density and complexity of structural remains encountered in my survey strongly impressed me with the potential for landscape archaeology on Yap. The built environment of stone constructions, and its integration with the textured mosaic of orchard gardens, swamp-taro cultivations, and grassland-savannas in the interior (the setting for clusters of burial mounds), would repay investigation from a landscape archaeology perspective. There is much scope for developing an archaeological history of this settlement pattern and its ecological, economic, and sociopolitical correlates.

FIGURE 6.14 A Yapese stone "money" disc of aragonitic limestone in a village plaza. (Photo by P. V. Kirch.)

Development of Sociopolitical Complexity in the Caroline High Islands

In the Caroline archipelago, complex societies—marked by elaborate ranking or stratification, and by economic specialization—developed exclusively on the high islands. This reflects the extreme resource limitations and restricted land area of atolls, which prohibited the buildup of sizable populations. Whatever one's theoretical position regarding the causal role of population in sociopolitical change (whether as prime mover, secondary stimulus, or simply inconsequential), there can be little doubt that a certain minimal threshold of population size is a necessary (although not necessarily sufficient) condition for the rise of social complexity. Thus in the Pacific islands generally, atoll societies—always ranging in the low hundreds of persons at most—never exhibited complex hierarchy, although some were involved in complex external exchange relationships, as in the *sawei*. But on high islands such as Pohnpei and Kosrae, populations numbering in the thousands were in place by the end of the first

millennium A.D., if not earlier. The history of amalgamation and organization of these sizable—and very dense—populations under various forms of hierarchical and centralized control is a story now beginning to be tackled by archaeology. Other approaches, such as analysis of indigenous oral traditions, provide complementary perspectives.

Because they have common origins in a late phase of Lapita expansion, the complex societies of Pohnpei and Kosrae may be compared with the classic high-island chiefdoms of Polynesia (see Chapter 8). Given such homologous relationships, structural similarities between these sets of societies may inform us about underlying processes of social change, either in response to demographic, environmental, or economic challenges and stimuli or as a result of structural contradictions inherent in the social formations themselves. These are issues to which I will return in Chapter 9.

Pohnpei and Nan Madol Pohnpei, at 310 square kilometers the largest high island in central-eastern Micronesia, has a nearly circular plan, with rugged mountains rising 550 meters above sea level and a radial pattern of stream drainages. High rainfall and fertile soils supported an agricultural system based on orchards of breadfruit and other tree crops, as well as root and tuber crops (especially yams), while an extensive barrier-reef and lagoon system provided rich fishing grounds. As with most Pacific islands that suffered massive depopulation after first contact with Europeans, the maximum population of Pohnpei is not certain, but Ayres et al. (1979, Table 17) estimate it to have been between 20,000 and 30,000 persons, certainly a size corresponding with many of the larger Polynesian chiefdoms. In early historic times, five independent districts (*wehi*) were each under the control of a diarchy of sacred and secular lords (the *nahmwarki* and the *nahnken,* respectively).[39] Each district was partitioned into smaller named land sections under the charge of lesser chiefs, who paid tribute to the dual paramounts through a seasonal round of feasts.[40] While this hierarchical sociopolitical system compares favorably with many of the midrange chiefdoms of Polynesia (for example, those of the southern Cook Islands or the Australs), there is evidence—both in Pohnpeian oral traditions and in archaeology—for an older system in which the entire island was unified under a single dynastic rule. The seat of this ancient Saudeleur dynasty is Nan Madol, adjacent to the small islet of Temwen in the district of Madolenihmw (Fig. 6.15).

William Morgan, a distinguished twentieth-century architect, claims that "no site in Oceania surpasses the dramatic beauty of ancient Nan Madol," which with its artificial islets and intervening canals has sometimes been called the "Venice of the Pacific." Morgan writes of how—despite having seen drawings and photos of the site beforehand—he was emotionally unprepared for the grandeur of the site when he first glimpsed it. The great tomb islet of Nandauwas (Fig. 6.16)

is "powerfully conceived, sensitively sited, and skillfully executed. . . . Passing jungle-covered islets on both sides of the canal, we caught our first glimpses of Nandauwas' southwest corner through the trees. A few moments later the canoe turned to the left, slowed, and stopped before the main entry landing of the west front. For several minutes I sat quietly in the boat, gazing at the magnificent west facade, the stately podium, the noble entryway, and the ascending steps that led to the interior courts, enclosures, and tombs" (Morgan 1988:68).

Nan Madol covers 81 hectares of sheltered reef area off the southern side of Temwen Island and comprises no fewer than 93 artificial islets constructed of stone with coral and rubble fill, the entire complex bounded on the west, south, and east by massive seawalls or breakwaters, some of them also incorporating islets. German ethnographer Paul Hambruch made the first accurate map of Nan Madol in 1910 (see Hambruch 1911, 1936), and his cartography still forms the basis for modern surveys, which have added much fine-grained detail.[41] Morgan (1988:66–67) provides a "provisional" map of Nan Madol incorporating Hambruch's data and later information.[42]

Nan Madol is laid out formally, as seen in the site plan (Fig. 6.17), and while it developed over a long period of time, some degree of overall planning is evident. As the administrative center of the Saudeleur polity, the islets functioned primarily as the residences and burial facilities for members of the Saudeleur elite. Nan Madol was divided into two named sectors (this ethnographic information was obtained by Hambruch and other investigators): Madol Pah to the west (with 34 islets) and Madol Powe to the east (with 58 islets). Four large, square islets dominate Madol Pah, a residential ward. Madol Powe, in classic binary structural opposition, was a ritual ward incorporating several large tombs as well as priestly residences. At

FIGURE 6.15 An aerial view of part of the Nan Madol site on Pohnpei, with the Nandauwas islet and tomb complex visible in the foreground. (Photo courtesy Steve Athens.)

the southeast corner of Nan Madol and dominating Madol Powe is Nandauwas, the massive royal mortuary compound of the Saudeleurs (Fig. 6.18).

Part of what makes Nan Madol so architecturally impressive—aside from its massive scale—is the use of large columnar basalt stones in wall construction. On some islets, the construction technique consisted of dry-fitting large basalt boulders, while on others a highly distinctive method of wall construction using columnar basalt slabs in a header-stretcher technique was employed. This latter technique was used in the Nandauwas tomb complex. Nandauwas islet has a base or podium measuring 79 by 63 meters; the outer enclosing walls, set back from the podium facing, rise 7.6 meters above the canal level. Within the enclosing

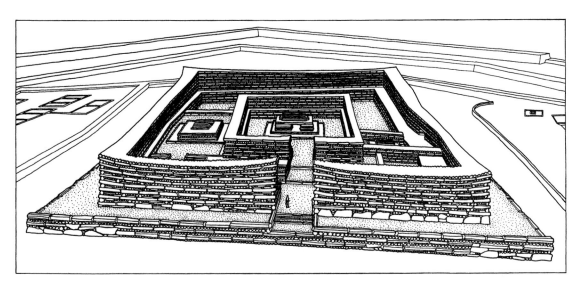

FIGURE 6.16 Perspective view of the Nandauwas tomb complex at Nan Madol, Pohnpei. (From Morgan 1988.)

walls are crypts, including a main central crypt, covered with columnar basalt lintel stones. Unfortunately, unsystematic digging by European explorers and by later Japanese archaeologists (prior to World War II) disturbed the interiors of these mortuary features, resulting in the loss of valuable information.

It will take many years of comprehensive archaeological study to map and record Nan Madol thoroughly, but recent fieldwork by Steve Athens, Bill Ayres, and others has produced accurate maps of many of the islets, detailed surface collection data on artifact distributions, and limited test excavations into islet fill. Based on their research, a tentative chronology for the construction of the Nan Madol complex is emerging. Initial occupation at the site was coeval with human colonization of Pohnpei itself, around A.D. 1. This is possibly one reason that Nan Madol became such an important ritual center: it may be the "ur-settlement" of the island. It is conceivable that the first occupation at Nan Madol, which has been revealed by ceramic-bearing deposits within the tidal zone under artificial islet fill, consisted of stilt-houses of Lapita type situated over the reef flat. By A.D. 900–1100 construction of artificially elevated islets had commenced, although this probably did not involve megalithic construction. A phase of truly megalithic building has been dated to A.D. 1200–1600, correlating with the Saudeleur period as recorded in Pohnpei oral traditions (Bath and Athens 1990). There was continued use of Nan Madol, and more construction, after A.D. 1650, but by the time of European visits in the mid-nineteenth century, the vast complex had been abandoned, with the Pohnpei people greatly fearing and respecting this sacred place.

Nan Madol is remarkable for its close correlations between oral traditions and archaeology.[43] Pohnpei history is indigenously conceived as falling into four successive ages: The Age of People, the Age of Saudeleur, the Age of Nahnmwarki, and the Age of Foreigners (the period of historic contact with Europeans). Primarily associated with

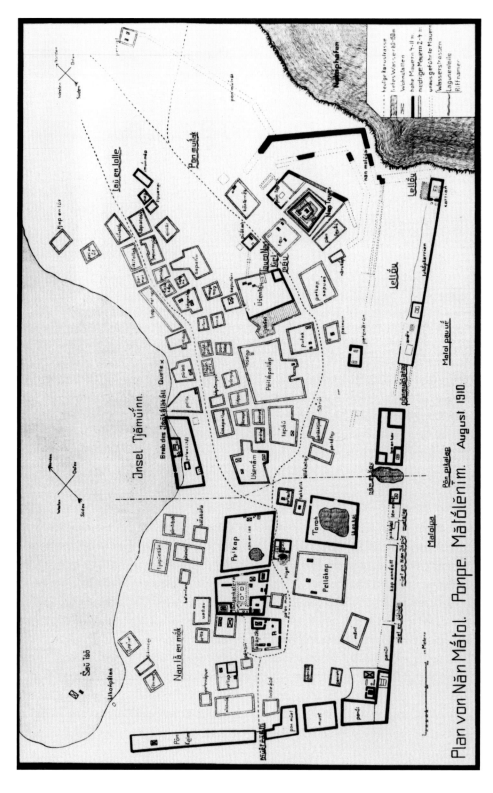

FIGURE 6.17 Map of the Nan Madol site complex by the early German ethnographer Paul Hambruch. (From Hambruch 1911.)

FIGURE 6.18 View of the Nandauwas tomb complex from the adjacent canal. Note the distinctive style of construction using prismatic basalt columns. (Photo courtesy Steve Athens.)

the Age of Saudeleur, Nan Madol is said to have been constructed by two brothers who built it as their place of prayer, using supernatural powers. Tradition records a succession of eight Saudeleur rulers, who held supreme power over the entire island, with the different districts providing tribute. The Saudeleurs resided on Pahnkedira islet, and they were interred in Nandauwas after death. Among the rituals enacted within the sacred sector of Nan Madol were a ceremonial turtle sacrifice and the care of a sacred eel kept in a pond in Ideht islet. Excavations by Smithsonian Institution archaeologists in the 1960s, in a mound of oven debris (the Ideht Mound) resulting from

successive turtle sacrifices, yielded three radiocarbon ages ranging between 770 and 520 B.P. Re-excavation of this mound in 1984 by Steve Athens and David Welch (as yet unpublished) produced a basal radiocarbon age of 700 ± 30 B.P. (uncalibrated) and an upper age of 355 ± 50 B.P. near the top of the mound. These dates, when calibrated, indicate that the ritual turtle sacrifices spanned a period from roughly A.D. 1300 to 1600.[44]

The Age of Saudeleur and its dynasty came to an end when the last ruler, infused with arrogance, attempted to capture one of the gods, Nan Sapwe; the latter escaped to a place in the sky

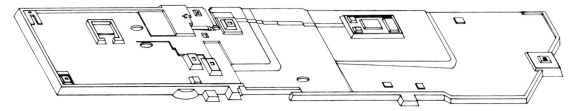

FIGURE 6.19 Perspective rendering of the Sapwtakai site in the Kiti District, Pohnpei. (After Bath and Athens 1990.)

called Katau,[45] where he inseminated a woman who bore him a son named Isokelekel. Isokelekel, after coming of age, voyaged to Pohnpei with a magical contingent of 333 warriors and engaged the last Saudeleur in battle, defeating him. Isokelekel is credited with instituting the modern chiefly system with its dual sacred-secular positions of Nahnmwarki and Nahnken.

Archaeological surveys in parts of Pohnpei outside Nan Madol, such as in the Awak Valley and the Kiti District, have added data on the distribution of megalithic architecture of "Nan Madol style" (e.g., using columnar basalt construction) and on the presence of administrative or ritual centers below the level of Nan Madol itself. Joyce Bath (1984a, 1984b) investigated the ridgetop center of Sapwtakai in the Kiti District, shown in perspective view in Figure 6.19. Sapwtakai incorporates columnar basalt in its construction, with a major central tomb structure similar to that of Nan Madol. Radiocarbon dates indicate occupation at Sapwtakai from about A.D. 1325 to 1700, roughly the same time span as that for the major development of Nan Madol.

Although the rise of complex sociopolitical structures on Pohnpei was largely a matter of internal processes, the possibility of external inputs or influences cannot be discounted. Ayres and Mauricio (1987) pointed to an unusual basalt adz from Nan Madol with closest parallels in Type I/III adz forms in Samoa, possibly an import from

Western Polynesia. Pohnpei and Kosrae are the only two islands in Micronesia where kava is consumed, and the Pohnpei term for this psychoactive plant, *sakaw*, is almost certainly a Polynesian borrowing (from *te kava*, with the article *te* being fossilized in the Pohnpeian loan word; Geraghty 1994). Rehg (n.d.) has identified more than 30 possible Polynesian loan words in Pohnpeian. In short, that there was contact between Western Polynesia (most likely Samoa) and Pohnpei seems likely, although determining the cultural impact of such external contact is more problematic.

Several prehistorians have advanced models for the development, evolution, or transformation of Pohnpeian society over the course of two millennia. Ayres (1990) and Bryson (1989) have explored "peer-polity interaction" theory, drawing upon the concept developed by Colin Renfrew (1982). According to Ayres, "The primary hypothesis is that Nan Madol's development as a chiefly and priestly center reflects an evolving chiefdom that controlled a Pohnpei polity from ca. A.D. 1000 to 1500" (1990:202), although the significance of "religious motivation [i.e., ideology] versus commanded labor [coercion]" is unclear to Ayres. Peoples (1990) inclines against a "functionalist" model in which chiefs increased their power through administrative control, in favor of a coercive model. "Multilevel political structures evolved as a consequence of the geographic expansion of power of some local groups led by chiefs"

(1990:299). Bath and Athens (1990), integrating Pohnpeian oral traditions with archaeological evidence, opine that there may have been a phase of centralized power (the Saudeleur period) with a four-level hierarchy, which failed to sustain itself and collapsed back to a three-level system, with independent districts. There are parallels in this scenario with the Hawaiian chiefdoms, which went through cycles of territorial expansion and retraction (Sahlins 1972; see Chapter 8). My own view is that future research in Pohnpei must achieve greater control over the demographic and economic contexts within which sociopolitical transformation occurred. Although Ayres and Haun (1985, 1990) have pointed to agricultural intensification as a significant aspect of the Pohnpeian economy, more information on the chronology of such intensification could provide critical evidence for interpreting the megalithic centers, as would better control over prehistoric population sizes and rates of change. These exciting research avenues should energize new generations of archaeologists working in Micronesia.

Kosrae and Lelu Some 550 kilometers east-south-east of Pohnpei and closer to the equator lies Kosrae, a high island with rugged mountains (the highest peak is 629 meters above sea level), at 109 square kilometers somewhat smaller than Pohnpei. Fringing reefs encase its narrow coastal flats, but Kosrae lacks a lagoon. Fertile volcanic soils support an agroforest subsistence system with breadfruit as the staple and significant plantings of giant swamp taro (*Cyrtosperma chamissonis*) under the orchard canopy.[46] Politically, the island is divided into four districts, each corresponding to a major drainage basin. At initial contact with Europeans in 1824, a single paramount chief controlled Kosrae, under whom subchiefs managed individual land units called *facl*, which ran from the mountains to the reef.[47] The contact

population of Kosrae is debated, as it is with the majority of Pacific islands (see Chapter 9). Most estimates have ranged around 3,000 persons, but these probably underestimate the maximum population prior to the ravages of European-introduced disease; a figure of 6,000 may be more accurate (Ritter 1981).

In 1824, *La Coquille* under the command of Louis Duperrey arrived off the eastern coast of Kosrae. The French explorers were taken to a remarkable stone-walled "city" situated on the point of a small islet named Lelu, capital and chiefly center of the Kosrae polity. In the words of First Officer Dumont d'Urville: "As we approached the shores of Lelu, a new scene presented itself to us: beautiful houses enclosed by high walls, well-paved streets, and on the beach was gathered the entire population of Lelu, at least 800 people, who had come to be present at our disembarkation" (quoted in Cordy 1993:54). The French could hardly believe the scale of construction, as remarked by the ship's doctor, René Lesson: "We observed with total bewilderment a wall, composed of blocks, of truly cyclopean size, and we wondered how and why they had been able to erect such masses to a 15 foot height. The elegant houses of these islanders lined the streets on elevated mounds" (in Cordy 1993:55). A view of these houses from a later Russian expedition is shown in Figure 6.20.

Similar to Nan Madol in its construction on a reef flat, the presence of canals, and its megalithic construction, yet different in other important details, Lelu was the residence of the paramount Kosrae chief and of the *facl* subchiefs who were required to live with him. Fortunately, much ethnographic information about Lelu and its occupants was obtained from the visits not only of *La Coquille* but also of later European ships, such as that of the Russian explorer Fyedor Lütke in 1827.[48] By the late nineteenth century, Kosrae

FIGURE 6.20 A residential compound at Lelu, Kosrae, as recorded during the early nineteenth-century Russian visit of Lütke. (From Lütke 1835.)

was severely depopulated, the traditional socio-political structure had collapsed, and Lelu had become an abandoned ruin.

In its newly ruined state, Lelu was visited by F. W. Christian (1899) in the mid-1890s, and he drew the first map of the site. In 1909–10, the German Südsee Expedition explored Kosrae, and Paul Hambruch (1919) accurately mapped the ruins and excavated in some of the tombs, while Ernst Sarfert (1919–20) obtained much additional "salvage" ethnographic material. These early studies have been expanded in recent years with a thorough survey by Cordy (1985a, 1993) and deep stratigraphic excavations by Athens (ed., 1995), which yielded early CST pottery at the base of

several residential compounds. Morgan (1988) describes the site from an architect's viewpoint.

The ruins of Lelu, covering 27 hectares, are made up of a series of walled compounds, most of which were residential, but some of which contain tombs. A canal traverses the center of the site: "Navigable throughout at high tide, the canal system gave maritime access to many of the compounds and numerous boat landings. Tribute of food and goods from the land sections on Kosrae were brought by boat to Leluh daily" (Morgan 1988:97). Excavations by Cordy and Athens, and the radiocarbon dates they obtained, outline a sequence for the construction of Lelu, as shown in Figure 6.21. Initial occupation or use of the area

Lelu: A.D. 1250-1400

Lelu: A.D. 1400-1600

Lelu: A.D. 1600-1650

Lelu: A.D. 1650-1800

FIGURE 6.21 The construction sequence for the Lelu site, as determined by Ross Cordy. (After Cordy 1993.)

around the first century A.D. is indicated by the early pottery, and it is possible that there was a stilt-house village in this vicinity. However, construction of the artificial islets and walled compounds did not commence until about A.D. 1250–1400, in the Finlas sector. From A.D. 1400–1600 there was a major building effort, with two components. One set of compounds (the Finbota to Katem area) was built using stacked prismatic basalt walls, while a western extension on the north end of the island was also constructed. Walls enclosing the Kinyeir and Lurun compounds rose to heights of 6 meters. This left an open space in the middle of the site, which was filled in during the next phase from about A.D. 1600 to 1650. A change in construction style ensued, incorporating rounded basalt boulders, and with walls constructed to heights as great as 4–5 meters. Finally, the remaining compounds were constructed from A.D. 1650 to 1800, using mixed coral stones and with low wall height (1–1.4 m).

Lelu, which required a great deal of labor to build and which also evinces centralized planning, holds a key to understanding the development of a complex chiefdom polity on Kosrae. Cordy (1993) proposed a model for the evolution of Kosraen society in which an older (pre–A.D. 1000) system with only two social strata (local chiefs and commoners) was first transformed through district-level unification and the addition of a third tier. Finally, through islandwide consolidation, a fourth tier was imposed, that of the island paramount. Cordy links this final change to the period of greatest construction at Lelu, between A.D. 1400 and 1600. Cordy sees population growth leading to resource imbalance, combined with competition between district-level polities, as key processes underlying these sociopolitical changes. In his own words:

I suggest that certain areas included more land (e.g., a larger valley) enabling the growth of a larger population center and thus providing more warriors. Such areas would have advantages in competing society situations and could eventually incorporate neighbors (through conquest, marriage, etc.). As geographic area would increase, local chiefs needed to supervise (to collect information for the ruler and to disseminate information for the ruler). This need for a lower decision-making level would lead to three strata (ruler, local chief, and commoner).

I suggest some of these "district" society areas would also have more contiguous flat, fertile land, enabling greater populations to build up. Lelu and Utwe particularly fit this pattern. Population imbalances among the competing "district" societies would in turn be critical factors in war. I suggest they tipped the balance in favor of Utwe and Lelu, and finally in favor of Lelu. With island-wide conquest, territorial and population sizes would increase requiring three decision-making levels (king, high chiefs controlling many [facl], their managers controlling individual [facl]). Accordingly, four [social] strata would form. (Cordy 1993:259)

Cordy calls his model a "competition hypothesis" in which "population imbalances" are the key variable leading to territorial conquest, a model in many respects similar to one proposed by Peoples (1990). Ueki (1990, Fig. 2) advances a similar model for the evolution of Kosraen society and social stratification, in which "population size and density increase" triggered an "increase in complexity of land management" on the one hand, and simultaneously an "increase in competition over rights to land and sea." The latter in turn led to conflict and territorial conquest, and ultimately the "emergence or appointment of a new managerial class."

A definitive test of the Cordy-Peoples-Ueki model requires evidence from sites other than Lelu itself; a broad settlement-pattern approach

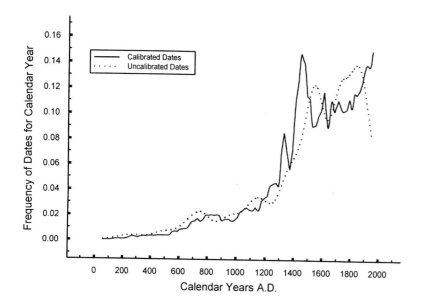

FIGURE 6.22 Radiocarbon frequency distribution for Kosrae Island. (After Athens 1995.)

throughout Kosrae is necessary. Ueki (1990: 311–12) discusses some limited evidence of this kind, based on a survey in the Utwa Valley, where he identified the Nefalil site as a district-level center dating to between A.D. 940 and 1470. Athens's (ed., 1995) landscape archaeology approach also provides evidence to test the Kosrae model, with evidence for population growth and for agricultural intensification and changing patterns of land use. Based on 109 radiocarbon dates from Kosrae Island, Athens derived a cumulative frequency plot of the calibrated age probabilities (Fig. 6.22). While such a plot does not *directly* track human population numbers, it may reflect general occupation density over a landscape. Athens observes that "the earliest inflection point [in the curve] just after 500 A.D. is interpreted to represent the first indication that population is starting to grow on the main island. This rate of growth continues, with perhaps something of a spurt about 800 A.D., until about A.D. 1200. At A.D. 1200 the frequency of radiocarbon dates increases sharply, suggesting a rapidly growing population" (1995:27). The fit

between this proxy population curve and the Lelu construction chronology is remarkably good, with the major inflection in the curve and the onset of megalithic construction both occurring around A.D. 1200–1300. This finding offers strong support for population growth playing an important role in the transformation of Kosrae society.

External influence possibly affected the course of sociopolitical evolution on Kosrae. Several scholars have pointed to similarities between Nan Madol and Lelu, suggesting that there was a connection between the two groups of people responsible for their construction. For example, the mythical Isokelekel—overthrower of the Saudeleur dynasty of Nan Madol—has been identified in some sources as coming from Kosrae. But the name used for Isokelekel's homeland in the Pohnpei traditions is "Katau," which refers to a mythical "sky world" and not to any particular island. Indeed, Goodenough suggests that if anything, the direction of influence may have been the other way around: "If the massive stone structures at Lele on Kosrae have any connection with those of Nan Madol on Ponape, the direction of influence must have been . . . from Ponape, perhaps along with the introduction of kava drinking" (1986:562). Now that construction chronologies have been archaeologically determined for the two sites, this scenario seems more likely, since the major construction phase at Lelu lags behind that at Nan Madol by one to two centuries. Hence in addition to internal demographic and social pressures within Kosrae itself, there may have been external connections between Kosrae and Pohnpei that played some role in Kosrae's history of sociopolitical transformation. Certainly the possibility cannot be wholly discounted.[49]

Chuuk　The third and final high island within the Carolines, Chuuk poses a striking contrast to Pohnpei and Kosrae, exhibiting none of the megalithic architecture or other material manifestations of stratified, complex chiefdoms found in the latter two islands. Ethnographically, Chuuk society was not strongly hierarchical and had a low degree of political integration. Peoples (1990:294) points out that the typical autonomous political unit in Chuuk was small, about 0.8 square kilometer in area and containing perhaps 100 people; there were many such units distributed throughout the islands of Chuuk Lagoon. Archaeological evidence supports the idea that this kind of system also was in place in prehistory. As King and Parker write, "We see no evidence in the archaeological record known thus far to indicate that efforts to impose a three or four strata society in Truk, if they occurred, were ever successful" (1984:456). What one does clearly see in the Chuuk archaeological record is the pervasiveness of raiding and interpolity warfare, manifested in numerous forts and in residential sites situated in naturally defensive positions (Rainbird 1996).

Why did Chuuk society not follow the same kinds of pathways of sociopolitical change leading to increasing integration and hierarchy that we see in Pohnpei and Kosrae? Peoples (1990) suggests that the answer lies in Chuuk's geography of many small, dispersed islands rather than one larger island, which permitted defeated groups simply to flee to another island. "The warring 'mini-chiefdom' stage persisted on Truk because no [one] chiefdom was in a position to permanently incorporate and subordinate its neighbors. Losing groups had other choices as well as a chance to acquire allies on other islands for a reconquest" (Peoples 1990:298). Moreover, due to the small size and resource limitations of the individual Chuuk high islands, none ever amassed a critically large population base.

CHAPTER 7

Polynesia

Origins and Dispersals

Earlier historical theories explained diversity in Polynesia from diffusion—from supposed waves of immigrants, each bringing in new cultural traditions and new levels of complexity; all present evidence, whether from genetics, linguistics, or culture, including ethnology and archaeology, converges towards the conclusion that the major Polynesian diversities have arisen from internal differentiation.

Goldman (1970:xxiii)

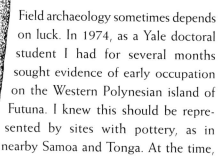

Field archaeology sometimes depends on luck. In 1974, as a Yale doctoral student I had for several months sought evidence of early occupation on the Western Polynesian island of Futuna. I knew this should be represented by sites with pottery, as in nearby Samoa and Tonga. At the time, however, Pacific archaeologists lacked the nuanced understanding they now possess regarding the dynamism of islands, including effects of sea-level change, or accelerated erosion and deposition resulting from shifting cultivation, which can bury or obliterate sites (see Chapter 2). Following conventional survey strategies, I had meticulously searched likely localities, such as beach terraces, for early sites, but I was having no success in realizing my goal.

One Sunday, the Futunan family with whom I resided decided to have a picnic at Tavai on the island's northwest coast, an abandoned village where the fishing is good and where people raise pigs. The morning passed pleasantly as we speared octopus and gathered *'alili* mollusks on the reef flats, and prepared the *umu*, or earth oven. Around midday, waiting for the oven to render its contents "from raw to cooked," as my companions settled down on the sand for a nap, I sauntered along the beachfront, again looking for signs of prehistoric occupation. To my amazement, a short distance up the beach from where we were camped I began to encounter potsherds. As far as I could ascertain, these were not eroding out of the beach terrace (where I had expected to find them) but became more frequent as I approached the mouth of a small stream that had deeply incised itself into the coastal plain.

Wading up the little creek with its steep banks cut into the volcanic clay, I kept tracing the potsherds in the stream bottom, hoping to locate the in situ context from which they were eroding. The channel became narrower and deeper, choked with rotten *Hibiscus* branches and debris, until, nearly 250 meters from the beachfront where my friends were listlessly resting, I detected the top of a distinctly blackish layer at the base of the bank, capped by thick reddish-brown clay. Pulling debris aside, I saw that this layer was indeed the source of the many potsherds I had been stuffing into my pockets. Needless to say, the contentment I felt that evening had as much to do with my discovery up the muddy little creek as with the delicious feast we later enjoyed on the beach as the afternoon stretched languorously into a glorious Pacific sunset.

Over the next few weeks, I returned to Tavai to excavate properly a *sondage* 3.5 meters deep into the creek bank, revealing the potsherd-rich occupation layer buried under 2.5 meters of alluvium (Fig. 7.1). Radiocarbon samples would later date the Tavai site (FU-11) to about 200 B.C. My work at Tavai was significant in two respects. First, it brought home to me how dramatically island landscapes can change in only a few thousand years, with a beachfront village at the end of the first millennium B.C. now deeply buried under tons of alluvium, invisible save for the little stream that had literally cut a window into the past. This revelation inspired me, in later expeditions, to take a fresh perspective on the geoarchaeology of Pacific sites.[1] Second, Tavai occupies a critical niche in the prehistory of Polynesia, for it represents the time at which a distinct "Ancestral Polynesian" culture emerged out of its Lapita predecessor. Along with similar sites dating to the late first millennium B.C., Tavai provides essential evidence for the development of Polynesian culture in the Western Polynesian "homeland" region.

Polynesian Origins

This view that the Polynesian homeland lies within the Polynesian Triangle itself, in the region of the Tongan and Samoan archipelagoes (along with Futuna and 'Uvea), contradicts that held by generations of earlier scholars (see Chapter 1). Throughout the nineteenth century and on into the first half of the twentieth, researchers had sought to resolve the "problem of Polynesian origins" by searching for some *external* homeland, usually in Asia, or in the case of some theorizers, in the Americas.[2] Te Rangi Hiroa, for example, believed that the Polynesian "Vikings of the Sunrise" had migrated in substantial fleets out from an Asiatic homeland, passing through Micronesia to enter the Polynesian Triangle via Samoa and on to the Society Islands, the "hub" of the Triangle (Hiroa 1938a; see Chapter 1). Most scholars agreed with some version of Hiroa's thesis, including an Asiatic homeland, although a few, such as Thor Heyerdahl (1952), believed that the Polynesians had originated in the Americas, with separate migrations from the Northwest Coast to Hawai'i, and from Peru to Easter Island and the southeastern archipelagoes. What all of these theories had in common was a notion of Polynesian culture as preexisting in all its essential elements in some other region of the world—to either side of the Pacific basin—at an earlier point in time.[3] Little consideration was given to the possibility that Polynesian cultures had developed within the Pacific; instead, one or more migrations were invoked to bring Polynesians into the Pacific, and culture change was thought to be the result of an overlaying of successive waves of migration.[4]

The discovery of Lapita, and the tracing of continuous archaeological sequences within Western

FIGURE 7.1 More than 2.5 meters of alluvium had to be removed before the early Polynesian occupation level at Tavai, Futuna (site FU-11) could be reached. (Photo by P. V. Kirch.)

Polynesia that begin with Lapita and emerge as typically Polynesian in their material culture, totally altered these older migrationist theories. Kenneth Emory, originally schooled in the migrationist paradigm, later in his career grasped the significance of the new archaeological finds from Fiji, Tonga, and Samoa when he wrote that the origins of the Polynesians would be found "in a western archipelago in the Polynesian area about 1500 B.C." (1959:34). As Jack Golson, Roger Green, and their students began to excavate in Samoa and Tonga in the late 1950s and 1960s, they uncovered evidence that distinctly "Polynesian" cultural traits had emerged within these archipelagoes over more than a thousand years. Green summarized this new understanding of Polynesian origins: "Thus there never was a Polynesian migration from elsewhere; becoming Polynesian took place

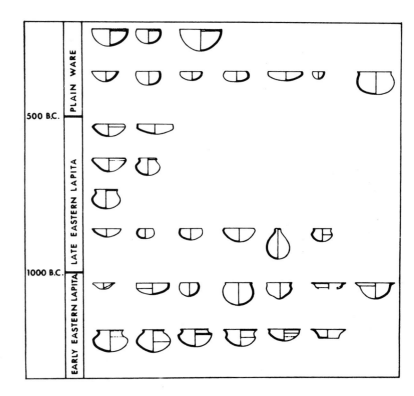

FIGURE 7.2 The gradual transition from Early Eastern Lapita to Polynesian Plain Ware ceramics took place over more than one millennium. This diagram shows changes in vessel forms. (Courtesy Roger C. Green.)

in Polynesia itself as the archaeology of Tonga and Samoa over the last 3,000 years readily attests. One begins with Eastern Lapita, and ends with Polynesian" (1967a:237).

The dispersal of some groups of Lapita pottery-making peoples from the southeastern Solomons and/or northern Vanuatu, across the 850-kilometer water gap and on into the Fiji archipelago, occurred around 1200–1000 B.C. (see Chapter 4). While Fiji was the first archipelago encountered in this Eastern Lapita expansion, the Lau Islands and then the Tongan archipelago were also quickly discovered, explored, and colonized. Samoa too was settled by around 1000 B.C., as were the isolated islands of Futuna, 'Uvea, and Niuatoputapu. The similarities in Early Eastern Lapita ceramics on all of these islands, as well as direct evidence for transport of obsidian, chert, and stone adzes between communities, reveal a network of con-

tinuing communication between these newly founded settlements.[5] Over time, however, "breaks" in this chain of Lapita communities arose, first between Fiji and Tonga, and later between Tonga and Samoa.[6] Such breaks were not final or absolute, for interaction between the peoples of the Fiji-Tonga-Samoa region continued throughout prehistory. But sufficient isolation developed during the first millennium B.C. that we can detect localized variation, especially in ceramics (Kirch 1988a). Out of such partial isolation, combined with adaptation to new environmental and social conditions, a distinctively Polynesian culture emerged.

The pottery sequences of Western Polynesia demonstrate that the later Polynesian cultures developed gradually out of their Eastern Lapita ancestor, as seen in changes in vessel forms (Fig. 7.2). The ceramics from Tavai in Futuna provide an important link, a phase between the Early Eastern Lapita assemblages, which still retain distinctive dentate-stamped designs, and the later Polynesian Plain Ware ceramics, which have no decoration and consist only of thickware bowls.[7] But change is also apparent in the gradual development of Polynesian adz forms out of Lapita prototypes, in part as a response to the need to produce adzes from the tough basalt stone found exclusively on such high islands as 'Uvea and Samoa.[8] Other aspects of material culture, such as shell ornaments and fishing gear, show continuity. In short, the branch of Oceanic-speaking peoples whom we designate as Polynesians had their origins in the Eastern Lapita expansion, to become distinctly Polynesian during the course of the first millennium B.C., within the archipelagoes of Western Polynesia. Here, in Tonga and Samoa and their close neighbors like Futuna, is the immediate Polynesian homeland—what generations of later Polynesian peoples would call, in their myths and traditions, *Havaiki.*[9]

Polynesia as a Phyletic Unit

Although Dumont d'Urville subdivided the Oceanic peoples into "Polynesian," "Melanesian," and "Micronesian" in his early-nineteenth-century scheme (see Chapter 1), only Polynesia has stood the test of time as *a meaningful unit for culture-historical analysis.* Melanesia is a geographic space whose human history is exceedingly complex, extending back in time 36,000 years or more, incorporating peoples of highly diverse origins, genetic makeup, linguistic affiliation, and cultural patterns. It makes no sense whatsoever to speak of a unified "Melanesian culture," for the peoples and cultures of Melanesia are strongly *multiphyletic.*[10] Micronesia does not have the same degree of complexity, but even there we find peoples speaking languages from two major subgroups

of the Austronesian family (Oceanic and Western Malayo-Polynesian), and at least four population movements into the region can be identified linguistically and archaeologically. Only in Polynesia do we find a robust grouping, one that is meaningful in terms of a set of peoples and cultures *who share a common history.*[11] That is to say, all of the Polynesian cultures known ethnographically (and the languages spoken by them) have arguably derived from a common ancestral culture (and proto-language) over a period of about 2,500 years (Kirch and Green 1987, in press). It is in this sense that one can speak of Polynesia as a *phyletic* unit, a "segment of cultural history" to which a *phylogenetic approach* to historical anthropology may properly be applied.[12]

That the Polynesians constitute a phylogenetic unity—in which the various Polynesian groups are all more closely related to each other than to any external population—was first recognized from their languages. Beginning with Captain James Cook, astute explorers remarked on the similarity of languages as far-flung as New Zealand Maori, Rapanui, and Hawaiian. Lieutenant King of H.M.S. *Resolution* put lexical evidence to the fore when he wrote that "the same language . . . hardly requires any other proof of those who speak it being the same people, and originating from the same country" (Beaglehole 1967:1392). J. R. Forster, naturalist on Cook's second voyage, was more systematic in his observations, publishing a "comparative table of the various languages in the isles of the South-Sea" (Forster 1996 [1778]:188–89). Today we would not call Rapanui, Maori, and Hawaiian a *single* language; rather, we regard them as *closely related* languages sharing a high degree of cognate vocabulary, as well as similar patterns of syntax. But it was precisely this relatedness of speech that allowed Cook, King, Banks, and other early observers to recognize that the Polynesian languages were all of one "stock."

Exhaustive linguistic research, especially in the latter part of the twentieth century, has borne fruit in a fine-grained understanding of the *subgrouping* or internal relationships of the Polynesian languages. Although refinements continue to be made, the linguistic phylogeny for Polynesian has been well understood for some time, since the pioneering work of Biggs, Green, and Pawley.[13] As a group, the 36 extant or recorded Polynesian languages[14] are most closely related to Fijian and Rotuman, with which they form the next higher-order subgroup of Oceanic languages, Central Pacific. Proto Central-Pacific must have been the language spoken by the Eastern Lapita colonists of the Fiji-Tonga-Samoa area, and at first it would have formed a continuous dialect chain throughout this region. Fairly quickly, however, "weak links" where speech communication was less frequent led to sound and word changes across the dialect chain, and Proto Central-Pacific began to differentiate into distinct Proto Fijic and Proto Tokalau-Polynesian languages (Geraghty 1983). Continued change within the latter linkage would lead to successive language interstages within the Tonga-Samoa region.

Figure 7.3 shows the internal relationships of the extant Polynesian languages, graphed as a tree. Two points relevant to prehistory are evident. First, all known Polynesian languages can be traced back to the Proto Polynesian interstage, confirming on linguistic grounds that we are dealing with a monophyletic unit. Second, the branching structure of the tree provides a kind of model for successive stages in the differentiation of Polynesian subgroups. While the early split of Proto Polynesian into Proto Tongic and Proto Nuclear Polynesian branches must have occurred within the Western Polynesian homeland, subsequent splits in the tree presumably occurred as populations expanded out of this core region,

specifically into the central Eastern Polynesian area, and later into more distant and isolated islands and archipelagoes. Of course, this model must be *independently* tested against the evidence of archaeology if it is to provide a basis for historical reconstruction.

One must be careful not to overinterpret such a linguistic tree, deriving implications that are not valid. For example, that there are two main branches of Eastern Polynesian—Tahitic and Marquesic—tells us that at an early stage in the settlement of the Eastern Polynesian region there was some differentiation—presumably along geographic lines—between two speech communities that may at first have been part of a continuous and interacting dialect chain. What does *not* necessarily follow is that these communities were located in Tahiti and the Marquesas, respectively. They could have been situated in *any* of the islands where Tahitic or Marquesic languages are currently spoken, or distributed across several of these. Thus the "homeland" of the Marquesic languages (including Mangarevan and old Rapan) could as likely have been in Mangareva or the Austral chain as in the Marquesas. (Later in this chapter I shall advance just such a proposition.) Overinterpretation of linguistic evidence has led some archaeologists to be skeptical of linguistic models; yet, properly used, such models offer a powerful source of historical hypotheses that may be tested on independently constituted archaeological data.

To return to the issue of Polynesia as a robust phyletic grouping, the skeptic may point to the anthropological truism that "race" (i.e., biology), language, and culture are independent and need not covary. Simply because a historical unity can be established for the Polynesian languages does not mean, a priori, that the populations who speak those languages share common origins. Let

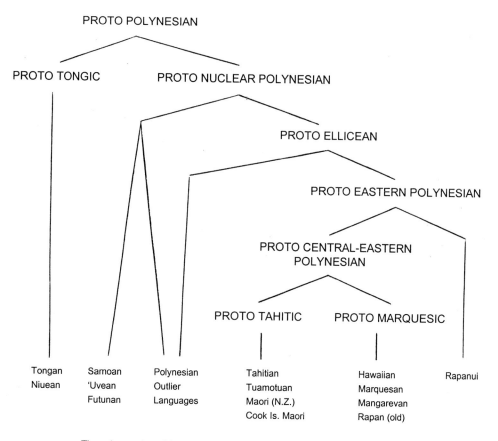

FIGURE 7.3 The subgrouping of the Polynesian languages. (After Marck 1999.)

us briefly consider the evidence of biological anthropology. The homogeneity of Polynesian populations has long been noted. Morphologically, despite variation, many features denote a common Polynesian phenotype, such as large body size and a high incidence of the "rocker jaw" and of a strongly "pentagonally" shaped cranium (Houghton 1996). Studies using both metrical and nonmetrical traits, measured on living Polynesians as well as on skeletal populations, yield statistical groupings in which Polynesian samples consistently link more closely with each other than with external populations.[15] One example is

shown in Figure 7.4. Recent genetic studies, including mitochondrial DNA sequencing, reinforce this homogeneity within the Polynesian genotype.[16] A well-documented example is the extremely high frequency among all Polynesians of a characteristic 9-base-pair deletion in their mtDNA. The likely explanation for this high degree of biological homogeneity—reflected both phenotypically and genotypically—is that the parental population from which all Polynesian groups derive went through a "bottleneck" associated with the initial colonization of Fiji and Western Polynesia (Kelly 1996; Martinson 1996;

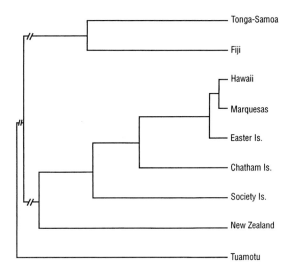

FIGURE 7.4 A dendrogram of Polynesian biological populations, based on anthropometric analysis, mirrors the Western-Eastern Polynesian division suggested by linguistic and cultural comparison. (From Pietrusewsky 1996.)

Martinson et al. 1993). This genetic bottleneck resulted from the well-known "founder effect."[17] In short, biological evidence reinforces the linguistic model of a robust phyletic grouping for the Polynesian populations.[18]

Turning to comparative ethnography—a third line of independent evidence—one finds that the historically documented Polynesian cultures share a core set of systemic cultural patterns also indicating descent from a common ancestor. Marshall Sahlins, in a now-classic comparative analysis of Polynesian cultures, invoked a biological metaphor when he wrote that "the Polynesian cultures derive from a common source; they are members of a single cultural genus that has filled in and adapted to a variety of local habitats" (Sahlins 1958:ix). Common systemic patterns include the basic kinds of social groups (the *kainanga* and the *kainga*) and land tenure patterns,

the concepts of *mana* and *tapu*, cosmogonic origin myths, and the ubiquitous presence of hereditary chiefs (all called by some variant of the word *ariki*), as well as more prosaic aspects of material culture (Burrows 1938).

Arguments adduced from the independent evidence of linguistics, biological anthropology, and comparative ethnography converge on an interpretation of Polynesia as a phyletic unit, in which the region's modern languages, populations, and cultures descended from a common proto-language, parental population, and ancestral culture. Differentiation out of this ancestral group occurred over two and a half millennia, resulting from geographic expansion out of an original homeland and from a variety of evolutionary processes and historical contingencies (Kirch 1984a; Kirch and Green 1987). Archaeology positions the primary geographic homeland of the parental population in the Tonga-Samoa archipelagoes and their smaller neighbors, including Futuna, 'Uvea, and Niuatoputapu. It also specifies the time of the emergence of the ancestral culture out of Early Eastern Lapita: the middle of the first millennium B.C.

Western and Eastern Polynesia, referred to previously, require formal definition, for they have much historical significance. The distinction was first critically examined by Edwin G. Burrows (1938), who noted that aspects of material culture, systemic social structures, and religious beliefs displayed consistent geographic distributions, with one group incorporating Tonga, Samoa, Futuna, 'Uvea, and Tokelau (Western Polynesia), the other encompassing both the central and the marginal islands, such as the Societies, Cooks, Australs, Marquesas, Tuamotus, Hawai'i, Easter Island, and New Zealand (Eastern Polynesia). In religion, for example, the Eastern Polynesian cultures share a pantheon of first-order, functionally differentiated, anthropomorphic gods—including Tane, Tu,

Rongo, and Tangaloa—whereas only one of these (Tangaloa) is known in Western Polynesia (Marck 1999). Similarly, the *marae* as a formal temple with enclosed court and raised altar (*ahu*) is exclusively an Eastern Polynesian phenomenon; in Western Polynesia the *malae* is an open-air assembly area.[19] From his systematic ethnographic comparisons, Burrows inferred that this east-west division among Polynesian cultures encapsulates the essentials of history, with the Western Polynesian cultures being those that developed in the region of the Polynesian homeland, and the Eastern Polynesian cultures those deriving from later migration and expansion out of that homeland. Archaeology has now confirmed this.

That the Eastern Polynesian cultures share many traits, as well as innovations in language, indicates that there was similarly an Eastern Polynesian homeland prior to the settlement of the more remote archipelagoes, where these innovations were developed. Such an Eastern Polynesian homeland need not have been a single island or even archipelago, and it could have encompassed most of the tropical core of central Eastern Polynesia, given extensive interisland voyaging and communication (Rolett 1996; Walter 1996). Evidence for such voyaging is now emerging in the form of artifacts, especially basalt adzes, that can be traced to particular source localities.[20]

The divergence of the Polynesian cultures from a common ancestor does not imply that cultural change within the region occurred solely as a result of successive "branchings," or that increasing isolation was invariably the agent of change. Linguists can demonstrate borrowing between languages, the result of contact between speech communities (Marck 1999). Likewise, oral traditions and ethnohistoric as well as archaeological evidence indicate some long-distance contacts between islands and archipelagoes at various times in prehistory and proto-history (Weisler,

ed., 1997). Such contacts were sometimes significant, as in Tonga, where the proto-historic polity relied on a prestige-good economy of long-distance exchange to reinforce its hegemony. But contrary to detractors of the "phylogenetic model," the existence of interisland linkages does not obviate Polynesia's basic phyletic structure, nor does it require a "tangled bank" metaphor for cultural history.

Ancestral Polynesia

As a phyletic unit, Polynesia is well suited to a "methodological framework for phylogenetic analysis of cultural groups, that is, a method for inferring cultural history . . . , establishing phylogeny, and permitting the disentanglement of homology [common origins of a trait] from analogy [independent origins of a trait]" (Kirch and Green 1987:434). A key aspect of the phylogenetic approach is a "triangulation" method, in which independent lines of evidence from historical linguistics, comparative ethnology, archaeology, and biological anthropology are applied to the reconstruction of an ancestral stage in the history of a group of related cultures (Kirch and Green, in press). To use a simple example, we could infer the presence of stone adzes in Ancestral Polynesia solely from the ubiquitous distribution of such adzes in all Polynesian cultures as ethnographically documented, assuming therefore that the use of stone adzes was a *homologous* trait, a matter of shared inheritance. But it is possible to cross-check this inference, first by using the comparative method of historical linguistics to reconstruct a Proto Polynesian word for adz, **toki*, from at least 30 cognates in contemporary Polynesian languages (e.g., Hawaiian *ko'i*, Tahitian *to'i*, or Tongan *toki*). Moreover, the archaeological record for this time period has produced numerous adz specimens, primarily of a type with a plano-convex cross section. By combining all three lines of evidence, not only can we be confident that the early Polynesians used stone adzes, we can also know the word used for these objects and their precise morphology.

Not all aspects of culture are supported by all of these lines of evidence. In the case of early Polynesian religious beliefs, there are no archaeological data (except the negative evidence of the absence of formal temple structures), and the triangulation method must rely primarily on linguistic and comparative ethnographic data. Despite such limitations, by using the triangulation method—within a phylogenetic model in which the internal relationships of the descendant cultures have been specified—it is feasible to produce cultural histories that are more detailed and nuanced than what could be achieved relying exclusively on archaeological data.

Green and Kirch (in press) apply a phylogenetic model and the triangulation method to Ancestral Polynesian culture and its constituent societies. Ancestral Polynesian culture was shared by people who inhabited the Western Polynesian homeland (Tonga, Samoa, Futuna, 'Uvea, Niuatoputapu) from the middle to the end of the first millennium B.C., and who spoke Proto Polynesian. We use the plural *societies* because a number of geographically localized communities had certainly emerged by this time. Because these societies were in regular communication through interisland voyaging, linguistic and cultural innovations were mostly shared. Archaeologically, more than 25 sites dating to this time period have been identified (Fig. 7.5), each representing a social community. All are small hamlets or villages, situated on or near the coast, although inland settlements also existed, as in the Falefa Valley on 'Upolu, Samoa.

Ancestral Polynesian communities were supported by much the same mixed horticultural-maritime economy as their Lapita ancestors, culti-

FIGURE 7.5 Excavation through a large earthen mound (SU-Va-2) at Vailele, 'Upolu Island, Western Samoa. (Photo courtesy Roger C. Green.)

vating tuber and root crops, including taro and yams, and tree crops such as coconut, breadfruit, bananas, vi apple, and Tahitian Chestnut. We have no evidence—archaeological or linguistic—for large-scale canal or pondfield irrigation at this early date, but there is good lexical evidence for shifting cultivation. Most likely, shifting cultivation was used for field crops such as taro, yams, and bananas, while tree crops were planted in and around villages and along coastal plains. These early Polynesians kept pigs, dogs, and chickens, but only chickens are well represented in the archaeological deposits. Fish and shellfish provided most of the protein in the Ancestral Polynesian diet, augmented by hunting or catching birds. Linguistic reconstructions indicate a wide range of fishing methods, as well as more than 150 terms for different kinds of fish (Clark 1991; Hooper 1994).

Ancestral Polynesian material culture included ubiquitous plain ware pottery (largely simple bowls

FIGURE 7.6 Artifacts from Ancestral Polynesian sites include simple *Turbo*-shell fishhooks, *Conus*-shell rings and beads, sea urchin abraders, adzes of *Tridacna* shell, hammerstones with pecked finger grips, and simple flake tools of obsidian. The assemblage shown here is from excavations on Niuatoputapu Island. (Photo by P. V. Kirch.)

and cups), adzes of *Tridacna* shell and (increasingly over time) of basalt, one-piece fishhooks of *Turbo* shell, beads and rings of *Conus* shell, hammerstones, files or abraders of sea-urchin spine and of coral or pumice, and amorphous scrapers or other ad hoc tools made from flakes of basalt or obsidian (Fig. 7.6). A great deal of this material culture, being made of wood or vegetable fibers, did not preserve in the archaeological record.

The triangulation method permits us to enumerate much of the missing inventory, even though we have no examples from excavations.[21] Entering an Ancestral Polynesian dwelling, one might have expected to find mats woven from coconut and *Pandanus* leaves, wooden bowls and containers, coconut water bottles, baskets, and clothing (loincloths and skirts) made from paper mulberry bark (*Broussonetia papyrifera*) and other plants. Fishing gear stored among the rafters included lines and poles, and several kinds of nets made from *Pipturus* bark cordage. Gardeners used digging sticks (which often doubled as coconut-husking poles) and transported the harvest back to their cookhouses with carrying poles. Dwellings and cookhouses alike were fashioned with timber posts and rafters, with thatch from sago palm or other kinds of leaves (such as *Pandanus*). Fleshing out the full range of Ancestral Polynesian material culture using the triangulation method, one becomes acutely aware of the limitations of any archaeological sample.

With respect to kinship, social organization, and religion, the archaeological record is largely mute, demanding that we rely on the Proto Polynesian lexical reconstructions, aided by comparative ethnography to flesh out specific semantic history hypotheses (Dyen 1985; Green 1994). Nonetheless, we can infer a good deal about these archaeologically invisible aspects of Ancestral Polynesian culture. Marck (1999), for example, has reconstructed Proto Polynesian kinship, informing us that relatives were classified principally on a generational basis, and that birth order (i.e., senior/junior distinctions) and gender distinctions were significant. The primary social group in Ancestral Polynesia was denoted by the word *kainanga* (recall that the asterisk denotes a reconstructed term), which indicated a unilineal descent group whose members traced their lineage back to a founding ancestor (*tupunga*). At the head of such a *kainanga* was the *qariki, probably in most cases a senior (ranking) male, who served as the group's secular and ritual leader.[22] Nothing suggests, at this early stage in the development of Polynesian societies, a separate status category of priest. There are, however, special terms for an expert or knowledgeable craftsperson (*tufunga), sea expert or navigator (*tautai), and warrior (*toa). A lower-level social group was the *kainga, a co-residential group holding an estate of land as well as other tangible and intangible property and rights.

While ethnographic cognates of the term *qariki (such as Hawaiian *ali'i) are associated in proto-historic Polynesian societies with chiefship, we cannot naively project back onto Ancestral Polynesian societies a notion of complex social stratification or rigid hierarchy. Rather, simple ranking based on the hereditary principle of seniority (birth order) seems to have been key, and given the small size of these communities (as indicated by the archaeological settlements), it is reasonable to think of them as *heterarchical* rather than hierarchical.[23] Nonetheless, subtle differences in ranking and access to resources by different *kainga and *kainanga and their leaders provided the structural basis for the evolution of hierarchy and stratification once large and dense populations had developed on particular islands, and after competition for land and resources intensified. This is an issue taken up in Chapter 8.

What of Ancestral Polynesian religious concepts, their calendar, and their ritual cycle? The pan-Polynesian concepts of *tapu (sacredness) and *mana (spiritual power) were central to their belief system (Shore 1989). *Mana flowed to this world from the spirit world, particularly via the efficacy of ancestors (*tupuna); indeed, ancestors were arguably at the core of Ancestral Polynesian ritual life. Functionally diversified anthropomorphic gods—such as Tane, Tu, and Rongo, so well known from Eastern Polynesian societies (e.g., Hawaiian Lono)—had not yet been invented, for these were decidedly a later, early Eastern Polynesian innovation, accompanied by changes in ritual architecture and the beginnings of a formal priesthood. Only Tangaloa seems to have been known as a deity to the Ancestral Polynesians, and his import is not clear. They also told tales of a culture hero, Maui, who performed magical feats to do with bringing order—and culture—into the world.[24]

Ritual activity in Ancestral Polynesian communities was most likely conducted in a house (*fare) much like an ordinary dwelling—perhaps the residence of the *qariki or ritual elder—and on an open, cleared space (called the *malaqe) to the seaward side of that house. Either key posts within the house or simple upright stones placed around the perimeter of the *malaqe, or both, represented specific ancestors or spirits, to whom prayers and invocations were directed. Deceased ancestors were probably buried beneath the house floor. The psychoactive kava plant (Piper methysticum), domesticated in Vanuatu and likely brought to the Western Polynesian homeland by the first Lapita colonizers, certainly played a role in Ancestral Polynesian ritual, presumably because it induced a trancelike state among those who partook of it.[25] We can only guess about other ceremonies, although there are at least ten Proto Polynesian words for kinds of ritual, prayer, and rite. There is a hint of an important ceremonial feast, perhaps a first-fruits ritual. The year itself was organized around a lunar calendar of thirteen months, indexed to the rising and setting of the star cluster Pleiades (*Mata-liki) and to the annual spawning of the reproductive segments of a sea-worm, the *palolo. The lunar month names are concerned in large part with an annual ecological rhythm, particularly the wet-dry seasonality critical to the timing of the yam crop.

Such was the culture of the small communities occupying the scattered islands of Tonga, Samoa, and their immediate neighbors. In presenting this portrait, I have ignored or glossed over indications of local variation, especially toward the end of the first millennium B.C. As the centuries passed, there can be no doubt that the Ancestral Polynesians in Tongatapu or Ha'apai or Samoa developed distinctive local variations in speech and in cultural practice, different from those in 'Uvea or Futuna. By the end of the first millen-

nium B.C., if not slightly earlier, a sufficient number of lexical innovations had occurred at the southern and northern ends of the Proto Polynesian dialect chain, resulting in distinct Proto Tongic and Proto Nuclear Polynesian languages. I turn now to that history of differentiation and cultural change within Western Polynesia, as evidenced primarily through archaeology.

Cultural Sequences in Western Polynesia

In 1956 Jack Golson (1961) pioneered stratigraphic excavation in Tonga and Samoa (Map 11), discovering the first pottery in Samoa and showing that in both archipelagoes ceramics defined the earliest cultural stages.[26] Golson's efforts were followed by a multiyear settlement-pattern study in Western Samoa, directed by Roger Green, and by Jens Poulsen's excavations on Tongatapu.[27] For a time, it was thought that Tonga had been settled as much as a millennium before Samoa, leading Les Groube (1971) to propose Tonga as the original Polynesian homeland. Then, an accidental discovery of Lapita pottery at Mulifanua, on 'Upolu in Western Samoa, demonstrated that the lack of Lapita sites in Samoa was a problem of archaeological "visibility" due to coastal submergence, and thus an issue of sampling error.[28]

Subsequent studies have extended our knowledge of the Samoan archaeological record, with work on Tutuila and in the Manu'a group of American Samoa, as well as continued research in 'Upolu and Savai'i.[29] In the Kingdom of Tonga, I investigated Niuatoputapu Island in 1976, Tom Dye reconnoitered Ha'apai, and David Burley has directed a long-term project throughout the Ha'apai group.[30] My initial efforts in the French territory of Wallis ('Uvea) and Futuna were amplified by a French team under the direction of Daniel Frimigacci.[31] We can now define cultural sequences for most islands in Western Polynesia,

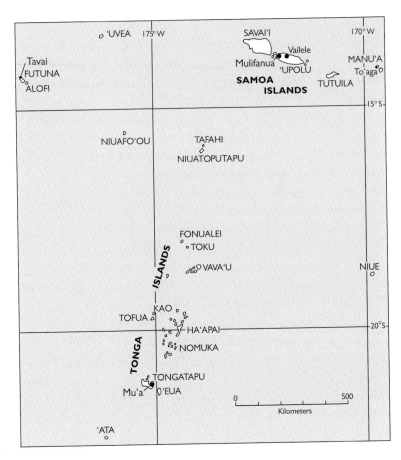

MAP 11 The islands of Western Polynesia, showing the location of key archaeological sites.

beginning with initial Lapita settlement through the development of Ancestral Polynesian culture, to the emergence of regionally distinctive cultures in later prehistory.[32] Some of the key sites are summarized in Table 7.1.

In both Tongatapu and Samoa, the sequences commence with Early Eastern Lapita pottery, as they do in the smaller islands of the Ha'apai group and in Niuatoputapu, Futuna, and 'Uvea. Throughout the first millennium B.C.—the period during which Ancestral Polynesian culture emerged—the region's ceramic sequences show parallel changes. Despite local differences in vessel forms (such as a distinctive handled, narrow-necked jar in Niuatoputapu and Futuna) and surface treatment, all of the

ceramic sequences go through the following succession of stages: Early Eastern Lapita (ca. 1100–700 B.C.), Late Eastern Lapita (ca. 700–300 B.C.), and Polynesian Plain Ware (ca. 300 B.C.–A.D. 300), as shown in Figure 7.2. Moreover, in all of these groups—and in striking contrast to nearby Fiji—the manufacture and use of pottery disappear early in the first millennium A.D.[33]

Ceramics are one of the most important inventions of preindustrialized humans, and to give them up willingly strikes most of us as peculiar. The loss of pottery among Polynesians cannot be explained by the absence of suitable clay or temper, because ceramics were, in fact, manufactured in Western Polynesia using local materials for

TABLE 7.1
Selected Archaeological Sites in Western Polynesia

Island	Site	Site Type	Age Range (B.P.)[a]	References
SAMOA (SAVAI'I)	Pulemelei	Stone mound	Undated	Green and Davidson, eds., 1969
SAMOA ('UPOLU)	Folasa-a-Lalo	Inland habitation complex	500–200	Green and Davidson, eds., 1974
	Luatuanu'u	Inland fortification	1,500	Green and Davidson, eds., 1969
	Mount Olo	Settlement complex	1,500–250	Jennings and Holmer, eds., 1980
	Mulifanua	Submerged coastal site	3,000	Green and Davidson, eds., 1974
	Sasoa'a	Inland occupation	2,000–1,800	Green and Davidson, eds., 1974
	Vailele	Mound site	2,000–recent	Green and Davidson, eds., 1969
SAMOA (TUTUILA)	'Aoa Valley	Settlement complex, various sites	3,000–recent	Clark and Herdrich 1993; Clark and Michlovic 1996
	Tatangamatau	Adz quarry and fortification	1,800–recent	Leach and Witter 1987, 1990
SAMOA (MANU'A)	To'aga	Coastal habitation complex	3,000–recent	Kirch and Hunt, eds., 1993; Kirch et al. 1990
TONGATAPU	'Atele	Burial mounds	500?	Davidson 1969
	Ha'amonga-a-Maui	Megalithic trilithon	Undated	McKern 1929
	Mu'a	Megalithic mound complex	1,500–200?	McKern 1929
HA'APAI GROUP	Mala'e Lahi	Burial mound	Proto-historic	Burley 1994
NIUATOPUTAPU	Houmafakalele	Megalithic burial complex	500	Kirch 1988a
	Lolokoka	Early Eastern Lapita midden	3,000–1,500	Kirch 1988a
	Lotoaa	Polynesian Plain Ware midden	2,500–1,500	Kirch 1988a
	Niutoua	Aceramic midden	1,500–recent	Kirch 1988a
	Pome'e-Nahau	Late Eastern Lapita midden	2,000–1,200	Kirch 1988a

(continued)

TABLE 7.1 (*continued*)

Island	Site	Site Type	Age Range (B.P.)[a]	References
FUTUNA AND ALOFI	Asipani	Buried ceramic midden	2,800–2,400?	Sand 1993b
	Lalolalo	Inland habitation and ceremonial complex	Proto-historic	Kirch 1994
	Loka (Alofi Island)	Late prehistoric village complex	Proto-historic	Kirch 1994
	Tavai	Buried ceramic midden	2,100	Kirch 1981
'UVEA (WALLIS)	Kolonui	Walled fortification complex	Proto-historic	Frimigacci and Hardy 1997
	Petania	Burial mound	Proto-historic	Sand and Valentin 1991

[a] Age ranges given are approximations based on available series of radiocarbon dates. Refer to the references cited for individual radiocarbon dates associated with specific sites.

more than a thousand years. Thus, we must seek nontechnological reason(s). Early changes in the ceramic sequences included the abandonment of decorated vessels, which, as argued in Chapter 4, were used in long-distance exchange. Probably these early ceramic changes were responses to innovation in exchange systems; pottery may have become "proletarianized," as Doug Yen once suggested. Once decorated pottery had been lost, and ceramics no longer figured as prestige goods or high-status items, they would have become strictly utilitarian. The Ancestral Polynesians did not need pottery for cooking (they preferred the earth oven), and they had an abundant supply of coconut shells for water storage and wooden bowls for food serving and pudding preparation. Wooden bowls are more durable than pottery, and one can readily stone-boil liquids such as coconut cream in them. Thus the abandonment of pottery was probably linked with the nature of the Polynesian culinary complex (Leach 1982).

The period after the abandonment of ceramics in Western Polynesia, but prior to the development of later sites with monumental architecture, corresponds roughly with the first millennium A.D. and has been called the "dark ages" (e.g., Davidson 1979:94–95), reflecting a dearth of excavated sites and lack of information. In part, this is a direct consequence of the abandonment of pottery, because sites become less "visible" on the archaeological landscape. However, a few sites are known, such as Niutoua on Niuatoputapu, and the Luatuanu'u complex on 'Upolu, and these suggest much cultural continuity. But there were also changes during the first millennium A.D., such as innovations in the Samoan adz kit, particularly the new triangular and trapezoidal-sectioned forms made in basalt, which began to replace older plano-convex sectioned types.[34] On the whole, the first millennium A.D. in Western Polynesia is a period that calls for more primary excavation.

Sites dating to the last thousand years, or what Davidson termed the "recent period" in Western Polynesia (1979:95–107), are more frequent and better studied. In virtually all islands, specialized, monumental architecture marks this period, linked

FIGURE 7.7 Perspective sketch of a Samoan star mound, at Vaito'omuli, Savai'i Island. (Courtesy Roger C. Green.)

with the rise of complex chiefdoms based on large populations and intensified forms of food production. From oral traditions and ethnohistoric sources, augmented by archaeology, we know that toward the end of the second millennium A.D. the Western Polynesian islands were linked by a long-distance prestige-good exchange network, with its center of gravity in Tongatapu.

In Samoa, settlement-pattern surveys have shown that the ethnographic pattern of coastal villages was a post-1830s adaptation to European contact, particularly depopulation and missionization. Prior to European contact, there was dense inland habitation in some areas, such as in the Falefa Valley on 'Upolu or in the Mount Olo tract. In these late prehistoric settlements, individual household units are delineated by elevated stone or earthen foundation mounds, sometimes separated by walls or pathways. Houses were paved with floors of rounded river or beach gravel ('ili'ili), and excavations at Folasa-a-Lalo revealed repeated occupations with successive pavings. Such densely settled landscapes included intensive agricultural production systems, as in the drained garden-island taro cultivation features on the swampy floor of the Falefa Valley.

Associated with these dense habitation landscapes are large mounds of specialized function. Many have a "star" plan with spokes radiating out from a central platform (Herdrich 1991). Some star mounds (Fig. 7.7) were the foundations for god houses, while others were used for the chiefly sport of pigeon snaring. The great rectangular mound of Pulemelei on Savai'i Island, incorporating 30,000 cubic meters of stone (Fig. 7.8), is an impressive construction indeed. Fortifications are another class of Samoan field monument; these consist of ridges defensified by the construction of transverse trenches (fosses) or other earthworks (Fig. 7.9). Other than Luatuanu'u, few forts have been excavated or dated, but the Tatangamatau site on Tutuila, incorporating fortified habitation terraces and adz-quarrying facilities, has been in use for at least two millennia (Leach and Witter 1987, 1990).

The late prehistoric period in Tonga is characterized by monumental architecture, although the forms differ from those in Samoa (Burley 1998). Several kinds of mounds were constructed, some

FIGURE 7.8 The massive Pulemelei Mound in Western Samoa is one of the largest monumental structures in Western Polynesia. (Courtesy Roger C. Green.)

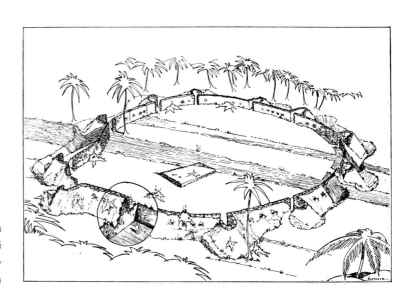

FIGURE 7.9 Perspective sketch of a walled fortification at Uliamoa, Savai'i Island, Western Samoa. (Courtesy Roger C. Green.)

(called *sia heu lupe*) for use by chiefs in their sport of snaring pigeons, others as sitting places or for elite burial. Davidson (1969) excavated two burial mounds at 'Atele on Tongatapu and showed that these had grown in size and elevation through several periods of use. Yet another class of burial mound was reserved for the interment of chiefs; typically rectangular in plan, these were faced with cut and dressed slabs of coral limestone. Quarrying and transporting the facing slabs required substantial labor, especially for the largest mounds (known as *langi*), in which the highest-ranking elite were buried, including the Tu'i Tonga or sacred paramount. The chiefly residential center of Mu'a on Tongatapu incorporated 26 *langi* mounds (Fig. 7.10), the largest fronting a great ceremonial plaza,

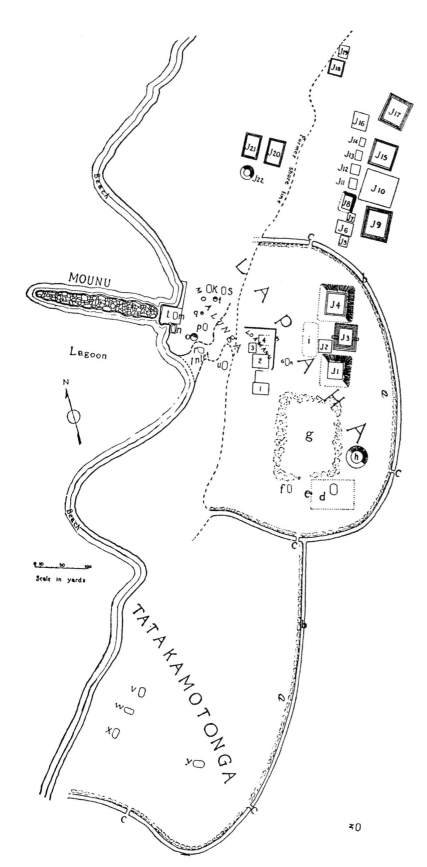

FIGURE 7.10 Archaeological plan of the Mu'a site, Tongatapu Island, seat of the Tu'i Tonga in late prehistoric and proto-historic times. (After McKern 1929.)

FIGURE 7.11 In 1777, Captain James Cook and his crew arrived at Tongatapu in time to witness the annual tribute presentations on the great plaza fronting the burial mounds of the Tu'i Tonga at Mu'a. Engraving after drawing by John Webber for the atlas of Cook's third voyage. (Collection of the author.)

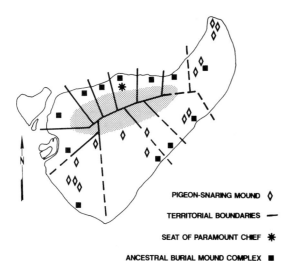

PIGEON-SNARING MOUND ◇

TERRITORIAL BOUNDARIES —

SEAT OF PARAMOUNT CHIEF ✳

ANCESTRAL BURIAL MOUND COMPLEX ■

FIGURE 7.12 The settlement pattern map of Niuatoputapu Island shows a distribution of burial mounds and other monuments, suggesting that the island was subdivided into several territorial units. (After Kirch 1988a.)

where in A.D. 1777 Captain Cook and his crew witnessed the annual rites of tribute called 'inasi (Fig. 7.11). A massive trilithon, the Ha'amonga at Hahake on Tongatapu, probably functioned as a gateway to an elite compound, and it may predate Mu'a. The importance of warfare or raiding is suggested by fortified villages; Mu'a itself was defended by ring-ditch earthworks.

In 1976 I mapped the settlement pattern of Niuatoputapu, a northern "outlier" of the Tongan Kingdom (Kirch 1988a). Niuatoputapu had an independent polity prior to about A.D. 1550 but in the centuries prior to European contact came under Tongan political hegemony. During this late period mounds of various kinds were constructed throughout the island, as shown in Figure 7.12. Their distribution suggests that the island was subdivided into several territories, each with its

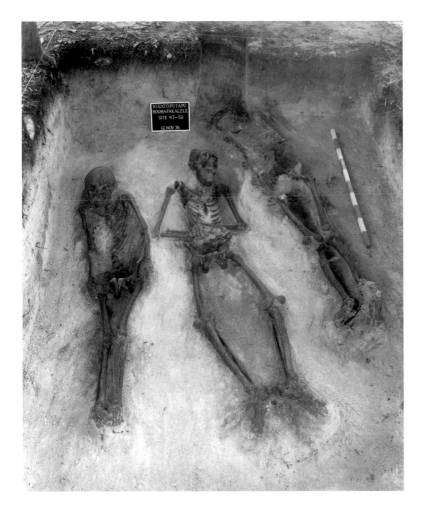

FIGURE 7.13 The Houmafakalele burial mound site on Niuatoputapu Island, a chiefly burial mound of Tongan style with cut and dressed facing stones of quarried limestone, contained several extended burials. (Photo by P. V. Kirch.)

own elite burial facilities, pigeon-snaring mounds, and chiefly sitting mounds. With permission of local Tongan authorities, I excavated a large stone-faced burial mound at Houmafakalele, dating its construction to the fifteenth century A.D. (Fig. 7.13). This mound contained the extended skeletons of at least four adults, buried without grave goods. Black stains surrounded the skeletons, suggesting burial in charcoal-blackened mats, a practice known ethnographically.

On the smaller, isolated islands there were also changes in settlement pattern and architecture paralleling those in Samoa and Tonga. On Futuna and Alofi, extensive taro pondfield irrigation systems were being constructed in the Sigave valleys by about A.D. 700, while walled field systems for dryland yam cultivation began to cover parts of the Alo District and Alofi.[35] Fortifications also appeared, such as the defended hilltop site of Mauga overlooking Nuku and the Sausau Valley. Monumental architecture is more limited in Futuna-Alofi, although the Loka village site on Alofi Island includes a *malae* plaza with an alignment of cut and dressed limestone backrest slabs,

FIGURE 7.14 The ceremonial plaza (*malae*) of the late prehistoric village site at Loka on Alofi Island is lined on one side with an alignment of quarried limestone slabs, which served as backrests for the high chiefs during *kava* ceremonies. (Photo by P. V. Kirch.)

a large chiefly house foundation, and several elite tombs (Fig. 7.14).

'Uvea Island was an independent polity in its earlier history, but like Niuatoputapu it fell under the hegemonic expansion of the Tongan chiefs in late prehistory (Sand 1998b). This Tongan domination is reflected linguistically, since 'Uvean is a Nuclear Polynesian language that borrowed heavily from Tongan. Archaeological evidence puts the oral traditions of Tongan conquest in a material perspective, with various monumental sites, including Tongan-style chiefly burial mounds and large fortifications. One of the most remarkable is the Petania burial mound, measuring 18.5 by 16 meters, with a central coral slab–lined vault.

Surrounding this vault (Fig. 7.15), which held one or more chiefly burials, were no fewer than 150 other individuals, "buried in six successive stratigraphic levels, placed in circles around the burial vault. . . . Most of them had been placed one body partially over another, that is, the head of one person was placed over the femora of the skeleton behind and below" (Sand and Valentin 1991: 239–41). Most, if not all, of the individuals were interred at the same time, possibly as a mass sacrificial offering to the high-ranking individual in the central vault.

Daniel Frimigacci (Frimigacci and Hardy 1997) studied fortifications in the southern part of 'Uvea Island, including Lanutavake (which encloses a

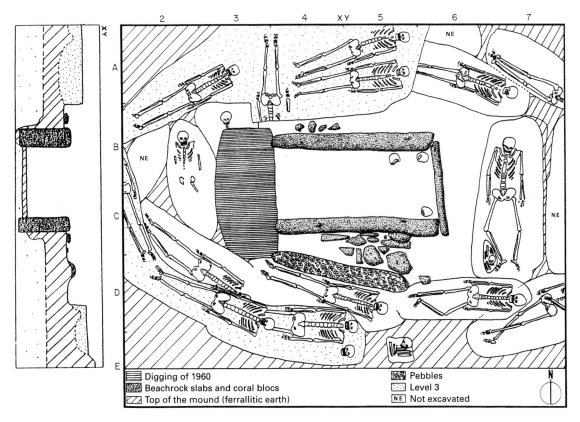

FIGURE 7.15 The Petania burial mound on 'Uvea Island has a central vault surrounded by no fewer than 150 burials in circular arrangement. (From Sand and Valentin 1991; courtesy C. Sand.)

crater lake), Makahu, Atuvalu, and the remarkable site of Kolonui. Kolonui ("Great Fort") has defensive walls of stacked basalt boulders up to 15 meters wide and 4 meters high enclosing a large area, with a chiefly residential complex (Talietumu) in the southwest corner. These sites testify that protohistoric Tongan and 'Uvean societies were strongly hierarchical, with chiefs who could command the labor of large numbers of subordinates and, at times, exert absolute power over life and death.

In the cultural sequences of Western Polynesia —despite distinctive regional and local differences —the main trends are remarkably parallel, and similar processes of change must have been at work throughout the entire region. In part, the synchronous nature of cultural change in Western Polynesia reflects continued interisland contact and the sharing of cultural and social innovations. There was also the imposition of cultural practice by conquest and force, particularly through the late expansion of the Tongan polity in the final centuries prior to European contact, as in Niuatoputapu and 'Uvea. But other changes reflect the gradual buildup of large and densely settled populations in Samoa, Tonga, Futuna, and 'Uvea, and the intensification of agricultural production, accompanied by increased hierarchy and political centralization. Warfare and force played a role in political change, evidenced by fortifications throughout the region. These are matters that will be explored in greater detail in Chapter 8, when the transformation of Polynesian sociopolitical structures is considered.

The Settlement of Eastern Polynesia

Archaeologists, historical linguists, and comparative ethnographers concur in identifying Western Polynesia as the immediate Polynesian homeland, where a distinctive Polynesian culture and language emerged during the first millennium B.C. When it comes to the timing and sequence of subsequent dispersals out of this homeland into the archipelagoes of Eastern Polynesia, however, debate is rampant. Not that a movement from Western Polynesia into Eastern Polynesia is in doubt, or that the central Eastern islands were settled before such "marginal" or remote archipelagoes as Hawai'i and New Zealand. Yet the particulars of sequence and chronology remain unresolved to the general satisfaction of most scholars.

In part, this debate reflects a lack of primary archaeological fieldwork in many Eastern Polynesian islands; for example, the Austral Island chain, one possible corridor of early expansion into southeastern Polynesia, remains largely unexplored. Method is also at issue; what kinds of evidence are admissible for establishing the chronology of human settlement on islands?[36] Some archaeologists, such as Atholl Anderson, insist that only artifactual evidence—that found at a primary habitation site—can pin down the date of human colonization of an island. Others, such as Steve Athens and I, argue that a range of environmental evidence for human disturbance on fragile island ecosystems (including increased charcoal influxes in sediment cores, pollen evidence for forest clearance and expansion of grass- or fernlands, or the appearance of synanthropic animals such as the Pacific Rat [*Rattus exulans*][37] or garden snails) can provide acceptable proxy indicators of human arrival. On large islands (such as Hawai'i or New Zealand), where finding physical remains of the first settlements may be exceedingly difficult (or on islands where geomorphological processes have led to site destruction, submergence, or deep burial under later sediments), environmental indicators may offer a better means of tracking the chronology of human arrival. As paleoecologist David Burney observes, "The earliest stratigraphic proxy evidence for initial human impacts (including increased charcoal particle influx to sediments, first appearance of exotic pollen, increase in ruderal pollen, and paleolimnological evidence for cultural eutrophication of lake waters) generally confirms *but sometimes predates the earliest conventional archaeological evidence for human activity*" (1997:437, emphasis added).

In the 1960s, as archaeological excavations commenced in central Eastern Polynesia, Kenneth Emory and Yosihiko Sinoto developed a model of Polynesian dispersals that privileged the Marquesas Islands as the first archipelago to be settled by voyagers moving from Western Polynesia.[38] As seen in Figure 7.16A, their model had successive dispersals radiating out from the Marquesas to the Society Islands, and then from both of these archipelagoes out to the other Eastern Polynesian groups. This "orthodox scenario" reflected the richness of the early Marquesan archaeological record and the lack of adequate samples from other islands.[39] In 1984, I proposed an alternative model, shown in Figure 7.16B, in which the Society and Marquesas Islands together formed an *Eastern Polynesian homeland region*, linked by regular contact. However, this model too has its shortcomings, and indeed both models shown in Figure 7.16 are insufficient to account for the emerging archaeological data. We have yet to replace them with alternatives that are acceptable to all. Later in this

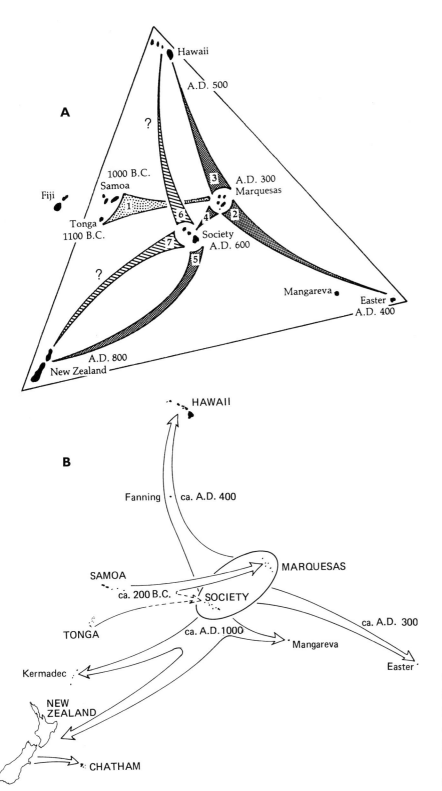

A

1000 B.C.
Samoa

Fiji

Tonga
1100 B.C.

Hawaii

A.D. 500

?

3 A.D. 300
Marquesas

1

6

4

2

7

Society
A.D. 600

5

Mangareva

Easter
A.D. 400

?

A.D. 800
New Zealand

B

HAWAII

Fanning · ca. A.D. 400

SAMOA

ca. 200 B.C.

SOCIETY

MARQUESAS

TONGA

ca. A.D. 1000

Mangareva

ca. A.D. 300

Easter

Kermadec

NEW ZEALAND

CHATHAM

FIGURE 7.16 (A) The model of Polynesian dispersals proposed by Emory and Sinoto (1965) based on initial results of excavations in Eastern Polynesia. (B) Kirch's revised model of Polynesian dispersals (Kirch 1984a).

chapter, I will suggest a new possibility, but first it is necessary to review recent developments in historical linguistics, experimental voyaging, and archaeology.

The "Long Pause" and Chronological Debates   Debate regarding Eastern Polynesian settlement revolves around what is called the "long pause." Lapita expansion into Remote Oceania occurred quickly, and the Eastern Lapita movement into Fiji, Tonga, and Samoa took place so rapidly that it virtually forms an archaeological "instant" (see Chapter 4). While Tonga, Samoa, and other Western Polynesian islands were colonized by 1000 B.C., the earliest known archaeological assemblages from Eastern Polynesia date to around 200 B.C.–A.D. 1 (in the northern Cooks and the Marquesas), and even these dates are disputed. Unequivocal radiocarbon dates for central Eastern Polynesian assemblages are no earlier than about A.D. 600.[40] This leaves a pause in the eastward expansion of people beyond Tonga-Samoa of as much as 1,600 years, followed by a sudden burst of exploration and discovery that, if correct, would take people into virtually every other island and archipelago within a mere four centuries (i.e., by A.D. 1000). The unanswered questions are: Did this pause really occur? Is it, at least in part, an artifact of sampling error and problems with radiocarbon dating? If it did occur, what was its true duration?

Most scholars believe that some pause did occur. Historical linguists such as Pawley (1996) argue for a period of common development in the Western Polynesian homeland—prior to later dispersals—in order to explain the many innovations in Proto Polynesian language (approximately 1,300 lexical innovations have been cataloged) and to allow time for the differentiation of Proto Tongic and Proto Nuclear Polynesian languages (see Figure 7.3). How many centuries were required

for such language changes is not precisely known. But if the pause was as long as some maintain, this leaves an insufficient period of time for similar innovations to arise in Proto Eastern Polynesian language and culture, once the expansion out of the Western Polynesian homeland had commenced. If the settlement of all of Eastern Polynesia did not begin until around A.D. 600, as Spriggs and Anderson (1993) assert, an amazing rate of fertility and population increase must be inferred to fuel such an unprecedented demographic expansion.

Resolution of these issues will ultimately come from the hard evidence of archaeology, combined with paleoenvironmental indicators of human presence on islands. Paleoenvironmental evidence from Mangaia may indicate human activity in the southern Cooks as early as 2,500–2,000 years ago.[41] In the northern Cook Islands, radiocarbon dates from Pukapuka Atoll range from 2310 ± 65 to 1540 ± 70 B.P., suggesting an early population movement out of Western Polynesia by around A.D. 1 (Chikamori 1996; ed., 1998; Chikamori and Yoshida 1988). In the Marquesas, the radiocarbon chronology is almost hopelessly confused, with early dates of between about 200 B.C. and A.D. 300 at the Ha'atuatua, Hane, Hanatekua, and Anapua sites contradicted by later age determinations, sometimes from the same stratigraphic contexts (Table 7.2). At the key sand dune site of Hane, suites of dates by two different laboratories yielded completely contradictory sequences![42] For the Society Islands, the oldest known habitation sites (Vaito'otia-Fa'ahia on Huahine, and Maupiti) date to around A.D. 800–1200, but the coastal terraces of the Societies have undergone much subsidence and alluviation, making the discovery of early sites problematic. In the 'Opunohu Valley on Mo'orea, Lepofsky et al. (1992) discovered a domesticated variety of coconuts dating to A.D. 600

buried under later alluvium, and paleoenvironmental evidence from 'Opunohu indicates that human-induced landscape changes were already under way by that time (Lepofsky et al. 1996).

Elsewhere in central and southeastern Polynesia (e.g., the Cooks, Australs, Mangareva, Pitcairn, and Easter Island) human settlements were well established by A.D. 900–1000, but this date probably does not represent initial discovery, colonization, and settlement. For example, M. S. Allen (1998) presents evidence that the earliest known sites on Aitutaki, dated to A.D. 1000, are *not* the earliest human occupations, since these contained already-depleted avifaunal assemblages as well as Polynesian floral and faunal introductions. The same situation holds with the Anai'o site on Ma'uke Island, which despite being the oldest known site on that island yielded almost no endemic or indigenous bird bones, and is therefore "not indicative of an early phase site" (Walter 1998:74). The Hawaiian Islands were settled no later than A.D. 800 based on both archaeological and paleoenvironmental evidence, but some radiocarbon dates suggest the possibility of earlier human arrival, perhaps by A.D. 300 (Hunt and Holsen 1991; Kirch 1985a). And for New Zealand, while there are no archaeological sites unequivocally dated before about A.D. 1000 (Anderson 1991), recent dates on bones of the Pacific Rat (*Rattus exulans*) raise the issue of whether humans introduced this commensal species to New Zealand as early as 2,000 years ago (Holdaway 1996).[43]

These thorny chronological issues will not be resolved without expanded archaeological and paleoenvironmental fieldwork, especially in the southern Cooks, Australs, and Society Islands. With respect to the "long" and "short" chronology models for Eastern Polynesian settlement, Geoff Irwin has written that "if the former remains difficult to prove, then the second is difficult to explain" (1998:136). Whereas proponents of the early model place much stock in context, advocates of the late-settlement model "may be trying to explain something that has already happened before they recognize it in the evidence." Time—and more hard fieldwork—will tell.

Early Settlement Sites in Eastern Polynesia   Leaving aside unresolved chronological issues, a number of early Eastern Polynesian sites have been excavated, and some of the most important are enumerated in Table 7.2. In contrast to later Polynesian settlement patterns in which habitation sites are typically dispersed (with a few exceptions, such as New Zealand and Rapa), these early sites were mostly nucleated hamlets or small villages, usually on or near the coast. This settlement pattern reflects long-term continuity from Lapita through Ancestral Polynesian times. On the tropical and subtropical high islands, early communities chose to situate their hamlets or villages in favorable ecological zones, such as well-watered windward coasts adjacent to freshwater streams and close to reef and lagoon resources.

Many of the early Eastern Polynesian sites (Table 7.2) are found in sand dune or beach terrace geomorphological contexts, such as Ureia on Aitutaki, Hane on Ua Huka, and Halawa on Moloka'i. The stratigraphy in such sites is often complex (Fig. 7.17), and it can be confusing since there is the potential for reworking and redeposition of deposits, as may have happened at Ha'atuatua on Nukuhiva, where despite much excavation, the occupation sequence and chronology still pose unresolved problems (Rolett and Conte 1995; Suggs 1961). The Vaito'otia-Fa'ahia site on Huahine (Society Islands) occupies low-lying terrain that was part of an infilling lagoon, and hence its deposits are waterlogged, with anaerobic preservation of wooden artifacts (Sinoto 1979b; Sinoto

TABLE 7.2
Selected Early Eastern Polynesian Archaeological Sites

Island/Group	Site (Island)	Site Type	Age Range (B.P.)[a]	References
COOK ISLANDS	Anai'o (Ma'uke)	Habitation site	1,075–950	Walter 1990, 1998
	Pukapuka	Stratified middens	2,300–1,500, 450–200	Chikamori, ed., 1998; Chikamori and Yoshida 1988
	Tangatatau (Mangaia)	Rockshelter	1,000–300	Kirch et al. 1995
	Ureia (Aitutaki)	Coastal midden	1,050–500	Allen and Steadman 1990
SOCIETY ISLANDS	Maupiti	Burial site on offshore islet	1,100	Emory and Sinoto 1964
	'Opunohu (Mo'orea)	Waterlogged sediments with preserved coconuts	1,400–1,200	Lepofsky et al. 1992, 1996
	Vaito'otia-Fa'ahia (Huahine)	Waterlogged habitation site	1,200–800	Sinoto 1979b; Sinoto and McCoy 1975
MARQUESAS	Anapua (Ua Pou)	Rockshelter	2,150?	Ottino 1992
	Ha'atuatua (Nuku Hiva)	Sand dune habitation	2,000–1,900, 1,300–1,100	Rolett and Conte 1995; Suggs 1996
	Hanamiai (Tahuata)	Sand dune habitation	1,250–600	Rolett 1989, 1992
	Hanatekua (Hiva Oa)	Rockshelter	1,900–1,250	Sinoto, unpublished data; see Kirch 1986a
	Hane (Ua Huka)	Sand dune habitation	1,900–650	Sinoto 1966, 1970, 1979a
PITCAIRN GROUP	Henderson	Rockshelters	1,100–200	Weisler 1994, 1995, 1996a
MANGAREVA	Kamata Island	Rockshelter	?	R. Green, unpublished data
EASTER ISLAND (RAPA NUI)	Anakena	Sand dune habitation	1,000–600	Steadman et al. 1994
	Poike Ditch	Artificially modified depression	1,600	Heyerdahl and Ferdon, eds., 1961
EQUATORIAL ISLANDS	Fanning	Midden site	1,560	A. Sinoto 1973

(continued)

TABLE 7.2 (*continued*)

Island/Group	Site (Island)	Site Type	Age Range (B.P.)[a]	References
HAWAIIAN ISLANDS	Bellows Dune (Oʻahu)	Sand dune habitation	1,600–700	Pearson et al. 1971
	Halawa Dune (Molokaʻi)	Sand dune habitation	1,380–820	Kirch and Kelly, eds., 1975
	Kawainui (Oʻahu)	Open habitation site	1,500	Kirch 1985a
	Puʻu Aliʻi (Hawaiʻi)	Sand dune habitation	1,600?	Emory et al. 1959; Kirch 1985a
	Waiahukini (Hawaiʻi)	Rockshelter	1,200	Emory et al. 1969
NEW ZEALAND	Mt. Camel	Stratified midden	550–800	Shawcross 1972
	Papatowai	Stratified midden	850–550	Anderson and Smith 1992
	Shag River	Stratified midden	1,000–600	Anderson et al., eds., 1996
	Wairau Bar	Midden and burial ground	850–600	Duff 1956
	Washpool	Stratified midden	800–450	Leach and Leach, eds., 1979

[a] Age ranges given are approximations based on available series of radiocarbon dates. Refer to the references cited for individual radiocarbon dates associated with specific sites.

and Han 1981; Sinoto and McCoy 1975). In addition to wooden bowls, a hafted adz, and cordage, this remarkable site yielded wooden planks that were probably part of a large canoe, and the framing timbers of a wooden storage hut.

These communities seemed to have separate dwelling and cooking spaces, and a variety of domestic architecture. Some dwellings were raised on low stone pavements, as at Hane in the Marquesas (Fig. 7.17), while others had gravel floors. Rectangular and perhaps also round-ended house forms are indicated. There is no firm evidence for religious or ceremonial architecture, although historical linguistic evidence suggests that the initial stages of the Eastern Polynesian *marae* probably developed at this time (Kirch and Green, in press). These sites provide evidence for horticulture and domestic animals (especially dogs and pigs, as well as chickens), and the colonization strategies originally worked out during the Lapita expansion into Remote Oceania were successfully continued in Eastern Polynesia. The early Eastern Polynesian colonists experimented with fishing techniques, developing a wider range of fishing gear than had been present in immediately preceding Ancestral Polynesian communities in Samoa or Tonga (Fig. 7.18). Early sites in the Marquesas, the Cook Islands, Mangareva, and the Hawaiian group display a remarkable diversity of one-piece fishhook types as well as trolling rigs; both angling and trolling hooks were made from pearl shell (*Pinctada* sp.) where available, but also from bone. Where good-quality shell was not available, larger angling hooks were manufactured (usually from

FIGURE 7.17 Excavations at the sand dune site of Hane on Ua Huka, Marquesas Islands, exposed simple pavements of waterworn stones on which dwellings were erected. (Photo courtesy Y. H. Sinoto.)

bone) by a clever two-piece method, with the point and shank carved of separate pieces lashed together at the bend.

Many new stylistic innovations set off the material culture of these early Eastern Polynesian sites from that found in older Ancestral Polyne-

sian contexts. For example, new forms of basalt adzes were invented, with incipient tangs to assist in lashing and with a variety of cross sections (triangular, trapezoidal, quadrangular). There is a range of ornaments (including whale's-tooth pendants or necklaces), tattooing needles, coconut-

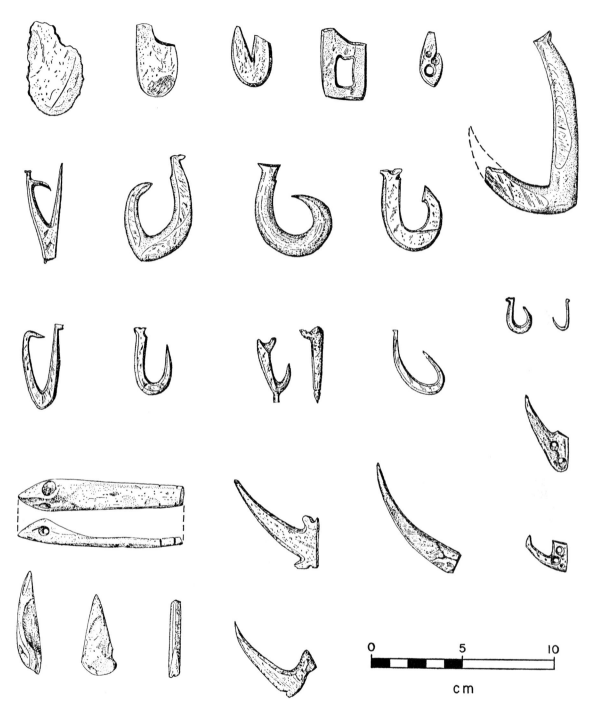

FIGURE 7.18 Early Eastern Polynesian fishhooks from the Marquesas Islands. (After Suggs 1961.)

POLYNESIA: ORIGINS AND DISPERSALS

grater heads in pearl shell and basalt, and net sinkers and weights (Fig. 7.19). Sinoto (1970, 1983, 1996b) labeled these distinctive early Eastern Polynesian assemblages as an Archaic Phase (see also Walter 1996). However, not all of the artifact forms are shared by all assemblages.

Polynesian Voyaging Debates concerning the settlement of Polynesia have long revolved around voyaging and indigenous navigational capabilities. The first Europeans to explore Polynesia had no doubts that the Pacific peoples arrived in the islands through purposive voyaging, for they witnessed firsthand the remarkable seagoing double-hulled and outrigger canoes, such as that encountered on the open ocean between Tonga and Samoa by the Dutch voyagers Schouten and Le Maire in 1616 (Fig. 7.20). But in the early nineteenth century indigenous Polynesian canoe-building industries collapsed, and traditional navigational lore was almost completely lost. By the mid-twentieth century a new generation of scholars was proposing that the Polynesians had arrived in the islands primarily by chance, riding prevailing winds and currents. Thor Heyerdahl (1952) pushed this idea with his *Kon-Tiki* raft voyage from South America to the Tuamotus, arguing that the Polynesian ancestors were American Indians who drifted into Polynesia from the Northwest Coast and from Peru. Though widely acclaimed in the popular press, Heyerdahl's theory was never taken seriously by scholars, since it ignores the mass of linguistic, ethnographic, ethnobiological, and archaeological evidence in support of a western (Asiatic) origin for the Polynesians.[44] Another theorist who proposed that the Polynesians had settled their islands by drifting was Andrew Sharp (1956). He did not derive the Polynesians from the Americas but argued that they were incapable of long-distance purposive navigation against prevailing winds and currents, and had colonized the eastern

Pacific islands through a lengthy succession of chance or drift voyages.

Sharp's thesis was tested in an early application of high-speed computing by Levison et al. (1973). Using a massive probability matrix of current and wind speed and force for specific areas of the Pacific Ocean obtained from naval hydrographic records, these geographers ran 101,016 simulated computer drift "voyages" from many Polynesian islands. Although the simulations showed that there is a good possibility of successful drift from east to west, as would account for the settlement of the Polynesian Outliers (see Chapters 5 and 6), it is virtually impossible to go in the opposite direction without purposive sailing. Not a single simulated voyage out of 16,000 computer trials from various starting points in central Eastern Polynesia managed to end up in Hawai'i. Thus Levison et al. concluded that Hawai'i had been colonized "by crews who *intended* to follow a northerly course, which implies a motive such as seeking new lands" (1973:53, emphasis added).

Of course, intentionality in voyaging had long been indicated by Polynesian oral traditions, rich in accounts of the discovery of certain archipelagoes and subsequent interarchipelago return trips.[45] Hawaiian traditions speak of great navigators such as Moikeha and Pa'ao, who made round-trip voyages between the ancestral lands of "Kahiki" and the Hawaiian group. Pa'ao quarreled with his older sibling Lonopele in Kahiki and fled to new lands in the north, introducing the cult of the war god Tu (Ku in Hawaiian), along with human sacrifice.

Archaeologist Geoff Irwin (1989, 1990, 1992), a deep-water yachtsman, has built on the pioneering work of Levison et al. to develop a sophisticated theory of Polynesian voyaging and colonization. Irwin argues that the purposive colonization of Eastern Polynesia was the final stage in a long process of Pacific exploration, enabled by a gradual

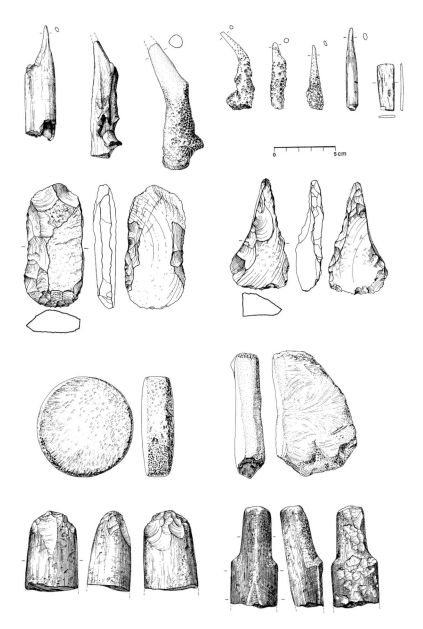

FIGURE 7.19 Artifacts from the Tangatatau Rockshelter site on Mangaia Island, including basalt adzes, bone tattooing needles, coral and sea urchin spine abraders, and a gaming stone of coral. (Drawings by Judith Ogden.)

FIGURE 7.20 A Polynesian double-hulled canoe at sea between Tonga and Samoa, as seen by the Dutch voyagers Schouten and Le Maire in 1616. (From Burney 1806.)

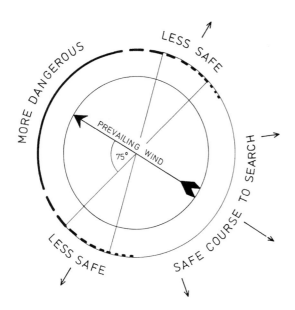

FIGURE 7.21 Geoff Irwin's model of survival sailing strategy. (Courtesy G. Irwin.)

improvement in voyaging skills, originating in the "voyaging nursery" of the Bismarck Archipelago (see Chapter 3) and elaborated during the Lapita expansion into Remote Oceania. A key element in this process was a "survival sailing strategy" (Fig. 7.21). Taking advantage of predictable westerly reversals of the prevailing east-to-west trades (Finney 1988, 1994), Pacific peoples learned to sail eastward in search of new landfalls, always able to depend on regular trade winds to bring them back to their home island. They discovered that they could fix latitude by the stars, enabling them to run back to a home island on the proper latitude; in this strategy, knowing longitude was not necessary. Effectively, exploration and the discovery of new islands proceeded as a series of "arcs of exploration," becoming wider in angle and deeper in their distance of penetration into the unknown as canoe technology and navigational skills improved with accumulated experience (Fig. 7.22).

Based on his model, Irwin (1992) questions the reality of a "long pause" in the settlement of Polynesia. Rather, he suggests that there may have been continuous attempts at eastward exploration out of Tonga and Samoa. However, given the ocean gap between Western Polynesia and the Cooks (and the fact that the northern Cook atolls would have been awash until about 2,000 years ago), effective discovery and settlement might not have occurred until several centuries after the first Lapita settlements in Tonga and Samoa. Based on this theory of "systematic voyaging," Irwin predicts the following sequence of island settlement in Eastern Polynesia: (1) southern Cooks–Australs chain ca. 700 B.C.; (2) northern Cooks–Tokelau ca. 300 B.C.; (3) Society-Tuamotu archipelagoes ca. 600 B.C.; (4) Marquesas ca. 100 B.C.; (5) Easter Island ca. A.D. 300; (6) Hawaiian Islands ca. A.D. 200; and (7) New Zealand ca. A.D. 800.[46] The late settlement of the margins of Eastern Polynesia correlates with the great difficulty of achieving these landfalls, where the search arcs become very large indeed, or in the case of Hawaii, where one must sail right outside the southern atmospheric circulation gyre, across the doldrums, and into the Northern Hemisphere. Irwin's proposed chronology agrees well with the controversial early radiocarbon dates for Mangaia, the Marquesas, and Hawai'i as mentioned earlier. Only further fieldwork will confirm or reject his model.

Computer simulations and theoretical models can also be tested through practical experiment, as has been done by an energetic group of young Hawaiians in the Polynesian Voyaging Society, with the encouragement of anthropologist Ben Finney.[47] In 1976, the Pacific world took notice when the replicated 19-meter Polynesian voyaging canoe *Hokule'a* (Fig. 7.23) made a successful round-trip voyage between Hawai'i and Tahiti. Subsequent voyages, many made without the aid of any Western navigational devices, have covered the seaways between Samoa and central Polynesia, Rarotonga and New Zealand, and Hawai'i and central Polynesia. A major voyage to Easter Island (Rapa Nui) by the *Hokule'a* was successfully completed in October 1999. These voyages constitute a kind of "experimental archaeology," adding insight into the seaworthiness of traditional Polynesian watercraft and the effectiveness of noninstrumental navigation. The voyages have had a dual effect, for as Finney writes, "In addition to helping to make voyaging once [again] more central to the study of Polynesian prehistory, our experimental initiative has also led to a voyaging renaissance whereby empowered Polynesians are now seeking to learn about their maritime past by sailing *Hokule'a* and other reconstructed canoes over the sea roads pioneered by their ancestors" (1996b:372).

Recent studies of Polynesian voyaging, combined with archaeological discoveries, have turned the tables on Thor Heyerdahl's theory of an American origin for the Polynesians, suggesting instead that it was the *Polynesians* who reached the coast of South America and successfully returned, bringing both the sweet potato (*Ipomoea batatas*) and the *Lagenaria* gourd with them (Green 1998). The sweet potato was domesticated in South America (Yen 1974a), but for a long while it was uncertain whether it had been introduced to Polynesia by early Spanish explorers. When late-eighteenth-century explorers such as the botanists Solander and Forster on Cook's voyages began to document the flora of Polynesia, they found that the sweet potato was intensively cultivated, especially in Hawai'i, Easter Island, and New Zealand (Merrill 1954). In 1989, excavating in the Tangatatau Rockshelter on Mangaia Island, I recovered carbonized

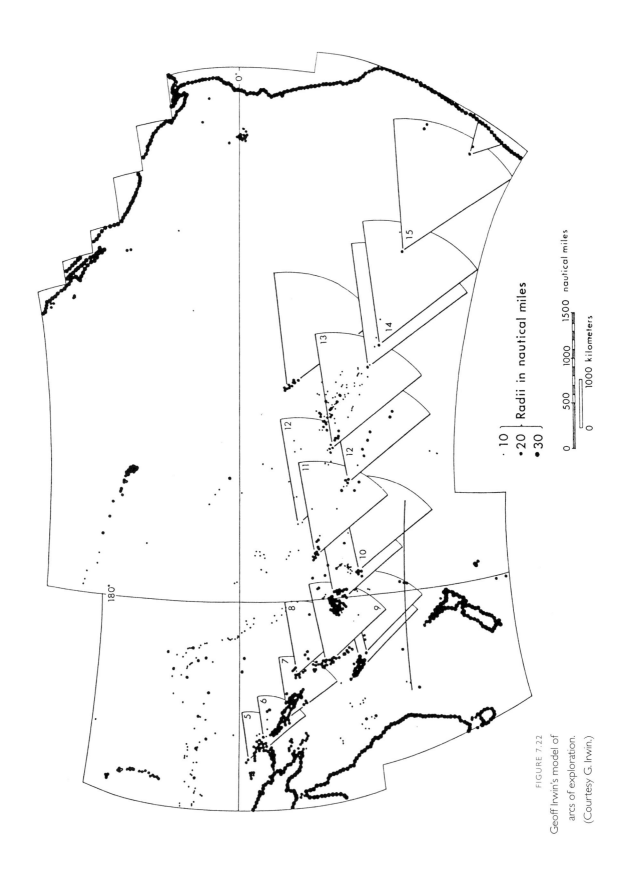

FIGURE 7.22
Geoff Irwin's model of
arcs of exploration.
(Courtesy G. Irwin.)

Radii in nautical miles

·10
·20
·30

0   500   1000   1500 nautical miles

0   1000 kilometers

FIGURE 7.23 The replicated voyaging canoe *Hokule'a* has sailed on numerous experimental voyages throughout Polynesia. (Photo courtesy Bishop Museum.)

pieces of sweet potato tubers, identified by archaeobotanist Jon Hather and radiocarbon dated to around A.D. 1000 (Hather and Kirch 1991). These materials, along with slightly later carbonized tubers from New Zealand and Hawai'i, prove that the sweet potato was introduced into Eastern Polynesia in prehistory. The probable transferors of this crop plant, as Yen (1974a) originally suggested, were the seafaring Polynesians.

Interaction Spheres in Eastern Polynesia When stratigraphic archaeology commenced in Eastern Polynesia in the 1950s and 1960s, connections between island groups had to be inferred on the basis of stylistic similarities between classes of artifacts. In the absence of pottery (except for a few sherds in early Marquesan sites[48]), fishhooks and adzes were the main artifacts on which comparisons were based.[49] These hinted at a close relationship between early sites in the Marquesas and Hawai'i, and similar linkages between the Society Islands and New Zealand, as well as the possibility of a later connection between Hawai'i and the Society Islands (Emory and Sinoto 1965). Despite trial experimentation with petrographic analysis of adz rock, however, there was no effort to trace the physical movement of individual artifacts between islands.

The development of high-precision methods of spectrochemical characterization and sourcing of stone, particularly energy-dispersive and wavelength-dispersive X-ray fluorescence (ED-XRF, WD-XRF), now provides the means to determine the source localities of basalt adzes and adz flakes, as well as of oven stones.[50] Marshall Weisler and I (1996) demonstrated that a few of the adz flakes in the deeper levels of the Tangatatau Rockshelter on Mangaia had originated at the large Tatangamatau quarry on Tutuila Island in American Samoa, a distance of some 1,600 kilometers. That the early Mangaian population was linked into a long-distance interisland exchange network was also suggested by quantities of pearl shell (*Pinctada margaritifera*), used to make fishhooks and other artifacts. Pearl shell does not occur locally on Mangaia and would have had to be imported from an island with a lagoon, perhaps Aitutaki, or one of the Tuamotu atolls. Imported basalt and pearl shell also occur on Ma'uke Island and on Aitutaki.[51] On these southern Cook Islands, the early patterns of extra-local linkages and importation of exotic materials gave way in later prehistory to replacements with strictly local materials (such as the use of inferior *Turbo setosus* shell for fishhooks on Mangaia). Thus an early period of interaction gradually shifted to a later phase of increased isolation.

More dramatic evidence for long-distance movement of lithic materials has been obtained using the ED-XRF and WD-XRF techniques on adzes and oven stones from Mangareva and Pit-

cairn in southeastern Polynesia and from Mo'orea in the Society Islands (Weisler 1993, 1998a). Weisler documented regular transport of oven stones from Mangareva and of basalt and pitchstone (a kind of volcanic glass) from Pitcairn to the remote makatea island of Henderson, between about A.D. 800 and 1450. Adz stone quarried from Eiao in the Marquesas was transported to Mo'orea in the Society chain and to Mangareva in the Australs (Weisler 1998a). These results provide the hard data necessary to track specific interaction spheres within Polynesia. Among other implications, they suggest that the central Eastern Polynesian archipelagoes were in regular communication during the earlier prehistoric period.

Another innovative approach to the study of prehistoric interaction in Eastern Polynesia uses the sequencing and comparison of mitochondrial DNA in populations of the Pacific Rat (*Rattus exulans*). Recent work by Matisoo-Smith et al. (1998) with populations of this commensal species—which was widely spread by the Polynesians—implies that there were multiple contacts between some island groups. On the other hand, certain islands (such as the remote Chathams) have only a single rat lineage, implying isolation. Matisoo-Smith's work also shows a link between the Hawaiian and Marquesan rat populations, confirming independent archaeological and linguistic evidence for the initial settlement of Hawai'i from the Marquesas.

A Possible Model of Eastern Polynesian Dispersals I conclude this discussion of the debate and issues surrounding the settlement of Eastern Polynesia by proposing a new model, one that incorporates the changing picture of Eastern Polynesian language relationships (Marck 1999; Pawley 1996), Irwin's (1992) model of continuous, strategic voyaging, and the emerging evidence for long-distance interaction spheres (Weisler, ed., 1997).

Rather than a single population movement into one island or archipelago of central Eastern Polynesia, which then served as a primary dispersal center (such as Ra'iatea in Te Rangi Hiroa's theory [see Chapter 1], or the Marquesas in Emory and Sinoto's "orthodox scenario"), I suggest that the process of expansion out of the Ancestral Polynesian homeland was more complex, involving at least three separate movements, each resulting in interaction spheres and dialect chains that persisted over significant time periods. All of these movements, I would argue, commenced in the late first millennium B.C. and were certainly under way by about A.D. 1. However, the full interaction spheres that subsequently developed may not have been achieved until around A.D. 600–800.

The first expansion may have been out of Western Polynesia into the Tuvalu (Ellice) and Tokelau archipelagoes. Linguistically, this is indicated by the Ellicean language subgroup, which differentiated early from Proto Nuclear Polynesian (see Figure 7.3). This early northern expansion probably gave rise—perhaps rather rapidly—to the movement of populations westward into Micronesia and northern Melanesia, as the founding populations of some Polynesian Outliers, especially Kapingamarangi and Nukuoro, as well as Sikaiana. Another group may have expanded eastward into the newly stabilized atolls of the northern Cooks, and possibly also into the Equatorial Islands (which were later devoid of human populations). These drought-prone equatorial atolls have not been adequately studied by archaeologists, although a site on Fanning Island yielded a radiocarbon date of 1560 ± 85 B.P., consistent with this interpretation of early Eastern Polynesian settlement.[52] From the northern Cooks, the Society Islands and the western Tuamotus[53] could have been quickly dis-

covered and settled, with all of these island communities remaining in regular voyaging contact. This would have formed one interaction sphere as well as a dialect chain, linguistically represented by the distinctive Proto Tahitic subgroup of Eastern Polynesian languages.

At roughly the same time, we may postulate a third expansion out of Western Polynesia, into the high volcanic islands of the southern Cooks (such as Rarotonga and Mangaia) and, following a strategy of exploratory voyaging, continuing gradually down the Austral Island chain as far as Mangareva. Mangarevan and some of the poorly recorded languages of the eastern Tuamotus make up, along with Marquesan and Hawaiian, the Marquesic subgroup of Eastern Polynesian languages. It is probable that a second interaction sphere and dialect chain thus linked the Australs and Mangareva (and the Pitcairn group beyond it) to the Marquesas via the eastern Tuamotus.[54] It was presumably from this Proto Marquesic sphere that Hawai'i was first settled (although Tahitic loan words in Hawaiian support the notion of a secondary population intrusion from the "Tahitic" sphere). The Rapanui language, on remote Easter Island, split off early, and thus it may represent an early branch of the Australs-Mangareva interaction sphere that became isolated from the rest, not sharing in later linguistic and cultural innovations.[55]

Such a hypothetical settlement sequence, in my view, makes the best sense of the available linguistic, archaeological, and comparative ethnographic evidence bearing both on Eastern Polynesian dispersals and on the settlement of the Polynesian Outliers. Testing this model, however, will require a concentrated field effort in islands and even whole archipelagoes that still remain archaeological *terra incognita*.

CHAPTER 8

The Polynesian Chiefdoms

It must be understood that I have not . . . imagined that I was tracing out what actually had been the history of these main features of Polynesian political organization;
this is a thing which presumably no one will ever be able to do. I have merely been
suggesting what seems to me to be a reasonably possible explanation of it.

Williamson (1924:428)

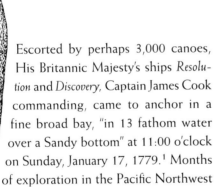

Escorted by perhaps 3,000 canoes, His Britannic Majesty's ships *Resolution* and *Discovery*, Captain James Cook commanding, came to anchor in a fine broad bay, "in 13 fathom water over a Sandy bottom" at 11:00 o'clock on Sunday, January 17, 1779.[1] Months of exploration in the Pacific Northwest had battered Cook's ships; his sea-worn crews yearned for rest. The reception accorded them by the Hawaiians was enthusiastic: "They express'd the greatest Joy & satisfaction, by Sing^g & Jumping, of our coming to Anchor," wrote Lt. King (Beaglehole 1967:503). Never before in his three Pacific expeditions had the veteran navigator Cook witnessed such a welcome. "I have no where in this Sea seen such a number of people assembled at one place, besides those in the Canoes all the

Shore of the bay was covered with people and hundreds were swimming about the Ships like shoals of fish" (1967:490–91). The *Discovery* heeled dangerously from the weight of hundreds of Hawaiians hanging off her side.

A delegation of priests and chiefs boarded the flagship. Draping a red cloth—symbol of divinity and kingship—over Cook's shoulders and offering him a small pig, the aged priest Koa "kept repeating a pretty long oration or prayer" (1967:504). Later Cook was received on the beach—the large multitude now at a distance and "prostrate" on their faces—by three or four elite men "who held wands tipt with dogs hair, & who kept repeating a sentence, wherein the word Erono was always mention'd." Cook and his fellow officers were conducted to the summit of a large stone temple platform, upon which further solemn rites commenced,

FIGURE 8.1 The paramount chief of Hawai'i Island, Kalaniopu'u, arrives in Kealakekua Bay to greet Captain James Cook in 1779. Engraving after drawing by John Webber for the atlas of Cook's third voyage. (Collection of the author.)

notably the ceremony of *hanaipu*, the "feeding of the god," part of the annual Makahiki fertility rituals.[2]

On that day in the sacred bay of Ke-ala-ke-[a]kua, "The Path of the God," Cook encountered in full Polynesia's most hierarchical chiefdom; indeed, he was actively incorporated into the Hawaiian mytho-praxis and made a part of that society by the Hawaiian chiefs and priests. Proclaiming Cook as "O Rono"—manifestation of the thunder and rain god Lono—and insisting that the assembled populace perform the requisite *kapu moe*, the prostrating taboo, the Hawaiian elite moved immediately to incorporate these strange new beings into the sphere of their political aspirations. Only later would Cook meet face to face the reigning Hawaiian paramount himself, Kalaniopu'u, at that moment absent on a war of con-

quest directed against his arch-rival Kahekili, paramount of neighboring Maui Island (Fig. 8.1). Within a few short weeks, the sequence of events initiated on the beach at Kealakekua would impel Cook and Kalaniopu'u on a cultural collision course, leading to Cook's death, but simultaneously to his deification within the pantheon of Hawaiian gods. For some years afterward, Cook's sennit casket–bound bones would be annually paraded around the island of Hawai'i, during the Makahiki rites of Lono.[3]

Until his fatal encounter with Kalaniopu'u, Cook interacted smoothly with the Hawaiian chiefs and priests; indeed, he thought he understood them well. This is not surprising, since Cook himself was at the pinnacle of one of the most hierarchical and rigidly defined "societies" of the Western world: the confined microcosm of a British naval vessel.[4] His command was iron-clad, unquestioned, backed by the threat of force and physical punishment. Cook oversaw a rigidly stratified society: the sailing master and other ship's officers, the petty officers, the marines, and finally the able-bodied seamen. No wonder that the Hawaiians had no trouble recognizing the "paramount chief" of this floating island, its command structure visually marked by insignia, uniforms, and protocols. At Kealakekua, one chiefdom met another, recognizing in the other the essential structures of hierarchy and power.

The Hawai'i Island chiefdom under Kalaniopu'u counted at least 60,000 persons within its borders (possibly as many as 150,000) and was arguably the most complex of any indigenous polity ever to develop within Oceania. But other Polynesian islands and archipelagoes also had seen hierarchical sociopolitical structures develop over the centuries since they were discovered and colonized. The range of variation within Polynesian chiefdoms is considerable, and rather than all being on some parallel evolutionary pathway, this diversity more likely reflects a myriad of historical trajectories. This chapter explores some key findings of modern archaeology with regard to the development of the Polynesian chiefdoms.[5]

Polynesian Chiefdoms: Ethnographic Background and Anthropological Significance

When evolutionary anthropologists attempted to synthesize the diversity of sociopolitical structures found throughout the world, they turned to the ethnographically documented societies of Polynesia as "type" examples of what are called *ranked societies* or more commonly *chiefdoms*.[6] Chiefdoms typically incorporate a few thousand up to a few tens of thousands of people, who exhibit social ranking or stratification. They are headed by *chiefs* who come to the chiefship by virtue of birth, that is, they inherit the chiefly title because their genealogies link them directly to eponymous ancestors, and above them to the gods. Chiefs control the power to organize labor and receive tribute. With the chiefdom stage of sociopolitical evolution, human organization moved from a strictly "domestic mode of production," inherently anti-surplus, to what some Marxist scholars have called an "Asiatic mode of production," a political economy in which a steady surplus is extracted from the society's producers to finance and support the activities and political aspirations of its elite.[7] In larger chiefdoms such economies are highly specialized, with functional differentiation of farmers, fishermen, craftspersons, and warriors. Frequently, their systems of production have become intensified through increased application of labor, or through the construction of landesque capital improvements such as terraces and canals.

Yet ethnographic studies of Polynesian chiefdoms reveal a great range of variation in these social formations. In the simplest Polynesian societies, particularly those of the atolls and some of the smaller high islands, distinctions between chief and commoner were minimal, all being linked as kinsmen. Tribute was limited to ritual "first-fruits" offerings, and production was only rarely organized on a suprahousehold level (usually in response to a communitywide disaster). The chief (in Proto Polynesian called the **qariki*, and varied forms derived from it, such as Hawaiian *ali'i*) was both the head of the local lineage or descent group (the **kainanga*) and its spiritual leader. Contrast this simple chiefdom mode with that of Hawai'i, where the chiefly class regarded themselves as directly descended from the gods and were internally ranked into seven or eight different grades, in which the highest chiefs practiced sibling or half-sibling marriage to concentrate the blood line; where *corvée* labor was mobilized on a massive scale to build temples and irrigation works; where tribute consisted of daily food supplies offered to the extended household and entourage of the paramount chief; where insignia of rank such as feathered cloaks and finely carved food bowls were highly elaborated; and where land was alienated from the common people, who held rights of usufruct only by virtue of regular tribute offerings to their chiefs. Between these extremes lay a range of intermediate societies, so that within the Polynesian region virtually the entire range of variation possible within a chiefdom social formation is evidenced.

Marshall Sahlins's classic *Social Stratification in Polynesia* (1958), which classified Polynesian societies according to their degree of hierarchy or stratification, offered an evolutionary explanation for these differences. The smallest-scale societies (Type III) were represented by atolls such as Pukapuka, Ontong-Java, and Tokelau, with populations of a few hundred up to perhaps 2,000 persons. In the midrange (Types IIA and IIB) were societies with two levels of chiefs (typically a paramount and subchiefs), generally situated on the smaller or midsized high islands, such as Futuna, 'Uvea, Mangaia, and Mangareva. At the pinnacle of Sahlins's classification (Type I) were Tonga, Hawai'i, the Society Islands, and Samoa, all with polities encompassing from 10,000 to 40,000 (or more) individuals, with marked indices of stratification. Sahlins regarded differences in social stratification as linked to adaptation to environment. Degree of stratification was directly related to productivity: "the greater the productivity, the greater the differentiation between distributors (chiefs) and producers (nonchiefs)" (1958:249).

While Sahlins stressed the role of ecology and differential resource distribution within a redistributive economic system, a similar comparative and evolutionary study by Irving Goldman (1970) focused on chiefly competition or "status rivalry."

Goldman offered his own tripartite classification of the Polynesian chiefdoms: Traditional, Open, and Stratified. The Traditional chiefdoms (which included Tokelau, Tikopia, Futuna, and others) were conservative, retaining an older Polynesian style of organization in which the chief combined both secular and sacred duties, and were "given stability by a religiously sanctioned gradation of worth" (1970:20). In the Open societies, the "system is more strongly military and political than religious and stability in it must be maintained more directly by the exercise of secular powers." Open chiefdoms included Easter Island, Mangaia, and the Marquesas. Finally, the Stratified chiefdoms (Tonga, Hawai'i, the Society Islands, and Mangareva) were "characterized by clearcut breaks in status that are far-reaching in their impact on everyday life." In these social formations, "high rank holds the rule and possesses the land title: commoners are subject and landless."

Sahlins and Goldman wrote during the heyday of mid-twentieth-century evolutionary anthropology, and their classifications and models might appear outmoded from the perspective of contemporary interpretative anthropology and postprocessual archaeology. Yet these classics retain much value, not as strictly evolutionary models but as analytical dissections of the range of synchronic variation in a phyletically related group of societies. Sahlins and Goldman worked primarily with ethnographic data from the European-contact period. Their studies offer intriguing hypotheses regarding underlying processes (redistribution of resources, status rivalry) that may have been influential in transforming the structure of Polynesian societies. Polynesian archaeology was in its infancy when Sahlins and Goldman carried out their research; today we control a diversity of direct, temporally precise evidence relating to the rise of increasingly complex, hierarchical sociopolitical structures in various Polynesian islands. Rather than force these data into a unilinear model of evolution, they are best seen as a series of sometimes parallel or convergent, sometimes divergent, historical trajectories, all ultimately springing from the common basis of Ancestral Polynesian culture (see Chapter 7).

In a synthesis of research on chiefdom-level societies, Timothy Earle (1997) draws attention to the different sources or kinds of *power* that emerging chiefly elites draw upon to enforce their authority. In Polynesia, authority was already inherent in the Ancestral Polynesian status category of **qariki*, the hereditary leader of a **kainanga* descent group, by virtue of birth order and hence direct access to spiritual power, or *mana* (see Chapter 7). However, as Polynesian chiefdoms became larger and more hierarchic in structure, mere ties of kinship were not a sufficient basis on which to build the power relations necessary to command labor and tribute, or to exercise—as was the case in some societies—the right of life and death over others. Earle identifies three "primary sources of power—economic, military, and ideological" (1997:6). All three sources played significant roles among Polynesian chiefdoms, but the emphasis or mix given to any of these varied with local circumstances and the contingencies of history.

Sociopolitical Transformation in the Open Societies

The Open societies, in Goldman's terminology, offer a fruitful field for archaeological studies of sociopolitical transformation in Polynesia. Goldman implied that these Open societies lay midway on an evolutionary continuum from Traditional to Stratified. But it is more productive to envisage them as headed not toward increased hierarchy but toward something different: to a more "fluid" social structure in which there was intense competition between different social groups and categories. Moreover, all of the Open societies share certain environmental features and ecological conditions which, it appears, influenced their histories. These societies all arose on midsized islands,[8] on which substantial populations (in the low thousands) could develop, but they were also resource restricted. Ecologically, such islands were fragile, and the combination of limited land and ecological vulnerability meant that these islands were prime locations for intensive resource competition once a "full-land" population density had been achieved. Rather than attempt to theorize them further, let us review their individual histories as revealed by archaeology. (Selected archaeological sites are listed in Table 8.1.)

Mangaia (Southern Cook Islands)   Mangaia, southernmost of the Cook Islands (Map 12), possesses one of the most unique geological structures in all of Oceania, rendering it ideal for paleoenvironmental studies. A smallish island of about 52 square kilometers, it has an ancient volcanic core (now deeply weathered to laterite) entirely surrounded by a rampart of elevated reef limestones, up to 2 kilometers wide (Fig. 8.2). Solution caves and caverns riddle this makatea limestone, and they were used as fortified refuges during frequent intertribal wars or as burial places. Narrow streams are incised into the volcanic hillsides (the island was traditionally subdivided into six districts corresponding to these valleys), to become entrapped by the makatea rampart, ponding against the sheer limestone wall. Although some streamflow escapes to the ocean in underground passages through the makatea, sediments brought down in the water channels settle in these low-lying basins, creating deep sedimentary sequences that encode a proxy record of environmental events occurring on this landscape over the millennia. The potential for decoding this sedimentary record enticed David

TABLE 8.1
Selected Later Prehistoric Sites in Eastern Polynesia

Island/Group	Site (Island)	Site Type	Age Range (B.P.)[a]	References
COOK ISLANDS	Maungaroa (Rarotonga)	Inland settlement complex	500–200	Bellwood 1978
	Tau Tua (Mangaia)	Refuge cave	200–100	Kirch 1997c
MARQUESAS	Hanapete'o (Hiva Oa)	Rockshelter	400–recent	Skjølsvold 1972
	Hane Valley (Ua Huka)	Inland settlement complex	500–recent?	Kellum-Ottino 1971
	Paeke (Nuku Hiva)	Megalithic statue complex	450–500	Heyerdahl and Ferdon, eds., 1965
	Vahangeku'a (Nuku Hiva)	*Tohua* complex	Undated	Suggs 1961
AUSTRAL ISLANDS	Morongo Uta (Rapa)	Fortified hilltop village	300–200	Heyerdahl and Ferdon, eds., 1965; Stokes, ms., a
EASTER ISLAND (RAPA NUI)	Ahu A Kivi	Inland statuary temple	700–400	Mulloy and Figueroa 1978
	Ahu Naunau	Megalithic temple with stone statues	800–200	Skjølsvold, ed., 1994
	Ahu Vinapu	Megalithic temple with stone statues	700–200	Heyerdahl and Ferdon, eds., 1961
	Orongo	Ceremonial village with subterranean houses	600–200	Heyerdahl and Ferdon, eds., 1961
	Rano Raraku	Statue quarry	800–200	Heyerdahl and Ferdon, eds., 1961
NEW ZEALAND	Galatea Bay	Coastal shell midden	250	Shawcross 1967
	Kauri Point	Wet site with preserved wooden artifacts	400–250	Shawcross 1976
	Maioro	Fortified village		Fox and Green 1982
	Tiromoana Pa	Fortified ridge settlement	550–250	Fox 1978
SOCIETY ISLANDS	Matairea Hill (Huahine)	Habitation and *marae* complex	500–recent?	Sinoto 1996a
	'Opunohu Valley (Mo'orea)	Inland settlement complex	700–recent	Descantes 1990; Green 1961; Green et al. 1967; Lepofsky 1994
	Taputapuatea (Ra'iatea)	*Marae* temple	Undated	Emory 1933

(continued)

TABLE 8.1 (*continued*)

Island/Group	Site (Island)	Site Type	Age Range (B.P.)[a]	References
HAWAIIAN ISLANDS	Anahulu Valley (O'ahu)	Inland settlement complex; pre- to postcontact	800–100	Kirch and Sahlins 1992
	Halawa (Moloka'i)	Windward valley settlement complex	1,400–recent	Kirch and Kelly, eds., 1975; Riley 1975
	Kahikinui (Maui)	Leeward settlement complex	600–100	Kirch, ed., 1997
	Kalahuipua'a (Hawai'i)	Leeward fishing settlement	800–200	Kirch 1979
	Kane'aki Heiau (Makaha Valley, O'ahu)	Stone temple, excavated sequence	400–200	Green 1980
	Kawela (Moloka'i)	Leeward settlement complex	400–100	Weisler and Kirch 1985
	Lapakahi (Hawai'i)	Leeward settlement complex and dryland field system	1,000–100	Pearson, ed., 1968; Rosendahl 1972, 1994; Tuggle and Griffin, eds., 1973
	Pi'ilanihale Heiau (Maui)	Stone temple	700–200	Kolb 1991
	Puako (Hawai'i)	Petroglyphs	Undated	Cox and Stasack 1970

[a] Age ranges given are approximations based on available series of radiocarbon dates. Refer to the references cited for individual radiocarbon dates associated with specific sites.

Steadman and me to bring an interdisciplinary team of researchers to Mangaia in 1989 and 1991.[9] Before our results are discussed, the Mangaia chiefdom polity as recorded in the early nineteenth century must be briefly described.[10]

Mangaia's population, which numbered at least 3,000 prior to the ravages of introduced diseases, was organized into six districts (see Fig. 8.2), each under the control of a chief (the *pava*), while the entire island was controlled by a paramount chief named *Te Mangaia* (Hiroa 1934). The latter position was not hereditary; it was achieved through war and legitimated by human sacrifice offered at the principal temple of Orongo. This sacrifice was directed to Rongo, a dual god of war and agriculture. Oral histories recount the succession of 42 Te Mangaia prior to European contact. These paramount war leaders were assisted by a triad of priest-chiefs called *ariki* (the Inland High Priest, the Shore High Priest, and the Ruler of Food), who enforced the religious ideology that legitimated the rule of Te Mangaia.

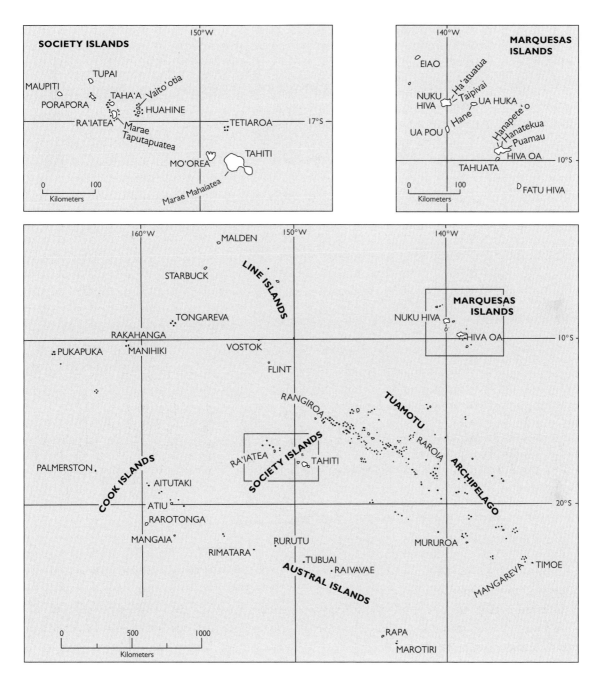

MAP 12 The central Eastern Polynesian archipelagoes and islands. Insets show the Society Islands and the Marquesas Islands, with the location of key archaeological sites.

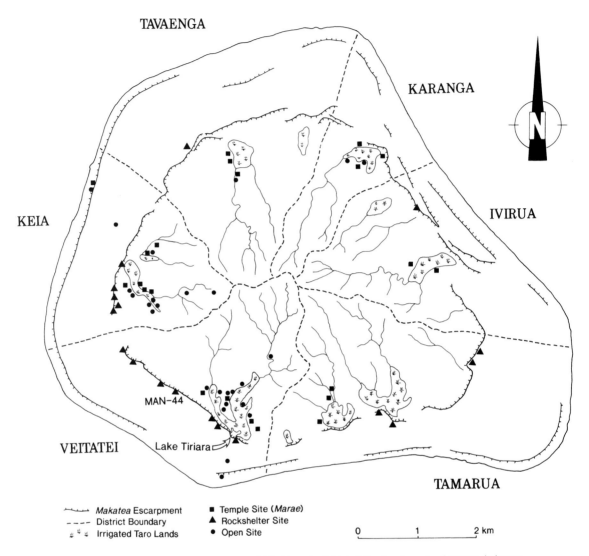

FIGURE 8.2 The island of Mangaia was traditionally subdivided into six districts, following the natural stream drainages. This settlement pattern map shows archaeological sites mapped in 1989 and 1991. (Map by P. V. Kirch.)

This fluid sociopolitical system—in which war was a necessary condition for political succession and groups were disenfranchised from prime lands and relegated to subservient status—was based upon a highly intensive production system. Most coveted were the swampy valley bottoms, modified through terracing and canalization of streams into reticulate pondfields yielding the main staple crop, taro. War victors seized control of these *puna* lands, along with garden lands on hillsides and orchards of breadfruit, Tahitian Chestnut, and coconuts. Defeated groups struggled to make a living on the karst makatea, cultivating yams and sweet potatoes with difficulty.

In proto-historic Mangaian society, competition for limited agricultural (and other) resources was intense, and the political as well as religious system directly reflected this situation. The severe limitation of prime agricultural land was critical: only 2 percent of the landscape could be irrigated, and productive dryland agriculture could be practiced on perhaps another 18 percent. This is because much of the makatea consists of pinnacle karst, and most of the central volcanic hill and ridges consist of highly degraded laterite, on which only a pyrophytic fern (*Dicranopteris linearis*), scrub *Pandanus*, and scattered ironwood trees will grow. But the island was not always environmentally impoverished, as our paleoenvironmental research demonstrated.

The deep cores that we extracted from the valley and lake bottoms yielded a 7,000-year-long history of vegetation and geomorphological changes. Along with archaeological materials from a well-stratified rockshelter (the Tangatatau site, MAN-44), these tell a story of human impact on a vulnerable island ecosystem (see Fig. 2.8). When Polynesians first set foot on Mangaia—perhaps between 2,500 and 2,000 years ago based on the pollen and charcoal evidence—they found the central volcanic hills well forested, probably ideal for shifting cultivation. However, once this old forest began to be cleared with the use of fire it was unable to regenerate, possibly because of a lack of phosphorus in the depleted laterite. Over several centuries the thin organic soil layer blanketing the hill slopes was eroded down into the valley bottoms. The hills, now covered in ferns and increasingly worthless for agriculture, became a kind of no-man's-land while the narrow valleys were converted through terracing into the main centers of agricultural production. Meanwhile, the island's population increased to a density of perhaps 150 persons per square kilometer, taxing the island's increasingly restricted resources.

Stress occurred not only in the agricultural sector; the faunal record from Tangatatau rockshelter (Fig. 8.3) reveals a parallel reduction of the terrestrial and marine food supply. A rich bird fauna—including many species of rails, doves, pigeons, and lorikeets, as well as nesting seabirds—was severely reduced through direct human predation, as well as through the indirect impacts of habitat reduction. Whereas 19 species of land birds and 12 species of seabirds were present on the island in A.D. 1000, only 5 and 6 of these species, respectively, have survived into the historic period. The marine fauna—never lush due to a limited reef lacking a lagoon—was also heavily exploited, leading to a severe reduction in the numbers and sizes of mollusks and fish.

Mangaia's late prehistoric settlement patterns reflect the Open chiefdom that had developed on the island in response to environmental changes set in motion by the land use and resource exploitation strategies of earlier generations. Residence was concentrated in clusters of terraced habitations on ridges just above and adjacent to irrigated taro fields, with *marae* or lineage temples as central foci. These *marae* were not architecturally elaborate but consisted of earthen terraces paved with coral gravel, with upright speleothems (stalactites and stalagmites) removed from makatea caverns placed as godstones. During warfare or raiding, groups fled from their exposed residential complexes into refuge caves in the makatea. One refuge cavern, Tau Tua, was studied by our team; it contained stone house foundations and cooking areas. A telling index of the ferocity of intertribal raiding and war was human sacrifice (Hiroa 1934). The archaeological record suggests that cannibalism, or cannibal-like practices such as the roasting and dismembering of captured enemies, if not their outright consumption, occurred with increased frequency in late prehistory (Anton and Steadman 1997).

FIGURE 8.3 The large Tangatatau Rockshelter in Veitatei District, Mangaia, contains a well-stratified sequence of occupation deposits. (Photo by P. V. Kirch.)

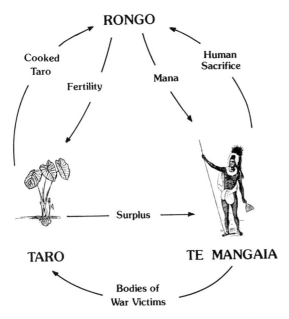

FIGURE 8.4 A complex set of ideological relationships linked the paramount chief of Mangaia (Te Mangaia) to the god Rongo in proto-historic Mangaian society. (From Kirch 1997c.)

With archaeology revealing something of the historical trajectory lying behind the ethnographic Mangaian sociopolitical formation, what emerges is not a society at an imagined midpoint along an evolutionary continuum toward ever-increasing hierarchy, but one that had followed its own distinctive trajectory, constrained by the cumulative actions of previous generations. The Mangaian polity had moved away from a rigid hierarchy based on hereditary power to one in which overt military power was to the fore. The Mangaian elite used ideological control, to be sure, as in the mytho-praxis that put the Janus-like god of war and taro, Rongo, at the center of the principal cult (Fig. 8.4). But there was little material elaboration of ideology (such as monumental temples or sculpture) as seen in other Polynesian societies. Perhaps the Mangaians could not afford such a luxury; their backs were up against a wall, with a severely resource-limited environment in which—lacking sufficient cultural controls on population growth—the only outlet appeared to be intense competition for land. Late precontact Mangaian society became, to a pervasive degree, a society based on terror (see Kirch 1997d).

The "Land of Men" Te Fenua 'Enata—the "land of men"—is the name given by the Polynesians to the Marquesas Islands (Map 12), a group of seven midsized volcanic high islands lying northeast of Tahiti and the Tuamotus. Collectively, the islands have a land area of 1,048 square kilometers, 330 of those on the largest island of Nuku Hiva. The cold Humboldt Current bears down on the islands from Peru, inhibiting coral growth, and the Marquesas lack lagoons or fringing reefs. Valleys descend to deep bays, with rocky headlands and cliffs separating one valley from another (Fig. 8.5). The fertile volcanic terrain supports most Polynesian crops, but periodic droughts beset the archipelago, sometimes for years. These environmental factors influenced the historical trajectory of Marquesan society.

The archipelago was never politically unified, even though its people share a common language and culture.[11] On individual islands the occupants of particular valleys typically formed independent polities, which were frequently at war with one other. As in Mangaia, the social structure at the proto-historic "endpoint" of indigenous development was fluid, although there was no paramount chief comparable to the Te Mangaia.[12] Power was shared, uneasily, among three main status groups: the hereditary chiefs (*haka'iki*), the inspirational priests (*tau'a*), and the warriors (*toa*). The exercise of force was pervasive, and *toa* made frequent raids

into neighboring valleys, seeking human victims to sacrifice at memorial feasts for deceased chiefs and priests; if the accounts are accurate, their flesh was consumed in cannibalistic rites (Handy 1923: 218–21). Arboriculture dominated the subsistence economy, with breadfruit as the main orchard crop. The Marquesans elaborated pit ensilage and fermentation of breadfruit to a greater level than anywhere else in Remote Oceania, digging storage pits with capacities of up to 200 cubic meters. Located in the interiors of valleys or in fortified locations, these *ma* pits provided food reserves in times of drought and famine.

The Marquesan archaeological record is among the most thoroughly investigated in Eastern Polynesia, its prehistoric sequence well defined in spite of controversies about the date of first colonization (see Chapter 7).[13] Robert Suggs (1961) divided Marquesan prehistory into four stages or periods, and his basic sequence, with modification and amplification, has withstood the test of additional research (Fig. 8.6).

Dates for the Settlement Period are still in dispute; Suggs (1961:181) suggested 150 B.C.– A.D. 100, while others have argued that initial colonization did not commence until A.D. 300 (Sinoto 1979a; Spriggs and Anderson 1993). Resolving the controversy will require more primary fieldwork and many more radiocarbon dates on a variety of materials. Other aspects of this early period are less controversial. Settlement was confined to coastal hamlets at the mouths of the larger and more fertile valleys (Fig. 8.7), with some use of rockshelters by fishermen (e.g., the Hanatekua rockshelter [Sinoto 1970], or possibly the Anapua site [Ottino 1992]). The earliest levels have a typical Eastern Polynesian material culture, with one-piece fishhooks of pearl shell, plano-convex and incipiently tanged basalt adzes, abraders of *Porites* coral, and other objects. Slightly later strata display

FIGURE 8.5 The Marquesas Islands lack developed reefs and have amphitheater-headed valleys with deep bays, as seen in this view of Ua Pou Island. (Photo by P. V. Kirch.)

a full range of "Archaic Eastern Polynesian" arti-facts (see Chapter 7). Plain ware pottery has been found at four sites, but in limited quantities. The sherds at Ha'atuatua were imports from Fiji, but other vessels were manufactured locally (Dick-inson and Shutler 1974; Dickinson et al. 1998; Kirch et al. 1988). This is the only local pottery thus far identified from Eastern Polynesia.[14]

The Developmental Period, which Suggs dated from A.D. 100 to 1100 but which may have been of somewhat shorter duration, continued the cultural pattern set in the preceding Settlement Period. Rolett (1998) found little evidence of artifactual change between the two periods in the Hanamiai site (Fig. 8.8) and sees them as forming a continuity. There were, however, changes in resource exploitation, particularly toward the later part of the Developmental Period. As in Mangaia, reductions in the frequency of endemic and in-digenous land birds and seabirds occurred, includ-ing the extirpation and extinction of numerous species, especially among the land birds. A decline

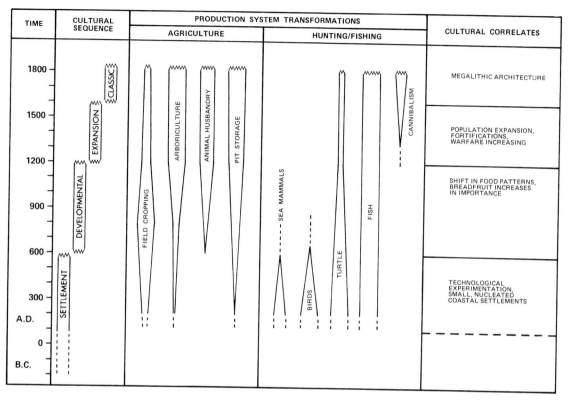

FIGURE 8.6 Diagrammatic summary of the Marquesan cultural sequence. (From Kirch 1984a.)

in sea mammal and turtle bones between early (Settlement or early Developmental) contexts and later deposits is also evident.[15] At the same time, the bones of domestic pigs begin to appear in some quantity in late Developmental Period sites. These changes speak to a reduction in wild food resources—reflecting the fragile ecology of oceanic islands—and to efforts at establishing more intensive agricultural production systems, including pig husbandry.

Particularly good evidence for these changes in environment and resource exploitation comes from Rolett's research in the Hanamiai Valley on Tahuata Island, supporting a model of human colonization and environmental change for tropical Polynesia proposed by Kirch (1984a:159–60). In the Hanamiai sequence there is a faunal succession in the land snail assemblages (with a shift in dominance from endemic and indigenous species to introduced species) that reflects the Polynesian establishment of a "transported landscape" (Rolett 1992). Also evident in the Hanamiai sequence is a pattern of bird extinctions and extirpations (affecting both land birds and seabirds), with the greatest impact occurring within the first 300 years after human settlement of the valley (ca. A.D. 1025–1300; Steadman and Rolett 1996). Rolett comments on these changes as follows:

Local increases in the density of human populations occurred rapidly, and simultaneously with the local depletion of wild species originally abundant

FIGURE 8.7 Artist's reconstruction of the early Eastern Polynesian settlement at Ha'atuatua Bay, Nuku Hiva, based on the 1956–57 excavations of Robert Suggs. Some aspects of this reconstruction would be contested today, but the scene nonetheless evokes some idea of what early coastal hamlets in Eastern Polynesia might have looked like. (Drawing by Nicholas Amorosi; courtesy Robert C. Suggs.)

in newly settled valleys. In the absence of a well developed food production system based on agriculture and domestic animals, the declining availability of wild species presumably stimulated human populations to seek out new resources. Population shifts to previously unsettled valleys would have alleviated pressure on subsistence systems in both old and new communities, prolonging the viability of a broad spectrum subsistence strategy. The initial

settlement of Hanamiai, around A.D. 1000–1100, apparently represents one such population movement in this process of range expansion. (1996:538)

The Expansion Period (A.D. 1100–1400 in Suggs's chronology) was unquestionably the phase of greatest transformation in Marquesan society, setting the stage for the Open society documented in the proto-historic era. Suggs (1961:182) wrote that "the population of Nuku Hiva, which had been increasing in the large verdant valleys on the south and east coasts, suddenly broke out," with sites now appearing not only near the mouths of the fertile valleys but everywhere, even in marginal areas. Rolett (1989:108) concurs that the "settlement pattern of this period reflects rapid population growth." Various cultural changes are evident. In material culture, basalt adzes distinctive to the Marquesas now appear in quantity, as well as the jabbing form of pearl-shell fishhook, which replaced a wider diversity of hook forms in earlier periods. New kinds of architecture make their appearance in the Expansion Period, including ridgetop fortifications (often with breadfruit storage pits), stone house platforms (*paepae*), and several types of ceremonial structures, including temple foundations (*me'ae*) and dance or feast centers (*tohua*). The *tohua* are rectangular courts (Fig. 8.9), often constructed as leveled terraces, surrounded by house platforms and other structures (and sometimes incorporating *me'ae*). As Suggs observes, "The construction of such ceremonial centers by subtribes marks the beginning of the intergroup rivalry that was so marked in the Historic period" (1961:183).

Suggs had little doubt that the causes of the "sudden appearance and proliferation of settlements in the marginal areas," while complex, were fundamentally linked with the population explosion occurring during this phase. This demographic transition coincided with the depletion of

FIGURE 8.8 The Hanamiai dune site on Tahuata Island yielded important information on the early phases of the Marquesan cultural sequence. Note the exposed stone pavement. (Photo courtesy Barry Rolett.)

wild faunal resources, and food stress would have been periodically exacerbated by the droughts for which the islands are noted. Certainly the Marquesan population was making substantial efforts at this time to intensify and augment agricultural production, evidenced in the development of cultivation terraces (some irrigated) and food storage pits throughout the valleys. However, the appearance of fortifications signals territorial aggression and raiding, the dark side of a society that increasingly pushed the ability of its island ecosystem to sustain a burgeoning population.

During the Classic Period (A.D. 1400–1790), patterns that arose during the Expansion Period came to florescence. Settlement distribution remained widespread and dispersed, with one

FIGURE 8.9 A view of the central ceremonial plaza on the Ta'a'oa *tohua* site on Hiva Oa Island, Marquesas. (Photo by P. V. Kirch.)

exception: "the beaches were generally shunned, and the entire population seemed to gravitate inland, moving up high into the valley heads for protection from increased raiding from the sea" (Suggs 1961:185). Architecture became more elaborate and larger in the Classic Period, reflecting the power of chiefs, inspirational priests, and war-riors to command the labor of their followers. *Tohua* platforms, for example, reached truly massive proportions, such as in the Vahangeku'a site in Taipivai Valley or Ta'a'oa on Hiva Oa (Fig. 8.10). On some *tohua*, or on *me'ae* temples where the inspirational priests officiated, anthropomorphic statues, some of considerable size, were erected

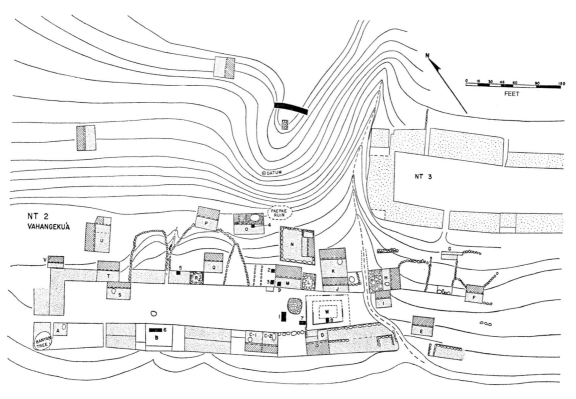

FIGURE 8.10 Plan map of the Vahangeku'a *tohua* site in Taipivai Valley, Nuku Hiva, Marquesas. (From Suggs 1961.)

(Fig. 8.11).[16] House platforms were now frequently constructed in a "megalithic" style (Fig. 8.12). Associated with these constructions were many breadfruit storage pits, some of them with truly cavernous capacities. The material arts of the Classic Period attest to a florescence of craft specialization by experts (*tohunga*) under elite patronage. Chiefs and warriors sported finely carved bone ornaments, such as ear plugs and hair spools, and anthropomorphic designs graced the heads of food (*popoi*) pounders. Early European accounts and drawings reveal that tattooing reached an artistic apogee during the Marquesan Classic Period.

The historical trajectory of the Marquesas in many respects parallels that of Mangaia, but there are important differences, particularly the elabo-

ration of status rivalry and its manifestation in the material arts, including architecture. Common factors in both cases were limiting constraints of the environment (including the effects of human-induced resource reduction), combined with population growth to a high-density level, spurring intense competition for land and other resources. In the social arena of everyday life, this competition played itself out in continuous prestige rivalry between the hereditary elite and the achieved-status elite of warriors and inspirational priests. Suggs, nonetheless, reminds us that there was a deeper level of causation: "The cause of the intense prestige rivalry may be seen in the relation of the population to the habitable land. As the population increased beyond the point at which all

FIGURE 8.11 A large anthro-pomorphic statue, carved from red volcanic tuff, at Puamau, Hiva Oa Island, Marquesas. (Photo by P. V. Kirch.)

FIGURE 8.12 During the Classic Period, Marquesan dwellings were frequently constructed upon massive stone platforms, with separate sleeping spaces and paved verandahs. (From Suggs 1961.)

possible ecological niches became filled, intergroup conflicts over land would have increased. . . . The need to acquire and hold the land necessary for existence and to increase the areas held to accommodate population increases intensified to an extreme the rivalry apparently present in most Polynesian societies" (1961:186).[17] In an analysis of the Marquesan sequence, I characterized what happened in the later prehistoric periods as a kind of "competitive involution," in which "a dynamic context of rapid population growth, pervasive environmental hazards (especially drought), ecological degradation, and acute competition over productive resources fostered rivalry between inherently contradictory hereditary and achieved status positions. The result was an involuted cycle of prestige rivalry and competition that led as often to the destruction of the very means of production which were the objects of competition" (Kirch 1991b:144).

Comparing the archaeological records of Mangaia and the Marquesas, both Open societies in Goldman's conception, many similarities as well as striking differences are evident. In both cases, initial human actions led to resource depletion, partially offset by intensification of agricultural production. Population growth and, eventually, high density levels unquestionably played an important role in the transformation of both societies. In both cases, military power, exercised by a warrior class (*toa*), came to challenge the traditional authority of the hereditary chiefly elite, and both warriors and chiefs vied with the spiritual authority of priests. In Mangaia, however, while a unifying polity—if always a fragile and temporary one— was achieved through conquest, there was none of the material elaboration of visual power displays, whether in personal ornamentation (including tattooing as well as mobiliary art) or in standing architecture, that characterizes the Marquesas. This may be primarily a matter of scale and of the available resource base. During hard times of drought and famine the Marquesans found themselves in difficult straits, yet at other times they had a sufficiently robust economy to support a level of craft specialization, as well as labor investment in monumental public works, that was never present in Mangaia, a much smaller island and one far more constrained by its unique geological history. Parallels, yet differences: in such contrasts we seek to tease out the essentials of Polynesian history.

Rapa, Mangareva, and the Pitcairn Group   The Austral Islands (Map 12) define the southern fringe of central Eastern Polynesia (Rimatara, Rurutu, Tubuai, Raivavae, and Rapa), and beyond them to the east lies the Mangareva (Gambier) group; even farther eastward lie Pitcairn Island (of *Bounty* mutineer fame) and Henderson. The latter two are among the so-called "mystery islands" of Polynesia (Kirch 1988f), some 12 generally small islands with archaeological traces of Polynesian habitation, but that were unoccupied at the time of early European exploration.[18] This southeastern lineament of islands, stretching altogether more than 2,000 kilometers, has been little explored archaeologically. However, recent work in Tubua'i, Mangareva, Pitcairn, and Henderson is beginning to reveal that all of these were at one time linked through a regular interaction sphere (see Chapter 7). Moreover, late prehistoric social upheavals—particularly in Mangareva—may have precipitated the final collapse of such long-distance interaction.

The most complete data at present come from the extreme eastern end of this old interaction network, from Henderson Island, where Weisler (1994, 1995, 1996a, 1998b) carried out intensive archaeological surveys and excavations in 1990–92. Henderson is a highly tenuous human habitat, consisting of an upraised makatea block with limited reef (much of the coast consists of sea cliffs) and almost no soil; surface water is entirely lacking. Yet well-stratified deposits in rockshelters and one beach site testify to a continuous Polynesian presence on Henderson from about A.D. 900 until perhaps 1500. Throughout most of this period, the archaeological deposits contain significant quantities of exotic imports (pearl shell for fishhook manufacture, basalt and pitchstone for adzes and flake tools, and volcanic oven stones). Weisler has shown, through X-ray fluorescence sourcing methods, that the volcanic imports derived from nearby Pitcairn and from Mangareva,

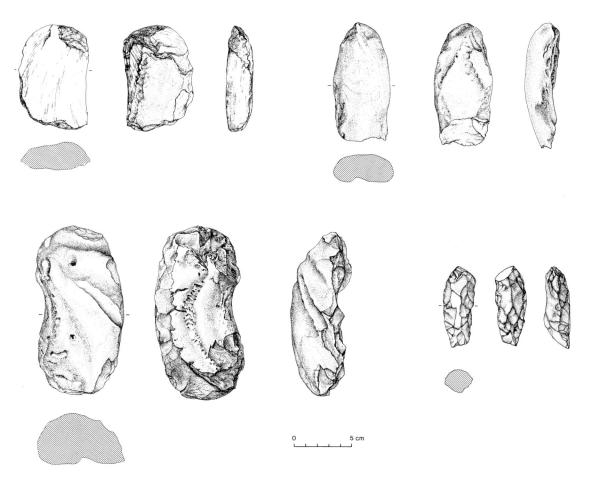

FIGURE 8.13 Late prehistoric occupation deposits on Henderson Island contain crude adzes made from locally available fossilized *Tridacna* shell. (Courtesy Marshall Weisler.)

some 400 kilometers distant. But at around A.D. 1450, these imported items suddenly disappear from the upper levels of sites on Henderson. The uppermost strata instead contain distinctive artifacts utilizing locally available materials (inferior *Isognomon* shell for fishhooks, fossilized *Tridacna* shell for adzes) reflecting an effort to adapt to strictly local resources (Fig. 8.13). But the sites were soon abandoned, and the island was devoid of people when first sighted by Europeans.

What happened on Henderson—or for that matter on Pitcairn, an island somewhat larger and better endowed with soil and water, but which was also unoccupied when, in 1790, the *Bounty* mutineers came ashore to seek refuge from the long arm of the British Admiralty? The answer may lie in Mangareva, the larger node to which these outposts were for several centuries vitally linked. As Weisler argues, these "so-called 'mystery islands' with their marginal ecological conditions and isolation taxed the capabilities of Polynesian colonization strategies to the physical and social limits" (1996a:627). Only through continued interaction with larger Mangareva—source not only of the oven stone that we see in the archaeological record but presumably also of continuing economic, demographic, and social support that has not left direct material traces—could human existence on these isolates be sustained for long periods. When that lifeline was severed, the human populations on Pitcairn and Henderson soon perished or abandoned the struggle.

What then transpired on Mangareva? The answer is not yet clear, for archaeological work on Mangareva is still in its infancy.[19] Mangareva is one of the most severely degraded islands in all of Polynesia, its volcanic slopes completely denuded of forest (although sedimentary deposits containing endemic arboreal land snails indicate the former presence of such forest). Hiroa's (1938b) salvage ethnography describes a proto-historic society in which food was frequently scarce, war endemic, and cannibalism not uncommon. While Goldman (1970) classified Mangareva as a Stratified society, a closer reading of the ethnohistoric texts suggests an alternative interpretation: a society that had at an earlier time undergone transformation toward hierarchy, but which in late prehistory plunged into a phase of social turmoil and upheaval (hence, an Open society). This internal strife presumably led the Mangarevans to abandon their long-distance voyaging to remote Pitcairn and Henderson. Future research in Mangareva will doubtless yield a much more complete, and doubtless fascinating, account of the transformation of this southeastern Polynesian society.

One other island in the Austral group should be mentioned: Rapa, where limited surface surveys and the intensive excavation of one large fortified village site (Morongo Uta) provide some indications of yet another variant on the Open society theme of intensification of production combined with territorial competition. On Rapa the main productive zones were the alluvial valley bottoms, which were converted into intensive taro pondfield

irrigation systems (not unlike those of Mangaia). The island's population developed a unique settlement pattern of fortified ridgetop villages, with 25 hill forts occupying defensive positions on the island's circular volcanic crater rim. The Morongo Uta hill fort was excavated by the Norwegian Archaeological Expedition in 1956 (Heyerdahl and Ferdon, eds., 1965) (Fig. 8.14). This large site, which was radiocarbon dated to the proto-historic period (310–210 B.P.), has a central tower surrounded by tiers of stone-faced terraces. Habitation terraces, on which were found large numbers of basalt adzes and *poi* pounders, extend outward along three ridges. Much more work will be necessary on Rapa before the sequence of development, of both the intensive production system and the fortified settlement pattern, can be understood in full.[20]

Rapa Nui: "Navel of the World" Although I had previously visited legendary Easter Island—Rapa Nui as it is known in the language of its Polynesian inhabitants—nothing prepared me for the sight that I now beheld at Tongariki, on a warm October afternoon in 1996. Chilean archaeologists Claudio Cristino and Patricia Vargas had driven us over the dusty road from Hangaroa to this bay on the island's southern coast, where for several years they had directed the restoration of the largest monumental construction ever erected in the Pacific islands. (The site had been ripped apart by a tsunami, and the task of restoration was truly daunting, requiring the use of a large crane shipped to the island; see Cristino and Casanova 1998.) The *ahu* or temple of Tongariki, with its 14 anthropomorphic statues now replaced upright on a massive elongated platform faced with finely cut and dressed basalt slabs, literally runs from one side of the valley to the other, a distance of 145 meters (Fig. 8.15).[21] On its seaward face, the platform itself rises to a height of 4 meters, and

FIGURE 8.14 The fortified ridgetop village site of Morongo Uta, Rapa Island, after the completion of excavations by the Norwegian Archaeological Expedition in 1956. Note the stone-faced terraces and the central tower. (From Heyerdahl and Ferdon, eds., 1965; courtesy Kon Tiki Museum, Oslo.)

the largest statues stand another 6 meters above that. Standing in the shadow of this incredible construction, watching the sun set behind the craggy outline of Rano Raraku—the volcano where these stone giants were quarried—I found mere adjectives inadequate to express my emotions. "Immense," "megalithic," "awe-inspiring"—such terms only poorly convey the thoughts evoked by this *mémoire de pierre*, this imposing stone text that suggests a thousand human sagas.

The island itself is known by various appellations. "Easter" was bestowed on this remote locality by the Dutch voyager Jacob Roggeveen, who arrived there on Easter Day 1722. More evocative, however, is the islanders' own name,

Te Pito-te-henua, deriving from the Polynesian words for "land" (*henua*) and for "navel" (*pito*). The name has thus sometimes been translated "Navel of the World," although given an alternative meaning for *pito* as "end," a reading as "Land's End" might be more appropriate (Métraux 1940: 34–35; Routledge 1919:209–10). Rapa Nui is the name commonly used for the island today, although there is much reason to believe that this name arose in the nineteenth century, in order to distinguish Easter Island from Rapa Iti in the Austral chain. (To make matters more confusing, the name of the language spoken by the Polynesian inhabitants of Rapa Nui is typically spelled Rapanui.)

FIGURE 8.15 The restored *ahu* of Tongariki, the largest statue temple ever constructed on Rapa Nui. The temple platform supports 14 *moai* or statues. (Photo by P. V. Kirch.)

Ever since the island's discovery in 1722, questions have been raised about the history of the unique statues of Rapa Nui (Map 13) and the origins of the people who carved and erected them. The more bizarre theories invoked space aliens or the survivors of an oceanic Atlantis called Mu; Thor Heyerdahl (1952) would have them be the legacy of Inca kings who sailed to Rapa Nui on balsa rafts. Yet the Rapa Nui people know that these statues were the work of their own Polynesian ancestors, and their oral traditions contain extensive information on the statue cult and its role in their ancient society. We might have learned a good deal more from the Rapa Nui themselves were it not for the decimation of disease and slave raiding, which had robbed the society of its

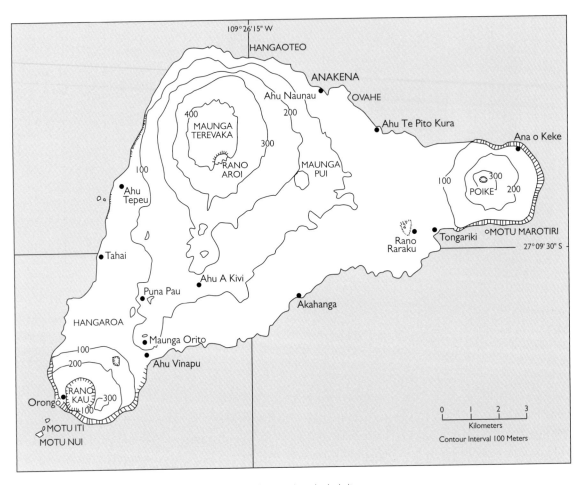

MAP 13 Easter Island (Rapa Nui), showing the location of key archaeological sites.

learned elders by the beginning of the present century. Thus it has fallen to archaeology, combined with "salvage" ethnography, to write a history of this most remote Polynesian island.

The early work of Katherine Scoresby Routledge (1919) in 1914–15 (see Chapter 1) was followed by the irreplaceable ethnography of Alfred Métraux (1940) and Père Sabastian Englert (1948, 1970), but not until the Norwegian Archaeological Expedition of 1955–56 were modern stratigraphic excavation techniques brought to bear on

the enigmas of Easter Island history. A great deal of intensive work has followed, which, combined with radiocarbon dating, provides the outline of a prehistoric sequence for the island.[22] A multiyear intensive survey of the island's archaeological sites, commenced by Patrick McCoy but carried out especially by the University of Chile team under Claudio Cristino and Patricia Vargas, has now recorded more than 20,000 sites in a state-of-the-art computerized database.[23] A major survey and analysis of the island's stone statues was

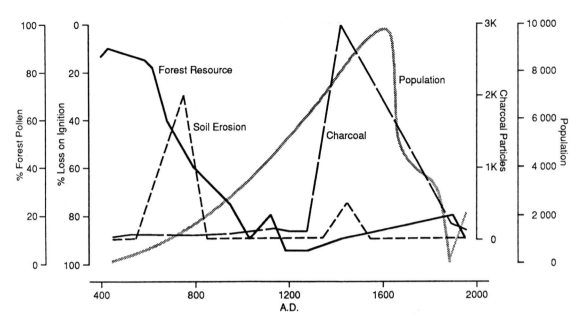

FIGURE 8.16 The cultural sequence of Easter Island was marked by major changes in the local environment, resulting from human land use. (Adapted from Bahn and Flenley 1992; courtesy John Flenley.)

conducted by Van Tilburg (1986, 1987, 1988) and Vargas (1988). Paleoecological research also provides a critical history of human-induced environmental change.[24]

It is not known when Rapa Nui was first colonized, but a pollen core from Rano Kau suggests the onset of human-induced forest clearance by 1630 ± 130 B.P. (A.D. 147–676, calibrated), consistent with a radiocarbon date on charcoal from the Poike Ditch of A.D. 235–615. Such early dates mesh well with linguistic evidence that the Rapanui language diverged early from the Proto Eastern Polynesian language subgroup (Green 1988b). Excavations at Anakena Bay, seaward of the Ahu Naunau temple, exposed deposits dating to A.D. 900, containing abundant seabird bones representing no fewer than 25 species, of which only a single species survives on the island today. These, combined with the pollen and preserved

seed evidence, testify to an originally forested island (with one dominant tree being a large, erect palm of the genus *Jubea*), completely different from the treeless landscape that greets modern visitors.

While Rapa Nui's history of ecological change is still incomplete, some key changes are evident (Fig. 8.16). Over the course of Polynesian occupation, the original forest cover was eliminated, with consequences that are only partly understood. The removal of all large trees had negative repercussions for fuel and construction needs, and certainly also for timber with which to transport the statues. More critical may have been the exposure of the island's landscape to erosion by wind and sheet wash, reducing soil fertility and agricultural productivity. The Anakena excavations revealed a substantial reduction in an original wild food resource: nesting or roosting seabirds. Given that Easter Island has almost no reef and an

FIGURE 8.17 A kneeling statue, rather different in form from the classic Rapa Nui *moai* and more similar to Marquesan sculpture, during its excavation at the Rano Raraku quarry during the 1955–56 Norwegian Archaeological Expedition. (From Heyerdahl and Ferdon 1965; courtesy Kon Tiki Museum, Oslo.)

impoverished marine fauna, birds were probably a key protein source in the early years of human colonization, one that was virtually eliminated by the later prehistoric periods.

This sequence of ecological change parallels that of Mangaia, and the similarities are notable. However, Rapa Nui, at 160 square kilometers, is more than three times the size of Mangaia, and virtually all of its land surface (except the crater lakes) is arable. Thus, whereas a maximal population of perhaps 3,000 struggled to produce sufficient food on Mangaia, the population of Rapa Nui at its peak certainly was much larger. No firm population estimate for prehistory has been established, but given the density of archaeological remains that literally cover the island's surface, a figure of 10,000 persons (a density of 62.5 per square kilometer) or possibly more is not unreasonable. Indeed, it is difficult to conceive of the scale of monumental public construction works undertaken on the island as feasible without a labor force on that order of magnitude.[25]

Just when statue carving first began is not known, but by A.D. 1100 small statues were already being quarried from the soft tuff of Rano Raraku volcano (Fig. 8.17) and transported to and erected on temple platforms (*abu*), ushering in the Ahu Moai Period (ca. A.D. 1100–1500). The earliest *abu* were small and utilized much natural stone in their construction, while later temples (at many *abu* there is a stratified construction sequence) were larger and more elaborate, and used cut and dressed basalt and red scoria in their facings. At the apogee of this local sequence of architectural development stand such magnificent constructions as Tongariki and the famous Ahu Vinapu (Fig. 8.18), whose closely fitted slabs have erroneously been compared with Inca stonework. Ultimately some 245 *abu* were constructed, primarily on the coast around the island's perimeter (although there are a few inland *abu*), and 324 statues were erected on them (another 200-odd statues remain unfinished in the Rano Raraku quarry).

The oldest *abu*—those which through continued rebuilding and enlargement gradually became the largest, with the greatest number of statues—are found at the best embayments around the island. Each of these marked the center of a territorial unit (a *kainga*) constituting the estate of a "tribe" or descent group (Métraux 1940, 1957). As

FIGURE 8.18 Extremely fine stonework marks the facing of Ahu Vinapu on Rapa Nui. (Photo by P. V. Kirch.)

these social groups fissioned, subsidiary temples were built at distances to either side flanking the coast, marking subgroup territories. The statues represented deified ancestors, and the chiefly elite constructed their houses with foundations of cut and dressed basalt immediately inland of the *ahu* plazas, to be literally under the gaze of the ancestors.[26]

Stretching inland from these elite centers—dominating the bays and visually "controlling" access to the limited marine resources—were the habitations and gardens of the common people. Typically these were clusters of small round, oval, or rectangular houses with rough stone foundations, a cooking facility marked by a stone-outlined oven, and cultivation features such as *manavai*, walled pits that protected bananas or other plants

from incessant winds (Yen 1988). Sweet potato fields dominated the agricultural landscape, able to produce high yields even in poor soil conditions and fueling a political economy bent on a spiraling competition of architectonic display.

The statue cult came to an end, and the island plunged into a state of intense intertribal raiding and warfare, during the Huri Moai[27] or Decadent Phase, from about A.D. 1500 to 1722. In all likelihood, this transition was not abrupt, for the incorporation of older (frequently broken) statues into the foundations of later temples suggests that raiding and overthrowing of the ancestral figures began even while the carving of new and ever-larger statues continued. However, the rise of endemic warfare—and of a kind of social terror far greater than that witnessed in the other Open

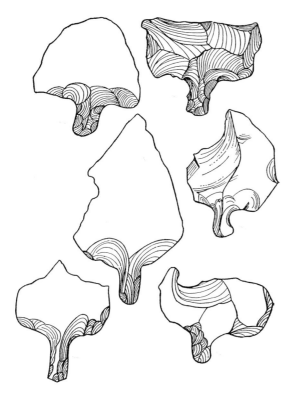

FIGURE 8.19 *Mata'a*, obsidian spearheads, were used in the frequent intertribal conflicts of late prehistoric Rapa Nui. (After Métraux 1957.)

societies—is well marked in the late prehistoric archeological record. The finely worked basalt foundation slabs of elite houses were pulled apart and used to fortify subterranean lava tubes and caves. Late-period sites are replete with obsidian spearheads (*mata'a*); lashed to short sticks, these could lacerate an enemy in close combat (Fig. 8.19). Late-period middens have a sickeningly high frequency of charred and fractured human bones, many of them from juveniles, archaeological signals of anthropophagy (Steadman, pers. comm., 1992). Whatever economic power the hereditary elite once commanded, inducing their people to erect ideologically legitimating symbols of their and their ancestors' glory, became thor-

oughly eroded. Power now fell to the warrior class, the *matatoa*, or as they were figuratively called, *tangata rima toto*, the "men with bloody hands."

By the proto-historic period, quarrying and erection of new statues came to a complete halt, although some statues were still standing when the first Europeans arrived. Moreover, the religious and ritual system had undergone a major transformation. While the *ahu* still held some importance, and the dead were buried in crude stone-faced crypts erected under and between fallen statues, the island's ritual focus now shifted to a narrow ridge on the crater rim of Rano Kau volcano, high above the sea, overlooking the offshore islets of Motu Iti and Motu Nui. These islets were the last refugia of the island's once vast seabird populations, and a bizarre cult of the *manutara* (the Sooty Tern, *Sterna fuscata*) arose, with its ceremonial center at Orongo on the crater rim. At Orongo, in a complex of subterranean stone houses, the representatives of the island's tribes would gather annually to await the arrival and first egg-laying of the *manutara* on the islets below. The first young contestant to retrieve such an egg and return with it to Orongo was proclaimed the *tangata manu*, the "bird man," bringing prestige and privilege to his people. The "bird man" himself would be secluded for one year in a special house at the now-silent statue quarry of Rano Raraku. Grant McCall has summarized this remarkable religious transformation: "It is not surprising that the Rapanui, faced with an ecological crisis that threatened their entire social order, if not their very lives, should take the initiative to fashion a new religion more suited to their precarious times. Instead of a king for life, they opted for one elected by ordeal. Instead of many ancestors who descended from many ancestors, they propounded a single god [Makemake], whose image they carved in deserted rocks, on the bases of feud-toppled figures, and even around water-holes" (1980:38–39).

One final aspect of Rapa Nui culture is the enigmatic *rongorongo* script, preserved primarily on wooden boards, but which also appears on other objects, such as staffs, pectorals, and statuettes (Barthel 1974; Fischer 1997). Given that the script does not appear on precontact stonework, it is likely to have been a proto-historic invention, possibly inspired by Rapa Nui elite being "made to witness, in pen and ink, the Spaniards' deed of cession on 20 November 1770" (Fischer 1997:552). The script, nonetheless, is strictly an indigenous invention, with the individual glyphs probably originating in the "inventory of the island's rock art" (1997:553). The *rongorongo* texts, which were presented in a singing voice, encapsulated ritual or sacred recitations, including procreation chants. It is telling that the word *rongorongo* has cognates in other Eastern Polynesian languages, such as those of Mangareva and the Marquesas, where the related terms refer to genealogical chants (Kirch 1984a:273–74).

There is much that we do not fully understand about the unique past of Rapa Nui, this "land's end" (*te pito o te henua*), an isolated world in the vastness of the eastern Pacific. The intricacies of its history demand more decades of careful fieldwork to decode. This much is certain: more than any of the Open chiefdoms, Rapa Nui's history repulses any attempt to pigeonhole it into some neat evolutionary cubicle. Seemingly tending toward hierarchy and increased centralization at one phase, it transformed itself into an almost anarchistic state. In the end, the relations of power that underwrote the construction of the most incredible monuments the ancient Pacific world has ever seen were not sufficient to survive the pressures they put upon the very ecosystem that those ideological symbols were meant to dominate and control.

Aotearoa: The "Long White Cloud"   In 1642, the Dutch explorer Abel Tasman came upon a great "conti-nental" land which he took to be an extension of Australia, naming it Staten Land, later changed to Zeelandia Nova or New Zealand (Map 14). Its Polynesian inhabitants, the Maori, had for many centuries called the land Ao-tea-roa, the "Long White Cloud." Not until Cook's navigations, almost a century and a half after Tasman, would the West learn that New Zealand consisted of two great islands, encompassing between them 501,776 square kilometers. Truly continental in their geography, North and South Islands are partly made up of fragments of the ancient Gondwanaland that broke apart from Australia millions of years ago and gradually migrated eastward (see Chapter 2). What the Polynesians who ventured south in their exploring canoes must have thought upon first reaching these shores we can never know, but this new land—this *whenua hou*—confronted them and their descendants with wondrous surprises as well as formidable challenges.

Aotearoa is temperate, the only part of Polynesia lying outside the tropical-subtropical zone in which Ancestral Polynesian culture developed. While the climate of the northern part of North Island is relatively mild—frosts, for example, are rare except in the central areas—climatic conditions become increasingly harsh as one moves south. For Polynesians with a tropical horticultural economy, this temperate climate posed a tremendous agronomic challenge, one successfully met only in parts of North Island and marginally in the northern part of South Island. Most Polynesian crops did not survive transplantation to New Zealand, and those that did (taro, *Dioscorea* yam, bottle gourd, paper mulberry, *Cordyline fruticosum*, and sweet potato) were confined to the milder regions of North Island, with one great exception: the sweet potato. A South American domesticate introduced prehistorically into central Eastern Polynesia (see Chapter 7), *Ipomoea batatas* was "preadapted" to a temperate climate, in part due to

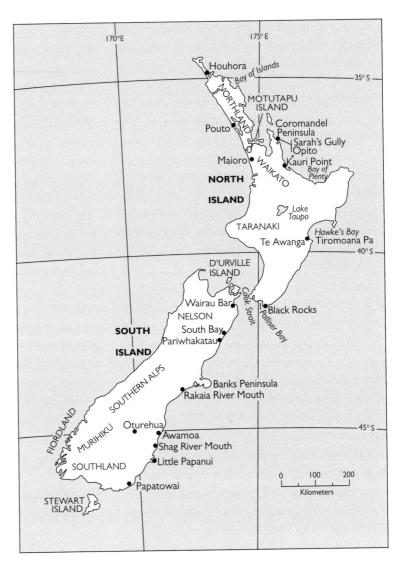

MAP 14 New Zealand, or Aotearoa, showing the location of key archaeological sites.

its seasonal growth habit and the annual dormancy of its tuber, permitting over-winter storage. The sweet potato became the principal basis of Maori economy where horticulture was feasible. Of the Polynesian domestic animals, only the dog was transferred to New Zealand.

The colonizing Polynesians did not confine themselves to those parts of Aotearoa where cultivation was feasible. Certain groups settled areas lying beyond the limits of sweet potato farming and eventually occupied even the harshest parts of South Island, such as the magnificent fjord country. In a reversal of the general cultural evolutionary trend from hunting and gathering to agriculture, these Polynesians gave up an agricultural existence for a life based on hunting and intensive collecting, particularly of rich maritime resources. What made this economic shift possible in the first place was the presence of a remarkable food resource: several species of flightless birds known collectively as *moa* (see Chapter 2). Another group split off from New Zealand around A.D. 1200 to sail 860 kilometers eastward and settle the Chatham Islands (Sutton 1980), where they developed a unique adaptation to a "cold water atoll." Evidence from the mtDNA of Polynesian rats on the Chathams (Matisoo-Smith et al. 1998) suggests that there was but a single colonization of these remote islands, which were thereafter isolated until European contact. The indigenous Chatham Islanders, called Moriori, were largely exterminated by their Maori cousins in a devastating raid in 1835.

This story of Polynesian migration from a tropical homeland to a challenging temperate landscape, filled with giant birds and strange plants, has gradually unfolded through a history of archaeological research that is one of the longest in Oceania. As early as 1848, W. B. Mantell observed the co-occurrence of *moa* bones and artifacts at Awamoa in South Island. In the 1870s, Sir Julius Von Haast investigated sites around Canterbury, developing a theory that the "Moahunters" had been a Paleolithic people responsible for exterminating the *moa*, who were replaced much later by the Neolithic Maori (Von Haast 1872). Twentieth-century ethnologists (who also undertook archaeological excavations) such as H. D. Skinner (1923–24) and David Teviotdale demonstrated that the "Moahunter" phase culture was actually of Polynesian origin and that there was no break between the Moahunters and the later Classic Maori.

While there was much unsystematic digging in New Zealand prior to the 1950s, Jack Golson and Roger Green revolutionized the study of Maori archaeology, in terms of both field methods and conceptual frameworks (e.g., Golson 1959; Green 1963b; see Chapter 1).[28] With a firm academic base at the University of Auckland, followed by

the establishment of a second strong archaeology program at the University of Otago and continued research out of the museums in Dunedin, Wellington, Canterbury, and Auckland, a great deal of primary field and laboratory work has now been carried out. More recently, a vigorous program of cultural resource management (CRM) or "contract" archaeology has been added to this academic program, largely funded by the Department of Conservation.[29]

The New Zealand sequence is classically divided into two broad phases or periods—the Archaic and the Classic Maori—although it is possible to delineate further subdivisions in particular regions, such as Green's sequence (1963b) for the Auckland Province or that proposed by Leach (1981) for the southern Wairarapa (Table 8.2). Archaic assemblages are early Eastern Polynesian in style, including tanged adzes, one- and two-piece fishhooks, bone reels, tooth pendants, and tattooing needles (Fig. 8.20). They point to an immediate homeland for Aotearoa's colonizing population somewhere in central Eastern Polynesia, possibly the southern Cook Islands or the Australs (Green 1975; Sutton, ed., 1994). The date of this colonization is generally put at not earlier than about A.D. 1000 (Anderson 1991), possibly as late as A.D. 1200,[30] making Aotearoa one of the last places on earth to be settled by preindustrialized humans.

The Archaic Phase is especially well documented in South Island, where colonizing Polynesians made a rapid transition from a horticultural to a hunting and gathering economy. With this new economic base, population size and density in South Island remained relatively small, but sizable multifunction base villages were established at the mouths of river valleys, such as at Shag River Mouth, Wairau Bar, Murdering Beach, Papatowai, and Little Papanui.[31] From these permanent base settlements, some of which covered several hectares, the interior regions were seasonally exploited

TABLE 8.2

The Prehistoric Cultural Sequence of the Southern Wairarapa Region, North Island, New Zealand[a]

Period	Dates (A.D.)	Characteristics
I. Successful Colonization	1000–1250	Valley-based communities established ca. A.D. 1050–1200; exchange links continued with communities to the north (obsidian imported); considerable experimentation with local stone sources; kumara and gourd successfully cultivated; bush birds and littoral-marine resources exploited.
II. Regional Consolidation	1250–1450	Population along coastal areas reached carrying capacity; trading contacts highly developed, with rich variety of imported stone types; reasonable economic stability; littoral-marine resources continued to be exploited; decline in forest birds.
III. Economic and Environmental Decline	1450–1550	Environmental decline caused by a combination of natural climatic shift (brief climatic recession) and high sediment loads in rivers due to inland deforestation; siltation in coastal areas led to decline in shellfish beds; decline in trade; skeletal remains suggest periodic malnutrition or near-starvation.
IV. Abandonment	1550–1625	Period of depopulation brought on by economic poverty and worsening climate.
V. New Colonization	1625–1769	Area resettled by the Ngati-Kahungunu from Poverty Bay area; significant habitation commenced in main alluvial valley and river and lakes district; coastal resources utilized intermittently; fernroot became an important food resource.
VI. Early Protohistoric	1769–1840	Captain Cook arrived at Palliser Bay, February 9, 1770; period of great upheaval ensued; considerable social unrest and intergroup conflict; many fortified *pa* sites constructed during this time.
VII. Late Protohistoric	1840–1853	Treaty of Waitangi signed in 1840; European squatters began to settle the region ca. 1844, more intensively after 1853; European crops began to be extensively cultivated.

[a] After Leach (1981).

for *moa* and other resources (including stone from nephrite and silcrete quarries). The *moa*, primary targets of this hunting strategy, included about 13 species ranging in size from smallish birds about the size of a brush turkey up to *Dinornis giganteus*, which stood perhaps 3 meters tall (Fig. 8.21).

Within a few centuries, the *moa* had been virtually exterminated through direct predation combined with extensive habitat disturbance. Fire was a main cause of habitat change, and fires were probably lit as a hunting strategy. Vast tracts of the South Island landscape were transformed from forest to grassland, as revealed in many pollen sequences.[32] South Island settlement patterns changed in response, with a shift from the permanent village settlements to a more transient settlement pattern (Anderson and Smith 1996).

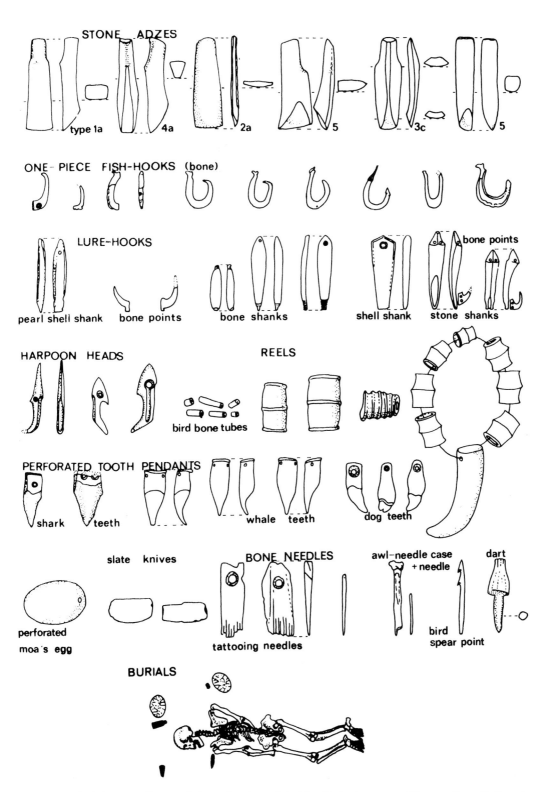

STONE ADZES

type 1a   4a   2a   5   3c   5

ONE-PIECE FISH-HOOKS (bone)

LURE-HOOKS   bone points

pearl shell shank   bone points   bone shanks   shell shank   stone shanks

HARPOON HEADS   REELS

bird bone tubes

PERFORATED TOOTH PENDANTS

shark   teeth   whale   teeth   dog teeth

slate knives   BONE NEEDLES   awl-needle case + needle   dart

perforated moa's egg   tattooing needles   bird spear point

BURIALS

FIGURE 8.20 Archaic-type artifacts mark the earlier phase of the New Zealand sequence. (Courtesy Roger C. Green.)

FIGURE 8.21 The largest *moa* birds towered over their Polynesian hunters. (After Cumberland 1962.)

Over most of South Island, human population never reached high densities, with a total overall population on the order of 3,000–10,000 persons, all that its hunting and gathering economy could sustain. In North Island, with a horticultural economy based on sweet potato production, the situation was entirely different, with a sigmoidal population growth curve (Fig. 8.22). North Island's maximal population prior to Tasman's visit is still controversial. Davidson (1984:58) favors a figure of 125,000, but authorities such as Lewthwaite (1950) have argued for as many as 250,000 people. Archaeological surveys in the more agriculturally favorable parts of North Island reveal an amazing density of sites, and *locally* it would seem that population densities of 60 persons or more per square kilometer were frequently achieved (Jones and Law 1987). As elsewhere in the Pacific, establishing the precontact population of Aotearoa is an archaeological problem urgently calling out for new methodologies.

North Island's larger population was directly related to the development of a horticultural economy, fueled by the sweet potato. Prehistoric Maori gardening systems, such as those at Palliser

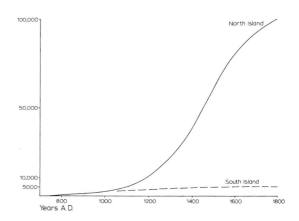

FIGURE 8.22 A probable population growth curve for the Maori, as reconstructed by Janet Davidson. (From Davidson 1984.)

Bay and in the Auckland region,[33] were frequently intensive, involving permanent stone and earthen field boundaries, mounds, and various kinds of mulch (including artificial gravel mulches). The sweet potato growing season lasted from 6 to 7 months, dictating that the harvested tubers be stored for 5–6 months. The Maori stored their crop in subterranean pits of various

FIGURE 8.23 A hilltop *pa* site in the Pouto region of North Island, New Zealand. (From Irwin 1985b.)

shapes and sizes, often with internal drains and roofed over with thatched roofs supported by wooden posts.

This horticultural economy, combined with dense settlement and the need to store key food resources during the winter months, led to a unique settlement pattern dominated by fortified hamlets or villages, known as *pa*.[34] Displaying great variation in size and specifics of construction, *pa* were situated on naturally defensible hills, ridges, or headlands, modified by the excavation of ditches and other earthworks and by the erection of palisades (Fig. 8.23). Such defense works typically enclosed a complex of storage pits, dwelling houses, cooking areas, and other activity spaces (Fig. 8.24). There were also undefended settlements, however, as well as defensive positions enclosing clusters of storage pits (such as Taniwha Pa; see Kirch 1984a, Fig. 66).[35]

The temporal development of *pa* has been studied by archaeologists over the past three decades.[36] At several sites, unfortified hilltop settlements incorporating storage pits preceded the construction of earthworks and palisades. Groube (1970) asserted that fortified *pa* were in evidence by about

A.D. 1300 and began to proliferate over the landscape in succeeding centuries. Irwin's study of the Pouto region provides data on the temporal development of *pa* and their relationship to environmental resources. As Irwin (1985b:77) observes, "In the Pouto study area *pa* are dense; there is approximately one per square kilometer." Based on the excavation and radiocarbon dating of 12 *pa*, Irwin found "the clear possibility that a majority of them were occupied at once," between about A.D. 1650 and 1800 (Irwin 1985b, Fig. 47). He suggests that "at some point late in the prehistory of Pouto, the settlement system passed through some kind of stress threshold which resulted in a spate of *pa* building" (1985b:98). Such a threshold could have been the advent of a "full-land" situation, as I argued (Kirch 1988g), based on Robert Carneiro's general model of "social circumscription" in chiefdom-level polities.[37]

Schmidt (1996) reviewed all radiocarbon dates from *pa* sites and argues for a shorter chronology of *pa* construction, commencing around A.D. 1500. His analysis, however, rejects—on a variety of criteria—no fewer than 257 out of 317 available radiocarbon dates, leaving only 60 "acceptable"

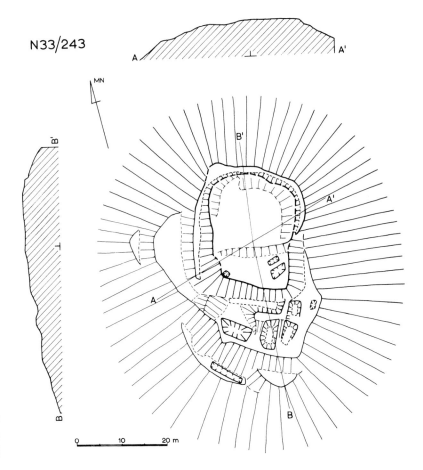

N33/243

FIGURE 8.24 Plan of a *pa* site in
the Pouto region of North Island,
New Zealand. (From Irwin 1985b.)

dates, a process that eliminates the statistical "tail" of earlier dates. This may be a case of overzealous application of "chronometric hygiene" (see Spriggs 1989a), and Groube's date of A.D. 1300 for the onset of *pa* construction may yet prove to be closer to the mark.

North Island settlement patterns, dominated by defensive settlements distributed through an intensified horticultural landscape, correlate with ethnographic descriptions of proto-historic Maori warfare in which raiding frequently escalated to full-scale wars of territorial conquest. Vayda (1960, 1961) interpreted such warfare as a response to population pressure and competition for the best

agricultural lands, a process that intensified once a region was fully occupied and territorially claimed by contending social groups (see also Kirch 1988g). Roger Duff, a longtime scholar of Maori prehistory and ethnography, viewed the critical causal linkages this way: "If we have to assign a specific reason for the evolution of warfare in the North Island rather than in the South or the Chathams, we can find it in the buildup of population which followed the adaptation of *kumara* [sweet potato] growing to a still marginal environment. If we have to explain the distinctively chronic nature of Classic Maori warfare, we may seek it in the inherent competition for good *kumara* land and in the one-crop season" (1967: 116). Yet as Mark W. Allen (1996:178) rightly argues, there was also a sociopolitical and economic aspect to *pa* development, not just a demographic and ecological context. Allen believes that "participation in regional polity formation, *pa* construction, and increased investment in horticulture and storage" consisted of "a negotiated partnership between ambitious leaders and wary but worried groups of followers."

Despite the sizable population of North Island in late prehistory, the Maori never amalgamated into large polities, nor did they undergo a sociopolitical transformation from a simple chiefdom level of organization to a complex, hierarchical social formation, as seen in Hawai'i or the Society Islands. The main social group above the level of the extended family was the *bapu* ("clan" or "subtribe," actually a cognatic descent group), usually numbering a few hundred individuals. The higher-level *iwi* ("tribe") rarely if ever acted as a unified political entity, although limited regional alliances did at times form. Thus Goldman (1970) classified Maori society as another instance of an Open chiefdom in which social relations were fluid and marked by intense competition between status groups. Davidson writes:

> Maori society in the eighteenth century was small-scale and fragmented, and there is no reason to suppose that it was different in earlier times. . . . In later times, particularly in northern regions, groups of up to several hundred people sometimes lived and worked together, at least for a time, and built and maintained fortifications for their own protection. However, the society was inherently unstable, and closely related groups quarreled among themselves when they were not united against a more distant enemy. *(1984:178)*

Aotearoa adds yet another variant in the range of Open Polynesian societies, one in which eco-

logical constraints were posed not by island size but by a marginal climatic regime that challenged traditional Oceanic horticulture. In a manner quite analogous to Mangaia, the Marquesas, and Rapa Nui, the convergence of high population density, intensive agricultural production, and social competition and conflict (especially over arable land) led in Aotearoa not to an evolutionary process favoring increased hierarchy and the development of large polities, but to an inherently unstable and oscillating social formation.

The Emergence of Stratified Chiefdoms

Whereas in the Open societies of Polynesia hierarchy tended to be fluid, spurring competition between status groups (hereditary elite, priests, warriors) for control of resources and the exercise of power, in the Stratified societies elite power became ever more concentrated, and the distinctions between elites and commoners increasingly pronounced. These stratified Polynesian societies exemplify what evolutionary anthropologists call "complex chiefdoms," and in the case of Hawai'i, perhaps an "archaic state." Critical environmental distinctions distinguish Open from Stratified societies, the latter situated in the larger and resource-rich archipelagoes, where ecological constraints (size or climatic limitations) were less pronounced. This does not mean that the rise of stratification was in some crude way environmentally "determined," for the social formations that arose in each archipelago were distinctive.

Tahiti and the Society Islands　No island society was more influential in forming eighteenth-century European conceptions of Polynesia and the "noble savage" than "Otaheite," purported isle of love and salubrious existence where nature's bounty made work unnecessary (Bougainville dubbed it *Nouvelle Cythère*).[38] Old ideas die hard, and Tahiti and the Society Islands have long been regarded by ethnographers as something of an exception or anomaly within Polynesia, a hierarchical and "aristocractic" society lacking an intensified economic base.[39] Recent archaeological research is finally dispelling such notions.

Tahiti, a double volcano of 1,040 square kilometers, dominates the Society Islands archipelago (Map 12), totaling 11 islands with a combined land area of 1,628 square kilometers. Tahiti, along with Mo'orea and the smaller islands of Me'etia, Maiao, and the atoll of Tetiaroa, comprise the windward isles. The leeward isles of Ra'iatea, Taha'a, Huahine, Porapora, Tupai, and Maupiti, while drought-prone, played an important role in late prehistoric political relations. The population of the archipelago prior to European contact—and before the ravages of disease that such contact inevitably wrought—has invoked great differences of opinion. Oliver (1974) suggests a population for Tahiti of 35,000 persons, but given the density of archaeological remains revealed by recent surveys (such as that of the Papeno'o Valley; see Orliac 1997), I suspect that this is too low, and Forster's original 1774 estimate of 120,000 may be closer to the mark.

Oliver's masterful synthesis (1974) of the ethnohistoric record reveals a rigidly hierarchical sociopolitical formation with three social classes: *ari'i* or principal chiefs; *ra'atira* or lesser chiefs, who were the titleholders to estates; and *manahune* or commoners, many of whom were landless. Chiefs held considerable power, and in Earle's (1997) terms much of this power was economic, such as tribute payments of food, barkcloth, and other materials or artifacts owed by the *manahune* to the elite. Maohi chiefs also exercised military and ideological power, manifest in the cult of the war-god Oro, to whom regular human sacrifices were made. Although it is the largest island in the archipelago, Tahiti was not the center of political or religious power, which was focused on Ra'iatea, where Oro was said to have been born of the god Ta'aroa, and where the most sacred temple (*marae*) Taputapuatea was located (Fig. 8.25).

Archaeological work in the Society Islands commenced in the 1920s with Emory's surface survey of stone ruins (1933), primarily *marae* temple foundations. From 1960 to 1962, Roger Green carried out the first systematic settlement-pattern study for Polynesia, in the 'Opunohu Valley of Mo'orea, also excavating *marae* and round-ended elite residences (Green 1961; Green et al. 1967). Garanger (1967) studied *marae* in the Tautira region of Tahiti. Aside from excavations at a few coastal sites such as Maupiti and Fa'ahia-Vaito'otia (see Chapter 7), the majority of archaeological work has focused on *marae*. Renewed settlement-pattern surveys by several French archaeologists from the Tahitian Département d'Archéologie, as well as studies of prehistoric agricultural systems and land use by Lepofsky (1994, 1995), are beginning to broaden our understanding of the Society Islands archaeological record.[40] Nonetheless, the archipelago's prehistory is less documented than that of many other Polynesian islands.

A cultural sequence for the Society Islands as a whole has yet to be proposed and would probably be premature.[41] However, Green (1996b) outlined a local sequence for the 'Opunohu Valley (Mo'orea Island)[42] that encapsulates some major changes predictable for the archipelago at large. The Pre-Atiro'o Phase (A.D. ??–1000) is only dimly reflected in deeply buried deposits in the valley's swampy floor (Lepofsky et al. 1996), but it certainly included among its agronomic strategies shifting cultivation on the interior slopes, leading to significant erosion and alluvial deposition toward the end of the phase. In the Atiro'o Phase (A.D. 1000–1650) we have the first evidence of stone structures in the valley interior, such as streamside agricultural terraces and associated simple *marae* in the

FIGURE 8.25 A view of part of the Taputapuatea temple (*marae*) complex on the island of Ra'iatea, seat of the Oro cult. (Photo by P. V. Kirch.)

Tupauruuru area (e.g., site OPU-159). The existence of both rectangular and round-ended houses in the Amehiti area suggests "a well-established community with status individuals" toward the later part of the Atiro'o Phase (Green 1996b:218). Lepofsky's data indicate the development of an arboricultural complex including large orchard stands of

Tahitian Chestnut (*Inocarpus fagiferus*) during this phase, as well as extensive dryland and irrigated terracing.

The onset of the Marama Phase (A.D. 1650–1788) correlates with the conquest of the 'Opunohu Valley, as described in oral traditions, by the Marama line of coastal-dwelling chiefs. By this

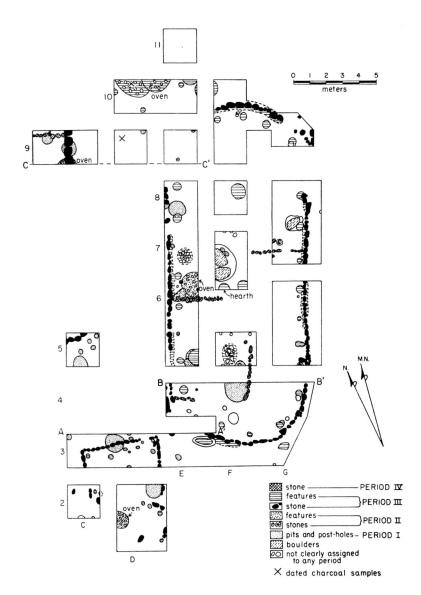

FIGURE 8.26 Plan of Site ScMo-103, a large round-ended house in the 'Opunohu Valley, Mo'orea, excavated by Roger Green. (From Green et al. 1967; courtesy Roger C. Green.)

time, the valley was politically divided into the Tupauruuru and Amehiti sectors, with the Marama elite centering their attention on Tupauruuru. During this phase, elaborate *marae* were constructed, along with numerous household *marae* and round-ended houses (with associated storage pits), which were the residences of the elite. An example of the settlement patterns of this phase is

Site ScMo-103, with a cluster of *marae* and a round-ended house (Fig. 8.26). The presence of a high-ranking titleholder in the valley is indicated by the complex *marae* forms, with stepped *ahu* or altars (Fig. 8.27). The final Pomare Phase (A.D. 1788–1812) reflects the tumultuous events of the early contact period, during which 'Opunohu became a refuge for chiefs who resisted European intrusion,

FIGURE 8.27 A stepped *marae* in the interior of the 'Opunohu Valley, Mo'orea. (Photo by P. V. Kirch.)

ending with the conversion of Pomare II to Christianity in 1812.

The 'Opunohu Valley sequence shows that changes in settlement pattern—and the increased hierarchization of society that these reflect—went hand in hand with increased intensification of the local agricultural production system. The extent of agricultural terracing, which Lepofsky (1995) has radiocarbon dated as commencing around A.D. 1200, speaks to a highly intensive system of land use, combined with orchard gardens focused on breadfruit and Tahitian Chestnut. Such intensified production replaced an earlier, more extensive system based largely on shifting cultivation. Other aspects of economic intensification during the Atiro'o and Marama Phases include an emphasis on breadfruit storage pits associated with elite residences. The 'Opunohu Valley sequence thus correlates enhancement of economic power with the rise of a social elite. Yet the role of ideology is manifest in the proliferation of temples, their architectonic elaboration a kind of index to the progressive transformation of society.

Not directly evident in the archaeological record of 'Opunohu, but playing a key role in the history of Society Islands polities during the later prehistoric and proto-historic phases, were war and territorial conquest. Emory (1933:45) mentions fortifications, but these were not elaborated as in some Open societies. But we know from oral traditions and early ethnohistoric sources that interdistrict and interisland rivalries and wars of conquest were prominent. Tellingly, the aggressive war cult of Oro arose not in the larger, resource-rich and populous islands of Tahiti or Mo'orea, but in the leeward group, especially on Porapora and Ra'iatea (Oliver 1974, vol. II:890–912). Oliver remarks that "the low productivity of Porapora seems to have predisposed its inhabitants to the foreign conquests which led to their chiefs' political superiority over nearby lands" (1974, vol. II:1131). The Society Islands thus provide an important instance of a fundamental tension between "wet" and "dry" production systems, the former emphasizing landesque capital intensification (primarily taro irrigation) and the latter the labor-intensive cultivation of dryland crops, such as yams and sweet potatoes. Militarily aggressive polities in Polynesia tend to be correlated with "dry" economic systems, although they consistently sought resource-rich "wet" systems as the spoils of war (Kirch 1994).

The Tongan "Maritime Empire"   In Chapter 7 I reviewed the culture-historical sequences of Western Polynesia. We saw that proto-historic Tonga constituted another highly stratified chiefdom, in which the bases of power were different from those of the Society Islands chiefdoms or that of Hawai'i.[43] Political power in proto-historic Tonga centered on the large island of Tongatapu, some 257 square kilometers in area. Although of makatea geology, Tongatapu has fertile soils enriched by volcanic ash falls and organic nutrients, as well as an extensive lagoon-reef ecosystem on its northern coast. Tongatapu's terrestrial resources (as well as those of nearby 'Eua Island) were not as rich as those of some other high islands, but they were sufficient to permit the growth of a prehistoric population numbering at least 40,000 persons. Tongan oral traditions, augmented by archaeology, suggest that three or more independent and competing chiefdoms on the island gradually amalgamated into a single polity, largely through territorial conquest.

By proto-historic times, there were at least two distinct levels of chiefs: the *hou'eiki* or lesser chiefs, who were in charge of managing local estates, and the Tu'i Tonga, or sacred paramount lord of Tonga and his immediate household. Moreover, the commoner population seems to have become alienated from direct control of the land, holding usufruct rights by virtue of regular tribute payments to the *hou'eiki* and through them to the Tu'i Tonga (a situation similar to that of Hawai'i).

Tongan oral traditions inform us that the chiefly apparatus became significantly elaborated in the final centuries prior to European contact. Following the reign of the 23rd Tu'i Tonga (Takalaua by name), his senior son Kauulufonuafekai (later the 24th Tu'i Tonga) initiated a campaign of territorial conquest extending beyond Tongatapu to encompass the Ha'apai and Vava'u groups, as well as farther-flung Niuatoputapu and even 'Uvea. Archaeological remains on Niuatoputapu and 'Uvea (Frimigacci and Hardy 1997; Kirch 1988a; Sand 1993c, 1998b; Sand and Valentin 1991) reveal extensive evidence of a Tongan intrusion around A.D. 1500–1600, in the form of elaborate Tongan-style burial mounds, pigeon-snaring mounds, and fortifications. To return to the oral histories, Kauulufonuafekai implemented a significant structural change in the chiefship, reserving for himself (and subsequent Tu'i Tonga titleholders) the sacred authority of the kingship, but simultaneously creating the office of the *hau*, or secular paramount, who became known as the Tu'i Ha'a Takalaua. The first titleholder of the *hau*-ship was Kauulufonuafekai's younger brother Moungamotu'a. This diarchy of sacred and secular leaders came to an end with the 39th and final Tu'i Tonga, Laufilitonga, who passed away in A.D. 1865.

The residential and ritual center of these political elites was at Mu'a, fronting the Tongatapu lagoon. There the dual paramounts occupied separate residential compounds, and successive generations of Tu'i Tonga and their kinfolk were interred in massive burial mounds (*langi*) faced with slabs hewn from coral limestone. At Mu'a, a stone pier or dock projects 200 meters into the lagoon, a material symbol of the external power base that the Tongan elite had achieved through their wars of interisland conquest. Each year double-hulled canoes brought tribute to Mu'a from these outlying islands, to be offered up to the Tu'i Tonga at the *'inasi* ceremony on his ceremonial plaza (see Figs. 7.10 and 7.11).

The proto-historic Tongan chiefdom had evolved into a kind of "maritime empire," maintained by emplacing junior-ranking members of the Tongatapu elite on outlying, conquered islands. These junior chiefs, removed from Mu'a where they might potentially threaten or subvert the power of the Tu'i Tonga or of the *hau*, married local chiefly women of the islands they governed and enforced the authority of Tongatapu. This elite system established connections ranging beyond the Tongan archipelago, into Fiji to the west and Samoa to the east. Regular long-distance voyaging to these foreign islands—along with carefully arranged chiefly marriages—assured a flow of prestige goods (fine mats, feathers, sandalwood, barkcloth, canoes, pottery) into Tongatapu. These goods provided "wealth finance" that underwrote the political strategies of the Tongan elite (see Earle 1997:73). Thus while the makatea environment of Tonga might seem insufficient to underwrite a strongly hierarchic, centralized polity, through the integration of an entire archipelago (along with external sources of prestige goods)—initially through military conquest—the Tongan chiefs transformed their social formation into one of the most highly stratified in Polynesia.

Hawai'i: An "Archaic State"? Anthropologists have long regarded proto-historic Hawai'i as the most highly stratified of all Polynesian chiefdoms, a stage in cultural evolution approaching the formative levels of such "archaic states" as the old Fertile Crescent civilizations or of the Olmec of Mesoamerica. Summarizing his lengthy research into Hawaiian society and economy at the period of initial European contact, Marshall Sahlins writes:

> Everything looks as if Hawaiian society had been through a history in which the concepts of lineage—of a classic Polynesian sort, organizing the relations of persons and tenure of land by seniority of descent—had latterly been eroded by the development of chiefship. Intruding on the land and people from outside, like a foreign element, the chiefship usurps the collective rights of land control and in the process reduces the lineage order in scale, function, and coherence. Of course, no one knows

when, how, or if such a thing ever happened. (*Sahlins in Kirch and Sahlins 1992, I:192*)

Sahlins points to a fundamental distinction between Hawai'i and most other Polynesian societies, in which land and resources were controlled by structures of *kinship*. In Hawai'i a structure of *kingship* had emerged in late prehistory (although some would argue that this was not fully developed until the early postcontact period). In an earlier work, Sahlins had put the matter this way: "The threshold which [Hawaiian society] had reached but could not cross was the boundary of primitive society itself" (1972:148). Restricted to the evidence of comparative ethnography, historical anthropologists such as Sahlins inevitably confront the problem of knowing "when, how, or if" such a transformation from kinship to kingship occurred. Rich oral traditions of chiefly marriages and alliances, wars and conquests, and other political events add much information (Kamakau 1961). But only archaeology provides direct historical evidence to track such fundamental changes through time, even though the processes underlying change must be inferred from material correlates of social action.

Hawai'i boasts the richest archaeological record for any Pacific archipelago.[44] Pre–World War II surface surveys defined the range of variation in monumental stone architecture, especially the numerous and structurally varied *heiau* or temple sites.[45] During the 1950s and 1960s, major excavation programs of the Bishop Museum and the University of Hawai'i outlined a material-culture sequence,[46] later augmented by settlement-pattern studies and increased attention to socio-political, economic, and demographic changes.[47] Aggressive economic development in Hawai'i, spurred by statehood in 1959, led to hundreds of CRM projects; while variable in quality and research orientation, these have created masses of

new data, such as extensive suites of radiocarbon dates.[48] The archaeological record from Hawai'i is so extensive that, as with New Zealand, an entire book-length treatment is required to do it justice (see Kirch 1985a); the following overview merely touches on a few highlights.

Excepting temperate New Zealand, the Hawaiian Islands, with 16,692 square kilometers of land area, constitute the largest archipelago in Polynesia (Map 15). Hawai'i enjoys a subtropical climate and fertile volcanic soils, making the islands ideal for the transference of the Oceanic root, tuber, and tree crops. This environment posed none of the environmental constraints to the rise of large, complex societies that we see in other Polynesian islands. And the precontact population of Hawai'i correlates with such environmental possibilities, for even by the most conservative estimates there were at least 250,000 indigenous Hawaiians when Cook arrived in 1778–79, and quite likely a good many more.[49]

Individual Hawaiian islands vary greatly in their environmental characteristics, influencing cultural developments in important ways. Because the archipelago has a linear age progression (owing to its hot-spot origin; see Chapter 2), the older islands of Kaua'i, O'ahu, and Moloka'i, along with the western half of Maui, display deeply weathered and dissected landforms, with valleys and permanent streams well suited to irrigated terrace agriculture. These older islands have more developed coastal reefs, with better fishing and the potential to construct large fishponds for aquaculture. In striking contrast, geologically younger East Maui and Hawai'i—while they account for 74 percent of the total land area—mostly lack permanent streams and have large tracts of young lava flows (e.g., Kirch, ed., 1997). I will return to the significance of these environmental contrasts later.

Several archaeologists have synthesized the Hawaiian cultural sequence, and despite minor dif-

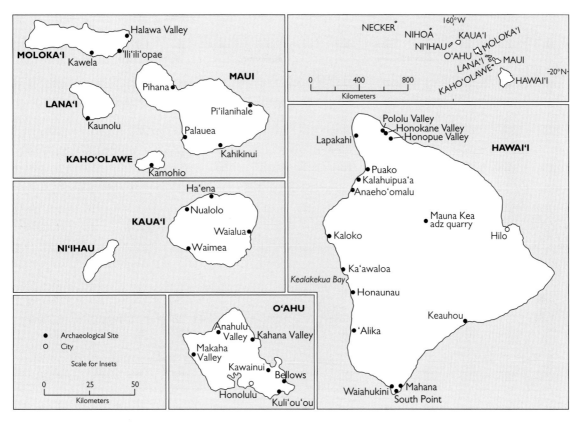

MAP 15 The Hawaiian Islands, showing the location of key archaeological sites.

ferences in terminology or periodization, they mostly concur.[50] Here I use my own formulation (Kirch 1985a:298–308), depicted in Figure 8.28. The Colonization Period (A.D. 300–600) remains controversial, for it is not well attested by direct archaeological evidence. Some archaeologists put the date of initial settlement of the archipelago as late as A.D. 750–800, although there are sufficient indications of earlier human presence that I would withhold judgment.[51] Whatever the date of first settlement, the Marquesas Islands are the posited immediate source for the first Hawaiian colonizers, both on the evidence of material culture (fish-hooks, adz forms) and on linguistic grounds (Green 1966; Marck 1999). However, Hawai'i did not become immediately isolated from central Eastern Polynesia, and Hawaiian oral traditions speak of a "voyaging period" in which great navigator-chiefs such as Moikeha and Pa'ao made return voyages to "Kahiki" and back.[52] The appearance of new fishhook styles in Hawaiian sites around A.D. 1200 may indicate contact between Hawai'i and the Society Islands, and there is linguistic evidence for Tahitic borrowings into Hawaiian language.[53] While long-distance voyaging certainly took place, it ceased after about A.D. 1300, after which the Hawaiian Islands became completely isolated from the rest of Polynesia. "Kahiki" became a mythic homeland from which the great anthropomorphic god Lono returned each year during

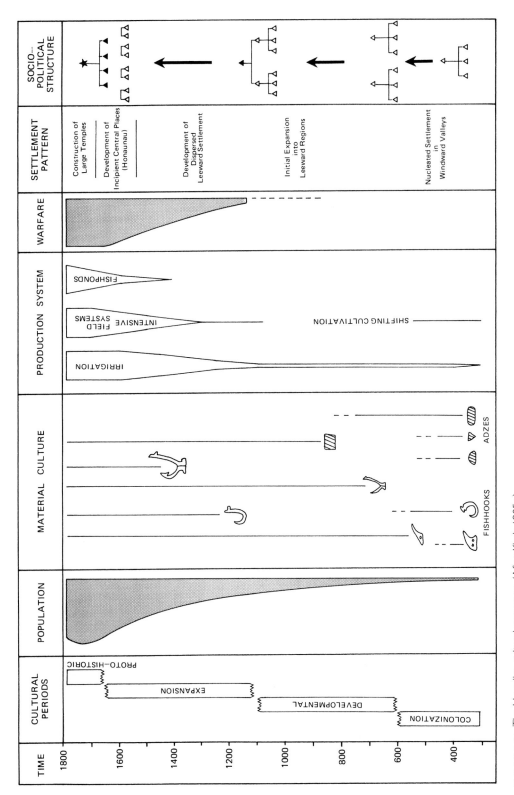

FIGURE 8.28 The Hawaiian cultural sequence. (After Kirch 1985a.)

FIGURE 8.29 The A1-3 dune site at the mouth of Halawa Valley, Moloka'i, with small round-ended house structures under excavation in 1970. (Photo by P. V. Kirch.)

the Makahiki to ritually fertilize and renew the land.[54]

Much better attested in the archaeological record, the Developmental Period (A.D. 600–1100) is represented by sites such as the A1-3 sand dune at the mouth of Halawa Valley, Moloka'i (Fig. 8.29), the upper levels in the Waimanalo dune (site O18), and sites at Waiahukini, Hawai'i Island.[55] Fishhooks, basalt adzes, ornaments, and other artifacts (Fig. 8.30) exhibit local stylistic elements, differentiating them from styles in central Eastern Polynesia. Settlements were nucleated hamlets in coastal settings, and domestic architecture differed somewhat from that of later periods. In the Halawa dune site, round-ended house foundations were preserved (whereas later prehistoric Hawaiian dwellings were characteristically rectangular in form), and at Waimanalo the dead were interred under house pavements (a practice that ceased in later times). Pigs, dogs, and chickens were all present, and pollen and microcharcoal evidence from sediment cores on O'ahu indicates that forest clearance for agriculture was under way as early as A.D. 800.[56]

The period of greatest change—the Expansion Period (A.D. 1100–1650)—spanned the next five and a half centuries. This was a time both of exponential growth of the archipelago's population and of its expansion out of the most ecologically favorable areas (what Rob Hommon has termed the "salubrious cores") into more marginal regions. During this dynamic period, production systems were intensified, ritual architecture was elaborated, and a system of hierarchical territorial land units was formalized. All of these changes—in tandem—radically transformed Hawaiian society.

The demographic transition of the Expansion Period is better attested in Hawai'i than for almost any other Polynesian group, thanks to a large sample of dated sites. Initial modeling of this demographic transition, based on sites in west Hawai'i Island, suggested a sigmoidal or logistic growth curve, generated from the kind of data plotted in Figure 8.31.[57] In such a logistic growth pattern, population at first increased at an exponential rate but later began to slow as density-dependent factors, such as the occupation of all arable lands, took effect. Cumulative radiocarbon

FIGURE 8.30 Artifacts from the early Bellows sand dune site (O18) at Waimanalo, O'ahu Island, included pearl-shell fish-hooks, coral and sea urchin–spine abraders, ornaments, a coconut grater, a bracelet of pig tusks, basalt adzes, and a basalt awl. (Photo by P. V. Kirch.)

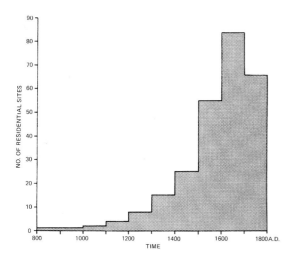

FIGURE 8.31 Hawaiian population growth as reflected in numbers of dated habitation sites. (After Kirch 1985a.)

date curves have recently been used as proxy records of the intensity of human activities on a landscape (and hence of population numbers), and they also display this kind of S-shaped sequence.[58] Figure 8.32 shows such curves for samples of agricultural and habitation sites. While it is difficult to convert these curves into actual population estimates (cf. Dye and Komori 1992), it is nonetheless evident that after about A.D. 1200, and continuing until at least A.D. 1600, the Hawaiian population expanded at a remarkable pace. Doubling times were probably on the order of a century or less. Such rapid demographic change inevitably spurred sociopolitical transformation.

Intensification of production went hand in glove with this demographic transition during the Expansion Period; indeed, these were arguably interlinked processes (see Kirch 1994:310–12). In the western islands—where topography and hydrology permitted—valley floors and lower hillsides were converted to terraced pondfields, irrigated by diverting streamflow into stone-lined canals (Fig. 8.33). In the geologically younger eastern

islands, irrigation was feasible only in limited areas, but vast volcanic flowslopes were in places gradually developed into intensive agricultural landscapes dominated by reticulate grids of stone walls, field systems that broke up the terrain into individual garden plots. In the Kohala region of Hawai'i Island, initial stages of field systems are recognizable by A.D. 1300, and they became increasingly intensified after A.D. 1450.[59] The later Expansion Period also witnessed the construction of large fishponds for aquacultural production of mullet and milkfish (Kikuchi 1976; Summers 1964) wherever coastal conditions permitted (Fig. 8.34).

Irrigation works in the western isles, and dryland field systems in the eastern group, both constitute forms of landesque capital intensification, but with rather different socioeconomic outcomes due to their differential labor input-to-yield ratios and their abilities to produce a surplus above individual household requirements. With irrigation, higher yields could be produced per unit of labor and greater surpluses extracted by the chiefs. In the dryland regions, greater labor inputs were required and the limits to intensification were more quickly approached, making the extraction of a surplus that could be put to political purposes more contentious. Two contrastive pathways to political (and ideological) transformation emerged.[60] The chiefly elite of the western islands invested heavily in irrigation works, while their religious system emphasized Kane, god of flowing waters and procreation. On Maui and Hawai'i Island, in contrast, the chiefs exercised a cycle of territorial conquest, promulgating a legitimating ideology based on the cult of Ku, a human sacrifice–demanding god of war, who seasonally alternated with Lono, god of rain and thunder (Valeri 1985).

Increased hierarchization of the Hawaiian chiefly class, and the use of religious ideology to legitimate chiefly dominance over the common

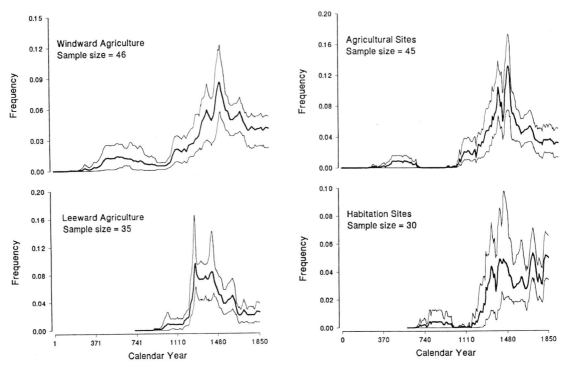

FIGURE 8.32 Radiocarbon date curves from Hawai'i have also been used as proxy indications of population growth. The two left-hand diagrams are for samples of radiocarbon dates from windward and leeward agricultural sites on Kaua'i, O'ahu, Moloka'i, and Hawai'i Islands. The right-hand diagrams are for agricultural and habitation sites on O'ahu Island. (After Jane Allen 1992 and Williams 1992.)

people (the *maka'ainana*), is best reflected in the archaeological record through the temple (*heiau*) system, which became more and more elaborated during the later Expansion Period (Kolb 1991, 1992, 1994). Diachronic studies of *heiau* are less common than surface surveys, but recent excavations document successive rebuildings of *heiau* over time, incorporating successively more elaborate architecture and greater size (both area and volume of stone).[61] Michael Kolb's study of *heiau* on Maui Island suggests that temples with stone terraces or enclosures of significant size first began to be constructed during the early Expansion Period. Major phases of *heiau* building or rebuilding on Maui took place from the late Expansion to

early Proto-Historic Periods. The largest chiefly *heiau*, such as Pi'ilanihale in the Hana District, eventually covered as much as 12,126 square meters, incorporating massive volumes of stone fill. *Heiau* became functionally differentiated, with local agricultural temples (*heiau ho'oulu'ai*) marking individual land units (Fig. 8.35) and much larger *luakini* temples associated with paramount chiefs and the cult of war.

It was presumably in the late Expansion Period that the proto-historic Hawaiian system of land tenure—the so-called *ahupua'a* system—developed. *Ahupua'a* (literally "pig altar") were territorial units that ran from the mountain ridges down to the sea, cross-cutting the ecological grain of an island

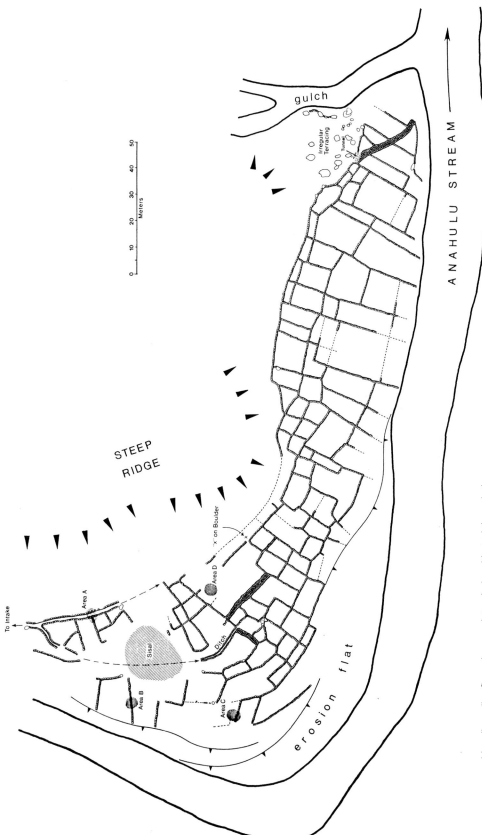

FIGURE 8.33 Hawaiian valley floors became intensively cultivated through the construction of pondfield irrigation systems, such as the one depicted in this archaeological plan from the Anahulu Valley, O'ahu. (After Kirch and Sahlins 1992.)

gulch

ANAHULU STREAM

Irregular Terracing

Tunnel

STEEP RIDGE

'X' on Boulder

To Intake

Area A

Area D

Sisal

Ditch

Area B

Area C

erosion flat

Meters
0 10 20 30 40 50

FIGURE 8.34 Another form of landesque capital intensification in later Hawaiian prehistory was the construction of large fishponds on reef flats, such as this pond on the southern shore of Moloka'i Island. (Photo by Thérèse Babineau.)

and incorporating all of its main resource zones (Cordy and Kaschko 1980). In proto-historic Hawai'i, such units were not the territory of a corporate descent group as in most other Polynesian systems but were each under the control of a lesser chief (the *ali'i 'ai ahupua'a*), who in turn held this territory at the pleasure of the paramount chief (*ali'i 'ai moku*) to whom he owed material support, especially in times of war. All of the *ahupua'a* under a paramount chief constituted the kingdom at large, called in Hawaiian terminology the *moku*, derived from the old Polynesian term for "island." The commoners, for their part, held rights of usufruct to work lands within an *ahupua'a* in return for tributary payments of produce and labor to the chief. Thus land became alienable, and the entire system one of enfeudation, tied together by re-

ciprocal rights of tribute and protection (Kirch and Sahlins 1992).

Another transformation of the later Expansion to Proto-Historic Periods was the elaboration of the *kapu* system, a complex set of prohibitions and cultural practices that differentiated among Hawaiians by gender and by rank. The highest-ranking chiefs, for example, were accorded the *kapu moe* or "prostrating taboo" by the commoners. Women were forbidden to eat certain foods, such as pig, bananas, and some fish, and had to prepare their food in separate earth ovens. Late precontact habitation sites in the Kahikinui region of Maui exhibit archaeological evidence of such separate cooking facilities (Van Gilder and Kirch 1997). Ladefoged argues that precontact Hawaiian houses, household clusters, and chiefly *heiau* all display certain

FIGURE 8.35 An aerial view of a midsized temple *(heiau)* in the *ahupua'a* of Kipapa, Kahikinui, Maui. (Photo by P. V. Kirch.)

structural similarities in their spatial layout, reflecting pervasive "organizational principles predicated upon notions of ritual offerings and the observance of the *kapu* system" (1998:70).

By the Proto-Historic Period (A.D. 1650–1795) the *ahupua'a* and *kapu* systems were well established,

to become increasingly entrenched and elaborated. Because we are able to draw upon a large and rich body of indigenous oral traditions relating to these final centuries prior to European contact, as well as upon the material evidence of archaeology, a great deal is known of the political history of this period, including the economic, military, and religious forms of power employed by the chiefly class. Social stratification had reached a level at which the chiefs (*ali'i*) distinguished themselves as a class from the commoners (*maka'ainana*), and although endogamy was not absolute, it was strongly encouraged. Chiefs claimed descent from the gods and internally differentiated among themselves through elaborate genealogies and a ranked gradation of levels. Not only did the chiefly class control the land and material apparatus of production, they encouraged and supported craft specialists who produced sumptuary items that visually reinforced their status. Most remarkable among these material symbols were finely executed feathered girdles, helmets, capes, and cloaks.

Increasing wars of territorial aggression between competing chiefdoms and a progressive amalgamation of formerly independent polities into ever-larger chiefdoms dominate the political history of the Proto-Historic Period (e.g., Cordy 1996). By the late seventeenth century, four main polities had emerged, focused on the main islands of Kaua'i, O'ahu, Maui, and Hawai'i, with the fought-over smaller islands being incorporated into one or another of the main units. However, the political dynamism of Hawai'i in late prehistoric and early historic times emanated primarily from the two largest and youngest islands, Maui and Hawai'i. Sahlins put this in social terms in *Islands of History*, when he observed that "the oldest and most senior [chiefly] lines are in the western islands, Kaua'i and O'ahu, whence originate also the highest tabus. But then, the historical dynamism of the system is in the east, among Maui and Hawai'i chiefs, who are able to differentiate themselves from local competitors, or even from their own dynastic predecessors, by appropriating ancestry from the ancient western sources of legitimacy" (1985:20). The Maui and Hawai'i chiefs coveted the generously endowed production systems based on irri-

gation that these western islands offered. Not long before Cook's fateful visit in 1778–79, the Maui paramount Kahekili expanded his polity to encompass all of the islands to the west and was engaged in a fierce succession of wars with his arch-rival Kalaniopu'u of Hawai'i. After the fateful encounter with the West, Kalaniopu'u's successor—the famous Kamehameha I—made shrewd use of Western arms to incorporate the entire archipelago under his hegemony.

After Kamehameha's consolidation of the Hawaiian Kingdom in the first decades of the eighteenth century, this Polynesian society could only be classified as a "state." Did it take the impetus of an engagement with the expanding world system of the West to make the fundamental transition from a complex chiefdom to a state, to cross the "boundary of primitive society itself"? The question may be more rhetorical than theoretically informative, a matter of semantic categories. From a generalizing evolutionary perspective, however, it is worth asking. My own opinion has changed subtly over the years and increasingly weighs in on the side of those such as Hommon (1976) who have argued that even prior to Cook, Hawaiian society constituted an "archaic state." The development of class stratification, as well as the alienation of land rights from the producers, not to mention the forms of absolutizing religious ideology (including the war cult of human sacrifice) and the regular exercise of military force, are all typical of state-level social formations. Some will demur, pointing to the absence of incipient urbanism or of a writing system. The debate will continue, and because its terms cannot be fixed, it will have no final conclusion. But one thing is clear: in late precontact Hawai'i, Oceanic society at large—which had commenced with the Lapita expansion into Remote Oceania—witnessed its most far-reaching transformation.

Summary

In the quotation that heads this chapter R. E. Williamson—a pioneer in the comparative study of Polynesian societies—regrets that it would not be possible to ever trace out "what actually had been the history" of these Polynesian societies. Writing in an era when archaeology had scarcely commenced in the Pacific—restricted in its methods to surface surveys with no temporal controls—Williamson believed that it would be impossible to obtain direct evidence of the history of Polynesian social transformations. He was wrong. Williamson could not envisage that the material remains of those societies themselves encapsulated a historical "text," which in time would be accessible with improved methods and with more sophisticated theoretical paradigms enabling its interpretation. We still have much to learn of the sociopolitical histories of the Polynesian chiefdoms, but we have traveled a great distance from Williamson's speculative "history" based solely on comparative ethnography.

What makes the historical study of the Polynesian chiefdoms so intellectually engaging, in part, is the opportunity to compare both the varied outcomes—the specific social formations, whether Traditional, Open, or Stratified—as well as the underlying processes and trajectories responsible for those outcomes, all of which derived from a common Ancestral Polynesian culture over the course of two and a half millennia. Because Polynesia constitutes a well-defined phyletic unit (see Chapter 7), it offers possibilities of comparative analysis not often found elsewhere. I have sketched some of the historical sequences of sociopolitical transformation that archaeology has begun to reveal and pointed out a few of the fundamental contexts, constraints, and processes that have influenced such changes. Some might prefer a greater emphasis on social agency to the focus I have given to environmental, demographic, and economic factors. However, I have also endeavored to show how specific elite social groups used alternative forms of power—economic, military, and ideological—in their attempts to exercise authority and control over society at large. There is much scope for alternative—one hopes mutually enlightening, rather than competitive—models of social change in Polynesia. After a half-century of study, the search is becoming truly exciting.

Big Structures and Large Processes in Oceanic Prehistory

Historically grounded huge comparisons of big structures and large processes help establish what must be explained, attach the possible explanations to their context in time and space, and sometimes actually improve our understanding of those structures and processes.

Charles Tilly (1984:145)

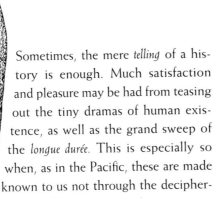

Sometimes, the mere *telling* of a history is enough. Much satisfaction and pleasure may be had from teasing out the tiny dramas of human existence, as well as the grand sweep of the *longue durée*. This is especially so when, as in the Pacific, these are made known to us not through the deciphering of eyewitness chronicles—for there were no indigenous scribes to pen such accounts—but by learning to "read" material "texts" that are the sedimented accumulations of countless everyday lives. From this perspective, the preceding chapters stand fully on their own, requiring no further summation or exegesis. But I have claimed this to be a work of *anthropological* history, that adjective carrying the weight of a proud tradition of comparative analysis. For anthropology's history (as opposed, with much deference to Greg Dening, to "history's

anthropology"[1]) can have no special claim on historical understanding sans comparison. And so, in this final chapter, I take my stance—as an anthropologist—to offer some observations on the long run of Pacific history, observations not tied to any one time or place, because indeed there are trends and movements that transcend the particular. It is in these "big structures" and "large processes" that any deeper insights may be discovered. They invite us to embark on a voyage beyond time to see—in the common experiences of human existence—some larger truths that might in small ways enlighten us.

Voyaging and the Human "Conquest" of the Pacific

The history of the Pacific is more than anything a history of voyages, and all that word entails:

curiosity, courage, skill, technique, stamina, doubt, hope, and more. In their initial expansion out of Africa, commencing perhaps 100,000 years ago, our ancestors—modern *Homo sapiens sapiens*—moved on foot, spreading into the Near East, Europe, the Indian subcontinent, and Asia. Their expansion may have paused, for a time, on Asiatic shores now drowned beneath the warm waters of the Sunda Sea. But neither curiosity nor ingenuity could be kept in check forever; in due course some of those coastal-dwelling people invented the means to begin moving out beyond the continental margins, into the island world of the Pacific. In reality, we know next to nothing about this earliest phase in the history of seafaring technology, other than that it had developed at least by 40,000 years ago. But the explosive appearance of human populations throughout Sahul and Near Oceania at this time can only be explained by the existence of some forms of simple watercraft. Bark-boats, rafts, simple dugouts—all of these are possibilities; to say more is sheer speculation. Whatever the technology, it was sufficient to move people across water gaps of 90 kilometers or more. In most cases, the voyaging targets were visible from the starting shore: the object loomed above the horizon, enticing them with promises of a rainforest rich in edible marsupials, birds, and reptiles, or of pristine reefs on which to gather tasty mollusks and sea urchins.

Further development of voyaging technology and skills was painfully slow. Twenty thousand years after the first humans moved into the Bismarck Archipelago and the Solomons, we have the simplest hints that advances in voyaging (or at least in the frequency of movement between islands) may have occurred. The evidence is indirect and highly inferential: the appearance of obsidian hundreds of kilometers beyond its source and of animals "translocated" from their endemic homes. But something more profound is hinted at, a subtle difference in the way that people were beginning to perceive their island environments as well as themselves. As Chris Gosden has observed, rather than now always moving themselves to new resources, people were beginning to apply voyaging technology to the movement of resources. The idea seems simple, almost trivial, but it underlies all that would come later, for the "conquest" of Remote Oceania could never have been accomplished without the ability to transport an arkful of biotic resources, from dogs and pigs to taro and breadfruit seedlings.

Transport distances in Remote Oceania are an order of magnitude greater than those within the Near Oceanic "voyaging nursery." They could never be successfully crossed with the crude technology we infer for early humans in the Pleistocene, or even the early Holocene. Sophisticated open-water craft were called for, and insofar as we can reconstruct its history, the sailing outrigger canoe complex emerged in the relatively calm waters of island Southeast Asia, perhaps between 4000 and 2000 B.C. The early Austronesian voyaging canoe, the *wangka*, which we reconstruct from linguistic and comparative ethnographic evidence since no material remains have yet been uncovered, was a marvel of "neolithic" technology. Its hull was probably a simple dugout (perhaps with greater freeboard achieved by lashing on separate washstrakes), while the addition of a float gave it both stability and the possibility of carrying added cargo (on platforms lashed to the outrigger booms). The lanteen sail made of plaited mats meant it could harness the wind, freed from mere drifting currents. The sailing outrigger canoe became a sharp instrument of exploration, discovery, and colonization, in the space of a few short millennia propelling people to the farthest ends of the Pacific Ocean.

More than just new and vastly improved technology underwrote the great expansion of

Austronesian-speaking voyagers into Remote Oceania, after about 1500 B.C. There was as well a new ideology, a different way of looking at the ocean, of envisioning lands the eye could not see but which the mind could populate with generations of descendants. This was the vision not of hunter-gatherers always moving on to new resources but of horticultural people tied to the land, for whom cultivated territory was always the fundamental basis of social life. This was, moreover, an ideology bound to a particular kind of social structure, one in which siblings were ranked by birth order and elder brothers became founders of descent lines, claiming the best lands and other resources as their own. Thus while the human settlement of Oceania is often thought of in maritime terms, as constituting a succession of great voyaging feats, these voyages were primarily means to an end: the discovery of new landscapes that could be claimed, named, divided, planted, and inherited.

Islanders were not content to always sit at home and tend their crops, or fish the reefs and lagoons of the inshore waters. In exploring and populating the Pacific, they gradually built up another ideology, one of the sea as highway, with a myriad of routes connecting one's own island to many others. Sometimes these highways were so long and the voyages necessary to traverse them so arduous that the desire or ability to keep up contacts with one's relations on other islands gradually waned. Thus the most remote islands and archipelagoes of the Pacific (such as Rapa Nui or Hawai'i) after a time became isolated worlds unto themselves. But throughout much of the Pacific, a complex network of interconnections developed, maintained by seafarers and navigators who became transportation specialists, keepers of esoteric knowledge of star paths and wind compasses, such as Tupaia, who met Captain Cook, or the modern Satawal navigator Mau Piailug. These networks were not

random; indeed, they became highly regularized through repeated economic and social transactions. By the time Europeans entered the Pacific, most (but not all) of its islands were connected to at least some other islands through network after network.

However, the reticulate grid of complex voyaging networks linking many Pacific islands in late prehistory should not mislead us to conclude that everything was in cultural flux, that the deeper history of cultural, linguistic, and biological differentiation among Pacific peoples had been wholly swamped by a frenzy of social (or, for that matter, sexual) intercourse.[2] Contact was important, for trade and exchange, and sometimes for marriage partners. Most often, contact was with nearby islanders who shared a common history and who were closely related—linguistically, biologically, and culturally. Thus Tongans voyaged to Samoa and Fiji; the people of Nendö interacted mostly with those of nearby Utupua, Vanikoro, and the Reefs; the Yapese went to Palau or the closer atolls of the central Carolines. Moreover, interisland connections, although frequently valorized in song and myth, were the purview of a privileged few; most members of Oceanic societies commanded neither the skills nor the physical equipment (voyaging canoes being expensive items of property) to make overseas voyages themselves. Further, would-be voyagers were not always welcomed at their intended destinations: the Mangaians, for example, aggressively repulsed efforts at contact. A great deal of linguistic, cultural, and biological distinctiveness was thus maintained— and often consciously enhanced—by the peoples of the many Pacific islands.

In fundamental ways the history of Oceanic voyaging mirrors the larger history of modern humans, from hunter-gatherers moving footstep by footstep across the land they exploited to food producers whose populations swelled rapidly and for whom the search for new lands to plant and control became a driving force of cultural change. Paradoxical as it might seem, the major advances in Pacific maritime technology can be correlated with the advent of a food-producing, horticultural economy, for they were partly stimulated by enhanced ability to find new land. Then too, a gradual development of craft and economic specialization can be read in the history of Pacific voyaging, whether the emergence of a class of navigator-chiefs (as in Tonga or Tahiti) or of social regimes rooted deeply in exchange and trade of commodities (as with Mailu and the Massim). To read the history of Pacific voyaging is to begin to grasp some of the essential structures of the Oceanic *longue durée*. The same great cultural transformations that made the premodern world what it was likewise made Oceania.

History Written in the Present: Correlations between Language, Biology, and Culture

A fundamental tenet of twentieth-century anthropology holds that race (i.e., human biological variation), language, and culture are independent. Yet since at least Sapir (1916) it has been evident to historical anthropologists that for many regions of the world, and for certain periods of time, biology, language, and culture have significantly covaried. In a seminal application of phylogenetic models in anthropology, Kimball Romney argued:

> Physical type and language, we would say, have no causal relationship; there is no functional reason why a given physical type should occur with a given language family. Therefore, when these two variables do show significant concordance in their distribution this may well represent an important historical fact, namely that the explanation for their concordance can be traced to a common point somewhere in the past. A demonstration that these two factors are also uniquely accompanied by a systemic culture

pattern . . . would strengthen the belief in a common origin. (1957:36)

Romney called this kind of concordance between biological, linguistic, and cultural patterns a "segment of cultural history" and went on to argue that the Uto-Aztecan-speaking peoples of North America constituted just such a segment.

Whether or not such segments of cultural history (or, as I have called them in this book, "phyletic units") can be identified in the Pacific and, if so, what they have to tell us about human history in Oceania have invoked controversy and debate for more than a century. The greatest agreement focuses on the Polynesians, whose linguistic and cultural unity was observed well before anthropology became an academic discipline, and whose biological homogeneity has been extensively documented. The many Polynesian societies and cultures together form a robust phyletic unit—all speaking genetically related languages, with common cultural patterns and a high degree of biological similarity—who descended from a common ancestral group. The application of a phylogenetic model to Polynesia is therefore not particularly controversial, and even scholars who are skeptical of such models admit its application to Polynesia (Moore 1994).

When it comes to other regions within Oceania, the degree to which biology, language, and culture are correlated remains hotly contested.[3] The debate centers around the issue of whether the patterns of distribution and relationship among the Austronesian and Non-Austronesian languages of Oceania correspond, in any significant manner, with patterns of human biological variation, and with systemic cultural patterns, particularly as these are reflected in archaeological cultures.

Many pioneering ethnographers and linguists who worked in the western Pacific thought that they could detect such correlations. W. H. R.

Rivers, who attempted a historical reconstruction based solely on comparative ethnography (a Pacific archaeological record did not exist in his day), was well aware of the "great variety of physical characters of the Melanesian people," opining that they displayed "a greater variety than the peoples of Europe" (1914, I:582). Rivers explained this variation largely as a "result of mixture of peoples differing widely from one another in physical character." Likewise, he recognized that language and biology can have radically different outcomes in the course of interaction between two groups, as in the case of a large local population adopting the language of a small (but socially dominant) immigrant group, yet having "relatively little effect on the physical appearance of those among whom they settled" (1914, I:594). His particular narrative of an ancient "dual people" who were successively influenced by new immigrant groups (the "kava-people" and the "betel-people") strikes us today as quaint, yet given his limited comparative data Rivers's speculative "history" makes considerable sense; when its antique terminology is recast in modern terms, his sequence bears much in common with modern syntheses. The German linguist Otto Dempwolff (1934–38) developed similar ideas, and he thought that the initial spread of Austronesian language speakers could be correlated with certain biological populations, although he argued that where malaria was rife, the malaria-resistant genes of the original, "darker-skinned and frizzy-haired" populations tended to dominate. Dempwolff, Rivers, and others of their day were greatly constrained in their ability to refine and test their theories, both by the lack of an archaeological record and by the "typological" (indeed, racist) approach then dominant in physical anthropology.

Some contemporary scholars argue that continued efforts to correlate biological, linguistic, and cultural patterns of variation in Melanesia or elsewhere in the western Pacific merely perpetuate an outdated paradigm of anthropology (e.g., Terrell 1986:63; Terrell et al. 1997). But historical anthropologists have not been deterred by such nay-saying, venturing to apply new and more powerful analytical and comparative tools than were available to Dempwolff, Rivers, or their peers, and testing phylogenetic hypotheses that "segments of cultural history" can be delineated in Melanesia. Their results strongly support the notion that even in Melanesia—where the degree of biological, linguistic, and cultural variation is enormous—historically meaningful patterns of covariance do exist and can be detected.[4]

Some of the strongest evidence for correlations between language groups and biological variation in Melanesia has come from the long-term Solomon Islands Project (Friedlaender, ed., 1987), which examined patterns of human variation among eight populations including both Austronesian- and Non-Austronesian-speakers. Summarizing a wealth of detailed biometric and genetic evidence, Friedlaender (1987:354–57) draws several noteworthy conclusions. First, the large island of Bougainville, which includes Non-Austronesian language groups and which "from a biogeographical perspective, is a logical place for relic populations to persist," in fact exhibits the greatest range of variation, with a "very distinctive biological population." Second, the biological diversity of Bougainville, and to some extent that of its nearest neighbors, "suggests that the pre-Austronesian settlements in Island Melanesia are very old, and possibly are the result of a number of separate migrations, and subsequent significant differentiation in situ of a lesser magnitude."[5] Third, the "Austronesian-speaking populations in Melanesia tend to show biological similarities in spite of their strong resemblances to immediately neighboring groups." For example, there are virtually perfect correspondences between the presence or absence of certain Gm alleles and the distribution of Austronesian and Papuan languages. Likewise, fingerprint patterns show clear-cut distinctions that correlate with these major language distinctions (Froehlich 1987); and again, tooth sizes (odontometric patterns) "lend strong support to the . . . interpretation that [Non-Austronesian]-speaking peoples of Bougainville Island have an origin and history in Oceania significantly different from that of the more recent [Austronesian]-speakers" (Harris and Bailil 1987:259). Thus Friedlaender concludes that in Melanesia, "although the correspondence is hardly perfect, biologic and linguistic variation are often reflections (sometimes sharp, sometimes dim) of migrational histories" (1987: 356–57). Friedlaender modestly says that he is simply "restating a now obvious truth of anthropology," yet it seems that such truths need to be periodically revalidated with empirical evidence for each new generation of anthropologists.

If the Solomon Islands Project's results are not sufficient to convince some that the patterns of biological and linguistic variation in Melanesia encapsulate a "migrational history" (which is to say that they are a kind of "text" of that history), there are ample validating data from recent genetic studies, including analyses of HLA genes, blood genetic systems, and mitochondrial DNA.[6] A completely different kind of evidence—not biological but cultural—consists of a large museum artifact database that has allowed the testing of the degree to which differences or similarities in material culture correlate with linguistic groups (Welsch et al. 1992). In several brilliant reanalyses of this data set, Carmella Moore and Kimball Romney have shown that "language and distance account for almost identical amounts of variation among material culture assemblages" (1994:387; see also Moore and Romney 1996; Roberts et al. 1995).

The point I would emphasize—the big structure that we must grasp—is that the cultural, bio-

logical, and linguistic patterns characteristic of Oceania (and not just of Polynesia) are far from random. They are, indeed, highly structured and, despite the complexities of their patterning, display regular correlations and concordances. This is precisely because they reflect a real history of human movements or migration into the Pacific, and of dispersal or diaspora over its many islands. That such movements must have occurred, and were responsible for regularities in cultural patterning, was only roughly grasped by the pioneering ethnographers and linguists of the early twentieth century. What they lacked were the more sophisticated methodologies at our disposal today and—even more critically—a direct archaeological record. They struggled to infer a "migrational history" solely from synchronic patterns of variation, from history written in the present. It has been the contribution of archaeology, in the closing decades of the twentieth century, to provide the properly *diachronic* evidence of human history in Oceania, against which the *synchronic* patterns in language, culture, and biology can be more fully interpreted. Knowing now that the history of Near Oceania runs deep indeed—well into the Pleistocene—we can finally explain the great genetic and linguistic diversity that already existed in this region when the Austronesian-speaking peoples voyaged into the Bismarck Sea around 1500 B.C. The discovery of the Lapita cultural complex as well provides the archaeological signature of that particular human diaspora, which not only added to the heterogeneity and complexity of Melanesia but also was responsible for the peopling of the vastness of Remote Oceania.[7]

The Role of Demographic Change in Oceanic History

I turn now, in Tilly's phrasing, from large structures to big processes, commencing with a demographic cycle that backgrounds the histories of a great many (possibly the majority of) Oceanic societies. First, however, we must revisit a critical contrast between the population structures of Near Oceania and those of Remote Oceania, a striking difference demanding a historical explanation. According to their ethnohistoric and archaeological records, the large archipelagoes of the Bismarcks, Solomons, and Vanuatu never supported high-density human populations, other than in very local areas.[8] Vast parts of these islands remained in climax rainforests, which, while hardly pristine (for low-density human settlements are dispersed within them), were largely untransformed by human activities, despite thousands of years of human presence. The absence of large populations in these fertile islands—even after indigenous food production systems arose in the Holocene—poses a real contradiction. In Remote Oceania beyond Vanuatu the situation is the opposite. Human populations again and again reached high density levels over relatively short time spans, even on such large land masses as New Caledonia and Fiji. And these dense populations wrought enormous and sometimes irrevocable changes in vegetation and other aspects of the environment.[9]

Why this difference in population structures between the large archipelagoes of the western Pacific and those of Remote Oceania? What could possibly account for the disparity in population densities? Malaria—probably combined with other kinds of parasitic and infectious diseases. The geographic distribution of malaria in the Pacific corresponds closely to the distribution of the population structures just observed: it is found in lowland and midaltitude Near Oceania, and within Remote Oceania only in the Santa Cruz Islands group and in Vanuatu. The effects of this disease, which one expert in the field claims has "probably resulted in more mortality in human populations than any other disease" (Livingstone

1984:413), is not to be underestimated. The one place within Near Oceania where malaria is absent—the New Guinea Highlands—is also the only region in which large and dense human populations did arise following the development of intensive agricultural production. In short, on a broad canvas the demographic history of Oceania has been intimately linked with the history of disease, especially malaria.

Once human populations began to expand into Remote Oceania, they found themselves in a significantly healthier environment. While some *Plasmodium* parasites would at first have been carried in their bloodstreams, there were no *Anopheles* mosquitoes to act as vectors, and the chain of malarial transmission was broken. These more isolated islands also lacked the diverse intestinal protozoa, bacteria, hookworms, and other disease-causing microorganisms of Near Oceania. The key conditions that had held human growth rates in check in Near Oceania were now lifted. In addition, the new islands discovered by the Lapita colonizers and their descendants were devoid of other human occupants; there were no others to claim or defend territory. Rich in natural food resources (especially birds and seafoods), the high islands were well suited to planting food crops. In addition to the lack of epidemiological or environmental constraints on population increase, there were strong cultural pressures favoring high reproduction rates. With founding populations on new islands being initially small (in many cases possibly consisting of the complement of a single voyaging canoe), the risks of extinction were substantially lessened with each new birth.[10] In short, conditions prevailing during the initial phases of human expansion into Remote Oceania—both environmental and cultural—almost ideally favored high rates of population increase.[11]

Some years ago, I outlined a model for human demographic transitions on Polynesian islands

(Kirch 1980, 1984a), equally applicable throughout Remote Oceania (except Santa Cruz and Vanuatu, which lay within the malarious zone, and the temperate, nonagricultural cases of South Island and the Chathams). In the early stages of island colonization and settlement, given a lack of constraints on population growth, reinforced by the obvious social advantage of increasing one's own population (and economic production) base, a high intrinsic growth rate arguably resulted, combined with relatively low mortality. After some time, however (and this would vary greatly depending upon local conditions, especially island size and resources), Remote Oceanic populations consistently grew to the point at which increased human numbers began to exert various kinds of pressure. These need not have been limited to direct pressure on food supply, which could often be offset through the implementation of intensive methods of cultivation. The social marking and claiming of all available territory brought to bear another kind of pressure. That is to say, people begin to perceive population pressure due to such socially and culturally defined criteria well before any absolute biological limits of food supply are reached. In any event, during the later time periods on many Polynesian and Remote Oceanic islands, human populations had reached quite large numbers (in the hundreds of thousands on larger islands and archipelagoes) and—more significantly—high densities per area of arable land. Population densities of 100 persons per square kilometer or more seem to have been quite common on many islands, and in some cases densities were much higher. Under these conditions, high intrinsic rates of population increase could no longer be tolerated, and cultural controls on population growth began to be implemented. As ethnographically documented, such controls included means of reducing fertility (celibacy, contraception, abortion), as well as of increasing

mortality (infanticide, suicide voyaging, war, expulsion of certain groups, ritual sacrifice, and even cannibalism).[12] The later stages in the demographic cycle of most Remote Oceanic islands are thus characterized by a reduced rate of population increase, in many cases probably oscillating around periods of growth and decline, and in at least some instances (such as Rapa Nui) with dramatic decline following an actual overshoot of a diminishing or degraded resource base (Fig. 9.1).

This kind of demographic cycle, known as logistic growth, is well demonstrated in natural populations of all kinds and is graphically defined by a sigmoidal or S-shaped curve.[13] While a perfect logistic curve is rarely if ever seen in natural populations, some variant of it is ubiquitous. In 1984, I tested this logistic growth model against empirical archaeological evidence for human population growth as indicated by proxy measures of dated habitation sites in Hawai'i, finding a reasonably good fit (Kirch 1984a:104–11). Despite some initial skepticism (e.g., Sutton and Molloy 1989), more than a decade of additional paleodemographic modeling has reinforced my argument. Especially for the Hawaiian archipelago, some form of logistic population growth cycle now seems incontestable based on a wealth of well-dated samples from both habitation and agricultural sites,[14] even though we recognize that there were locally important variations in rates and densities.[15] Logistical growth cycles have now been suggested for such diverse Remote Oceanic islands as Kosrae (Athens 1995), New Caledonia (Sand 1995), and New Zealand (Brewis et al. 1990; Davidson 1984).

I remain convinced that some form of logistic growth process was probably the norm on virtually all Remote Oceanic islands, even though there must have been innumerable variations on this overall theme (see Green 1993:229–30). A demographic transition from high-growth, "density-

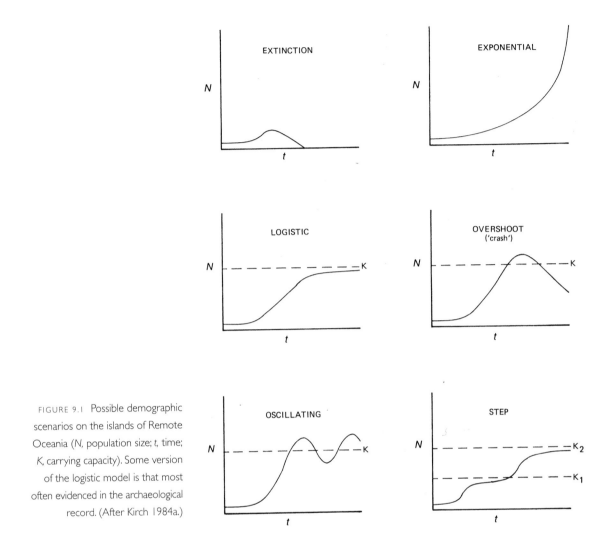

FIGURE 9.1 Possible demographic scenarios on the islands of Remote Oceania (N, population size; t, time; K, carrying capacity). Some version of the logistic model is that most often evidenced in the archaeological record. (After Kirch 1984a.)

independent" to lowered-growth, "density-depen-dent" populations is, I would assert, one of the big processes underlying the history of hundreds of Oceanic societies. I am *not*, however, asserting that the particular demographic histories of islands were ever identical, for everything depends on local conditions of founding group size, land and resources, elapsed time, and particular cultural and social behaviors within which reproduction and death are embedded. But I am convinced that the underlying cycle, and hence processes, were

often equivalent and had structurally similar consequences and outcomes. Among these were heightened competition for land and resources, technological and social measures to increase pro-duction, and increased impacts on the natural biota and landscapes of islands.

In highlighting a logistic population cycle as a big process of Oceanic history, I nonetheless emphatically reject a simplistic demographic deter-minism, a unicausal explanation for what hap-pened in Oceanic societies. Population growth can never provide a *sufficient* prime mover for cultural change; what it offers is a *necessary* condition without which other kinds of social, technological, ideological, or political changes are highly unlikely to occur. Here I draw insight from Ernst Mayr, whose clearheadedness has more than once enlightened evolutionary thinking, and who observes that there are nearly always both a *proximate* and an *ultimate* cause for any given phenomenon. What is more, "many famous controversies in the history of biology came about because one party considered only proximate causations and the other party considered only evolutionary [ultimate] ones" (Mayr 1997:67). In my view, the logistic cycle of population growth that has now been empirically demonstrated for at least some Remote Oceanic islands (and will probably soon be documented for many others) provides one fundamental kind of ultimate causation in the history of Oceanic peoples.[16] But it is hardly the full story, for there are many forms of proximate causation as well, equally important and just as fascinating.

Oceanic Populations on the Eve of European Contact

If paleodemographic studies support the notion that many (if not most) of the environmentally favorable high islands of Remote Oceania experienced a logistic growth cycle leading to large, high-density populations in late prehistory, estimating the actual sizes of those populations is another matter. The dean of Oceanic ethnography, Douglas Oliver, writes that "estimating the number of pre-European inhabitants of Oceania is like trying to photograph a fast-moving train broadside, with a Brownie camera" (1989:27). Yet this has not stopped historical demographers from "playing the numbers," by reworking the estimates and rough census counts made by the early European explorers and missionaries. Demographers

and statisticians such as McArthur (1968), Rallu (1990), and Schmitt (1968, 1973) expended much effort deriving estimates of Oceanic island populations prior to the advent of Europeans. Their estimates necessarily reflect the assumptions they bring to this work. Among these are a presumption that the earliest European accounts (usually made by explorers who had only limited contact with the islands they "discovered") are typically inflated, and that the depopulation that occurred following European contact (due primarily to the introduction of diseases for which the indigenous peoples had little or no resistance), while substantial, was not acute. Much greater reliability has been placed on the head-counts made by missionaries who, unlike explorers, lived among their converts for extended periods and were often obsessed with quantifying the number of "pagan souls" to be saved. But in most island groups these missionaries arrived decades—and in some cases, a century or more—after initial contact with Europeans,[17] leaving what happened during the intervening period a matter of dispute.[18]

As Pacific archaeologists increasingly turned their attention to the distribution of sites over whole landscapes, and to paleodemography, these issues have come to the fore. Consider the case of New Caledonia. One of the largest islands in Remote Oceania, La Grande Terre has much of its landscape covered in vestiges of former intensive habitation and cultivation (see Chapter 5). The island was "discovered" by Cook in 1774, yet the first attempt at census-taking did not occur until 1887, with an estimate of 42,519 persons (Rallu 1990:272). (The island's population had clearly been on the decline for some time, and by 1921 it reached a low of 27,100.) Despite a total absence of data on what happened between 1774 and 1887, historical demographers have been content to estimate the 1774 population of La Grande Terre at somewhere between 40,000 (Shineberg

1983) and possibly as high as 80,000 (Rallu 1990). Only the geographer Roux (1990), based on an evaluation of land and traditional subsistence practices, has cautiously extended the precontact population estimate as high as 100,000. Christophe Sand (1995:281–309) directly challenges the veracity of all these estimates and suggests that even the 100,000 figure is too low. He argues that the effects of epidemic disease have been grossly underestimated, and that the demographic collapse suffered by the inhabitants of La Grande Terre after 1774 was truly catastrophic. How much greater than 100,000 Sand thinks the real precontact population might have been he does not say, but clearly this has become an issue that archaeology must address.

Spriggs (1997:253) echoes Sand's comments for the rest of island Melanesia, pointing to the "archaeological evidence of massive population disruption and decline attendant upon European contact." Among the archaeological signals of "catastrophic collapse" that Spriggs sees in the Melanesian archaeological record are "the abandoned village sites deep in the forests, the disused irrigation systems and other manifestations of once-intensive agricultural systems, and the marked discontinuity in settlement pattern often found between sites with European artifacts on them and those from the period immediately before contact" (1997:253–54). Such evidence occurs throughout Remote Oceania.

In Samoa, settlement pattern surveys reveal extensive and dense inland occupations, extending in some cases right up to the ridgetops.[19] Yet the earliest missionary accounts of Samoa paint a landscape portrait of coastal villages with vacant interiors, and their estimates and census counts (made decades after first contact) have been invoked to suggest a maximum population for Western Samoa ('Upolu and Savai'i Islands) of no more than about 38,000 (McArthur 1968:115).[20]

This figure represents a population density of only 13 persons per square kilometer on these fertile volcanic islands, an absurdly low figure given the high density of inland settlement revealed by archaeological survey. Ethnographically documented Polynesian subsistence agriculture regularly supported population densities of 100 persons per square kilometer, and at times as high as 242 persons per square kilometer in favorable environmental situations (Kirch and Yen 1982:56). Thus it hardly seems conceivable—especially in light of the archaeological evidence for dense inland settlement—that the maximum population of Samoa was less than 100,000, and it might have been as great as 300,000 or more prior to European contact.[21] To be sure, this hypothesis must be tested with further research.[22]

For no other Pacific archipelago has debate over the size of the indigenous population on the eve of Western contact become so intense as Hawai'i, due to the scholarly gauntlet thrown down by David Stannard in his book *Before the Horror* (1989). Lieutenant King, officer on Cook's expedition at first contact in 1778–79, estimated 400,000 persons for the total population of Hawai'i. Later demographic scholarship by Schmitt (1968, 1973) reduced this to 250,000–300,000, a widely quoted number. In a carefully crafted argument, however, Stannard reverses Schmitt: "All the evidence available to us regarding the credibility of King's 1778 population estimate points in precisely the opposite direction from that which most subsequent writers have alleged: King's 400,000 estimate was, if anything, a serious *under* estimate of the actual figure. But how short was he?" (1989:27). Stannard answers his own rhetorical question by contending that the pre-1778 Hawaiian population reached a maximum of at least 800,000, and perhaps more than one million persons (1989:30).

Stannard's argument turns largely on archaeological evidence, especially for dense inland agricultural field systems and settlements, and for a high windward regional population. Indeed, not only Stannard, but also those who strongly disagree with his views, all invoke *archaeological* evidence as key aspects of their arguments. Eleanor Nordyke, a noted authority on Hawaiian demography, insists that she will reject Stannard's figures "until an anthropologic or archaeological assessment verifies" his claims (1989:112–13). Two archaeologists, Tom Dye and Eric Komori (1992; Dye 1994), have offered just such an assessment, but rather than backing up either Stannard's or the conventional Schmitt estimate of 250,000–300,000, they would *lower* the estimated population at contact to a mere 120,000![23]

Where does all this leave us? Must we abandon any hope of ever knowing the "real" population numbers of Pacific islands prior to contact with the West? Stannard urges us to take these questions seriously: "It makes an enormous difference to the work of anthropologists and archaeologists, as well as to cultural, intellectual, social, and political historians—to say nothing of the Hawaiian people today—whether there were a quarter of a million Hawaiians in 1778 or three-quarters of a million. Or more" (Stannard 1989:143). I strongly agree, and I believe that continued scholarship on this problem is one of the most significant contributions that historical anthropologists can make to Oceanic studies. These are matters that mean a great deal to the indigenous peoples of the Pacific, and they challenge us to seek new evidence, new methods, and new models. The old "numbers game" of historical demography—based on endless reassessments of historical estimates and census reports—has long since played out. Continuing that line of debate will get us nowhere. The ball is now in the archaeologists' court; it is up to us to seize the challenge and apply all of the lines of material evidence at our command to break out of the old debates. Paleo-

demography as adduced from archaeological evidence is a relatively new field, but it has great promise. Whether the contentions of Stannard, Spriggs, or Sand—that the Pacific archaeological record holds the clues to a far more catastrophic impact of the West on Oceania than has hitherto been imagined—will prove true can only be tested through empirical field research and careful analysis. One thing is certain: our work will be closely watched by contemporary Pacific islanders, for whom this aspect of their history is most crucial.

The Political Economy of Dynamic Landscapes

If the Remote Oceanic islands were in most instances densely populated at the time of European intrusion in the sixteenth to eighteenth centuries—and the archaeological record increasingly confirms that this was the case—their landscapes were also irrevocably transformed by generations of human activity. In Near Oceania, landscape transformation seems not to have been so pronounced (although the New Guinea Highlands with their anthropogenic grasslands and intensively cultivated valley floors are more like Remote Oceania in this regard), for as I have argued, population densities in the Near Oceanic region generally did not reach the levels seen in Remote Oceania. Even in the Bismarcks and Solomons, however, the hand of *Homo sapiens* left its mark in many ways, from the extinction of bird species, to the translocation of the cuscus and other animals, to the modification of lowland vegetation communities. In Remote Oceania, impacts wrought by human populations on island ecosystems were often far-reaching and—if viewed from the perspective of the natural biota—frequently disastrous. The wholesale decimation and extinction of many species of sea- and land birds from these islands, the removal of vast tracts of indigenous forest and their replacement with pyrophytic

FIGURE 9.2 The fern-covered hills of Mangaia Island, dotted here and there with scrub ironwood trees, typify the pyrophytic, degraded landscapes of many tropical Pacific islands. Note the coconut palms, which are restricted to the narrow valley bottom. (Photo by P. V. Kirch.)

grass- and fernlands (Fig. 9.2), erosion and alluviation in valleys and along coastal plains—these and other impacts are now well documented for many islands (Kirch and Hunt, eds., 1997). In part, such cultural modifications of the natural ecology of islands stemmed directly from the food-getting and food-producing activities of Pacific islanders, whether hunting birds or clearing forest for shifting cultivation. Other impacts were indirect and followed from the introduction of domestic plants and animals, and of "weed species" (like the ubiquitous Pacific Rat). Cumulatively and incrementally, even small inroads to natural biotic communities had far-reaching effects over time. Islands such as Mangareva and Rapa Nui were largely denuded of all arboreal vegetation prior to European contact, and even on large high islands such as Viti Levu the lower-elevation vegetation communities were thoroughly modified (Ash 1992). We are again in the presence of a big process, an ecological process with enormous consequences for island landscapes and for island cultures.

Remarkably, the scale and nature of human modification of island landscapes were not recognized until fairly recently. For most anthropologists throughout the twentieth century, island environments seemed as changeless as the timeless "ethnographic present" they invented in their monographs. Such Rousseauian thinking is a legacy of Enlightenment notions about "the peoples without history," which historical anthropology struggles to shed (Kirch 1997b). Indeed, establishing a paleoenvironmental record for the Pacific islands— one that includes the role of indigenous human populations as major players in the transformation of insular ecologies—has been one of the more significant contributions of Oceanic archaeology, in collaboration with the natural sciences. Not only has Pacific archaeology overthrown the old ethnographic bias of "static" island cultures (in which change derived primarily from migration; see Chapter 1), it has demonstrated that in the process of transforming themselves, island cultures forever changed their microcosmic worlds (Kirch 1997d).

The outcomes of ecological change on islands differ radically depending on whether these are viewed from the perspective of the natural flora and fauna, or of the people who initiated these changes. For many a species of flightless rail or native lorikeet, or for an endemic lobeloid or palm, the outlook after the arrival of humans on its island home was frankly bleak. It is no exaggeration to say that among the Remote Oceanic islands, the "biodiversity crisis" began not recently but 3,500 years ago with the Lapita expansion. It now seems likely that literally hundreds, if not thousands, of endemic species of plants and animals (especially birds, insects, and land snails, as well as vascular plants and ferns) underwent extinction or local extirpation as a consequence— direct and indirect—of the "human conquest" of the Pacific islands.[24]

Viewed from the perspective of the human "conquerors," the transformation of island landscapes was altogether different, for the most part a highly desirable series of modifications, improvements, innovations, and intensifications that quite literally made the islands inhabitable. For indeed, oceanic islands—despite their famously salubrious climates, lack of disease-inducing organisms, and physical beauty—were not naturally well suited to supporting large human populations. True, many islands abounded in birds, fish, and shellfish, which offered ample supplies of protein (at least in the early phases of colonization when human numbers were relatively low), but vegetable foods—especially the staple starches upon which every complex society has ultimately been built—were entirely lacking. It was truly essential, as human populations burgeoned on these islands, that their landscapes increasingly undergo a transformation from natural to cultural, from merely extractive to highly productive resource bases.

On many islands, the process of creating a productive infrastructure of gardens and fields was highly successful, evoking admiration from anyone who has ever struggled to wrest food from the ground, whether in an urban backyard plot or on a grander rural scale. The agroforests or "orchard gardens" of Tikopia and Kosrae are marvels of "sustainable agriculture" (Athens et al. 1996; Kirch 1997d; Kirch and Yen 1982), while the irrigated taro pondfields of Hawai'i or Mangaia were so efficient and successful that they continue to be used by contemporary farmers virtually without modification.[25] The development of these and other innovative and intensified production systems literally fueled the rise of large and complex societies throughout the oceanic world. Processes that could be so destructive to nature (in its "pristine" manifestation) were simultaneously the foundation of culture.

But not every experiment in the conversion of island ecosystems to productive economies was entirely successful; in some cases, there were outright failures.[26] Rapa Nui has become a highly publicized instance in which the anthropogenic transformation of an island went too far, in which initial success led to a population expansion that overwhelmed the island's capacity to sustain it (Bahn and Flenley 1992; Van Tilburg 1994). Rapa Nui's history is mixed in its successes and failures, including great artistic and cultural accomplishments (of which the statue complex is only one) combined with dark and terrible moments inscribed in the archaeological record of endless obsidian spearheads, fortified refuge caves, and middens evidencing cannibalism. Yet the Rapa Nui people inevitably survived all this (and even more terrible deeds done to them at the hands of Europeans after their isolated world was shattered), and today they aspire to rebuild the greatness of their island culture.[27] Similar narratives could be related for other island peoples, in which the endless struggle to produce and reproduce, and to build a life rich in cultural meaning, has more than once embraced severe challenges. For most Mangaians in late prehistory, theirs was a world of lurking terror punctuated by fierce intertribal wars for control of land (Hiroa 1934). Other stories have yet to be

told. For example, why were the vast sculptured landscapes of Palau abandoned well before European contact? What history of human effort gone awry in the face of environmental constraints might be encapsulated in those *Miscanthus* grasslands covering rank after rank of terraces? Such unanswered questions simultaneously chasten and challenge us.

Some historical trajectories seem to have been greatly influenced by fundamental contrasts in island environments, such as those provided by different geological origins and ages, or different climatic and seasonal regimes. One such underlying contrast is between "wet" and "dry" environmental zones, a structural aspect of environment with great significance for agricultural production, as Barrau (1965a) insightfully recognized. Interactions between "the wet and the dry" in many islands constituted a dynamic cycle that fundamentally influenced the course of sociopolitical change (Kirch 1994). These contrasts might be played out as well on different scales and in different configurations, ranging from the windward/leeward distinctions that mark Viti Levu and many other islands to contrasts on the scale of an entire archipelago. Consider the geological age progression of the Hawaiian Islands, where the largest yet youngest islands had only limited possibilities for intensive irrigation, feeding the aspirations of their chiefly rulers for territorial conquest. In these large environmental "structures" one seeks clues to certain big processes of political economy.

To assert that the history of Oceanic cultures is intimately bound up with the historical ecology of island landscapes is emphatically not to espouse an environmentally determined model of change. Island environments posed *constraints*, and some of these were impossible to overcome given the limitations of a "neolithic" technology; the "reversion" of South Island Maori to a hunting and gathering mode of existence is a case in point. Other constraints were hardly absolute. Productive landscapes could be created in many environments—given sufficient labor—often under the aegis of increasingly hierarchical social formations. Most often, Pacific landscapes were what people made of them. By the end of "prehistory" the Pacific world was a constructed world, an ocean full of thoroughly modified, transformed, anthropogenic islands. In this respect too the Pacific would offer a lesson for the larger history of our species.

Intensification and Specialization in Island Economies

Peering down the dim corridor of the *longue durée*, one glimpses yet other reflections of large structures and big processes; one is a proclivity for island economies to undergo both *intensification* and *specialization* over time. These are indeed big concepts in anthropology and archaeology, and I cannot review here all of the nuanced theoretical arguments that scholars have advanced regarding such processes and their significance in prehistory.[28] But no overview of grand patterns in Oceanic history would be adequate without at least some consideration of these trends.

Building on work by Boserup (1965), Brookfield (1972, 1984), Yen (1971, 1973), and others, the variety of changes in economic systems (and here we are concerned especially, though not exclusively, with agricultural systems) usually subsumed under the rubric *intensification* may be parsed into several kinds of rather different processes (Kirch 1994). When we speak of intensification, what is usually implied is some increased level of output (usually crop yield), typically measured against a constant area of land. But increased yields per unit

area can be achieved in many ways. For example, higher-yielding varieties of crops may be developed, and this is not a phenomenon limited to modern plant breeders or genetic engineering. For thousands of years, gardeners and farmers improved their crops through the simple process of selection (sometimes called "Burbankian selection," after the famed California orchardist Luther Burbank). This was certainly the case in the Pacific, with well-documented examples of selection for improved cultivars (e.g., Lepofsky et al. 1998; Yen 1974a, 1974b). Yields may also be increased through improved technology or by new agronomic methods. While these changes result in higher yields, it may be best to think of them as *innovations* rather than as intensification proper (Kirch 1994:18–19, Fig. 5).

Distinguishing innovation from intensification allows us to reserve the latter term for processes involving increased input of human effort—in a word, *labor*—to achieve the desired goal of increased yields. But even so, two significantly different kinds of intensification can be identified, and both were operative in Pacific island economies. The first involves the construction of agronomic *facilities*, permanent modifications to the landscape that result in higher levels of agricultural production. Excellent examples are the irrigated pondfield terraces and canals constructed on many islands, including Kolombangara, Aneityum, New Caledonia, Fiji, Futuna, Rapa, Mangaia, Hawai'i, and elsewhere in Oceania (Fig. 9.3). Less well known are the dryland field systems of Hawai'i, New Zealand, and other areas, or the yam mounds of New Caledonia. The extensive nonirrigated terraces of Palau are yet another case. This kind of intensification has been called *landesque capital intensification* because it involves a permanent modification of the landscape (Blaikie and Brookfield, eds., 1987). What is frequently

FIGURE 9.3 Irrigated taro pondfields of Tamarua Valley, Mangaia Island. Such intensive agricultural landscapes were developed in late prehistory on many Pacific islands. (Photo by P. V. Kirch.)

overlooked about landesque capital intensification, however, is that while substantial labor inputs may be required to construct terraces, canals, field boundaries, or other facilities, once in place the labor required to maintain them may be relatively low. This is especially true for pondfield irrigation of *Colocasia* taro, which produces significantly higher yields than dryland cultivation but does not require greater labor once the terraced pondfields have been constructed (Kirch 1994).[29]

Contrasting with landesque capital intensification is *cropping cycle intensification*, the classic Boserupian mode of intensification (Boserup 1965) through reduction of fallow length and increased application of labor, especially in such activities as weeding and mulching (Kirch 1994). Here labor must be invested not in permanent improvements to an agricultural landscape but in seasonally repetitive activities, in order to gain increased yields per unit area. This kind of intensification was commonly present in Pacific island economies and is precisely the sort of process we would reconstruct for Rapa Nui and for the dry, leeward parts of Hawai'i Island (Kirch 1984a:181–92; Yen 1988), to name just two cases.

Demonstrating the occurrence of innovation and intensification in the history of island economies is significant, but the topic becomes more intriguing when we begin to link these processes with other patterns in a search for more general explanations. Why did Pacific islanders undertake major projects of landesque capital intensification that even today leave their indelible marks on island landscapes? Why, when the construction of physical infrastructure was not possible due to environmental constraints or other reasons, did people feel compelled to invest greater and greater labor in agricultural production? Were these kinds of intensification linked to particular sorts of economic or social or political structures? These are big questions—and complex at that—but they go to the core of Oceanic cultural history.

The simplest explanation for intensification of island economies would be demographic, invoking increased populations as the underlying "cause" for change, and indeed at a basic level population pressure was probably in most cases an "ultimate" form of causation (again, see Mayr 1997:67). As island populations burgeoned, increased food production was surely a necessary consequence. But to leave the explanation at this level would both ignore the fact that population is not a wholly *independent* variable (for, after all, people have many cultural and social means for regulating population growth) and miss what is all the more interesting from an anthropological perspective: the linkages between production and power.

Here it is instructive to invoke Brookfield's (1972) concept of "social production," as differentiated from "production for use" (i.e., that which is necessary merely to keep the population fed and healthy, and able to reproduce itself). The idea of social production is that in virtually any complex social formation there are invariably demands on the household economy that go beyond immediate production for consumption by its members. Contributions to village feasts (Fig. 9.4), tribute offerings to chiefs, taro and pigs for religious ceremonies, production for external exchange—all of these combine to create an economy of surplus, or perhaps we should say, of the ceaseless extrac-

tion of surplus from individual households that otherwise might be thought of as intrinsically antisurplus. As Marshall Sahlins put it, a "society's economic destiny is played out in its relations of production, especially the political pressures that can be mounted on the household economy" (1972:82). Moreover, "the development of rank and chieftainship becomes, *pari passu*, development of the productive forces" (1972:140). Brookfield noted this equation too, and he observed that throughout the Pacific islands the development of intensified agricultural systems always correlated with the creation of a surplus, which indeed seems to have been the principal objective. And furthermore, all these cases "seem to have been accompanied by social differentiation, if not also stratification" (Brookfield 1984:23). While increased population numbers provided a necessary condition for intensification (and also a requisite labor force that could be controlled by political leaders), and thus an ultimate form of causation, the more immediate, proximal causes of intensification were typically social and political. Power flowed from production and in turn encouraged greater efforts at intensification.

Intensification too has its limits, and long before these are reached the burdens of intensified labor can become enormously oppressive. It is in such considerations that the most significant relations of production in ancient Oceanic societies may be discovered. Consider once again the case of Rapa Nui. At some early stage in the island's history, social groups were clearly able to produce sufficient surpluses to underwrite the enormous tasks of quarrying, sculpting, transporting, and erecting multiton statues that glorified collective ancestors and marked lineage territories. The island's weathered volcanic surface and reasonably fertile soils favored the high-yielding sweet potato, cultivated in a short-fallow rotation. But as the island's population grew ever larger, the *margin* between

FIGURE 9.4 A *katoanga* or village feast in Sigave District, Futuna Island, in 1974. Each basket contains yams and a roasted pig. Note the rows of kava plants in front of the house, where the chiefs and lineage elders are assembled for a ritual kava ceremony. (Photo by P. V. Kirch.)

production and simple autoconsumption (what we call "surplus") dwindled,[30] even as chiefs and priests felt compelled to exhort their followers to undertake yet grander works. The people were pressed to produce an ever-greater surplus—requiring increased labor inputs in a classic mode of cropping cycle intensification—at the same time that the ability of the island's somewhat marginal environment to give up ever-higher yields was pushed to its limit. Its elasticity exceeded, the system snapped. Not all at once, presumably, but certainly within the span of a few short generations, all statue carving had ceased, and Rapa Nui society was plunged into a period of endemic warfare, raiding, and general social terror.

Rapa Nui is, to be sure, a unique case, lying at one end of a spectrum. In many island societies intensification was very much an ongoing process when European contact interrupted the pace of history, primarily through the introduction of foreign diseases that undermined economies, decimating their population bases. But it is often through the lens provided by a Rapa Nui that certain key structures—as well as the dialectical contradictions inherent in them—can be all the more clearly glimpsed. So it is with the relations between power and production.

I have said little thus far about specialization, as distinct from intensification, but this too deserves at least a comment. During the early stages of

Lapita expansion into Remote Oceania (as certainly in the long pre-Lapita period before it), there is but slight indication of specialization within island economies. Some craft specialization at the village or hamlet level was present in Lapita communities, for it has been inferred that some communities were ceramic producers and others manufacturers of shell objects, and that networks of exchange linked these into larger systems of economic integration. But for the most part Lapita communities appear to have been self-sufficient, certainly as regards food production, if not the production of every manner of material goods. When we turn to the ethnohistoric record of island societies at the time of early European contact, however, we find many examples of highly specialized economies, particularly in the western Pacific, where shorter interisland distances made communication and transport relatively feasible. This is certainly the case with the specialized trading societies of the Papuan coast and the Massim, or the Siassi traders. In some cases, specialization of production resulted in significant dependence for food supplies on external sources. Archaeology has just begun to trace the specific and localized histories whereby such specialization arose, and whether there are common conditions that might provide a convincing causal model for specialization only further work will tell. But specialization is certainly a big process within the history of island societies, one that will doubtless repay sustained research with added insight.

Transformations of Status and Power

In thinking about intensification, we have already raised the issue of power in relation to production and have seen how the two are inextricably intertwined. But the transformation of sociopolitical structures in Oceania was surely more than just a matter of economics, and the topic deserves

closer consideration. At one time, it was maintained that the sociopolitical structures found in Polynesia and Melanesia were of distinct types, *chiefdoms* in the former and *big-man systems* in the latter (Sahlins 1963). This dichotomy has not held up to closer scrutiny, however, and much of island Melanesia as well as Micronesia was also characterized by various structures of chiefship (Scaglion 1996). Although we should be wary of replacing one outmoded overgeneralization with another, we might cautiously suggest that if there is a major distinction between political "types" in Oceania, it would be between the societies of the Austronesian-speaking peoples and the Non-Austronesians. The former are typically characterized by principles of hereditary ranking, which is probably an ancient aspect of Austronesian societies in general (Bellwood 1996b; Blust 1996; Fox 1994, 1995). The social structures of the Papuan speakers are more varied, but it is among them that classic big-man structures of achieved (rather than inherited) status are typically found.

The varied sociopolitical formations found throughout Austronesian-speaking Near Oceania and Remote Oceania can be seen as transformations of an original structure, which Friedman (1981) inferred to have been hierarchical and based on asymmetric exchange. That these societies should share fundamental structural features is not surprising, since they are almost all ultimately descended from the Lapita cultural complex. The nature of Lapita society itself is still uncertain, although I have argued that it may have been more heterarchical than hierarchical. But with some principle of ranking inherent, the basis for "status rivalry" (as Goldman [1970] called it) was presumably already present in Lapita society, between junior and senior siblings and more widely between junior and senior branches of a lineage. This is the structural germ that could give rise to hierarchy again and again once societies increased in size from small groups, in which everyone was known to each other, face to face as kinsmen, to larger groups of a few thousand up to tens of thousands, in which a small self-selected elite could gain control over a vast populace.

Historical linguistic research is beginning to define some of the lexically marked kinds of social groups, and status positions, that were present in Ancestral Oceanic societies (that is, those made up of speakers of Proto Oceanic language and reflected archaeologically by the Lapita cultural complex). One important Proto Oceanic term is **kainanga*, which probably denoted an exogamous group (quite possibly matrilineal) made up of the descendants of an eponymous ancestor, who collectively controlled an estate of land (Kirch and Green, in press). Cognates of this word are found throughout much of Remote Oceania today, indicating the persistence of this kind of social unit over thousands of years. Also present in Proto Oceanic were specific terms for the leader of such a corporate descent group and for the first-born son of this leader (**adiki*), which implies some kind of hereditary principle for succession of leadership (Lichtenberk 1986; Pawley 1982). (The POC term **adiki* is reflected in later Polynesian languages by the widespread term *ariki* or *aliki*, meaning "chief.") Through careful semantic reconstruction of such terms for social groups and statuses, and comparison of these with later transformations in descendant societies throughout Remote Oceania, it is possible to gain considerable insight into the changing nature of social organization in those cultures and societies that originally derived from the first Lapita colonists into Remote Oceania. One example of this kind of research is the detailed reconstruction of Ancestral Polynesian social organization (as well as religion) undertaken by Kirch and Green (in press).

As with the processes of intensification, the growth of large and dense populations was linked to the rise of increasingly hierarchical and stratified societies. It can be empirically demonstrated that the level of stratification in Polynesian chiefdoms is significantly correlated with both population density and the size of the maximal political unit (Kirch 1984a:98–99, Fig. 26). But a correlation is not necessarily a cause, and it is probably best to regard the growth of large populations as a necessary condition for sociopolitical transformation—again perhaps an *ultimate* cause—but certainly not a proximal cause or determining factor.

What then can we posit as the immediate or proximal causes or mechanisms leading to the rise of hierarchical, stratified societies, not only in Polynesia but also on many of the Micronesian high islands (especially Pohnpei and Kosrae) and in various parts of Melanesia (e.g., Fiji, New Caledonia, and parts of the Solomons)? Various explanations have been advanced by comparative ethnologists, such as Sahlins's (1958) model of "redistribution" and chiefs as economic regulators, Goldman's (1970) model of "status rivalry," or Friedman's (1981) model of an economic transformation from prestige-good exchange to agricultural intensification. Indeed, each of these helps to explain certain aspects of particular historical sequences.

In Chapter 8, I referred to Timothy Earle's contention that "chiefs shape their positions from three primary power media—economy, military, and ideology" (1997:193), and it may be instructive to reconsider this paradigm. Earle contends that elites or "ruling segments" use particular "power strategies" to achieve their political goals. The three main sources of power are "intertwined and interdependent" (1997:207), and particular combinations were variously used by chiefs to create an economic surplus (thus fueling the political economy), to control labor or seize territory (by armed force), and to legitimate their position in society.

We have already examined economic power as developed through various forms of intensification or specialization of production. Fundamentally, all transformations in Oceanic sociopolitical formations had to be based on some form of control of economic production, and on the extraction of a surplus, although the specific ways in which this was achieved vary endlessly. When environmental or other conditions set limits to such control, or to the continued ability of a system to yield sufficient surplus, chiefly power was undermined. When such conditions did arise, as in most of the "Open" chiefdoms of central Polynesia, a considerable struggle for power ensued, with overt military power strategies becoming dominant. Military power was not exercised just in situations of ecological crisis, however. Territorial conquest was a major power strategy used throughout Oceania, a means for elites to capture that which was most essential to production: land.

Most interesting archaeologically—because it is manifested in the most striking forms of monumental architecture—is *ideological* power. The ranking inherent in Austronesian social structures automatically placed senior lines "closer" to the sources of supernatural power, which initially were probably deified ancestors. (The whole *mana* [supernatural power] and *tapu* [sacred] ideological complex is an extension of this basic principle.) As some societies grew larger, and senior lines were able increasingly to distance and differentiate themselves, ancestors became gods, and chiefly elites the direct descendants of those deities. Such was the ideology used by the Hawaiian kings to legitimate their rule, and by other Oceanic chieftains as well (to greater or lesser degrees). But ideology is more powerful when it can be physically manifested, through symbolically charged architecture and objects. Much of the monumental architecture of Oceanic societies was constructed precisely for this purpose. The Tongan *langi* tombs, the Easter Island statue temples, the Hawaiian *heiau*, and the tomb islets of Nan Madol are all reminders

of the powerful role of ideology in the legitimation of a sociopolitical structure (Fig. 9.5).

On Comparison: A Closing Comment

Paradoxically, the act of ending a book is, for me, the most difficult part of its making. Whether this stems from an inner hesitation to let the satisfying process of book-making come to a close, or whether it is inherent in the structure of a book itself (how to succinctly terminate a complexly interwoven chain of assertion and argument?) I cannot judge; perhaps it is some combination of both. For this book, I close merely with a comment. It might have been no more than a footnote did I not feel so passionately about its significance for historical anthropology.

My reference is again to archaeology and historical anthropology as explicitly "historical sciences" in the same sense that geology and biology (at least evolutionary ecology and paleobiology) are largely historical sciences, quite distinct in their epistemologies—as well as their modes of investigation and explanation—from the "experimental sciences" (Gould 1989; Mayr 1982, 1997). More particularly, I draw attention to the importance of *comparison* in our historical science, for through comparison we move beyond the particular, the local, and the time-bound, to what is generalizing and sometimes global. Comparison reveals similarity as well as difference, exposing patterns that lurk beneath variation. Ultimately, comparison yields general principles (not "laws"), and it is these which allow us to make of our historical narratives not merely "just so stories" but robust explanations of historical phenomena.

Comparison is especially productive in contexts in which history has provided sets of parallel "experiments." We cannot rerun the real experiments of history; therefore, we must look for the closest analogues history provides. Historical

FIGURE 9.5 A human sacrifice being offered to the god Oro on a *marae* or temple in Tahiti, Society Islands. Engraving after drawing by John Webber for the atlas of Cook's third voyage. (Collection of the author.)

sociologists do this by comparing the contexts, processes, and outcomes of various social movements (revolutions, for example), seeking to hold one or another factor "constant" and thus gain insights into underlying causes (Tilly 1981, 1984, 1997). Evolutionary biologists do the same when they seek "natural experiments," such as the defaunation and recolonization of landscapes created by glaciation or volcanic eruptions. Mayr writes that "much progress in the observational sciences is due to the genius of those who have discovered, critically evaluated, and compared such natural experiments in fields where a laboratory experiment is highly impractical, if not impossible" (1997:28–29).

The Pacific islands provide precisely such fertile intellectual terrain, in which comparison is facilitated and deeper understanding possible. I am certainly not the first to recognize or say this.

Ward Goodenough made the point succinctly decades ago when he argued that Oceania "is the logical place to work out the problems of cultural reconstruction of related cultures" (1957:154).[31] This analogy with the experimental sciences, this particular quality of Oceania—its suitedness for controlled comparisons—has sometimes led researchers to write of the Pacific as a kind of "laboratory" for historical social science (e.g., Kirch 1984a; Vayda and Rappaport 1963). But the Pacific as "laboratory" is only an analogy, and given other possible connotations, perhaps one that is best dropped. Semantics aside, what matters is that in the Pacific history has given us an unparalleled opportunity to compare what literally hundreds of societies have wrought, at times in highly similar environments, at other times in strikingly different ones. And it is not only the range of environmental variation among Pacific islands that enhances the possibilities for controlled comparison, but also the demonstrable fact that many of these societies had common origins. To be sure, we must not delude ourselves about the complexities; these are human societies after all, replete with all kinds of messy complications. Nor was every island an isolated world unto itself. People moved about, they interchanged ideas, words, genes. But as Raymond Fosberg once wrote, "isolation . . . [is] basic to insularity" (1963a:5), and the relative isolation of islands is what renders them such marvelous microcosms—such wonderful natural and cultural experiments—of history. Among these islands of history, Clio sets her course by the road of the winds.

Notes

Introduction

1. For samples of indigenous Pacific oral literature, including the voyaging sagas described in this paragraph, see Beckwith (1970), Grimble (1933–34), Luomala (1955), and Stimson (1957).

2. The accounts of Fornander (1878) or S. Percy Smith (1921), for example, were largely based on Polynesian oral traditions.

3. My reference is to Wolf (1982), whose marvelous book of the same title refers to the myriad non-European cultures of the premodern, preindustrialized world as the "people without history."

4. My approach falls within the long tradition stemming from such pioneering twentieth-century historical anthropologists as Sapir (1916), strongly influenced by the more recent engagement of history and anthropology in the Pacific, as promulgated by such scholars as Greg Dening (1992) and Marshall Sahlins (1985).

5. The story of the Manila galleons is expertly recounted in Schurz (1959).

6. On "Tupaia's map," as drawn by Cook and including 74 islands, see Finney (1994:31–34, Fig. 3). Cook's own comments on Tupaia's map are given in Beaglehole (1968:29194). Dening (1962) discusses indigenous Polynesian geographical knowledge.

7. *Polynesia* derives from the Greek πολν, "many," and νησοζ, "island"; *Micronesia* from μικροζ, "small," and νησοζ, "island"; and *Melanesia* from μελαζ, "black," and νησοζ, "island." The term *Polynesia* was already in use well before Dumont d'Urville, usually attributed to de Brosses (1756). De Brosses, however, used the term in a more inclusive sense than Dumont d'Urville to encompass all the Pacific islands beyond Australia. It was thus Dumont d'Urville who gave Polynesia its modern sense.

8. The single exception is languages of the Reef–Santa Cruz Islands (Nendö) in the southeastern Solomons, regarded by most linguists as Non-Austronesian (Green 1997).

9. The most useful overview is Oliver's *Oceania* (1989). Houghton (1996) deals with human biological variation, although he emphasizes Remote Oceania; see also Howells (1973). On languages in Oceania, see Foley (1986) on Papuan and Pawley and Ross (1993, 1995) on Austronesian (including its Oceanic branch).

10. As examples, see Dixon (1929) and Sullivan (1924).

11. Despite the growing recognition by philosophers of science that there are deep distinctions between the "experimental" and "historical" sciences (see, e.g.,

Chalmers 1982; Gould 1987; Mayr 1982, 1997), and the realization of many archaeologists that our discipline, along with paleontology, falls into the latter category, there are some who cling to a Hempelian model. Thus imagine my incredulity at finding myself chastised by a Pacific colleague (Hunter-Anderson 1991:20) for "indulging in prehistorical narrations," something she evidently regards as nonscientific!

Chapter 1

1. The one exception was New Zealand, where stratigraphic evidence for cultural change had been noted as early as Von Haast (1872) and was developed in the mid-twentieth century by scholars such as Duff (1942, 1947) and Lockerbie (1940, 1959); see also Green (1993:218).

2. Theories of Polynesian origins generated by missionaries and other colonials are covered, in much greater detail, by Howard (1967).

3. Rivers belonged to the British "diffusionist" school (see Harris 1968:380–81), theoretically opposed to the historical particularists in the United States, especially Boas.

4. Among those who disagreed with the *Kulturkreise* school were Haddon and Hornell (1936–38, 3:69), who used detailed distributional studies of canoe technology to assess historical relationships between Oceanic peoples and cultures.

5. In his magnum opus on Cook Islands material culture, Hiroa (1944) critiqued Handy's "two-strata" model of Polynesian origins and, following Burrows (1938), argued for the importance of internal cultural processes.

6. Piddington later modified his views, and as chairman of the University of Auckland's department of anthropology hired its first archaeologist, Jack Golson (R. Green, pers. comm., 1998).

7. An excellent overview of fieldwork carried out during the pre–World War II period in Polynesia is Hiroa (1945).

8. At this time the Eugenics movement was at its height in the United States, and such prominent Americans as Theodore Roosevelt spoke of the "Yellow Peril" and other problems they associated with immigration and "racial impurity." Stocking (1968:297–98) discusses the expansion of "serious modern American anthropological interest in the Pacific" in the context of the scientific interest in race prevalent in the 1920s, including the close intellectual connections between the members of the National Research Council (including the Bishop Museum's H. E. Gregory) and the planners of the Bayard Dominick Expeditions.

9. Hiroa published under both Te Rangi Hiroa and Peter H. Buck, using the latter name for his popular account of Polynesian ethnography written for a North American audience (Hiroa 1938a). He clearly preferred his Polynesian surname.

10. Hiroa wrote of his background: "I am binomial, bilingual, and inherit a mixture of two bloods that I would not change for a total of either" (1938a: 260).

11. Hiroa's exact birth date was never recorded; he himself said it was 1880, but Sorrenson (ed., 1986–88, I:12) says it is more likely to have been 1877.

12. In 1931, Hiroa wrote to his close friend Sir Apirana Ngata: "We have entered into competition with people of western culture and must be prepared for disparaging comment based on their past superiority" (Sorrenson, ed., 1986–88, II:233). Further views regarding White and Native relations were expressed in a letter of July 1934: "Western culture has accepted an axiom that any member of their race or races is superior by that very fact to any member of a Native race no matter how gifted that Native may be in his own culture. . . . The Native is a fine fellow so long as he accepts an inferior position" (Sorrenson, ed., 1986–88, III:163).

13. Eventually, in 1946, Hiroa was made a knight commander of the Order of St. Michael and St. George.

14. In 1943 a House of Representatives concurrent resolution (No. 42) was passed asking Congress to confer U.S. citizenship on Prof. Buck, to no avail. A prominent member of the Bishop Museum Trustees, C. Montague Cooke, Jr., wrote to Joseph

R. Farrington, the delegate to Congress from the Territory of Hawaii, that Buck "feels keenly the fact that he has not been able to procure American citizenship" (Cooke to Farrington, May 21, 1943, Archives, Bishop Museum). In the same letter, Cooke argued that "the Polynesians are of Caucasoid stock, closely related to the original stock of western Europe, and thus ought to be eligible for American citizenship."

15. In the same letter to Ngata, Hiroa commented on a trip to Pago Pago with the American Samoan Commission: "The job was to show that the Samoan was a Polynesian of Caucasian descent and quite distinct from the negroid division of mankind" (Sorrenson, ed., 1986–88, II:78). On Hiroa's use of physical anthropological data (somatology), and also on his views regarding Samoa, see J. S. Allen (1994).

16. In another passage, Hiroa writes: "Sufficient for the day is the fact that a tall, athletic people without woolly hair or a Mongoloid eyefold had the ability and courage to penetrate into the hitherto untraversed seaways of the central and eastern Pacific" (1938a:18).

17. In his 1944 monograph on Cook Islands material culture, Hiroa wrote that the Polynesian ancestors "retrogressed from the stone age to what may be termed a shell age." Upon reaching the Society Islands, however, "the shell age Polynesians had the raw material with which to rise again into the stone age" (1944:474).

18. The Micronesian route theory was resurrected, unsuccessfully, by Howells (1973).

19. Hiroa's view on archaeology was not charitable: "Archaeology . . . is a dry subject but the details must be recorded for subsequent comparative study" (Sorrenson, ed., 1986–88, III:160). See also Hiroa (1944:500) on the limited value of Polynesian archaeology.

20. Spoehr (1952:460) felt that his Marianas results lent support to Hiroa's "Micronesian route" and proposed the concept of "Micro-Polynesia." "Grouping Micronesia and Polynesia together in a larger area . . . assumes . . . that the main migration route of the Polynesians was through Micronesia. This I believe to have been the case."

21. On Emory's remarkable career, see Krauss (1988) and Kirch (1992).

22. In his first annual report as Bishop Museum director, Spoehr opined that "despite the reams that have been written on the early migrations of Pacific peoples, the one discipline from which most valid conclusions must derive has barely been utilized. This discipline is archaeology" (1954:24). Spoehr mentioned the new excavations in Fiji, New Caledonia, and Palau, and he pressed Emory to develop an archaeological research program in Hawai'i.

23. Although a full account of them was not published until 1950, the Wairau excavations actually commenced in 1939 and a preliminary account was published in 1942; see Duff (1968) for a useful historical account of the development of archaeological research in New Zealand.

24. Spoehr (1957:178) commented: "Most important of all is the nature of culture change encompassed by the chronology derived from our present carbon 14 dates. Here the answer can only come from careful excavation in key island areas. Since World War II, an excellent beginning has been made, yet much remains to be done."

25. On Thor Heyerdahl and his contribution to Pacific prehistory, see Kirch (1997g).

26. Willey first applied the settlement pattern approach in his study of the Viru Valley, Peru, in 1947, and continued this in his Mesoamerican research in the 1950s.

27. Examples of such research on prehistoric agriculture include Jane Allen (1991, 1992), Ayres and Haun (1985, 1990), Earle (1980), Golson (1977, 1988, 1990), Kirch (1977a, 1991a, 1997c, 1997d), Leach (1984), Leach and Leach (1979), Lepofsky (1994), Yen (1976a, 1988), and Yen et al. (1972).

28. The five-year Tri-Institutional Pacific Program (TRIPP), launched in 1953 with a major grant from the Carnegie Corporation, included archaeology within its purview, providing funding for the work of Osborne in Palau and Golson in Samoa (Spoehr 1955:28, 1958:8), although most of its

emphasis was on contemporary culture change. The Bishop Museum, one of the three TRIPP institutions (along with Yale and the University of Hawaii), became a key center for the expanding range of U.S. science in the Pacific, housing the office of the Pacific Science Board of the National Research Council, and in 1954 receiving its first major NSF grant, for an entomological survey of Micronesia (Spoehr 1956:20, 27).

29. The recommendation to appoint Golson had been made by John Mulvaney (1993:19), himself the pioneer of modern stratigraphic archaeology in Australia. In 1960, Mulvaney commenced excavations in Kenniff Cave (Queensland), which would shortly push the known sequence for human occupation of the Australian continent back into the Pleistocene.

30. In 1969 Golson was promoted to the title of Chair of Prehistory in a new ANU department focused exclusively on archaeology. Sadly, the department of prehistory was closed by the ANU administration in 1997.

31. These studies were published as Egloff (1979), Irwin (1985a), Lauer (1970, 1971), and White (1972).

32. Smart's work was never completed; see Poulsen (1968, 1983, 1987) and Specht (1968a).

33. The first phase of the SSICHP was summarized in Green and Cresswell (eds., 1976) and by Yen (1982); significant results of the second phase include Green (1978, 1987), Kirch and Yen (1982), and McCoy and Cleghorn (1988). See also Foana'ota (1996).

34. An example of how extreme and narrow such claims can get is the recent comment by Kennedy (1997), in which Theodore Schwartz's model for areal integration within the Admiralty (Manus) Islands—a geographic space less than 200 kilometers from one end to the other—is advanced as an appropriate paradigm for the entire Pacific Ocean. To hold that the closely linked trading systems of Manus resembled the diversity of literally thousands of societies stretching from Palau to Easter Island is absurd.

Chapter 2

1. This was the "lost continent of Mu" theory: that the Pacific islands were the tips of former continental mountain ranges and that the Pacific peoples were remnants of a formerly more extensive race of people who had constructed monumental sites, such as Nan Madol on Pohnpei, and carved the Easter Island statues.

2. Coleman (ed., 1973) deals with the island-arc geology of the western Pacific, while Menard (1986) provides a highly readable account of island geology of all types. Nunn (1994) is a valuable summary of the physical geography of oceanic islands.

3. Flannery (1994) provides an account of the unique biota of these ancient Gondwana-derived lands.

4. Discussions of hot spot islands can be found in Menard (1986) and Nunn (1994).

5. On Hawaiian geology and island evolution, see Macdonald and Abbott (1970).

6. In some cases, there are complexities beyond the evolutionary cycle described for the Hawaiian-Emperor Chain, as in Samoa (Dickinson and Green 1998).

7. An alternative myth of Hawaiian island origins concerns the great culture-hero Maui, who pulled the islands up from the sea with his magic fishhook (Luomala 1955). Again, Maui pulled them in the correct geological order.

8. An excellent overview of the human geography of the Melanesian island-arcs is Brookfield with Hart (1971); see also Winslow (ed., 1977).

9. Obsidian and geochemically related volcanic glasses are typical products of island-arc volcanism and occur on the Willaumez Peninsula (Talasea) of New Britain, in the Manus group, in the Banks Islands of Vanuatu, in New Zealand, and on Easter Island (Shackley, ed., 1998). Obsidian obtained from certain of these sources was widely traded and exchanged throughout the southwest Pacific.

10. The definitive treatment of atoll ecology, including the role of humans, remains Wiens (1962). Davis (1928) provides much useful data on coral

reefs and atolls. The series *Atoll Research Bulletin*, formerly edited by F. R. Fosberg and still published by the Smithsonian Institution, contains numerous valuable monographs on atoll geography, biology, and ecology.

11. See Stoddart et al. (1985) and McNutt and Menard (1978) on the process of "lithospheric flexure" and on makatea islands in general.

12. The makatea island of Henderson was intensively studied by an interdisciplinary team during the early 1990s, including an investigation of its archaeology and prehistory (Benton and Spencer, eds., 1995).

13. The presence of this ice cap had an interesting consequence: a summit eruption on Mauna Kea produced a basalt lava flow under the glacier, which was then supercooled, resulting in a uniquely fine-grained rock highly suitable for stone adz production. This lava flow, at about 3,500 meters above sea level, was discovered by the ancient Hawaiians and heavily quarried by them (Cleghorn 1986).

14. More detailed treatments of Pacific climate may be found in Nunn (1994) and Thomas (1963). On rainfall variability see Taylor (1973).

15. In Hawaiian, the terms are *kona* and *ko'olau*, which appear throughout the archipelago as various district names or other toponyms.

16. The volume edited by Diaz and Markgraf (eds., 1992) contains much valuable information on the historical aspects of El Niño; see also Nunn (1994: 160-64).

17. Carlquist (1974) remains a classic treatment on island biota and biogeography. On island biogeography, see Fosberg (ed., 1963), Gressitt (ed., 1963), MacArthur and Wilson (1967), Radovsky et al. (eds., 1984), Wagner and Funk (eds., 1995), and Williamson (1981).

18. A classic summary of Oceanic flora and vegetation is Merrill (1945); see also van Balgooy (1971). The vegetation zonation on a highly complex island, New Guinea, is treated by Paijmans (ed., 1976), while that of Hawai'i is well summarized in Wagner et al. (1990) and in Zimmerman (1948).

19. See Parkes (1997) on evidence for the coconut on Atiu Island by 7820 ± 70 B.P. Lepofsky et al. (1992) discuss finds of anaerobically preserved domesticated coconuts in the Society Islands, dated to A.D. 600.

20. On Pacific region mammals, see Carter et al. (1945); Mayr (1945) provides the classic synthesis on Pacific birds, updated by numerous regional manuals.

21. On the biogeography of the tropical Pacific, see Stoddart (1992).

22. For an insightful account of the role of disease in history, see McNeill (1976).

23. I will never forget the frightful pallor of a young Mussau woman suffering from acute anemia, who died within hours from an attack of cerebral *P. falciparum* malaria.

24. See Blong (1982), Eissen et al. (1994), Machida et al. (1996), and Robin et al. (1993, 1994).

25. Kirch (1997b) discusses the history of Western perspectives on human impacts on island environments.

26. There is a tendency even today to hold to such naive Rousseauian notions. Some "green" activists and popular writers would draw a distinction between traditional, non-Western peoples, whom they see as natural conservationists, and ecologically destructive industrialized peoples. In my view, such distinctions mistake differential impact of technology and population density for different cultural views of nature.

27. Two volumes that provide overviews of this new evidence are Dodson (ed., 1992) and Kirch and Hunt (eds., 1997); see also Kirch (1982b, 1983b, 1997d).

28. Roberts (1991) discusses the Pacific Rat, and Matisoo-Smith et al. (1998) present a study of *R. exulans* mtDNA variation and its implications for Polynesian voyaging. See Kirch (1983b, 1984a) for further discussion of "transported landscapes" in the Pacific.

29. On Pacific agricultural systems in general, see Barrau (1965a, 1965b), Kirch (1991a), and Yen (1971, 1973). Kirch (1994) provides a case study

of Polynesian agriculture and its relation to island ecology.

30. See Sand (1995, 1996a) on New Caledonia, Osborne (1966, 1979) on Palau, and Kirch (1977a) on the Hawaiian systems. The significance of "landesque capital intensification" is explored in some depth by Kirch (1994).

31. See papers by Athens (1997), Athens and Ward (1993, 1995, 1997), Athens et al. (1992), Bussell (1988), Dodson and Intoh (1999), Elliot et al. (1995), Ellison (1994), Kirch and Ellison (1994), Flenley and King (1984), Flenley et al. (1991), Hope and Hope (1976), Hope and Spriggs (1982), Hughes et al. (1979), McGlone and Basher (1995), Parkes (1997), Stevenson (1998), and Stevenson and Dodson (1995). On paleoecological consequences of human colonization for islands in general, see Burney (1997).

32. Vegetation changes are indicated by other kinds of evidence as well, such as sequences of change in native land snail populations (Christensen and Kirch 1981, 1986) that are sensitive to vegetation communities, and the direct evidence of wood charcoal, increasingly being used in Hawai'i, New Zealand, and Mangaia (e.g., Kirch et al. 1992).

33. The Easter Island pollen sequence is detailed by Flenley and King (1984) and Flenley et al. (1991) and is summarized more generally by Bahn and Flenley (1992); see also Fischer (ed., 1993) and Van Tilburg (1994).

34. See Jane Allen (1991, 1992), Dickinson et al. (1998), Kirch (1981, 1994, 1996b), and Lepofsky et al. (1996).

35. Steadman (1989, 1995, 1997) provides excellent overviews of the newly acquired evidence for Polynesian bird extinctions (see also Steadman and Justice 1998; Steadman and Kirch 1990; Steadman and Pahlavan 1992; Steadman and Rolett 1996; Steadman et al. 1990). See James (1995), James et al. (1987), Moniz (1997), and Olson and James (1982a, 1982b, 1984) on the evidence from Hawai'i, and Cassells (1984) and Worthy and Holdaway (1995) for the New Zealand avifaunal extinction record. An avifaunal record for Near

Oceania is just beginning to be developed, but it also suggests considerable human impacts (Steadman and Kirch 1998; Steadman et al. 1999).

36. The Tangatatau excavations and avifaunal assemblage analyses are reported in Kirch (1996b, 1997c), Kirch et al. (1992), Steadman (1995, 1997), and Steadman and Kirch (1990).

37. The definitive work on *moa* and *moa* hunting is by Anderson (1989a; see also 1989b, 1997).

38. There was also significant impact on the New Zealand marine fauna, especially large marine mammals such as seals (Smith 1989).

39. See Kirch (1997d) on the environmental histories of Mangaia and Tikopia, and for a discussion of the possibilities and limitations of "sustainability" in island ecosystems.

40. Some may question even this assertion, for it is possible that low-density hunting and gathering populations played a major role in the extinction of large birds and mammals in Australia and the Americas (Martin 1990; Steadman and Martin 1984). Not all accept this scenario, of course.

Chapter 3

1. The Huon finds are reported in Groube (1986) and Groube et al. (1986); Groube (1989) discusses implications of the "waisted blades." On the U/Th dating of the Huon reef series, and sea levels, see Chappell (1974, 1993) and Chappell et al. (1994).

2. Similar waisted axes are found in other parts of Sahul, such as North Queensland, and on Kangaroo Island (Lourandos 1997:81, 84).

3. On the biogeography of Sahul, Wallacea, and adjacent Southeast Asia, and its relevance to human history, see Bellwood (1985) and Golson (1972a, 1972b).

4. Chappell (1993) summarizes the evidence for Pleistocene sea levels and changing shorelines in the Sahul region.

5. See Roberts et al. (1990, 1995) for putative early dates for Sahul colonization, and contrary views by J. Allen (1994) and Allen and Holdaway (1995).

6. Important overviews on Pleistocene Sahul include Allen (1993), Bowdler (1977), Lourandos (1997), and White and Allen (1980). See also Smith et al. (eds., 1993).

7. We should not be too pessimistic about ultimately recovering such evidence, for early watercraft might conceivably be preserved in anaerobic contexts along the drowned coasts of New Guinea or other localities.

8. The Kilu site is reported by Wickler and Spriggs (1988).

9. The Pamwak site is reported by Fredericksen et al. (1993). The 13,000 B.P. date from Pamwak comes from a depth of about 1.7 meters; the basal occupation levels remain undated (Ambrose 1994; Fredericksen et al. 1993; Spriggs 1997:49).

10. The Matenkupkum faunal remains are reported in Gosden and Robertson (1991).

11. Since this book is about Oceania, I do not deal further with the prehistory of Australia or Tasmania, although their Pleistocene sequences are related to those of New Guinea. For summaries of Australian and Tasmanian Pleistocene finds, see Allen (1993), Flood (1983), Lourandos (1997), and Smith et al. (eds., 1993).

12. For a summary of Papua New Guinea prehistory, see Lilley (1992). Swadling (1981) provides excellent illustrations of sites and artifacts. The archaeology of Irian Jaya remains little known.

13. On pollen records from the New Guinea Highlands see Haberle (1996), Haberle et al. (1991), Hope and Golson (1995), Hope and Hope (1976), and Hope et al. (1983).

14. Here we may have a sampling problem, in that much of the material culture of Highlands peoples was probably made in perishable wood, fiber, bark, or leaves, which do not survive in the open sites and rockshelters so far discovered and excavated.

15. On the Lapita Homeland Project and its main results, see Allen (1984a), Allen and Gosden (eds., 1991), Allen and White (1989), and Gosden et al. (1989).

16. Syntheses of these new data from Pleistocene sites in the Bismarcks include Allen (1996), Allen and Gosden (1996), Allen et al. (1989), Enright and Gosden (1992), Gosden (1993), Gosden and Robertson (1991), and Spriggs (1997).

17. See Loy et al. (1992), but note that the techniques and methods of residue analysis in archaeology remain contested and experimental.

18. There is a substantial literature on the obsidian sources of New Britain and their exploitation in Pleistocene and later (especially Lapita) contexts. See Allen and Bell (1988), Kirch (1991c), Shackley (ed., 1998), Summerhayes and Allen (1993), Summerhayes and Hotchkis (1992), and Summerhayes et al. (1998).

19. On the marsupial fauna of Near Oceania see Carter et al. (1945) and Flannery (1995). Another introduction—evidently purposeful—of the small wallaby *Thylogale brownii* from New Guinea to New Ireland occurred around the end of the Pleistocene. Flannery et al. (1988) discuss archaeological evidence for faunal changes in the Holocene period, and Flannery and White (1991) discuss animal translocations.

20. From a site in the Sepik-Ramu area of New Guinea, dated to 14,000 B.P., Yen (1990:262) reports the presence of *Canarium* nut shells, suggestive of initial efforts to domesticate this important Melanesian tree crop.

21. On New Guinea and the Near Oceanic region as a center for plant domestication, see Barrau (1965a, 1965b) and Yen (1971, 1973, 1990, 1991, 1995), and additional references cited therein.

22. On the origins of *Colocasia esculenta*, see Yen and Wheeler (1968) for cytological evidence and Matthews (1991) for karyotype analyses. Yen (1991) discusses the origins of Pacific taro and its possible role in the early New Guinea agricultural landscape.

23. On the indigenous development of agriculture in Near Oceania, see Golson (1988, 1990, 1991a), Spriggs (1993a, 1993b), and Yen (1990, 1995).

24. These complex drainage systems have been described many times in the anthropological literature (e.g., Feil 1987; Pospisil 1963).

25. A full account of the Kuk excavations has yet to be published, but tentative syntheses are available in

a succession of papers (Bayliss-Smith and Golson 1992; Golson 1977, 1988, 1990, 1991a, 1997; Golson and Gardner 1990; Wilson 1985); see also Feil (1987).

26. Spriggs (1997:73–82) provides a more elaborate discussion of these sites.

27. Swadling et al. (1989) report key geomorphological and radiometric data, and further details are provided in Swadling et al. (1991) and in Swadling (1997a). Color photos of the sites and some finds are provided in Swadling et al. (1988).

28. Yen (1991:84, Fig. 6) notes that P. Gorecki recovered *Canarium* remains from a mid-Sepik site that may indicate domestication of this tree crop in the late Pleistocene.

29. One unresolved issue regarding these pre-Lapita subsistence economies in lowland Near Oceania is the presence of the domestic pig. Gorecki et al. (1991) report pig bones "throughout the deposit" of the Taora shelter on the Vanimo coast of New Guinea, dated to the mid-Holocene. In the Bismarcks, the only claim for pre–Lapita period pigs is by Allen (1996:22–23), for two pig teeth from levels dated by charcoal samples to 8000 and 6000 B.P., in Matenbek. Allen (pers. comm., 1998) believes these are in situ finds, although one cannot entirely discount the possibility that they are intrusive. An attempt to date one of the two teeth directly by the accelerator mass spectrometer ^{14}C method yielded an age of "modern," bolstering the argument for intrusion, although Allen (pers. comm., 1998) suggests "contamination."

30. For Taora, Gorecki et al. (1991:120–21) report that 78 sherds were recovered, but that "most are in the upper levels," with an associated radiocarbon age of 2250 ± 70 B.P. (which postdates Lapita). Although they note the "possible vertical displacement of artefacts" in the site, they remain "confident that pottery first appears at Taora about 5400 years ago." Judgment is best reserved until the promised additional analysis is provided. Similarly, the claims of Swadling et al. (1989) for pottery dated to 5600 B.P. in the Ramu area lack conclusive

dating of their stratigraphic contexts and full ceramic analysis and description.

31. Our present knowledge of the frequency and distribution of small, aceramic inland sites on the larger islands of Near Oceania may be imperfect, given the difficulties of site survey under dense rainforest.

32. Of these, the most notable is the α-thalassemia deletion, ubiquitous in Near Oceanic populations, which must already have been present there by 3500 B.P., because it was transferred to certain Austronesian-speaking groups who subsequently migrated into Remote Oceania and Polynesia (Hill et al. 1985; Martinson 1996).

Chapter 4

1. A comprehensive review of the Lapita cultural complex, and an exhaustive bibliography, can be found in Kirch (1997a), to which the reader is referred for elaboration and amplification. For other overviews of Lapita, see Golson (1971), Gosden (1991b), Green (1978, 1979a, 1991b, 1992, 1997), Kirch (1988d), Kirch and Hunt (eds., 1988), and Spriggs (1984, 1997).

2. Buried midden sites dating to ca. 6000–5000 B.P. in the Sepik-Ramu river basin, such as Dongon (Swadling et al. 1991), may be an exception, but their areal extent has yet to be determined.

3. This diversity may have been even greater ca. 2000 B.C., because Non-Austronesian languages once spoken throughout the Bismarck and Solomon groups have doubtless been replaced by Austronesian languages or gone extinct entirely.

4. On the α-thalassemia deletion and its significance, see Allen et al. (1997), Boyce et al. (1995), and Hill et al. (1985).

5. The corpus of radiocarbon dates from Lapita sites was first analyzed by Green (1979a), and later by Kirch and Hunt (eds., 1988), Specht and Gosden (1997), and Spriggs (1989a, 1990a).

6. For the indigenous, island-Melanesian model of Lapita origins, see Allen (1984a), Allen and White (1989), and White et al. (1988).

7. It is likely that over-water contacts between Near Oceania and island Southeast Asia occurred sporadically throughout prehistory and into historic times (see Swadling 1997b).

8. Among his key writings on Lapita in relation to island Southeast Asian culture history, see Bellwood (1985, 1992, 1993, 1998).

9. For overviews of Austronesian linguistics, see Blust (1985, 1996, 1999), Pawley and Ross (1993, 1995), and Ross (1989).

10. Dendritic or "tree" models are by no means the only kinds used by Austronesian and Oceanic linguists, who have developed sophisticated dialect chain and linkage models as well (see Pawley and Ross 1993, 1995; Ross 1995, 1997). The importance of linkage joining and breaking models for Oceanic culture history is discussed by Kirch and Green (in press).

11. An asterisk before a word indicates that it is a reconstruction rather than a cognate of the proto-lexeme in a descendant language. In the case of Proto-Austronesian *tales (taro), a few of the reflexes occurring in modern Austronesian languages are: Bunan (Taiwan) taiʔ, Tongan talo, and Hawaiian kalo.

12. This deletion was incorporated into the gene pool of Lapita populations who expanded eastward into then-unoccupied Remote Oceania, so that this genetic marker shows up even today in low frequency in Polynesian populations (Hill et al. 1985).

13. See also Gosden (1991c, 1992b) and Kirch (1996a, 1997a).

14. On radiocarbon dates from Lapita sites, see Green (1979a), Kirch (1997a, Table 3.1), Kirch and Hunt (1988), Sand (1997), Specht and Gosden (1997), and Spriggs (1989a, 1990a).

15. This shows how nonsensical is the proposition made by some scholars that there was a "fast train to Polynesia" (Diamond 1988; cf. Allen 1984a).

16. This is not to say that Lapita voyagers did not explore or camp temporarily prior to organizing a voyage of colonization. Charcoal from beach sands underlying the earliest permanent settlement horizon on Tikopia Island, dated to 3360 ±

130 B.P., may represent such an exploratory camp (Kirch and Yen 1982:312–14).

17. David Anthony (1990) distinguishes between these two kinds of factors in his review of migration theories in archaeology.

18. For linguistic evidence bearing on early Austronesian and Proto Oceanic social organization, see Bellwood (1996b), Fox (1994), Lichtenberk (1986), and Pawley (1982).

19. See, for example, Hawaiian myths cited in Beckwith (1970) and Luomala (1955).

20. On Oceanic languages and their relationships, see Pawley and Green (1973, 1984), Pawley and Ross (1993, 1995), and Ross (1988, 1989).

21. Two exceptions in Micronesia are the languages of Palau and the Marianas, which are Austronesian (specifically Western Malayo-Polynesian) languages, but not Oceanic. See Chapter 6 for further discussion.

22. Malcolm Ross (1988, 1989) discusses the high-order subgrouping of Oceanic languages in Near Oceania, and the breakup of the Proto Oceanic dialect chain into the Admiralties Cluster, North New Guinea Cluster, Meso-Melanesian Cluster (New Ireland and Solomons), Papuan Tip Cluster (Massim and Papuan regions), and possibly a separate Mussau Cluster. On the difference between linguistic divergence by *dialect differentiation* and by *separation*, see Ross (1995, 1997).

23. On the notions of foundation cultures and languages, see Pawley and Green (1973, 1984).

24. The exceptions to this are the Reef–Santa Cruz Islands and the western fringe of Micronesia (also part of Remote Oceania), where the founding populations were not Lapita but from a related group of ceramic-using peoples in the Philippines-Sulawesi region (see Chapter 6).

25. Space limitations dictate that I gloss over many fine points in these arguments; the reader is referred to Chapter 4 of Kirch (1997a) for a more definitive treatment.

26. See, for example, the essays in the volumes edited by Pawley and Ross (eds., 1994) and Ross et al. (eds., 1998). Blust (1987) outlines methodological

aspects of lexical and semantic reconstruction. Kirch and Green (in press) use the "triangulation method," drawing upon historical linguistics, archaeology, and comparative ethnology to reconstruct the culture and societies of Ancestral Polynesia.

27. See Kirch (1997a:100–17) for a more extensive discussion.

28. On the 9-base-pair deletion, see Hagelberg (1997), Hertzberg et al. (1989), and Merriwether et al. (1999).

29. Some key papers on the "genetic trail" include the chapters in Hill and Serjeantson (eds., 1989), as well as papers by Lum (1998), Lum and Cann (1998), Lum et al. (1998), Martinson (1996), Melton et al. (1998), Merriwether et al. (1999), Serjeantson and Gao (1995), and Serjeantson et al. (1982).

30. Some of this ceramic variation is treated in greater detail in Kirch (1997a:118–61).

31. On sand tempers in Pacific pottery, and their significance for tracing interisland movement of pottery, see Dickinson (1998), Dickinson and Shutler (1979), and Dickinson et al. (1996).

32. Key references on Lapita pottery decoration include Anson (1983, 1986), Donovan (1973), Golson (1971), Green (1976a, 1978, 1979a, 1979b, 1990), Kirch (1978, 1988a, 1997a), Mead et al. (1975), Sharp (1988, 1991), Shaw (1975), and Summerhayes (1997).

33. This argument is put forward in Kirch (1988c).

34. On Lapita anthropomorphic designs, see Kirch (1997a:132–40) and Spriggs (1990b, 1993c).

35. The argument that Lapita dentate-stamping originated in tattooing of the human body is laid out in Kirch (1997a:141–44).

36. The distinction between pervasive and partitive art styles is from De Boer (1991).

37. On the mid-Holocene higher sea level, see Kirch and Hunt (eds., 1993).

38. On the Mulifanua site and its geological context, see Dickinson and Green (1998).

39. I base these estimates on ethnographic information for house sizes in Oceania, with roughly 50 square meters for a "typical" dwelling, surrounded by another 500 square meters of open activity space, incorporating cook sheds or other ancillary structures.

40. Details of the important RF-2 site have been reported in Green (1976a, 1986, 1987, 1991c), Sheppard (1992, 1993) and Sheppard and Green (1991).

41. This argument was set out by Groube (1971) and countered in articles by Green (1979a) and Kirch (1979a).

42. On linguistic evidence for Proto Oceanic crops and horticulture, see French-Wright (1983), Osmond (1998), and Ross (1996a). Lichtenberk (1994) deals with food preparation methods. The linguistic evidence for horticulture and food preparation is contrasted with archaeological evidence in Kirch (1997a:192–217).

43. On plant remains from Lapita sites, see Gosden (1992a, 1995) and Kirch (1989b).

44. The plant remains from Talepakemalai are described in Kirch (1989b), and a detailed analysis of their morphology and metrical characteristics is given in Lepofsky et al. (1998).

45. See Gosden and Webb (1994:46); this erosional layer has an associated radiocarbon date of 2870 ± 70 B.P.

46. Diffusion of terracing and irrigation technology out of Asia was argued by Spriggs (1982) but countered on archaeological and linguistic evidence by Kirch and Lepofsky (1993).

47. The pig (Sus scrofa) may have entered the large island of New Guinea by about 5000 B.P., 1,500 years prior to the earliest Lapita sites. To date, however, no pig bones have been found in sites of the Bismarck Archipelago or Solomons in unequivocal pre-Lapita contexts. Dog and chicken bones are also first attested in Lapita sites.

48. Also transported in Lapita voyaging canoes was the little Pacific Rat (Rattus exulans), the bones of which have been found in many Lapita sites. This was presumably an inadvertent introduction in most cases, although purposive transport cannot be ruled out (Matisoo-Smith et al. 1998).

49. Marine faunal remains from Lapita sites are discussed by Butler (1988, 1994), Green (1986), Nagaoka (1988), and Swadling (1986). Kirch and Dye (1979) and Walter (1989a) treat aspects of Lapita fishing.

50. Oceanic peoples widely use the grated or pounded roots or bark of such plants as *Barringtonia asiatica* and *Derris elliptica* as narcotics to stupefy fish in shallow waters. The names of these plants can be reconstructed for Proto Oceanic, and their narcotic properties were probably known to the Lapita peoples.

51. On the *Sylviornis* remains, see Balouet and Olson (1989) and Sand (1995).

52. On the extinct iguana, see Pregill and Dye (1989); Steadman (1993b) discusses the extinct megapodes of Samoa (see also Steadman 1993a).

53. On the *kula*, see Leach and Leach (1983), Malinowski (1922), and Weiner (1992). Davenport (1962) discusses the Santa Cruz exchange network. Aspects of these networks are formally analyzed by Hage and Harary (1991, 1996).

54. On sourcing and material evidence for Lapita exchange, see Allen and Bell (1988), Ambrose and Green (1972), Bellwood (1992), Bellwood and Koon (1989), Best (1987), Dickinson et al. (1996), Galipaud (1990), Green (1974a, 1987, 1992, 1996a), Kirch (1990a, 1990b, 1991c, 1996a), Lilley (1986, 1988), Sheppard (1993), Spriggs (1984, 1991a), Summerhayes (1997), Summerhayes and Hotchkis (1992), Summerhayes et al. (1998), and Wickler (1990). The argument for shell valuables was advanced by Kirch (1988c, 1997a:236–39).

55. Detailed evidence for material exchanges in and out of Mussau will be presented in a forthcoming monograph (Kirch, ed., forthcoming); see also Kirch (1987, 1988b, 1990a) and Kirch et al. (1991).

56. In keeping with the terminology proposed by Kirch and Green (1987), I would distinguish between *Ancestral* Oceanic culture and societies, the *Proto* Oceanic language they spoke, and the *Parental* Oceanic populations (as biological entities). In this sense, Lapita is the archaeological manifestation of Ancestral Oceanic *culture.*

57. See papers by Lichtenberk (1986) and Pawley (1982).

58. The concept of heterarchy has been elaborated by several archaeologists in recent years (e.g., Ehrenreich et al., eds., 1995).

59. Most likely, these basic social groups constituted some form of what Austronesian scholars now refer to as a "house," based on the "house society" concept (*sociétés à maison*) of Claude Lévi-Strauss (1982) and other works; see Carsten and Hugh-Jones (1995) and Fox (1995).

Chapter 5

1. Overviews of Melanesian archaeology include Spriggs (1993b, 1997) and White and Allen (1980).

2. Classic ethnographic accounts of these trade and exchange networks include Barton (1910), Malinowski (1922), Seligman (1910), and Williams (1932).

3. Allen (1972) excavated at Nebira and did extensive work at Motupore Island, a major trading center (Allen 1977, 1984b; Allen et al. 1997). Bulmer (1971, 1975) provides settlement pattern and ceramic data on the Port Moresby area. Mailu was intensively studied by Irwin (1974, 1978a, 1978b, 1985a; Irwin and Holdaway 1996). The early site of Oposisi has been reported in summary form by Vanderwal (1978). Bickler (1997), Frankel and Rhoads (1994), and Rhoads (1980) deal with the Gulf of Papua.

4. Reconnaissance data are reported by Egloff (1978) and Lauer (1970, 1971), while stratigraphic excavations at Collingwood Bay are reported by Egloff (1979). Irwin (1983) provides additional perspective on the prehistory of the *kula* region.

5. This hypothesis is supported by the occurrence of one piece of Fergusson Island obsidian in a Lapita site in the Reef–Santa Cruz Islands (Green and Bird 1989), suggesting that Lapita peoples had some connection to the Massim region.

6. For a summary of these methods see Kirch (1991c: 141–44). Shackley (ed., 1998) includes papers dealing with recent advances in the sourcing of Oceanic obsidian.

7. Some influences may have filtered into the Highlands via the Sepik-Ramu drainages. If the arrival of the pig in Near Oceania was in fact associated with the expansion of Austronesian-speakers, then its presence in the Highlands—where it became the economic foundation of social exchanges—would constitute a significant impact.

8. The main sources for this period in the Highlands are the pioneering study by Bulmer and Bulmer (1964), White's (1972; White and Thomas 1972) excavations at four rockshelters, Watson and Cole's (1977; Cole 1996) excavations at eight open sites in Kainantu, Christensen's (1975) work at four rockshelters in the Manim Valley, and Golson's study of the Kuk agricultural site (Bayliss-Smith and Golson 1992; Golson 1977, 1988, 1990, 1991a, 1997; Golson and Gardner 1990). On connections between the Highlands and the north coast, see Gorecki and Gillieson (eds., 1989) and Swadling (1997).

9. See Haberle (1996), Haberle et al. (1991), and Walker and Hope (1982) for summaries of the pollen sequences and their implications for changing vegetation patterns.

10. White and O'Connell (1982, Table 6.5) summarize these data.

11. On Highlands trade, see the historical ethnographic synthesis by Hughes (1977).

12. Goodenough (1997a) disagrees with aspects of Ross's model for Proto Oceanic, suggesting that a Proto Kimbe language, which "was part of a chain of Eastern Oceanic dialects that were linked together in the Lapita trade network," broke up into several dialect groups after the W-K2 Witori volcanic eruption.

13. A monograph on the Mussau ceramic assemblages is in preparation (Kirch, ed., forthcoming), but an overview may be found in Kirch et al. (1991).

14. On Lossu see White (1992) and White and Downie (1980); on the Lasigi excavation and ceramics see Golson (1991b), and on Fissoa see White and Murray-Wallace (1996).

15. Watom was the site of Otto Meyer's discovery of Lapita (Meyer 1909, 1910). It was reinvestigated by Specht (1968a), and by Green and Anson (1987, 1991) as part of the Lapita Homeland Project.

16. On Manus ceramics, see Ambrose (1991).

17. See Ambrose (1988, 1991) and the discussion in Spriggs (1997:162–65, Plate 24).

18. The Sabah obsidian is reported by Bellwood and Koon (1989).

19. The ethnographic system is described by Harding (1967).

20. There are additional indications of contacts between Mussau and Micronesia, such as the presence of the backstrap loom in both localities and possible Micronesian loan words into Mussau (Blust 1984; Ross 1988).

21. Peter Sheppard (pers. comm., 1997) reports that a newly discovered site on the intertidal flats of Honiavasa Island has Lapita (i.e., dentate-stamped) sherds, and other sites in the Roviana and Marovo Lagoons of the New Georgia group may prove to be of Lapita age.

22. Specht (1968b) initially defined the Buka ceramic sequence, while new work has been carried out by Wickler (1990, 1995). The Nissan sequence is reported by Spriggs (1991b, 1997). Terrell (1986) incorporates data from the large island of Bougainville.

23. Chikamori (1967) reconnoitered New Georgia, followed in 1971 by work by Yen, Rosendahl, and myself on Kolombangara Island (see Yen 1976a). Miller (1979, 1980) carried out site surveys in the Western Solomons in the late 1970s. The Panaivili site is reported by Reeve (1989).

24. Davenport (1972) reports on an excavation on Santa Ana Island; the radiocarbon dates from this site were reinterpreted by Black and Green (1977). Green (1976b, 1976c), Hendren (1976), Kaschko (1976), and Ward (1976) provide archaeological and ethnoarchaeological reports from Uki and Ulawa. Swadling (1991) studied walled gardens on Santa Ana.

25. The first phase (1970–71) of the SSICHP was summarized in Green and Cresswell (eds., 1976). No final report of the second (1977–78) phase was produced, but key results are presented by Kirch (1983a), Kirch and Yen (1982), McCoy and Cleghorn (1988), and Yen (1982).

26. The classic ethnographic account of Vanuatu is Speiser (1923). A well-illustrated overview of the culture and arts of Vanuatu societies is provided in Bonnemaison et al. (1996). For an overview of Vanuatu archaeology see Spriggs (1996); recent results from Erromango, Malakula, and Efate Islands are reported by Bedford et al. (1998).

27. On pottery traditions of Vanuatu, see Galipaud (1996b, 1996c). Ward (1979) excavated in the Banks Islands, where he found ceramics at the Pakea site.

28. The site was masterfully excavated by Garanger (1972a, 1972b, 1996).

29. Congruence between oral traditions and archaeology in the late period of Tikopia is discussed by Kirch and Yen (1982). On Vanuatu oral traditions and archaeology see Rivierre (1996).

30. See Robin et al. (1994) and Spriggs (1997: 215–18).

31. For a cultural and linguistic summary of the Polynesian Outliers, see Bayard (1976). Pawley (1967) considered the linguistic relationships of the Polynesian Outlier languages. The Micronesian Outliers of Nukuoro and Kapingamarangi are discussed in Chapter 6.

32. Firth, a student of Bronislaw Malinowski, applied a British structural-functionalist approach, authoring a classic series of monographs on Tikopia culture and society, of which the best known is *We, the Tikopia* (Firth 1936).

33. For Tikopia, Firth (1961) documents oral traditions regarding the origins of lineages from various sources, mostly to the west. The most famous of these involves the Taumako clan, tracing its ancestry to a reputed offspring of the Tu'i Tonga or paramount chief of Tonga. See Kirch and Yen (1982:362–68) for a discussion of these traditions in relation to the archaeological record.

34. This was part of the study of drift voyaging probabilities in the Pacific by Levison et al. (1973); see also Ward et al. (1973).

35. On Nukuoro, see Davidson (1967a, 1967b, 1971). The Anutan archaeological sequence presented by Kirch and Rosendahl (1973, 1976) was revised by Kirch (1982d). Poulsen (1972) excavated on Bellona, while Chikamori (1975; Chikamori and Takasugi 1985) studied Rennell. Other work on the Outliers of Futuna, Fila, and Aniwa in Vanuatu is reported by Shutler and Shutler (1965, 1968), and excavations on Mele Island by Garanger (1972a).

36. Archaeological sequences from the Outliers are synthesized by Kirch (1984b).

37. Key archaeological results from Tikopia are presented in Kirch and Yen (1982); see also Kirch (1986b, 1997d) and Steadman et al. (1990).

38. Possible earlier human visitation(s) are indicated by a charcoal deposit in the beach sand underlying the oldest cultural horizon in the Sinapupu site, dated to 3360 ± 130 B.P.

39. Dickinson (in Kirch and Yen 1982:372) examined these sherds petrographically; they are similar to Mangaasi-style sherds from Emo in Vanikoro. Both the Tikopia and Vanikoro pottery wares were probably imported from Vanuatu (possibly Santo).

40. As discussed by Kirch and Yen (1982:355–59), the absence of turtles, sharks, and rays from the faunal record of the Sinapupu Phase cannot be explained by environmental factors and must reflect cultural practices. These species are ethnographically known as totemic animals in Banks Island and Vanuatu societies.

41. The genetic evidence is provided in Blake et al. (1983), although its cultural historical significance was first pointed out by Kirch (1985b).

42. I draw in this section from my review essay on New Caledonian prehistory (Kirch 1997f).

43. On the extinct biota of New Caledonia, see Balouet and Olson (1989), Flannery (1995), and Sand (1995).

44. Classic ethnographic summaries of New Caledonian societies include Guiart (1963), Leenhardt

(1937), and Sarasin (1917). On linguistic diversity, see Kasarherou (1989).

45. New Caledonia is comparable on a micro scale to New Guinea, which is likewise ethnographically remarkable for its small-scale social differentiation. Margaret Mead (1967) offered some thoughtful suggestions regarding the "heterogeneity" of these Melanesian regions, as opposed to the evident "homogeneity" of Polynesia.

46. For example, French ethnographer Maurice Leenhardt maintained that the Kanak peoples were a "paleo-mélanésien" group, even retaining traits "plus primitifs que ceux de l'Australien . . . et que ceux de l'homme de Néanderthal" (1937:12–13)!

47. See Chevalier (1963) and Golson (1963) on these "tumuli," and Green's (1988a) interpretation of these as nonhuman artifacts associated with the extinct megapode (*Sylviornis neocaledoniae*). The question of a "paleolithic" or preceramic presence may have been spurred by the biological diversity of the indigenous Kanak population, some of whom have been regarded as being related more closely to Australian aboriginal populations than to other island Melanesians (Howells 1973:35).

48. This view of two parallel ceramic wares was developed by Green and Mitchell (1983) in their reworking of Gifford and Shutler's data, followed as well by Frimigacci (1975).

49. In addition to Gifford and Shutler (1956), Green and Mitchell (1983), and a recent reanalysis of the Gifford–Shutler collections by Kirch et al. (eds., 1997), important works on New Caledonian and Loyalty Island archaeology and prehistory include the doctoral dissertations of Frimigacci (1975), Galipaud (1988; see also Galipaud 1990, 1992, 1995, 1996a), and Sand (1993a, 1994, 1995; see also Sand 1996a, 1996b, 1996c, 1996d, 1998c). Sand's bibliography (1995) encompasses more specialized articles and reports. Sand (1996a) offers an English-language overview of New Caledonian archaeology. The Service Territorial des Musées et du Patrimoine of New Caledonia publishes a monograph series, *Les Cahiers de l'Archéologie en Nouvelle-Calédonie*, with six volumes up to 1996.

50. The birds responsible were either the large *Sylviornis neocaledoniae*, whose association with the Megapodidae is controversial, or the extinct *Megapodius molistructor*. Golson (1996a) provides details on the mounds based on his excavations, although he does not accede to Green's view that these are megapode incubation sites.

51. On the paddle-impressed pottery, see Galipaud (1988, 1990, 1992, 1996a).

52. Galipaud (1995:101–3) makes important observations on the role of ceramics in defining the major periods of the New Caledonian sequence.

53. Sand and Ouétcho (1993) define Puen Ware. Galipaud (1995:102–3), however, is more reserved about the validity of this typological category.

54. The tradition takes its name from Gifford and Shutler's site 26, Oundjo village, the ceramic assemblages of which are reanalyzed in Kirch et al. (eds., 1997).

55. The term "landesque capital intensification" is from Blaikie and Brookfield (eds., 1987).

56. These highly intensive agricultural systems are described in Barrau (1956).

57. The Païta work is described by Sand and Ouétcho (1993; see also Sand 1995:138–40, 171–81).

58. On the independent development of irrigation technology in Oceania, see Kirch and Lepofsky (1993).

59. Such suggestions are contrary to the historical demographic accounts, such as those of Rallu (1990:280) for New Caledonia specifically or of McArthur (1968) for Oceania generally. For the Hawaiian Islands, Stannard (1989) has raised an identical question.

60. On the history of the Fijian languages, see Geraghty (1983); Pawley and Sabaya (1971) discuss dialectical variation in Fijian.

61. Classic ethnographic works on Fiji include Seemann (1862), B. Thompson (1908), and Williams (1884). On the Lau Islands, see Hocart (1929) and Thompson (1940).

62. In addition to Gifford (1951), see Birks (1973) on the Sigatoka excavations, Shaw (1967) on a reanalysis of Gifford's collections, and Davidson

and Leach (1993) and Davidson et al. (1990) on the early Lapita site at Natunuku. The early Lapita site on Naigani Island is reported by Kay (1984). Anderson and Clark (1999) discuss radiocarbon dates for initial Fijian settlement.

63. Parry (1977, 1981, 1984, 1987) used aerial photography in his study of fortifications and agricultural features. Frost (1974, 1979) reports on ceramic typology as well as fortifications. Rechtman (1992) excavated two fortified sites on Wakaya Island, while Best (1984) traces the cultural sequence of Lakeba from Lapita colonization to the early contact period. Palmer (1969) reports fortified sites on Viti Levu. Parke (1998) describes recent rescue excavations at the Navatanitawake ceremonial mound on Bau Island, a proto-historic and early postcontact chiefly center.

64. Ethnographic accounts of traditional Fijian pottery making include Geraghty (1996), MacLachlan (1940), Palmer and Shaw (1968), and Thompson (1938).

65. Shaw (1967) modified a few aspects of Green's sequence; see also Babcock (1977). Rossitto (1995) discusses ceramic change in the postcontact Ra Phase.

66. Linguistically, a dialect chain probably linked the main islands of Fiji, Lau, and Tonga-Samoa (Geraghty 1983).

67. Bellwood relates Vunda Phase developments to the arrival of a historical figure, named Lutunasobasoba, a prominent ancestor in Fijian oral traditions (1979:264).

68. See Parry (1977, 1981, 1987) for analysis of such sites and landscapes based on aerial photo interpretation.

69. Parry (1987, Plate 20) illustrates extensive flights of such terraces in an aerial photo of the Nabala Creek region, Sigatoka Valley.

70. Arens (1979) discounts cannibalism in general but ignores the evidence from Fiji or other Pacific islands. For ethnographic and ethnohistoric accounts of Fijian cannibalism, see Rechtman (1992). Sahlins (1982) provides a structuralist account of the role of cannibalism as one of the

"great things" of Fijian culture; see also Carneiro (1990).

71. David DeGusta (1999) reanalyzed Gifford's material, curated in the P. A. Hearst Museum of Anthropology, Berkeley, using criteria developed by T. D. White for the analysis of cannibalized assemblages.

72. Rotuman, along with Fijian and Polynesian, is a key independent witness for the reconstruction of the Proto Central-Pacific interstage in the diversification of the Eastern Oceanic languages (Geraghty 1983).

73. For sedimentological and palynological evidence of these human-induced environmental changes, see Bayliss-Smith et al. (1988) and Hughes et al. (1979).

74. Kirch (1988a) recovered Fijian sherds on Niuatoputapu, while Dye (1988) noted the same for sites in the Ha'apai group. See also Davidson (1977) and Green (1996a) regarding prehistoric contacts between these archipelagoes.

75. The "Tongan maritime empire" has been discussed by various authors, including Guiart (1963), Kaeppler (1978), and Kirch (1984a); see further discussion in Chapter 8.

76. One example is the elaboration of kava ritual as an overtly political activity. In technology, another example may be the diffusion of pondfield terracing from Fiji to Futuna (see Kirch 1994).

77. The terms *exchange* and *trade* are not well defined or differentiated by archaeologists. I use the former for systems in which economic transactions underwrite, or are accompanied by, other kinds of social relations (such as marriage), where the transactions are ritualized and the return "gift" need not be immediate. Trade, in contrast, I see as more overtly economic or commercial, with an immediate transaction of goods expected. Specialized trade, such as occurred in the Papuan *hiri* system, was often characterized by high volumes of goods passing through the networks. From the archaeological record alone, it is not always evident whether one is dealing with exchange or trade.

78. On these points, see Kirch (1994).

79. Here I call attention to the facile distinction often drawn between Polynesia and Melanesia (in part, based on Sahlins 1963), that the former is characterized by chiefdoms and the latter by "big-man" political structures. In fact, many of the Austronesian-speaking societies of island Melanesia (as opposed to the New Guinea Highlands, where the big-man model is probably accurate) fit well within the chiefdom paradigm (see Scaglion 1996). Part of the confusion resulted from social collapse and "devolution" of complex political structures following initial European contact, in part due to massive depopulation.

Chapter 6

1. Alkire (1977) presents an overview of Micronesian peoples and cultures.

2. Christian (1899), Hambruch (1911, 1919, 1936), and Kubary (1874) made early contributions to archaeology on Pohnpei and Kosrae. In the 1920s, Commander J. C. Thompson and H. G. Hornbostel excavated in the Marianas, sending their collections to the Bishop Museum, where they were analyzed by L. M. Thompson (1932). Chapman (1964) provides a survey of pre–World War II German and Japanese work, as well as sources up to the early 1960s. Periodic overviews of Micronesian archaeology include Cordy (1980, 1982), Craib (1983), Davidson (1988), and Rainbird (1994). Intoh (1992) summarizes Micronesian ceramic traditions; see also Takayama (1984).

3. For a geoarchaeological study of how cyclones can affect the archaeological record of atolls, see Dye (ed., 1987).

4. See the bibliography in Rainbird (1994), as well as the symposium proceedings edited by Hanson and Pietrusewsky (eds., 1997) and by Hunter-Anderson (ed., 1990).

5. The linguistic classification of Yapese, along with that of Nauru, has been in flux. Bender and Wang (1985:54) were unable "to make a definitive statement on the relationship of either to the unquestionably nuclear Micronesian languages." Ross

(1996b) argues that Yapese is Oceanic but has been influenced by no fewer than four phases of borrowing, two from Non-Oceanic languages.

6. The one exception may be Nauruan (see Bender and Wang 1985:54).

7. Some might protest that I am confusing archaeological and linguistic evidence and categories, but the correlation of Lapita with Oceanic is sufficiently strong that I have no qualms about referring to the Lapita expansion and the Oceanic dialect chain in the same sentence. The arguments supporting this view are presented in detail in Kirch (1997a).

8. For the tortured history of Spoehr's Chalan Piao oyster shell date, see Butler (1994) and Kurashina and Clayshulte (1983).

9. On the Chalan Piao site, see Amesbury et al. (1996) and Spoehr (1957:60–65). Investigations at Tarague Beach are reported by Athens (1986) and by Kurashina and Clayshulte (1983) and Kurashina et al. (1984).

10. Robert Blust (pers. comm., 1998) is skeptical of Starosta's hypothesis, which is also contradicted by Zobel's (1997) analysis of Chamorro verb morphology and morphosyntax.

11. A third coring site, Lake Hagoi on Tinian Island, has produced a date for human presence at about 3444 B.P. (Athens and Ward 1998).

12. Coconuts had naturally dispersed into parts of Remote Oceania prior to human colonization (e.g., in the Cook Islands; Parkes 1997), but the total absence of coconut pollen in the deeper levels of cores from the Pago swamp, as well as from coring sites in Palau, may imply that wild coconuts were not present in western Micronesia before humans. This problem requires more intensive research to resolve.

13. While lime-infilled, incised ceramics have not been found in Palau, a team directed by Steve Athens (pers. comm., 1998) has defined "an early thin black ware type of pottery," which occurs around 2000 B.P. on Babeldaob Island.

14. The earliest radiocarbon date reported by Takayama (1982:91) for the Pemrang site is 360 ±

80 B.C., which, as in the Marianas, is associated with CST pottery quite different from the later Yapese "laminated" ware. At the Rungruw site, Intoh and Leach (1985:68) obtained a radiocarbon date of 1905 ± 65 B.P. in association with CST pottery.

15. The classic case is Samoa, where despite a concerted archaeological program in the 1960s, the first third of the cultural sequence remained invisible until the accidental discovery of a submerged Lapita site at Mulifanua (Green and Davidson 1974). A similar situation may obtain on Mangaia, where palynological and geomorphological evidence suggests human settlement by 2500 B.P., but where no archaeological sites older than 1000 B.P. have yet been discovered (Kirch and Ellison 1994).

16. On the ceramic finds at Nan Madol, see Athens (1990a) and Bryson (1989); on the Lelu pottery, see Athens (1990b).

17. Regarding Nan Madol, Bath and Athens (1990: 280) write that "radiocarbon dates of islet fill indicate an initial occupation on sand beaches, bars or possibly on stilt houses over the reef as early as A.D. 1."

18. Athens (ed., 1995:267; see also Athens 1990b) indicates that Kosrae pottery is different from that of Pohnpei and more like ceramics from Chuuk. However, all three assemblages fall within the range of variation known for late Lapita ceramics in the southeastern Solomons.

19. The literature in support of this higher sea-level stand is too extensive to cite here, but see the summaries in Athens (ed., 1995:239–51) and in Kirch and Hunt (eds., 1993).

20. For the Majuro and Arno sites, see Dye (ed., 1987; Riley 1987); the Maloelap date is from Weisler (1999). Streck (1990) reported an anomalously early date of 3450 ± 60 B.P. from Bikini Atoll, which is rejected here. His other dates of 2380 ± 290 and 2575 ± 210 B.P. are probably acceptable, especially as their large error ranges bring them into line with the other Marshall Islands dates. See also Beardsley (1994) and Shun and Athens (1990) for archaeological studies of Kwajalein Atoll.

21. For additional information on Marianas prehistory, see Amesbury et al. (1996), Bonhomme and Craib (1987), B. Butler (ed., 1988; 1992), Craib (1986), Dye and Cleghorn (1990), Graves (1986a, 1986b, 1991), Hunter-Anderson and Butler (1995), Reinman (1966, n.d.), Russell (1998), Russell and Fleming (1986), Takayama and Egami (1971), Takayama and Intoh (1976), and Thompson (1932).

22. On Palau prehistory, see Gumerman et al. (1981), Lucking and Parmentier (1990), Masse (1989, 1990), Masse et al. (1984), Morgan (1988), Osborne (1966, 1979), and Van Tilburg (1991).

23. On Chuuk archaeology, see Brooks (1984), Clune (1974), Knudson (1990), Parker and King (1984), Takayama and Intoh (1978, 1980), Takayama and Seki (1973), and Takayama and Shutler (1978).

24. On Pohnpei archaeology, see Athens (1980, 1983, 1984a, 1984b, 1990a), Ayres (1992), Ayres and Haun (1985, 1990), Ayres and Mauricio (1987), Ayres et al. (1979, 1983), Bath (1984a, 1984b), Bath and Athens (1990), Christian (1899), Hambruch (1911, 1936), and Kubary (1874).

25. As noted in Chapter 5, *Terebra*-shell adzes also appear in island Melanesian sequences in the last 1,000 years.

26. Athens (pers. comm., 1998) would revise Ayres's sequence with a start date for the Nan Madol Phase at A.D. 1200, and that for the Isohkelekel Phase at A.D. 1600.

27. Key works on Micronesian atoll archaeology include Beardsley (1994), Craib (1984), Davidson (1967a, 1967b, 1992), Davidson and Leach (1996), Dye (ed., 1987), Fujimura and Alkire (1984), Intoh (1984, 1986, 1991, 1992, 1996), Leach and Davidson (1988), Leach and Ward (1981), Moir (1989), Rosendahl (1987), Streck (1990), and Weisler (1999).

28. Kiribati remains a major gap in the archaeological record for Micronesia. Some excavations were conducted by Takayama, but only preliminary accounts are available (Takayama and Takasugi 1987; Takayama et al. 1989, 1990). Di Piazza (1999) reports on two dated earth ovens from Nikunau Island.

29. On Nukuoro archaeology, see Davidson (1967a, 1967b, 1992), and on Kapingamarangi see Leach and Ward (1981). Leach and Davidson (1988) discuss faunal evidence for prehistoric fishing on both islands.

30. The best overview of atoll environments, including human ecology, remains Wiens (1962). The *Atoll Research Bulletin* includes important studies of human ecology on atolls.

31. The land snail faunas of atolls reveal the extent to which these islands have been influenced by human agency and are dominated by synanthropic species transported by people (such as *Gastrocopta pediculus, Lamellaxis gracilis,* and *Assiminea nitida*). Harry (1966) provides an informative account of the snail fauna of Ulithi Atoll.

32. For a classic ethnographic description of traditional navigation, see Gladwin (1970); see also Goodenough and Thomas (1987).

33. In addition to Spoehr (1957) and Thompson (1932), important archaeological surveys or excavations of *latte* sites include Butler (ed., 1988; 1992), Craib (1986), and Reinman (n.d.). Graves (1986b) synthesizes data pertaining to *latte*, while Morgan (1988) offers an architect's viewpoint. Cordy (1983; see also 1986) also discusses Chamorro sociopolitical organization (but see Graves 1986a).

34. Butler (1992:223) lends cautious support to Craib's position, based on independent data from Aguiguan Island.

35. In a study of a terrace complex at Uluang, Lucking and Parmentier (1990) found that an ethnographically documented village had been constructed on top of considerably earlier terraces.

36. Osborne (1966, 1979) included many of these sites in his survey and excavated at Bairulchau; Van Tilburg (1991) documented 38 monoliths. Morgan (1988:13–17) provides additional information on the Melekeok and Bairulchau sites.

37. Intoh (1991) raises the possibility of cultural contacts with the Solomon Islands. Specifically, shell fishhooks from Fais are of distinctive Solomon Island forms.

38. Labby's suggestions regarding changing patterns of agricultural production find support in the paleo-environmental sequence of Dodson and Intoh (1999).

39. Reisenberg (1968) analyzed the traditional sociopolitical system of Pohnpei, and additional ethnographic material of relevance to the archaeological record is contained in Christian (1899) and Hambruch (1936). See also Hanlon (1988) and Petersen (1990).

40. Pohnpei is ethnobotanically noted for its specialized agronomic techniques for producing giant yams (*Dioscorea alata*), the focus of competitive tributary feasts.

41. An 1849 map of Madolenihmw Harbor by M. J. de Rosamel shows Nan Madol, but in a stylized manner. For an annotated bibliography of early references to Nan Madol, see Athens (1981).

42. For archaeological studies at Nan Madol, see Athens (1980, 1983, 1984a, 1990a), Ayres (1992), Ayres et al. (1983), and Bryson (1989).

43. The main source for Pohnpei oral traditions is *The Book of Luelen* (Bernart 1977); see also the summary by Maurico in Ayres et al. (1983), and Mauricio (1987).

44. I thank Steve Athens for permission to publish these dates.

45. Katau has sometimes been identified as Kosrae Island, but as Goodenough (1986) argues, the term refers to a mythical "sky world."

46. This kind of arboriculture, or what Athens et al. (1996) call an "agroforest," is similar to that found in the southeast Solomon Islands (Yen 1974b), such as on Tikopia (Kirch and Yen 1982). Given that Kosrae was probably settled from the southeast Solomons, these arboricultural systems may have a common origin in Lapita subsistence practices.

47. Systems of radial land division are widespread in Oceania, as in the well-known *ahupua'a* system of Hawai'i (see Chapter 8). Given the concentric zonation of resources on high islands, a radial system that cross-cuts and incorporates segments of each major ecological zone is the most efficient method of resource segmentation.

48. These accounts have been summarized and analyzed by Cordy (1993).

49. Steve Athens (pers. comm., 1998), who has worked at both Nan Madol and Lelu, does not favor any kind of interaction between these sites. He cites the absence of archaeological materials from either island that can be traced to the other, and he notes that both island societies lacked oceangoing canoes at the time of European contact. He thus argues for insularity and isolation, and would "let those that disagree have the burden of presenting the hard evidence to the contrary."

Chapter 7

1. As a consequence of the Futunan work I began to implement a transect sampling strategy in subsequent archaeological excavations on Niuatoputapu (Kirch 1988a), Tikopia (Kirch and Yen 1982), and Mussau (Kirch, ed., forthcoming). By aligning transects so that they cross-cut and sample a sequence of geomorphological features, one can often discover cultural deposits even when these are deeply buried and there are no surface indications, as for example at To'aga on Ofu Island (Kirch and Hunt, eds., 1993). Moreover, cultural strata can be interpreted in terms of a broader landscape history.

2. For a review of Polynesian origin and migration theories, see Howard (1967).

3. One of the more farfetched of such *Kulturkreise* theories held that the Polynesians originated in the Indus Valley of Pakistan, based on supposed similarities between the enigmatic Indus Valley script and the *rongorongo* tablets of Easter Island.

4. A classic example of accounting for cultural change through a layering of migrations is Handy's theory for the Society Islands (1930b).

5. On interisland relationships, see Best (1984, 1987), Davidson (1979), Green (1996a), Green and Kirch (1997), and Kirch (1988a).

6. Geraghty (1983) provides a network or chain model of linguistic differentiation among Fijian and Polynesian languages.

7. On the ceramic sequences of Western Polynesia, see Burley (1998), Dye (1988, 1996a), Green (1974b), Kirch (1978, 1988a), Kirch and Hunt (eds., 1993), Poulsen (1983, 1987), and Sand (1990, 1992).

8. Green (1971, 1974b) discusses the development of the Polynesian adz kit.

9. On the Polynesian "homeland," see Green (1981).

10. It is nonetheless possible, as Kirch and Green (in press) argue, to delineate some phylogenetic units within the Melanesian region, such as Fiji or New Caledonia, or the Trans–New Guinea linguistic group in the Highlands.

11. Archaeological overviews of Polynesia include Bellwood (1987), Green (1993), Jennings (ed., 1979), and Kirch (1982a, 1984a, 1989a).

12. The phrase "segment of cultural history" is from Romney (1957), one of the originators of the phylogenetic model; see also Bellwood (1996a), Bellwood et al. (1995), Kirch and Green (1987, in press), and Vogt (1964, 1994).

13. On the internal subgrouping of Polynesian, see Biggs (1971), Clark (1979), Green (1966), Marck (1996, 1999), Pawley (1966), and Wilson (1985).

14. A number of Polynesian languages have gone extinct, such as Moriori in the Chatham Islands, or been replaced, such as the languages of the Austral chain (largely replaced by Tahitian). Some Polynesian languages, such as Mangaian, remain inadequately recorded.

15. Such statistical analyses have been carried out by, among others, Howells (1970) and Pietrusewsky (1970, 1990, 1994).

16. On genetic data, see the volume edited by Hill and Serjeantson (eds., 1989), and Merriwether et al. (1999).

17. In a controversial theory, Houghton (1991) argues that critical selection pressures on the Polynesian genotype resulted from the risks of long-distance voyaging, with its exposure of the human body, at sea level, to prolonged periods of cold.

18. For an unconventional interpretation of Polynesian biological origins, see Katayama (1996).

19. Kirch (1990f) discusses differences between the temple architecture of Tonga (a Western Polynesian culture) and Hawai'i (Eastern Polynesian).

20. On adz sourcing in Polynesia, see Best et al. (1992), Weisler (1993, 1998a; ed., 1997), and Weisler and Kirch (1996).

21. Osmond (1996, 1998) makes the same point for reconstructions of fishing and hunting gear in Proto Oceanic.

22. *Qariki became the word for "chief" in most Polynesian cultures.

23. On the concept of *heterarchy* in social organization, and its significance for the evolution of complex societies, see Ehrenreich et al. (eds., 1995).

24. Maui is best known to the Western world through the island in the Hawaiian chain named in his honor, where according to Hawaiian mythology, he snared the sun from the peak of Haleakala ("House of the Sun"), slowing its path across the sky sufficiently that crops could grow (see Beckwith 1970 for the entire myth).

25. The domestication of kava, based on botanical and ethnographic evidence, is discussed by Lebot and Levesque (1989).

26. McKern (1929) found pottery, some of it Early Eastern Lapita, in Tonga in 1920, but in the absence of radiocarbon dating interpreted this as a late, protohistoric variant of Fijian ware (see Chapter 1).

27. The Samoan research was published in a two-volume monograph edited by Green and Davidson (eds., 1969, 1974); see also Davidson (1977, 1979). On the Tongatapu excavations, see Poulsen (1968, 1983, 1987).

28. On the Mulifanua site, see Green and Davidson (eds., 1974), as well as Dickinson and Green (1998).

29. See J. T. Clark (1996), Clark and Herdrich (1993), Clark and Michlovic (1996), Herdrich (1991), Jennings and Holmer (eds., 1980), Jennings et al. (1976), Kirch and Hunt (eds., 1993), and Kirch et al. (1990).

30. On Tongan archaeology, see Burley (1994, 1998), Dickinson et al. (1994, 1996), Dye (1988, 1996a), Kirch (1988a), Shutler et al. (1994), and Spennemann (1989).

31. On Futunan archaeology, see Frimigacci (1990), Kirch (1981, 1994), and Sand (1990, 1993b). Results from 'Uvea are reported in Frimigacci and Hardy (1997), Sand (1998b), and Sand and Valentin (1991); Burrows (1937) discusses 'Uvean oral traditions.

32. On Western Polynesian prehistory in general, see Davidson (1977, 1979) and Green (1968). The prehistory of Niue Island remains a lacuna in our knowledge of Western Polynesia, despite a brief survey by Trotter (ed., 1979). Recent work by Atholl Anderson (pers. comm., 1998) may correct this. Also little known is the Tokelau Group, but see Best (1988).

33. The chronology of ceramic loss in Western Polynesia is debated. Green (1974b) suggested that pottery was abandoned in Samoa by around A.D. 300–400, while Clark and Michlovic (1996; Clark et al. 1997) argue—on the basis of evidence from the 'Aoa Valley—that it persisted much later, until ca. A.D. 1500. For Niuatoputapu, I believe the evidence supports a date of ca. A.D. 800–900 for terminal pottery use (Kirch 1988a).

34. On changes in adz forms, see Green (1971, 1974b) and Green and Davidson (eds., 1969).

35. On the development of Futunan agricultural systems, see Di Piazza (1990), Frimigacci (1990), and Kirch (1994).

36. On these methodological issues, see Athens (1997), Burney (1997), Kirch (1986a), Kirch and Ellison (1994), and Spriggs and Anderson (1993).

37. An unresolved controversy concerns the arrival in New Zealand of the Pacific Rat around 2000 B.P. (Holdaway 1996), based on direct accelerator mass spectrometer dating of rat bones. Recent archaeological interpretations hold that initial settlement did not occur until A.D. 1000–1200 (Anderson 1991).

38. This model was proposed by Emory and Sinoto (1965) and elaborated in Emory (1968) and Sinoto (1967, 1970, 1983). Finney (1985) proposed that a direct voyage from Western Polynesia to the Marquesas may have been facilitated by periodic wind shifts associated with El Niño weather patterns.

39. The "orthodox scenario" was critiqued by Kirch (1986a); see also Irwin (1981), Rolett (1993), and Sutton (1987).

40. On these chronological issues and dates, see Irwin (1992, 1998), Kirch (1986a), Kirch and Ellison (1994), and Spriggs and Anderson (1993).

41. On Mangaia, see Ellison (1994), Kirch (1996b, 1997c), Kirch and Ellison (1994), and Kirch et al. (1992). Palynological evidence from Rarotonga (Peters 1994) has been interpreted to support a late settlement chronology, but it could be interpreted differently.

42. On the Marquesan chronology, see Kirch (1986a), Rolett (1993, 1996, 1998), Sinoto (1966, 1979a), and Suggs (1961).

43. Some *R. exulans* bones have been found in secure stratigraphic contexts underlying the massive Taupo ashfall dated to ca. A.D. 150. This raises the possibility that there was an attempted human colonization of New Zealand around 2,000 years ago (Holdaway 1999), which was either abandoned or exterminated by this massive volcanic event. Matisso-Smith et al. (1997) are exploring the use of ancient DNA from Polynesian rats as proxy indicators of Polynesian migration routes.

44. For a review of Heyerdahl's theory, and its impact on Polynesian archaeology, see Kirch (1997g).

45. On voyaging traditions, see Beckwith (1970), Luomala (1955), and Thrum (ed., 1916–20).

46. These dates are based on Irwin (1992, Figs. 24 and 83).

47. The experimental voyages of the *Hokule'a* and the work of the Polynesian Voyaging Society are discussed in Babayan et al. (1987), Finney (1977, 1988, 1996a, 1996b), and Finney et al. (1986, 1989).

48. The problems of pottery in the Marquesas, and of whether the sherds found at four sites on three islands are the product of local manufacture or were exotic imports, remain contentious. For various positions, see Dickinson and Shutler (1974), Green (1974a), Kirch et al. (1988), Sinoto (1966, 1979a), and Suggs (1961). Dickinson et al. (1998:119) assert that while potsherds from the Ha'atuatua site were without doubt manufactured on the Rewa Delta of Viti Levu, Fiji, sherds from other sites on Nuku Hiva, Hiva Oa, and Ua Huka "contain contrasting quartz-free basaltic temper sands compatible with local derivation from Marquesan volcanic assemblages."

49. On Eastern Polynesian fishhooks, see M. S. Allen (1992, 1996b), Duff (1956), Emory et al. (1959), Sinoto (1962, 1991), Suggs (1961), and Walter (1989b). On adzes, see Duff (1956), Emory (1968), and Green (1971).

50. On basalt sourcing, see Best et al. (1992) and Weisler (1993; ed., 1997).

51. On Ma'uke, see Walter (1989b, 1990); on Aitutaki see M. S. Allen (1996a), Allen and Schubel (1990), and Allen and Steadman (1990).

52. On archaeological sites in the Equatorial Islands, see Emory (1934b); A. Sinoto (1973) excavated on Fanning Island.

53. Archaeological research in the Tuamotu Group has been spotty and deals primarily with ceremonial structures (*marae*); see Chazine (1977), Conte (1988), Conte and Dennison (1995), and Emory (1947).

54. While Rarotongan language falls within the Tahitic group, it does not encompass the range of linguistic variation within the southern Cooks. The Mangaian language is quite distinctive, but it has never been adequately recorded or described.

55. On the linguistic position of Rapanui, see Green (1988b).

Chapter 8

1. The estimate of canoes is from Ledyard (1963: 103), who calculated that at least 15,000 people greeted Cook's expedition as it entered Kealakekua Bay on Hawai'i Island.

2. On the Makahiki and other Hawaiian rituals of kingship, see Valeri (1985).

3. On Cook as Lono, see the masterful work of Sahlins (1981, 1995).

4. Dening (1992) discusses British naval organization and compares it to Polynesian chiefdoms.

5. A more exhaustive treatment will be found in Kirch (1984a; see also Kirch 1988e, 1988g, 1990d, 1991b; ed., 1986), although the present chapter benefits from the results of new research.

6. See Fried (1967), Renfrew (1984), and Service (1967) for overviews of evolutionary paradigms incorporating a chiefdom stage. Earle (ed., 1991) reviews archaeological perspectives on chiefdoms, and Carneiro (1981) summarizes the evolutionary significance of chiefdoms.

7. On the "domestic mode of production" and its significance for chiefdoms, see Sahlins (1972). Friedman and Rowlands (1978) present an "epigenetic model" of sociopolitical evolution in which the chiefdom stage figures prominently.

8. The exception is New Zealand, where resource restriction was due not to size limitation but to a temperate climate that posed great challenges to the ancestral Polynesian production system based on a tropical horticultural complex.

9. The results of the Mangaia Project are reported by Ellison (1994), Kirch (1996b, 1997c, 1997d), Kirch et al. (1991, 1992, 1995), Steadman (1997), and Steadman and Kirch (1990). An earlier archaeological survey of *marae* sites is contained in Bellwood (1978). Trotter (ed., 1974) reports on similar *marae* sites elsewhere in the southern Cook Islands, and Chikamori et al. (1995) on *marae* on the northern Cook Islands (Tongareva).

10. The major ethnographic source for Mangaia is Hiroa (1934), who relied on early missionary accounts as well as his own field research.

11. There are cultural and dialectical differences between the Northern and Southern Marquesas, probably owing to the difficulty of voyaging between Ua Pou and Hiva Oa.

12. Handy (1923) remains the classic source on Marquesan ethnography, augmented by the historical work of Dening (1980) and Thomas (1990).

13. Linton (1925) pioneered surface survey throughout the Marquesas, while Suggs (1961) conducted the first stratigraphic excavations on Nuku Hiva and outlined the prehistoric sequence. Excavations by Rolett (1989, 1992, 1998), Rolett and Conte (1995), and Sinoto (1966, 1970, 1979a, 1996b) have amplified the artifactual and faunal record (see also Kirch 1973), while settlement-pattern studies by Bellwood (1972), Kellum-Ottino (1971), and Ottino (1985, 1990a, 1990b) added critical information on architecture and land use. Millerstrom (1997) reports on petroglyphs. Anderson et al. (1994) reanalyzed the Hane sequence based on Sinoto's excavations.

14. Rolett (1998:60) believes that the Ha'atuatua pottery dates to the midpoint of the Marquesan sequence, ca. A.D. 1300–1650, and thus "represents relatively late prehistoric interarchipelago voyaging."

15. The Marquesan faunal sequence was first outlined by Kirch (1973), augmented by Dye (1990, 1996b) and Rolett (1992). Steadman (1989, 1997) and Steadman and Rolett (1996) summarize the avifaunal record.

16. Although Marquesan statue styles differ somewhat from those of Easter Island, they exhibit some similarities (particularly to certain aberrant Easter Island types), and there is a parallel in the use of red tuff in both cases for statues and as an architectural element, such as for facings on platforms. Although a direct connection has not been established, it seems to me that the statue complex in the Marquesas may have been influenced by immigrants from Easter Island, perhaps arriving in the Marquesas on one or more voyages from the former. The near impossibility of sailing or drifting from the Marquesas to Easter Island makes the reverse scenario improbable.

17. I refer here to the distinction, so ably drawn by Ernst Mayr (1997), between *proximate* and *ultimate* causation. Prestige rivalry in the social arena can readily be identified as a proximate cause for aspects of Classic Period Marquesan culture (such as the elaboration of material arts that were elite sumptuary items). Underlying such a proximate cause one can identify other ultimate causes, including resource restriction, periodic environmental perturbations (drought), and high population density.

18. For discussion of the "mystery islands," and a complete listing of these, see Kirch (1984a:89–92, Table 9).

19. See, however, Weisler (1996b) for a reconnaissance survey, as well as the earlier surface survey of Emory (1939).

20. The Austral Islands represent a major gap in our knowledge of Eastern Polynesian archaeology. For additional references to this group, see Aitken (1930), Edwards (1998), Stokes (ms. a, b), and Vérin (1969).

21. Ahu Tongariki was illustrated by Routledge (1919: Figs. 33, 34) and is described by Cristino and Casanova (1998) and by Van Tilburg (1986:532–40); see also metric data in Martinsson-Wallin (1994).

22. The Norwegian Archaeological Expedition results were published in Heyerdahl and Ferdon (eds., 1961, 1965); see also Golson (1965). Important excavation reports include Ayres (1973), Mulloy and Figueroa (1978), and Skjølsvold (ed., 1994). Van Tilburg (1994) provides a masterful synthesis and excellent bibliography; see also McCoy (1979). Lee (1992) describes the island's notable rock art. On the statue cult, see especially Gonzalez et al. (1988), Van Tilburg (1986, 1988), and Vargas (1988). The volumes edited by Casanova (ed., 1998) and Fischer (ed., 1993) also contain much valuable information.

23. McCoy's survey (1976) of several quadrangles in the Rano Kau area was completely analyzed. Preliminary results of the more extensive University of Chile survey may be found in Casanova (1998), Casanova et al. (1998), Cristino and Vargas (1980), Cristino et al. (1981), and Vargas (1993).

24. Palynological studies and vegetation history are presented by Flenley (1996), Flenley and King (1984), Flenley et al. (1991), and Orliac and Orliac (1998), while significant new avifaunal data are presented by Steadman et al. (1994). See also the more popularly oriented book by Bahn and Flenley (1992).

25. Note that this labor force included not just the stone workers in Rano Raraku, Puna Pau, and other quarries, but also those who kept the former supplied with food and with such materials as great lengths of sturdy rope and a continual supply of basalt picks.

26. I draw attention to this gaze deliberately, for the emphasis accorded the eye in the Rapa Nui statues is clear. Only recently have archaeologists recovered the actual coral and obsidian eyes that were originally placed in the sockets, and which gave the images a visual presence that must be seen to be appreciated.

27. The term literally means "statue-toppling."

28. An important exception to the unsystematic nature of excavations prior to Golson is Duff's (1956) work at the Wairau Bar site. The careful excavations and analysis of the Wairau Bar assemblages established the Eastern Polynesian origins of Maori culture.

29. Davidson's synthesis of New Zealand prehistory (1984; see also Davidson 1993) is now dated and in need of revision, although it remains the best overview. See also the collection of essays edited by Prickett (ed., 1982), and Wilson (ed., 1987).

30. There are nagging objections to this late date, and in my view the possibility of earlier settlement, especially in North Island, should not be entirely rejected. This issue has been brought to the fore by accelerator mass spectrometer ^{14}C dating of the bones of *Rattus exulans*, the Pacific Rat, almost certainly a human introduction to New Zealand, with ages as old as 2155 ± 130 B.P. (Holdaway 1996). Some pollen sequences and paleoenvironmental indicators in North Island could be interpreted as evidence of human disturbance prior to A.D. 1000 (Elliot et al. 1995; Sutton 1987). One possibility is that North Island was settled around 2000 B.P., but that the fledgling population either was wiped out or fled in the wake of the massive Taupo eruption around A.D. 150, one of the most violent volcanic events in Holocene world history. Holdaway (1996:226) has dated a rat dentary sealed under Taupo ash at 1775 ± 93 B.P.

31. For key site reports and analyses of such South Island Archaic sites, see Anderson (1982, 1989a),

Anderson and Smith (1992, 1996), Anderson et al. (eds., 1996), and Duff (1956).

32. On the environmental transformation of South Island through fire and other human actions, see Cumberland (1962) and McGlone (1983, 1989).

33. On prehistoric Maori gardening, see Barber (1989), Best (1925), Jones (1986, 1989, 1991), Leach (1984), Leach and Leach (eds., 1979), and Sullivan (1985).

34. On *pa* variation, classification, and distribution, see Bellwood (1971), Best (1927), Davidson (1984), Fox (1976), and Groube (1965). For examples of excavated *pa* sites, see Fox (1978), Fox and Green (1982), McFadgen and Sheppard (1984), Phillips (1986), and Shawcross (1976).

35. The linkage between *pa* and a horticultural economy is made clear by the absence of *pa* sites in South Island south of the Banks Peninsula. According to Davidson (1984:193), virtually all of the approximately 100 *pa* recorded for South Island are concentrated in "the area in which Polynesian horticulture was marginally possible."

36. Key studies on the temporal development of *pa* and *pa*-based settlement patterns include Irwin (1985b), Schmidt (1996), and Sutton (ed., 1990, 1993); see also Sutton (1990).

37. Barber (1996:877) also suggests that *pa* construction "is consistent with a heightened concern for territorial visibility and, as a corollary, the physical and spiritual maintenance of local production and harvest by cognate groups."

38. On early European myths of man and nature, see Kirch (1997b).

39. This view carries over into Oliver's discussion of subsistence in his definitive Society Islands historical ethnography, in which he claims that "the physical environment of these Islands imposed no serious restraints on Maohi subsistence" (1974:254); for an alternative interpretation, see Lepofsky (1994).

40. In addition to the references cited here, important contributions include: Descantes's (1990) analysis of Green's 'Opunohu Valley settlement pattern data; Eddowes (1991) on *marae*; Emory and Sinoto's var-

ious studies (Emory 1979; Emory and Sinoto 1965; Sinoto 1979b, 1996a; Sinoto and McCoy 1975), Wallin (1993); and the paleoenvironmental analyses of Lepofsky et al. (1992, 1996), Orliac (1997), and Parkes (1997).

41. Lepofsky (1995) and Lepofsky et al. (1992, 1996) report human-induced environmental changes as early as A.D. 600, predating habitation sites such as Vaito'otia-Fa'ahia on Huahine (Sinoto 1979b).

42. Green's sequence was based on an earlier proposal by Descantes (1990:89–97).

43. For a more detailed analysis of the Tongan case, see Kirch (1984a:217–42).

44. For a synthesis of Hawaiian archaeology up to the early 1980s, see Kirch (1985a; also 1990c, 1990d, 1990e) and Tuggle (1979).

45. Key early works include Bennett (1931), Emory (1921, 1924, 1928), McAllister (1933a, 1933b), and Stokes (1991). Hawaiian rock art is surveyed by Cox and Stasack (1970) and Lee and Stasack (1999).

46. Some of the classic culture-historical works in Hawaiian archaeology include Emory et al. (1959, 1969), Emory and Sinoto (1961), and Pearson (ed., 1969).

47. See, for example, Allen and McAnany (1994), Barrera (1971), Cordy (1981), Earle (1978, 1980), Green (1980), Hommon (1976, 1986), Kirch (1977a, 1979b, 1990d, 1990e; ed., 1997), Kirch and Kelly (eds., 1975), Kirch and Sahlins (1992), Kolb (1991, 1992, 1994), Pearson (ed., 1968), Tainter and Cordy (1977), Tuggle and Griffin (eds., 1973), and Weisler and Kirch (1985). A comprehensive bibliography of Hawaiian archaeology, complete up to 1986, is provided by Spriggs and Tanaka (1988).

48. On changes in Hawaiian archaeological practice, and some of the political problems this has engendered, see Graves and Erkelens (1991), Kirch (in press), and Spriggs (1989b). For important examples of archaeological research generated by CRM contracts, see Clark and Kirch (eds., 1983), Dixon et al. (1995), Kirch (1979b), Schilt (1984), and Weisler and Kirch (1985).

49. The 250,000 population estimate is from Schmitt (1968), but this has been challenged by Stannard (1989), who argues for as many as 800,000 prior to the introduction of syphilis and other diseases (see also Bushnell 1993).

50. See Cordy (1974a, 1974b), Hommon (1986), Kirch (1985a, 1990d), Kolb (1991, 1992), and Weisler (1989).

51. For perspectives on the dating of the initial Polynesian settlement in Hawai'i, see Athens (1997), Graves and Addison (1996), and Kirch (1985a).

52. On these voyaging traditions, see Cachola-Abad (1993) and Thrum (ed., 1916–20), and the discussion in Finney (1996b).

53. The linguistic evidence is discussed by Green (1966) and Marck (1999).

54. This later prehistoric isolation is reflected in changes in Hawaiian canoe design. At European contact, the Hawaiians did not fabricate canoes capable of long-distance, open-ocean travel.

55. See Emory et al. (1969), Kirch and Kelly (eds., 1975), and Pearson et al. (1971) for reports on these sites.

56. See Athens (1997), Athens and Ward (1993), and Athens et al. (1992).

57. On such demographic modeling, see Clark (1988), Cordy (1981), Hommon (1976, 1986), and Kirch (1984a:104–16).

58. See, for example, J. Allen (1992), Williams (1992), Spear (1992), and Weisler (1989).

59. On Hawaiian irrigation systems, see Jane Allen (1991, 1992), Earle (1978, 1980), Kirch (1977a, 1984a, 1992), Riley (1975), Tuggle and Tomonari-Tuggle (1980), and Yen et al. (1972). On the dryland field systems of Hawai'i Island, see Kirch (1984a, 1994), Ladefoged et al. (1996), and Rosendahl (1972, 1994).

60. The argument is advanced in detail in Kirch (1994).

61. On the temporal development of Hawaiian *heiau*, see Kolb (1991, 1992, 1994, 1999), as well as the overview in Kirch (1985a), and references cited therein to specific *heiau* site studies. Other important *heiau* studies include Bennett (1931), Dixon et al. (1995), Emory (1921, 1924, 1928), McAllister

(1933a, 1933b), Masse et al. (1991), Stokes (1991), and Weisler and Kirch (1985).

Chapter 9

1. Greg Dening (e.g., 1992) has done much to bring anthropology and history closer together, but his own approach is that of a particularistic history informed by anthropology, rather than a generalizing anthropology informed by the details of history.

2. Contra Terrell et al. (1997).

3. See, for example, Terrell (1986), Terrell et al. (1997), and Welsch et al. (1992), with contrary views by Howells (1987), Kirch (1997e), Moore and Romney (1994), and Roberts et al. (1995).

4. In response to Terrell et al. (1997), Goodenough writes: "If we are to pay attention to history, we need to get our history straight" (1997b:178). I concur.

5. This conclusion was independently supported by the archaeological results of the Lapita Homeland Project in 1985; see Chapter 3.

6. See, for example, Hill et al. (1985), Hill and Serjeantson (eds., 1989), Merriwether et al. (1999), Serjeantson and Gao (1995), and Serjeantson et al. (1982).

7. All this merely demonstrates the analytical power of a truly holistic anthropology that combines the data and methods of comparative ethnography, biological anthropology, historical linguistics, and archaeology; Sapir (1916) said so too, but he would have marveled at how much more sophisticated our "time perspectives" have become. To quote Kent Flannery, "If evolution is what you are interested in, then anthropology includes archaeology or it is nothing" (1983:362).

8. One area in which there were fairly dense populations in late prehistory, and where landesque capital intensification is also present, is the New Georgia group in the Solomons. Significantly, the New Georgia archaeological landscape is also dominated by fortified, nucleated hilltop settlements.

9. The significant exception to this generalization would be New Zealand, but only for South Island,

since where intensive sweet potato cultivation was feasible in North Island relatively high population densities were also achieved, in less than 1,000 years.

10. McArthur et al. (1976) show the striking differences in extinction probabilities that result from small increases in the size of the founding population. For example, a founding group of three couples (six people) in which the only marriage rule is a ban on incest have an extinction probability of 77 percent, whereas increasing that founding group to seven couples lowers the extinction probability to only 19 percent.

11. The speed at which even a small founding group can quickly produce a dense population on Oceanic high islands with good agricultural resources is shown by the case of Pitcairn Island, settled by the *Bounty* mutineers and their Tahitian accomplices in 1790. The founding population of 28 had given rise to 193 descendants by 1856, when the British government stepped in to remove them to Norfolk Island because of overcrowding and a shortage of agricultural land. The net rate of intrinsic increase during this period had been about 3.7 percent.

12. The classic ethnographic account of population control in Oceania is certainly that of Firth for Tikopia (Borrie et al. 1957; Firth 1936; see also Kirch and Yen 1982; Kirch 1997d).

13. The classic logistic growth curve is given by the well-known Verhulst-Pearl equation: $dN/dt = rN(K - N)/K$, where N is the population size, r is the intrinsic rate of population increase, and K is carrying capacity. See Hutchinson (1978) and Pianka (1974) for further discussion of the concept and its application in population biology.

14. See, for example, the data presented in Jane Allen (1992), Dye (1994), Dye and Komori (1992), Spear (1992), and Williams (1992).

15. In leeward areas, especially on Hawai'i Island and East Maui, population pressure may have reached more acute levels than on such islands as Kaua'i and O'ahu, where intensive irrigation was feasible (Kirch 1994; Kirch and Sahlins 1992).

16. This is, presumably, what Douglas Yen had in mind when he wrote that "human population level may be regarded as the primary incentive to technological development or adoption of greater intensity in production methods" (1973:80).

17. In the case of Hawai'i, initial European contact occurred with Cook's 1778–79 voyage, when the population was estimated by Lieutenant King at around 400,000. The earliest missionary "census" (a rough estimate, really) was carried out 53 years later, and it suggested a total population of around 130,000 for the archipelago (Schmitt 1973). A decline from 400,000 to 130,000 in five decades is regarded by many historical demographers as too abrupt, and thus King's estimate was reduced to 250,000 at first contact (Schmitt 1968; but see Stannard 1989). In the case of certain Western Polynesian islands such as Tongatapu, Niuatoputapu, and Futuna, "first contact" dates to the voyages of Tasman (1643) and Schouten and Le Maire (1616), with the first serious attempts at population estimate not made until some two centuries later. In these latter cases there would have been time for major population collapse, but also for possible recovery.

18. Consider the case of Tahiti. In one of the earliest attempts at estimating Oceanic island populations, Johann Reinhold Forster, who had sailed with Cook in 1772–75, devoted a section of his famous *Observations* to a disquisition on "the numbers of inhabitants in the South-Sea-Isles" (1996 [1778]:145–52). Forster used estimates of naval forces as well as a carefully argued calculation of agricultural carrying capacity to estimate 150,000 persons for Tahiti and Emeo Islands, and 200,000 for the rest of the Society Islands. Oliver (1974:35) calls Forster's estimates "pure fantasy," but it is not evident that Oliver's reduced estimate of about 35,000 for Tahiti is any more accurate.

19. See Green and Davidson (eds., 1969, 1974), Jennings et al. (1976), and Leach and Witter (1987, 1990).

20. The U.S. Exploring Expedition under the command of Commodore Wilkes estimated the Samoan

population at 56,600 in 1839 (McArthur 1968, Table 18), decades after first contact. Yet McArthur's view was that there had been "no very great decrease in population numbers in Samoa before mid-century" because "sporadic wars, famines, and outbreaks of disease checked its growth" (1968:115).

21. Green and Davidson (eds., 1974:281–82) briefly discuss the matter of pre-European population in Samoa. Without giving their own estimate, they aver that "only a population twice the size of that in the 1840s [i.e., around 80,000] . . . would require the amount of arable land which archaeology indicates was once in use." In a long-unpublished manuscript, Green (pers. comm., 1998) argued the case for a precontact Samoan population of about 200,000.

22. Another example of the gap between population estimates based on historical texts and those based on archaeological evidence is the Marquesas, where Suggs (1961:192) proposed a figure of 100,000 for the archipelago, but Rallu (1990) would go no higher than 43,000. For Tahiti in the Society Islands, there is tremendous disagreement, ranging from McArthur's (1968) low estimate of 17,000–19,000, to Oliver's (1974:34) cautious 35,000, up to Rallu's (1990) estimate of 70,000. Archaeology has yet to weigh in on the Tahitian case, but given the recent indications of dense settlement even in the farthest interior reaches of large valleys such as the Papeno'o, one wonders whether Forster's 1778 estimate of 150,000 may not yet be resurrected.

23. Dye and Komori's estimates are based on a proxy model of population growth derived from radiocarbon dates, which in their view demonstrates that Hawaiian population reached a maximum around A.D. 1400 and stayed low after that. However, linking a radiocarbon date–generated growth curve to actual population numbers involves critical assumptions that Dye and Komori (1992) do not make explicit, and I am dubious regarding their overall estimate. Moreover, the shape of the curve that they generate may be strongly affected by an underrepresentation of contact-period and postcontact sites (Komori, pers. comm., 1995).

24. This is by no means to single out the Pacific islanders as in any way more—or less—destructive in their actions that any other populations of *Homo sapiens* elsewhere on the planet. The record of preindustrial human impacts on local and regional ecologies (which in the aggregate constitute "global" change) is only now beginning to be investigated by archaeologists and paleoecologists. But it certainly includes major episodes of faunal extinction, as well as forest clearance, throughout all major zones of both the Old and New Worlds, long before the Industrial Revolution.

25. In 1989, while carrying out research on Mangaia Island, I encountered an irrigation agronomist working under contract to the World Bank, which had engaged him to study how the traditional taro irrigation systems of the island might be improved through the application of modern technology. After several months of study, he confided to me that he couldn't see any way in which the indigenous system could be "improved" at all!

26. The "failures" would presumably include attempts to colonize some of the minute or otherwise ecologically marginal islands, such as the Equatorial Islands, Nihoa, the Kermadecs, Pitcairn, Henderson, and others that had been abandoned by the time of European arrival in the Pacific; see Kirch (1988f) for one perspective on such cases.

27. I will long remember a conversation with a young Rapa Nui stone carver, on the plaza of the great Ahu Tepeu, as he spoke emotionally of the day when all the *moai* would stand once again upon their temple foundations.

28. For a review of some of the literature and ideas regarding intensification, see Morrison (1994, 1996); on specialization see Brumfiel and Earle (eds., 1987).

29. One reason for this is that the flooded pondfield is "self-weeding" as long as the water level is kept up, whereas in dryland taro cultivation constant weeding (and usually mulching as well) is required. For Futuna Island (Kirch 1994), I estimated that the

yield of irrigated pondfields was between four and eight times greater than that of shifting cultivation (per unit area).

30. For a more elaborate discussion of the theory invoked here, and the production-function model upon which it builds, see Kirch (1984a:160–67).

31. In response to a recent attack against the research agenda of controlled comparison in the Pacific (Terrell et al. 1997), Goodenough writes that "I see no reason to retract what I argued in 1957" (1997b:178). Bravo.

References

Aitken, R. T. 1930. *Ethnology of Tubuai*. Bernice P. Bishop Museum Bulletin 70. Honolulu.

Alkire, W. H. 1965. *Lamotrek Atoll and Inter-Island Socio-economic Ties*. Illinois Studies in Anthropology No. 5. Urbana: University of Illinois Press.

———. 1977. *An Introduction to the Peoples and Cultures of Micronesia*, 2d ed. Menlo Park: Cummings.

———. 1980. Technical knowledge and the evolution of political systems in the central and western Caroline Islands of Micronesia. *Canadian Journal of Anthropology* 1:229–37.

Allen, Jane. 1991. The role of agriculture in the evolution of the pre-contact Hawaiian state. *Asian Perspectives* 30:117–32.

———. 1992. Farming in Hawai'i from colonization to contact: Radiocarbon chronology and implications for cultural change. *New Zealand Journal of Archaeology* 14:45–66.

Allen, Jim. 1970. Prehistoric agricultural systems in the Wahgi Valley: A further note. *Mankind* 7:177–83.

———. 1972. Nebira 4: An early Austronesian site in central Papua. *Archaeology and Physical Anthropology in Oceania* 7:92–124.

———. 1977. Sea traffic, trade and expanding horizons. In J. Allen, J. Golson, and R. Jones, eds., *Sunda and Sahul*, pp. 387–417. London: Academic Press.

———. 1982. Pre-contact trade in Papua New Guinea. In R. J. May and H. Nelson, eds., *Melanesia: Beyond Diversity*, Vol. I, pp. 193–205. Canberra: Australian National University.

———. 1984a. In search of the Lapita homeland. *Journal of Pacific History* 19:186–201.

———. 1984b. Pots and poor princes: A multidimensional approach to the study of pottery trading in coastal Papua. In S. E. van der Leeuw and A. Pritchard, eds., *The Many Dimensions of Pottery: Ceramics in Archaeology and Anthropology*, pp. 407–63. Amsterdam: Inst. Prae-Protohist.

———. 1993. Notions of the Pleistocene in Greater Australia. In M. A. Smith, M. Spriggs, and B. Fankhauser, eds., *Sahul in Review: Pleistocene Archaeology in Australia, New Guinea and Island Melanesia*, pp. 139–51. Occasional Papers in Prehistory No. 24. Canberra: Department of Prehistory, Australian National University.

———. 1994. Radiocarbon determinations, luminescence dating and Australian archaeology. *Antiquity* 68:339–43.

———. 1996. The pre-Austronesian settlement of island Melanesia: Implications for Lapita archaeology. In W. H. Goodenough, ed., *Prehistoric Settlement of the Pacific*, pp. 11–27. *Transactions of the American Philosophical Society* 86(5).

Allen, J., and C. Gosden. 1996. Spheres of interaction and integration: Modelling the culture history of the Bismarck Archipelago. In J. Davidson, G. Irwin, F. Leach, A. Pawley, and D. Brown, eds., *Oceanic Culture History: Essays in Honour of Roger Green*, pp. 183–97. New Zealand Journal of Archaeology Special Publication. Dunedin North: New Zealand Journal of Archaeology.

Allen, J., and C. Gosden, eds. 1991. *Report of the Lapita Homeland Project*. Occasional Papers in Prehistory No. 20. Canberra: Department of Prehistory, Australian National University.

Allen, J., C. Gosden, and J. P. White. 1989. Human Pleistocene adaptations in the tropical island Pacific. *Antiquity* 63:548–61.

Allen, J., and S. Holdaway. 1995. The contamination of Pleistocene radiocarbon determinations in Australia. *Antiquity* 69:101–12.

Allen, J., S. Holdaway, and R. Fullagar. 1997. Identifying specialisation, production and exchange in the archaeological record: The case of shell bead manufacture on Motupore Island, Papua. *Archaeology in Oceania* 32:13–38.

Allen, J., and P. White. 1989. The Lapita homeland: Some new data and an interpretation. *Journal of the Polynesian Society* 98:129–46.

Allen, J. S. 1994. Te Rangi Hiroa's physical anthropology. *Journal of the Polynesian Society* 103:11–28.

Allen, M. S. 1992. Temporal variation in Polynesian fishing strategies: The Southern Cook Islands in regional perspective. *Asian Perspectives* 31:183–204.

———. 1996a. Patterns of interaction in Southern Cook Island prehistory. In I. C. Glover and B. Bellwood, eds., *Indo-Pacific Prehistory: The Chiang Mai Papers*, Vol. 2, pp. 13–22. Canberra: Australian National University.

———. 1996b. Style and function in East Polynesian fish-hooks. *Antiquity* 70:97–116.

———. 1998. Holocene sea-level change on Aitutaki, Cook Islands: Landscape change and human response. *Journal of Coastal Research* 12:10–22.

Allen, M. S., and G. Bell. 1988. Lapita flaked stone assemblages: Sourcing, technological, and functional studies. In P. V. Kirch and T. L. Hunt, eds., *Archaeology of the Lapita Cultural Complex: A Critical Review*, pp. 83–98. Thomas Burke Memorial Washington State Museum Research Report No. 5. Seattle: Burke Museum.

Allen, M. S., and P. A. McAnany. 1994. Environmental variability and traditional Hawaiian land use patterns: Manuka's cultural islands in seas of lava. *Asian Perspectives* 33:19–56.

Allen, M. S., and S. E. Schubel. 1990. Recent archaeological research on Aitutaki, southern Cooks: The Moturakau shelter. *Journal of the Polynesian Society* 99:265–96.

Allen, M. S., and D. W. Steadman. 1990. Excavations at the Ureia site, Aitutaki, Cook Islands: Preliminary results. *Archaeology in Oceania* 25:24–36.

Allen, M. W. 1996. Pathways to economic power in Maori chiefdoms: Ecology and warfare in prehistoric Hawke's Bay. *Research in Economic Anthropology* 17:171–225.

Allen, S. J., A. O'Donnell, N. D. E. Alexander, M. P. Alpers, T. E. A. Peto, J. B. Clegg, and D. J. Weatherall. 1997. α-Thalassemia protects children against disease caused by infections as well as malaria. *Proceedings of the National Academy of Sciences, USA* 94:14,736–41.

Ambrose, W. R. 1988. An early bronze artefact from Papua New Guinea. *Antiquity* 62:483–91.

———. 1991. Lapita or not Lapita: The case of the Manus pots. In J. Allen and C. Gosden, eds., *Report of the Lapita Homeland Project*, pp. 103–12. Canberra: Australian National University.

———. 1994. Obsidian hydration dating of a Pleistocene age site from the Manus Islands, Papua New Guinea. *Quaternary Geochronology* 13:137–42.

———. 1997. Contradictions in Lapita pottery: A composite clone. *Antiquity* 71:525–38.

Ambrose, W. R., and R. C. Green. 1972. First millennium BC transport of obsidian from New Britain to the Solomon Islands. *Nature* 237:31.

Amesbury, J. R., D. R. Moore, and R. L. Hunter-

Anderson. 1996. Cultural adaptations and late Holocene sea level change in the Marianas: Recent excavations at Chalan Piao, Saipan, Micronesia. In I. C. Glover and B. Bellwood, eds., *Indo-Pacific Prehistory: The Chiang Mai Papers,* Vol. 2, pp. 53–70. Canberra: Australian National University.

Anderson, A. 1982. A review of economic patterns during the Archaic Phase in Southern New Zealand. *New Zealand Journal of Archaeology* 4:45–75.

———. 1989a. *Prodigious Birds: Moas and Moa-Hunting in Prehistoric New Zealand.* Cambridge: Cambridge University Press.

———. 1989b. Mechanics of overkill in the extinction of New Zealand Moas. *Journal of Archaeological Research* 16:137–51.

———. 1991. The chronology of colonization in New Zealand. *Antiquity* 65:767–95.

———. 1997. Prehistoric Polynesian impact on the New Zealand environment: Te whenua hou. In P. V. Kirch and T. L. Hunt, eds., *Historical Ecology in the Pacific Islands: Prehistoric Environmental and Landscape Change,* pp. 271–83. New Haven, Conn.: Yale University Press.

Anderson, A., B. Allingham, and I. Smith, eds. 1996. *Shag River Mouth: The Archaeology of an Early Southern Maori Village.* Research Papers in Archaeology and Natural History No. 27. Canberra: Australian National University.

Anderson, A., and G. Clark. 1999. The age of Lapita settlement in Fiji. *Archaeology in Oceania* 34:31–39.

Anderson, A., H. Leach, I. Smith, and R. Walter. 1994. Reconsideration of the Marquesan sequence in East Polynesian prehistory, with particular reference to Hane (MUH1). *Archaeology in Oceania* 29:29–52.

Anderson, A., and I. Smith. 1992. The Papatowai site: New evidence and interpretations. *Journal of the Polynesian Society* 101:129–58.

———. 1996. The transient village in southern New Zealand. *World Archaeology* 27:359–71.

Anderson, E. 1952. *Plants, Man, and Life.* Berkeley: University of California Press.

Anson, D. 1983. Lapita Pottery of the Bismarck Archipelago and Its Affinities. Ph.D. dissertation, University of Sydney (Australia).

———. 1986. Lapita pottery of the Bismarck archipelago and its affinities. *Archaeology in Oceania* 21:157–65.

Anthony, D. W. 1990. Migration in archaeology: The baby and the bathwater. *American Anthropologist* 92:895–914.

Anton, S., and D. W. Steadman. 1997. Cannibals in the Cooks? Island biogeography and hominid behavior. Paper presented at the American Association of Physical Anthropology Annual Meeting, Salt Lake City.

Arens, W. 1979. *The Man-Eating Myth.* New York: Oxford University Press.

Ash, J. 1992. Vegetation ecology of Fiji: Past, present, and future perspectives. *Pacific Science* 46:111–27.

Athens, J. S. 1980. Pottery from Nan Madol, Ponape, Eastern Caroline Islands. *Journal of the Polynesian Society* 89:95–99.

———. 1981. *The Discovery and Archaeological Investigation of Nan Madol, Ponape, Easter Caroline Islands: An Annotated Bibliography.* Micronesian Archaeological Survey Report No. 3. Saipan: Micronesian Archaeological Survey.

———. 1983. The megalithic ruins of Nan Madol. *Natural History* 92(12):50–61.

———. 1984a. Surface artefact distributions at the Nan Madol site: A preliminary assessment of spatial patterning. *New Zealand Journal of Archaeology* 6:129–52.

———. 1984b. A stone adze from Ponape, Eastern Caroline Islands. *Asian Perspectives* 24:43–46.

———. 1986. *Archaeological Investigations at Tarague Beach, Guam.* Honolulu: J. S. Athens, Archaeological Consultant.

———.1990a. Nan Madol pottery, Pohnpei. In R. L. Hunter-Anderson, ed., *Recent Advances in Micronesian Archaeology: Selected Papers from the Micronesian Archaeology Conference, September 9–12, 1987. Micronesica,* Supplement 2, pp. 17–32.

———. 1990b. Kosrae pottery, clay, and early settlement. In R. L. Hunter-Anderson, ed., *Recent Advances in Micronesian Archaeology: Selected Papers from the Micronesian Archaeology Conference, September 9–12, 1987. Micronesica,* Supplement 2, pp. 171–86.

———. 1997. Hawaiian native lowland vegetation in prehistory. In P. V. Kirch and T. L. Hunt, eds.,

Historical Ecology in the Pacific Islands: Prehistoric Environmental and Landscape Change, pp. 248–70. New Haven, Conn.: Yale University Press.

Athens, J. S., ed. 1995. *Landscape Archaeology: Prehistoric Settlement, Subsistence, and Environment of Kosrae, Eastern Caroline Islands, Micronesia.* Honolulu: International Archaeological Research Institute.

Athens, J. S., and J. V. Ward. 1993. Environmental change and prehistoric Polynesian settlement in Hawai'i. *Asian Perspectives* 32:205–23.

———. 1995. Paleoenvironment of the Orote Peninsula, Guam. *Micronesica* 28:51–76.

———. 1997. The Maunawili core: Prehistoric inland expansion of settlement and agriculture, O'ahu, Hawai'i. *Hawaiian Archaeology* 6:37–51.

———. 1998. *Paleoenvironment and Prehistoric Landscape Change: A Sediment Core Record from Lake Hagoi, Tinian, CNMI.* Honolulu: International Archaeological Research Institute.

Athens, J. S., J. V. Ward, and G. M. Murakami. 1996. Development of an agroforest on a Micronesian high island: Prehistoric Kosraean agriculture. *Antiquity* 70:834–46.

Athens, J. S., J. Ward, and S. Wickler. 1992. Late Holocene lowland vegetation, O'ahu, Hawai'i. *New Zealand Journal of Archaeology* 14:9–34.

Attenborough, R. D., and M. P. Alpers, eds. 1992. *Human Biology in Papua New Guinea: The Small Cosmos.* Oxford: Clarendon Press.

Ayres, W. S. 1973. The Cultural Context of Easter Island Religious Structures. Unpublished Ph.D. dissertation, Tulane University.

———. 1990. Pohnpei's position in eastern Micronesian prehistory. In R. L. Hunter-Anderson, ed., *Recent Advances in Micronesian Archaeology: Selected Papers from the Micronesian Archaeology Conference, September 9–12, 1987. Micronesica,* Supplement 2, pp. 187–212.

———. 1992. Nan Madol, Micronesia. *Society for American Archaeology Bulletin* 10:4–5.

Ayres, W. S., and A. E. Haun. 1985. Archaeological perspectives on food production in eastern Micronesia. In I. S. Farrington, ed., *Prehistoric Intensive Agriculture in the Tropics,* pp. 455–73. B.A.R. International Series 232. Oxford: British Archaeological Reports.

———. 1990. Prehistoric food production in Micronesia. In D. E. Yen and J. M. J. Mummery, eds., *Pacific Production Systems: Approaches to Economic Prehistory,* pp. 211–30. Occasional Papers in Prehistory No. 18. Canberra: Department of Prehistory, Australian National University.

Ayres, W. S., A. E. Haun, and R. Mauricio. 1983. Nan Madol Archaeology: 1981 Survey and Excavations. Typescript report.

Ayres, W. S., A. E. Haun, and C. Severance. 1979. *Settlement and Subsistence on Ponape, Micronesia.* Interim Report 78-2, Ponape Archaeology Survey. Eugene: Department of Anthropology, University of Oregon.

Ayres, W. S., and R. Mauricio. 1987. Stone adzes from Pohnpei, Micronesia. *Archaeology in Oceania* 22:27–30.

Babayan, C., B. Finney, B. Kilonsky, and N. Thompson. 1987. Voyage to Aotearoa. *Journal of the Polynesian Society* 96:161–200.

Babcock, T. 1977. A re-analysis of pottery from fortified sites on Taveuni, Fiji. *Archaeology and Physical Anthropology in Oceania* 12:112–34.

Bahn, P., and J. Flenley. 1992. *Easter Island: Earth Island.* London: Thames and Hudson.

Ballard, C. 1993. Stimulating minds to fantasy? A critical etymology for Sahul. In M. A. Smith, M. Spriggs, and B. Fankhauser, eds., *Sahul in Review: Pleistocene Archaeology in Australia, New Guinea and Island Melanesia,* pp. 17–23. Occasional Papers in Prehistory No. 24. Canberra: Department of Prehistory, Australian National University.

Balouet, J. C., and S. L. Olson. 1989. *Fossil Birds from Late Quaternary Deposits in New Caledonia.* Smithsonian Contributions to Zoology 469. Washington, D.C.: Smithsonian Institution.

Barber, I. G. 1989. Of boundaries, drains, and crops: A classification system for traditional Maori horticultural ditches. *New Zealand Journal of Archaeology* 11:23–50.

———. 1996. Loss, change, and monumental landscaping: Towards a new interpretation of the "Classic" Maaori emergence. *Current Anthropology* 37:868–80.

Barrau, J. 1956. *L'Agriculture Vivrière Autochtone de la Nouvelle-Calédonie.* Noumea, New Caledonia: Commission du Pacifique Sud.

————. 1965a. L'humide et le sec: An essay on ethnobiological adaptation to contrastive environments in the Indo-Pacific area. *Journal of the Polynesian Society* 74:329–46.

————. 1965b. Histoire et préhistoire horticoles de l'Océanie tropicale. *Journal de la Société des Océanistes* 21:55–78.

Barrera, W., Jr. 1971. *Anaeho'omalu: A Hawaiian Oasis.* Pacific Anthropological Records 15. Honolulu: Bernice P. Bishop Museum.

Barthel, T. S. 1974. *Das Achte Land: Die Entdeckung und Besiedlung der Osterinsel nach Eingeborenentraditionen Übersetzt und Erläutert.* Munich: Klaus Renner Verlag. [1978 English translation published as *The Eighth Land* by University of Hawaii Press, Honolulu.]

Barton, F. R. 1910. The annual trading expedition to the Papuan Gulf. In C. G. Seligman, *The Melanesians of British New Guinea,* pp. 96–120. Cambridge: Cambridge University Press.

Bath, J. E. 1984a. *Sapwtakai: Archaeological Survey and Testing.* Micronesian Archaeological Survey Report 14. Saipan: Historic Preservation Office.

————. 1984b. A Tale of Two Cities: An Evaluation of Political Evolution in the Eastern Caroline Islands of Micronesia Since A.D. 1000. Unpublished Ph.D. dissertation, University of Hawaii (Manoa).

Bath, J. E., and J. S. Athens. 1990. Prehistoric social complexity on Pohnpei: The Saudeleur to Nahnmwarki transformation. In R. L. Hunter-Anderson, ed., *Recent Advances in Micronesian Archaeology: Selected Papers from the Micronesian Archaeology Conference, September 9–12, 1987. Micronesica,* Supplement 2, pp. 275–90.

Bayard, D. T. 1976. *The Cultural Relationships of the Polynesian Outliers.* University of Otago Studies in Prehistoric Anthropology 9. Dunedin, New Zealand: Department of Anthropology, University of Otago.

Bayliss-Smith, T., R. Bedford, H. C. Brookfield, and M. Latham. 1988. *Islands, Islanders, and the World.* Cambridge: Cambridge University Press.

Bayliss-Smith, T., and J. Golson. 1992. A Colocasian revolution in the New Guinea Highlands? Insights from Phase 4 at Kuk. *Archaeology in Oceania* 27:1–21.

Beaglehole, J. C., ed. 1967. *The Journals of Captain James Cook on his Voyages of Discovery. The Voyage of the Resolution and Discovery, 1776–1780.* 2 vols. Cambridge: Cambridge University Press for the Hakluyt Society.

————. 1968. *The Journals of Captain James Cook on His Voyages of Discovery. The Voyage of the* Endeavor, *1768–1771.* Cambridge: Cambridge University Press for the Hakluyt Society.

————. 1969. *The Journals of Captain James Cook on his Voyages of Discovery. The Voyage of the* Resolution *and* Adventure, *1772–1775.* Cambridge: Cambridge University Press for the Hakluyt Society.

Beardsley, F. R. 1994. *Archaeological Investigations on Kwajalein Atoll, Marshall Islands.* Honolulu: International Archaeological Research Institute.

Beckwith, M. W. 1970. *Hawaiian Mythology.* Honolulu: University Press of Hawaii.

Bedford, S., M. Spriggs, M. Wilson, and R. Regenvanu. 1998. The Australian National University–National Museum of Vanuatu Archaeology Project: A preliminary report on the establishment of cultural sequences and rock art research. *Asian Perspectives* 37:165–93.

Bellwood, P. 1971. Fortifications and economy in prehistoric New Zealand. *Proceedings of the Prehistoric Society* 37:56–95.

————. 1972. *Settlement Pattern Survey, Hanatekua Valley, Hiva Oa, Marquesas Islands.* Pacific Anthropological Records 17. Honolulu: Bernice P. Bishop Museum.

————. 1978. *Archaeological Research in the Cook Islands.* Pacific Anthropological Records 27. Honolulu: Bernice P. Bishop Museum.

————. 1979. *Man's Conquest of the Pacific: The Prehistory of Southeast Asia and Oceania.* New York: Oxford University Press.

————. 1985. *Prehistory of the Indo-Malaysian Archipelago.* Sydney: Academic Press.

————. 1987a. The prehistory of island southeast Asia: A multidisciplinary review of recent research. *Journal of World Prehistory* 1:171–224.

————. 1987b. *The Polynesians.* London: Thames and Hudson.

————. 1992. New discoveries in Southeast Asia relevant for Melanesian (especially Lapita) prehistory. In J.-C. Galipaud, ed., *Poterie Lapita et Peuplement: Actes du Colloque LAPITA,* pp. 49–66. Noumea, New Caledonia: ORSTOM.

———. 1993. Crossing the Wallace Line—with style. In M. A. Smith, M. Spriggs, and B. Fankhauser, eds., *Sahul in Review: Pleistocene Archaeology in Australia, New Guinea and Island Melanesia*, pp. 152–63. Occasional Papers in Prehistory No. 24. Canberra: Department of Prehistory, Australian National University.

———. 1996a. Phylogeny vs. reticulation in prehistory. *Antiquity* 70:881–90.

———. 1996b. Hierarchy, founder ideology and Austronesian expansion. In J. J. Fox and C. Sather, eds., *Origins, Ancestry and Alliance: Explorations in Austronesian Ethnography*, pp. 18–40. Canberra: Australian National University.

———. 1998. The archaeology of Papuan and Austronesian prehistory in the Northern Moluccas, Eastern Indonesia. In R. Blench and M. Spriggs, eds., *Archaeology and Language II: Correlating Archaeological and Linguistic Hypotheses*, pp. 128–40. London: Routledge.

Bellwood, P., J. Fox, and D. Tryon. 1995. The Austronesians in history: Common origins and diverse transformations. In P. Bellwood, J. Fox, and D. Tryon, eds., *The Austronesians: Historical and Comparative Perspectives*, pp. 1–16. Canberra: Australian National University.

Bellwood, P., and P. Koon. 1989. Lapita colonists leave boats unburned! The question of Lapita links with Island Southeast Asia. *Antiquity* 63:613–22.

Bellwood, P., G. Nitihaminoto, G. Irwin, Gunadi, A. Waluyo, and D. Tanudirjo. 1998. 35,000 years of prehistory in the northern Moluccas. In G.-J. Bartstra, ed., *Bird's Head Approaches: Irian-Jaya Studies—A Programme for Interdisciplinary Research*, pp. 233–75. Rotterdam: A. A. Balkema.

Bender, B. W., and J. W. Wang. 1985. The status of Proto-Micronesian. In A. Pawley and L. Carrington, eds., *Austronesian Linguistics at the 15th Pacific Science Congress*, pp. 53–92. Pacific Linguistics C-88. Canberra: Australian National University.

Bennett, W. C. 1931. *Archaeology of Kauai.* Bernice P. Bishop Museum Bulletin 80. Honolulu: Bernice P. Bishop Museum.

Benton, T. G., and T. Spencer, eds. 1995. The Pitcairn Islands: Biogeography, ecology and prehistory. *Biological Journal of the Linnaean Society* 56(1–2):1–463.

Bernart, L. 1977. *The Book of Luelen.* Pacific History Series No. 8. Honolulu: University of Hawaii Press.

Best, E. 1925. *Maori Agriculture.* Dominion Museum Bulletin 9. Wellington, New Zealand: Dominion Museum.

———. 1927. *The Pa Maori.* Dominion Museum Bulletin 6. Wellington, New Zealand: Dominion Museum.

Best, S. 1984. Lakeba: The Prehistory of a Fijian Island. Unpublished Ph.D. dissertation, University of Auckland.

———. 1987. Long-distance obsidian travel and possible implications for the settlement of Fiji. *Archaeology in Oceania* 22:31–32.

———. 1988. Tokelau archaeology: A preliminary report of an initial survey and excavations. *Bulletin of the Indo-Pacific Prehistory Association* 8:104–18.

Best, S., P. Sheppard, R. Green, and R. Parker. 1992. Necromancing the stone: Archaeologists and adzes in Samoa. *Journal of the Polynesian Society* 101:45–85.

Bickler, S. H. 1997. Early pottery exchange along the south coast of Papua New Guinea. *Archaeology in Oceania* 32:151–62.

Biggs, B. 1971. The languages of Polynesia. In T. A. Sebeok, ed., *Current Trends in Linguistics*, Vol. 8, Part 1, pp. 466–505. The Hague: Mouton.

Birks, L. 1973. *Archaeological Excavations at Sigatoka Dune Site, Fiji.* Bulletin of the Fiji Museum No. 1. Suva: Fiji Museum.

Birks, L., and H. Birks. 1967. Archaeological excavations at Site VL 16/81, Yanuca Island, Fiji. Oceanic Prehistory Records 6. Auckland, New Zealand: Department of Anthropology, University of Auckland.

Black, S. J., and R. C. Green. 1977. Radiocarbon dates from the Solomon Islands to 1975. Oceanic Prehistory Records 4 (microfiche). Auckland, New Zealand: Department of Anthropology, University of Auckland.

Blaikie, P., and H. C. Brookfield, eds. 1987. *Land Degradation and Society.* London: Methuen.

Blake, N., M. B. Hawkins, R. Kirk, K. Bhatia, P. Brown, R. M. Garruto, and D. C. Gajdusek. 1983. A population genetic study of the Banks and Torres Islands (Vanuatu) and of the Santa Cruz Islands and Polynesian Outliers (Solomon Islands). *American Journal of Physical Anthropology* 62:343–61.

Blong, R. J. 1982. *The Time of Darkness: Local Legends and Volcanic Reality in Papua New Guinea*. Seattle: University of Washington Press.

Blust, R. 1984. A Mussau vocabulary, with phonological notes. *Pacific Linguistics* A-69:159–208.

———. 1985. The Austronesian homeland: A linguistic perspective. *Asian Perspectives* 26:45–67.

———. 1987. Lexical reconstruction and semantic reconstruction: The case of Austronesian "house" words. *Diachronica* 4(1–2):79–106.

———. 1995. The prehistory of the Austronesian-speaking peoples: A view from language. *Journal of World Prehistory* 9:453–510.

———. 1996. Austronesian culture history: The windows of language. In W. H. Goodenough, ed., *Prehistoric Settlement of the Pacific*, pp. 28–35. *Transactions of the American Philosophical Society* 86(5).

———. 1999. Subgrouping, circularity and extinction: Some issues in Austronesian comparative linguistics. In E. Zeitoun and P. Jen-kuei Li, eds., *Selected Papers from the Eighth International Conference on Austronesian Linguistics*, pp. 31–94. Symposium Series of the Institute of Linguitics, Academia Sinica, No. 1. Taipei: Academia Sinica.

Bonhomme, T., and J. Craib. 1987. Radiocarbon dates from Unai Bapot, Saipan—Implications for the prehistory of the Mariana Islands. *Journal of the Polynesian Society* 96:95–106.

Bonnemaison, J., K. Huffman, and D. Tryon, eds. 1996. *Vanuatu–Océanie: Arts des Îles de Cendre et de Corail*. Paris: Editions de la Réunion des Musées Nationaux.

Borrie, W. D., R. Firth, and J. Spillius. 1957. The population of Tikopia, 1929 and 1952. *Population Studies* 10:229–52.

Boserup, E. 1965. *The Conditions of Agricultural Growth: The Economics of Agrarian Change under Population Pressure*. Chicago: Aldine.

Bowdler, S. 1977. The coastal colonisation of Australia. In J. Allen, J. Golson, and R. Jones, eds., *Sahul and Sunda*, pp. 205–46. London: Academic Press.

Boyce, A. J., R. M. Harding, and J. J. Martinson. 1995. Population genetics of the α-globin complex in Oceania. In A. J. Boyce and V. Reynolds, eds., *Human Populations: Diversity and Adaptation*, pp. 217–32. Oxford: Oxford University Press.

Braudel, F. 1980. *On History*. S. Matthews, trans. Chicago: University of Chicago Press.

Brewis, A., M. A. Molloy, and D. G. Sutton. 1990. Modeling the prehistoric Maori population. *American Journal of Physical Anthropology* 81:343–56.

Brigham, W. T. 1902. *Stone Implements and Stone Work of the Ancient Hawaiians*. Bernice P. Bishop Museum Memoir 1(5). Honolulu: Bernice P. Bishop Museum.

Brookfield, H. C. 1972. Intensification and disintensification in Pacific agriculture: A theoretical approach. *Pacific Viewpoint* 13:30–48.

———. 1984. Intensification revisited. *Pacific Viewpoint* 25:15–44.

Brookfield, H. C., with D. Hart. 1971. *Melanesia: A Geographical Interpretation of an Island World*. London: Methuen.

Brooks, C. C. 1984. A contribution to the geoarchaeology of Truk, Micronesia. *Asian Perspectives* 24:27–42.

Brown, P. 1978. *Highland Peoples of New Guinea*. Cambridge: Cambridge University Press.

Brumfiel, E., and T. Earle, eds. 1987. *Specialization, Exchange, and Complex Societies*. Cambridge: Cambridge University Press.

Bryson, R. U. 1989. Ceramic and Spatial Archaeology at Nan Madol, Pohnpei. Unpublished Ph.D. dissertation, University of Oregon.

Buck, P. H. *See* Hiroa, T. R.

Bulmer, S. 1971. Prehistoric settlement patterns and pottery in the Port Moresby area. *Journal of the Papua and New Guinea Society* 5:28–91.

———. 1975. Settlement and economy in prehistoric Papua New Guinea: A review of the archaeological evidence. *Journal de la Société des Océanistes* 31(46): 7–75.

Bulmer, S., and R. Bulmer. 1964. The prehistory of the Australian New Guinea Highlands. *American Anthropologist* 66:29–76.

Burley, D. V. 1994. As a prescription to rule: The royal tomb of Mala'e Lahi and 19th-century Tongan kingship. *Antiquity* 68:504–17.

———. 1997. Archaeological Research, Sigatoka Dune

National Park, June 1996. Report submitted to the Fiji Museum, Suva.

———. 1998. Archaeology and the Tongan past, 2850–150 B.P. *Journal of World Prehistory* 12:337–92.

Burley, D. V., D. E. Nelson, and R. Shutler, Jr. 1999. A radiocarbon chronology for the Eastern Lapita frontier in Tonga. *Archaeology in Oceania* 34:59–70.

Burney, D. A. 1997. Tropical islands as paleoecological laboratories: Gauging the consequences of human arrival. *Human Ecology* 25:437–57.

Burney, J. 1806. *A Chronological History of the Voyages and Discoveries in the South Sea or Pacific Ocean.* London: Luke Hansard and Sons.

Burrows, E. G. 1937. *Ethnology of Uvea.* Bernice P. Bishop Museum Bulletin 145. Honolulu: Bernice P. Bishop Museum.

———. 1938. *Western Polynesia: A Study in Cultural Differentiation.* Ethnological Studies No. 7. Gothenburg, Sweden: n.p.

Burton, J. 1987. Exchange pathways at a stone axe factory in Papua New Guinea. In G. de G. Sieveking and M. H. Newcomer, eds., *The Human Uses of Flint and Chert*, pp. 183–91. Cambridge: Cambridge University Press.

Bushnell, O. A. 1993. *The Gifts of Civilization: Germs and Genocide in Hawai'i.* Honolulu: University of Hawaii Press.

Bussell, M. R. 1988. Mid and late Holocene pollen diagrams and Polynesian deforestation, Wanganui District, New Zealand. *New Zealand Journal of Botany* 26:431–51.

Butler, B. M. 1992. *An Archaeological Survey of Aguiguan (Aguijan), Northern Marianas Islands.* Micronesian Archaeological Survey Report No. 29. Saipan: Division of Historic Preservation.

———. 1994. Early prehistoric settlement in the Marianas Islands: New evidence from Saipan. *Man and Culture in Oceania* 10:15–38.

Butler, B. M., ed. 1988. *Archaeological Investigations on the North Coast of Rota, Mariana Islands.* Center for Archaeological Investigations, Occasional Paper No. 8. Carbondale: Southern Illinois University.

Butler, V. L. 1988. Lapita fishing strategies: The faunal evidence. In P. V. Kirch and T. L. Hunt, eds., *Archae-ology of the Lapita Cultural Complex: A Critical Review*, pp. 99–116. Thomas Burke Memorial Washington State Museum Research Report No. 5. Seattle: Burke Museum.

———. 1994. Fishing feeding behavior and fish capture: The case for variation in Lapita fishing strategies. *Archaeology in Oceania* 29:81–90.

Cachola-Abad, C. K. 1993. Evaluating the orthodox dual settlement model for the Hawaiian Islands: An analysis of artefact distribution and Hawaiian oral traditions. In M. W. Graves and R. C. Green, eds., *The Evolution and Organization of Prehistoric Society in Polynesia*, pp. 13–32. New Zealand Archaeological Association Monograph 19. Auckland: New Zealand Archaeological Association.

Carlquist, S. 1974. *Island Biology.* New York: Columbia University Press.

Carneiro, R. 1981. The chiefdom as precursor to the state. In G. Jones and R. Krautz, eds., *The Transition to Statehood in the New World*, pp. 37–79. Cambridge: Cambridge University Press.

———. 1990. Chiefdom-level warfare as exemplified in Fiji and the Cauca Valley. In J. Haas, ed., *The Anthropology of War*, pp. 190–211. Cambridge: Cambridge University Press.

Carsten, J., and S. Hugh-Jones. 1995. Introduction. In J. Carsten and S. Hugh-Jones, eds., *About the House: Lévi-Strauss and Beyond*, pp. 1–46. Cambridge: Cambridge University Press.

Carter, T. D., J. E. Hill, and G. H. H. Tate. 1945. *Mammals of the Pacific World.* New York: Macmillan.

Casanova, P. V. 1998. Rapa Nui settlement patterns: Types, function and spatial distribution of household structural components. In P. V. Casanova, ed., *Easter Island and East Polynesian Prehistory*, pp. 110–30. Santiago: Instituto de Estudios Isla de Pascua, Universidad de Chile.

Casanova, P. V., ed. 1998. *Easter Island and East Polynesian Prehistory.* Santiago: Instituto de Estudios Isla de Pascua, Universidad de Chile.

Casanova, P. V., R. Izaurieta, C. Cristino, and C. Arias. 1998. New approaches to settlement pattern studies: A GIS based analysis of the Easter Island archaeological survey data. In P. V. Casanova, ed., *Easter*

Island and East Polynesian Prehistory, pp. 147–52. Santiago: Instituto de Estudios Isla de Pascua, Universidad de Chile.

Cassels, R. 1984. Faunal extinction and prehistoric man in New Zealand and the Pacific islands. In P. Martin and R. Klein, eds., *Quaternary Extinctions: A Prehistoric Revolution,* pp. 741–67. Tucson: University of Arizona Press.

Cattani, J. A. 1992. The epidemiology of malaria in Papua New Guinea. In R. D. Attenborough and M. P. Alpers, eds., *Human Biology in Papua New Guinea: The Small Cosmos,* pp. 302–12. Oxford: Clarendon Press.

Chalmers, A. F. 1982. *What Is This Thing Called Science?* St. Lucia, Australia: University of Queensland Press.

Chapman, P. S. 1964. Micronesian Archaeology: An Annotated Bibliography. Unpublished M.A. thesis, Stanford University, Stanford, California.

Chappell, J. 1974. Geology of coral terraces, Huon Peninsula, New Guinea: A study of Quaternary tectonic movements and sea-level changes. *Bulletin of the Geological Society of America* 85:553–70.

———. 1993. Late Pleistocene coasts and human migrations in the Austral Region. In M. Spriggs, D. E. Yen, W. Ambrose, R. Jones, A. Thorne, and A. Andrews, eds., *A Community of Culture: The People and Prehistory of the Pacific,* pp. 43–48. Occasional Papers in Prehistory No. 21. Canberra: Department of Prehistory, Australian National University.

Chappell, J., A. Omura, M. McCulloch, T. Esat, Y. Ota, and J. Pandolfi. 1994. Revised late Quaternary sea levels between 70 and 30 Ka from coral terraces at Huon Peninsula. In Y. Ota, ed., *Study on Coral Reef Terraces of the Huon Peninsula, Papua New Guinea: Establishment of Quaternary Sea Level and Tectonic History,* pp. 155–65. Yokohama: Department of Geography, Yokohama National University.

Chazine, J.-M. 1977. Prospections archéologiques à Takapoto. *Journal de la Société des Océanistes* 56–57: 191–214.

Chevalier, L. 1963. Le problème des tumuli en Nouvelle-Calédonie. *Études Mélanésiennes N.S.* 14–17:24–42.

Chikamori, M. 1967. Preliminary report on the archaeological researches in Western Solomon Islands. In M. Chikamori and S. Itoh, eds., *Eiryo*

Solomon Shoto ni Okeru Kokogaku-teki, Minzokugakuteki Choza Ryakuho. Privately published by Kaimeido, Tokyo (in Japanese).

———. 1975. *The Early Polynesian Settlement on Rennell Island, British Solomon Islands Protectorate.* Occasional Papers of the Department of Archaeology and Ethnology, Keio University, No. 1. Tokyo: Keio University.

———. 1996. Development of coral reefs and human settlement: Archaeological research in the northern Cook Islands and Rarotonga. In I. C. Glover and B. Bellwood, eds., *Indo-Pacific Prehistory: The Chiang Mai Papers,* Vol. 2, pp. 45–52. Canberra: Australian National University.

Chikamori, M., ed. 1998. *Archaeological Studies on the Cook Islands, Series 2.* Occasional Papers of the Department of Archaeology and Ethnology, Keio University, No. 12. Tokyo: Keio University.

Chikamori, M., and H. Takasugi. 1985. *Archaeology on Rennell Island.* Occasional Papers of the Department of Archaeology and Ethnology, Keio University, No. 5. Tokyo: Keio University.

Chikamori, M., and S. Yoshida. 1988. *An Archaeological Survey of Pukapuka Atoll, 1985.* Occasional Papers of the Department of Archaeology and Ethnology, Keio University, No. 6. Tokyo: Keio University.

Chikamori, M., S. Yoshida, and T. Yamaguchi. 1995. *Archaeological Studies of the Cook Islands, Series 1.* Occasional Papers of the Department of Archaeology and Ethnology, Keio University, No. 10. Tokyo: Keio University.

Christensen, C., and P. V. Kirch. 1981. Nonmarine mollusks from archaeological sites on Tikopia, Southeastern Solomon Islands. *Pacific Science* 35:75–88.

———. 1986. Non-marine mollusks and ecological change at Barbers Point, O'ahu, Hawai'i. *Bishop Museum Occasional Papers* 26:52–80.

Christensen, O. A. 1975. Hunters and horticulturalists: A preliminary report of the 1972–4 excavations in the Manim Valley, Papua New Guinea. *Mankind* 10: 24–36.

Christian, F. W. 1899. *The Caroline Islands: Travel in the Sea of the Little Lands.* London: Methuen.

Churchill, W. 1911. *The Polynesian Wanderings.* Carnegie

Institution of Washington Publication 134. Washington, D.C.: Carnegie Institution.

Clark, J. T. 1988. Paleodemography in leeward Hawaii. *Archaeology in Oceania* 23:22–30.

———. 1996. Samoan prehistory in review. In J. Davidson, G. Irwin, F. Leach, A. Pawley, and D. Brown, eds., *Oceanic Culture History: Essays in Honour of Roger Green*, pp. 445–60. New Zealand Journal of Archaeology Special Publication. Dunedin: New Zealand Journal of Archaeology.

Clark, J. T., and A. O. Cole. 1997. Environmental Change and Human Prehistory in the Central Pacific: Archaeological and Palynological Investigations on Totoya Island, Fiji. Report submitted to the Fiji Museum, Suva.

Clark, J. T., and D. J. Herdrich. 1993. Prehistoric settlement system in eastern Tutuila, American Samoa. *Journal of the Polynesian Society* 102:147–86.

Clark, J. T., and K. M. Kelly. 1993. Human genetics, paleoenvironments, and malaria: Relationships and implications for the settlement of Oceania. *American Anthropologist* 95:612–30.

Clark, J., and P. V. Kirch, eds. 1983. *Archaeological Investigations in the Mudlane–Waimea–Kawaihae Road Corridor, Island of Hawaii: An Interdisciplinary Study of an Environmental Transect.* Department of Anthropology Report No. 83-1. Honolulu: Bernice P. Bishop Museum.

Clark, J. T., and M. G. Michlovic. 1996. An early settlement in the Polynesian homeland: Excavations at 'Aoa Valley, Tutuila Island, American Samoa. *Journal of Field Archaeology* 26:151–68.

Clark, J. T., P. Sheppard, and M. Jones. 1997. Late ceramics in Samoa: A test using hydration-rim measurements. *Current Anthropology* 38:898–904.

Clark, R. 1979. Language. In J. Jennings, ed., *The Prehistory of Polynesia*, pp. 249–70. Cambridge, Mass.: Harvard University Press.

———. 1991. Fingota/Fangota: Shellfish and fishing in Polynesia. In A. Pawley, ed., *Man and a Half: Essays in Pacific Anthropology and Ethnobiology in Honour of Ralph Bulmer*, pp. 78–83. Auckland, New Zealand: Polynesian Society.

———. 1996. Linguistic consequences of the Kuwae eruption. In J. Davidson, G. Irwin, F. Leach, A. Pawley, and D. Brown, eds., *Oceanic Culture History: Essays in Honour of Roger Green*, pp. 275–85. New Zealand Journal of Archaeology Special Publication. Dunedin: New Zealand Journal of Archaeology.

Cleghorn, P. 1986. Organizational structure at the Mauna Kea Adze Quarry Complex, Hawai'i. *Journal of Archaeological Science* 13:375–87.

Clune, F. J., Jr. 1974. Archaeological survey of Truk, Micronesia. *Micronesica* 10:205–6.

Cole, J. D. 1996. Function and development in the East New Guinea Highlands. *Archaeology in Oceania* 31:12–18.

Coleman, P. J., ed. 1973. *The Western Pacific: Island Arcs, Marginal Seas, Geochemistry.* Nedlands: University of Western Australia Press.

Condliffe, J. B. 1971. *Te Rangi Hiroa: The Life of Sir Peter Buck.* Christchurch, New Zealand: Whitcombe and Tombs.

Conte, E. 1988. L'Exploitation Traditionelle des Ressources Marines à Napuka (Tuamotu–Polynésie Française). Ph.D. dissertation, University of Paris I (Panthéon-Sorbonne).

Conte, E., and J. Dennison. 1995. An anthropological study of the burials in Marae Te Tahata, Tepoto (Tuamotu Archipelago, French Polynesia). *Journal of the Polynesian Society* 104:397–427.

Cordy, R. 1974a. Cultural adaptation and evolution in Hawaii: A suggested new sequence. *Journal of the Polynesian Society* 83:180–91.

———. 1974b. Complex rank cultural systems in the Hawaiian Islands: Suggested explanations for their origin. *Archaeology and Physical Anthropology in Oceania* 9:89–109.

———. 1980. Archaeology in Micronesia. *Journal of the Polynesian Society* 89:359–65.

———. 1981. *A Study of Prehistoric Social Change: The Development of Complex Societies in the Hawaiian Islands.* New York: Academic Press.

———. 1982. A summary of archaeological work in Micronesia since 1977. *Bulletin of the Indo-Pacific Prehistory Association* 3:118–28.

———. 1983. Social stratification in the Mariana Islands. *Oceania* 53:272–76.

————. 1985a. Investigations of Leluh's stone ruins. *National Geographic Research* 1:255–63.

————. 1985b. Settlement patterns of complex societies in the Pacific. *New Zealand Journal of Archaeology* 7:159–82.

————. 1986. Relationships between the extent of social stratification and population in Micronesian polities at European contact. *American Anthropologist* 88:136–42.

————. 1993. *The Lelu Stone Ruins (Kosrae, Micronesia): 1978–1981 Historical and Archaeological Research.* Asian and Pacific Archaeology Series No. 10. Honolulu: Social Science Research Institute, University of Hawaii.

————. 1996. The rise and fall of the O'ahu kingdom: A brief overview of O'ahu's history. In J. Davidson, G. Irwin, F. Leach, A. Pawley, and D. Brown, eds., *Oceanic Culture History: Essays in Honour of Roger Green,* pp. 591–613. New Zealand Journal of Archaeology Special Publication. Dunedin: New Zealand Journal of Archaeology.

Cordy, R. H., and M. W. Kaschko. 1980. Prehistoric archaeology in the Hawaiian Islands: Land units associated with social groups. *Journal of Field Archaeology* 7:403–16.

Cox, J. H., and E. Stasack. 1970. *Hawaiian Petroglyphs.* Special Publication No. 60. Honolulu: Bernice P. Bishop Museum.

Craib, J. L. 1983. Micronesian prehistory: An archaeological overview. *Science* 219:922–27.

————. 1984. Settlement on Ulithi Atoll, Western Caroline Islands. *Asian Perspectives* 24:47–56.

————. 1986. Casas de los Antiguos: Social Differentiation in Protohistoric Chamorro Society, Marianas Islands. Unpublished Ph.D. dissertation, University of Sydney.

Cristino, C., and P. V. Casanova. 1998. Archaeological excavations and restoration of Ahu Tongariki. In P. V. Casanova, ed., *Easter Island and East Polynesian Prehistory,* pp. 153–58. Santiago: Instituto de Estudios Isla de Pascua, Universidad de Chile.

Cristino, C., and P. Vargas. 1980. Prospección arqueólogica de Isla de Pascua. *Anales de la Universidad de Chile* 161–62:191–215.

Cristino, C., P. Vargas, and S. Izaurieta. 1981. *Atlas Arqueólogica de Isla de Pascua.* Santiago: Faculty of Architecture and Urban Studies, University of Chile.

Crosby, A. W. 1986. *Ecological Imperialism: The Biological Expansion of Europe, 900–1900.* Cambridge: Cambridge University Press.

Cumberland, K. B. 1962. Moas and men: New Zealand about A.D. 1250. *The Geographical Review* 52:151–73.

Damon, A. 1974. Human ecology in the Solomon Islands: Biomedical observations among four tribal societies. *Human Ecology* 2:191–215.

Darwin, C. 1842. *Structure and Distribution of Coral Reefs.* London: Smith, Elder.

Davenport, W. H. 1962. Red feather money. *Scientific American* 206(3):94–103.

————. 1972. Preliminary excavations on Santa Ana Island, Eastern Solomon Islands. *Archaeology and Physical Anthropology in Oceania* 7:165–83.

Davidson, J. M. 1967a. An archaeological assemblage of simple fishhooks from Nukuoro Atoll. *Journal of the Polynesian Society* 76:177–96.

————. 1967b. Archaeology on coral atolls. In G. A. Highland, R. W. Force, A. Howard, M. Kelly, and Y. H. Sinoto, eds., *Polynesian Culture History: Essays in Honor of Kenneth P. Emory,* pp. 363–75. Special Publication 56. Honolulu: Bernice P. Bishop Museum.

————. 1969. Archaeological excavations in two burials mounds at 'Atele, Tongatapu. *Records of the Auckland Institute and Museum* 6:251–86.

————. 1971. *Archaeology on Nukuoro Atoll: A Polynesian Outlier in the Eastern Caroline Islands.* Auckland Institute and Museum Bulletin 9. Auckland, New Zealand: Auckland Institute and Museum.

————. 1977. Western Polynesia and Fiji: Prehistoric contact, diffusion and differentiation in adjacent archipelagoes. *World Archaeology* 9:82–94.

————. 1979. Samoa and Tonga. In J. Jennings, ed., *The Prehistory of Polynesia,* pp. 82–109. Cambridge, Mass.: Harvard University Press.

————. 1984. *The Prehistory of New Zealand.* Auckland: Longman Paul.

————. 1988. Archaeology in Micronesia since 1965: Past achievements and future prospects. *New Zealand Journal of Archaeology* 10:83–100.

———. 1992. New evidence about the date of colonisation of Nukuoro Atoll, a Polynesian Outlier in the Eastern Caroline Islands. *Journal of the Polynesian Society* 101:293–98.

———. 1993. Issues in New Zealand prehistory since 1954. In M. Spriggs, D. E. Yen, W. Ambrose, R. Jones, A. Thorne, and A. Andrews, eds., *A Community of Culture: The People and Prehistory of the Pacific*, pp. 239–58. Occasional Papers in Prehistory No. 21. Canberra: Department of Prehistory, Australian National University.

Davidson, J. M., E. Hinds, S. Holdaway, and F. Leach. 1990. The Lapita site of Natunuku, Fiji. *New Zealand Journal of Archaeology* 12:121–55.

Davidson, J. M., and F. Leach. 1993. The chronology of the Natunuku site, Fiji. *New Zealand Journal of Archaeology* 15:99–105.

———. 1996. Fishing on Nukuoro Atoll: Ethnographic and archaeological viewpoints. In M. Julien, M. Orliac, and C. Orliac, eds., *Mémoire de Pierre, Mémoire d'Homme: Tradition et Archéologie en Océanie*, pp. 183–202. Paris: Publications de la Sorbonne.

Davis, W. M. 1928. *The Coral Reef Problem*. American Geographic Society Special Publication No. 9. New York: American Geographic Society.

DeBoer, W. R. 1991. The decorative burden: Design, medium, and change. In W. A. Longacre, ed., *Ceramic Ethnoarchaeology*. Tucson: University of Arizona Press.

De Brosses, C. 1756. *Histoire des Navigations aux Terres Australes*. Paris: Durand.

DeGusta, D. 1999. Fijian cannibalism: Osteological evidence from Navatu. *American Journal of Physical Anthropology* 110:215–41.

Dempwolff, O. 1934–38. *Vergleichende Lautlehre des Austronesischen Wortschatzes*. 3 vols. Beihefte zur Zeitschrift für Eingeborenen-Sprachen 15, 17, 19. Berlin: Dietrich Reimer.

Dening, G. 1962. The geographical knowledge of the Polynesians and the nature of inter-island contact. In J. Golson, ed., *Polynesian Navigation*, pp. 102–32. Polynesian Society Memoir 34. Wellington, New Zealand: Polynesian Society.

———. 1980. *Islands and Beaches: Discourse on a Silent Land, Marquesas 1774–1880*. Honolulu: University of Hawaii Press.

———. 1992. *Mr. Bligh's Bad Language: Passion, Power and Theatre on the Bounty*. Cambridge: Cambridge University Press.

Descantes, C. 1990. Symbolic Stone Structures: Protohistoric and Early Historic Spatial Patterns of the 'Opunohu Valley, Mo'orea, French Polynesia. M.A. thesis, University of Auckland.

———. 1998. Integrating Archaeology and Ethnohistory: The Development of Exchange Between Yap and Ulithi, Western Caroline Islands. Unpublished Ph.D. dissertation, University of Oregon (Eugene).

Diamond, J. 1988. Express train to Polynesia. *Nature* 336:307–8.

Diaz, H. F., and V. Markgraf, eds. 1992. *El Niño: Historical and Paleoclimatic Aspects of the Southern Oscillation*. Cambridge: Cambridge University Press.

Dickinson, W. R. 1984. Indigenous and exotic sand tempers in prehistoric potsherds from the central Caroline Islands. In Y. H. Sinoto, ed., *Caroline Islands Archaeology*, pp. 131–35. Pacific Anthropological Records 35. Honolulu: Bernice P. Bishop Museum.

———. 1998. Prehistoric temper provinces of prehistoric pottery in Oceania. *Records of the Australian Museum* 50:263–76.

Dickinson, W. R., D. V. Burley, P. D. Nunn, A. Anderson, G. Hope, A. de Biran, C. Burke, and S. Matararaba. 1998. Geomorphic and archaeological landscapes of the Sigatoka Dunes Site, Viti Levu, Fiji: Interdisciplinary investigations. *Asian Perspectives* 37:1–32.

Dickinson, W. R., D. V. Burley, and R. Shutler, Jr. 1994. Impact of hydro-isostatic Holocene sea-level change on the geologic context of island archaeological sites, northern Ha'apai group, Kingdom of Tonga. *Geoarchaeology* 9:85–111.

Dickinson, W. R., and R. C. Green. 1998. Geoarchaeological context of Holocene subsidence at the Ferry Berth site, Mulifanua, Upolu, Western Samoa. *Geoarchaeology* 13:239–63.

Dickinson, W. R., B. V. Rolett, Y. H. Sinoto, M. E.

Rosenthal, and R. Shutler, Jr. 1988. Temper sands in exotic Marquesan pottery and the significance of their Fijian origin. *Journal de la Société des Océanistes* 107:119–33.

Dickinson, W. R., and R. Shutler, Jr. 1974. Probable Fijian origin of quartzose temper sands in prehistoric pottery from Tonga and the Marquesas. *Science* 185:454–57.

———. 1979. Petrography of sand tempers in Pacific Island potsherds. *Bulletin of the Geological Society of America* 90:993–95, 1644–1701.

Dickinson, W. R., R. Shutler, Jr., R. Shortland, D. V. Burley, and T. S. Dye. 1996. Sand tempers in indigenous Lapita and Lapitoid Polynesian Plainware and imported protohistoric Fijian pottery of Ha'apai (Tonga) and the question of Lapita tradeware. *Archaeology in Oceania* 31:87–98.

Di Piazza, A. 1990. Les jardins enfouis de Futuna: une ethno-archéologie de l'horticulture. *Journal de la Société des Océanistes* 91:151–62.

———. 1999. Te Bakoa site: Two old earth ovens from Nikunau Island (Republic of Kiribati). *Archaeology in Oceania* 34:40–42.

Dixon, B., A. Carpenter, F. Eble, C. Mitchell, and M. Major. 1995. Community growth and heiau construction: Possible evidence of political hegemony at the site of Kaunolu, Lana'i, Hawai'i. *Asian Perspectives* 34:229–56.

Dixon, R. B. 1929. The peopling of the Pacific. *Philippine Magazine* 26:195–97, 244–45.

Dodson, J., ed. 1992. *The Naive Lands: Prehistory and Environmental Change in Australia and the Southwest Pacific.* Melbourne: Longman Cheshire.

Dodson, J., and M. Intoh. 1999. Prehistory and paleoecology of Yap, Federated States of Micronesia. *Quaternary International* 59:17–26.

Donovan, L. J. 1973. A Study of the Decorative System of the Lapita Potters in Reefs and Santa Cruz Islands. Unpublished M.A. research essay, University of Auckland.

Downie, J. E., and J. P. White. 1978. Balof Shelter, New Ireland: Report on a small excavation. *Records of the Australian Museum* 31:762–802.

Duff, R. 1942. Moa-hunters of the Wairau. *Records of the Canterbury Museum* 5:1–49.

———. 1947. The evolution of native culture in New Zealand: Moa hunters, Morioris, Maoris. *Mankind* 3:281–91, 313–22.

———. 1950. *The Moa Hunter Period of Maori Culture.* Wellington, New Zealand: Government Printer.

———. 1967. The evolution of Maori warfare. *New Zealand Archaeological Association Newsletter* 10:114–29.

———. 1968. A historical survey of archaeology in New Zealand. In W. G. Solheim II, ed., *Anthropology at the Eighth Pacific Science Congress*, pp. 167–90. Asian and Pacific Archaeology Series No. 2. Honolulu: Social Science Research Institute, University of Hawaii.

Dumont d'Urville, M. J. 1832. Notice sur les îles du Grand Océan et sur l'origine des peuples qui les habitent. *Société de Géographie Bulletin* 17:1–21.

Dye, T. S. 1988. Social and Cultural Change in the Prehistory of the Ancestral Polynesian Homeland. Unpublished Ph.D. dissertation, Yale University (New Haven).

———. 1989. Tales of two cultures: traditional historical and archaeological interpretations of Hawaiian prehistory. *Bishop Museum Occasional Papers* 29:3–22.

———. 1990. The causes and consequences of a decline in the prehistoric Marquesan fishing industry. In D. E. Yen and J. M. J. Mummery, eds., *Pacific Production Systems: Approaches to Economic Prehistory*, pp. 70–94. Occasional Papers in Prehistory No. 18. Canberra: Department of Prehistory, Australian National University.

———. 1994. Population trends in Hawai'i before 1778. *Hawaiian Journal of History* 28:1–20.

———. 1996a. Early Eastern Lapita to Polynesian Plainware at Tongatapu and Lifuka: An exploratory data analysis and comparison. In J. Davidson, G. Irwin, F. Leach, A. Pawley, and D. Brown, eds., *Oceanic Culture History: Essays in Honour of Roger Green*, pp. 461–73. New Zealand Journal of Archaeology Special Publication. Dunedin: New Zealand Journal of Archaeology.

———. 1996b. Assemblage definition, analytic methods, and sources of variability in the interpretation of Marquesan subsistence change. *Asian Perspectives* 35:73–88.

Dye, T. S., ed. 1987. *Marshall Islands Archaeology.* Pacific Anthropological Records 38. Honolulu: Bernice P. Bishop Museum.

Dye, T., and P. L. Cleghorn. 1990. Prehistoric use of the interior of southern Guam. In R. L. Hunter-Anderson, ed., *Recent Advances in Micronesian Archaeology: Selected Papers from the Micronesian Archaeology Conference, September 9–12, 1987. Micronesica,* Supplement 2, pp. 261–74.

Dye, T. S., and E. Komori. 1992. A pre-censal population history of Hawaii. *New Zealand Journal of Archaeology* 14:113–28.

Dyen, I. 1965. *A Lexicostatistical Classification of the Austronesian Languages.* International Journal of American Linguistics Memoir 19. Baltimore: Waverly Press.

——. 1985. Lexical reconstruction and the semantic history hypothesis. In A. Makkai and A. K. Melby, eds., *Linguistics and Philosophy: Essays in Honor of Rulon S. Wells,* pp. 343–91. Amsterdam: John Benjamins.

Earle, T. 1978. *Economic and Social Organization of a Complex Chiefdom: The Halelea District, Kaua'i, Hawaii.* Anthropological Papers No. 63. Ann Arbor: Museum of Anthropology, University of Michigan.

——. 1980. Prehistoric irrigation in the Hawaiian Islands: An evaluation of evolutionary significance. *Archaeology and Physical Anthropology in Oceania* 15:1–28.

——. 1997. *How Chiefs Come to Power: The Political Economy in Prehistory.* Stanford, Calif.: Stanford University Press.

Earle, T., ed. 1991. *Chiefdoms: Power, Economy, and Ideology.* Cambridge: Cambridge University Press.

Eddowes, M. D. 1991. Ethnohistorical Perspectives on the *Marae* of the Society Islands: The Sociology of Use. Unpublished M.A. thesis, Department of Anthropology, University of Auckland.

Edwards, E. 1998. The archaeological survey of Raivavae, Austral Islands, French Polynesia. In P. V. Casanova, ed., *Easter Island and East Polynesian Prehistory,* pp. 31–58. Santiago: Instituto de Estudios Isla de Pascua, Universidad de Chile.

Egloff, B. 1971. Archaeological research in the Col-

lingwood Bay area of Papua. *Asian Perspectives* 14:60–64.

——. 1978. The Kula before Malinowski: A changing configuration. *Mankind* 11:429–35.

——. 1979. *Recent Prehistory in Southeast Papua.* Terra Australis 4. Canberra: Australian National University.

Ehrenreich, R. M., C. Crumley, and J. E. Levy, eds. 1995. *Heterarchy and the Analysis of Complex Societies.* Archaeological Papers of the American Anthropological Association No. 6. Arlington, Va.: American Anthropological Association.

Eissen, J.-P., M. Monzier, and C. Robin. 1994. Kuwae, l'éruption volcanique oubliée. *La Recherche* 270:1200–2.

Elliot, M. B., B. Stiewski, J. R. Flenley, and D. G. Sutton. 1995. Palynological and sedimentological evidence for a radiocarbon chronology of environmental change and Polynesian deforestation from Lake Taumatawhana, Northland, New Zealand. *Radiocarbon* 37:899–916.

Ellis, W. 1830. *Polynesian Researches.* London: Fisher, Son, and Jackson.

Ellison, J. 1994. Palaeo-lake and swamp stratigraphic records of Holocene vegetation and sea-level changes, Mangaia, Cook Islands. *Pacific Science* 48:1–15.

Emory, K. P. 1921. An archaeological survey of Haleakala. *Bishop Museum Occasional Papers* 7:237–59.

——. 1924. *The Island of Lanai: A Survey of Native Culture.* Bernice P. Bishop Museum Bulletin 12. Honolulu: Bernice P. Bishop Museum.

——. 1928. *Archaeology of Nihoa and Necker Islands.* Bernice P. Bishop Museum Bulletin 53. Honolulu: Bernice P. Bishop Museum.

——. 1933. *Stone Remains in the Society Islands.* Bernice P. Bishop Museum Bulletin 116. Honolulu: Bernice P. Bishop Museum.

——. 1934a. *Tuamotuan Stone Structures.* Bernice P. Bishop Museum Bulletin 118. Honolulu: Bernice P. Bishop Museum.

——. 1934b. *Archaeology of the Pacific Equatorial Islands.* Bernice P. Bishop Museum Bulletin 123. Honolulu: Bernice P. Bishop Museum.

——. 1939. *Archaeology of Mangareva and Neighboring*

Atolls. Bernice P. Bishop Museum Bulletin 163. Honolulu: Bernice P. Bishop Museum.

———. 1946. Eastern Polynesia: Its Cultural Relationships. Unpublished Ph.D. dissertation, Yale University (New Haven).

———. 1947. *Tuamotuan Religious Structures and Ceremonies.* Bernice P. Bishop Museum Bulletin 191. Honolulu: Bernice P. Bishop Museum.

———. 1959. Origin of the Hawaiians. *Journal of the Polynesian Society* 68:29–35.

———. 1962. Archaeological investigation of Polynesia. Mimeographed proposal to the U.S. National Science Foundation. Honolulu: Bernice P. Bishop Museum.

———. 1963. East Polynesian relationships: Settlement pattern and time involved as indicated by vocabulary agreements. *Journal of the Polynesian Society* 72:78–100.

———. 1968. East Polynesian relationships as revealed through adzes. In I. Yawata and Y. Sinoto, eds., *Prehistoric Culture in Oceania,* pp. 151–69. Honolulu: Bishop Museum Press.

———. 1979. The Society Islands. In J. Jennings, ed., *The Prehistory of Polynesia,* pp. 200–21. Cambridge, Mass.: Harvard University Press.

Emory, K. P., W. J. Bonk, and Y. H. Sinoto. 1959. *Hawaiian Archaeology: Fishhooks.* Special Publication 47. Honolulu: Bernice P. Bishop Museum.

———. 1969. *Waiahukini Shelter, Site H8, Ka'u, Hawaii.* Pacific Anthropological Records 7. Honolulu: Bernice P. Bishop Museum.

Emory, K. P., and Y. H. Sinoto. 1961. *Hawaiian Archaeology: Oahu Excavations.* Special Publication 49. Honolulu: Bernice P. Bishop Museum.

———. 1964. Eastern Polynesian burials at Maupiti. *Journal of the Polynesian Society* 75:143–60.

———. 1965. Preliminary Report on the Archaeological Investigations in Polynesia. Mimeographed report to the National Science Foundation. Honolulu: Bernice P. Bishop Museum.

Englert, Père S. 1948. *La Tierra de Hotu Matu'a.* Santiago, Chile: Padre las Casas.

———. 1970. *Island at the Center of the World.* New York: Charles Scribner's Sons.

Enright, N. J., and C. Gosden. 1992. Unstable archipelagoes: South-west Pacific environment and prehistory since 30,000 B.P. In J. Dodson, ed., *The Naive Lands: Prehistory and Environmental Change in Australia and the Southwest Pacific,* pp. 160–98. Melbourne: Longman Cheshire.

Feil, D. K. 1987. *The Evolution of Papua New Guinea Societies.* Cambridge: Cambridge University Press.

Finney, B. R. 1977. Voyaging canoes and the settlement of Polynesia. *Science* 196:1277–85.

———. 1985. Anomalous westerlies, El Niño, and the colonization of Polynesia. *American Anthropologist* 87:9–26.

———. 1988. Voyaging against the direction of the trades: A report of an experimental canoe voyage from Samoa to Tahiti. *American Anthropologist* 90:401–5.

———. 1994. *Voyage of Rediscovery: A Cultural Odyssey Through Polynesia.* Berkeley: University of California Press.

———. 1996a. Colonizing an island world. In W. H. Goodenough, ed., *Prehistoric Settlement of the Pacific,* pp. 71–116. *Transactions of the American Philosophical Society* 86(5).

———. 1996b. Putting voyaging back into Polynesian prehistory. In J. Davidson, G. Irwin, F. Leach, A. Pawley, and D. Brown, eds., *Oceanic Culture History: Essays in Honour of Roger Green,* pp. 365–76. New Zealand Journal of Archaeology Special Publication. Dunedin: New Zealand Journal of Archaeology.

Finney, B., P. Frost, R. Rhodes, and N. Thompson. 1989. Wait for the west wind. *Journal of the Polynesian Society* 98:261–302.

Finney, B., B. J. Kilonsky, S. Somsen, and E. D. Stroup. 1986. Re-learning a vanishing art. *Journal of the Polynesian Society* 95:41–90.

Firth, R. 1936. *We, the Tikopia.* London: George Allen and Unwin.

———. 1961. *History and Traditions of Tikopia.* Wellington, New Zealand: Polynesian Society.

Fischer, S. R., ed. 1993. *Easter Island Studies: Contributions to the History of Rapanui in Memory of William T. Mulloy.* Oxbow Monograph 32. Oxford: Oxbow.

———. 1997. *Rongorongo, the Easter Island Script: History, Traditions, Texts.* Oxford: Clarendon Press.

Flannery, K. V. 1983. Archaeology and ethnology in the context of divergent evolution. In K. V. Flannery and J. Marcus, eds., *The Cloud People*, pp. 361–62. New York: Academic Press.

Flannery, T. F. 1994. *The Future Eaters: An Ecological History of the Australasian Lands and People*. New York: George Braziller.

Flannery, T. F., P. V. Kirch, J. Specht, and M. Spriggs. 1988. Holocene mammal faunas from archaeological sites in island Melanesia. *Archaeology in Oceania* 23:89–94.

Flannery, T. F., and J. P. White. 1991. Animal translocations: Zoogeography of New Ireland mammals. *National Geographic Research and Exploration* 7:96–113.

Flenley, J. R. 1996. Further evidence of vegetational change on Easter Island. *South Pacific Study* 16:135–41.

Flenley, J. R., and King, S. M. 1984. Late Quaternary pollen records from Easter Island. *Nature* 307:47–50.

Flenley, J., S. King, J. Jackson, C. Chew, J. Teller, and M. Prentice. 1991. The Late Quaternary vegetational and climatic history of Easter Island. *Journal of Quaternary Science* 6:85–115.

Flint, J., A. J. Boyce, J. J. Martinson, and J. B. Clegg. 1989. Population bottlenecks in Polynesia revealed by minisatellites. *Human Genetics* 83:257–63.

Flood, J. 1983. *Archaeology of the Dreamtime*. Honolulu: University of Hawaii Press.

Foana'ota, L. 1996. The development of archaeological work in the Solomon Islands. In J. Davidson, G. Irwin, F. Leach, A. Pawley, and D. Brown, eds., *Oceanic Culture History: Essays in Honour of Roger Green*, pp. 241–43. New Zealand Journal of Archaeology Special Publication. Dunedin: New Zealand Journal of Archaeology.

Foley, W. A. 1986. *The Papuan Languages of New Guinea*. Cambridge: Cambridge University Press.

Force, R. W. 1964. *Annual Report of the Director for 1962*. Honolulu: Bishop Museum Press.

———. 1965. Polynesian culture history. Mimeographed proposal to the U.S. National Science Foundation. Honolulu: Bernice P. Bishop Museum.

Fornander, A. 1878. *An Account of the Polynesian Race*. London: Trubner.

Forster, J. R. 1996 [1778]. *Observations Made during a Voyage Round the World*. N. Thomas, H. Guest, and M. Dettelbach, eds. Honolulu: University of Hawaii Press.

Fosberg, F. R. 1963a. The island ecosystem. In F. R. Fosberg, ed., *Man's Place in the Island Ecosystem: A Symposium*, pp. 1–7. Honolulu: Bishop Museum Press.

———. 1963b. Disturbance in island ecosystems. In J. L. Gressitt, ed., *Pacific Basin Biogeography*, pp. 557–61. Honolulu: Bishop Museum Press.

Fosberg, F. R., ed. 1963. *Man's Place in the Island Ecosystem*. Honolulu: Bishop Museum Press.

Fox, A. 1976. *Prehistoric Maori Fortifications*. Auckland, New Zealand: Longman Paul.

———. 1978. *Tiromoana Pa, Te Awanga, Hawke's Bay. Excavations 1974–5*. New Zealand Archaeological Association Monograph 8. Dunedin: New Zealand Archaeological Association.

Fox, A., and R. C. Green. 1982. Excavations at Maioro, N51/5, South Auckland, 1965–66. *Records of the Auckland Institute and Museum* 19:53–80.

Fox, J. J. 1994. Who's who in Ego's generation: Probing the semantics of Malayo-Polynesian kinship classification. In A. K. Pawley and M. D. Ross, eds., *Austronesian Terminologies: Continuity and Change*, pp. 127–40. Pacific Linguistics C-127. Canberra: Australian National University.

———. 1995. Austronesian societies and their transformations. In P. Bellwood, J. J. Fox, and D. Tryon, eds., *The Austronesians: Historical and Comparative Perspectives*, pp. 214–28. Canberra: Australian National University.

Frankel, D., and J. W. Rhoads. 1994. *Archaeology of a Coastal Exchange System: Sites and Ceramics of the Papuan Gulf*. Research Papers in Archaeology and Natural History No. 25. Canberra: Australian National University.

Fredericksen, C., M. Spriggs, and W. Ambrose. 1993. Pamwak rockshelter: A Pleistocene site on Manus Island, Papua New Guinea. In M. A. Smith, M. Spriggs, and B. Fankhauser, eds., *Sahul in Review: Pleistocene Archaeology in Australia, New Guinea and Island Melanesia*, pp. 144–54. Occasional Papers in Prehistory No. 24. Canberra: Department of Prehistory, Australian National University.

French-Wright, R. 1983. Proto-Oceanic Horticultural Practices. Unpublished M.A. thesis, University of Auckland.

Fried, M. 1967. *The Evolution of Political Society.* New York: Random House.

Friedlaender, J. S. 1987. Conclusion. In J. S. Friedlaender, ed., *The Solomon Islands Project: A Long-Term Study of Health, Human Biology, and Culture Change,* pp. 351–64. Oxford: Clarendon Press.

Friedlaender, J. S., ed. 1987. *The Solomon Islands Project: A Long-Term Study of Health, Human Biology, and Culture Change.* Oxford: Clarendon Press.

Friedlaender, J. S., and L. B. Page. 1987. Epidemiology. In J. S. Friedlaender, ed., *The Solomon Islands Project: A Long-Term Study of Health, Human Biology, and Culture Change,* pp. 89–121. Oxford: Clarendon Press.

Friedman, J. 1981. Notes on structure and history in Oceania. *Folk* 23:275–95.

Friedman, J., and M. Rowlands. 1978. Notes toward an epigenetic model of the evolution of "civilisation." In J. Friedman and M. Rowlands, eds., *The Evolution of Social Systems,* pp. 201–76. Pittsburgh: University of Pittsburgh Press.

Frimigacci, D. 1974. Les deux niveaux à poterie du site du Vatcha. *Journal de la Société des Océanistes* 30:25–70.

———. 1975. La Préhistoire Neo-Calédonien. Thèse de 3e cycle, University of Paris I.

———. 1990. *Aux Temps de la Terre Noire: Ethno-Archéologie des îles Futuna et Alofi.* Paris: Peeters.

Frimigacci, D., and M. Hardy. 1997. *Des Archéologues, des Conquérants, et des Forts. Talietumu: Résidence Tongienne d'Uvea.* Versailles: Art Lys.

Froehlich, J. W. 1987. Fingerprints as phylogenetic markers in the Solomon Islands. In J. S. Friedlaender, ed., *The Solomon Islands Project: A Long-Term Study of Health, Human Biology, and Culture Change,* pp. 175–214. Oxford: Clarendon Press.

Frost, E. L. 1974. *Archaeological Excavations of Fortified Sites on Taveuni, Fiji.* Asian and Pacific Archaeology Series No. 6. Honolulu: Social Science Research Institute, University of Hawaii.

———. 1979. Fiji. In J. Jennings, ed., *The Prehistory of Polynesia,* pp. 61–81. Cambridge, Mass.: Harvard University Press.

Fujimura, K., and W. H. Alkire. 1984. Archaeological test excavations of Faraulep, Woleai, and Lamotrek in the Caroline Islands of Micronesia. In Y. H. Sinoto, ed., *Caroline Islands Archaeology,* pp. 66–130. Pacific Anthropological Records 35. Honolulu: Bernice P. Bishop Museum.

Fullagar, R. L. K., D. M. Price, and L. M. Head. 1996. Early human occupation of northern Australia: Archaeology and thermoluminescence dating of Jinmium rock-shelter, Northern Territory. *Antiquity* 70: 751–74.

Galipaud, J. C. 1988. La Poterie Préhistorique Neo-Calédonien et ses Implications dans l'Étude du Processus de Peuplement du Pacifique Occidental. Thèse de doctorat. University of Paris I.

———. 1990. The physico-chemical analysis of ancient pottery from New Caledonia. In M. Spriggs, ed., *Lapita Design, Form and Composition,* pp. 134–42. Occasional Papers in Prehistory No. 19. Canberra: Department of Prehistory, Australian National University.

———. 1992. Un ou plusieurs peuples potiers en Nouvelle-Calédonie? Analyse physico-chimique des poteries préhistoriques de Nouvelle-Calédonie. *Journal de la Société des Océanistes* 95:185–200.

———. 1995. A revision of the archaeological sequence of southern New Caledonia. *New Zealand Journal of Archaeology* 17:77–109.

———. 1996a. New Caledonia: Some recent archaeological perspectives. In J. Davidson, G. Irwin, F. Leach, A. Pawley, and D. Brown, eds., *Oceanic Culture History: Essays in Honour of Roger Green,* pp. 297–305. New Zealand Journal of Archaeology Special Publication. Dunedin: New Zealand Journal of Archaeology.

———. 1996b. Poteries et potiers de Vanuatu. In J. Bonnemaison, K. Huffman, and D. Tryon, eds., *Vanuatu—Océanie: Arts des Iles de Cendre et de Corail,* pp. 98–103. Paris: Editions de la Réunion des Musées Nationaux.

———. 1996c. Le rouge et le noir: La poterie Mangaasi et le peuplement des îles de Mélansie. In M. Julien, M. Orliac, and C. Orliac, eds., *Mémoire de Pierre, Mémoire d'Homme: Tradition et Archéologie en Océanie,* pp. 115–30. Paris: Publications de la Sorbonne.

Garanger, J. 1967. Archaeology and the Society Islands. In G. A. Highland, R. W. Force, A. Howard, M. Kelly, and Y. H. Sinoto, eds., *Polynesian Culture History: Essays in Honor of Kenneth P. Emory*, pp. 377–96. Special Publication No. 56. Honolulu: Bernice P. Bishop Museum.

———. 1972a. *Archéologie des Nouvelles-Hébrides*. Publication de la Société des Océanistes No. 30. Paris: Société des Océanistes.

———. 1972b. Mythes et archéologie en Océanie. *La Recherche* 21:233–42.

———. 1996. Tongoa, Mangaasi, et Eretoka: Histoires d'une préhistoire. In J. Bonnemaison, K. Huffman, and D. Tryon, eds., *Vanuatu—Océanie: Arts des Iles de Cendre et de Corail*, pp. 68–75. Paris: Editions de la Réunion des Musées Nationaux.

Geraghty, P. 1983. *The History of the Fijian Languages*. Oceanic Linguistics Publication No. 19. Honolulu: University of Hawaii Press.

———. 1994. Linguistic evidence for the Tongan empire. In T. Dutton and D. T. Tryon, eds., *Language Contact and Change in the Austronesian World*, pp. 233–49. New York: Mouton de Gruyter.

———. 1996. Pottery in Fiji: A preliminary survey of locations and terminology. In J. Davidson, G. Irwin, F. Leach, A. Pawley, and D. Brown, eds., *Oceanic Culture History: Essays in Honour of Roger Green*, pp. 421–31. New Zealand Journal of Archaeology Special Publication. Dunedin: New Zealand Journal of Archaeology.

Gifford, E. W. 1951. *Archaeological Excavations in Fiji*. Anthropological Records 13:189–288. Berkeley: University of California Press.

Gifford, E. W., and D. S. Gifford. 1959. *Archaeological Excavations on Yap*. Anthropological Records 18, Part 2. Berkeley: University of California Press.

Gifford, E. W., and D. Shutler, Jr. 1956. *Archaeological Excavations in New Caledonia*. Anthropological Records 18, Part 1. Berkeley: University of California Press.

Gillieson, D. S., and J. M. Mountain. 1983. Environmental history of Nombe rockshelter, Papua New Guinea Highlands. *Archaeology in Oceania* 18:53–62.

Gilliland, C. L. C. 1975. *The Stone Money of Yap*. Smithsonian Studies in History and Technology 23. Washington, D.C.: Smithsonian Institution.

Gladwin, T. 1970. *East Is a Big Bird: Navigation and Logic on Puluwat Atoll*. Cambridge, Mass.: Harvard University Press.

Goldman, I. 1970. *Ancient Polynesian Society*. Chicago: University of Chicago Press.

Golson, J. 1959. Culture change in prehistoric New Zealand. In J. D. Freeman and W. R. Geddes, eds., *Anthropology in the South Seas*, pp. 29–74. New Plymouth, New Zealand: Avery.

———. 1961. Report on New Zealand, Western Polynesia, New Caledonia, and Fiji. *Asian Perspectives* 5:166–80.

———. 1963. Rapport sur les fouilles effectuées à l'Île des Pins (Nouvelle-Calédonie) de Décembre 1959 à Février 1960. *Études Mélanésiennes N.S.* 14–17:11–24.

———. 1965. Thor Heyerdahl and the prehistory of Easter Island. *Oceania* 36:38–83.

———. 1971. Lapita Ware and Its transformations. In R. C. Green and M. Kelly, eds., *Studies in Oceanic Culture History*, Vol. 2, pp. 67–76. Pacific Anthropological Records 12. Honolulu: Bernice P. Bishop Museum.

———. 1972a. Both sides of the Wallace Line: New Guinea, Australia, Island Melanesia, and Asian prehistory. In N. Barnard, ed., *Early Chinese Art and Its Possible Influence in the Pacific Basin*, pp. 533–95. New York: Intercultural Arts Press.

———. 1972b. The Pacific islands and their prehistoric inhabitants. In R. G. Ward, ed., *Man in the Pacific Islands: Essays on Geographical Change in the Pacific Islands*, pp. 5–33. Oxford: Oxford University Press.

———. 1977. No room at the top: Agricultural intensification in the New Guinea Highlands. In J. Allen, J. Golson, and R. Jones, eds., *Sunda and Sahul: Prehistoric Studies in Southeast Asia, Melanesia and Australia*, pp. 601–38. London: Academic Press.

———. 1988. The origins and development of New Guinea agriculture. In D. Harris and G. Hillman, eds., *Foraging and Farming: The Evolution of Plant Exploitation*, pp. 678–87. London: Unwin Hyman.

———. 1990. Kuk and the development of agriculture

in New Guinea: Retrospection and introspection. In D. E. Yen and J. M. J. Mummery, eds., *Pacific Production Systems: Approaches to Economic Prehistory*, pp. 139–47. Occasional Papers in Prehistory No. 18. Canberra: Department of Prehistory, Australian National University.

———. 1991a. Bulmer Phase II: Early agriculture in the New Guinea Highlands. In A. Pawley, ed., *Man and a Half: Essays in Pacific Anthropology and Ethnobiology in Honour of Ralph Bulmer*, pp. 484–91. Auckland, New Zealand: Polynesian Society.

———. 1991b. Two sites at Lasigi, New Ireland. In J. Allen and C. Gosden, eds., *Report of the Lapita Homeland Project*, pp. 244–59. Canberra: Australian National University.

———. 1996a. Roger Green: Early and late encounters. In J. Davidson, G. Irwin, F. Leach, A. Pawley, and D. Brown, eds., *Oceanic Culture History: Essays in Honour of Roger Green*, pp. 307–17. New Zealand Journal of Archaeology Special Publication. Dunedin: New Zealand Journal of Archaeology.

———. 1996b. New Guinea: The making of a history. In M. Julien, M. Orliac, and C. Orliac, eds., *Mémoire de Pierre, Mémoire d'Homme: Tradition et Archéologie en Océanie*, pp. 153–82. Paris: Publications de la Sorbonne.

———. 1997. From horticulture to agriculture in the New Guinea Highlands: A case study of people and their environments. In P. V. Kirch and T. L. Hunt, eds., *Historical Ecology in the Pacific Islands: Prehistoric Environmental and Landscape Change*, pp. 39–50. New Haven, Conn.: Yale University Press.

Golson, J., and D. Gardner. 1990. Agriculture and sociopolitical organization in New Guinea Highlands prehistory. *Annual Review of Anthropology* 19: 395–417.

Gonzalez, L., J. A. van Tilburg, and P. C. Vargas. 1988. Easter Island statue type, part two: the moai as sociopolitical feature. In C. Cristino, P. Vargas, R. Izaurieta, and R. Budd, eds., *First International Congress, Easter Island & East Polynesia*, Vol. 1: *Archaeology*, pp. 150–63. Santiago: University of Chile.

Goodenough, W. H. 1957. Oceania and the problem of controls in the study of cultural and human evolution. *Journal of the Polynesian Society* 66:146–55.

———. 1986. Sky world and this world: The place of Kachaw in Micronesian cosmology. *American Anthropologist* 88:551–68.

———. 1997a. Proto-Kimbe: A new analysis. *Oceanic Linguistics* 36:247–311.

———. 1997b. Comment [on Terrell et al. 1997]. *Current Anthropology* 38:177–78.

Goodenough, W. H., and S. D. Thomas. 1987. Traditional navigation in the Western Pacific. *Expedition* 29:3–14.

Gorecki, P. P., and D. S. Gillieson, eds. 1989. *A Crack in the Spine: Prehistory and Ecology of the Jimi-Yuat Valley, Papua New Guinea*. Townsville, Australia: Division of Anthropology and Archaeology, James Cook University of North Queensland.

Gorecki, P., M. Mabin, and J. Campbell. 1991. Archaeology and geomorphology of the Vanimo Coast, Papua New Guinea: Preliminary results. *Archaeology in Oceania* 26:119–22.

Gosden, C. 1989. Prehistoric social landscapes of the Arawe Islands, West New Britain Province, Papua New Guinea. *Archaeology in Oceania* 24:45–58.

———. 1991a. Towards an understanding of the regional archaeological record from the Arawe Islands, West New Britain, Papua New Guinea. In J. Allen and C. Gosden, eds., *Report of the Lapita Homeland Project*, pp. 205–16. Occasional Papers in Prehistory No. 20. Canberra: Department of Prehistory, Australian National University.

———. 1991b. Learning about Lapita in the Bismarck Archipelago. In J. Allen and C. Gosden, eds., *Report of the Lapita Homeland Project*, pp. 260–68. Occasional Papers in Prehistory No. 20. Canberra: Department of Prehistory, Australian National University.

———. 1991c. Long-term trends in the colonisation of the Pacific: Putting Lapita in its place. In P. Bellwood, ed., *Indo-Pacific Prehistory 1990: Proceedings of the 14th Congress of the Indo-Pacific Prehistory Association*, pp. 333–38. Canberra: Indo-Pacific Prehistory Association.

———. 1992a. Production systems and the colonization of the Western Pacific. *World Archaeology* 24:55–69.

———. 1992b. Dynamic traditionalism: Lapita as a long term social structure. In J.-C. Galipaud, ed., *Poterie Lapita et Peuplement: Actes du Colloque LAPITA*, pp. 21–26. Noumea, New Caledonia: ORSTOM.

———. 1993. Understanding the settlement of Pacific islands in the Pleistocene. In M. A. Smith, M. Spriggs, and B. Fankhauser, eds., *Sahul in Review: Pleistocene Archaeology in Australia, New Guinea and Island Melanesia*, pp. 131–36. Occasional Papers in Prehistory No. 24. Canberra: Department of Prehistory, Australian National University.

———. 1995. Arboriculture and agriculture in coastal Papua New Guinea. *Antiquity* 69 (special number 265):807–17.

Gosden, C., J. Allen, W. Ambrose, D. Anson, J. Golson, R. Green, P. Kirch, I. Lilley, J. Specht, and M. Spriggs. 1989. Lapita sites of the Bismarck Archipelago. *Antiquity* 63:561–86.

Gosden, C., and N. Robertson. 1991. Models for Matenkupkum: Interpreting a late Pleistocene site from Southern New Ireland, Papua New Guinea. In J. Allen and C. Gosden, eds., *Report of the Lapita Homeland Project*, pp. 20–45. Occasional Papers in Prehistory No. 20. Canberra: Department of Prehistory, Australian National University.

Gosden, C., and J. Webb. 1994. The creation of a Papua New Guinean landscape: Archaeological and geomorphological evidence. *Journal of Field Archaeology* 21:29–51.

Gosden, C., J. Webb, B. Marshall, and G. R. Summerhayes. 1994. Lolmo Cave: A mid- to late Holocene site, the Arawe Islands, West New Britain Province, Papua New Guinea. *Asian Perspectives* 33:97–120.

Gould, S. J. 1987. Evolution and the triumph of homology, or why history matters. *American Scientist*, Jan.-Feb., pp. 60–69.

———. 1989. *Wonderful Life: The Burgess Shale and the Nature of History*. New York: W. W. Norton and Company.

Gräbner, F. 1905. Kulturkriese und Kulturschichten in Ozeanien. *Zeitschrift für Anthropologie, Ethnologie und Urgeschichte* 37:28–53, 84–90.

Graves, M. W. 1986a. Late prehistoric social complexity on Lelu: Alternatives to Cordy's model. *Journal of the Polynesian Society* 95:479–90.

———. 1986b. Organization and differentiation within late prehistoric ranked social units, Mariana Islands, Western Pacific. *Journal of Field Archaeology* 13:139–54.

———. 1991. Architectural and mortuary diversity in late prehistoric settlements at Tumon Bay, Guam. *Micronesica* 24:169–94.

Graves, M. W., and D. Addison. 1996. Models and methods for inferring the prehistoric colonisation of Hawai'i. In I. C. Glover and B. Bellwood, eds., *Indo-Pacific Prehistory: The Chiang Mai Papers*, Vol. 2, pp. 3–8. Canberra: Australian National University.

Graves, M. W., and C. Erkelens. 1991. Who's in control? Method and theory in Hawaiian archaeology. *Asian Perspectives* 30:1–18.

Green, R. C. 1961. Moorea archaeology: A preliminary report. *Man* 61:169–73.

———. 1963a. A suggested revision of the Fijian sequence. *Journal of the Polynesian Society* 72:235–53.

———. 1963b. *A Review of the Prehistoric Sequence of the Auckland Province*. New Zealand Archaeological Association Monograph 2. Auckland: New Zealand Archaeological Association.

———. 1966. Linguistic subgrouping within Polynesia: The implications for prehistoric settlement. *Journal of the Polynesian Society* 75:6–38.

———. 1967a. The immediate origins of the Polynesians. In G. A. Highland, R. W. Force, A. Howard, M. Kelly, and Y. H. Sinoto, eds., *Polynesian Culture History*, pp. 215–40. Honolulu: Bishop Museum Press.

———. 1967b. Settlement patterns: Four case studies from Polynesia. In W. G. Solheim II, ed., *Archaeology at the Eleventh Pacific Science Congress*, pp. 101–32. Asian and Pacific Archaeology Series No. 1. Honolulu: Social Science Research Institute, University of Hawaii.

———. 1968. West Polynesian prehistory. In I. Yawata and Y. H. Sinoto, eds., *Prehistoric Culture in Oceania*, pp. 99–110. Honolulu: Bishop Museum Press.

———. 1971. Evidence for the development of the early Polynesian adz kit. *New Zealand Archaeological Association Newsletter* 14:12–44.

———. 1974a. Sites with Lapita pottery: Importing and voyaging. *Mankind* 9:253–59.

———. 1974b. A review of portable artifacts from

Western Samoa. In R. C. Green and J. Davidson, eds., *Archaeology in Western Samoa*, Vol. 2, pp. 245–75. Auckland, New Zealand: Auckland Institute and Museum.

———. 1975. Adaptation and change in Maori culture. In G. Kuschel, ed., *Biogeography and Ecology in New Zealand*, pp. 591–641. The Hague: W. Junk.

———. 1976a. Lapita sites in the Santa Cruz group. In R. C. Green and M. M. Cresswell, eds., *Southeast Solomon Islands Cultural History: A Preliminary Survey*, pp. 245–65. Royal Society of New Zealand Bulletin 11. Wellington: Royal Society of New Zealand.

———. 1976b. A late prehistoric settlement in Star Harbour. In R. C. Green and M. Cresswell, eds., *Southeast Solomon Islands Cultural History: A Preliminary Survey*, pp. 133–47. Royal Society of New Zealand Bulletin 11. Wellington: Royal Society of New Zealand.

———. 1976c. A late prehistoric sequence from Su'ena Village, Uki. In R. C. Green and M. Cresswell, eds., *Southeast Solomon Islands Cultural History: A Preliminary Survey*, pp. 181–91. Royal Society of New Zealand Bulletin 11. Wellington: Royal Society of New Zealand.

———. 1976d. An introduction to the Southeast Solomons Culture History Programme. In R. C. Green and M. Cresswell, eds., *Southeast Solomon Islands Cultural History: A Preliminary Survey*, pp. 9–17. Royal Society of New Zealand Bulletin 11. Wellington: Royal Society of New Zealand.

———. 1978. *New Sites with Lapita Pottery and their Implications for an Understanding of the Settlement of the Western Pacific*. Working Papers in Anthropology No. 51. Auckland: Department of Anthropology, University of Auckland.

———. 1979a. Lapita. In J. Jennings, ed., *The Prehistory of Polynesia*, pp. 27–60. Cambridge, Mass.: Harvard University Press.

———. 1979b. Early Lapita art from Polynesia and island Melanesia: Continuities in ceramic, barkcloth, and tattoo decorations. In S. Mead, ed., *Exploring the Visual Art of Oceania*, pp. 13–31. Honolulu: University of Hawaii Press.

———. 1980. *Makaha before 1880 A.D.* Pacific Anthro-

pological Records 31. Honolulu: Bernice P. Bishop Museum.

———. 1981. Location of the Polynesian homeland: A continuing problem. In J. Hollyman and A. Pawley, eds., *Studies in Pacific Languages and Cultures*, pp. 133–58. Auckland: Linguistic Society of New Zealand.

———. 1986. Lapita fishing: The evidence of site SE-RF-2 from the main Reef Islands, Santa Cruz group, Solomons. In A. Anderson, ed., *Traditional Fishing in the Pacific*, pp. 19–35. Pacific Anthropological Records 37. Honolulu: Bernice P. Bishop Museum.

———. 1987. Obsidian results from the Lapita sites of the Reef/Santa Cruz Islands. In W. R. Ambrose and J. M. Mummery, eds., *Archaeometry: Further Australasian Studies*, pp. 239–49. Canberra: Australian National University.

———. 1988a. Those mysterious mounds are for the birds. *Newsletter of the New Zealand Archaeological Association* 31:153–58.

———. 1988b. Subgrouping of the Rapanui language of Easter Island in Polynesian and its implications for East Polynesian prehistory. In C. Cristino, P. Vargas, R. Izaurieta, and R. Budd, eds., *First International Congress, Easter Island & East Polynesia*, Vol. 1: *Archaeology*, pp. 37–58. Santiago: University of Chile.

———. 1990. Lapita design analysis: The Mead System and its use, a potted history. In M. Spriggs, ed., *Lapita Design, Form and Composition*, pp. 33–52. Occasional Papers in Prehistory No. 19. Canberra: Department of Prehistory, Australian National University.

———. 1991a. Near and Remote Oceania: Disestablishing "Melanesia" in culture history. In A. Pawley, ed., *Man and a Half: Essays in Pacific Anthropology and Ethnobiology in Honour of Ralph Bulmer*, pp. 491–502. Auckland, New Zealand: Polynesian Society.

———. 1991b. The Lapita Cultural Complex: Current evidence and proposed models. In P. Bellwood, ed., *Indo-Pacific Prehistory 1990: Proceedings of the 14th Congress of the Indo-Pacific Prehistory Association*, pp. 295–305. Canberra: Indo-Pacific Prehistory Association.

———. 1991c. A reappraisal of the dating for some Lapita sites in the Reef/Santa Cruz Group of the southeast Solomons. *Journal of the Polynesian Society* 100:197–208.

————. 1992. Definitions of the Lapita cultural complex and its non-ceramic component. In J.-C. Galipaud, ed., *Poterie Lapita et Peuplement: Actes du Colloque LAPITA*, pp. 7–20. Noumea, New Caledonia: ORSTOM.

————. 1993. Tropical Polynesian prehistory—Where are we now? In M. Spriggs, D. E. Yen, W. Ambrose, R. Jones, A. Thorne, and A. Andrews, eds., *A Community of Culture: The People and Prehistory of the Pacific*, pp. 218–38. Occasional Papers in Prehistory No. 21. Canberra: Department of Prehistory, Australian National University.

————. 1994. Archaeological problems with the use of linguistic evidence in the reconstruction of rank, status and social organization in ancestral Polynesian society. In A. K. Pawley and M. D. Ross, eds., *Austronesian Terminologies: Continuity and Change*, pp. 171–84. Pacific Linguistics C-127. Canberra: Australian National University.

————. 1995. Linguistic, biological, and cultural origins of the initial inhabitants of Remote Oceania. *New Zealand Journal of Archaeology* 17:5–27.

————. 1996a. Prehistoric transfers of portable items during the Lapita horizon in Remote Oceania: A review. In I. C. Glover and B. Bellwood, eds., *Indo-Pacific Prehistory: The Chiang Mai Papers*, Vol. 2, pp. 119–30. Canberra: Australian National University.

————. 1996b. Settlement patterns and complex society in the Windward Society islands: Retrospective commentary from the 'Opunohu Valley, Mo'orea. In M. Julien, M. Orliac, and C. Orliac, eds., *Mémoire de Pierre, Mémoire d'Homme: Tradition et Archéologie en Océanie*, pp. 209–28. Paris: Publications de la Sorbonne.

————. 1997. Linguistic, biological, and cultural origins of the initial inhabitants of Remote Oceania. *New Zealand Journal of Archaeology* 17:5–27.

————. 1998. Rapanui origins prior to European contact: The view from Eastern Polynesia. In P. V. Casanova, ed., *Easter Island and East Polynesian Prehistory*. Santiago: Instituto de Estudios Isla de Pascua, Universidad de Chile.

Green, R. C., and D. Anson. 1987. The Lapita site of Watom: New evidence from excavations in 1985. *Man and Culture in Oceania* 3:121–32.

————. 1991. The Reber-Rakival Lapita site on Watom. Implications of the 1985 excavations at the SAC and SDI localities. In J. Allen and C. Gosden, eds., *Report of the Lapita Homeland Project*, pp. 170–81. Occasional Papers in Prehistory No. 20. Canberra: Department of Prehistory, Australian National University.

Green, R. C., D. Anson, and J. Specht. 1989. The SAC burial ground, Watom Island, Papua New Guinea. *Records of the Australian Museum* 41:215–22.

Green, R. C., and J. R. Bird. 1989. Fergusson Island obsidian from the D'Entrecasteaux Group in a Lapita site of the Reef Santa Cruz Group. *New Zealand Journal of Archaeology* 11:87–99.

Green, R. C., and M. M. Cresswell, eds. 1976. *Southeast Solomon Islands Cultural History: A Preliminary Survey*. Royal Society of New Zealand Bulletin 11. Wellington: Royal Society of New Zealand.

Green, R. C., and J. Davidson, eds. 1969. *Archaeology in Western Samoa*, Vol. I. Bulletin of the Auckland Institute and Museum 6. Auckland, New Zealand: Auckland Institute and Museum.

————. 1974. *Archaeology in Western Samoa*, Vol. II. Bulletin of the Auckland Institute and Museum 7. Auckland, New Zealand: Auckland Institute and Museum.

Green, R. C., K. Green, R. Rappaport, A. Rappaport, and J. Davidson. 1967. *Archaeology on the Island of Mo'orea, French Polynesia*. Anthropological Papers of the American Museum of Natural History 51(2). New York: American Museum of Natural History.

Green, R. C., and P. V. Kirch. 1997. Lapita exchange systems and their Polynesian transformations: Seeking explanatory models. In M. I. Weisler, ed., *Prehistoric Long-Distance Interaction in Oceania: An Interdisciplinary Approach*, pp. 19–37. New Zealand Archaeological Association Monograph 21. Auckland: New Zealand Archaeological Association.

Green, R. C., and J. S. Mitchell. 1983. New Caledonian culture history: A review of the archaeological sequence. *New Zealand Journal of Archaeology* 5:19–68.

Green, R. C., and A. Pawley. 1998. Architectural forms and settlement patterns. In M. Ross, A. Pawley, and M. Osmond, eds., *The Lexicon of Proto Oceanic: The Culture and Environment of Ancestral Oceanic Society*, pp. 37–65. Pacific Linguistics C-152. Canberra: Australian National University.

Green, W., and J. F. Doershuk. 1998. Cultural resource management and American archaeology. *Journal of Archaeological Research* 6:121–68.

Gregory, H. E. 1921. Report of the director for 1920. *Occasional Papers of the Bernice P. Bishop Museum* 8(1):1–28.

[Gregory, H. E.], ed., 1921. *Proceedings of the First Pan-Pacific Scientific Conference.* Bernice P. Bishop Museum Special Publication 7. Honolulu: Bishop Museum Press.

Gressitt, J. L., ed. 1963. *Pacific Basin Biogeography.* Honolulu: Bishop Museum Press.

Grimble, A. 1933–34. *The Migrations of a Pandanus People.* Polynesian Society Memoir 12. Wellington, New Zealand: Polynesian Society.

Groube, L. M. 1964. Settlement Patterns in Prehistoric New Zealand. Unpublished M.A. thesis, University of Auckland.

———. 1965. *Settlement Patterns in New Zealand Prehistory.* Occasional Papers in Archaeology No. 1. Dunedin, New Zealand: University of Otago.

———. 1970. The origin and development of earthwork fortification in the Pacific. In R. C. Green and M. Kelly, eds., *Studies in Oceanic Culture History,* Vol. 1, pp. 133–64. Pacific Anthropological Records 11. Honolulu: Bishop Museum Press.

———. 1971. Tonga, Lapita pottery, and Polynesian origins. *Journal of the Polynesian Society* 80:278–316.

———. 1986. Waisted axes of Asia, Melanesia, and Australia. In G. K. Ward, ed., *Archaeology at ANZAAS Canberra,* pp. 168–77. Canberra: Department of Prehistory and Anthropology, Australian National University.

———. 1989. The taming of the rain forests: A model for late Pleistocene forest exploitation in New Guinea. In D. R. Harris and D. C. Hillman, eds., *Foraging and Farming: The Evolution of Plant Exploitation,* pp. 292–304. London: Unwin Hyman.

———. 1993a. Contradictions and malaria in Melanesian and Australian prehistory. In M. A. Smith, M. Spriggs, and B. Fankhauser, eds., *Sahul in Review: Pleistocene Archaeology in Australia, New Guinea and Island Melanesia,* pp. 164–86. Occasional Papers in Prehistory No. 24. Canberra: Department of Prehistory, Australian National University.

———. 1993b. "Dig up those moa bones, dig." Golson in New Zealand, 1954–1961. In M. Spriggs, D. E. Yen, W. Ambrose, R. Jones, A. Thorne, and A. Andrews, eds., *A Community of Culture: The People and Prehistory of the Pacific,* pp. 6–17. Occasional Papers in Prehistory No. 21. Canberra: Department of Prehistory, Australian National University.

Groube, L. M., J. Chappell, J. Muke, and D. Price. 1986. A 40,000 year-old human occupation site at Huon Peninsula, Papua New Guinea. *Nature* 324:453–55.

Guiart, J. 1963. *La Chefferie en Mélanésie du Sud.* Paris: Institut d'Ethnologie, Musée de l'Homme.

Gumerman, G. J., D. Snyder, and W. B. Masse. 1981. *An Archaeological Reconnaissance of the Palau Archipelago, Western Caroline Islands, Micronesia.* Research Paper 23. Carbondale: Southern Illinois University Center for Archaeological Investigations.

Haberle, S. 1993. Late Quaternary Environmental History of the Tari Basin, Papua New Guinea. Unpublished Ph.D. thesis, Australian National University (Canberra).

———. 1996. Paleoenvironmental change in the eastern highlands of Papua New Guinea. *Archaeology in Oceania* 31:1–11.

Haberle, S., G. Hope, and Y. DeFretes. 1991. Environmental change in the Bliem Valley, montane Irian Jaya, Republic of Indonesia. *Journal of Biogeography* 18:25–40.

Haddon, A. C., and J. Hornell. 1936–38. *Canoes of Oceania.* 3 vols. Special Publications 27–29. Honolulu: Bernice P. Bishop Museum.

Hage, P. In press. Reconstructing Proto-Oceanic society. *Current Anthropology.*

Hage, P., and F. Harary. 1991. *Exchange in Oceania: A Graph Theoretic Analysis.* Oxford: Clarendon Press.

———. 1996. *Island Networks: Communication, Kinship, and Classification Structures in Oceania.* Cambridge: Cambridge University Press.

Hagelberg, E. 1997. Ancient and modern mitochondrial DNA sequences and the colonization of the Pacific. *Electrophoresis* 18:1529–33.

Hale, H. 1846. *Ethnography and Philology.* United States Exploring Expedition, Vol. VI. Philadelphia: Sherman.

Hambruch, P. 1911. Die "sogenannten Ruinen" von Matolenim auf Ponape. *Deutsche Gesellschaft für Anthropologie, Ethnologie, und Urgeschichte* 42:128–31.

———. 1919. Die Ruinen von Lolo. In E. G. Sarfert, *Kusae*, Vol. I: *Allgemeiner Teil und Materielle Kultur*, pp. 261–96. In G. Thilenius, ed., *Ergebnisse der Südsee-Expedition, 1908–1910*, II, *Ethnographie: B, Mikronesien*, Vol. 4. Hamburg: L. Friederichsen, de Gruyter.

———. 1936. *Ponape*. In G. Thilenius, ed., *Ergebnisse der Südsee-Expedition, 1908–1910*, II, *Ethnographie: B, Mikronesien*, Vol. 7. Hamburg: L. Friederichsen, de Gruyter.

Handy, E. S. C. 1923. *The Native Culture in the Marquesas*. Bernice P. Bishop Museum Bulletin 9. Honolulu: Bernice P. Bishop Museum.

———. 1930a. The problem of Polynesian origins. *Bernice P. Bishop Museum Occasional Papers* 9:1–27.

———. 1930b. *History and Culture in the Society Islands*. Bernice P. Bishop Museum Bulletin 79. Honolulu: Bernice P. Bishop Museum.

Hanlon, D. 1988. *Upon a Stone Altar: A History of the Island of Pohnpei to 1890*. Honolulu: University of Hawaii Press.

Hanson, D. B., and M. Pietrusewsky, eds. 1997. *Prehistoric Skeletal Biology in Island Ecosystems: Current Status of Bioarchaeological Research in the Marianas Archipelago*. *American Journal of Physical Anthropology* 104(3; special issue):267–425.

Harding, T. G. 1967. *Voyagers of the Vitiaz Straits*. Seattle: University of Washington Press.

Harris, E. F., and H. L. Bailit. 1987. Odontometric comparisons among Solomon Islanders and other Oceanic peoples. In J. S. Friedlaender, ed., *The Solomon Islands Project: A Long-Term Study of Health, Human Biology, and Culture Change*, pp. 215–64. Oxford: Clarendon.

Harris, M. 1968. *The Rise of Anthropological Theory: A History of Theories of Culture*. New York: Thomas Y. Crowell.

Harry, H. W. 1966. Land snails of Ulithi Atoll, Caroline Islands: A study of snails accidentally distributed by man. *Pacific Science* 20:212–23.

Hassan, F. A. 1981. *Demographic Archaeology*. London: Academic Press.

Hather, J., and P. V. Kirch. 1991. Prehistoric sweet potato (*Ipomoea batatas*) from Mangaia Island, Central Polynesia. *Antiquity* 65:887–93.

Hedrick, J. D. 1971. Lapita-style pottery from Malo Island. *Journal of the Polynesian Society* 80:15–19.

Hendren, G. H. 1976. Recent settlement pattern changes on Ulawa, southeast Solomon Islands. In R. C. Green and M. Cresswell, eds., *Southeast Solomon Islands Cultural History: A Preliminary Survey*, pp. 149–59. Royal Society of New Zealand Bulletin 11. Wellington: Royal Society of New Zealand.

Herdrich, D. 1991. Towards an understanding of Samoan star mounds. *Journal of the Polynesian Society* 100:381–436.

Herle, A., and S. Rouse, eds. 1998. *Cambridge and the Torres Strait: Centenary Essays on the 1898 Anthropological Expedition*. Cambridge: Cambridge University Press.

Hertzberg, M., K. P. N. Mickleson, S. W. Serjeantson, J. F. Prior, and R. J. Trent. 1989. An Asian-specific 9-bp deletion of mitochondrial DNA is frequently found in Polynesians. *American Journal of Human Genetics* 44:504–10.

Heyerdahl, T. 1952. *American Indians in the Pacific: The Theory behind the Kon-Tiki Expedition*. London: Allen and Unwin.

Heyerdahl, T., and E. N. Ferdon, Jr., eds. 1961. *Reports of the Norwegian Archaeological Expedition to Easter Island and the East Pacific*, Vol. 1: *Archaeology of Easter Island*. Monographs of the School of American Research 24(1). Santa Fe, N.M.: School of American Research.

———. 1965. *Reports of the Norwegian Archaeological Expedition to Easter Island and the East Pacific*, Vol. 2: *Miscellaneous Papers*. Monographs of the School of American Research 24(2). Santa Fe, N.M.: School of American Research.

Hill, A. V. S., D. K. Bowden, R. J. Trent, D. R. Higgs, S. J. Oppenheimer, S. L. Thein, K. N. P. Mickleson, D. J. Weatherall, and J. B. Clegg. 1985. Melanesians and Polynesians share a unique α-thalassemia mutation. *American Journal of Human Genetics* 37:571–80.

Hill, A. V. S., and S. W. Serjeantson, eds. 1989. *The Colonization of the Pacific: A Genetic Trail*. Oxford: Clarendon Press.

Hiroa, T. R. (P. H. Buck). 1934. *Mangaian Society*. Bernice P. Bishop Museum Bulletin 122. Honolulu: Bernice P. Bishop Museum.

———. 1938a. *Vikings of the Sunrise*. New York: Frederick Stokes.

———. 1938b. *Ethnology of Mangareva*. Bernice P. Bishop Museum Bulletin 157. Honolulu: Bernice P. Bishop Museum.

———. 1944. *Arts and Crafts of the Cook Islands*. Bernice P. Bishop Museum Bulletin 179. Honolulu: Bernice P. Bishop Museum.

———. 1945. *An Introduction to Polynesian Anthropology*. Bernice P. Bishop Museum 187. Honolulu: Bernice P. Bishop Museum.

Hocart, A. M. 1922. The cult of the dead in Eddystone of the Solomons. *Journal of the Royal Anthropological Institute of Great Britain and Ireland* 52:71–112, 259–305.

———. 1929. *Lau Islands, Fiji*. Bernice P. Bishop Museum Bulletin 62. Honolulu: Bernice P. Bishop Museum.

Hoeningswald, H. 1960. *Language Change and Linguistic Reconstruction*. Chicago: University of Chicago Press.

———. 1973. The comparative method. In T. A. Sebeok, ed., *Current Trends in Linguistics III*, pp. 51–62. The Hague: Mouton.

Holdaway, R. N. 1996. Arrival of rats in New Zealand. *Nature* 384:225–26.

———. 1999. A spatio-temporal model for the invasion of the New Zealand archipelago by the Pacific rat *Rattus exulans*. *Journal of the Royal Society of New Zealand* 29:91–105.

Hommon, R. J. 1976. The Formation of Primitive States in Pre-Contact Hawaii. Unpublished Ph.D. dissertation, University of Arizona (Tucson).

———. 1986. Social evolution in ancient Hawai'i. In P. V. Kirch, ed., *Island Societies: Archaeological Approaches to Evolution and Transformation*, pp. 55–68. Cambridge: Cambridge University Press.

Hooper, R. 1994. Reconstructing Proto Polynesian fish names. In A. K. Pawley and M. D. Ross, eds., *Austronesian Terminologies: Continuity and Change*, pp. 185–230. Pacific Linguistics C-127. Canberra: Australian National University.

Hope, G. S., and J. Golson. 1995. Late Quaternary change in the mountains of New Guinea. *Antiquity* 69 (special number 265):818–30.

Hope, G., J. Golson, and J. Allen. 1983. Palaeoecology and prehistory in New Guinea. *Journal of Human Evolution* 12:37–60.

Hope, J., and G. Hope. 1976. Palaeoenvironments for man in New Guinea. In R. Kirk and A. Thorne, eds., *The Origin of the Australians*, pp. 28–54. Human Biology Series 6. Canberra: Australian Institute of Aboriginal Studies.

Hope, J., and M. Spriggs. 1982. A preliminary pollen sequence from Aneityum Island, Southern Vanuatu. *Bulletin of the Indo-Pacific Prehistory Association* 3:88–94.

Horridge, A. 1987. *Outrigger Canoes of Bali and Madura, Indonesia*. Special Publication 77. Honolulu: Bernice P. Bishop Museum.

Houghton, P. 1991. The early human biology of the Pacific. *Journal of the Polynesian Society* 100:167–96.

———. 1996. *People of the Great Ocean: Aspects of Human Biology of the Early Pacific*. Cambridge: Cambridge University Press.

Howard, A. 1967. Polynesian origins and migrations. In G. A. Highland, R. W. Force, A. Howard, M. Kelly, and Y. H. Sinoto, eds., *Polynesian Culture History*, pp. 45–101. Special Publication 56. Honolulu: Bishop Museum Press.

Howe, K. R. 1984. *Where the Waves Fall: A New South Seas History from First Settlement to Colonial Rule*. Sydney: George Allen and Unwin.

Howells, W. W. 1970. Anthropometric grouping analysis of Pacific peoples. *Archaeology and Physical Anthropology in Oceania* 5:192–217.

———. 1973. *The Pacific Islanders*. New York: Charles Scribner's Sons.

———. 1987. Introduction. In J. S. Friedlaender, ed., *The Solomon Islands Project: A Long-Term Study of Health, Human Biology, and Culture Change*, pp. 3–13. Oxford: Clarendon Press.

Hughes, I. 1977. *New Guinea Stone Age Trade: The Geography and Ecology of Traffic in the Interior*. Terra Australis 3. Canberra: Australian National University.

Hughes, P., G. Hope, M. Latham, and M. Brookfield. 1979. Prehistoric man-induced degradation of the Lakeba landscape: Evidence from two inland swamps. In H. Brookfield, ed., *Lakeba: Environmental Change,*

Population Dynamics, and Resource Use, pp. 93–110. Paris: UNESCO.

Hunt, T. L., and R. M. Holsen. 1991. An early radiocarbon chronology for the Hawaiian Islands: A preliminary analysis. *Asian Perspectives* 30:147–62.

Hunter-Anderson, R. L. 1983. *Yapese Settlement Patterns: An Ethnoarchaeological Approach.* Agana, Guam: Micronesian Area Research Center.

———. 1984. Recent observations on traditional Yapese settlement patterns. *New Zealand Journal of Archaeology* 6:95–106.

———. 1991. A review of traditional Micronesian high island horticulture in Belau, Yap, Chuuk, Pohnpei, and Kosrae. *Micronesica* 24:1–56.

Hunter-Anderson, R. L., ed. 1990. *Recent Advances in Micronesian Archaeology: Selected Papers from the Micronesian Archaeology Conference, September 9–12, 1987. Micronesica*, Supplement 2. Guam: University of Guam Press.

Hunter-Anderson, R. L., and B. M. Butler. 1995. *An Overview of Northern Marianas Prehistory.* Micronesian Archaeological Survey Report No. 31. Saipan: Division of Historic Preservation.

Hunter-Anderson, R. L., and Y. Zan. 1996. Demystifying the *sawei*, a traditional interisland exchange system. *Isla: A Journal of Micronesian Studies* 4:1–45.

Hutchinson, G. E. 1978. *An Introduction to Population Biology.* New Haven, Conn.: Yale University Press.

Intoh, M. 1984. Reconnaissance archaeological research on Ngulu Atoll in the Western Caroline Islands. *Asian Perspectives* 24:69–80.

———. 1986. Pigs in Micronesia: Introduction or reintroduction by the Europeans. *Man in Oceania* 2:1–26.

———. 1988. Changing Prehistoric Yapese Pottery Technology: A Case Study of Adaptive Transformation. Unpublished Ph.D. thesis, University of Otago.

———. 1990. Ceramic environment and technology: A case study in the Yap Islands in Micronesia. *Man in Oceania* 6:35–52.

———. 1991. *Archaeological Research on Fais Island: Preliminary Report.* Prepared for Historic Preservation Office, Yap State. Hokkaido, Japan: Tokai University.

———. 1992. Pottery traditions in Micronesia. In J.-C. Galipaud, ed., *Poterie Lapita et Peuplement*, pp. 67–82. Noumea, New Caledonia: ORSTOM.

———. 1992. Why were pots imported to Ngulu Atoll? A consideration of subsistence strategies. *Journal of the Polynesian Society* 101:159–68.

———. 1996. Multi-regional contacts of prehistoric Fais islanders of Micronesia. In I. C. Glover and B. Bellwood, eds., *Indo-Pacific Prehistory: The Chiang Mai Papers*, Vol. 2, pp. 111–18. Canberra: Australian National University.

———. 1997. Human dispersals into Micronesia. *Anthropological Science* 105:15–28.

Intoh, M., and F. Leach. 1985. *Archaeological Investigations in the Yap Islands, Micronesia: First Millennium B.C. to the Present Day.* B.A.R. International Series 277. Oxford: British Archaeological Reports.

Irwin, G. 1972. An Archaeological Survey in the Shortland Islands, B.S.I.P. Unpublished M.A. thesis, University of Auckland.

———. 1974. The emergence of a central place in coastal Papuan prehistory: A theoretical approach. *Mankind* 9:268–72.

———. 1978a. The development of Mailu as a specialized trading and manufacturing centre in Papuan prehistory: The causes and the implications. *Mankind* 11:406–15.

———. 1978b. Pots and entrepots: A study of settlement, trade and the development of economic specialization in Papuan prehistory. *World Archaeology* 9:299–319.

———. 1981. How Lapita lost its pots: The question of continuity in the colonisation of Oceania. *Journal of the Polynesian Society* 90:481–94.

———. 1983. Chieftainship, kula, and trade in Massim prehistory. In J. W. Leach and E. Leach, eds., *The Kula: New Perspectives on Massim Exchange*, pp. 29–72. Cambridge: Cambridge University Press.

———. 1985a. *The Emergence of Mailu.* Terra Australis 10. Canberra: Australian National University.

———. 1985b. *Land, Pa and Polity.* New Zealand Archaeological Association Monograph 15. N.p.: New Zealand Archaeological Association.

———. 1989. Against, across and down the wind: The

first exploration of the Pacific Islands. *Journal of the Polynesian Society* 98:167–206.

———. 1990. Human colonisation and change in the Remote Pacific. *Current Anthropology* 31: 90–94.

———. 1991. Pleistocene voyaging and the settlement of Greater Australia and its Near Oceanic neighbors. In J. Allen and C. Gosden, eds., *Report of the Lapita Homeland Project*, pp. 9–19. Occasional Papers in Prehistory No. 20. Canberra: Department of Prehistory, Australian National University.

———. 1992. *The Prehistoric Exploration and Colonisation of the Pacific*. Cambridge: Cambridge University Press.

———. 1993. Voyaging. In M. A. Smith, M. Spriggs, and B. Fankhauser, eds., *Sahul in Review: Pleistocene Archaeology in Australia, New Guinea and Island Melanesia*, pp. 73–87. Occasional Papers in Prehistory No. 24. Canberra: Department of Prehistory, Australian National University.

———. 1998. The colonisation of the Pacific: Chronological, navigational and social issues. *Journal of the Polynesian Society* 107:111–44.

Irwin, G., and S. Holdaway. 1996. Colonisation, trade and exchange: From Papua to Lapita. In J. Davidson, G. Irwin, F. Leach, A. Pawley, and D. Brown, eds., *Oceanic Culture History: Essays in Honour of Roger Green*, pp. 225–35. New Zealand Journal of Archaeology Special Publication. Dunedin: New Zealand Journal of Archaeology.

Jackson, F. H. 1986. On determining the external relationships of the Micronesian languages. In P. Geraghty, L. Carrington, and S. A. Wurm, eds., *FOCAL II: Papers from the Fourth International Conference on Austronesian Linguistics*, pp. 201–38. Pacific Linguistics C-94. Canberra: Australian National University.

James, H. F. 1995. Prehistoric extinctions and ecological changes on oceanic islands. *Ecological Studies* 115: 87–102.

James, H. F., T. Stafford, W. D. Steadman, S. Olson, P. Martin, A. Jull, and P. McCoy. 1987. Radiocarbon dates on bones of extinct birds from Hawaii. *Proceedings of the National Academy of Sciences, USA* 84: 2350–54.

Jennings, J., ed. 1979. *The Prehistory of Polynesia*. Cambridge, Mass.: Harvard University Press.

Jennings, J., and R. Holmer, eds. 1980. *Archaeological Excavations in Western Samoa*. Pacific Anthropological Records 32. Honolulu: Bernice P. Bishop Museum.

Jennings, J., R. Holmer, J. Janetski, and H. Smith. 1976. *Excavations on 'Upolu, Western Samoa*. Pacific Anthropological Records 25. Honolulu: Bernice P. Bishop Museum.

Jones, K. L. 1986. Polynesian gardening and settlement in two river catchments of the eastern North Island. *New Zealand Journal of Archaeology* 8:5–32.

———. 1989. Settlement chronology, pa and environment of Tolaga Bay, East Coast, North Island, New Zealand. In D. G. Sutton, ed., *Saying So Doesn't Make it So: Papers in Honour of B. Foss Leach*, pp. 233–57. New Zealand Archaeological Association Monograph 17. Auckland: New Zealand Archaeological Association.

———. 1991. Maori settlement and horticulture on the Rangitaiki Plains, Bay of Plenty, New Zealand. *New Zealand Journal of Archaeology* 13:143–75.

Jones, K. L., and R. G. Law. 1987. Prehistoric population estimates for the Tolaga Bay vicinity, East Coast, North Island, New Zealand. *New Zealand Journal of Archaeology* 9:81–114.

Kaeppler, A. 1978. Exchange patterns in goods and spouses: Fiji, Tonga, and Samoa. *Mankind* 11:246–52.

Kamakau, S. 1961. *Ruling Chiefs of Hawaii*. Honolulu: Kamehameha Schools Press.

Kasarherou, E. 1989. La Calédonie pré-coloniale: Populations et Aires Linguistiques. Chapter 14, *Atlas de la Nouvelle-Calédonie*. Noumea, New Caledonia: Editions du Cagou.

Kaschko, M. W. 1976. An archaeological consideration of the ethnographic fishhook set on Uki Island, southeast Solomon Islands. In R. C. Green and M. Cresswell, eds., *Southeast Solomon Islands Cultural History: A Preliminary Survey*, pp. 193–201. Royal Society of New Zealand Bulletin 11. Wellington: Royal Society of New Zealand.

Katayama, K. 1996. Polynesians, the hypermorphic Asiatics: A scenario on prehistoric Mongoloid dispersals into Oceania. *Anthropological Science* 104:15–30.

Kay, R. M. A. 1984. Analysis of Archaeological Material from Naigani. Unpublished M.A. thesis, University of Auckland.

Kellum-Ottino, M. 1971. *Archéologie d'une Vallée des Iles Marquises.* Publications de la Société des Océanistes 26. Paris: Société des Océanistes.

Kelly, K. M. 1996. The end of the trail: The genetic basis for deriving the Polynesian peoples from Austronesian speaking paleopopulations of Melanesian Near Oceania. In J. Davidson, G. Irwin, F. Leach, A. Pawley, and D. Brown, eds., *Oceanic Culture History: Essays in Honour of Roger Green,* pp. 355–64. New Zealand Journal of Archaeology Special Publication. Dunedin: New Zealand Journal of Archaeology.

Kelly, R. C. 1988. Etoro suidology: A reassessment of the pig's role in the prehistory and comparative ethnology of New Guinea. In J. G. Weiner, ed., *Mountain Papuans: Historical and Comparative Perspectives from New Guinea Fringe Highlands Societies,* pp. 116–86. Ann Arbor: University of Michigan Press.

Kennedy, J. 1983. On the prehistory of western Melanesia: The significance of new data from the Admiralty Islands. *Australian Archaeology* 16:115–22.

———. 1997. On social life in the Pacific. *Current Anthropology* 38:659–60.

Kikuchi, W. K. 1976. Prehistoric Hawaiian fishponds. *Science* 193:295–99.

King, T. F., and P. Parker. 1984. *Pisekin Noomw Noon Tonaachaw: Archaeology in the Tonaachaw Historic District, Moen Island.* Occasional Paper 3. Carbondale: Southern Illinois Center for Archaeological Investigations.

Kirch, P. V. 1973. Prehistoric subsistence patterns in the northern Marquesas Islands, French Polynesia. *Archaeological and Physical Anthropology in Oceania* 8: 24–40.

———. 1977a. Valley agricultural systems in prehistoric Hawaii: An archaeological consideration. *Asian Perspectives* 20:246–80.

———. 1977b. Archaeological Reconnaissance of the Proposed Yap Airport Alternate Sites, Yap District, Western Caroline Islands. Report prepared for Federal Aviation Administration. Honolulu: Bernice P. Bishop Museum.

———. 1978. The Lapitoid period in West Polynesia: Excavations and survey in Niuatoputapu, Tonga. *Journal of Field Archaeology* 5:1–13.

———. 1979a. Subsistence and ecology. In J. Jennings, ed., *The Prehistory of Polynesia,* pp. 286–307. Cambridge, Mass.: Harvard University Press.

———. 1979b. *Marine Exploitation in Prehistoric Hawai'i: Archaeological Excavations at Kalahuipua'a, Hawai'i Island.* Pacific Anthropological Records 29. Honolulu: Bernice P. Bishop Museum.

———. 1980. Polynesian prehistory: Cultural adaptation in island ecosystems. *American Scientist* 68:39–48.

———. 1981. Lapitoid settlements of Futuna and Alofi, Western Polynesia. *Archaeology in Oceania* 16:127–43.

———. 1982a. Advances in Polynesian prehistory: Three decades in review. *Advances in World Archaeology* 1:51–87.

———. 1982b. The impact of the prehistoric Polynesians on the Hawaiian ecosystem. *Pacific Science* 36: 1–14.

———. 1982c. Mangaasi-style ceramics from Tikopia and Vanikoro and their implications for east Melanesian prehistory. *Bulletin of the Indo-Pacific Prehistory Association* 3:67–76.

———. 1982d. A revision of the Anuta sequence. *Journal of the Polynesian Society* 91:245–54.

———. 1983a. An archaeological exploration of Vanikoro, Santa Cruz Islands, eastern Melanesia. *New Zealand Journal of Archaeology* 5:69–113.

———. 1983b. Man's role in modifying tropical and subtropical Polynesian ecosystems. *Archaeology in Oceania* 18:26–31.

———. 1984a. *The Evolution of the Polynesian Chiefdoms.* Cambridge: Cambridge University Press.

———. 1984b. The Polynesian outliers: Continuity, change, and replacement. *Journal of Pacific History* 19: 224–38.

———. 1985a. *Feathered Gods and Fishhooks: An Introduction to Hawaiian Archaeology and Prehistory.* Honolulu: University of Hawaii Press.

———. 1985b. On the genetic and cultural relationships of certain Polynesian Outlier populations. *American Journal of Physical Anthropology* 66:381–82.

———. 1986a. Rethinking East Polynesian prehistory. *Journal of the Polynesian Society* 95:9–40.

———. 1986b. Exchange systems and inter-island contact in the transformation of an island society: The

Tikopia case. In P. V. Kirch, ed., *Island Societies: Archaeological Approaches to Evolution and Transformation*, pp. 33–41. Cambridge: Cambridge University Press.

———. 1987. Lapita and Oceanic cultural origins: Excavations in the Mussau Islands, Bismarck Archipelago, 1985. *Journal of Field Archaeology* 14:163–80.

———. 1988a. *Niuatoputapu: The Prehistory of a Polynesian Chiefdom.* Thomas Burke Memorial Washington State Museum Monograph No. 5. Seattle: Burke Museum.

———. 1988b. The Talepakemalai site and Oceanic prehistory. *National Geographic Research* 4:328–42.

———. 1988c. Long-distance exchange and island colonisation: The Lapita case. *Norwegian Archaeological Review* 21:103–17.

———. 1988d. A brief history of Lapita archaeology. In P. V. Kirch and T. L. Hunt, eds., *Archaeology of the Lapita Cultural Complex: A Critical Review*, pp. 1–8. Thomas Burke Memorial Washington State Museum Research Report No. 5. Seattle: Burke Museum.

———. 1988e. The transformation of Polynesian societies: Archaeological issues. In C. Cristino, P. Vargas, R. Izaurieta, and R. Budd, eds., *First International Congress, Easter Island & East Polynesia*, Vol. 1: *Archaeology*, pp. 1–12. Santiago: University of Chile.

———. 1988f. Polynesia's mystery islands. *Archaeology* 41:26–31.

———. 1988g. Circumscription and sociopolitical evolution in Polynesia. *American Behavioral Scientist* 31:416–27.

———. 1989a. Prehistory. In A. Howard and R. Borofsky, eds., *Developments in Polynesian Ethnology*, pp.13–46. Honolulu: University of Hawaii Press.

———. 1989b. Second millennium B.C. arboriculture in Melanesia: Archaeological evidence from the Mussau Islands. *Economic Botany* 43:225–40.

———. 1990a. Specialization and exchange in the Lapita complex of Oceania (1600–500 B.C.). *Asian Perspectives* 29:117–33.

———. 1990b. La colonisation du Pacifique. *La Recherche* 21:1226–35.

———. 1990c. Regional variation and local style: A neglected dimension in Hawaiian prehistory. *Pacific Studies* 13:41–54.

———. 1990d. The evolution of socio-political com-plexity in prehistoric Hawaii: An assessment of the archaeological evidence. *Journal of World Prehistory* 4:311–45.

———. 1990e. Production, intensification, and the early Hawaiian Kingdom. In D. E. Yen and J. M. J. Mummery, eds., *Pacific Production Systems: Approaches to Economic Prehistory*, pp. 190–210. Occasional Papers in Prehistory No. 18. Canberra: Department of Prehistory, Australian National University.

———. 1990f. Monumental architecture and power in Polynesian chiefdoms: A comparison of Tonga and Hawaii. *World Archaeology* 22:206–22.

———. 1991a. Polynesian agricultural systems. In P. A. Cox and S. A. Banack, eds., *Islands, Plants, and Polynesians: An Introduction to Polynesian Ethnobotany*, pp. 113–34. Portland: Dioscorides Press.

———. 1991b. Chiefship and competitive involution: The Marquesas Islands of eastern Polynesia. In T. Earle, ed., *Chiefdoms: Power, Economy and Ideology*, pp. 119–45. Cambridge: Cambridge University Press.

———. 1991c. Prehistoric exchange in Western Melanesia. *Annual Review of Anthropology* 20:141–65.

———. 1992. Kenneth Pike Emory, 1897–1992. *Asian Perspectives* 31:1–8.

———. 1994. *The Wet and the Dry: Irrigation and Agricultural Intensification in Polynesia.* Chicago: University of Chicago Press.

———. 1995. The Lapita culture of western Melanesia in the context of Austronesian origins and dispersals. In P. Li, C. Tsang, Y. Huang, D. Ho, and C. Tseng, eds., *Austronesian Studies Relating to Taiwan*, pp. 255–94. Taipei: Academia Sinica.

———. 1996a. Lapita and its aftermath: Austronesian settlement of Oceania. In W. H. Goodenough, ed., *Prehistoric Settlement of the Pacific*, pp. 57–70. *Transactions of the American Philosophical Society* 86(5).

———. 1996b. Late Holocene human-induced modifications to a central Polynesian island ecosystem. *Proceedings of the National Academy of Sciences, USA* 93:5296–5300.

———. 1997a. *The Lapita Peoples: Ancestors of the Oceanic World.* Oxford: Blackwell.

———. 1997b. Introduction: The environmental history of Oceanic islands. In P. V. Kirch and T. L.

Hunt, eds., *Historical Ecology in the Pacific Islands: Prehistoric Environmental and Landscape Change*, pp. 1–21. New Haven, Conn.: Yale University Press.

————. 1997c. Changing landscapes and sociopolitical evolution in Mangaia, Central Polynesia. In P. V. Kirch and T. L. Hunt, eds., *Historical Ecology in the Pacific Islands: Prehistoric Environmental and Landscape Change*, pp. 147–65. New Haven, Conn.: Yale University Press.

————. 1997d. Microcosmic histories: Island perspectives on "global" change. *American Anthropologist* 99: 30–42.

————. 1997e. Comment [on Terrell et al. 1997]. *Current Anthropology* 38:181–82.

————. 1997f. New Caledonia and Melanesian prehistory: Resolving the enigmas. *Asian Perspectives* 36: 232–44.

————. 1997g. Le voyage du *Kon-Tiki* et son impact sur l'archéologie Polynésienne. *Bulletin de la Société des Études Océaniennes* 275:53–59.

————. 1999. Hawaiian archaeology: Past, present, and future. *Hawaiian Archaeology* 7:60–73.

Kirch, P. V., ed. 1986. *Island Societies: Archaeological Approaches to Evolution and Transformation*. Cambridge: Cambridge University Press.

————. 1997. *Na Mea Kahiko O Kahikinui: Studies in the Archaeology of Kahikinui, Maui*. Oceanic Archaeology Laboratory, Special Publication No. 1. Berkeley: Archaeological Research Facility, University of California.

————. Forthcoming. *Lapita and Its Transformations in Near Oceania: Archaeological Investigations in the Mussau Islands, Papua New Guinea, 1985–88*. Archaeological Research Facility Contribution. Berkeley: University of California.

Kirch, P. V., W. R. Dickinson, and T. L. Hunt. 1988. Polynesian plainware sherds from Hivaoa and their implications for early Marquesan prehistory. *New Zealand Journal of Archaeology* 10:101–8.

Kirch, P. V., and T. S. Dye. 1979. Ethnoarchaeology and the development of Polynesian fishing strategies. *Journal of the Polynesian Society* 88:53–76.

Kirch, P. V., and J. Ellison. 1994. Palaeoenvironmental evidence for human colonization of remote Oceanic islands. *Antiquity* 68:310–21.

Kirch, P. V., J. Flenley, D. Steadman, F. Lamont, and S. Dawson. 1992. Ancient environmental degradation. *National Geographic Research and Exploration* 8: 166–79.

Kirch, P. V., and R. C. Green. 1987. History, phylogeny, and evolution in Polynesia. *Current Anthropology* 28: 431–56.

————. In press. *Hawaiki: Ancestral Polynesia. An Essay in Historical Anthropology*. Cambridge: Cambridge University Press.

Kirch, P. V., and T. L. Hunt. 1988. Radiocarbon dates from the Mussau Islands and the Lapita colonization of the southwestern Pacific. *Radiocarbon* 30:161–69.

Kirch, P. V., and T. L. Hunt, eds. 1988. *Archaeology of the Lapita Cultural Complex: A Critical Review*. Thomas Burke Memorial Washington State Museum Research Report No. 5. Seattle: Burke Museum.

————. 1993. *The To'aga Site: Three Millennia of Polynesian Occupation in the Manu'a Islands, American Samoa*. Archaeological Research Facility Contribution No. 51. Berkeley: University of California.

————. 1997. *Historical Ecology in the Pacific Islands*. New Haven, Conn.: Yale University Press.

Kirch, P. V., T. L. Hunt, L. Nagaoka, and J. Tyler. 1990. An Ancestral Polynesian occupation site at To'aga, Ofu Island, American Samoa. *Archaeology in Oceania* 25:1–15.

Kirch, P. V., T. L. Hunt, M. Weisler, V. Butler, and M. S. Allen. 1991. Mussau Islands prehistory: Results of the 1985–86 excavations. In J. Allen and C. Gosden, eds., *Report of the Lapita Homeland Project*, pp. 144–63. Occasional Papers in Prehistory No. 20. Canberra: Department of Prehistory, Australian National University.

Kirch, P. V., and M. Kelly, eds. 1975. *Prehistory and Ecology in a Windward Hawaiian Valley: Halawa Valley, Molokai*. Pacific Anthropological Records 24. Honolulu: Bernice P. Bishop Museum.

Kirch, P. V., and D. Lepofsky. 1993. Polynesian irrigation: Archaeological and linguistic evidence for origins and development. *Asian Perspectives* 32:183–204.

Kirch, P. V., and P. H. Rosendahl. 1973. Archaeological investigations of Anuta. In D. E. Yen and J. Gordon, eds., *Anuta: A Polynesian Outlier in the Solomon Islands*, pp. 25–108. Pacific Anthropological Records 21. Honolulu: Bernice P. Bishop Museum.

————. 1976. Early Anutan settlement and the position of Anuta in the prehistory of the southwest Pacific. In R. C. Green and M. Cresswell, eds., *Southeast Solomon Islands Cultural History: A Preliminary Survey*, pp. 225–44. Royal Society of New Zealand Bulletin 11. Wellington: Royal Society of New Zealand.

Kirch, P. V., and M. Sahlins. 1992. *Anahulu: The Anthropology of History in the Kingdom of Hawaii.* 2 vols. Chicago: University of Chicago Press.

Kirch, P. V., D. W. Steadman, V. L. Butler, J. Hather, and M. I. Weisler. 1995. Prehistory and human ecology in Eastern Polynesia: Excavations at Tangatatau rockshelter, Mangaia, Cook Islands. *Archaeology in Oceania* 30:47–65.

Kirch, P. V., and M. I. Weisler. 1994. Archaeology in the Pacific Islands: An appraisal of recent research. *Journal of Archaeological Research* 2:285–328.

Kirch, P. V., M. I. Weisler, and E. Casella, eds. 1997. *Towards a Prehistory of the Koné Region, New Caledonia: A Reanalysis of the Pioneering Archaeological Excavations of E. W. Gifford.* Kroeber Anthropological Society Papers 82.

Kirch, P. V., and D. E. Yen. 1982. *Tikopia: The Prehistory and Ecology of a Polynesian Outlier.* Bernice P. Bishop Museum Bulletin 238. Honolulu: Bernice P. Bishop Museum.

Knudson, K. E. 1990. Social complexity on Truk and in the Marianas: Lack of correspondence between anthropological models and historical evidence. In R. L. Hunter-Anderson, ed., *Recent Advances in Micronesian Archaeology: Selected Papers from the Micronesian Archaeology Conference, September 9–12, 1987. Micronesica,* Supplement 2, pp. 117–124.

Kolb, M. J. 1991. Social Power, Chiefly Authority, and Ceremonial Architecture in an Island Polity, Maui, Hawaii. Unpublished Ph.D. dissertation, University of California (Los Angeles).

————. 1992. Diachronic design changes in *heiau* temple architecture on the island of Maui, Hawai'i. *Asian Perspectives* 31:9–38.

————. 1994. Monumentality and the rise of religious authority in precontact Hawai'i. *Current Anthropology* 35:521–48.

————. 1999. Monumental grandeur and political efflorescence in pre-contact Hawai'i: Excavations at Pi'ilanihale Heiau, Maui. *Archaeology in Oceania* 34: 71–82.

Krauss, B. 1988. *Keneti: South Seas Adventures of Kenneth Emory.* Honolulu: University of Hawaii Press.

Kubary, J. S. 1874. Die Ruinen von Nanmatal auf der Insel Ponope (Ascension), nach J. Kubary's brieflichen Mittheilungen. *Journal des Museums Godeffroy* 3: 123–31.

Kurashina, H., and R. N. Clayshulte. 1983. Site formation processes and cultural sequence at Tarague, Guam. *Bulletin of the Indo-Pacific Prehistory Association* 4:114–22.

Kurashina, H., D. Moore, O. Kataoka, R. Clayshulte, and E. Ray. 1984. Prehistoric and protohistoric cultural occurrences at Tarague, Guam. *Asian Perspectives* 24:57–68.

Labby, D. 1976. *The Demystification of Yap: Dialectics of Culture on a Micronesian Island.* Chicago: University of Chicago Press.

Ladefoged, T. N. 1992. Intergroup Aggression and Political Integration in Traditional Rotuman Society. Unpublished Ph.D. dissertation, University of Hawaii (Manoa).

————. 1998. Spatial similarities and change in Hawaiian architecture: The expression of ritual offering and *kapu* in *luakini heiau*, residential complexes, and houses. *Asian Perspectives* 37:59–73.

Ladefoged, T. N., M. W. Graves, and R. P. Jennings. 1996. Dryland agricultural expansion and intensification in Kohala, Hawai'i Island. *Antiquity* 70:861–80.

Lauer, P. 1970. Amphlett Islands' pottery trade and the kula. *Mankind* 7:165–76.

————. 1971. Changing patterns of pottery trade to the Trobriand Islands. *World Archaeology* 3:197–209.

Leach, B. F. 1981. The prehistory of the southern Wairarapa. *Journal of the Royal Society of New Zealand* 11:11–33.

Leach, B. F., and J. M. Davidson. 1988. The quest for the rainbow runner: Prehistoric fishing on Kapinga-marangi and Nukuoro Atolls, Micronesia. *Micronesica* 21:1–22.

Leach, B. F., and H. Leach, eds. 1979. *Prehistoric Man in Palliser Bay.* National Museum of New Zealand Bulletin 21. Wellington: National Museum of New Zealand.

Leach, B. F., and G. K. Ward. 1981. *Archaeology on Kapingamarangi Atoll, A Polynesian Outlier in the Eastern Caroline Islands.* Privately published.

Leach, H. 1982. Cooking without pots: Aspects of prehistoric and traditional Polynesian cooking. *New Zealand Journal of Archaeology* 4:149–56.

———. 1984. *1,000 Years of Gardening in New Zealand.* Wellington, New Zealand: Reed.

Leach, H., and R. C. Green. 1989. New information for the Ferry Berth Site, Mulifanua, Western Samoa. *Journal of the Polynesian Society* 98:319–30.

Leach, H. M., and D. C. Witter. 1987. Tataga-Matau "rediscovered." *New Zealand Journal of Archaeology* 9: 33–54.

———. 1990. Further investigations at the Tataga-matau site, American Samoa. *New Zealand Journal of Archaeology* 12:51–83.

Leach, J. W., and E. Leach. 1983. *The Kula: New Perspectives on Massim Exchange.* Cambridge: Cambridge University Press.

Leavesley, M., and J. Allen. 1998. Dates, disturbance and artefact distributions: Another analysis of Buang Merabak, a Pleistocene site on New Ireland, Papua New Guinea. *Archaeology in Oceania* 33:63–82.

Lebot, V., and J. Levesque. 1989. *The Origin and Distribution of Kava* (Piper methysticum *Forst. f., Piperaceae): A Phytochemical Approach.* Allertonia 5(2). Lawai, Hawaii: National Tropical Botanical Garden.

Ledyard, J. 1963. *John Ledyard's Journal of Captain Cook's Last Voyage.* Corvallis: Oregon State University Press.

Lee, G. 1992. *The Rock Art of Easter Island: Symbols of Power, Prayers to the Gods.* Monumenta Archaeologica 17. Los Angeles: Institute of Archaeology, University of California.

Lee, G., and E. Stasack. 1999. *Spirit of Place: Petroglyphs of Hawai'i.* Los Osos, Calif.: Easter Island Foundation.

Leenhardt, M. 1937. *Gens de la Grande Terre,* 9th ed. Paris: Gallimard.

Lepofsky, D. 1988. The environmental context of Lapita settlement locations. In P. V. Kirch and T. L. Hunt, eds., *Archeology of the Lapita Cultural Complex: A Critical Review,* pp. 33–48. Thomas Burke Memorial Washington State Museum Research Report No. 5. Seattle: Burke Museum.

———. 1994. Prehistoric Agricultural Intensification in the Society Islands, French Polynesia. Unpublished Ph.D. dissertation, University of California (Berkeley).

———. 1995. A radiocarbon chronology for prehistoric agriculture in the Society Islands, French Polynesia. *Radiocarbon* 37:917–30.

Lepofsky, D., H. C. Harries, and M. Kellum. 1992. Early coconuts on Mo'orea Island, French Polynesia. *Journal of the Polynesian Society* 101:299–308.

Lepofsky, D., P. V. Kirch, and K. Lertzman. 1996. Stratigraphic and paleobotanical evidence for prehistoric human-induced environmental disturbance on Mo'orea, French Polynesia. *Pacific Science* 50:253–73.

———. 1998. Metric analyses of prehistoric morphological change in cultivated fruits and nuts: An example from Island Melanesia. *Journal of Archaeologial Science* 25:1001–14.

Levison, M., R. Ward, and J. Webb. 1973. *The Settlement of Polynesia: A Computer Simulation.* Minneapolis: University of Minnesota Press.

Lévi-Strauss, C. 1982. *The Way of the Masks.* Translated by Sylvia Modelski. Seattle: University of Washington Press.

Lewthwaite, G. R. 1950. The population of Aotearoa: Its number and distribution. *New Zealand Geographer* 6:35–52.

Li, K. C. 1983. *Report of Archaeological Investigations in the O-Luan-Pi Park at the Southern Tip of Taiwan.* Taipei: Department of Anthropology, National Taiwan University.

Lichtenberk, F. 1986. Leadership in Proto-Oceanic society: Linguistic evidence. *Journal of the Polynesian Society* 95:341–56.

———. 1994. The raw and the cooked: Proto Oceanic terms for food preparation. In A. K. Pawley and

M. D. Ross, eds., *Austronesian Terminologies: Continuity and Change*, pp. 267–88. Pacific Linguistics C-127. Canberra: Australian National University.

Lilley, I. 1986. Prehistoric Exchange across the Vitiaz Strait, Papua New Guinea. Unpublished Ph.D. thesis, Australian National University (Canberra).

———. 1988. Prehistoric exchange across the Vitiaz Strait, Papua New Guinea. *Current Anthropology* 20: 513–16.

———. 1991a. Lapita sites in the Duke of York Islands. In J. Allen and C. Gosden, eds., *Report of the Lapita Homeland Project*, pp. 164–69. Occasional Papers in Prehistory No. 20. Canberra: Department of Prehistory, Australian National University.

———. 1992. Papua New Guinea's human past: The evidence of archaeology. In R. D. Attenborough and M. P. Alpers, eds., *Human Biology in Papua New Guinea: The Small Cosmos*, pp. 150–71. Oxford: Clarendon Press.

Lingenfelter, S. G. 1975. *Yap: Political Leadership and Culture Change in an Island Society*. Honolulu: University of Hawaii Press.

Linton, R. 1923. *The Material Culture of the Marquesas Islands*. Memoirs of the Bernice P. Bishop Museum VIII(5). Bayard Dominick Expedition Publication No. 5. Honolulu: Bernice P. Bishop Museum.

———. 1925. *Archaeology of the Marquesas Islands*. Bernice P. Bishop Museum Bulletin 23. Honolulu: Bernice P. Bishop Museum.

Liston, J., M. W. Kaschko, and D. J. Welch. 1998. *Archaeological Inventory Survey for the Capitol Relocation Project, Melekeok, Republic of Palau*. Honolulu: International Archaeological Research Institute.

Livingstone, F. B. 1984. The Duffy blood groups, vivax malaria, and malaria selection in human populations: A review. *Human Biology* 56:413–25.

Lockerbie, L. 1940. Excavations at King's Rock, Otago, with a discussion of the fish-hook barb as an ancient feature of Polynesian culture. *Journal of the Polynesian Society* 49:393–446.

———. 1959. From Moa-hunter to classic Maori in Southern New Zealand. In J. D. Freeman and W. R. Geddes, eds., *Anthropology in the South Seas*, pp. 75–110. New Plymouth, New Zealand: Avery.

Lourandos, H. 1997. *Continent of Hunter-Gatherers: New Perspectives in Australian Prehistory*. Cambridge: Cambridge University Press.

Loy, T. H., M. Spriggs, and S. Wickler. 1992. Direct evidence for human use of plants 28,000 years ago: Starch residues on stone artifacts from the northern Solomon Islands. *Antiquity* 66:898–912.

Lucking, L. J., and R. J. Parmentier. 1990. Terraces and traditions of Uluang: Ethnographic and archaeological perspectives on a prehistoric Belauan site. In R. L. Hunter-Anderson, ed., *Recent Advances in Micronesian Archaeology: Selected Papers from the Micronesian Archaeology Conference, September 9–12, 1987. Micronesica*, Supplement 2, pp. 125–36.

Lum, J. K. 1998. Central and eastern Micronesia: Genetics, the overnight voyage, and linguistic divergence. *Man and Culture in Oceania* 14:69–80.

Lum, J. K., and R. L. Cann. 1998. mtDNA and language support a common origin of Micronesians and Polynesians in Island Southeast Asia. *American Journal of Physical Anthropology* 105:109–19.

Lum, J. K., R. L. Cann, J. J. Martinson, and L. B. Jorde. 1998. Mitochondrial and nuclear genetic relationships among Pacific Island and Asian populations. *American Journal of Human Genetics* 63:613–24.

Luomala, K. 1955. *Voices on the Wind: Polynesian Myths and Chants*. Honolulu: Bishop Museum Press.

Lütke, F. 1835. *Voyage Autour du Monde*. Paris: Didot.

MacArthur, R. H., and E. O. Wilson. 1967. *The Theory of Island Biogeography*. Monographs in Population Biology No. 1. Princeton, N.J.: Princeton University Press.

Macdonald, G. A., and A. T. Abbott. 1970. *Volcanoes in the Sea: The Geology of Hawai'i*. Honolulu: University of Hawaii Press.

Machida, H., R. J. Blong, J. Specht, H. Moriwaki, R. Torrence, Y. Hayakawa, B. Talai, D. Lolok, and C. F. Pain. 1996. Holocene explosive eruptions of Witori and Dakataua Caldera volcanoes in West New Britian, Papua New Guinea. *Quaternary International* 34–36:65–78.

MacLachlan, R. R. C. 1940. The native pottery of the Fiji Islands. *Journal of the Polynesian Society* 49:243–71.

Malinowski, B. 1922. *Argonauts of the Western Pacific*. London: Routledge and Kegan Paul.

Marck, J. 1996. Eastern Polynesian subgrouping today. In J. Davidson, G. Irwin, F. Leach, A. Pawley, and D. Brown, eds., *Oceanic Culture History: Essays in Honour of Roger Green*, pp. 491–511. New Zealand Journal of Archaeology Special Publication. Dunedin: New Zealand Journal of Archaeology.

———. 1999. Polynesian Language and Culture History. Unpublished Ph.D. thesis, Australian National University (Canberra).

Marshall, B., and J. Allen. 1991. Excavations at Panakiwuk Cave, New Ireland. In J. Allen and C. Gosden, eds., *Report of the Lapita Homeland Project*, pp. 59–91. Occasional Papers in Prehistory No. 20. Canberra: Department of Prehistory, Australian National University.

Martin, P. S. 1990. 40,000 years of extinction on the "planet of doom." *Palaeogeography, Palaeoclimatology, Palaeoecology* 82:187–201.

Martinson, J. J. 1996. Molecular perspectives on the colonisation of the Pacific. In A. J. Boyce and C. G. N. Mascie-Taylor, eds., *Molecular Biology and Human Diversity*, pp. 171–95. Cambridge: Cambridge University Press.

Martinson, J. J., R. M. Harding, G. Philippon, F. Flye Sainte-Marie, J. Roux, A. J. Boyce, and J. B. Clegg. 1993. Demographic reductions and genetic bottlenecks in humans: Minisatellite allele distributions in Oceania. *Human Genetics* 91:445–50.

Martinsson-Wallin, H. 1994. *Ahu—The Ceremonial Stone Structures of Easter Island. Analyses of Variation and Interpretation of Meanings.* Aun 18. Uppsala, Sweden: Societas Archaeologica Upsaliensis.

Masse, W. B. 1989. The Archaeology and Ecology of Fishing in the Belau Islands, Micronesia. Ph.D. dissertation, Southern Illinois University (Carbondale).

———. 1990. Radiocarbon dating, sea-level change and the peopling of Belau. In R. L. Hunter-Anderson, ed., *Recent Advances in Micronesian Archaeology: Selected Papers from the Micronesian Archaeology Conference, September 9–12, 1987. Micronesica*, Supplement 2, pp. 213–30.

Masse, W. B., L. A. Carter, and G. F. Somers. 1991. Waha'ula *Heiau*: The regional and symbolic context of Hawai'i Island's "red mouth" temple. *Asian Perspectives* 30:19–56.

Masse, W. B., D. Snyder, and G. J. Gumerman. 1984. Prehistoric and historic settlement in the Palau Islands, Micronesia. *New Zealand Journal of Archaeology* 6:107–28.

Matisoo-Smith, E., J. S. Allen, T. N. Ladefoged, R. M. Roberts, and D. M. Lambert. 1997. Ancient DNA from Polynesian rats: Extraction, amplification and sequence from single small bones. *Electrophoresis* 18:1534–37.

Matisoo-Smith, E., R. M. Roberts, G. J. Irwin, J. S. Allen, D. Penny, and D. M. Lambert. 1998. Patterns of prehistoric human mobility revealed by mitochondrial DNA from the Pacific rat. *Proceedings of the National Academy of Sciences, USA* 95:15145–50.

Matthews, P. 1991. A possible tropical wild type taro: *Colocasia esculenta* var. *aquatilis. Bulletin of the Indo-Pacific Prehistory Association* 11:69–81.

Mauricio, R. 1987. Peopling of Pohnpei Island: Migration, dispersal and settlement themes in clan narratives. *Man in Oceania* 3:47–72.

Mayr, E. 1945. *Birds of the Southwest Pacific.* New York: Macmillan.

———. 1982. *The Growth of Biological Thought: Diversity, Evolution, and Inheritance.* Cambridge, Mass.: Harvard University Press.

———. 1997. *This Is Biology: The Science of the Living World.* Cambridge, Mass.: Harvard University Press.

McAllister, J. G. 1933a. *Archaeology of Oahu.* Bernice P. Bishop Museum Bulletin 104. Honolulu: Bernice P. Bishop Museum.

———. 1933b. *Archaeology of Kahoolawe.* Bernice P. Bishop Museum Bulletin 115. Honolulu: Bernice P. Bishop Museum.

McArthur, N. 1968. *Island Populations of the Pacific.* Canberra: Australian National University Press.

McArthur, N., I. Saunders, and R. Tweedie. 1976. Small population isolates: A micro-simulation study. *Journal of the Polynesian Society* 85:307–26.

McCall, G. 1980. *Rapanui: Tradition and Survival on Easter Island.* Honolulu: University Press of Hawaii.

McCoy, P. C. 1976. *Easter Island Settlement Patterns in the Late Prehistoric and Proto-Historic Periods.* International Fund for Monuments, Easter Island Committee, Bulletin 5. New York: International Fund for Monuments.

———. 1979. Easter Island. In J. Jennings, ed., *The Prehistory of Polynesia*, pp. 135–66. Cambridge, Mass.: Harvard University Press.

McCoy, P. C., and P. C. Cleghorn. 1988. Archaeological excavations on Santa Cruz (Nendö), Southeast Solomon Islands: Summary report. *Archaeology in Oceania* 23:104–15.

McEldowney, P. H. 1995. Subsistence Intensification in the Late Prehistory of Manus. Unpublished Ph.D. dissertation, Australian National University (Canberra).

McFadgen, B. G., and R. A. Sheppard. 1984. *Ruahihi Pa: A Prehistoric Defended Settlement in the South-Western Bay of Plenty.* National Museum of New Zealand Bulletin 22. Wellington: National Museum of New Zealand.

McGlone, M. S. 1983. Polynesian deforestation of New Zealand: A preliminary synthesis. *Archaeology in Oceania* 18:11–25.

———. 1989. The Polynesian settlement of New Zealand in relation to environmental and biotic changes. *New Zealand Journal of Ecology* 12(suppl.): 115–30.

McGlone, M. S., and L. R. Basher. 1995. The deforestation of the upper Awatere catchment, inland Kaikoura Range, Malborough, South Island, New Zealand. *New Zealand Journal of Ecology* 19:53–66.

McGlone, M. S., and J. M. Wilmshurst. 1999. Dating initial Maori environmental impact in New Zealand. *Quaternary International* 59:5–16.

McKern, W. C. 1929. *Archaeology of Tonga.* Bernice P. Bishop Museum Bulletin 60. Honolulu: Bernice P. Bishop Museum.

McNeill, W. H. 1976. *Plagues and Peoples.* New York: Doubleday.

McNutt, M., and H. Menard. 1978. Lithospheric flexure and uplifted atolls. *Journal of Geophysical Research* 83:1206–12.

Mead, M. 1967. Homogeneity and hypertrophy: A Polynesian-based hypothesis. In G. A. Highland, R. W. Force, A. Howard, M. Kelly, and Y. H. Sinoto, eds., *Polynesian Culture History: Essays in Honor of Kenneth P. Emory,* pp. 121–40. Bernice P. Bishop Museum Special Publication 56. Honolulu: Bernice P. Bishop Museum.

Mead, S. M., L. Birks, H. Birks, and E. Shaw. 1975. *The Lapita Pottery Style of Fiji and Its Associations.* Polynesian Society Memoir No. 38. Wellington, New Zealand: Polynesian Society.

Melton, T., S. Clifford, J. Martinson, M. Batzer, and M. Stoneking. 1998. Genetic evidence for the Proto-Austronesian homeland in Asia: mtDNA and nuclear DNA variation in Taiwanese Aboriginal tribes. *American Journal of Human Genetics* 63:1807–23.

Menard, H. W. 1986. *Islands.* New York: Scientific American Library.

Merrill, E. D. 1945. *Plant Life of the Pacific World.* New York: Macmillan.

———. 1954. *The Botany of Cook's Voyages and Its Unsuspected Significance in Relation to Anthropology, Biogeography and History.* Chronica Botanica, Vol. 14. Waltham, Mass.: Chronica Botanica.

Merriwether, D. A., J. S. Friedlaender, J. Mediavilla, C. Mgone, F. Gentz, and R. E. Ferrell. 1999. Mitochondrial DNA variation is an indicator of Austronesian influence in Island Melanesia. *American Journal of Physical Anthropology* 110:243–70.

Métraux, A. 1940. *Ethnology of Easter Island.* Bernice P. Bishop Museum Bulletin 160. Honolulu: Bernice P. Bishop Museum.

———. 1957. *Easter Island: A Stone-Age Civilization of the Pacific.* Oxford: Oxford University Press.

Meyer, O. 1909. Funde prähistorischer Töpferei und Steinmesser auf Vuatom, Bismarck-Archipel. *Anthropos* 4:1093–95.

———. 1910. Funde von Menschen- und Tierknochen, von prähistorischer Töpferei und Steinwerkzeugen auf Vuatom, Bismarck-Archipel. *Anthropos* 5:1160–61.

Miller, D. 1979. *Report of the National Sites Survey: 1976–1978.* Honiara: Solomon Islands Museum.

———. 1980. Settlement and diversity in the Solomon Islands. *Man* 15:451–66.

Miller, L. J. 1997. Mollusk exploitation and paleoenvironmental change in the Kone Region: A reanalysis of the site 13 mollusk assemblages. *Kroeber Anthropological Society Papers* 82:25–37.

Millerstrom, S. N. 1997. Carved and painted rock images in the Marquesas Islands, French Polynesia. *Archaeology in Oceania* 32:181–96.

Moir, B. G. 1989. A review of Tridacnid ecology and some possible implications for archaeological research. *Asian Perspectives* 31:95–122.

Moniz, J. J. 1997. The role of seabirds in Hawaiian subsistence: Implications for interpreting avian extinction and extirpation in Polynesia. *Asian Perspectives* 36:27–50.

Moore, C., and K. Romney. 1994. Material culture, geographic propinquity, and linguistic affiliation on the north coast of New Guinea: A reanalysis of Welsch, Terrell, and Nadloski (1992). *American Anthropologist* 96:370–92.

———. 1996. Will the "real" data please stand up? Reply to Welsch (1996). *Journal of Quantitative Anthropology* 6:235–61.

Moore, J. 1994. Ethnogenetic theories of human evolution. *Research and Exploration* 10:10–23.

Morgan, W. N. 1988. *Prehistoric Architecture in Micronesia.* Austin: University of Texas Press.

Morrison, K. 1994. Intensification of production: Archaeological approaches. *Journal of Archaeological Method and Theory* 1:111–59.

———. 1996. Typological schemes and agricultural change: Beyond Boserup in precolonial South India. *Current Anthropology* 37:583–608.

Mountain, M.-J. 1983. Preliminary report on excavations at Nombe Rockshelter, Simbu Province, Papua New Guinea. *Bulletin of the Indo-Pacific Prehistory Association* 4:84–89.

———. 1991a. Landscape use and environmental management of tropical rainforest by pre-agricultural hunter-gatherers in northern Sahulland. *Bulletin of the Indo-Pacific Prehistory Association* 11:54–68.

———. 1991b. Bulmer Phase 1: Environmental change and human activity through the late Pleistocene into the Holocene in the Highlands of New Guinea: A scenario. In A. Pawley, ed., *Man and a Half: Essays in Pacific Anthropology and Ethnobiology in Honour of Ralph Bulmer,* pp. 510–20. Auckland, New Zealand: Polynesian Society.

Mulloy, W., and G. Figueroa. 1978. *The A Kivi-Vai Teka Complex and Its Relationship to Easter Island Architectural Prehistory.* Asian and Pacific Archaeology Series No. 8.

Honolulu: Social Science Research Institute, University of Hawaii.

Mulvaney, J. 1993. From Cambridge to the bush. In M. Spriggs, D. E. Yen, W. Ambrose, R. Jones, A. Thorne, and A. Andrews, eds., *A Community of Culture: The People and Prehistory of the Pacific,* pp. 18–26. Occasional Papers in Prehistory No. 21. Canberra: Department of Prehistory, Australian National University.

Murdock, G. P. 1963. Human influences on the ecosystem of high islands of the tropical Pacific. In F. R. Fosberg, ed., *Man's Place in the Island Ecosystem: A Symposium,* pp. 145–52. Honolulu: Bishop Museum Press.

Nagaoka, L. 1988. Lapita subsistence: The evidence of non-fish archaeofaunal remains. In P. V. Kirch and T. L. Hunt, eds., *Archaeology of the Lapita Cultural Complex: A Critical Review,* pp. 117–34. Thomas Burke Memorial Washington State Museum Research Report No. 5. Seattle: Burke Museum.

Nordyke, E. C. 1989. Comment. In D. Stannard, *Before the Horror: The Population of Hawai'i on the Eve of Western Contact,* pp. 105–13. Honolulu: Social Science Research Institute, University of Hawaii.

Nunn, P. D. 1994. *Oceanic Islands.* Oxford: Blackwell.

Oliver, D. L. 1974. *Ancient Tahitian Society.* 3 vols. Honolulu: University of Hawaii Press.

———. 1989. *Oceania: The Native Cultures of Australia and the Pacific Islands.* 2 vols. Honolulu: University of Hawaii Press.

Olson, S. L., and H. F. James. 1982a. Fossil birds from the Hawaiian Islands: Evidence for wholesale extinction by man before Western contact. *Science* 217: 633–35.

———. 1982b. Prodromus of the fossil avifauna of the Hawaiian Islands. *Smithsonian Contributions to Zoology* 365:1–59.

———. 1984. The role of Polynesians in the extinction of the avifauna of the Hawaiian Islands. In P. S. Martin and R. L. Klein, eds., *Quaternary Extinctions: A Prehistoric Revolution,* pp. 768–80. Tucson: University of Arizona Press.

Orliac, C., and M. Orliac. 1998. Evolution du couvert végétal à l'Île de Paques du 15è au 19è siècle. In P. V.

Casanova, ed., *Easter Island and East Polynesian Prehistory*, pp. 195–200. Santiago: Instituto de Estudios Isla de Pascua, Universidad de Chile.

Orliac, M. 1997. Human occupation and environmental modifications in the Papeno'o Valley, Tahiti. In P. V. Kirch and T. L. Hunt, eds., *Historical Ecology in the Pacific Islands: Prehistoric Environmental and Landscape Change*, pp. 200–29. New Haven, Conn.: Yale University Press.

Osborne, D. 1966. *The Archaeology of the Palau Islands: An Intensive Survey*. Bernice P. Bishop Museum Bulletin 230. Honolulu: Bernice P. Bishop Museum.

———. 1979. *Archaeological Test Excavations, Palau Islands: 1968–1969*. Micronesica, Supplement 1.

Osmond, M. 1996. Proto Oceanic terms for fishing and hunting implements. In J. Lynch and F. Pat, eds., *Oceanic Studies: Proceedings of the First International Conference on Oceanic Linguistics*, pp. 111–32. Pacific Linguistics C-133. Canberra: Australian National University.

———. 1998. Horticultural practices. In M. Ross, A. Pawley, and M. Osmond, eds., *The Lexicon of Proto Oceanic: The Culture and Environment of Ancestral Oceanic Society*, Vol. 1: *Material Culture*, pp. 115–42. Pacific Linguistics C-152. Canberra: Australian National University.

Ottino, P. 1985. Archéologie des Îles Marquises: Contribution à la Connaissance de l'Île de Ua Pou. 2 vols. Unpublished Ph.D. dissertation, University of Paris I (Panthéon-Sorbonne).

———. 1990a. L'habitat des anciens Marquisiens: Architecture des maisons, évolution et symbolisme des formes. *Journal de la Société des Océanistes* 90:3–15.

———. 1990b. *Hakao'hoka: Étude d'une Vallée Marquisienne*. Travaux et Documents Microédités 66. Paris: ORSTOM.

———. 1992. Anapua: Abri-sous-roche de pêcheurs. Étude des hameçons. *Journal de la Société des Océanistes* 94:57–79, 95:201–26.

Paijmans, K., ed. 1976. *New Guinea Vegetation*. Canberra: Australian National University Press.

Palmer, B. 1969. Ring-ditch fortifications on windward Viti Levu, Fiji. *Archaeology and Physical Anthropology in Oceania* 4:181–97.

Palmer, B., and E. Shaw. 1968. Pottery-making in Nasama Village. *Records of the Fiji Museum* 1:48–67.

Parke, A. 1998. Navatanitawake ceremonial mound, Bau, Fiji: Some results of 1970 investigations. *Archaeology in Oceania* 33:20–27.

Parker, P. L., and T. F. King. 1984. Recent and current archaeological research on Moen Island, Truk. *Asian Perspectives* 24:11–26.

Parkes, A. 1997. Environmental change and the impact of Polynesian colonization: Sedimentary records from Central Polynesia. In P. V. Kirch and T. L. Hunt, eds., *Historical Ecology in the Pacific Islands: Prehistoric Environmental and Landscape Change*, pp. 166–99. New Haven, Conn.: Yale University Press.

Parry, J. T. 1977. *Ring-Ditch Fortifications in the Rewa Delta, Fiji: Air Photo Interpretation and Analysis*. Fiji Museum Bulletin No. 3. Suva: Fiji Museum.

———. 1981. *Ring-Ditch Fortifications in the Navua Delta, Fiji: Air Photo Interpretation and Analysis*. Fiji Museum Bulletin No. 7. Suva: Fiji Museum.

———. 1984. Air photo interpretation of fortified sites: Ring-ditch fortifications in southern Viti Levu, Fiji. *New Zealand Journal of Archaeology* 6:71–94.

———. 1987. *The Sigatoka Valley: Pathway into Prehistory*. Fiji Museum Bulletin No. 9. Suva: Fiji Museum.

Pavlides, C. 1993. New archaeological research at Yombon, West New Britain, Papua New Guinea. *Archaeology in Oceania* 28:55–59.

Pavlides, C., and C. Gosden. 1994. 35,000-year-old sites in the rainforests of West New Britain, Papua New Guinea. *Antiquity* 68:604–10.

Pawley, A. 1966. Polynesian languages: A subgrouping based on shared innovations in morphology. *Journal of the Polynesian Society* 75:39–64.

———. 1967. The relationships of Polynesian Outlier languages. *Journal of the Polynesian Society* 76:259–96.

———. 1982. Rubbish-man, commoner, big-man, chief? Linguistic evidence for hereditary chieftainship in Proto-Oceanic society. In J. Siikala, ed., *Oceanic Studies: Essays in Honor of Aarne A. Koskinen*, pp. 33–52. Transactions of the Finnish Anthropological Society No. 11. Helsinki: Finnish Anthropological Society.

————. 1996. On the Polynesian subgroup as a problem for Irwin's continuous settlement hypothesis. In J. Davidson, G. Irwin, F. Leach, A. Pawley, and D. Brown, eds., *Oceanic Culture History: Essays in Honour of Roger Green*, pp. 387–410. New Zealand Journal of Archaeology Special Publication. Dunedin: New Zealand Journal of Archaeology.

Pawley, A., and R. C. Green. 1973. Dating the dispersal of the Oceanic languages. *Oceanic Linguistics* 12: 1–67.

————. 1984. The Proto-Oceanic language community. *Journal of Pacific History* 19:123–46.

Pawley, A., and M. Pawley. 1994. Early Austronesian terms for canoe parts and seafaring. In A. K. Pawley and M. D. Ross, eds., *Austronesian Terminologies: Continuity and Change*, pp. 329–61. Pacific Linguistics C-127. Canberra: Australian National University.

————. 1998. Canoes and seafaring. In M. Ross, A. Pawley, and M. Osmond, eds., *The Lexicon of Proto Oceanic: The Culture and Environment of Ancestral Oceanic Society*, Vol. 1: *Material Culture*, pp. 173–210. Pacific Linguistics C-152. Canberra: Australian National University.

Pawley, A. K., and M. Ross. 1993. Austronesian historical linguistics and culture history. *Annual Review of Anthropology* 22:425–59.

————. 1995. The prehistory of Oceanic languages: A current view. In P. Bellwood, J. J. Fox, and D. Tryon, eds., *The Austronesians: Historical and Comparative Perspectives*, pp. 39–74. Canberra: Australian National University.

Pawley, A. K., and M. Ross, eds. 1994. *Austronesian Terminologies: Continuity and Change*. Pacific Linguistics C-127. Canberra: Australian National University.

Pawley, A., and T. Sabaya. 1971. Fijian dialect divisions: Eastern and western Fiji. *Journal of the Polynesian Society* 80:405–36.

Pearson, R. J., ed. 1968. *Excavations at Lapakahi: Selected Papers*. Hawaii State Archaeological Journal 69-2.

————. 1969. *Archaeology on the Island of Hawaii*. Asian and Pacific Archaeology Series No. 3. Honolulu: Social Science Research Institute, University of Hawaii.

Pearson, R. J., P. V. Kirch, and M. Pietrusewsky. 1971. An early prehistoric site at Bellows Beach, Waimanalo, Oahu, Hawaiian Islands. *Archaeology and Physical Anthropology in Oceania* 6:204–34.

Peoples, J. G. 1990. The evolution of complex stratification in eastern Micronesia. In R. L. Hunter-Anderson, ed., *Recent Advances in Micronesian Archaeology: Selected Papers from the Micronesian Archaeology Conference, September 9–12, 1987*. Micronesica, Supplement 2, pp. 291–302.

Peters, C. 1994. Human Settlement and Landscape Change on Rarotonga, Southern Cook Islands. Unpublished Ph.D. thesis, University of Auckland.

Petersen, G. 1990. Some overlooked complexities in the study of Pohnpei social complexity. In R. L. Hunter-Anderson, ed., *Recent Advances in Micronesian Archaeology: Selected Papers from the Micronesian Archaeology Conference, September 9–12, 1987*. Micronesica, Supplement 2, pp. 137–52.

Phillips, C. 1986. Excavations at Raupa Pa (N53/37) and Waiwhau Village (N53/198), Paeroa, New Zealand, in 1984. *New Zealand Journal of Archaeology* 8:89–114.

Pianka, E. 1974. *Evolutionary Ecology*. New York: Harper and Row.

Pickering, R. B. 1990. An ethno-archaeological investigation of Yapese mortuary behavior. In R. L. Hunter-Anderson, ed., *Recent Advances in Micronesian Archaeology: Selected Papers from the Micronesian Archaeology Conference, September 9–12, 1987*. Micronesica, Supplement 2, pp. 153–70.

Piddington, R., ed. 1939. *Essays in Polynesian Ethnology, by Robert W. Williamson*. Cambridge: Cambridge University Press.

Pietrusewsky, M. 1970. An osteological view of indigenous populations in Oceania. In R. C. Green and M. Kelly, eds., *Studies in Oceanic Culture History*, Vol. 1, pp. 1–12. Pacific Anthropological Records 11. Honolulu: Bernice P. Bishop Museum.

————. 1990. Craniometric variation in Micronesia and the Pacific: A multivariate study. *Micronesica*, Supplement 2, pp. 373–402.

————. 1994. Lapita origins: An osteological perspective. In P. J. C. Dark and R. G. Rose, eds., *Artistic Heritage in a Changing Pacific*, pp. 15–19. Honolulu: University of Hawaii Press.

————. 1996. The physical anthropology of Polynesia: A review of some cranial and skeletal studies. In

J. Davidson, G. Irwin, F. Leach, A. Pawley, and D. Brown, eds., *Oceanic Culture History: Essays in Honour of Roger Green*, pp. 343–53. New Zealand Journal of Archaeology Special Publication. Dunedin: New Zealand Journal of Archaeology.

Pospisil, L. 1963. *Kapauku Papuan Economy.* Yale University Publications in Anthropology No. 67. New Haven, Conn.: Department of Anthropology, Yale University.

Poulsen, J. 1968. Archaeological excavations on Tongatapu. In I. Yawata and Y. H. Sinoto, eds., *Prehistoric Culture in Oceania*, pp. 85–92. Honolulu: Bernice P. Bishop Museum.

———. 1972. Outlier archaeology: Bellona. A preliminary report on field work and radiocarbon dates. *Archaeology and Physical Anthropology in Oceania* 7: 184–205.

———. 1983. The chronology of early Tongan prehistory and the Lapita ware. *Journal de la Société des Océanistes* 76:46–56.

———. 1987. *Early Tongan Prehistory.* 2 vols. Terra Australis 12. Canberra: Australian National University.

Pregill, G., and T. Dye. 1989. Prehistoric extinction of giant iguanas in Tonga. *Copeia* 1989:505–8.

Prickett, N., ed. 1982. *The First Thousand Years: Regional Perspectives in New Zealand Archaeology.* Palmerston North, New Zealand: Dunmore Press.

Radovsky, F. J., P. H. Raven, and S. H. Sohmer, eds. 1984. *Biogeography of the Tropical Pacific.* Bernice P. Bishop Museum Special Publication 72. Honolulu: Bishop Museum Press.

Rainbird, P. 1994. Prehistory in the northwest tropical Pacific: The Caroline, Mariana, and Marshall Islands. *Journal of World Prehistory* 8:293–349.

———. 1996. A place to look up to: A review of Chuukese hilltop enclosures. *Journal of the Polynesian Society* 105:461–78.

Rallu, J.-L. 1990. *Les Populations Océaniennes aux XIXe et XXe Siècles.* Travaux et Documents Cahier No. 128. Paris: Institut National d'Études Démographiques.

Rechtman, R. B. 1992. The Evolution of Sociopolitical Complexity in the Fiji Islands. Unpublished Ph.D. dissertation, University of California (Los Angeles).

Reeve, R. 1989. Recent work on the prehistory of the western Solomons, Melanesia. *Bulletin of the Indo-Pacific Prehistory Association* 9:46–67.

Rehbock, P. F. 1988. Organizing Pacific science: Local and international origins of the Pacific Science Association. In R. MacLoed and P. F. Rehbock, eds., *Nature in Its Greatest Extent: Western Science in the Pacific*, pp. 195–222. Honolulu: University of Hawaii Press.

Rehg, K. L. 1995. The significance of linguistic interaction spheres in reconstructing Micronesian prehistory. *Oceanic Linguistics* 34:305–26.

———. n.d. The linguistic evidence for prehistoric contact between Western Polynesia and Pohnpei. Manuscript.

Reid, L. A. 1999. Morphosyntactic evidence for the position of Chamorro in the Austronesian language family. Revised draft of a paper presented at the 16th Congress of the Indo-Pacific Prehistory Association, Melaka, Malaysia, July 1–7, 1998.

Reinman, F. R. 1966. Notes on an Archaeological Survey of Guam, Marianas Islands, 1965–66. Mimeographed preliminary report to the National Science Foundation. Chicago: Field Museum of Natural History.

———. n.d. [1966]. An Archaeological Survey and Preliminary Test Excavations on the Island of Guam, Marianas Islands, 1965–66. Mimeographed report. Los Angeles: California State University.

Reisenberg, S. H. 1968. *The Native Polity of Ponape.* Smithsonian Contributions to Anthropology 10. Washington, D.C.: Smithsonian Institution.

Renfrew, C. 1982. Polity and power: Interaction, intensification and exploitation. In C. Renfrew and M. Wagstaff, eds., *An Island Polity: The Archaeology of Exploitation in Melos*, pp. 264–90. Cambridge: Cambridge University Press.

———. 1984. *Approaches to Social Archaeology.* Cambridge, Mass.: Harvard University Press.

Rhoads, J. W. 1980. Through a Glass Darkly: Present and Past Land Use Systems among Papuan Sago-palm Users. Unpublished Ph.D. thesis, Australian National University (Canberra).

Riley, T. 1975. Survey and excavation of the aboriginal agricultural system. In P. V. Kirch and M. Kelly, eds., *Prehistory and Human Ecology in a Windward Hawaiian*

Valley: Halawa Valley, Molokai, pp. 79–115. Pacific Anthropological Records 24. Honolulu: Bernice P. Bishop Museum.

———. 1987. Archaeological survey and testing, Majuro Atoll, Marshall Islands. In T. S. Dye, ed., *Marshall Islands Archaeology,* pp. 169–270. Pacific Anthropological Records 38. Honolulu: Bernice P. Bishop Museum.

Ritter, P. L. 1981. The population of Kosrae at contact. *Micronesica* 17:11–28.

Rivers, W. H. R. 1914. *The History of Melanesian Society.* 2 vols. Cambridge: Cambridge University Press.

Rivierre, J.-C. 1996. Mythhistoire et archéologie dans le Centre-Vanuatu. In M. Julien, M. Orliac, and C. Orliac, eds., *Mémoire de Pierre, Mémoire d'Homme: Tradition et Archéologie en Océanie,* pp. 431–64. Paris: Publications de la Sorbonne.

Roberts, J. M., Jr., C. Moore, and A. K. Romney. 1995. Predicting similarity in material culture among New Guinea villages from propinquity and language: A log-linear approach. *Current Anthropology* 36:769–88.

Roberts, M. 1991. Origin, dispersal routes, and geographic distribution of *Rattus exulans,* with specific reference to New Zealand. *Pacific Science* 45:123–30.

Roberts, R. G., R. Jones, and M. A. Smith. 1990. Thermoluminescence dating of a 50,000 year-old human occupation site in northern Australia. *Nature* 345:153–56.

———. 1995. Beyond the radiocarbon barrier in Australian prehistory. *Antiquity* 68:611–16.

Robin, C., J.-P. Eissen, and M. Monzier. 1993. Giant tuff cone and 12-km-wide associated caldera at Ambrym Volcano (Vanuatu, New Hebrides Arc). *Journal of Volcanology and Geothermal Research* 55:225–38.

Robin, C., M. Monzier, and J.-P. Eissen. 1994. Formation of the mid-fifteenth century Kuwae Caldera (Vanuatu) by an initial hydroclastic and subsequent ignimbritic eruption. *Bulletin of Volcanology* 56:170–83.

Roe, D. 1992. Investigations into the prehistory of the central Solomons: Some old and some new data from Northwest Guadalcanal. In J.-C. Galipaud, ed., *Poterie Lapita et Peuplement: Actes du Colloque LAPITA,* pp. 91–102. Noumea, New Caledonia: ORSTOM.

———. 1993. Prehistory Without Pots: Prehistoric Settlement and Economy of North-west Guadalcanal, Solomon Islands. Unpublished Ph.D. dissertation, Australian National University (Canberra).

Rogers, G. 1974. Archaeological discoveries on Niuatoputapu Island, Tonga. *Journal of the Polynesian Society* 83:308–48.

Rolett, B. V. 1989. Hanamiai: Changing Subsistence and Ecology in the Prehistory of Tahuata (Marquesas Islands, French Polynesia). Unpublished Ph.D. dissertation, Yale University (New Haven).

———. 1992. Faunal extinctions and depletions linked with prehistory and environmental change in the Marquesas Islands. *Journal of the Polynesian Society* 101:86–94.

———. 1993. Marquesan prehistory and the origins of East Polynesian culture. *Journal de la Société des Océanistes* 96:29–47.

———. 1996. Colonisation and cultural change in the Marquesas. In J. Davidson, G. Irwin, F. Leach, A. Pawley, and D. Brown, eds., *Oceanic Culture History: Essays in Honour of Roger Green,* pp. 531–40. New Zealand Journal of Archaeology Special Publication. Dunedin: New Zealand Journal of Archaeology.

———. 1998. *Hanamiai: Prehistoric Colonization and Cultural Change in the Marquesas Islands (East Polynesia).* Yale University Publications in Anthropology No. 84. New Haven, Conn.: Department of Anthropology, Yale University.

Rolett, B. V., and E. Conte. 1995. Renewed investigation of the Ha'atuatua dune (Nukuhiva, Marquesas Islands): A key site in Polynesian prehistory. *Journal of the Polynesian Society* 104:195–228.

Romney, K. 1957. The genetic model and Uto-Aztecan time perspective. *Davidson Journal of Anthropology* 3:35–41.

Rose, R. 1980. *A Museum to Instruct and Delight: William T. Brigham and the Founding of the Bernice Pauahi Bishop Museum.* Bernice P. Bishop Museum Special Publication 68. Honolulu: Bishop Museum Press.

Rosendahl, P. H. 1972. Aboriginal Agriculture and Residence Patterns in Upland Lapakahi, Island of Hawaii. Unpublished Ph.D. dissertation, University of Hawaii.

———. 1987. Archaeology in Eastern Micronesia: A

Reconnaissance Survey in the Marshall Islands. In T. S. Dye, ed., *Marshall Islands Archaeology*, pp. 17–168. Pacific Anthropological Records 38. Honolulu: Bernice P. Bishop Museum.

————. 1994. Aboriginal Hawaiian structural remains and settlement patterns in the upland agricultural zone at Lapakahi, Island of Hawai'i. *Hawaiian Archaeology* 3:14–70.

Rosenfeld, A. 1997. Excavation at Buang Merabak, Central New Ireland. In P. Bellwood, ed., *Indo-Pacific Prehistory: The Chiang Mai Papers*, Vol. 3, pp. 213–24. Canberra: Indo-Pacific Prehistory Association.

Ross, M. D. 1988. *Proto Oceanic and the Austronesian Languages of Western Melanesia.* Pacific Linguistics C-98. Canberra: Australian National University.

————. 1989. Early Oceanic linguistic prehistory. *Journal of Pacific History* 24:135–49.

————. 1995. Some current issues in Austronesian linguistics. In D. T. Tryon, ed., *Comparative Austronesian Dictionary*, Part 1, pp. 45–120. Berlin: Mouton de Gruyter.

————. 1996a. Reconstructing food plant terms and associated terminologies in Proto Oceanic. In J. Lynch and F. Pat, eds., *Oceanic Studies: Proceedings of the First International Conference on Oceanic Linguistics*, pp. 163–221. Pacific Linguistics C-133. Canberra: Australian National University.

————. 1996b. Is Yapese Oceanic? In B. Nothofer, ed., *Reconstruction, Classification, Description: Festschrift in Honor of Isidore Dyen*, pp. 121–66. Hamburg: Abera Verlag Meyer.

————. 1997. Social networks and kinds of speech-community event. In R. Blench and M. Spriggs, eds., *Archaeology and Language I: Theoretical and Methodological Orientations*, pp. 209–61. London: Routledge.

Ross, M., A. Pawley, and M. Osmond, eds. 1998. *The Lexicon of Proto Oceanic: The Culture and Environment of Ancestral Oceanic Society*, Vol. 1: *Material Culture.* Pacific Linguistics C-152. Canberra: Australian National University.

Rossitto, R. 1995. Stylistic change in Fijian pottery. *Pacific Studies* 18:1–46.

Routledge, K. S. 1919. *The Mystery of Easter Island.* London: Sifton, Praed.

Roux, J.-C. 1990. Traditional Melanesian agriculture in New Caledonia and pre-contact population distribution. In D. E. Yen and J. M. J. Mummery, eds., *Pacific Production Systems: Approaches to Economic Prehistory*, pp. 161–73. Occasional Papers in Prehistory No. 18. Canberra: Department of Prehistory, Australian National University.

Russell, S. 1998. *Tiempon I Manmofo'na: Ancient Chamorro Culture and History of the Northern Mariana Islands.* Micronesian Archaeological Survey Report No. 32. Saipan: Divsion of Historic Preservation.

Russell, S., and M. Fleming. 1986. Archaeology in the north Northern Mariana Islands: An overview. *Journal of the Polynesian Society* 95:115–26.

Sahlins, M. 1958. *Social Stratification in Polynesia.* Seattle: American Ethnological Society.

————. 1963. Poor man, rich man, big-man, chief: Political types in Melanesia and Polynesia. *Comparative Studies in Society and History* 5:285–303.

————. 1972. *Stone Age Economics.* Chicago: Aldine-Atherton.

————. 1981. *Historical Metaphors and Mythical Realities: Structure in the Early History of the Sandwich Islands Kingdom.* Ann Arbor: University of Michigan Press.

————. 1982. Femmes crues, hommes cuits et autres "grandes choses" des îles Fidji. *Le Débat* 19:121–45.

————. 1985. *Islands of History.* Chicago: University of Chicago Press.

————. 1995. *How "Natives" Think: About Captain Cook, for Example.* Chicago: University of Chicago Press.

Sand, C. 1990. The ceramic chronology of Futuna and Alofi: An overview. In M. Spriggs, ed., *Lapita Design, Form and Composition*, pp. 123–33. Occasional Papers in Prehistory No. 19. Canberra: Department of Prehistory, Australian National University.

————. 1992. La différenciation des chronologies céramiques de Polynésie occidentale à partir d'une tradition culturelle commune issue du complexe culturel Lapita. In J.-C. Galipaud, ed., *Poterie Lapita et Peuplement: Actes du Colloque LAPITA*, pp. 207–18. Noumea, New Caledonia: ORSTOM.

————. 1993a. *Archéologie en Nouvelle-Calédonie.* Noumea: Agence de Développement de la Culture Kanak.

————. 1993b. Données archéologiques et géomorphologiques du site ancien d'Asipani (Futuna–Poly-nésie occidentale). *Journal de la Société des Océanistes* 97:117–44.

———. 1993c. A preliminary study of the impact of the Tongan maritime chiefdom on the late prehistoric society of 'Uvea, Western Polynesia. In M. W. Graves and R. C. Green, eds., *The Evolution and Organisation of Prehistoric Society in Polynesia*, pp. 43–51. New Zealand Archaeological Association Monograph 19. Auckland: New Zealand Archaeological Association.

———. 1994. La Préhistoire de la Nouvelle-Calédonie. Thèse de Préhistoire, Ethnologie, Anthropologie, Université Paris I (Panthéon-Sorbonne).

———. 1995. *"Le Temps d'Avant": La Préhistoire de la Nouvelle-Calédonie.* Paris: l'Harmattan.

———. 1996a. Recent developments in the study of New Caledonia's prehistory. *Archaeology in Oceania* 31:45–70.

———. 1996b. Archaeological structures, socio-political complexity and population density: New insight into the prehistory of the New Caledonian archipelago. In J. Davidson, G. Irwin, F. Leach, A. Pawley, and D. Brown, eds., *Oceanic Culture History: Essays in Honour of Roger Green*, pp. 287–95. New Zealand Journal of Archaeology Special Publication. Dunedin: New Zealand Journal of Archaeology.

———. 1996c. Structural remains as markers of complex societies in southern Melanesia during prehistory: The case of the monumental forts of Mare Island (New Caledonia). *Bulletin of the Indo-Pacific Prehistory Association* 15(2):37–44.

———. 1996d. *Le Début du Peuplement Austronésien de la Nouvelle-Calédonie: Données Archéologiques Récentes.* Les Cahiers de l'Archéologie en Nouvelle-Calédonie, Vol. 6. Noumea, New Caledonia: Service Territorial des Musées et du Patrimoine.

———. 1997. The chronology of Lapita ware in New Caledonia. *Antiquity* 71:539–47.

———. 1998a. Archaeological report on localities WKO013A and WKO013B at the site of Lapita (Koné, New Caledonia). *Journal of the Polynesian Society* 107:7–33.

———. 1998b. Archaeological research on 'Uvea Island, Western Polynesia. *New Zealand Journal of Archaeology* 18(1996):91–123.

———. 1998c. Recent archaeological research in the Loyalty Islands of New Caledonia. *Asian Perspectives* 37:194–223.

Sand, C., K. Coote, J. Bole, and A. Ouétcho. 1998. A pottery pit at locality WKO013A, Lapita (New Caledonia). *Archaeology in Oceania* 33:37–43.

Sand, C., and A. Ouétcho. 1993. Three thousand years of settlement in the South of New Caledonia: Some recent results from the region of Païta. *New Zealand Journal of Archaeology* 15:107–30.

Sand, C., and F. Valentin. 1991. First results of the excavation of the burial mound of Petania, 'Uvea, Western Polynesia. *Bulletin of the Indo-Pacific Prehistory Association* 11:236–46.

Sapir, E. 1916. *Time Perspective in Aboriginal American Culture: A Study in Method.* Department of Mines, Geological Survey Memoir 90, Anthropological Series No. 13. Ottawa: Government Printing Bureau.

Sarasin, F. 1917. *La Nouvelle-Calédonie et les Iles Loyalty.* Basle: Georg.

Sarfert, E. G. 1919–20. *Kusae.* 2 vols. In G. Thilenius, ed., *Ergebnisse der Südsee-Expedition, 1908–1910,* Part II(B):4. Hamburg: L. Friederichsen, de Gruyter.

Scaglion, R. 1996. Chiefly models in Papua New Guinea. *The Contemporary Pacific* 8:1–31.

Schilt, R. 1984. *Subsistence and Conflict in Kona, Hawai'i.* Department of Anthropology Report 84-1. Honolulu: Bernice P. Bishop Museum.

Schmidt, M. 1996. The commencement of pa construction in New Zealand prehistory. *Journal of the Polynesian Society* 105:441–51.

Schmitt, R. C. 1968. *Demographic Statistics of Hawaii: 1778–1965.* Honolulu: University of Hawaii Press.

———. 1973. *The Missionary Censuses of Hawaii.* Pacific Anthropological Records 20. Honolulu: Bernice P. Bishop Museum.

Schurz, W. L. 1959. *The Manila Galleon.* New York: E. P. Dutton.

Seemann, B. 1862. *Viti: An Account of the Government Mission to the Vitian or Fijian Islands in the Years 1860–1861.* Cambridge: Macmillan.

Seligman, C. G. 1910. *The Melanesians of British New Guinea.* Cambridge: Cambridge University Press.

Serjeantson, S. W., and X. Gao. 1995. *Homo sapiens* is an evolving species: Origins of the Austronesians. In P. Bellwood, J. J. Fox, and D. Tryon, eds., *The Austronesians: Historical and Comparative Perspectives*, pp. 165–80. Canberra: Australian National University.

Serjeantson, S. W., D. P. Ryan, and A. R. Thompson. 1982. The colonization of the Pacific: The story according to human leukocyte antigens. *American Journal of Human Genetics* 34:904–18.

Service, E. 1967. *Primitive Social Organization: An Evolutionary Perspective.* New York: Random House.

Shackley, M. S., ed. 1998. *Archaeological Obsidian Studies: Method and Theory.* New York: Plenum Press.

Sharp, A. 1956. *Ancient Voyagers in the Pacific.* Wellington: Polynesian Society.

Sharp, N. 1988. Style and substance: A reconsideration of the Lapita decorative system. In P. V. Kirch and T. L. Hunt, eds., *Archaeology of the Lapita Cultural Complex: A Critical Review*, pp. 61–82. Thomas Burke Memorial Washington State Museum Research Report No. 5. Seattle: Burke Museum.

———. 1991. Lapita as text: The meaning of pottery in Melanesian prehistory. In P. Bellwood, ed., *Indo-Pacific Prehistory 1990: Proceedings of the 14th Congress of the Indo-Pacific Prehistory Association*, pp. 323–32. Canberra: Indo-Pacific Prehistory Association.

Shaw, E. 1967. A Reanalysis of Pottery from Navatu and Vuda, Fiji. Unpublished M.A. thesis, Department of Anthropology, University of Auckland.

———. 1975. The decorative system of Natunuku, Fiji. In S. Mead, L. Birks, H. Birks, and E. Shaw, *The Lapita Style of Fiji and Its Associations*, pp. 44–55. Polynesian Society Memoir 38. Wellington: Polynesian Society.

Shawcross, W. 1967. An investigation of prehistoric diet and economy at a coastal site at Galatea Bay, New Zealand. *Proceedings of the Prehistoric Society* 33:107–31.

———. 1972. Energy and ecology: Thermodynamic models in archaeology. In D. L. Clarke, ed., *Models in Archaeology*, pp. 577–622. London: Methuen.

———. 1976. Kauri Point Swamp: The ethnographic interpretation of a prehistoric site. In G. de G. Sieveking, I. H. Longworth, and K. E. Wilson, eds., *Problems in Economic and Social Archaeology*, pp. 277–305. London: Duckworth.

Sheppard, P. J. 1992. A report on the flaked lithic assemblage from three Southeast Solomons Lapita sites. In J.-C. Galipaud, ed., *Poterie Lapita et Peuplement: Actes du Colloque LAPITA*, pp. 145–54. Noumea, New Caledonia: ORSTOM.

———. 1993. Lapita lithics: Trade/exchange and technology. A view from the Reefs/Santa Cruz. *Archaeology in Oceania* 28:121–37.

Sheppard, P. J., and R. C. Green. 1991. Spatial analysis of the Nenumbo (SE-RF-2) Lapita site, Solomon Islands. *Archaeology in Oceania* 26:89–101.

Shineberg, D. 1983. Un nouveau regard sur la démographie historique de la Nouvelle-Calédonie. *Journal de la Société des Océanistes* 39(76):33–43.

Shore, B. 1989. *Mana* and *tapu*. In A. Howard and R. Borofsky, eds., *Developments in Polynesian Ethnology*, pp. 137–73. Honolulu: University of Hawaii Press.

Shun, K., and J. S. Athens. 1990. Archaeological investigations on Kwajalein Atoll, Marshall Islands, Micronesia. In R. L. Hunter-Anderson, ed., *Recent Advances in Micronesian Archaeology: Selected Papers from the Micronesian Archaeology Conference, September 9–12, 1987. Micronesica*, Supplement 2, pp. 231–40.

Shutler, M. E., and R. Shutler, Jr. 1965. A Preliminary Report of Archaeological Explorations in the Southern New Hebrides. Mimeographed report, Department of Anthropology. Honolulu: Bernice P. Bishop Museum.

Shutler, R., Jr., D. V. Burley, W. R. Dickinson, E. Nelson, and A. K. Carlson. 1994. Early Lapita sites, the colonisation of Tonga and recent data from northern Ha'apai. *Archaeology in Oceania* 29:53–68.

Shutler, R., Jr., and J. C. Marck. 1975. On the dispersal of the Austronesian horticulturalists. *Archaeology and Physical Anthropology in Oceania* 10:81–113.

Shutler, R., Jr., and M. E. Shutler. 1968. Archaeological excavations in southern Melanesia. In I. Yawata and Y. H. Sinoto, eds., *Prehistoric Culture in Oceania*, pp. 15–17. Honolulu: Bishop Museum Press.

Sinoto, A. 1973. Fanning Island: Preliminary archaeological investigations of sites near the Cable Station. In K. Chave and E. Kay, eds., *Fanning Island Expedition*. Honolulu: Hawaii Institute of Geophysics.

Sinoto, Y. H. 1962. Chronology of Hawaiian fishhooks. *Journal of the Polynesian Society* 71:162–66.

————. 1966. A tentative prehistoric cultural sequence in the northern Marquesas Islands, French Polynesia. *Journal of the Polynesian Society* 75:287–303.

————. 1967. Artifacts from excavated sites in the Hawaiian, Marquesas, and Society Islands. In G. A. Highland, R. W. Force, A. Howard, M. Kelly, and Y. H. Sinoto, eds., *Polynesian Culture History*, pp. 341–61. Bernice P. Bishop Museum Special Publication 56. Honolulu: Bernice P. Bishop Museum.

————. 1970. An archaeologically based assessment of the Marquesas Islands as a dispersal center in East Polynesia. In R. C. Green and M. Kelly, eds., *Studies in Oceanic Culture History*, pp. 105–32. Pacific Anthropological Records 11. Honolulu: Bernice P. Bishop Museum.

————. 1979a. The Marquesas. In J. Jennings, ed., *The Prehistory of Polynesia*, pp. 110–34. Cambridge, Mass.: Harvard University Press.

————. 1979b. Excavations on Huahine, French Polynesia. *Pacific Studies* 3:1–40.

————. 1983. An analysis of Polynesian migrations based on the archaeological assessments. *Journal de la Société des Océanistes* 76:57–67.

————. 1991. A revised system for the classification and coding of Hawaiian fishhooks. *Bishop Museum Occasional Papers* 31:85–105.

————. 1996a. Mata'ire'a Hill, Huahine: A unique prehistoric settlement, and a hypothetical sequence of *marae* development in the Society Islands. In J. Davidson, G. Irwin, F. Leach, A. Pawley, and D. Brown, eds., *Oceanic Culture History: Essays in Honour of Roger Green*, pp. 541–53. New Zealand Journal of Archaeology Special Publication. Dunedin: New Zealand Journal of Archaeology.

————. 1996b. Tracing human movement in East Polynesia: A discussion of selected artifact types. In M. Julien, M. Orliac, and C. Orliac, eds., *Mémoire de Pierre, Mémoire d'Homme: Tradition et Archéologie en Océanie*, pp. 131–52. Paris: Publications de la Sorbonne.

Sinoto, Y. H., ed. 1984. *Caroline Islands Archaeology: Investigations on Fefan, Faraulep, Woleai, and Lamotrek*. Pacific Anthropological Records 35. Honolulu: Bernice P. Bishop Museum.

Sinoto, Y. H., and T. L. Han. 1981. Report on the Fa'ahia Site Excavations, Zone "A"–Section 5; Fare, Huahine, Society Islands, French Polynesia. Unpublished report on file. Honolulu: Department of Anthropology, Bernice P. Bishop Museum.

Sinoto, Y. H., and P. C. McCoy. 1975. Report on the preliminary excavation of an early habitation site on Huahine, Society Islands. *Journal de la Société des Océanistes* 47:143–86.

Skinner, H. D. 1923–24. Archaeology of Canterbury. *Records of the Canterbury Museum* 2:93–104, 151–62.

Skjølsvold, A. 1972. *Excavations of a Habitation Cave, Hanapete'o, Hiva Oa, Marquesas Islands*. Pacific Anthropological Records 16. Honolulu: Bernice P. Bishop Museum.

Skjølsvold, A., ed. 1994. *Archaeological Investigations at Anakena, Easter Island*. Kon-Tiki Museum, Occasional Papers, Vol. 3. Oslo: Kon-Tiki Museum.

Smith, B. 1985. *European Vision and the South Pacific*. New Haven, Conn.: Yale University Press.

Smith, I. W. G. 1989. Maori impact on the marine megafauna: Pre-European distributions of New Zealand sea mammals. In D. G. Sutton, ed., *Saying So Doesn't Make It So: Papers in Honour of B. Foss Leach*, pp. 76–108. New Zealand Archaeological Association Monograph 17. Auckland: New Zealand Archaeological Association.

Smith, M. A., and N. D. Sharp. 1993. Pleistocene sites in Australia, New Guinea and Island Melanesia: Geographic and temporal structure of the archaeological record. In M. A. Smith, M. Spriggs, and B. Fankhauser, eds., *Sahul in Review: Pleistocene Archaeology in Australia, New Guinea and Island Melanesia*, pp. 37–59. Occasional Papers in Prehistory No. 24. Canberra: Department of Prehistory, Australian National University.

Smith, M. A., M. Spriggs, and B. Fankhauser, eds. 1993. *Sahul in Review: Pleistocene Archaeology in Australia, New*

Guinea and Island Melanesia. Occasional Papers in Prehistory No. 24. Canberra: Department of Prehistory, Australian National University.

Smith, S. P. 1921 [1910]. *Hawaiki: The Original Home of the Maori, with a Sketch of Polynesian History,* 4th ed. Auckland, New Zealand: Whitcombe and Tombs.

Somers, G. F. 1991. The effects of rapid geological change on archaeology in Hawai'i. *Asian Perspectives* 30:133–47.

Sorrenson, M. P. K., ed. 1986–88. *Na To Hoa Aroha, From Your Dear Friend: The Correspondence Between Sir Apirana Ngata and Sir Peter Buck, 1925–50.* 3 vols. Auckland, New Zealand: Auckland University Press.

Spear, R. L. 1992. Settlement and expansion in an Hawaiian valley: The archaeological record of North Halawa, O'ahu. *New Zealand Journal of Archaeology* 14:79–88.

Specht, J. 1968a. Preliminary report on excavations on Watom Island. *Journal of the Polynesian Society* 77:117–34.

———. 1968b. Prehistoric and Modern Pottery Industries of Buka Island, T.P.N.G. Unpublished Ph.D. dissertation, Australian National University (Canberra).

———. 1972. The pottery industry of Buka Island, T.P.N.G. *Archaeology and Physical Anthropology in Oceania* 7:125–44.

———. 1974. Lapita pottery at Talasea, West New Britain, Papua New Guinea. *Antiquity* 48:302–6.

———. 1991. Kreslo: A Lapita pottery site in southwest New Britain, Papua New Guinea. In J. Allen and C. Gosden, eds., *Report of the Lapita Homeland Project,* pp. 189–204. Occasional Papers in Prehistory No. 20. Canberra: Department of Prehistory, Australian National University.

Specht, J., and C. Gosden. 1997. Dating Lapita pottery in the Bismarck Archipelago, Papua New Guinea. *Asian Perspectives* 36:175–99.

Specht, J., I. Lilley, and J. Normu. 1981. Radiocarbon dates from west New Britain, Papua New Guinea. *Australian Archaeology* 12:13–15.

Speiser, F. 1923. *Ethnographische Materialien aus den Neuen Hebriden und den Banks-Inseln.* Berlin: C. W. Kreidel's Verlag. [1996 English translation by D. Q. Stephen-

son published as *Ethnology of Vanuatu* by University of Hawaii Press, Honolulu.]

Spennemann, D. H. R. 1989. 'Ata 'a Tonga mo 'Ata 'o Tonga: Early and Later Prehistory of the Tongan Islands. Unpublished Ph.D. dissertation, Australian National University (Canberra).

Spoehr, A. 1952. Time perspective in Micronesia and Polynesia. *Southwestern Journal of Anthropology* 8:457–65.

———. 1954. *Bernice P. Bishop Museum, Annual Report 1953.* Honolulu: Bishop Museum Press.

———. 1955. *Museum at Work: Bernice P. Bishop Museum, Annual Report for 1954.* Honolulu: Bishop Museum Press.

———. 1956. *A Museum Is a Point of View: Bernice P. Bishop Museum, Annual Report for 1955.* Honolulu: Bishop Museum Press.

———. 1957. *Marianas Prehistory: Archaeological Survey and Excavations on Saipan, Tinian, and Rota.* Fieldiana: Anthropology 48. Chicago: Field Museum of Natural History.

———. 1958. *Concept of the Pacific: Bernice P. Bishop Museum, Annual Report for 1957.* Honolulu: Bishop Museum Press.

———. 1962. *Science and Education: Bernice P. Bishop Museum, Annual Report for 1961.* Honolulu: Bishop Museum Press.

———. 1973. *Zamboanga and Sulu: An Archaeological Approach to Ethnic Diversity.* Ethnology Monographs No. 1. Pittsburgh: Department of Anthropology, University of Pittsburgh.

Spriggs, M. 1981. Vegetable Kingdoms: Taro Irrigation and Pacific Prehistory. Unpublished Ph.D. dissertation, Australian National University (Canberra).

———. 1982. Taro cropping systems in the Southeast Asian-Pacific region. *Archaeology in Oceania* 17:7–15.

———. 1984. The Lapita Cultural Complex: Origins, distribution, contemporaries and successors. *Journal of Pacific History* 19:202–23.

———. 1986. Landscape, land use and political transformation in southern Melanesia. In P. V. Kirch, ed., *Island Societies: Archaeological Approaches to Evolution and Transformation,* pp. 6–19. Cambridge: Cambridge University Press.

———. 1989a. The dating of the Island Southeast

Asian Neolithic: An attempt at chronometric hygiene and linguistic correlation. *Antiquity* 63: 587–613.

———. 1989b. God's police and damned whores: Images of archaeology in Hawaii. In P. Gathercole and D. Lowenthal, eds., *Politics of the Past*, pp. 118–29. London: Unwin Hyman.

———.1990a. Dating Lapita: Another view. In M. Spriggs, ed., *Lapita Design, Form and Composition*, pp. 6–27. Occasional Papers in Prehistory No. 19. Canberra: Department of Prehistory, Australian National University.

———. 1990b. The changing face of Lapita: Transformation of a design. In M. Spriggs, ed., *Lapita Design, Form and Composition*, pp. 83–122. Occasional Papers in Prehistory No. 19. Canberra: Department of Prehistory, Australian National University.

———. 1991a. Lapita origins, distribution, contemporaries and successors revisited. In P. Bellwood, ed., *Indo-Pacific Prehistory 1990: Proceedings of the 14th Congress of the Indo-Pacific Prehistory Association*, pp. 306–12. Canberra: Indo-Pacific Prehistory Association.

———. 1991b. Nissan: The island in the middle. In J. Allen and C. Gosden, eds., *Report of the Lapita Homeland Project*, pp. 222–43. Canberra: Australian National University.

———. 1991c. Facing the Nation: Archaeologists and Hawaiians in the era of sovereignty. *The Contemporary Pacific* 3:380–92.

———. 1992a. What happens to Lapita in Melanesia? In J.-C. Galipaud, ed., *Poterie Lapita et Peuplement: Actes du Colloque LAPITA*, pp. 219–30. Noumea, New Caledonia: ORSTOM.

———. 1992b. Alternative prehistories for Bougainville: Regional, national, or micronational. *The Contemporary Pacific* 4:269–98.

———. 1993a. Pleistocene agriculture in the Pacific: Why not? In M. A. Smith, M. Spriggs, and B. Fankhauser, eds., *Sahul in Review: Pleistocene Archaeology in Australia, New Guinea and Island Melanesia*, pp. 137–43. Occasional Papers in Prehistory No. 24. Canberra: Department of Prehistory, Australian National University.

———. 1993b. Island Melanesia: The last 10,000 years. In M. A. Smith, M. Spriggs, and B. Fankhauser, eds., *Sahul in Review: Pleistocene Archaeology in Australia, New Guinea and Island Melanesia*, pp. 187–205. Occasional Papers in Prehistory No. 24. Canberra: Department of Prehistory, Australian National University.

———. 1993c. How much of the Lapita design system represents the human face? In P. J. C. Dark and R. G. Rose, eds., *Artistic Heritage in a Changing Pacific*, pp. 7–14. Honolulu: University of Hawaii Press.

———. 1995. The Lapita culture and Austronesian prehistory in Oceania. In P. Bellwood, J. J. Fox, and D. Tryon, eds., *The Austronesians: Historical and Comparative Perspectives*, pp. 112–33. Canberra: Australian National University.

———. 1996. L'archéologie du Vanuatu dans le contexte de l'Océanie. In J. Bonnemaison, K. Huffman, and D. Tryon, eds., *Vanuatu—Océanie: Arts des Iles de Cendre et de Corail*, pp. 76–81. Paris: Editions de la Réunion des Musées Nationaux.

———. 1997. *The Island Melanesians*. Oxford: Blackwell.

Spriggs, M. J. T., and A. Anderson. 1993. Late colonization of East Polynesia. *Antiquity* 67:200–17.

Spriggs, M. J. T., and P. L. Tanaka. 1988. *Na Mea 'Imi Ka Wa Kahiko: An Annotated Bibliography of Hawaiian Archaeology*. Asian and Pacific Archaeology Series No. 11. Honolulu: Social Science Research Institute, University of Hawaii.

Spriggs, M. J. T., and S. Wickler. 1989. Archaeological research on Erromango: Recent data on southern Melanesian prehistory. *Bulletin of the Indo-Pacific Prehistory Association* 9:68–91.

Stannard, D. 1989. *Before the Horror: The Population of Hawai'i on the Eve of Western Contact*. Honolulu: Social Science Research Institute, University of Hawaii.

Starosta, S. 1995. A grammatical subgrouping of Formosan languages. In P. Li, C.-H. Tsang, Y.-K. Huang, D.-A. Ho, and C.-Y. Tseng, eds., *Austronesian Studies Relating to Taiwan*, pp. 683–726. Taipei: Academia Sinica.

Steadman, D. W. 1989. Extinction of birds in Eastern Polynesia: A review of the record, and comparisons with other Pacific island groups. *Journal of Archaeological Science* 16:177–205.

———. 1993a. Biogeography of Tongan birds before

and after human impact. *Proceedings of the National Academy of Sciences, USA* 90(3):818–22.

———. 1993b. Birds from the To'aga Site, Ofu, American Samoa: Prehistoric loss of seabirds and megapodes. In P. V. Kirch and T. L. Hunt, eds., *The To'aga Site: Three Millennia of Polynesian Occupation in the Manu'a Islands, American Samoa*, pp. 217–28. Archaeological Research Facility Contribution No. 51. Berkeley: University of California.

———. 1995. Prehistoric extinctions of Pacific island birds: Biodiversity meets zooarchaeology. *Science* 267: 1123–30.

———. 1997. Extinctions of Polynesian birds: Reciprocal impacts of birds and people. In P. V. Kirch and T. L. Hunt, eds., *Historical Ecology in the Pacific Islands: Prehistoric Environmental and Landscape Change*, pp. 51–79. New Haven, Conn.: Yale University Press.

Steadman, D. W., and L. J. Justice. 1998. Prehistoric exploitation of birds on Mangareva, Gambier Islands, French Polynesia. *Man and Culture in Oceania* 14:81–98.

Steadman, D. W., and P. V. Kirch. 1990. Prehistoric extinction of birds on Mangaia, Cook Islands, Polynesia. *Proceedings of the National Academy of Sciences, USA* 87:9605–9.

———. 1998. Biogeography and prehistoric exploitation of birds in the Mussau Islands, Bismarck Archipelago, Papua New Guinea. *Emu* 98:13–22.

Steadman, D. W., and P. S. Martin. 1984. Extinction of birds in the late Pleistocene of North America. In P. S. Martin and R. G. Klein, eds., *Quaternary Extinctions: A Prehistoric Revolution*, pp. 466–77. Tucson: University of Arizona Press.

Steadman, D. W., and D. S. Pahlavan. 1992. Extinction and biogeography of birds on Huahine, Society Islands, French Polynesia. *Geoarchaeology* 7:449–83.

Steadman, D. W., D. Pahlavan, and P. V. Kirch. 1990. Extinction, biogeography, and human exploitation of birds on Tikopia and Anuta, Polynesian outliers in the Solomon Islands. *Bishop Museum Occasional Papers* 30:118–53.

Steadman, D. W., and B. Rolett. 1996. A chronostratigraphic analysis of landbird extinction on Tahuata, Marquesas Islands. *Journal of Archaeological Science* 23: 81–94.

Steadman, D. W., C. Vargas, and F. Cristino. 1994. Stratigraphy, chronology, and cultural context of an early faunal assemblage from Easter Island. *Asian Perspectives* 33:79–96.

Steadman, D. W., J. P. White, and J. Allen. 1999. Prehistoric birds from New Ireland, Papua New Guinea: Extinctions on a large Melanesian island. *Proceedings of the National Academy of Sciences, USA* 96:2563–68.

Stevenson, J. 1998. Late Quaternary Environmental Change and the Impact of Melanesian Colonisation in New Caledonia. Unpublished Ph.D. thesis, University of New South Wales (Sydney, Australia).

Stevenson, J., and J. R. Dodson. 1995. Palaeoenvironmental evidence for human settlement of New Caledonia. *Archaeology in Oceania* 30:36–41.

Stimson, J. F. 1957. *Songs and Tales of the Sea Kings: Interpretations of the Oral Literature of Polynesia.* Salem, Mass.: Peabody Museum.

Stocking, G. W., Jr. 1968. *Race, Culture, and Evolution: Essays in the History of Anthropology.* Chicago: University of Chicago Press.

Stoddart, D. R. 1992. Biogeography of the tropical Pacific. *Pacific Science* 46:276–93.

Stoddart, D., T. Spencer, and T. Scoffin. 1985. Reef growth and karst erosion on Mangaia, Cook Islands: A reinterpretation. *Zeitschrift für Geomorphologie, N.F.* 57:121–40.

Stokes, J. F. G. (Dye, T., ed.) 1991. *Heiau of the Island of Hawai'i: A Historic Survey of Native Hawaiian Temple Sites.* Bishop Museum Bulletins in Anthropology 2. Honolulu: Bernice P. Bishop Museum.

———. ms, a [1930]. Ethnology of Rapa. 5 vols. Library, Bernice P. Bishop Museum (Honolulu).

———. ms, b. Archaeology of Raivavae. Library, Bernice P. Bishop Museum (Honolulu).

Streck, C. S. 1990. Prehistoric settlement in eastern Micronesia: Archaeology on Bikini Atoll, Republic of the Marshall Islands. In R. L. Hunter-Anderson, ed., *Recent Advances in Micronesian Archaeology: Selected Papers from the Micronesian Archaeology Conference, September 9–12, 1987.* Micronesica, Supplement 2, pp. 247–60.

Suggs, R. C. 1960. *The Island Civilizations of Polynesia.* New York: Mentor.

———. 1961. *Archaeology of Nuku Hiva, Marquesas*

Islands, French Polynesia. Anthropological Papers of the American Museum of Natural History 49, Part 1. New York: American Museum of Natural History.

———. 1962. *The Hidden Worlds of Polynesia.* New York: Harcourt, Brace, and World.

Sullivan, A. 1985. Intensification in volcanic zone gardening in northern New Zealand. In I. S. Farrington, ed., *Prehistoric Intensive Agriculture in the Tropics,* pp. 475–89. B.A.R. International Series 232. Oxford: British Archaeological Reports.

Sullivan, L. R. 1924. Race types in Polynesia. *American Anthropologist* 26:22–26.

Summerhayes, G. R. 1997. Interaction in Pacific Prehistory: An Approach Based on the Production, Distribution and Use of Pottery. 2 vols. Unpublished Ph.D. thesis, La Trobe University (Bundoora, Australia).

Summerhayes, G. R., and J. Allen. 1993. The transport of Mopir obsidian to late Pleistocene New Ireland. *Archaeology in Oceania* 28:144–48.

Summerhayes, G. R., J. R. Bird, R. Fullagar, C. Gosden, J. Specht, and R. Torrence. 1998. Application of PIXE-PIGME to archaeological analysis of changing patterns of obsidian use in West New Britain, Papua New Guinea. In S. Shackley, ed., *Archaeological Obsidian Studies: Method and Theory,* pp. 129–58. New York: Plenum Press.

Summerhayes, G. R., and M. Hotchkis. 1992. Recent advances in Melansian obsidian sourcing: Results of the 1990 and 1991 PIXE/PIGME analyses. In J.-C. Galipaud, ed., *Poterie Lapita et Peuplement: Actes du Colloque LAPITA,* pp. 127–34. Noumea, New Caledonia: ORSTOM.

Summers, C. 1964. *Hawaiian Archaeology: Fishponds.* Bernice P. Bishop Museum Special Publication 52. Honolulu: Bernice P. Bishop Museum.

Sutton, D. G. 1980. A culture history of the Chatham Islands. *Journal of the Polynesian Society* 89:67–93.

———. 1987. A paradigmatic shift in Polynesian prehistory: Implications for New Zealand. *New Zealand Journal of Archaeology* 9:135–56.

———. 1990. Organization and ontology: The origins of the northern Maori chiefdom, New Zealand. *Man* (N.S.) 25:667–92.

Sutton, D. G., ed. 1990. *The Archaeology of the Kainga: A Study of Precontact Maori Undefended Settlements at Pouerua, Northland, New Zealand.* Auckland: Auckland University Press.

———. 1993. *The Archaeology of Peripheral Pa at Pouerua, Northland, New Zealand.* Auckland: Auckland University Press.

———. 1994. *The Origins of the First New Zealanders.* Auckland: Auckland University Press.

Sutton, D. G., and M. A. Molloy. 1989. Deconstructing Pacific paleodemography: A critique of density dependent causality. *Archaeology in Oceania* 24: 31–36.

Swadling, P. 1981. *Papua New Guinea's Prehistory: An Introduction.* Boroko, Papua New Guinea: National Museum and Art Gallery.

———. 1986. Lapita shellfishing: Evidence from sites in the Reef Santa Cruz group, Southeast Solomon Islands. In A. Anderson, ed., *Traditional Fishing in the Pacific,* pp. 137–48. Pacific Anthropological Records 37. Honolulu: Bernice P. Bishop Museum.

———. 1991. Garden boundaries as indicators of past land-use strategies: Two case studies from coastal Melanesia. In A. Pawley, ed., *Man and a Half: Essays in Pacific Anthropology and Ethnobiology in Honour of Ralph Bulmer,* pp. 550–57. Auckland: Polynesian Society.

———. 1997a. Changing shorelines and cultural orientations in the Sepik-Ramu, Papua New Guinea: Implications for Pacific prehistory. *World Archaeology* 29:1–14.

———. 1997b. *Plumes from Paradise: Trade Cycles in Outer Southeast Asia and Their Impact on New Guinea and Nearby Islands until 1920.* Boroko: Papua New Guinea National Museum.

Swadling, P., N. Araho, and B. Ivuyo. 1991. Settlements associated with the Sepik-Ramu Sea. In P. Bellwood, ed., *Indo-Pacific Prehistory 1990: Proceedings of the 14th Congress of the Indo-Pacific Prehistory Association,* pp. 92–112. Canberra: Indo-Pacific Prehistory Association.

Swadling, P., J. Chappell, G. Francis, N. Araho, and B. Ivuyo. 1989. A Late Quaternary inland sea and early pottery in Papua New Guinea. *Archaeology in Oceania* 24:106–9.

Swadling, P., B. H. Schaublin, P. Gorecki, and F. Tiesler.

1988. *The Sepik-Ramu: An Introduction.* Boroko: National Museum of Papua New Guinea.

Tainter, J. A., and R. Cordy. 1977. An archaeological analysis of social ranking and residence groups in prehistoric Hawaii. *World Archaeology* 9:95–112.

Takayama, J. 1982. A brief report on archaeological investigations of the southern part of Yap Island and nearby Ngulu Atoll. In M. Aoyagi, ed., *Islanders and Their Outside World,* pp. 77–104. Tokyo: Committee for Micronesian Research, Rikkyo University.

———. 1984. Early pottery and population movements in Micronesian prehistory. *Asian Perspectives* 24:1–10.

Takayama, J., and J. T. Egami. 1971. *Archaeology on Rota in the Mariana Islands.* Reports of Pacific Archaeological Survey No. 1. Hiratsuka, Japan: Tokai University.

Takayama, J., B. Eritaia, and A. Saito. 1987. Preliminary observation of the origins of the Vaitupuans in view of pottery. Reprinted from *Cultural Adaptation to Atolls in Micronesia and West Polynesia.*

Takayama, J., and M. Intoh. 1976. *Archaeological Excavation of Latte Site (M-13), Rota, in the Marianas.* Reports of Pacific Archaeological Survey No. 4. Hiratsuka, Japan: Tokai University.

———. 1978. *Archaeological Excavation at Chukienu Shell Midden on Tol, Truk.* Reports of Pacific Archaeological Survey No. 5. Nara City, Japan: Tezukayama University.

———. 1980. *Reconnaissance Archaeological Survey in the Lower Mortlocks, Truk State.* Reports of Pacific Archaeological Survey No. 6. Nara City, Japan: Tezukayama University.

Takayama, J., and A. Saito. 1987. The discovery of the Davidson Type Ia hooks on Vaitupu Island, Tuvalu. *Tezukayama University Review* 55:29–49.

Takayama, J., and T. Seki. 1973. *Preliminary Archaeological Investigations on the Island of Tol in Truk.* Reports of Pacific Archaeological Survey No. 2. Tokyo: Azuma Shuppan.

Takayama, J., and R. Shutler, Jr. 1978. Preliminary report of a pottery site on Fefan Island, Truk, Central Caroline Islands. *Archaeology and Physical Anthropology in Oceania* 13:1–9.

Takayama, J., and H. Takasugi. 1987. The significance of lure shanks excavated in the Utiroa site of Makin Island in the Gilberts. *Senri Ethnological Studies* 21: 29–41.

Takayama, J., H. Takasugi, and K. Kaiyama. 1989. The 1988 archaeological expedition to Kiribati: A preliminary report. *Tezukayama University Review* 63: 1–14.

———. 1990. Test excavation at the Nukantekaing site on Tarawa, Kiribati, Central Pacific. In I. Ushijima, ed., *Anthropological Research on the Atoll Cultures of Micronesia, 1988,* pp. 1–20. Tsukuba-shi, Japan: University of Tsukuba.

Taylor, R. C. 1973. *An Atlas of Pacific Islands Rainfall.* Hawaiian Institute of Geophysics Data Report No. 25 (HIG-73-9). Honolulu: Hawaii Institute of Geophysics.

Terrell, J. 1986. *Prehistory in the Pacific Islands.* Cambridge: Cambridge University Press.

Terrell, J. E., T. L. Hunt, and C. Gosden. 1997. The dimensions of social life in the Pacific: Human diversity and the myth of the primitive isolate. *Current Anthropology* 38:155–96.

Thilenius, G. 1902. *Ethnographische Ergebnisse aus Melanesien,* Vol. I: *Die Polynesischen Inseln an der Ostgrenze Melanesiens.* Halle, Germany: Erhardt Karras.

———. 1913–36. *Ergebnisse der Südsee-Expedition 1908–1910.* Pt. 1, *Allgemeines.* Pt. 2, *Ethnographie; A: Melanesien; B: Micronesien.* 15 vols. Hamburgische Wissenschaftliche Stiftung. Hamburg: L. Friederichsen.

Thomas, N. 1989. The force of ethnology: Origins and significance of the Melanesia/Polynesia division. *Current Anthropology* 30:27–41.

———. 1990. *Marquesan Societies: Inequality and Political Transformation in Eastern Polynesia.* Oxford: Clarendon Press.

Thomas, W. L., Jr. 1963. The variety of physical environments among Pacific islands. In F. R. Fosberg, ed., *Man's Place in the Island Ecosystem,* pp. 7–38. Honolulu: Bishop Museum Press.

Thompson, L. M. 1932. *Archaeology of the Mariana Islands.* Bernice P. Bishop Museum Bulletin 100. Honolulu: Bernice P. Bishop Museum.

———. 1938. The pottery of the Lau Islands, Fiji. *Journal of the Polynesian Society* 47:109–13.

———. 1940. *Southern Lau, Fiji: An Ethnography.* Bernice

P. Bishop Museum Bulletin 162. Honolulu: Bernice P. Bishop Museum.

———. 1945. *The Native Culture of the Marianas Islands.* Bernice P. Bishop Museum Bulletin 185. Honolulu: Bernice P. Bishop Museum.

Thomson, B. 1908. *The Fijians: A Study of the Decay of Custom.* London: William Heinemann.

Thrum, T., ed. 1916–20. *Fornander's Collection of Hawaiian Antiquities and Folk-lore.* 3 vols. Bernice P. Bishop Museum Memoirs 4, 5, and 6. Honolulu: Bernice P. Bishop Museum.

Tilly, C. 1981. *As Sociology Meets History.* New York: Academic Press.

———. 1984. *Big Structures, Large Processes, Huge Comparisons.* New York: Russell Sage Foundation.

———. 1997. *Durable Inequality.* Berkeley: University of California Press.

Torrence, R., and B. Boyd. 1997. Archaeological Fieldwork in West New Britain, PNG. June–August 1997. Report on file, Australian Museum, Sydney.

Torrence, R., C. Pavlides, P. Jackson, and J. Webb. In press. Volcanic disasters and cultural discontinuities in the Holocene of West New Britain, Papua New Guinea. *Geological Society of London,* Special Publication.

Torrence, R., J. Specht, and R. Fullagar. 1990. Pompeiis in the Pacific. *Australian Natural History* 23:3–16.

Torrence, R., and G. R. Summerhayes. 1997. Sociality and the short distance trader: Intra-regional obsidian exchange in the Willaumez region, Papua New Guinea. *Archaeology in Oceania* 32:74–84.

Trask, H.-K. 1993. *From a Native Daughter: Colonialism and Sovereignty in Hawai'i.* Monroe, Me.: Common Courage Press.

Trask, R. L. 1996. *Historical Linguistics.* London: Arnold.

Trigger, B. 1989. *A History of Archaeological Thought.* Cambridge: Cambridge University Press.

Trotter, M. M., ed. 1974. *Prehistory of the Southern Cook Islands.* Canterbury Museum Bulletin No. 6. Christchurch, New Zealand: Canterbury Museum.

———. 1979. *Niue Island Archaeological Survey.* Canterbury Museum Bulletin No. 9. Christchurch, New Zealand: Canterbury Museum.

Tsang, C.-H. 1992. *Archaeology of the P'eng-Hu Islands.* Institute of History and Philology Special Publication No. 95. Taipei: Academia Sinica.

Tuggle, H. D. 1979. Hawaii. In J. Jennings, ed., *The Prehistory of Polynesia,* pp. 167–99. Cambridge, Mass.: Harvard University Press.

Tuggle, H. D., and P. B. Griffin, eds. 1973. *Lapakahi, Hawaii: Archaeological Studies.* Asian and Pacific Archaeology Series No. 5. Honolulu: Social Science Research Institute, University of Hawaii.

Tuggle, H. D., and M. J. Tomonari-Tuggle. 1980. Prehistoric agriculture in Kohala, Hawaii. *Journal of Field Archaeology* 7:297–312.

Ueki, T. 1990. Formation of a complex society in an island situation. In R. L. Hunter-Anderson, ed., *Recent Advances in Micronesian Archaeology: Selected Papers from the Micronesian Archaeology Conference, September 9–12, 1987. Micronesica,* Supplement 2, pp. 303–16.

Valeri, V. 1985. *Kingship and Sacrifice: Ritual and Society in Ancient Hawaii.* Chicago: University of Chicago Press.

Van Balgooy, M. M. J. 1971. Plant geography of the Pacific. *Blumea* 6:1–222.

Vanderwal, R. L. 1978. Exchange in prehistoric coastal Papua. *Mankind* 11:416–26.

Van Gilder, C., and P. V. Kirch. 1997. Household archaeology in Kipapa and Nakaohu, Kahikinui. In P. V. Kirch, ed., *Na Mea Kahiko o Kahikinui: Studies in the Archaeology of Kahikinui, Maui,* pp. 45–60. Oceanic Archaeology Laboratory, Special Publication No. 1. Berkeley: University of California.

Van Heerkeren, H. R. 1972. *The Stone Age of Indonesia.* Verhandelingen van het Koninklijk Instituut voor Taal-, Land- en Volkenkunde 61. The Hague: Koninklijk Instituut voor Taal-, Land- en Volkenkunde.

Van Tilburg, J. A. 1986. Power and Symbol: The Stylistic Analysis of Easter Island Monolithic Sculpture. Unpublished Ph.D. dissertation, University of California (Los Angeles).

———. 1987. Symbolic archaeology on Easter Island. *Archaeology* 40:26–33.

———. 1988. Easter Island statue type, part three: The moai as ideological symbol. In C. Cristino, P. Vargas, R. Izaurieta, and R. Budd, eds., *First International Congress, Easter Island & East Polynesia,* Vol. 1: *Archaeology,* pp. 164–73. Santiago: University of Chile.

————. 1991. Anthropomorphic stone monoliths on the islands of Oreor and Babeldaob, Republic of Belau (Palau), Micronesia. *Bishop Museum Occasional Papers* 31:3–62.

————. 1994. *Easter Island: Archaeology, Ecology and Culture.* London: British Museum Press.

Vargas, P. 1988. Easter Island statue type, part one: The moai as archaeological artefact. In C. Cristino, P. Vargas, R. Izaurieta, and R. Budd, eds., *First International Congress, Easter Island & East Polynesia,* Vol. 1: *Archaeology,* pp. 133–49. Santiago: University of Chile.

————. 1993. The Easter Island prehistoric sequence and developments in its settlement patterns. In M. W. Graves and R. Green, eds., *The Evolution and Organization of Prehistoric Society in Polynesia,* pp. 103–5. New Zealand Archaeological Association Monograph No. 5. Auckland: New Zealand Archaeological Association.

Vayda, A. 1960. *Maori Warfare.* Polynesian Society Maori Monograph No. 2. Wellington, New Zealand: Polynesian Society.

————. 1961. Expansion and warfare among swidden agriculturalists. *American Anthropologist* 63:346–58.

Vayda, A., and R. Rappaport. 1963. Island cultures. In F. R. Fosberg, ed., *Man's Place in the Island Ecosystem,* pp. 133–42. Honolulu: Bishop Museum Press.

Vérin, P. 1969. *L'Ancienne Civilisation de Rurutu: La Periode Classique.* Mémoires ORSTOM 33. Paris: ORSTOM.

Veyne, P. 1984. *Writing History: Essay on Epistemology.* Translated by M. Moore-Rinvolucre. Middletown, Conn.: Wesleyan University Press.

Vogt, E. Z. 1964. The genetic model and Maya cultural development. In E. Z. Vogt and A. Ruz L., eds., *Desarrollo Cultural de los Mayas,* pp. 9–48. Mexico City: Universidad Nacional Autónoma de México.

————. 1994. On the application of the phylogenetic model to the Maya. In R. J. DeMallie and A. Ortiz, eds., *North American Indian Anthropology: Essays on Society and Culture,* pp. 377–414. Norman: University of Oklahoma Press.

Von Haast, J. 1872. Moas and moa hunters. *Transactions of the New Zealand Institute* 4:66–107.

Wagner, W. C., D. R. Herbst, and S. H. Sohmer. 1990. *Manual of the Flowering Plants of Hawai'i.* 2 vols. Bishop Museum Special Publication 83. Honolulu: University of Hawaii Press and Bishop Museum Press.

Wagner, W. L., and V. A. Funk, eds. 1995. *Hawaiian Biogeography: Evolution on a Hot Spot Archipelago.* Washington, D.C.: Smithsonian Institution Press.

Wahome, E. W. 1997. Continuity and change in Lapita and post-Lapita ceramics: A review of evidence from the Admiralty Islands and New Ireland, Papua New Guinea. *Archaeology in Oceania* 32:118–23.

Walker, D., and G. Hope. 1982. Late Quaternary vegetation history. In J. L. Gressitt, ed., *Biogeography and Ecology of New Guinea,* Vol. 1, pp. 263–85. The Hague: W. Junk.

Wallace, A. R. 1895. *Island Life, or the Phenomena and Causes of Insular Faunas and Floras, Including a Revision and Attempted Solution of the Problem of Geological Climates,* 3rd ed. London: Macmillan.

Wallin, P. 1993. *Ceremonial Stone Structures: The Archaeology and Ethnohistory of the Marae Complex in the Society Islands, French Polynesia.* Aun 18. Uppsala, Sweden: Societas Archaeologica Upsaliensis.

Walter, R. 1989a. Lapita fishing strategies: A review of the archaeological and linguistic evidence. *Pacific Studies* 31:127–49.

————. 1989b. An archaeological fishhook assemblage from the southern Cook Islands. *Man in Oceania* 5: 67–78.

————. 1990. The Southern Cook Islands in Eastern Polynesian Prehistory. Unpublished Ph.D. dissertation, University of Auckland.

————. 1996. What is the East Polynesian "Archaic"? A view from the Cook Islands. In J. Davidson, G. Irwin, F. Leach, A. Pawley, and D. Brown, eds., *Oceanic Culture History: Essays in Honour of Roger Green,* pp. 513–29. New Zealand Journal of Archaeology Special Publication. Dunedin: New Zealand Journal of Archaeology.

————. 1998. *Anai'o: The Archaeology of a Fourteenth Century Polynesian Community in the Cook Islands.* New Zealand Archaeological Association Monograph 22. Auckland: New Zealand Archaeological Association.

Ward, G. K. 1976. The archaeology of settlements

associated with the chert industry of Ulawa. In R. C. Green and M. M. Cresswell, eds., *Southeast Solomons Cultural History: A Preliminary Survey*, pp. 161–80. Royal Society of New Zealand Bulletin 11. Wellington: Royal Society of New Zealand.

———. 1979. Prehistoric Settlement and Economy in a Tropical Small Island Environment: The Banks Islands, Insular Melanesia. Unpublished Ph.D. thesis, Australian National University (Canberra).

Ward, J. V. n.d. A Holocene Pollen Record from the Pago River Valley, Guam. Report on file, Micronesian Archaeological Research Services, Guam.

Ward, J. V., J. S. Athens, and C. Hotton. 1998. Holocene pollen records from Babeldaob Island, Palau, Western Caroline Islands. Paper presented at the annual meeting of the Society for American Archaeology, Seattle, March 29, 1998.

Ward, R. G., J. W. Webb, and M. Levison. 1973. The settlement of the Polynesian Outliers: A computer simulation. *Journal of the Polynesian Society* 82:330–42.

Watson, J. B. 1965. From hunting to horticulture in the New Guinea Highlands. *Ethnology* 4:295–309.

Watson, V. 1986. *Obsidian as Tool and Trade: A Papua New Guinea Case*. Burke Museum Contributions to Anthropology and Natural History No. 4. Seattle: Burke Museum.

Watson, V., and J. D. Cole. 1977. *Prehistory of the Eastern Highlands of New Guinea*. Seattle: University of Washington Press.

Weiner, A. B. 1992. *Inalienable Possessions: The Paradox of Keeping-While-Giving*. Berkeley: University of California Press.

Weisler, M. I. 1989. Chronometric dating and late Holocene prehistory in the Hawaiian Islands: A critical review of radiocarbon dates from Moloka'i Island. *Radiocarbon* 31:121–45.

———. 1993. Long-Distance Inter-island Communication in Prehistoric Polynesia: Three Case Studies. Unpublished Ph.D. dissertation, Department of Anthropology, University of California (Berkeley).

———. 1994. The settlement of marginal Polynesia: New evidence from Henderson Island. *Journal of Field Archaeology* 21:83–102.

———. 1995. Henderson Island prehistory: Colonization and extinction on a remote Polynesian island. *Biological Journal of the Linnean Society* 56(1–2):377–404.

———. 1996a. Taking the mystery out of the Polynesian "mystery" islands: A case study from Mangareva and the Pitcairn group. In J. Davidson, G. Irwin, F. Leach, A. Pawley, and D. Brown, eds., *Oceanic Culture History: Essays in Honour of Roger Green*, pp. 615–29. New Zealand Journal of Archaeology Special Publication. Dunedin: New Zealand Journal of Archaeology.

———. 1996b. An archaeological survey of Mangareva: Implications for regional settlement models and interaction studies. *Man and Culture in Oceania* 12:61–85.

———. 1998a. Hard evidence for prehistoric interaction in Polynesia. *Current Anthropology* 39:521–32.

———. 1998b. Issues in the colonization and settlement of Polynesian islands. In P. V. Casanova, ed., *Easter Island and East Polynesian Prehistory*, pp. 73–86. Santiago: Instituto de Estudios Isla de Pascua, Universidad de Chile.

———. 1999. The antiquity of aroid pit agriculture and significance of buried A horizons on Pacific atolls. *Geoarchaeology* 14:621–54.

Weisler, M., ed. 1997. *Prehistoric Long-Distance Interaction in Oceania: An Interdisciplinary Approach*. New Zealand Archaeological Association Monograph 21. Auckland: New Zealand Archaeological Association.

Weisler, M., and P. V. Kirch. 1985. The structure of settlement space in a Polynesian chiefdom: Kawela, Moloka'i, Hawaiian Islands. *New Zealand Journal of Archaeology* 7:129–58.

———. 1996. Interisland and interarchipelago transport of stone tools in prehistoric Polynesia. *Proceedings of the National Academy of Sciences, USA* 93: 1381–85.

Welsch, R., ed. 1998. *An American Anthropologist in Melanesia: A. B. Lewis and the Joseph N. Field South Pacific Expedition, 1909–1913*. 2 vols. Honolulu: University of Hawaii Press.

Welsch, R. L., J. Terrell, and J. A. Nadloski. 1992. Language and culture on the North Coast of New Guinea. *American Anthropologist* 94:568–600.

White, J. P. 1972. *Ol Tumbuna: Archaeological Excavations in the eastern Central Highlands, Papua New Guinea*.

Terra Australis 2. Canberra: Australian National University.

———. 1992. New Ireland and Lapita. In J.-C. Galipaud, ed., *Poterie Lapita et Peuplement: Actes du Colloque LAPITA*, pp. 83–90. Noumea, New Caledonia: ORSTOM.

White, J. P., and J. Allen. 1980. Melanesian prehistory: Some recent advances. *Science* 207:728–34.

White, J. P., J. Allen, and J. Specht. 1988. Peopling the Pacific: The Lapita Homeland Project. *Australian Natural History* 22:410–16.

White, J. P., K. A. W. Crook, and B. P. Ruxton. 1970. Kosipe: A late Pleistocene site in the Papuan Highlands. *Proceedings of the Prehistoric Society* 36:152–70.

White, J. P., and J. Downie. 1980. Excavations at Lesu, New Ireland. *Asian Perspectives* 23:193–220.

White, J. P., T. F. Flannery, R. O'Brien, R. V. Hancock, and L. Pavlish. 1991. The Balof Shelters, New Ireland. In J. Allen and C. Gosden, eds., *Report of the Lapita Homeland Project*, pp. 46–58. Occasional Papers in Prehistory No. 20. Canberra: Department of Prehistory, Australian National University.

White, J. P., and C. V. Murray-Wallace. 1996. Site ENX (Fissoa) and the incised and applied pottery tradition in New Ireland, Papua New Guinea. *Man and Culture in Oceania* 12:31–46.

White, J. P., and J. F. O'Connell. 1982. *A Prehistory of Australia, New Guinea and Sahul*. Sydney: Academic Press.

White, J. P., and J. Specht. 1971. Prehistoric pottery from Ambitle Island, Bismarck Archipelago. *Asian Perspectives* 14:88–94.

White, J. P. and D. H. Thomas. 1972. What mean these stones? Ethnotaxonomic models and archaeological interpretations in the New Guinea Highlands. In D. L. Clarke, ed., *Models in Archaeology*, pp. 275–308. London: Methuen.

Wickler, S. 1990. Prehistoric Melanesian exchange and interaction: Recent evidence from the Northern Solomon Islands. *Asian Perspectives* 29:135–54.

———. 1995. Twenty-Nine Thousand Years on Buka: Long-Term Cultural Change in the Northern Solomon Islands. Unpublished Ph.D. dissertation, University of Hawaii (Manoa).

Wickler, S., and M. Spriggs. 1988. Pleistocene human occupation of the Solomon Islands, Melanesia. *Antiquity* 62:703–6.

Wiens, H. 1962. *Atoll Environment and Ecology*. New Haven, Conn.: Yale University Press.

Williams, F. E. 1932. Trading voyages from the Gulf of Papua. *Oceania* 3:139–66.

Williams, S. 1992. Early inland settlement expansion and the effect of geomorphological change on the archaeological record in Kane'ohe, O'ahu. *New Zealand Journal of Archaeology* 14:67–78.

Williams, T. 1884. *Fiji and the Fijians*. London: Charles H. Kelly.

Williamson, M. 1981. *Island Populations*. Oxford: Oxford University Press.

Williamson, R. W. 1924. *The Social and Political Systems of Central Polynesia*. 3 vols. Cambridge: Cambridge University Press.

Wilson, J., ed. 1987. *From the Beginning: The Archaeology of the Maori*. Auckland: Penguin.

Wilson, S. 1985. Phytolith analysis at Kuk, an early agricultural site in Papua New Guinea. *Archaeology in Oceania* 20:90–97.

Wilson, W. 1985. Evidence for an Outlier source for the Proto Eastern Polynesian pronominal system. *Oceanic Linguistics* 24:85–133.

Winslow, J. H., ed. 1977. *The Melanesian Environment*. Canberra: Australian National University Press.

Wolf, E. 1982. *Europe and the People Without History*. Berkeley: University of California Press.

Worthy, T. H., and R. N. Holdaway. 1995. Quaternary fossil faunas from caves on Mt. Cookson, North Canterbury, South Island, New Zealand. *Journal of the Royal Society of New Zealand* 25:333–70.

Yen, D. E. 1971. The development of agriculture in Oceania. In R. C. Green and M. Kelly, eds., *Studies in Oceanic Culture History*, Vol. 2, pp. 1–12. Pacific Anthropological Records 12. Honolulu: Bernice P. Bishop Museum.

———. 1973. The origins of Oceanic agriculture. *Archaeology and Physical Anthropology in Oceania* 8:68–85.

———. 1974a. *The Sweet Potato and Oceania: An Essay in Ethnobotany*. Bernice P. Bishop Museum Bulletin 236. Honolulu: Bernice P. Bishop Museum.

————. 1974b. Arboriculture in the subsistence of Santa Cruz, Solomon Islands. *Economic Botany* 28:247–84.

————. 1976a. Agricultural systems and prehistory in the Solomon Islands. In R. C. Green and M. Cresswell, eds., *Southeast Solomon Islands Cultural History: A Preliminary Survey*, pp. 61–74. Royal Society of New Zealand Bulletin 11. Wellington: Royal Society of New Zealand.

————. 1976b. Inland settlement on Santa Cruz Island (Nendö). In R. C. Green and M. Cresswell, eds., *Southeast Solomon Islands Cultural History: A Preliminary Survey*, pp. 203–24. Royal Society of New Zealand Bulletin 11. Wellington: Royal Society of New Zealand.

————. 1982. The Southeast Solomons Cultural History Programme. *Bulletin of the Indo-Pacific Prehistory Association* 3:52–66.

————. 1988. Easter Island agriculture in prehistory: The possibilities of reconstruction. In C. Cristino, P. Vargas, R. Izaurieta, and R. Budd, eds., *First International Congress, Easter Island & East Polynesia*, Vol. 1: *Archaeology*, pp. 59–82. Santiago: University of Chile.

————. 1990. Environment, agriculture and the colonisation of the Pacific. In D. E. Yen and J. M. J. Mummery, eds., *Pacific Production Systems: Approaches to Economic Prehistory*, pp. 258–77. Occasional Papers in Prehistory No. 18. Canberra: Department of Prehistory, Australian National University.

————. 1991. Polynesian cultigens and cultivars: The questions of origin. In *Islands, Plants, and Polynesians*, ed. P. A. Cox and S. A. Banack, pp. 67–98. Portland: Dioscorides Press.

————. 1995. The development of Sahul agriculture with Australia as a bystander. *Antiquity* 69(special number 265):831–47.

Yen, D. E., P. V. Kirch, P. Rosendahl, and T. Riley. 1972. Prehistoric agriculture in the upper Makaha Valley, Oahu. In D. E. Yen and E. Ladd, eds., *Makaha Valley Historical Project: Interim Report No. 3*, pp. 59–94. Pacific Anthropological Records 18. Honolulu: Bernice P. Bishop Museum.

Yen, D. E., and J. M. Wheeler. 1968. Introduction of taro into the Pacific: The indications of chromosome numbers. *Ethnology* 7:259–67.

Zimmerman, E. C. 1948. *Insects of Hawaii*, Vol. 1: *Introduction*. Honolulu: University of Hawaii Press.

Zobel, E. 1997. The position of Chamorro and Palauan in the Austronesian family tree: Evidence from verb morphology and morphosyntax. Paper presented at the Eighth International Conference on Austronesian Linguistics, Academia Sinica, Taipei, Taiwan.

Index

Figures are indicated by a suffixed -f, maps by a suffixed -m, and tables by a suffixed -t. Notes (suffixed -n) are referred to by number.

PATRICK VINTON KIRCH is the Class of 1954 Professor of Anthropology, and Director of the Phoebe A. Hearst Museum of Anthropology, at the University of California, Berkeley, and a member of the National Academy of Sciences.

Designer:	Nicole Hayward
Compositor:	Princeton Editorial Associates, Inc., Scottsdale, Arizona
Text:	Weiss
Display:	Weiss and Gill Sans
Printer and binder:	Friesens, Altona, Manitoba, Canada